THRIVING

Making Cities *Green, Resilient*, and *Inclusive* in a Changing Climate

THRIVING

Megha Mukim
Mark Roberts
Editors

CONTENTS

PART 2: WHAT DO WE KNOW?

PART 3: HOW DO WE GET IT DONE?

Boxes

Figures

Maps

Tables

Foreword

The past 50 years have seen both a quadrupling of global urban population and a rapidly changing climate, with rising surface temperatures and sea levels and increasing frequency of extreme weather events. Fast-growing cities—which offer a range of opportunities—can give rise to a wide variety of stresses, especially if their urbanization is not well-managed. An unpredictable and fast-changing climate compounds these underlying stresses. The impacts of climate change–related shocks on cities may be significant; for many households, they can be devastating. Cities, both small and large, in developing countries suffer disproportionately when confronted by extreme hot and dry weather events, as well as by tropical cyclones.

Using data from across 10,000 cities globally, this report asks four important questions: How green, resilient, and inclusive are cities today? How does climate change affect cities and people in cities? How does the growth of cities impact the climate and, more generally, the environment? And finally, what policies will help make cities greener, more resilient, and more inclusive?

Climate change is also a symptom of a larger problem—the erosion of natural capital, to which poorly managed urbanization contributes. This erosion contributes, in turn, to dangerously poor air quality in many cities, detrimental competition for water between urban and rural areas, unnecessary loss of fertile agricultural land, deforestation, and loss of biodiversity. These trends are playing themselves out against a backdrop of high and rising levels of inequality in many cities globally and stalled progress in the worldwide fight against extreme poverty. These trends both interact with and reinforce climate change–related stressors to affect the greenness, resilience, and inclusiveness of urban development.

This report provides a compass to help policy makers—both local and national—meet their objectives to make cities greener, more resilient, and more inclusive. It outlines what policy instruments are available; who wields these instruments; and how policy choices could be tailored, prioritized, and sequenced for effective implementation.

Policy makers can draw on five broad sets of policy instruments that constitute the "five I's": information, incentives, insurance, integration, and investments. Early warning information can help save lives, property, and infrastructure. Accurate information that reflects risks can help governments, individuals, and businesses make better decisions. Incentives are needed to motivate people and businesses to act on the available information and take account of the impacts of their own decisions on the environment and on others. Insurance can help minimize the financial impact of disasters, complementing adaptation strategies. Integration within cities, to which well-implemented planning is key, is good for the poor and good for budgets, helping minimize unnecessary sprawl and bringing people closer to jobs and opportunities. Integration across cities—through measures that help promote the movement of people, goods, and services—can have a dampening effect on shocks and stresses. Finally, investments can be used to anticipate, prevent, and respond to shocks, as well as to retrofit buildings and infrastructure in response to stresses.

It is well known that cities are "engines of growth" at both the local and national levels. However, less is known about how urban development and climate change are interacting, and this flagship report makes an important contribution to our collective understanding of cities and climate change. I firmly believe that the insights from this report will provide valuable guidance for the World Bank Group as we collaborate with partners and clients to help cities not only survive but also thrive in the face of the perils of climate change.

Action now is possible, action now is necessary and urgent, and action now is where we should focus our efforts.

Juergen Voegele
Vice President for Sustainable Development
World Bank

Acknowledgments

This report was prepared by a team led by **Mark Roberts** and **Megha Mukim**. The core team also consisted of **Paolo Avner, Paola Marcela Ballon Fernandez, Jonathan Bower, Vladimir Chlouba, Jose Antonio Cuesta Leiva, Maitreyi Das, Chandan Deuskar, Felipe Dizon, Benny Istanto, Remi Jedwab, Nicholas Jones, Lucia Madrigal, Shohei Nakamura, Sammy Ndayizamvye, Jane Park, Nerali Patel, Natalia Pecorari, Luis Quintero, Giuseppe Rossitti, Steven Rubinyi, Dmitry Sivaev, Benjamin Stewart, Rui Su, Eigo Tateishi, Zoe Trohanis, Aishwarya Venkat, Takahiro Yabe, Esha Zaveri,** and **Tianyu Zhang.** Additional written inputs into the report were provided by Gauteng City-Region Observatory researchers **Graeme Götz, Gillian Maree,** and **Laven Naidoo.**

The work was conducted under the general guidance of **Juergen Voegele** (Vice President, Sustainable Development), **Richard Damania** (Chief Economist, Sustainable Development), **Sameh Wahba** (Regional Director, Europe and Central Asia, Sustainable Development), and **Bernice Van Bronkhorst** (Global Director, Urban, Disaster Risk Management, Resilience, and Land).

The team was fortunate to receive excellent advice and guidance from the following peer reviewers at various points in the report preparation process: **Louise Cord, Marianne Fay, Matthew Kahn, Mark Lundell, Martin Rama, Harris Selod, Anna Wellenstein,** and **Ming Zhang.** These reviewers are not responsible for any remaining errors, omissions, or interpretations. The team also benefited greatly from the feedback provided by the report's external and internal panels of advisers at various key points during the report preparation process. External advisers to the report, who have not already been acknowledged, included **Gilles Duranton, Rema Hanna,** and **Esteban Rossi-Hansberg.** Internal advisers to the report included **Madhur Gautam, Stephane Hallegatte, Ruth Hill, Somik Lall,** and **Kanta Kumar Rigaud.**

Somik Lall also played an instrumental role in early discussions regarding the report's scope and the background research that should feed into it. The team further gratefully acknowledges the exceptional feedback provided on early drafts of the report's overview by **Thomas Farole, Francis Ghesquiere,** and **Catalina Marulanda.**

Preparation of the report also benefited greatly from the feedback received from the discussants and other participants during an authors' workshop that was held on February 24 and 28, 2022. Discussants who have not already been acknowledged were **Paula Restrepo Cadavid, Luc Christiaensen, Olivia D'Aoust, Mathilde Lebrand, Ellen Moscoe, Tanner Regan,** and **Forhad Shilpi.** The team is further grateful to the numerous other colleagues—including **Martin Heger, Angel Hsu, Ghazala Mansuri, Augustin Maria, Joanna Masic,** and **Craig Meisner**—who contributed insights during the team's conversations with them.

Sabra Ledent was the substantive editor, and **Nora Mara** was the copyeditor; **Voilà:** was responsible for the design, layout, and visualizations of the report's stand-alone Overview cover and text. **Mary Fisk, Jewel McFadden,** and **Deborah Appel-Barker** of the World Bank's formal publishing unit were responsible for the design, typesetting, printing, and dissemination of both the hard copy and digital versions of the full report, while also providing inputs into the production of the stand-alone Overview. Last, but not least, we thank **Sreypov Tep** and **Kai Xin Nellie Teo** for unfailing administrative support.

This work received generous financial and technical support from the **City Resilience Program** and the **Global Facility for Disaster Reduction and Recovery.**

Main Messages

Between 1970 and 2021, the number of people living in cities increased from 1.19 billion to 4.46 billion, while the Earth's surface temperature climbed by 1.19°C above its preindustrial level. Because of the prosperity they have helped generate, cities have been a major cause of this climate change. It is also in cities, however, that many of the solutions to the climate crisis will be found, not least because by 2050 almost 70 percent of the world's population will call cities home.

This report combines original empirical analysis of a global sample of more than 10,000 cities with insights from secondary literature to take stock of how green, how resilient, and how inclusive cities are today, and to examine the two-way interplay between cities and climate change. Informed by this analysis, the report provides a compass for policy makers on how to help their cities become greener, more resilient, and more inclusive—in other words, on how to help their cities thrive—in a changing climate.

A changing climate

- *Climate change is exposing cities to increasingly frequent extreme weather events*. From the 1970s to the period 2010–20, the frequency of extreme heat and dry events increased across cities globally, and the frequency of extreme wet events has increased since the 1990s. Global sea-level rise of about 0.125 millimeters per year is also increasing the risk of flooding for coastal cities.

How green, how resilient, and how inclusive are cities?

- *Cities in high- and upper-middle-income countries are major contributors to climate change, whereas the contribution of cities in lower-income countries is modest*. Globally, about 70 percent of anthropogenic greenhouse gas emissions, the bulk of which are fossil carbon dioxide (CO_2) emissions, emanate from cities. Cities in lower-income countries, however, accounted for only about 14 percent of all global urban CO_2 emissions in 2015, and cities in low-income cities contributed less than 0.20 percent. The mitigation challenge for cities in lower-income countries is to develop without following the historic CO_2 emissions trajectories of cities in higher-income countries.

- *Cities in low- and lower-middle-income countries face the highest exposure to projected climate change–related hazards*. Projected exposure for 2030–40 for these cities—based on a composite index that combines projections for six key hazards (floods, heat stress, tropical cyclones, sea-level rise, water stress, and wildfires)—is considerably higher than for cities in higher-income countries.

- *Cities in low- and lower-middle-income countries are less resilient to increasingly frequent climate change–related shocks and stresses*. These cities suffer larger negative impacts to their local levels of economic activity from extreme hot, dry, and wet weather events, as well as from tropical cyclones, than do cities in higher-income countries. The impacts of extreme weather for cities in lower-income countries are particularly pronounced when they reinforce a city's baseline climatic conditions.

- *Cities suffer indirect impacts of climate change, especially in low- and lower-middle-income countries.* These indirect impacts occur through a variety of channels. For example, when extreme weather events hit, people in the countryside often seek safe harbor in cities. Extended droughts in rural areas result in faster expansion of urban areas. The resulting new settlements are often informal and established on the outskirts of cities, in urban floodplains with limited access to services.

- *Construction in countries is gravitating toward cities that will be most affected by climate change.* Since the 1960s, construction in countries has increasingly gravitated toward cities projected to become unbearably hot because of climate change—the opposite of what would be expected in the face of intensifying changes in climate.

- *Lack of inclusiveness contributes to the lack of resilience of cities in low- and lower-middle-income countries.* This lack of resilience can be explained, in part, by these cities' higher rates of poverty and lower levels of access to basic services such as health care and education; water, electricity, and other utilities; solid waste management; digital and financial services; and emergency rescue services.

- *Cities in low- and middle-income countries are less green in terms of air pollution, and air pollution from key urban sectors presents a greater challenge for larger cities in countries at all income levels.* On average, concentrations of $PM_{2.5}$ (particulate matter of 2.5 microns or less in diameter) in both 2000 and 2015 were lower in cities in high-income countries than in cities in lower-income countries. And a city's $PM_{2.5}$ emissions in its residential and transportation sectors— sectors that urban planning and policies can most directly influence—tend to increase with its population.

- *Policies that improve air quality can help cities both mitigate and adapt to climate change.* Many of the activities that contribute to poor urban air quality, such as industrial activities and driving internal combustion engine vehicles, also contribute to global climate change. Consistent with this finding, across cities globally, for the residential and transportation sectors, a strong positive correlation exists between CO_2 and $PM_{2.5}$ emissions.

- *Cities that develop vertically consume less land, accommodate more people, and are more prosperous.* Across cities globally, a doubling of a city's total height leads to a roughly 16 percent long-run increase in its population and a 19 percent long-run reduction in its land area relative to other cities. These results are accompanied by a 4 percent long-run increase in the intensity of the city's nighttime lights per capita, which suggests increased prosperity.

- *Lack of vegetation, especially evident in large cities and cities in upper-middle-income countries, can exacerbate the impacts of extreme heat events in cities.* It does so because a lack of vegetation exacerbates the urban heat island effect, which can lead to urban land surface temperatures that are more than 10°C higher than the equivalent rural land surface temperatures.

A policy compass to help cities thrive

A thriving city is one that is green, resilient, and inclusive in the face of a changing climate. This report presents general conclusions related to the realization of this vision in the form of three questions policy makers should answer: What policy instruments are available? Who wields these instruments? How can policy choices based on these instruments be prioritized and sequenced for effective implementation?

- *WHAT*: Policy options take the form of five I's: information, incentives, insurance, integration, and investments. In many instances, the interdependencies between these sets of instruments play out in complementary ways, wherein policies across the bundles strengthen impacts when implemented together.

- *WHO*: Because "traditional" urban stresses interact with climate change–related stresses to determine outcomes, local governments are well-placed to drive climate action. Cities, working with other stakeholders including national governments, the private sector, and civil society, have an important policy wedge at their disposal.

- *HOW*: To ensure their cities thrive, policy makers will need to toggle between, and sandwich together, bundles of policy options drawn from the five I's. The combination of interventions, their sequencing, and the prioritization of outcomes will vary depending on the characteristics of cities, including their level of risk, level of development, and size.

Abbreviations

CO_2	carbon dioxide
CSO	civil society organization
EID	emerging infectious disease
EV	electric vehicle
FLLoCA	Financing Locally Led Climate Action (Kenya)
GDP	gross domestic product
GHG	greenhouse gas
GHS	Global Human Settlement
GRID	green, resilient, and inclusive development
IDP	internally displaced person
IV	instrumental variable
MDE	multidimensional exclusion
$\mu g/m^3$	micrograms per cubic meter
MTA	Metropolitan Transit Authority (New York)
OAP	outdoor air pollution
$PM_{2.5}$	particulate matter of 2.5 microns or less in diameter
PPD	public-private dialogue
SEDLAC	Socio-Economic Database for Latin America and the Caribbean
SSP	Shared Socioeconomic Pathway
TCIP	Turkish Catastrophe Insurance Pool
WHO	World Health Organization
WUI	wildland-urban interface

Overview

Introduction

For at least 50 years, the view that human activity has spurred the world's warming has been supported by scientific evidence, the weight of which is now beyond dispute (Benton 1970; IPCC 2021; Madden and Ramanathan 1980).[1] Globally during this time, the number of people living in cities has almost quadrupled[2] and the Earth's surface temperature has climbed by nearly 1.2°C above its preindustrial levels.[3] This warming has been associated with an increased frequency of extreme hot, dry, and wet events across cities worldwide.[4] Global sea-level rise has also increased the risk of flooding for many coastal cities.

Because of the prosperity they have helped generate, cities have been an important cause of this climate change (Kahn 2010).[5] At the same time, this prosperity has helped make cities more resilient to climate change–related shocks and stressors. Cities have also become increasingly vocal advocates of climate action;[6] however, in the race between climate change and climate action, climate change retains a commanding lead. Cities in high- and upper-middle-income countries, which account for the bulk of global urban carbon dioxide (CO_2) emissions, are not moving quickly enough toward net zero. Similarly, although their current contributions to climate change may be small, cities in lower-income countries are not acting fast enough to moderate their emissions trajectories. These trajectories, if left unchecked, will eventually offset any reductions in global emissions made by cities in higher-income countries. Poorly managed urbanization also contributes to an even larger problem—the more general erosion of natural capital.[7] This erosion takes the form not only of polluted skies but also of contaminated water bodies, destroyed natural habitats, and the loss of both plant and animal species.[8]

In addition to not acting quickly enough to mitigate climate change, cities, especially those in low- and lower-middle-income countries, are also not adapting quickly enough to its challenges. The residents of cities in lower- and even in higher-income countries may see climate change as a secondary concern, especially when pitted against poverty, inequality, and a lack of access to markets and services—problems that for some people and some cities have worsened over time. As illustrated by France's "yellow vest" protests, important trade-offs undoubtedly exist between such problems and certain policies that aim to tackle climate change.[9] The good news, however, is that complementary policies can help ease these trade-offs, as can policies that make cities more inclusive while simultaneously helping them become both greener and more resilient to climate change. In this context, how inclusive a city is today is also an important determinant of how well it can cope with the climate change–related shocks and stresses of the future.

To ensure that cities thrive in a world confronted by climate change, policy makers at both national and local levels need to work together to implement bold policies to address the interrelated stresses that arise from climate change and urban growth. These include the stresses arising from the pressure of a city's population on its supplies of land, housing, and basic services; its stock of infrastructure; and its environment.[10] If not well managed, such stresses can give rise to slums and sprawl, deteriorating levels and quality of basic service provision, streets gridlocked with polluting cars and motorcycles, the excessive conversion of fertile agricultural land to urban uses, choking air pollution, and heightened greenhouse gas (GHG) emissions.

Drawing on a wide variety of data sources, this report combines original empirical analysis with insights from a diverse range of secondary literature to take stock of how green, how resilient, and how inclusive cities are, and to shed light on the interaction of stresses related to urban growth with those related to climate change. To address those interrelated stresses, policy makers need to enlist the use of five broad sets of policy instruments—information, incentives, insurance, integration, and investments—in short, the five I's. The report provides a compass to help cities tailor the use of these instruments to their own circumstances and problems.

How green, how resilient, and how inclusive are cities today?

To take stock of how green, how resilient, and how inclusive cities are today, this report defines a global typology of more than 10,000 cities, measuring a city's greenness, resilience, and inclusiveness using a variety of indicators (box O.1). Based on the analysis of this typology and the indicators more generally, as well as on the report's other global analysis, 10 key findings emerge.

Box O.1

Defining a global typology of cities

This report measures a city's greenness, resilience, and inclusiveness using a variety of indicators. For greenness, these indicators include absolute and per capita production-based fossil fuel carbon dioxide emissions, emissions and concentrations of particulate matter of 2.5 microns or less in diameter, and measures of a city's level and extent of greenery or vegetation. For resilience, they include estimates of the size of impacts of weather events on a city's aggregate level of economic activity. Indicators of inclusiveness include levels of access to basic services such as improved sanitation and safely managed drinking water, poverty rates, and levels of intracity household income inequality.[a]

Although cities vary widely on these indicators, some general patterns are nevertheless evident, with many related to both a city's population size and its level of development. These patterns allow definition of a global typology that distinguishes between nine types of city—small, medium, and large cities in low- and lower-middle-, upper-middle-, and high-income countries (map BO.1.1)—and the relative severity of the greenness, resilience, and inclusiveness challenges they face. Chapter 2 offers a full discussion of this typology and the relative severity of challenges that different types of cities face.

a. In addition to these indicators, the report also discusses a range of other dimensions of the greenness, resilience, and inclusiveness of cities and how these dimensions relate to climate change (see also box O.2).

Map BO.1.1   Global typology of cities

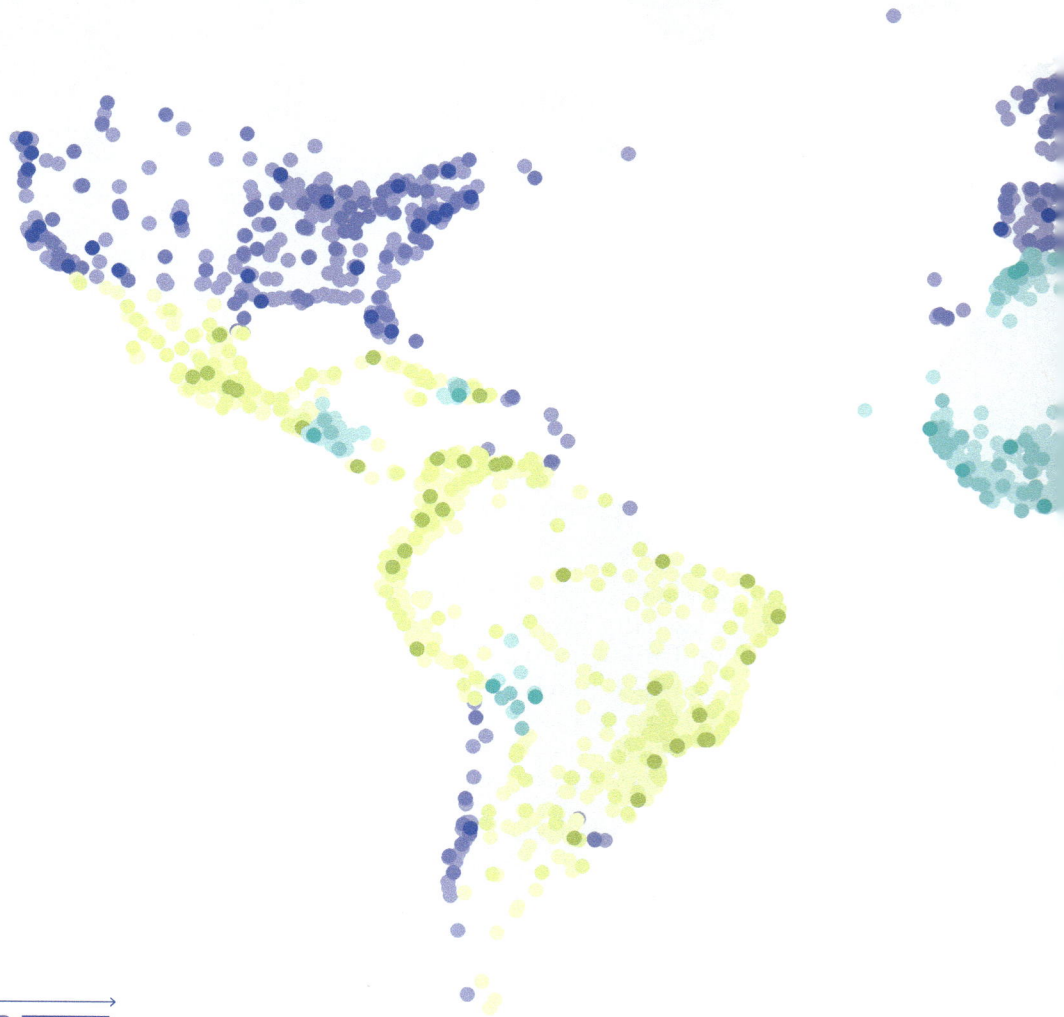

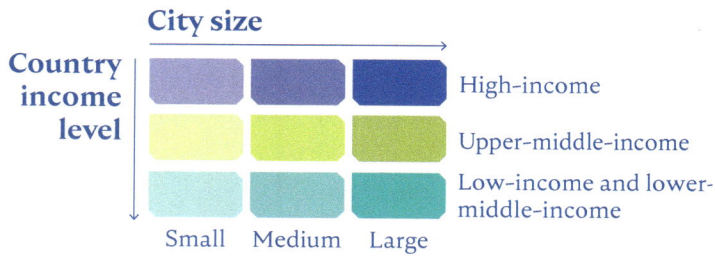

City size

Country income level

High-income

Upper-middle-income

Low-income and lower-middle-income

Small   Medium   Large

Source: World Bank calculations based on data from the European Commission's Global Human Settlement (GHS) Urban Centre Database R2019 (https://ghsl.jrc.ec.europa.eu/ghs_stat_ucdb2015mt_r2019a.php).

Note: Cities are defined as urban centers following the European Commission's degree of urbanization methodology (Dijkstra et al. 2021; Dijkstra and Poelman 2014). Small, medium, and large cities are those that in 2015 had a population of 50,000–199,999; 200,000–1.4999 million; and 1.5 million or more, respectively.

KEY FINDING 1

Cities in high- and upper-middle-income countries are the least green globally in terms of CO_2 emissions, whereas cities in lower-income countries barely contribute to global emissions.

Globally, about 70 percent of anthropogenic GHG emissions, the bulk of which are fossil CO_2 emissions, emanate from cities (Hopkins et al. 2016).[11] On a per capita basis, cities in high- and upper-middle-income countries have the highest fossil CO_2 emissions, and those in low-income countries have the lowest (figure O.1, panel a). Indeed, in 2015 average per capita emissions in cities in high-income countries were almost 18 times higher than those of cities in low-income countries, whereas those in cities in upper-middle-income countries were more than 21 times higher. Higher average per capita emissions in cities in high- and upper-middle-income countries also translate into higher shares of global urban CO_2 emissions (figure O.1, panel b). In 2015, these cities together accounted for nearly 86 percent of all global urban CO_2 emissions. Cities in lower-middle-income countries contributed almost 13 percent and cities in low-income countries less than 0.2 percent.

When focusing on just urban fossil CO_2 emissions from the residential and transportation sectors—the sectors that urban planning and policies can most directly influence—even stronger patterns emerge. In 2015, average per capita emissions from these sectors in cities in high-income countries were more than 76 times those in cities in low-income countries and more than 10 times those in cities in lower-middle-income countries (figure O.1, panel a). Whereas cities in high-income countries accounted for 48 percent of total global urban emissions from the residential and transportation sectors, cities in low-income countries accounted for less than 0.4 percent (figure O.1, panel b).[12]

The picture is clear: cities in high- and upper-middle-income countries are the major drivers of global urban CO_2 emissions and therefore of the urban contribution to global climate change. By contrast, cities in low-income countries barely register in terms of their contribution. Thus, from a mitigation perspective, the challenge facing cities in high- and upper-middle-income countries is how to reduce their high current levels of CO_2 emissions. Cities in low- and, to a lesser extent, lower-middle-income countries face a different challenge—how to develop without following the CO_2 emissions trajectories historically followed by cities in higher-income countries.

Figure O.2 depicts the importance of the challenge for cities in low- and lower-middle-income countries. It shows that—even if (and it is a very big if) high- and upper-middle-income countries can make a successful green transition consistent with net zero CO_2 emissions by 2050—global GHG emissions will remain above the level required to limit global warming to 1.5°C as long as low- and lower-middle-income countries follow their current policies.[13] Thus, a comparison of panel a of the figure with panel b reveals that total global GHG emissions in 2050 will remain 4.2 times the level required to keep warming within 1.5°C if current policies remain the same in low- and lower-middle-income countries while higher-income countries achieve net zero.

Even if lower-middle-income countries were also to achieve net zero by 2050 but low-income countries were to continue with their current policies, GHG emissions would remain 60 percent higher than required to limit global warming to 1.5°C.

Figure O.1 **Cities in high- and upper-middle-income countries emit the most CO$_2$ and contribute the most to global urban CO$_2$ emissions**

Average CO$_2$ emissions per capita and share of global CO$_2$ emissions generated in cities, by country income group, 2015

Residential and transportation ● ○ *All sources (restricted sample)*

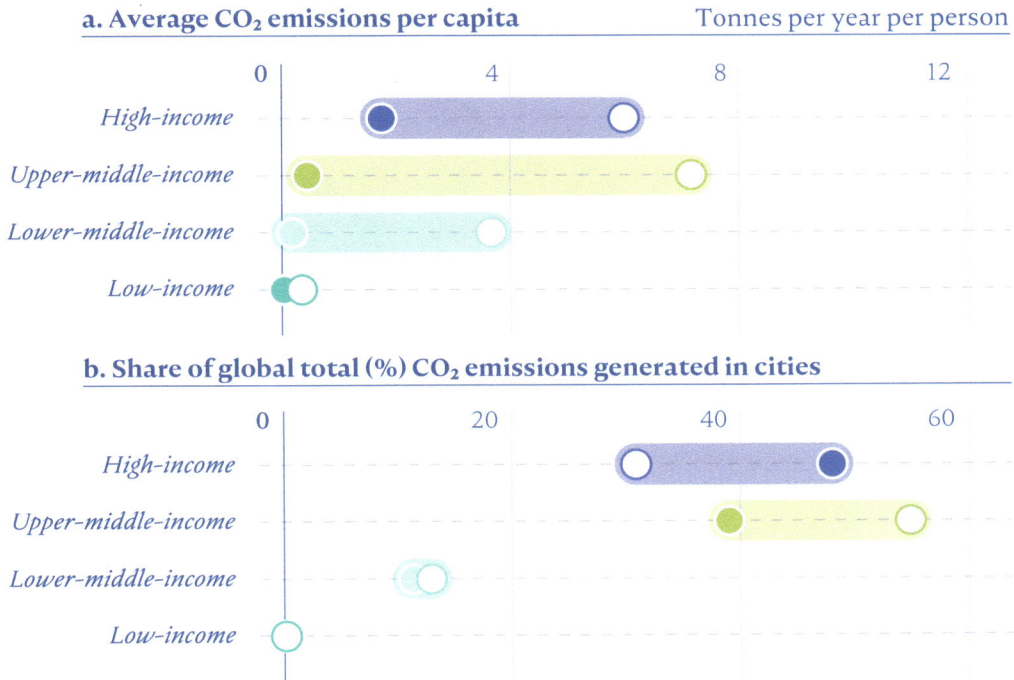

a. Average CO₂ emissions per capita — Tonnes per year per person

b. Share of global total (%) CO₂ emissions generated in cities

Source: World Bank analysis based on data from the European Commission's Global Human Settlement (GHS) Urban Centre Database R2019 (https://ghsl.jrc.ec.europa.eu/ghs_stat_ucdb2015mt_r2019a.php), which derives its carbon dioxide (CO$_2$) emissions data from the European Commission's Emissions Database for Global Atmospheric Research (EDGAR v5.0). For the residential and transportation sectors, the data cover 10,179 cities. For all sources of emissions, the data cover 3,148 cities.

Note: In panel a, each marker shows the unweighted average of long-cycle (fossil) CO$_2$ emissions per capita (measured in tonnes per year per person) of cities by country income group. In panel b, each marker shows the share of global urban long-cycle (fossil) CO$_2$ emissions generated in cities classified by country income group.

Figure 0.2 **Global GHG emissions will remain above the level required to limit global warming to 1.5°C if low- and lower-middle-income countries continue to follow their current policies**

Historical and projected aggregate GHG emissions trajectories under different scenarios, by country income group, 1990–2050

a. If all countries transition to net zero by 2050

b. If low- and lower-middle-income countries continue with current policies while the rest transition to net zero by 2050

GHG emissions (Mt CO₂e, thousands)

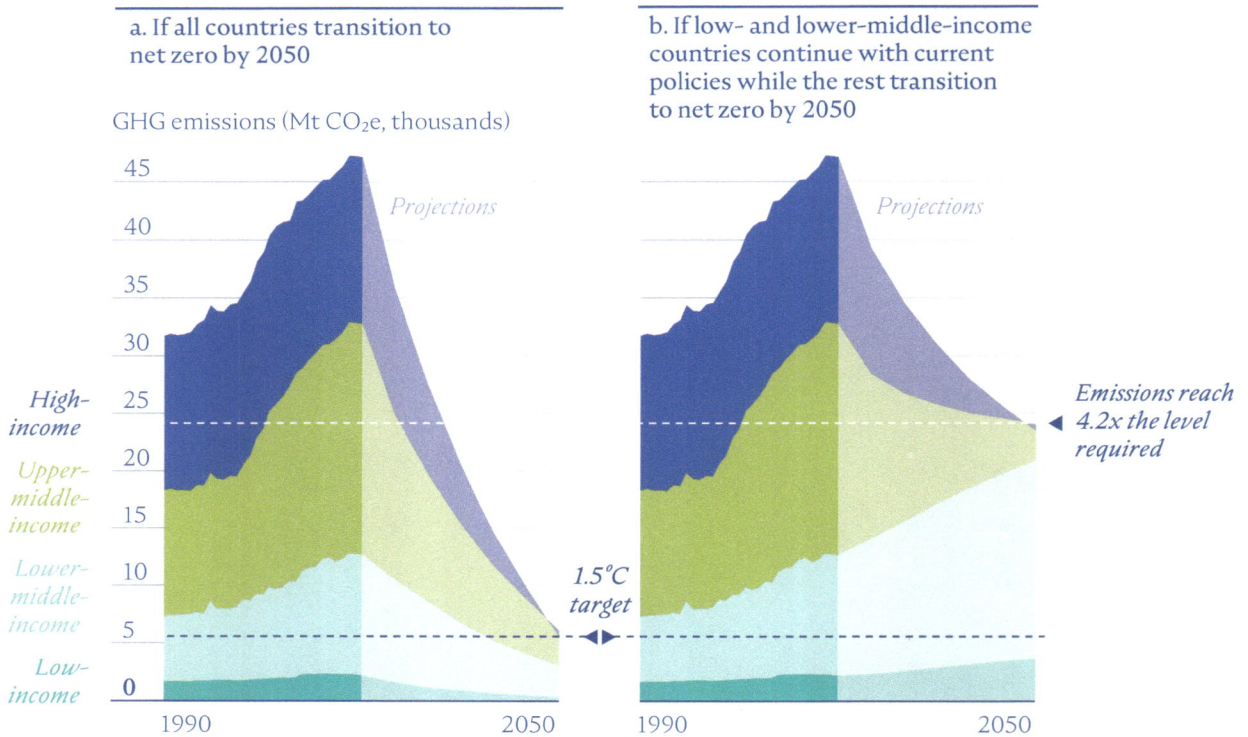

Source: World Bank analysis based on historical emissions data from Climate Watch (2022) and emissions projections from the Network of Central Banks and Supervisors for Greening the Financial System (NGFS) v. 2 scenarios data.

Note: GHG = greenhouse gas; Mt CO₂e = metric tons of carbon dioxide equivalent.

KEY FINDING 2

Cities in low- and lower-middle-income countries face the highest levels of projected climate change–related hazards.

Looking forward, although few cities globally will escape the effects of climate change, cities in low- and lower-middle-income countries face the highest overall levels of projected climate change–related hazards. Evidence of this situation is provided by an indicator that combines information on six key hazards—floods, heat stress, tropical cyclones, sea-level rise, water stress, and wildfires—projected forward to 2030–40.[14] Thus, among the nine types of city identified by this report's global typology (box O.1), large, medium, and small cities in low- and lower-middle-income countries have the highest average climate hazard exposure scores (figure O.3). For medium and large cities, these high average scores are driven mainly by projected flood hazards. For small and medium cities, they are driven by projected water, sea-level rise, and heat stress hazards. Wildfires also contribute to higher projected climate hazard scores for all sizes of city in low- and lower-middle-income countries.

Figure O.3   Projected climate change–related hazards are strongest for cities in low- and lower-middle-income countries

Average weighted overall climate change–related hazard exposure, by city size and country income group

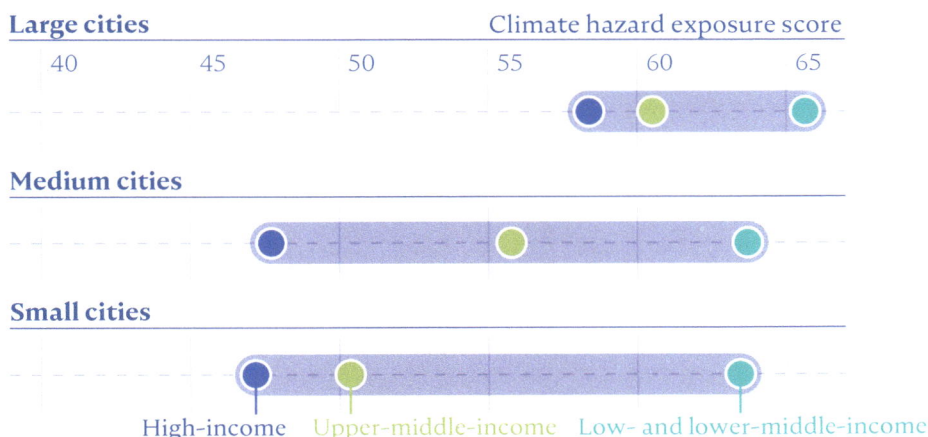

Source: World Bank analysis based on data from Moody's ESG Solutions, Sub-Sovereign Physical Climate Risk Scores, October 2021 (https://esg.moodys.io/climate-solutions).

Note: The figure reports the mean projected climate hazard exposure scores for cities that belong to a given type. The mean scores are estimated by regressing a city's score on a series of dummy variables for the different types of city. Small, medium, and large cities are those that in 2015 had a population of 50,000–199,999; 200,000–1.4999 million; and 1.5 million or more, respectively.

KEY FINDING 3

Cities in low- and lower-middle-income countries are less resilient to increasingly frequent climate change–related shocks and stresses.

Historically, cities have, with a few exceptions, exhibited remarkable long-run resilience[15] to many forms of physical, and even human capital, destruction. Their resilience includes that to events such as earthquakes, widespread flooding, major fires, pandemics, and even large-scale, including nuclear, bombing (Glaeser 2022).

Notwithstanding this impressive long-run resilience, however, it is estimated that cities in low- and lower-middle-income countries suffer larger negative impacts from extreme hot, dry, and wet weather events (or "anomalies"), as well as from tropical cyclones, on their local levels of economic activity than do cities in higher-income countries.[16] This disparity comes at a time when climate change is increasing both the frequency and intensity of extreme hot, dry, and wet events.[17] Thus, although extreme weather events have relatively little impact on the levels of economic activity of cities in high- and upper-middle-income countries (as proxied by their nighttime light intensities) in the months when those events occur, they have much larger negative impacts on cities in low- and lower-middle-income countries (figure O.4).[18]

Estimates also suggest that—for cities in low- and lower-middle-income countries—hot, wet, and dry weather anomalies have more severe negative impacts on economic activity when they mirror a city's baseline climate. Thus, hot, wet, and dry anomalies have larger negative impacts on cities with hot, wet, and dry baseline climates, respectively (figure O.5). This effect is most evident for dry anomalies in cities in low- and lower-middle-income countries with dry baseline climates. Such cities are particularly prevalent in the Middle East and North Africa and parts of Sub-Saharan Africa.

The increasing frequency of extreme dry events contributes to the growing number of cities globally experiencing near "day zero" events, whereby water supplies are only weeks or days from running out. In a worst-case scenario, estimates suggest that a warming world could make day zero–type droughts 100 times more likely than they were in the early twentieth century in certain regions (Pascale et al. 2020). Such dwindling water supplies can cost a city up to a 12-percentage-point loss in gross domestic product and lead to damaging competition between urban and rural areas for water supplies as cities encroach on surrounding areas to satisfy their thirst. In the absence of equitable legal arrangements, transfers of water from rural to urban areas can even be coercive, such as in Chennai, India (Singh et al. 2021; Varadhan 2019; Zaveri et al. 2021). In allocation decisions, most legal systems give higher priority to drinking water, and often to industrial water, than to agricultural water. Such prioritization can reduce the water available for irrigated urban and peri-urban agriculture (Hoekstra, Buurman, and van Ginkel 2018).

The fact that, in general, cities in low- and lower-middle-income countries experience more severe estimated negative impacts of weather anomalies than do cities in higher-income

Figure O.4   **Cities in low- and lower-middle-income countries are less resilient to climate change–related shocks and stresses**

Estimated impact of extreme weather (hot, dry, wet, and tropical cyclone) events on a city's level of nighttime light intensity, April 2012–December 2020

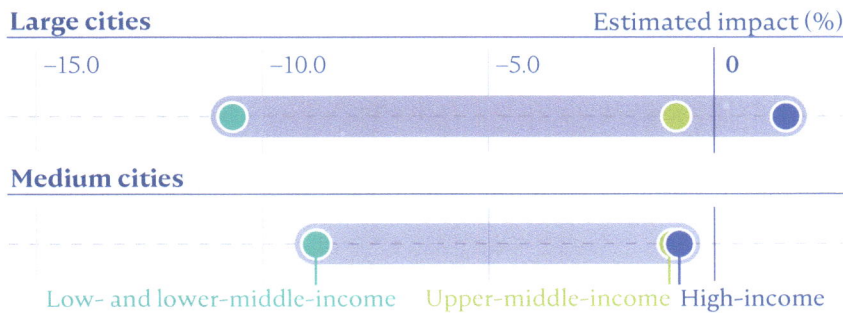

Source: Derived from Park and Roberts 2023. Results are based on analysis of monthly composites of nighttime lights derived from Visible Infrared Imaging Radiometer Suite (VIIRS) satellite data (https://payneinstitute.mines.edu/eog-2/viirs/), monthly weather data from Climatology Lab, TerraClimate (https://www.climatologylab.org/terraclimate.html), and tropical cyclone data from International Best Track Archive for Climate Stewardship (https://www.ncdc.noaa.gov/ibtracs/).

Note: The horizontal axis shows the unweighted average estimated impact of extreme hot, dry, and wet weather events and tropical cyclones on a city's nighttime light in the month when the event occurred. For any given month, an extreme hot, dry, or wet event is defined as one in which the weather variable (temperature or precipitation) deviates by at least 2 standard deviations from a city's own long-run historical average for that variable, with that average calculated using monthly data for the period January 1958–March 2012. A tropical cyclone is defined as a category 2 or stronger cyclone based on the Saffir-Simpson wind scale that occurs within 200 kilometers of a city's geographic center. Medium and large cities correspond to those that in 2015 had a population of 200,000–1.4999 million and 1.5 million or more, respectively. The colors of the markers for different types of cities correspond to the colors in map BO.1.1.

countries is consistent with a greater level of resilience on the part of the latter. These estimates paint a partial picture of resilience, however, because they consider only the immediate impacts of a weather shock while disregarding the subsequent path of recovery of economic activity, or the lack thereof. Nevertheless, related research that also uses lights data suggests a quicker rebound of economic activity for a city in an upper-middle- or high-income country in response to a flood event than for a city in a low- or lower-middle-income country. Thus, although economic activity is restored to its preshock level in a city in higher-income countries within one month, restoration in a city in a lower-income country will take two months (Gandhi et al. 2022; Lall et al., forthcoming).

Figure 0.5 **For cities in lower-income countries, dry, hot, and wet weather anomalies have larger negative impacts when they reinforce baseline climatic conditions**

Estimated impacts of dry, hot, wet, and cold anomalies on cities in low- and lower-middle-income countries with dry, hot, wet, and cold baseline climates, respectively, April 2012–December 2020

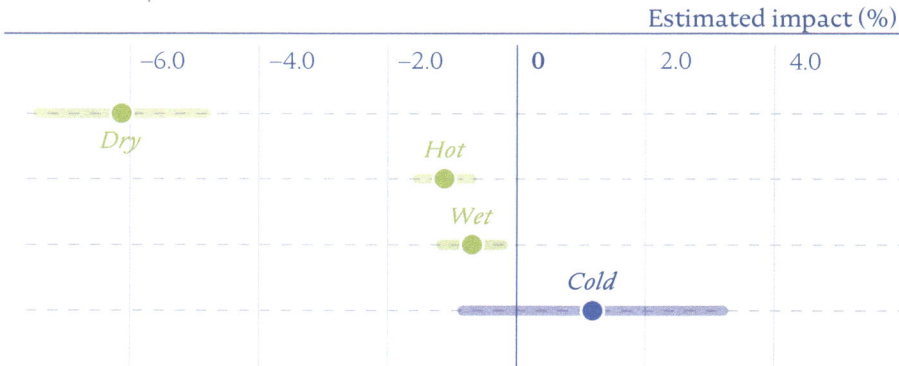

Source: Derived from Park and Roberts 2023. Results are based on the analysis of nighttime lights monthly composites derived from Visible Infrared Imaging Radiometer Suite (VIIRS) satellite data (https://payneinstitute.mines.edu/eog-2/viirs/) and monthly weather data from Climatology Lab, TerraClimate (https://www.climatologylab.org/terraclimate.html).

Note: Each marker shows the estimated impact on a city's nighttime light intensity of a 1-standard-deviation departure of the relevant weather variable (either temperature or precipitation) from a city's own monthly long-run average for that weather variable, with that average defined using monthly data for the period January 1958–March 2012. The horizontal lines indicate the upper and lower bounds of the 95 percent confidence interval associated with the corresponding estimated impact. Hot and wet cities are in the top half of the global distribution of the long-run mean monthly temperature and precipitation, respectively, and cold and dry cities are in the bottom half.

KEY FINDING 4

Construction in countries is gravitating toward cities that will be most affected by climate change.

In the face of intensifying climate change–related hazards, one might expect that construction in countries would move away from cities whose climatic conditions are projected to deteriorate (that is, "future bad locations") and toward cities whose climate will be less affected or may even improve. Since the 1960s, however, the opposite has occurred. Construction in countries has increasingly gravitated toward cities projected to become unbearably hot because of climate change.

Evidence of this finding appears in figure O.6, which, for any given year, shows the estimated effect of a future bad location index on the aggregated height of a city's buildings. Higher values of this index indicate that a city's average maximum temperature during its hottest season is projected to pass a threshold of 43°C sooner—for example, an index value of 0 indicates that a city is not projected to pass this threshold during the current century, whereas an index value of 5 (the maximum value) indicates that the city passed this threshold during the period 1995–2014. If construction were moving away from future bad locations, one would expect this index to have an increasingly negative impact on the aggregated height of a city's buildings as the reality of the transition to unbearably hot temperatures becomes more evident. Figure O.6 shows instead an increasingly positive impact of the future bad location index on the aggregated height of a city's buildings. Moreover, this trend is evident for buildings of all heights, from 55 meters (roughly 15 stories) or higher to 195 meters or higher, which includes the world's tallest skyscrapers. It is also evident for built-up area, which includes low-rise urban development more generally (Desmet and Jedwab 2022).

The trend of rising construction in cities deemed "future bad locations" (even as that future approaches) is emerging despite increasing public awareness of climate change and its potential impacts. Consistent with this finding, the major international conferences have had no discernible impact on construction trends. Such conferences include the 1985 Villach conference[19] and Conference of the Parties sessions held in Doha in 2012 (COP 18) and Paris in 2015 (COP 21), which increased global awareness of the threat posed by climate change. Adoption of the Kyoto Protocol in 1997 had no effect either. Moreover, not only has construction in countries been moving toward cities that are future bad locations, but also over the period 1985–2015 the global growth of urban built-up area in high-risk flood zones has outpaced that in low-risk flood zones. This trend has been most evident in middle-income countries, especially upper-middle-income countries (Rentschler et al. 2022).

These trends suggest a spatial misallocation of investments in buildings, with negative potential impacts on the future health, safety, and welfare of populations. Thus, because buildings, especially tall buildings, are durable structures that depreciate only slowly over decades, these construction patterns risk locking in urban development, and therefore urban populations, in suboptimal locations that will be most affected by climate change.

Figure 0.6 Within countries, construction of tall buildings of all heights is occurring fastest in cities that will be most affected by climate change ("future bad locations")

Estimated effects of "future bad location" index on construction
of buildings above various heights, 1920–2020

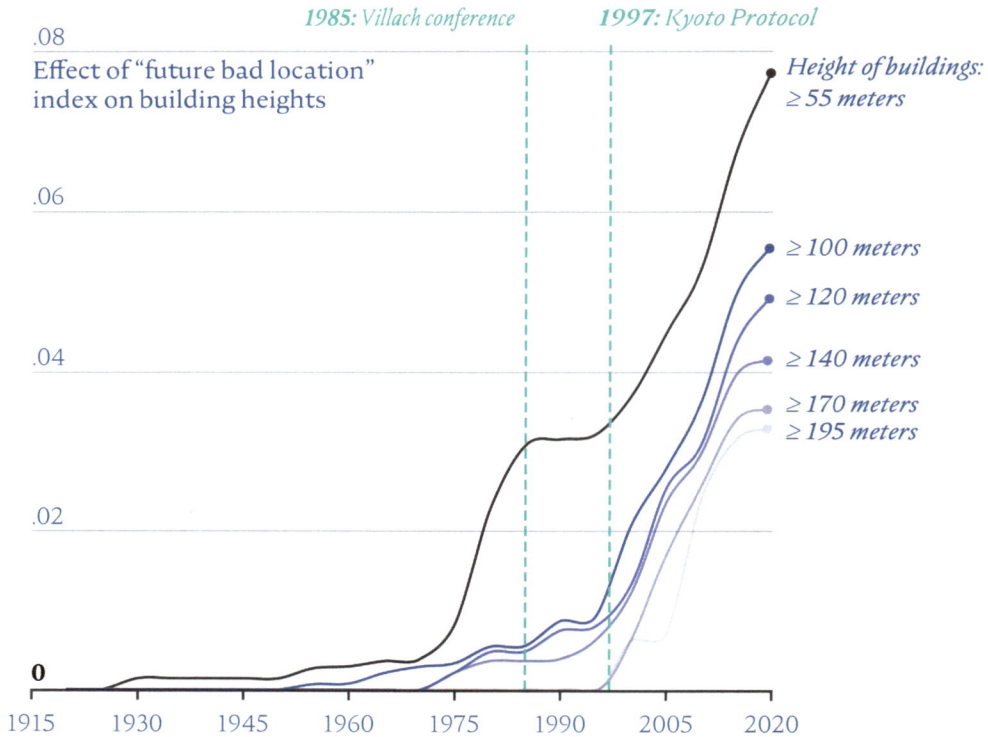

Source: Based on Desmet and Jedwab 2022, which uses data for cities from the European Commission's Global Human Settlement (GHS) Urban Centre Database R2019 (https://ghsl.jrc.ec.europa.eu/ghs_stat _ucdb2015mt_r2019a.php) and on building heights from the Emporis database.

Note: For each year shown on the horizontal axis, the vertical axis shows the estimated impact, relative to the base year of 1915, of a future bad location index on the aggregated height of a city's buildings above a certain specified height level (55 meters, 100 meters, 120 meters, 140 meters, 170 meters, and 195 meters). The future bad location index has a value between 0 and 5, where 0, 1, 2, 3, 4, and 5 indicate that a city is projected to surpass an average maximum temperature of 43°C after 2100, during 2080–99, during 2060–79, during 2040–59, during 2020–39, and during 1995–2014, respectively. A positive estimated impact indicates movement of construction toward cities that are future bad locations. The regression from which impacts are estimated includes both city fixed effects and country-year fixed effects.

KEY FINDING 5

Lack of inclusiveness contributes to the lack of resilience of cities in low- and lower-middle-income countries.

The movement of urban development in countries toward locations facing the greatest climate change–related hazards is particularly worrisome for low- and lower-middle-income countries because their cities lack resilience to the climate change–related shocks and stresses highlighted in key finding 3. This relative lack of resilience can be explained, in part, by these cities' higher rates of poverty and lower levels of access to basic services such as health care and education; water, electricity, and other utilities; solid waste management; digital and financial services; and emergency rescue services.

For example, households in cities in low- and lower-middle-income countries in East Asia and Pacific, Latin America and the Caribbean, South Asia, and Sub-Saharan Africa have lower levels of access to improved sanitation and safely managed drinking water than do households in cities in the upper-middle-income countries in these regions (figure O.7).[20] For improved sanitation, small and medium cities in low- and lower-middle-income countries have particularly low levels of access. More generally within income classes, larger cities tend to provide better access to services and, thus, in this sense at least, to be more inclusive. This finding stems in part from the fact that larger cities can spread over a greater population the fixed costs of the large-scale infrastructure that underpins the provision of such services.

More generally, *inclusion* can be defined as the ability and opportunity of all who reside in a city to fully participate in markets, services (including digital and financial services), and spaces (including political, physical, cultural, and social), thereby enabling them to lead their lives with dignity (box O.2). The ability of its residents to participate in markets, services, and spaces contributes to a city's resilience through a variety of channels. For example, participation in labor markets facilitates income growth, which helps provide households with the resources to invest in self-protection against climate change–related shocks, while also allowing them to accumulate savings that can act as a form of self-insurance against such shocks. Participation in financial markets can similarly assist households in buffering and insuring against shocks. Meanwhile, their ability to participate in political, physical, cultural, and social spaces helps provide a city's residents with voice. This voice can, in turn, lead to policies that are more inclusive of otherwise marginalized groups in society, thereby helping build their resilience.

Figure 0.7   **Access to improved sanitation and safely managed drinking water is worse in cities in** `low- and lower-middle-income` **countries**

Share of households with access to improved sanitation and safely managed drinking water by city type, circa 2015

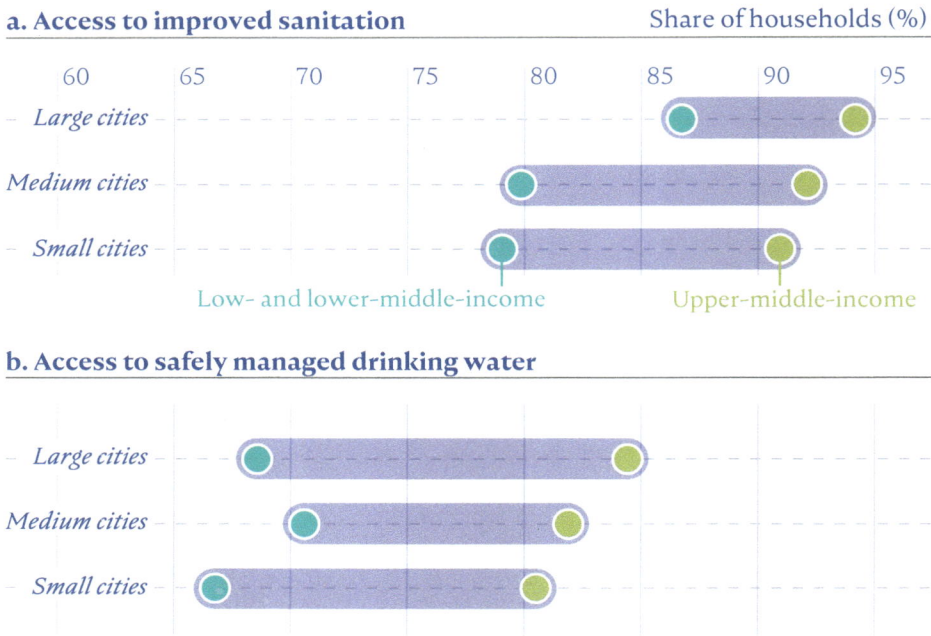

a. Access to improved sanitation   Share of households (%)

b. Access to safely managed drinking water

Source: World Bank calculations using data on household access to improved sanitation and safely managed drinking water from Henderson and Turner (2020) and downloaded from https://doi.org/10.7910/DVN/YZ46FJ.

Note: In both panels, the share of households is calculated for cities in 40 countries (3 in the East Asia and Pacific region, 5 in Latin America and the Caribbean, 3 in South Asia, and 29 in Sub-Saharan Africa). In panel b, safely managed drinking water is defined as all improved water sources that take zero minutes to collect or are on the premises. Improved water sources include all piped water and packaged water, protected wells or springs, boreholes, and rainwater. Small, medium, and large cities correspond to those that in 2015 had a population of 50,000–199,999; 200,000–1.4999 million; and 1.5 million or more, respectively. The colors of the markers for different types of cities correspond to the colors in map BO.1.1.

Box 0.2

How this report defines *inclusiveness*

In this report, inclusiveness is broadly considered in terms of (1) ability and opportunity and (2) outcomes. Inclusion is defined as the ability and opportunity of all who reside in a city to fully participate in markets, services, and spaces (including political, physical, cultural, and social), thereby enabling them to lead their lives with dignity (World Bank 2013). Consistent with that definition, this report variously discusses how cities differ globally in the access they provide to basic urban services, financial services, digital technologies, and labor market opportunities. It also shines a spotlight on multidimensional exclusion and touches on issues of voice.

As for outcomes, this report analyzes, among other things, how cities vary globally in terms of both their rates of poverty and their levels of income inequality; the levels of socioeconomic mobility they afford their residents, especially new migrants; gender-differentiated patterns of population displacement following climate-related natural disasters; and the differential impacts of exposure to extreme heat on segments of a city's workforce, including informal versus formal, female versus male, and older versus younger workers.

Despite this broad coverage, however, the report is silent on some important dimensions of inclusion. For example, because of the lack of adequate data, it does not discuss the impacts of climate change on city residents who live with disabilities or who belong to a racial or ethnic minority.

KEY FINDING 6

Cities in low- and middle-income-countries are less green in terms of air pollution, and air pollution from key urban sectors presents a greater challenge for larger cities in countries at all income levels

On average, concentrations of particulate matter of 2.5 microns or less in diameter ($PM_{2.5}$) in both 2000 and 2015 were lower in cities in high-income countries than in cities in lower-income countries. A city's average $PM_{2.5}$ concentration also tends to first increase and then decrease with its level of development, with air pollution at its worst for cities in lower-middle-income countries (figure O.8).[21] Meanwhile, evidence from regression analysis indicates that, controlling for the level of development of the country in which a city is located and for other determinants of pollution, a city's level of $PM_{2.5}$ emissions in its residential and transportation sectors tends to increase with its population. In other words, in the sectors that urban planning and policies can most directly influence, larger cities have higher emissions. This finding is consistent with higher levels of traffic congestion emanating from stronger urban stresses in larger cities.

Figure O.8 **Cities in low- and middle-income countries have worse air pollution than cities in high-income countries**

Average of $PM_{2.5}$ concentrations across cities, by country income group, 2000 and 2015

Average concentration of $PM_{2.5}$ (μg/m³)

2000 | 2015

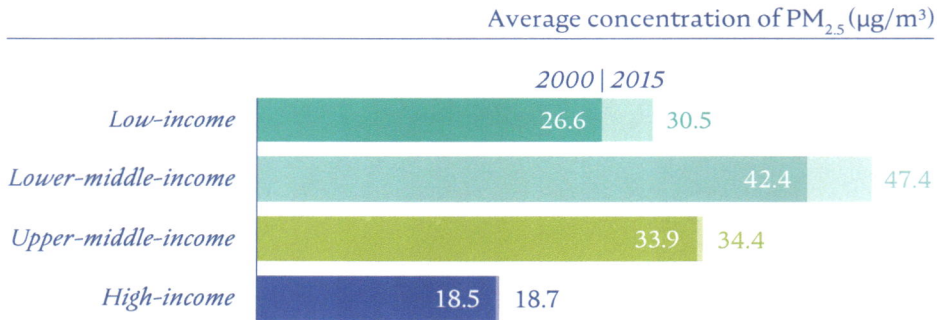

Low-income: 26.6 | 30.5
Lower-middle-income: 42.4 | 47.4
Upper-middle-income: 33.9 | 34.4
High-income: 18.5 | 18.7

Source: World Bank analysis based on data for 10,303 cities from the European Commission's Global Human Settlement (GHS) Urban Centre Database R2019 (https://ghsl.jrc.ec.europa.eu/ghs_stat_ucdb2015mt_r2019a.php), which derives its data on $PM_{2.5}$ concentrations from the Global Burden of Disease (GBD) 2017 database on ambient air pollution.

Note: The graph shows the weighted average $PM_{2.5}$ concentration for cities in each income classification, with weights given by city populations. μg/m³ = micrograms per cubic meter; $PM_{2.5}$ = particulate matter of 2.5 microns or less in diameter.

KEY FINDING 7

Policies that improve air quality can help cities both mitigate and adapt to climate change

Many of the activities that contribute to poor air quality in cities, including both industrial activities and driving internal combustion engine vehicles, also contribute to global climate change. The reason: emissions of local air pollutants such as $PM_{2.5}$ tend to accompany CO_2 emissions, as illustrated in figure O.9 for the residential and transportation sectors. Moreover, black carbon, a short-lived climate pollutant, constitutes a major part of $PM_{2.5}$. However, whereas local air pollution is, at least partially, a local negative externality of activities in a city, climate change is a global externality. As a result, a city's local policy makers have a greater incentive to address local air pollution—a problem they find more fixable—than to address global climate change, which requires collective action across cities globally. This is especially the case for cities in low-income countries, whose current collective contribution to global urban CO_2 emissions is negligible (figure O.1, panel b). As a result, at the local level cities may find the most politically effective approach to the mitigation of global climate change to be policies that aim to improve local air quality, but that carry climate change co-benefits.

Figure O.9   **$PM_{2.5}$ and CO_2 emissions are strongly positively correlated across cities globally**

Relationship between CO_2 and $PM_{2.5}$ emissions across cities globally, residential and transportation sectors, 2015

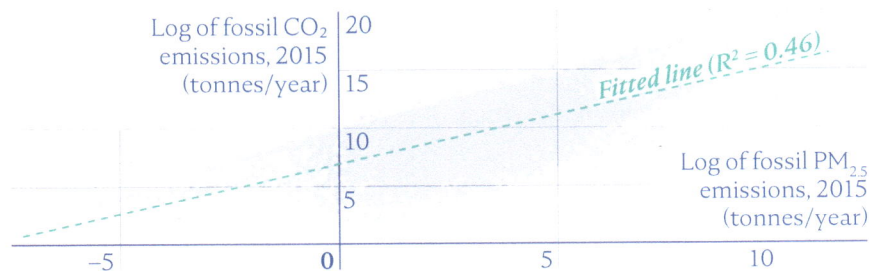

Source: World Bank analysis based on data for 10,303 cities from the European Commission's Global Human Settlement (GHS) Urban Centre Database R2019 (https://ghsl.jrc.ec.europa.eu/ghs _stat_ucdb2015mt_r2019a.php), which derives its data on $PM_{2.5}$ concentrations from the Global Burden of Disease (GBD) 2017 database on ambient air pollution.

Note: The graph is a scatterplot of the log of the sum of residential and transportation long-cycle CO_2 emissions in 2015 on the log of the sum of residential and transportation $PM_{2.5}$ emissions in the same year. CO_2 = carbon dioxide; $PM_{2.5}$ = particulate matter of 2.5 microns or less in diameter.

Less sprawling development is associated with lower CO_2 and $PM_{2.5}$ emissions from the residential and transportation sectors.

One particularly promising set of local policies for improving local air quality with significant climate change co-benefits comprises those that address urban sprawl and promote more compact urban development. Across this report's global sample of cities, the compactness of a city's development has a strong negative correlation with its levels of both $PM_{2.5}$ and CO_2 emissions from the transportation and residential sectors. Figure O.10 illustrates these negative associations for both the residential and the transportation sectors for $PM_{2.5}$ emissions and for the transportation sector only for CO_2 emissions. For both $PM_{2.5}$ and CO_2 emissions, more compact development is associated with lower emissions (comparing cities within countries at a given level of development and holding both a city's population and its built-up area constant). An important benefit of more compact development is that it tends to be associated with less driving and more transit-oriented development, both of which contribute to lower transportation sector emissions of local air pollutants and CO_2.

In this context, it is also important not to confound compact urban development with *overcrowded* urban development. Although both types of development involve high densities of population per square kilometer of built-up area, compact urban development involves accommodating this high density through more vertical development (that is, the construction of taller buildings). It thereby preserves, or even increases, the amount of living space per person. By contrast, overcrowded development involves the proliferation of slums and ever tighter living spaces that can contribute to, among other things, the faster spread of COVID-19 and other infectious diseases, not to mention less inclusive, and therefore less resilient, cities.

Local policies that improve local air quality can not only help mitigate climate change but also contribute to a city's adaptation to climate change. Better air quality generates significant health and productivity benefits (Kahn and Li 2020). These benefits, in turn, contribute to income growth, which helps make cities more resilient to climate change–related shocks and stresses.

Figure 0.10 **More compact development is associated with lower emissions from the residential and transportation sectors**

Relationship between city compactness and $PM_{2.5}$ and CO_2 emissions across cities globally, 2015

a. $PM_{2.5}$: estimated effect of various city characteristics on emissions

b. CO_2: transportation sector

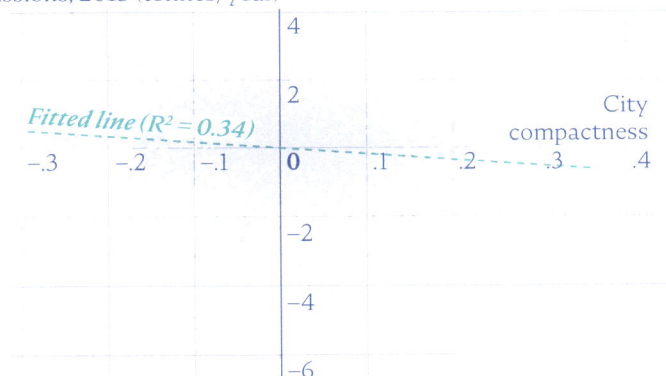

Source: World Bank analysis based on data for 2,785 cities with a 2015 population of over 200,000 from the European Commission's Global Human Settlement (GHS) Urban Centre Database R2019 (https://ghsl.jrc.ec.europa.eu/ghs_stat_ucdb2015mt_r2019a.php), which derives its emissions data from the European Commission's Emissions Database for Global Atmospheric Research (EDGAR v5.0).

Note: Panel a shows for each sector the estimated coefficients, together with the associated 95 percent confidence intervals, from a regression of a city's log $PM_{2.5}$ emissions in 2015 on the log of its population, the log of the GDP per capita of the country in which the city is located, the log of its built-up area, and a measure of the city's compactness (the Polsby-Popper Ratio compactness index). The regression also controls for a city's climate (precipitation, temperature, biome) and elevation, and it includes both a dummy variable that is equal to 1 if a city is in a high-income country (and to 0 otherwise) and its interaction with a country's log level of GDP per capita (results not shown). Panel b shows a partial scatterplot of log CO_2 emissions in 2015 on a measure of city compactness (the Polsby-Popper Ratio) controlling for the log of a city's population, the log of its built-up area, a city's climate (precipitation, temperature, biome) and elevation, and country fixed effects. CO_2 = carbon dioxide; GDP = gross domestic product; $PM_{2.5}$ = particulate matter of 2.5 microns or less in diameter.

🔍 **KEY FINDING 9** ──────────────────────────────────

Cities that develop vertically consume less land, accommodate more people, and are more prosperous.

Compact cities develop vertically, as well as through infill development, rather than horizontally. But, theoretically at least, more upward growth through increased mid- and high-rise development, as opposed to low-rise, does not necessarily lead to less outward growth of a city. By increasing the supply of available floor space, more vertical development makes housing and commercial space within a city more affordable. Affordability, in turn, helps attracts more people to a city, thereby boosting its population. If it has a sufficiently large inflow of population, a city may expand horizontally in response to its original vertical expansion. In practice, however, empirical analysis of data on building heights for this report's global sample of cities reveals that, although a city's vertical development does indeed lead to population growth, such growth is insufficient to also provoke outward expansion. A city's vertical development leads it to consume less land overall than it would otherwise, which, in turn, could preserve fertile agricultural land on a city's periphery—land that for many cities is a "leading source of nutritionally important fresh fruit and vegetables" (Acharya et al. 2021, xviii). Moreover, the type of density arising from vertical development generates powerful agglomeration economies while avoiding overcrowding, so it is associated with greater economic prosperity. Overall, averaging across estimates that result from the application of different empirical strategies, a doubling of a city's total height leads to a roughly 16 percent long-run increase in its population and a 19 percent long-run reduction in its land area relative to other cities. These results are accompanied by a 4 percent long-run increase in the intensity of the city's nighttime lights per capita, which suggests increased prosperity (figure O.11).

Although at any given level of development more compact cities tend to have lower CO_2 and $PM_{2.5}$ emissions in both the residential and transportation sectors, more vertical development does entail a dynamic trade-off when it comes to the mitigation of climate change. The construction of taller buildings tends to rely on materials such as concrete, steel, and glass, whose production entails high CO_2 emissions (Pomponi et al. 2021). Thus, a tall building constructed using current technologies embeds high up-front CO_2 emissions, which must be weighed against the future flow of lower CO_2 emissions associated with more compact urban development. This factor implies that, to transition to lower long-run emissions trajectories using a strategy of more compact urban development, policy makers in countries where such development is currently limited—because of, for example, dysfunctional land and property markets and failures in planning—may have to tolerate a short-run increase in emissions. Policy makers may, however, be able to soften this dynamic trade-off by combining policies that help facilitate more vertical development with complementary transportation investments and policies that both encourage a move toward less-polluting modes of transportation, including walking and cycling, and further promote compact and livable development. Technological innovations that reduce the carbon embedded in the production of concrete, steel, and glass will likewise soften the trade-off.[22]

Figure 0.11 **Cities that develop vertically accommodate more people, are more prosperous, and consume less land**

Estimated elasticities of population, nighttime light intensity, and land area with respect to total sum of tall building heights

Estimated elasticity with respect to total height of a city's buildings (%)

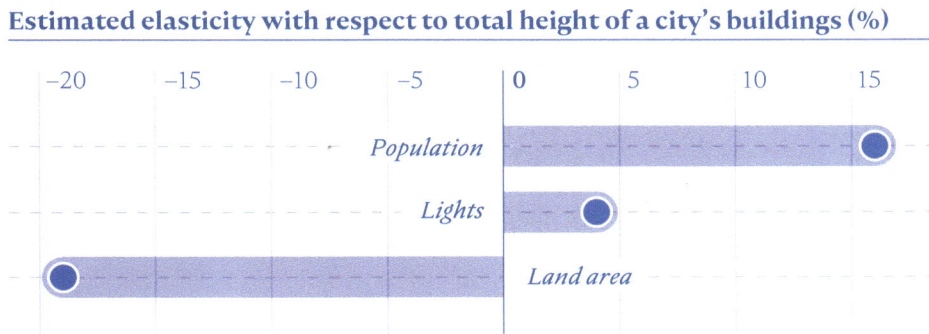

Source: World Bank analysis based on results from Ahlfeldt and Jedwab 2022. Their data for tall buildings come from Emporis.

Note: Figure shows the estimated percentage change in each variable resulting from a doubling of the total sum of tall building heights. For population and land area, these estimates are based on averaging results from across three different econometric (instrumental variable) estimation strategies (for details, see chapter 4 and Ahlfeldt and Jedwab 2022). For lights, the estimate is based on the application of an ordinary least squares estimation strategy, in which "lights" refers to the intensity of nighttime lights per capita within a city's extent. Nighttime light intensity is measured using radiance calibrated data derived from Defense Meteorological Satellite Program satellite sensors.

KEY FINDING 10

Lack of vegetation, especially evident in large cities and cities in upper-middle-income countries, and poor urban design can exacerbate the impacts of extreme heat events in cities.

Although discussion of a city's vertical development conjures up images of concrete and steel, few people wish to live in a concrete jungle. Indeed, defining characteristics of many of the world's most well-known and successful cities—think of Singapore with its lush vegetation or London with its majestic parks—include not only the height of their skylines but also their extensive urban greenery. The greenery in cities—that is, the trees and other vegetation in parks and elsewhere—comes with important benefits for a city's residents. Not only does greenery have an inherent amenity, but its presence can also play an important role in mitigating the urban heat island effect. This effect can lead to urban land surface temperatures that are more than 10°C higher than the equivalent rural land surface temperatures (Deuskar 2022).

The demand for land that comes with the growth of urban population can place development pressure on green spaces in a city, further exacerbating the impacts of extreme heat events, which are becoming both more frequent and more intense with climate change. Cities in upper-middle-income countries are noticeably less green, on average, than cities in low-, lower-middle-, and high-income countries. At the same time, within any income class, larger cities tend, on average, to be less green than smaller cities (figure O.12).

Lack of vegetation is not the only culprit behind the urban heat island effect. The depth of street canyons—that is, the ratio of the height of buildings along a street to the width of the street—can affect air temperatures through its impact on shade and ventilation. The orientation of streets also affects both shade and ventilation. Streets with an east-west orientation receive more prolonged exposure to the sun than do those with other orientations and thus experience more heat, especially in cities close to the equator (Lai et al. 2019). Heat from motorized vehicles and the widespread and excessive use of air-conditioning are additional factors contributing to the urban heat island effect.

Figure 0.12 **Average levels of vegetation are lowest for cities in upper-middle-income countries**

Average levels of greenness, by city type, 2014

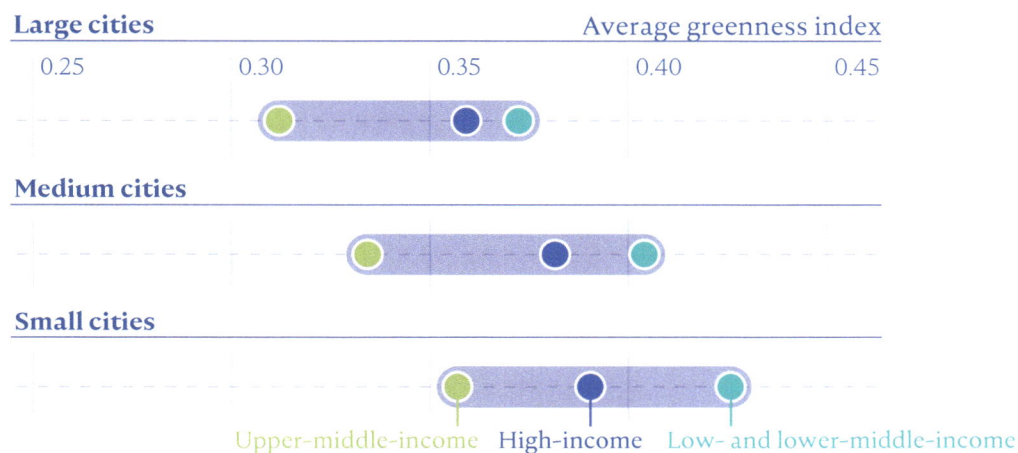

Large cities   Average greenness index

| 0.25 | 0.30 | 0.35 | 0.40 | 0.45 |

Medium cities

Small cities

Upper-middle-income   High-income   Low- and lower-middle-income

Source: World Bank analysis using data from the European Commission's Global Human Settlement (GHS) Urban Centre Database R2019 (https://ghsl.jrc.ec.europa.eu/ghs_stat_ucdb2015mt_r2019a.php).

Note: A city's average greenness is measured by the average greenness of the pixels in satellite imagery that fall within its urban extent. For each city type, the marker shows the unweighted average of the greenness index across cities of that type. The colors of the markers for different types of cities correspond to the colors in map BO.1.1.

The impacts of climate change on cities

Climate change–related shocks and stresses can affect the greenness, resilience, and inclusiveness of cities through a wide array of direct and indirect channels. Moreover, these shocks often do not occur in isolation and can be compounded by underlying urban challenges that arise from the pressure of growing urban populations on urban infrastructure, the supplies of basic services, land and housing, and the environment. Climate hazards can also cascade into cities from surrounding rural areas, as well as from areas on which a city might depend for its water supply. Inequalities within cities, which, especially for many cities in low- and lower-middle income countries, are already large, may be further exacerbated by climate change–related shocks and stresses. And while cities have traditionally been thought of as providing escalators out of poverty (Glaeser 2012), climate change may slow the speed of these escalators.

Climate hazards can be compounded by underlying urban challenges

The climate change–related shocks and stressors that affect green, resilient, and inclusive development in cities do not occur in isolation but often interact and compound, both with each other and with other urban stressors. Tropical cyclones and extreme heat events are related and often occur simultaneously. Poorly managed urban development pressures that lead to the removal of urban trees and destruction of urban wetlands could compound the effects of heat waves and floods. Losses in agricultural production from heat and drought, compounded both by the excessive loss of fertile agricultural land on the peripheries of cities due to sprawl associated with poorly managed urbanization and by heat-induced reductions in the productivity of workers, could affect the food supply. Risks can spill over across populations, places, and sectors, leading to cascading impacts. Rural migrants fleeing drought events can settle in precarious informal settlements in urban floodplains, with cascading risks for some groups of people and locations. Wildfires in agricultural regions can increase urban air pollution while also disrupting the supply, and thus prices, of essential food products. The general interdependence within cities of critical infrastructure, such as transportation systems and power grids, means that failure of one element or node could result in a cascade of adverse events. Thus, storm surges and extreme heat could lead to power outages. Other underlying stresses within cities—not necessarily related to climate change—can also exacerbate its effects. For example, high rates of informal dumping of waste worsen pluvial floods because of the accumulation of refuse in drains, waterways, and open spaces. According to the Intergovernmental Panel on Climate Change, multiple climate hazards will continue to occur simultaneously, thereby compounding overall risk and causing risks to cascade across sectors and regions (IPCC 2022).

Nevertheless, as highlighted in key finding 4, construction patterns show little sign of responding to the growing threats. This situation could result, in part, from public policy that encourages settlement in more hazard-prone areas. For example, in the United States, subsidized flood insurance and relief aid may have increased people's willingness to live in disaster-prone areas (Deryugina 2014; Gregory 2017). Likewise, free federal fire protection may have increased construction in areas with high fire risk (Baylis and Boomhower 2019).

Climate hazards can also cascade into cities

Climate change–related shocks in rural areas also indirectly affect cities. When extreme weather events hit, people in the countryside often seek safe harbor in cities. In background research for this report, Chlouba, Mukim, and Zaveri (2022) show that periods of extended drought in the rural hinterlands of cities result in faster growth of the urban built-up area, presumably because of push migration. The relationship between drought and growth of urban built-up areas is particularly pronounced in low- and middle-income-countries, which suggests that climate change may be one of the factors behind the rapid urbanization of many of these countries (figure O.13). Such climate-induced migration affects not just the pace of urban built-up expansion but also the nature of that expansion. Drought-driven urban expansion often takes the form of expanding informal settlements, where service delivery remains a challenge. When climate migrants arrive in urban areas, they often cluster in peripheral informal settlements. These settlements offer limited job opportunities, lack basic infrastructure, and have service delivery systems that remain in their infancy. Because the settlements are informal, settlers face the risk of eviction and forced relocation, creating secondary displacement because they no longer have the option to return to climate-decimated rural areas. Thus, climate-induced displacement can undermine the inclusiveness of urban development, leaving some of the most vulnerable members of society on the outskirts, both figuratively and literally.

Figure O.13 **Drought is associated with faster built-up area growth in low- and middle-income countries**

Heterogeneous impacts of droughts on built-up area across a global sample of cities, by country income group, 1985–2014

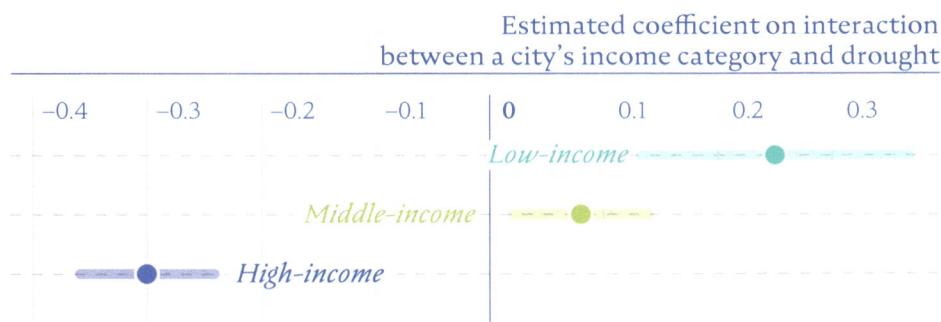

Estimated coefficient on interaction between a city's income category and drought

Source: Chlouba, Mukim, and Zaveri 2022.

Note: The circles represent the point estimates of coefficients of interactions between country income group and a spatially and temporally lagged grid cell measure of drought. The solid lines running through the circles indicate the lower and upper bounds of the 95 percent confidence intervals of the estimated coefficients.

Nevertheless, such urban expansion can also come with opportunities. Rapid urban population growth induced by climate change can strain cities by putting pressure on land, housing, infrastructure, and service delivery; but it can also fuel urban economies by providing a steady flow of new laborers to growing sectors such as manufacturing, construction, hotels and restaurants, and transportation. Urban environments also hold the potential to break down traditional gender barriers by bringing women into professions previously reserved for their male counterparts (World Bank 2021b). Although most people displaced or migrating because of climate impacts stay within their countries of origin, the accelerating trend of global displacement can increase cross-border movements as well, particularly where climate change interacts with conflict and violence.[23]

Water stresses also affect cities—even from afar. Cities have always relied on water imported from other, sometimes distant, areas. From the time of ancient Rome to Los Angeles in the early twentieth century to contemporary initiatives from Mexico City to Kathmandu, Nepal, water imports have offered a path to urban water security. But the scale and intensity of these water transfers have undergone rapid changes. Nowadays, cities often rely on dozens of water sources hundreds of kilometers away. Thus, a faraway drought may profoundly affect a city. In addition to creating water supply problems for cities, climate-related shocks and stressors affect rural food-producing areas. In their background paper prepared for this report, Venkat, Dizon, and Masters (2022) demonstrate that impacts spill over to cities via higher urban food prices. These impacts vary significantly by the types of shocks and stressors and by the type of food (such as more nutrient-dense perishables versus calorie-dense nonperishables). Better transportation networks help mitigate the impact of shocks and stressors,[24] allowing potentially more resilient food supply chains.

Climate change could also exacerbate inequalities

Around the world, urban slums are often found in precarious locations—on steep slopes, on floodable land, or near open drains and sewers. Research conducted for this report by Rossitti (2022) shows that, for a selected sample of 18 cities in South Asia and Sub-Saharan Africa, slums do not necessarily have more exposure to floods or excessive heat. When focusing only on the probability of a high-risk event, however, slums do appear to have relatively higher exposure than formal residential areas to such potentially more destructive events (Rossitti 2022). Location sorting—the tendency of people with similar characteristics to cluster together in certain neighborhoods within cities—can explain the overexposure of the poor in some cities. The choice to live in hazard-prone areas often reflects a difficult trade-off—better access to jobs and services against environmental risks. In such contexts, a lack of affordable housing often prices people out of safer, well-connected locations. It is also possible that poorer households are less able to acquire information on the environmental risks of specific locations, or that these households consist of migrants from rural areas who, as newcomers to a city, do not possess needed information. Indeed, prospective dwellers often do not have accurate information on the risks associated with different locations (Bakkensen and Barrage 2022; Votsis and Perrels 2016). Because poverty involves a series of distractions that reduce productivity as well as the chances to gather information (Banerjee and Mullainathan 2008), poorer, less educated individuals may face higher costs in acquiring hazard-proneness information than their richer counterparts.[25]

The poor may or may not have greater exposure to natural hazards, but they are often the hardest-hit when disaster does strike. In absolute terms, the rich often lose more because their assets are worth more; in relative terms, however, the opposite holds true. Poorer households also suffer disproportionally from the indirect effects of natural hazards through infrastructure disruption, such as being cut off from roads and public transportation, which limits their access to jobs and economic opportunities, and their water supply. Not only do poor urban dwellers suffer higher relative losses from climate change–related shocks, but they also have less ability to engage in adaptation and mitigation. In general, poorer households have less access to financial markets (Erman et al. 2019) and insurance markets. Moreover, they are less likely to benefit from public investments in infrastructure that mitigates the risk of natural hazards. Such investments can translate into higher property prices, thereby pricing the poor out of now-safer areas of a city (Nakagawa, Saito, and Yamaga 2007). Finally, many poor households engage in recurrent self-financed short-term measures (such as temporary structural improvements) that place a large financial burden on them (Patankar 2015).

Climate change–related stresses, such as excessively high temperatures, are also expected to have negative distributional impacts. For one thing, the effects will likely be concentrated in low- and middle-income countries. Cities in lower-income countries often depend more on sectors focused on outdoor work. More important, they have less ability to implement adaptation measures. Adaptation measures such as air-conditioning in the workplace could decouple high temperatures from worker productivity, but such measures can be relatively expensive. Moreover, climate change–related stresses will exacerbate inequality within countries when informal workers, who already have lower income levels, see sharper reductions in those incomes. In their background paper for this report, Jiang and Quintero (2022) evaluate the effects of both high average annual temperatures and number of extremely hot days on the productivity of workers in thousands of cities across eight countries in Latin America and the Caribbean.[26] They find that both significantly reduce worker productivity, as measured by wages. Thus, for example, a doubling of average annual temperature is associated with an estimated 14.1 percent drop in wages.

Cities have traditionally served as escalators out of poverty; however, more frequent climate change–related shocks may slow down these escalators. Urban residents remain vulnerable or chronically poor if deprived of access to economic opportunities, basic services, and amenities. The impacts of climate change–related and environmental shocks exacerbate such failures. For example, as noted earlier, the poor and vulnerable are more likely to suffer disruption from flooding and other climate change–related shocks. Poorer households also have limited financial buffers to cope with shocks. In their background research for this report, Abanokova et al. (2022) estimate the probabilities of exit from poverty for urban residents in five countries—Chile, Colombia, Ecuador, Indonesia, and Peru. Consistent with the hypothesis that cities act as escalators out of poverty, they find that many people have indeed escaped from poverty in urban areas. And that escape is more likely in larger cities. As flood risks rise in large cities, however, the probability of exit from poverty falls. For cities with large populations, households in areas at high risk of flooding have a substantially lower probability of escaping from poverty than do households in low-risk areas.

Policies for making cities greener, more resilient, and more inclusive in a world confronted by climate change

As the preceding sections have made clear, stresses associated with urban growth interact with climate change–related stresses through a variety of channels. In doing so, they act against productivity-enhancing agglomeration economies, adversely affecting the greenness, resilience, and inclusiveness of a city's development pathway (figure O.14).[27] It follows that, to improve development outcomes, policy makers at the national and local levels need to work together to target these inter-related stresses in a way that best addresses a city's specific greenness, resilience, and inclusiveness challenges, where these challenges vary with both a city's size and its level of development. To assist those efforts, this section lays out the general conclusions in three questions that policy makers should consider: What policy instruments are available? Who wields these instruments? How can policy choices be prioritized, sequenced, and financed for effective implementation?

Figure O.14 **A framework for making cities greener, more resilient, and more inclusive**

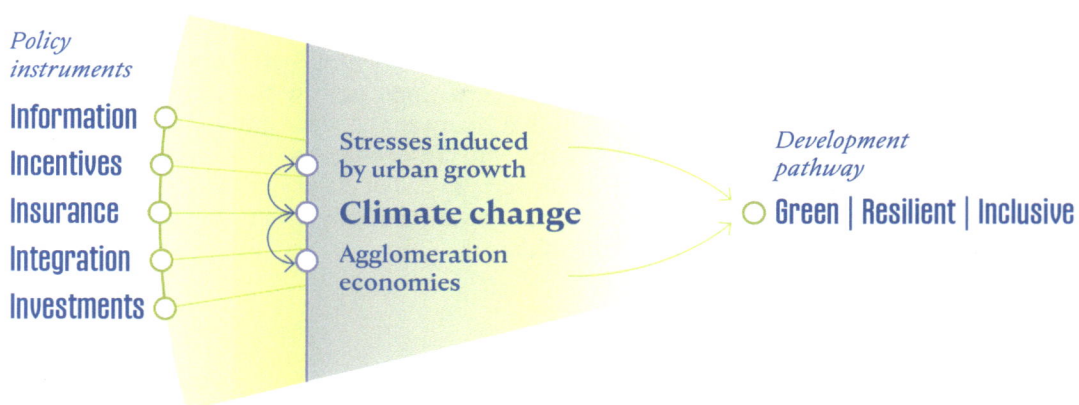

Source: World Bank.

What are the choices?

Policy makers can draw on five broad sets of policy instruments: information, incentives, insurance, integration, and investments—the five I's. Box O.3 summarizes these instruments, and the sections that follow provide more details on each.

Box 0.3

The five I's: Information, incentives, insurance, integration, and investments

This report distinguishes between the following five broad sets of instruments that policy makers can draw on in seeking to improve the greenness, resilience, and inclusiveness of a city's development in a world confronted by climate change.

Information | Policies and measures to improve the timely provision of credible information that helps people, businesses, and local governments better understand climate change–related risks both across and within cities, and, in doing so, helps promote both mitigation and adaptation.

Incentives | Policy instruments that provide incentives for individuals and businesses to internalize negative environmental externalities, as well as institutional and other types of reform that provide government officials with incentives to work better together to address green, resilient, and inclusive development challenges. Incentives also include the removal of fossil fuel subsidies and other incentives that encourage activities with negative environmental externalities.

Insurance | Policies and reforms that help people, businesses, and governments either to insure through the market or to self-insure against losses associated with climate change and other environmental shocks and stresses.

Integration | Policy interventions and reforms that promote more compact cities and better integration of cities both with each other and with rural areas as a means of facilitating adaptation through migration and trade.

Investments | Investments by national and local governments in green, resilient, and inclusive urban infrastructure, including nature-based solutions, as well as measures to promote the crowding-in of private sector finance for such investments.

Information

A necessary precondition for efficient decision-making by households and businesses that maximizes their expected well-being and profits, respectively, is complete and accurate information about all the potential risks they face. In this context, information comprises various policy instruments relating to both imminent threats, such as an impending extreme weather event, and the longer-term evolution of climate change–related hazards. Efforts surrounding information include disaster risk and risk management strategies or participatory initiatives that allow local, regional, and national authorities to convey information on climate change–related risks to urban residents, as well as vice versa.

Despite remarkable progress on the scientific front, some of the most vulnerable communities in climate change–threatened cities remain poorly informed about both looming extreme events that, if not adequately responded to, could spell disaster and slow-moving changes that affect everyday life. Availability of information, however, does not automatically translate into understanding, action, or even acceptance—after all, many people deny, dismiss, or cast unwarranted doubt on the scientific consensus around climate change.[28] Climate adaptation information, such as the results of climate modeling and future weather forecasts, constitutes a public good, providing a strong rationale for government provision or subsidization. The diffusion of information about risks can result in more efficient decisions by both households and businesses on, for example, where to live and invest, potentially countering the trend of construction in "future bad locations" and ensuring that households can accurately evaluate the trade-off between a location's environmental hazards and the access to job opportunities and services it provides. Such diffusion can also provide a city's residents with the information they need to hold their local elected officials accountable for addressing environmental hazards.

Information can take the form of early warning information and monitoring systems. Early warnings can provide huge benefits as a preventive measure, saving lives and, if issued sufficiently in advance, property. The earlier the warning, the more time a city's residents, businesses, and authorities have to prepare, including by protecting property and infrastructure and by positioning and reinforcing assets for protection and response. Often, coupling them with other preventive investments can maximize the benefits of early warning systems.[29] Even modest investments in such systems can have high returns.[30]

Finally, information entails regularly updated urban planning documents, building codes, and zoning regulations that help both guide and coordinate the decisions of households and businesses. It is also useful to think of information in the context of key urban markets—land, real estate, labor, and capital. The price of land is the primary element driving efficient land use in cities and decisions by households, developers, and businesses on how much to invest and on what type of structures in a particular location. A standard economic prescription is to provide transparent information that helps ensure that market prices accurately reflect both risk and supply and demand conditions (in the case of dynamically efficient volumetric water pricing, for example). Such transparency helps ensure that prices send the correct signals to economic agents making location, consumption, and investment decisions. Better information that facilitates the more transparent and efficient working of land markets could also contribute to climate change mitigation efforts with co-benefits in terms of, for example, the preservation of fertile agricultural land by lowering the costs of vertical construction. As research for this report by Ahlfeldt and Jedwab (2022) shows, vertical construction results in a more compact urban form (see also key finding 9).

Incentives

Although the provision of information helps households and businesses factor climate change–related risks into their own decisions, information in and of itself may not be sufficient to motivate them to take into account the impacts of their own decisions on the environment and on others. Cities therefore need incentives to motivate households and businesses to internalize externalities such as pollution. Incentives come in various guises, including pricing policies, such as taxes on dirty fuels,[31] and congestion charging, environmental taxes, charges, and subsidies. These policies can also carry significant climate change co-benefits— for example, congestion pricing reduces vehicle miles traveled and motor vehicle emissions, with a significant positive impact on health in the short term and even larger longer-term effects as a community evolves to a new lower pollution equilibrium level. By contrast, carbon pricing policies (such as emissions trading systems and carbon taxes) tend to occur more at the national level and aim at addressing global externalities.

Incentives can also involve removing or reducing subsidies that, although perhaps well intended when originally introduced, nevertheless have the unintended consequence of inducing overconsumption of goods and services or overinvestment in activities that entail negative environmental externalities. For example, the Arab Republic of Egypt initiated a fuel subsidy removal program aimed at targeting wasteful consumption and balancing the public fiscal burden. This program resulted in targeted fuel price increases in November 2016 and June 2017 that, depending on the fuel category and period, varied between 30 and 80 percent. Heger et al. (2019) estimate that, by reducing traffic below the levels that would have otherwise prevailed, these increases led to a 4 percent reduction in Greater Cairo's concentrations of particulate matter of 10 microns or less in diameter. The reform also gave the country an opportunity to establish a nationally defined social protection floor.

Quota control policies can be effective in reducing polluting activities, but they need to be carefully designed. An analysis of Singapore's vehicle quota control by Song, Feng, and Diao (2020) finds that vehicle quotas substantially limit vehicle ownership and usage. Consumers' desire to maximize their return on investment, however, yields higher usage by existing car owners, partially offsetting the mitigation effects of the quotas. Globally, countries are making pledges and committing to phase out the sale, production, and use of vehicles dependent on fossil fuels. For example, Rwanda is on track to gradually phase out the use of polluting vehicles by 2040, starting with a pilot program in Kigali to convert motorcycles to electric. Ahead of the Republic of Korea's 2030 target, Seoul's plan to phase out diesel vehicles from the public sector and mass transit fleets by 2025 also seeks to push ahead with fleet changeover in the taxi industry with strong subsidies.

As originally pointed out by Nobel economist Kenneth Arrow (1963), addressing a market failure such as inadequate information or negative externalities can often lead to more efficient and equitable market outcomes. This result occurs because such market failures typically affect poorer households more heavily. For example, those who walk to work because they cannot afford either cars or motorbikes also suffer most from the pollution and additional heat generated by the inefficiently high levels of private motor vehicle use in the absence of congestion pricing or, even worse, in the presence of fuel subsidies.

More generally, the design of policy packages that involve incentives must include careful attention to the distribution of burden and favor across economic or social groups. And, when possible, complementary policy measures should be introduced to compensate those who stand to lose. In the case of increased fuel duties or congestion charging, for example, such measures could involve the hypothecation of the revenue raised for investments in public transportation, which London did when it introduced a congestion charge in 2003

(Santos, Button, and Noll 2008). Meanwhile, failure to take into account the distributional impacts of new incentives and, more generally, any policy intended to help address climate change and other environmental issues may result in insurmountable political opposition to the policy. One recent high-profile example of this opposition is the French government's freezing of its carbon pricing policy following the "yellow vest" protest movement of 2018 (Rubin and Sengupta 2018).

Insurance

Insurance aims to minimize the financial impact of disasters through risk sharing and to help secure access to postdisaster financing quickly and efficiently, thereby ensuring rapid, cost-effective resources to finance recovery and reconstruction efforts. Governments can implement policy and regulatory reforms to deepen insurance markets and improve access for businesses and households to complement their adaptation and resilience strategies. Market insurance that reflects disaster risks is often touted, and with good reason, by economists as the first best option to internalize risks and minimize disaster impacts (World Bank 2017). At the same time, market insurance can be difficult to implement, especially in lower-income countries that have lacking or asymmetric information, weak regulation, and limited risk capital. Developing insurance markets in this context may require government interventions beyond simple policy prescriptions and subsidy mechanisms.

Information about hazards, vulnerability, and exposure is essential not only for the sound pricing of insurance but also for other (physical) mitigation actions. Government actions to generate and share such information have broad co-benefits, and those co-benefits should be at the core of adaptation strategies, including efforts to develop market insurance.

Catastrophe risk insurance can have high capital and administrative costs. When it sells specific coverage, an insurance company promises to compensate its client in case of a disaster. It must set aside reserves and buy reinsurance to cover such an eventuality and have systems in place to assess losses and pay claims promptly and in full. Holding financial reserves, buying reinsurance, and processing claims can add substantial cost to that related to the expected loss, particularly when the company must deal with many small claims at once. In addition, uncertainty related to the underlying risk, which is growing for climate-related disasters because of climate change, will be reflected in the insurance premium through uncertainty loading.

What are some ways to reduce the high costs? High deductibles to manage moral hazard and avoid "penny claims" and mechanisms to cover first loss (for example, through government guarantees) can help reduce the cost of insurance. Making insurance compulsory ensures wider distribution of the risk and better risk pooling. Parametric or index-based instruments can help accelerate and reduce the cost of claim processing if the underlying index used to calculate the payout has a high correlation with the actual loss. Such financial engineering can substantially reduce the cost of insurance, particularly for the poorest, who are generally the first affected by a disaster.

Finally, the development of catastrophe insurance markets in lower-income countries has often suffered from a lack of clarity on when and where the government intervenes. Businesses and individuals tend to assume that the government acts as the insurer of last resort and thus do not purchase insurance. Making insurance compulsory, even if doing so requires some subsidies or guarantees to reduce the cost to a minimum, is sometimes more efficient if it helps clarify responsibilities and encourages private actors to cover at least part of their risk.

Integration

Within cities. Between 2022 and 2050, the number of people living in cities globally is projected to grow from 4.53 billion to 6.68 billion.[32] With this growth will come heightened urban demand for housing, basic services, infrastructure, and amenities. This demand could increase pressures on land and real estate markets, resulting in development patterns that further undermine the greenness, resilience, and inclusiveness of cities. Reforms that strengthen formal institutions for titling and property transfer, along with flexible and effective urban planning that is properly coordinated with investments in infrastructure, can ensure that cities are not locked into suboptimal physical forms and investments.

One notable example of such a lock-in is overly sprawling car- and motorcycle-dependent urban development. As shown under key finding 8, such development is associated with higher levels of production-based CO_2 emissions in both the transportation and residential sectors, and with higher $PM_{2.5}$ emissions.[33] According to research prepared for this report by Ahlfeldt and Jedwab (2022), reforms that reduce the costs of vertical development can encourage cities to expand upward rather than outward, while generating economic growth (see also key finding 9). Ahlfeldt and Jedwab (2022) calculate that the welfare potential of tall buildings is highest for the largest cities. In low- and middle-income countries, these cities are precisely the ones hit hardest by the constraints to vertical development posed by dysfunctional land markets and failures.

Beyond sprawl and dependency on cars, further undesirable lock-ins include energy- or water-intensive building technologies and urban settlements located in vulnerable areas (see also key finding 4). Although retrofitting infrastructures and buildings will be essential to greener and more resilient growth, doing so can be costly. Early efforts at integrated planning, however, could help cities—especially smaller but rapidly growing ones in low- and middle-income countries—avoid such retrofitting.

Integration is good for the poor—and good for budgets. The poor may know the hazards they face, but they depend more than the wealthy on public services that are often inadequate. In places without coordinated land use and urban infrastructure and development decisions, households end up disconnected from labor markets and having to trade safety for accessibility. Local governments often struggle to provide essential urban infrastructure; until they succeed in doing so, the poor will remain vulnerable. More secure land and property rights would encourage investment in prevention measures. Equally, the provision of land and affordable housing in safer areas, with accessibility to jobs and essential services, would go a long way toward lowering the risk exposure of poor people. City leaders can underinvest in time spent on long-term planning when dealing with a series of emergencies, because pressing matters crowd out important matters. Through investments undertaken before settlement, cities can more easily and cost-effectively deliver interventions aimed at improving and increasing density.[34] Such projects are often more effective when jointly developed and implemented alongside the communities that stand to benefit, and often must include awareness-raising components to appropriately manage behaviors.[35]

Between cities. Climate change is forcing individuals, families, and even whole communities to seek more viable and less vulnerable places to live. Governments have resorted to specific legislation, regulations, and policies to discourage or restrict domestic migration. These policies include residential registration systems, such as China's Hukou and Vietnam's Ho Khau systems that explicitly restrict internal migration (Bosker et al. 2012; World Bank 2020). Migration may also be stymied by failures in planning and policy, such as a failure to provide secure land tenure and overly restrictive regulations on building heights, that contribute to an insufficiency of affordable housing in the face of a growing urban population.

In the specific case of climate change–induced migration, the overall economic effect on the receiving city is ambiguous and will depend on local conditions and the capacity of the city to absorb a larger labor force of lower-skilled workers. Even as the precise policy mix will vary across countries, the fundamental ingredient for easing such migration transitions would likely remain unchanged. For example, decision-makers could focus on integrating migrants into the city to both limit impacts on host communities and ensure inclusive opportunities for new migrants (Zaveri et al. 2021). This emphasis would involve building human capital and investing in worker productivity through education and labor market policies that build skills and provide training. Governments could also help reduce the costs of migration by, for example, fostering increased access to financial markets and thereby relaxing the credit constraint, lowering the barriers to assimilation in receiving areas, or providing better information on jobs and other opportunities in destinations with lower climate change–related risks.

Finally, the extent to which migration between cities can act as a viable adaptation strategy to climate change further depends on two factors: the number of cities and the variation in the strength of climate change–related hazards across those cities. For a large country such as Brazil, China, or the United States that boasts many cities across which the strength of projected climate change–related hazards varies greatly, migration from cities that are more exposed to high levels of hazard to those that are less exposed represents an important potential adaptation mechanism (figure O.15). However, for small Pacific and Caribbean Island nations, for example, which have only one or two major cities, intercity migration carries much less potential as an adaptation mechanism. The same holds true for large low- and middle-income countries such as Indonesia and Vietnam whose cities face uniformly strong projected climate change–related hazards.

Investments

Investments may come last in this list, but they are not least. Investments in infrastructure, when well designed, constructed, and maintained, can help cities prevent and respond to urban and climate change–related shocks and stressors, thereby reducing the probability of disasters and the associated loss of life and property. Infrastructure investments can include important prevention measures, such as flood control systems, construction of shelters, and protection of environmental buffers. Some infrastructure can serve multiple purposes. For example, safe schools in Bangladesh also serve as community cyclone shelters. Postdisaster investments can involve rehabilitation and reconstruction, including the repair and rebuilding of public and private property such as housing and infrastructure assets. Reconstruction may often include disaster-resistant measures for future prevention. Because the continued effectiveness of infrastructure will also depend on its quality, investment outlays must include maintenance, thereby boosting the resilience of infrastructure assets while reducing overall costs in the long run.

Investments in infrastructure that affect land use and a city's urban form can have implications far into the future. For example, investments in roads that promote motor vehicle over public transportation use, thereby encouraging sprawl, could significantly and permanently increase the costs of delivering basic services, such as water, sanitation, and electricity, and building social infrastructure, such as clinics and schools.[36] Indeed, investing in basic services in low-income cities represents a leap toward integration. It not only builds resilience in vulnerable communities but also enhances mobility by reducing migration barriers between them.

Figure 0.15 Ranges of projected climate change–related hazard scores across cities for selected countries

Urban exposure to combined climate change–related hazard score, selected countries, by country income group

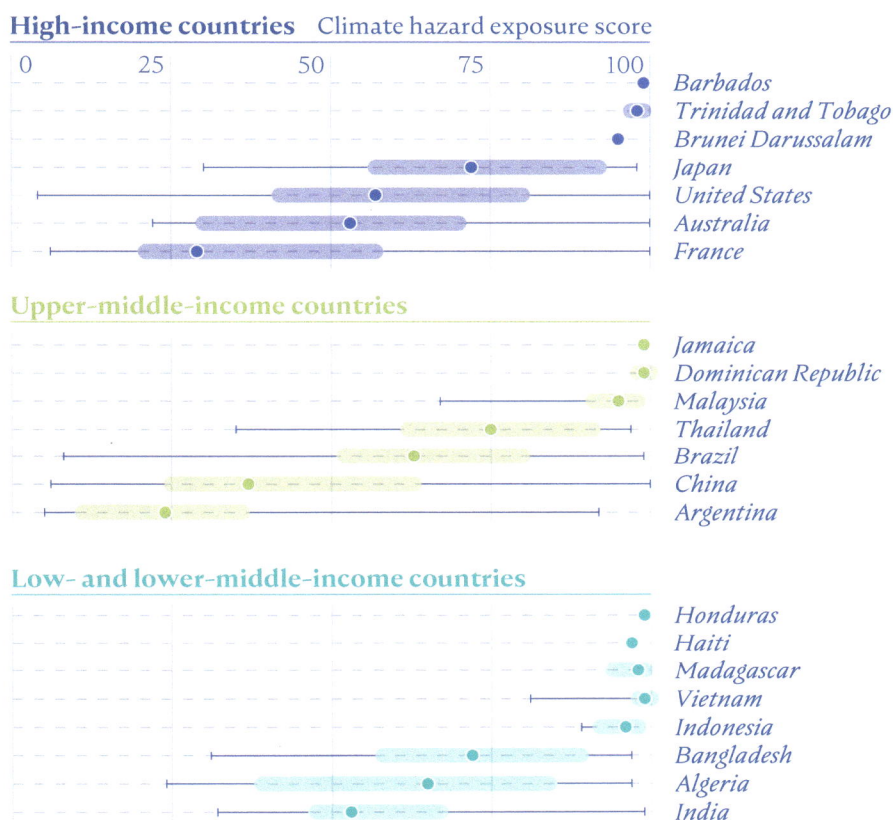

High-income countries Climate hazard exposure score
(Barbados, Trinidad and Tobago, Brunei Darussalam, Japan, United States, Australia, France)

Upper-middle-income countries
(Jamaica, Dominican Republic, Malaysia, Thailand, Brazil, China, Argentina)

Low- and lower-middle-income countries
(Honduras, Haiti, Madagascar, Vietnam, Indonesia, Bangladesh, Algeria, India)

Source: World Bank analysis based on data from Moody's ESG Solutions, Sub-Sovereign Physical Climate Risk Scores, October 2021 (https://esg.moodys.io/climate-solutions).

Note: The figure is organized in descending order of the average climate hazard exposure scores in each income group. The end points of the solid black lines indicate the maximum and minimum scores for each country. The solid horizontal colored line starts at the first quartile and ends at the third. The marker indicates the median value. Climate hazard exposure scores combine information on six key hazards—floods, heat stress, tropical cyclones, sea-level rise, water stress, and wildfires—projected to 2030–40.

Investments can also anticipate the impact of shocks and stresses. One of the great benefits of cities is that they create the density of demand that can justify large sunk investments such as public transportation systems, including, for sufficiently large cities, mass transit systems. These public transportation systems not only have importance for urban productivity, accessibility, and labor market outcomes but also act as a key lever to reducing emissions of both CO_2 and local air pollutants such as $PM_{2.5}$. In a study of the 58 subway system openings that occurred in cities globally between August 2001 and July 2016, Gendron-Carrier et al. (2022) find that, for cities with higher initial pollution levels, subway openings led to a significant reduction in pollution in the area surrounding a city center. Such subway openings have, in turn, generated significant health benefits for cities with higher initial pollution levels.

Meanwhile, this report demonstrates that urbanization in high-risk areas—whether measured by heat or floods—seems to be outpacing settlement growth in safe areas (Desmet and Jedwab 2022; Rentschler et al. 2022). Relocating or retrofitting these neighborhoods is difficult and costly, and can prove politically sensitive. Instead, anticipating urban growth and guiding it spatially can be a much more effective and cost-efficient option. Laying out basic infrastructure can act as a powerful signal for households to settle in areas that authorities have identified, away from high risks. The early stages of growth require only the most basic infrastructure—essentially rights-of-way for roads and well-demarcated land plots (Angel 2012). Scaling up the infrastructure can happen in a second phase once households have settled in. Michaels et al. (2021) find that in Tanzania modest infrastructure investments in greenfield areas where people subsequently built their own houses helped facilitate long-run neighborhood development in terms of larger, more regularly laid-out buildings and better-quality housing.

Finally, investments can be used to retrofit. For example, retrofitting of residential homes and buildings could have important impacts on greening through its effects on energy consumption. Making improvements to the existing housing stock can increase resilience to tropical cyclones, landslides, floods, and other natural hazards. However, retrofitting building structures and infrastructure in densely populated areas to help them adapt to natural hazards can be a costly solution, requiring large outlays of time and money. Nature-based investments may be more cost-effective in such situations. Narayan et al. (2016) carried out a survey of multiple nature-based projects aimed at defending coastal habitats, comparing them with investments in "gray infrastructure."[37] They find that nature-based investments can be highly cost-effective for protecting coastal settlements. Trees, wetlands, green spaces, and rivers can alleviate the urban heat island effect (Raj et al. 2020; Tan, Lau, and Ng 2016). Nature-based solutions also reduce the impact of natural hazards, such as flooding, erosion, landslides, and droughts, in cities—often by complementing gray infrastructure such as storm drains, embankments, and retaining walls.[38]

Who makes the choices?

Because cities will likely bear an outsized share of climate impacts, city leaders are probably the most motivated political actors to take on climate change. City leaders also have knowledge of local context and the ability to mobilize their communities. As such, they can influence and implement climate policies put in place by higher levels of government; design and implement city-specific policies and initiatives; and, crucially, help coordinate collective climate action in their cities (De Coninck et al. 2018).

Higher levels of government may need to commit to policy and investment approaches that support local governments and give them incentives to better plan for and invest in addressing the impacts of climate change. National governments can provide strategic oversight, facilitate access to climate finance, and exercise their capacity and authority to drive climate action by creating a supportive enabling environment. National programs on emissions and clean energy standards, carbon pricing mechanisms, appliance standards, and green financing are more likely to achieve economies of scale by creating larger markets for high- to low-tech cleaner technologies. Through policy and regulatory interventions, governments could spur economic restructuring by managing transition and enabling green growth. National governments play the leading role in embedding social protection into climate plans and should focus on climate risks within social policies (Costella et al. 2021). Moreover, they hold the key to setting policy frameworks for insurance and can provide cover for high levels of physical and business risks.

It is widely agreed that climate action will require multilevel involvement not only by city and national governments but also by nonstate actors such as multilateral institutions, large multinational corporations, small enterprises, and civil society groups. Private financial flows can contribute in several ways to tackling climate risks—from portfolio equity to direct investments, to commercial bank lending, to bond finance. At the grassroots level, communities often take the lead on climate action.

How can choices be made?

How do policy makers choose among the different bundles of policies in a way that will produce the greatest positive impact on the most people in the most efficient manner? They must toggle between and sandwich together the bundles of policy interventions in the five I's to arrive at greener, more resilient, and more inclusive outcomes.

Sequencing of the five I's

The ordering of the five I's is deliberate and represents a potential sequencing of instruments. It goes from addressing information failures and issues of externalities and missing markets to government-funded investments in green, resilient, and inclusive infrastructure. The reasoning underlying the sequencing melds efficiency and efficacy—that is, it balances the need to maximize the desired effects of a policy with the need to do it in the most economical way.

— Early and easy interventions linked to the provision of *information* could have large knock-on effects on improving market outcomes. With access to more information, households and businesses can better understand the benefits and costs of their actions, including location decisions, in well-regulated markets. Such improved decision-making could stem the need for expensive government interventions, including postdisaster recovery.

— In the same vein, well-implemented *incentives* can scale quickly (for example, by affecting behaviors) at relatively low costs. Economic incentives (such as tax rebates or subsidies) can have monetary implications that could lead to snowballing costs, but they could also take the form of disincentives through monetary fines, taxes, and the like. Removing fossil fuel and other subsidies that distort behavior in a way that contributes to climate change and other environmental ills such as local air pollution could also free up government expenditure.

— Well-functioning markets for *insurance* could lower risks to a point that would minimize the need for governments to make expensive interventions and reduce the need for postdisaster relief. Insurance could transfer and mitigate risks, helping allocate economic resources more efficiently, thereby stimulating growth.

— *Integration* includes better planning for cities, often and ideally before the building of urban settlements. Given the durability of urban investments, well-planned integration could have long-lasting effects, not least for the balance sheet. Integration includes policies and reforms to reduce barriers to migration between cities and between cities and rural areas, which, especially for countries with a large number of cities across which the severity of climate hazards vary, can help adaptation.

— Finally, *investments* in infrastructure often involve large public outlays, but they can help shape a city's form in a way that fundamentally affects its emissions of both CO_2 and local air pollutants. In many cases, investments also constitute the primary (and very necessary) response following disasters. Durable investments in mitigation and adaptation strategies are crucially important because of their implications for longer-term outcomes.

The policy instruments represented by the five I's provide a relatively simple approach to organizing the many policies available into distinct bundles. Nevertheless, many interdependencies exist between these sets of instruments. In some, the instruments play out in complementary ways, wherein some policies across the bundles have a stronger impact when implemented together. Examples include how information helps facilitate migration decisions and thus integration, and how information allows prices to better reflect risks, thereby better incentivizing behaviors. Large public investments themselves signal businesses and households (information) about the direction of future development. And incentives via prices or regulation can drive insurance markets more efficiently, affecting, in turn, investment decisions by households and businesses. Thus, decisions across the five I's are not made in isolation of each other but are, in fact, interrelated and compounding.

Tailoring of the five I's

Policy makers need to tailor the application of the five I's, and the specific policy instruments that fall within them, to a city's greenness, resilience, and inclusiveness challenges, keeping in mind that these challenges vary with both a city's size and its level of development. In that context, building on this report's global typology of cities (box O.1), annex OA provides a detailed matrix that maps the five I's policy options to the interrelated challenges arising from urban growth and climate change that confront small, medium, and large cities in all countries. Only with such tailoring can policy be effective—that is, one size does not fit all. However, even the tailoring presented in annex OA represents but a crude guide to the most appropriate policies for any given city, and policy makers will need to further tailor them on the basis of the specific local circumstances that confront a city of any given type.

Challenges related to climate change and urbanization are intensifying across cities globally, especially cities in low- and middle-income countries. To achieve green, resilient, and inclusive urban development, policy makers at both the national and local levels need to work together to address these interrelated challenges head-on. They can do so by drawing on the five I's suite of policy instruments. By acting now to apply these instruments in an appropriately tailored manner, policy makers can ensure that the world's cities not only survive but thrive in the face of the perils of climate change.

Tailored policy options by type of city and instrument

MAIN CHALLENGES

	Low- and lower-middle-income country			Upper-middle-income country			High-income country		
	City size								
	Small	*Med.*	*Large*	*Small*	*Med.*	*Large*	*Small*	*Med.*	*Large*
Resilience	●	●	●	○	○	○	○	○	
Poverty	●	●	○	●	○	○			
Basic services	●	●	●	○	○	○			
Inequality	○			●	●	●	○	○	●
Vegetation			○	○	●	●		○	○
Greenhouse gas (GHG)			○		○	●	○	○	●
Pollution	○	○	●	○	○	●			○

○ = Moderate | ● = Severe

Note: Med. = Medium.

INFORMATION INCENTIVES INSURANCE INTEGRATION INVESTMENTS

policy options to address challenges

	Low- and lower-middle-income country			Upper-middle-income country			High-income country		
	City size								
	Small	*Med.*	*Large*	*Small*	*Med.*	*Large*	*Small*	*Med.*	*Large*
Early warning systems; hazard mapping and assessment	●	●	●	●	●	●	●	●	●
Build institutional capacity	●	●	●						
Decentralized land administration services	●	●	●						
Participatory risk awareness	●	●		●					
Job fairs and local forums	●	●		●					
Greenhouse gas (GHG) emissions inventories						●	●	●	●
Pollution monitoring			●			●			
Better zoning of polluting industries			●			●			
Urban planning documents			●		●	●	●	●	●
Urban design guidelines					●	●	●	●	●
Building codes						●	●	●	●
Disaster risk-informed land value							●	●	●
Disaster-risk land development penalty									●

Note: For brevity, this table only covers policy options for severe challenges for low- and middle-income countries. Med. = Medium.

INFORMATION **INCENTIVES** INSURANCE INTEGRATION INVESTMENTS

policy options to address challenges

	Low- and lower-middle-income country			Upper-middle-income country			High-income country		
	City size								
	Small	*Med.*	*Large*	*Small*	*Med.*	*Large*	*Small*	*Med.*	*Large*
Phase out fossil fuel subsidies	●	●	●	●	●	●	●	●	●
Cash transfers	●	●		●					
Workfare programs	●	●		●					
Subsidized housing	●	●	●	●	●	●			
Congestion control schemes/pricing			●			●		●	●
Parking charges/reform			●			●		●	●
Reforms to reduce costs of vertical construction; relaxed height restrictions			●			●		●	●
Carbon taxes						●	●	●	●
Inclusionary zoning				●	●	●	●	●	●
Density bonus						●	●	●	●
Expedited permitting						●	●	●	●
Fast-track project review								●	●
Building retrofit and clean energy subsidies and tax credits						●	●		
Electric vehicle tax credit						●	●		
Performance zoning							●	●	●
Retrofit incentives								●	●
Linkage fees								●	●
Air rights program								●	●

Note: For brevity, this table only covers policy options for severe challenges for low- and middle-income countries. Med. = Medium.

INFORMATION INCENTIVES **INSURANCE** INTEGRATION INVESTMENTS

policy options to address challenges

	Low- and lower-middle-income country			Upper-middle-income country			High-income country		
	City size								
	Small	*Med.*	*Large*	*Small*	*Med.*	*Large*	*Small*	*Med.*	*Large*
Social protection	●	●	●	●	●				
Subsidized insurance (low-risk areas)	●	●	●	●	●				
Catastrophe insurance	●	●	●	●	●				
Incorporate climate risk considerations in asset (re-)pricing, new insurance product launches, and underwriting process						●	●	●	●

Note: For brevity, this table only covers policy options for severe challenges for low- and middle-income countries. Med. = Medium.

INFORMATION   INCENTIVES   INSURANCE   **INTEGRATION**   INVESTMENTS

policy options to address challenges

	Low- and lower-middle-income country			Upper-middle-income country			High-income country		
	City size								
	Small	*Med.*	*Large*	*Small*	*Med.*	*Large*	*Small*	*Med.*	*Large*
Integrate climate change adaptation and urban management; urban planning and regulation	●	●	●	●	●	●	●	●	●
Basic services; education	●	●	●						
Flexible urban planning				●	●	●	●	●	●
Connect to medium and large cities	●			●				●	
Lower migration barriers	●	●	●	●			●		
Laying-out of street network in anticipation of future expansion	●	●		●					
Secure land and property rights	●	●							
Integrated land use and transportation planning			●		●	●			
Transit-oriented development			●		●	●	●	●	●

Note: For brevity, this table only covers policy options for severe challenges for low- and middle-income countries. Med. = Medium.

INFORMATION   INCENTIVES   INSURANCE   INTEGRATION   **INVESTMENTS**

policy options to address challenges

	Low- and lower-middle-income country			Upper-middle-income country			High-income country		
	City size								
	Small	*Med.*	*Large*	*Small*	*Med.*	*Large*	*Small*	*Med.*	*Large*
Well-located affordable housing	●	●	●	●	●	●	●	●	●
Local bus services	●	●		●			●		
Land provision	●	●							
Improve building stock	●	●							
Climate adaptation infrastructure	●	●	●				●	●	
Nature-based solutions	●	●	●	●	●	●	●	●	●
Renewable energy	●	●	●	●	●	●	●	●	●
Bus rapid transit (BRT)			●		●	●	●	●	●
Mass rapid transit (MRT); light rail transit (LRT)			●			●	●	●	●
Energy-efficient retrofits			●			●	●	●	
Urban green space				●	●			●	
Mobility						●	●	●	●

Note: For brevity, this table only covers policy options for severe challenges for low- and middle-income countries. Med. = Medium.

Notes

1. The Earth's natural "greenhouse effect" was first described by French physicist Joseph Fourier in 1824. Swedish chemist Svante Arrhenius subsequently concluded in 1869 that industrial age coal burning enhances the natural greenhouse effect. In 1938, the British engineer Guy Callendar used records from 147 weather stations around the world to show that temperatures had increased over the previous century and that, over the same period, carbon dioxide (CO_2) emissions had also increased. On the basis of this correlation, he suggested that the increase in CO_2 emissions had been responsible for global warming (an effect referred to as the "Callendar effect"). For a "brief history of climate change," see BBC News (2013).

2. The global urban population climbed from 1.19 billion in 1970 to 4.53 billion in 2022. The urban population data cited here are drawn from the following database: United Nations, Department of Economic and Social Affairs, World Urbanization Prospects 2018 (revision), https://population.un.org/wup/.

3. The surface temperature is averaged across land and water. The preindustrial period is defined as 1880–1900. Data come from Lindsey and Dahlman (2021).

4. Conversely, extreme cold events have decreased in frequency since the 1970s.

5. Cities help generate prosperity both through the agglomeration economies to which they give rise and the structural transformation from agrarian to nonagrarian activities they help facilitate. Historically, this prosperity has, in turn, helped drive demand for energy and therefore fossil fuels. Causation has also historically run in the reverse direction, with the supply of fossil fuel energy helping spur the growth of industry and cities.

6. This is, in part, through networks such as the C40 Cities Climate Leadership Group, the World Mayors Council on Climate Change (WMCCC), and the Urban Climate Change Research Network (UCCRN).

7. Nature provides essential inputs for human life, health, and prosperity; economists therefore treat it as an asset, or *natural capital*.

8. The welfare impact of air, water, and soil pollution was estimated to have been equivalent to 6.2 percent of global output in 2015. Ninety-two percent of pollution-related deaths and the highest burden of economic losses were in low- and middle-income countries. Globally, poorly managed urbanization has been among the major drivers of pollution-related deaths (Landrigan et al. 2017).

9. France's "yellow vest" protests started in November 2018 as a response by motorists to the announcement that a green tax on fuel would go into effect on January 1, 2019, as part of the French government's environmental policy strategy. The original protestors, from peri-urban and rural areas, had to drive long distances daily. The protests quickly spread to Paris, however, and turned violent. The French government abandoned its planned introduction of the green tax in December 2018.

10. Economists refer to these stresses variously as congestion and crowding effects, and diseconomies of agglomeration.

11. Fossil CO_2 emissions accounted for 77 percent of the world's anthropogenic GHG emissions in 2015. Since 2000, their increase constitutes the main source of the global increase in GHG emissions (Crippa et al. 2019).

12. Additional regression analysis, discussed in chapter 1, shows that, for both the residential and transportation sectors, a statistically significant positive correlation remains between a city's CO_2 emissions and the income level of the country in which the city is located even after controlling for a city's own climate (temperature, precipitation, biome, and elevation). Thus, the relationships are not driven solely by differences in demand for heating and cooling associated with temperature.

13. On the basis of current policies, upper-middle- and high-income countries, as an aggregate, are not on course to achieve net zero emissions by 2050, according to version 2 scenario modeling by the Network of Central Banks and Supervisors for Greening the Financial System. According to these scenarios, if all countries maintain their current policies, global GHG emissions in 2050 will be almost 16 percent higher than they were in 2020. Even if upper-middle- and high-income countries achieve their nationally determined contributions while low- and lower-middle-income countries retain their current policies, global GHG emissions in 2050 will be only 8.2 percent lower than in 2020. This level falls far short of that required to limit global warming to 1.5°C.

14. The data on projected climate hazards cover 2,208 cities globally and come from Moody's ESG Solutions. Chapter 2 includes a description of the methodology on which the Moody's climate hazard scores is based.

15. *Resilience* is defined here as the ability of cities to recover their population levels and economic vitality after an adverse shock.

16. Tropical cyclones in the Atlantic are also referred to as "hurricanes"; in the Pacific they are also referred to as "typhoons."

17. For example, globally, the average number of days a year a city's temperature was extremely hot relative to its own historical experience increased from just under two days in the 1970s to more than 41 days over the period from 2010 to 2020—a staggering 21-fold increase in just four decades. Extreme heat events also increased in intensity over this period. Chapter 1 provides more details on the evolution of extreme weather events.

18. The results presented in figure O.4 are limited to cities with a 2015 population of at least 200,000.

19. The 1985 Villach conference, organized by the United Nations Environment Program, World Meteorological Organization, and International Science Council, was notable for its recognition that climate change was occurring much more rapidly than previously thought. The conference also issued the first call from the world's leading climate scientists for collaboration between scientists and policy makers to explore policy options for addressing climate change.

20. Data used for the calculations cited here cover 3 countries in East Asia and Pacific (Cambodia, Myanmar, and Timor-Leste); 5 countries in Latin America and the Caribbean (Colombia, Dominican Republic, Guatemala, Haiti, and Honduras); 3 countries in South Asia (Bangladesh, India, and Nepal); and 29 countries in Sub-Saharan Africa (East Africa: Burundi, Comoros, Ethiopia, Kenya, Malawi, Mozambique, Rwanda, Tanzania, Uganda, Zambia, and Zimbabwe; West Africa: Benin, Burkina Faso, Côte d'Ivoire, Ghana, Guinea, Liberia, Mali, Nigeria, Senegal, Sierra Leone, and Togo; Central Africa: Angola, Cameroon, Chad, Democratic Republic of Congo, and Gabon; southern Africa: Lesotho and Namibia).

21. This finding is suggestive of the so-called environmental Kuznets curve relationship.

22. For a description of a proposed technological innovation for reducing the CO_2 emissions embedded in Portland cement, the most widely used standard variety of cement, see Ellis et al. (2019).

23. The United Nations High Commissioner on Refugees estimates that 89.3 million people worldwide were forced to flee their homes in 2021 because of conflicts, violence, fear of persecution, and human rights violations. This number is more than double the 42.7 million people who remained forcibly displaced a decade ago and the most since World War II (https://www.unhcr.org/en-us/figures-at-a-glance.html).

24. However, even good transportation networks may not be able to mitigate the impacts of some nonclimate stressors, as illustrated by the conflict in Ukraine.

25. For example, a rich body of literature in development economics documents how the poor possess lower financial literacy and how the provision of financial information can have substantial positive welfare effects. See, among others, Hastings, Madrian, and Skimmyhorn (2013); Karlan, Ratan, and Zinman (2014); Lusardi and Mitchell (2014).

26. Jiang and Quintero (2022) define an extremely hot day as one in which the temperature during at least one hour during the day exceeds 35°C, even if the average temperature of the entire day is lower.

27. As figure O.14 indicates, climate change may also potentially interact with agglomeration economies. For example, more frequent extreme weather associated with climate change could make it less likely that people can mingle, thereby reducing the likelihood of knowledge spillovers, or it could interrupt dense local supply chains. In general, however, the mechanisms through which climate change may affect the strength of agglomeration economies are less well understood and researched and thus are downplayed in this report.

28. See *Guardian* article on whether climate reporting shifts viewpoints (Harvey 2022).

29. For example, Hong Kong SAR, China, has invested in housing improvements that allow for sheltering at home during tropical cyclones and in early warning systems that allow people to return safely to their homes using an adaptive public transportation system (Rogers and Tsirkunov 2010).

30. The 2019 Global Commission on Adaptation report finds that early warning systems provided a 10-fold return on investment—the greatest of any adaptation measure included in the report (GCA and WRI 2019).

31. In the presence of a low-price elasticity—such as suggested by the meta-analysis carried out by Galindo et al. (2015) in Latin America—a fuel tax will be inadequate to control rising consumption.

32. The urban population data cited here are drawn from the following database: United Nations, Department of Economic and Social Affairs, World Urbanization Prospects 2018 (revision), https://population.un.org/wup/.

33. See also evidence presented in chapter 1.

34. It has been estimated that the cost of proactive planning (such as via sites and services) for the provision of affordable and safe housing to accommodate the burgeoning population in Freetown, Sierra Leone, would cost approximately US$375 million (Mukim 2018). By contrast, the provision of a public housing scheme would cost almost nine times as much (US$3.2 billion).

35. In Jamaica, coastal hazard mapping is under way with the intent to update land use regulation, but in tandem local authorities continue to successfully enforce minimally intrusive and low-cost hurricane straps, which are connectors, often made of galvanized or stainless steel, used to strengthen wood-framed roofs and homes.

36. For African cities, Foster and Briceño-Garmendia (2010) estimate that doubling urban density reduces the per capita cost of a package of infrastructure improvements by about 25 percent.

37. *Gray infrastructure* refers to built structures and engineering equipment (such as reservoirs, embankments, and canals) that are embedded in watersheds or coastal ecosystems.

38. See World Bank (2021a) for an overview of the literature and examples in which such solutions can help cities target climate resilience.

References

Abanokova, K., H-A. Dang, S. Nakamura, S. Takamatsu, C. Pei, and D. Prospere. 2022. "Is Climate Change Slowing the Urban Escalator out of Poverty? Evidence from Indonesia and LAC." Background paper prepared for this report, World Bank, Washington, DC.

Acharya, G., E. Cassou, S. Jaffee, and E. K. Ludher. 2021. *RICH Food, Smart City: How Building Reliable, Inclusive, Competitive, and Healthy Food Systems Is Smart Policy for Urban Asia*. Washington, DC: World Bank.

Ahlfeldt, G. M., and R. Jedwab. 2022. "The Global Economic and Environmental Effects of Vertical Urban Development." Background paper prepared for this report, World Bank, Washington, DC.

Angel, S. 2012. *Planet of Cities*. Hollis, NH: Puritan Press, Inc.

Arrow, K. J. 1963. "Uncertainty and the Welfare Economics of Medical Care." *American Economic Review* 53 (5): 941–73.

Bakkensen, L. A., and L. Barrage. 2022. "Going Underwater? Flood Risk Belief Heterogeneity and Coastal Home Price Dynamics." *Review of Financial Studies* 35 (8): 3666–709.

Banerjee, A. V., and S. Mullainathan. 2008. "Limited Attention and Income Distribution." *American Economic Review* 98 (2): 489–93.

Baylis, P., and J. Boomhower. 2019. "Moral Hazard, Wildfires, and the Economic Incidence of Natural Disasters." NBER Working Paper w26550, National Bureau of Economic Research, Cambridge, MA. https://ssrn.com/abstract=3504434.

BBC News. 2013. "A Brief History of Climate Change." *BBC News*, September 20, 2013. https://www.bbc.com/news/science-environment-15874560.

Benton, G. 1970. "Carbon Dioxide and Its Role in Climate Change." *Proceedings of the National Academy of Sciences* 67: 898–91.

Bosker, M., S. Brakman, H. Garretsen, and M. Schramm. 2012. "Relaxing Hokou: Increased Labor Mobility and China's Economic Geography." *Journal of Urban Economics* 72 (2): 252–66.

Chlouba, V., M. Mukim, and E. Zaveri. 2022. "How Do Climate Change-Related Stressors Affect Urban Form?" Background paper prepared for this report, World Bank, Washington, DC.

Climate Watch. 2022. "GHG Emissions." World Resources Institute, Washington, DC. https://www.climatewatchdata.org/ghg-emissions.

Costella, C., A. McCord, M. van Aalst, R. Holmes, J. Ammoun, and V. Barca. 2021. "Social Protection and Climate Change: Scaling Up Ambition." Social Protection Approaches to COVID-19 Expert Advice Service (SPACE), Development Alternatives Incorporated (DAI) Global, LLC, Bethesda, MD.

Crippa, M., G. Oreggioni, D. Guizzardi, M. Muntean, E. Schaaf, E. Lo Vullo, E. Solazzo, et al. 2019. *Fossil CO$_2$ and GHG Emissions of All World Countries*. EUR 29849 EN. Luxembourg: Publications Office of the European Union.

De Coninck, H., A. Revi, M. Babiker, P. Bertoldi, M. Buckeridge, A. Cartwright, W. Dong, et al. 2018. "Strengthening and Implementing the Global Response." In *Global Warming of 1.5°C,* edited by V. Masson-Delmotte, P. Zhai, H.-O. Pörtner, D. Roberts, J. Skea, P. R. Shukla, A. Pirani, et al. Geneva: Intergovernmental Panel on Climate Change.

Deryugina, T. 2014. "The Fiscal Cost of Hurricanes: Disaster Aid versus Social Insurance." *American Economic Journal: Economic Policy* 9 (3): 168–98.

Desmet, K., and R. Jedwab. 2022. "Are We Over-building in 'Bad' Locations Globally? Future Climate Change and Durable Real Estate." Background prepared paper for this report, World Bank, Washington, DC.

Deuskar, C. 2022. "Beating the Heat: Measuring and Mitigating Extreme Heat in East Asian Cities." Unpublished manuscript.

Dijkstra, L., A. Florczyk, S. Freire, T. Kemper, M. Melchiorri, M. Pesaresi, and M. Schiavina. 2021. "Applying the Degree of Urbanisation to the Globe: A New Harmonised Definition Reveals a Different Picture of Global Urbanisation." *Journal of Urban Economics* 125: 103312.

Dijkstra, L., and H. Poelman. 2014. "A Harmonised Definition of Cities and Rural Areas: The New Degree of Urbanization." Regional Working Paper, Directorate-General for Regional and Urban Policy, European Commission, Brussels.

Ellis, L.D., A. F. Badel, M. L. Chiang, and Y.-M. Chiang. 2019. "Toward Electrochemical Synthesis of Cement-An Electrolyzer-Based Process for Decarbonating CaCO$_3$ while Producing Useful Gas Streams." *PNAS* 117 (23): 12584–91.

Erman, A., M. Tariverdi, M. Obolensky, X. Chen, R. C. Vincent, S. Malgioglio, J. Rentschler, et al. 2019. "Wading Out the Storm: The Role of Poverty in Exposure, Vulnerability and Resilience to Floods in Dar es Salaam." Policy Research Working Paper 8976, World Bank, Washington, DC.

Foster, V., and C. Briceño-Garmendia. 2010. *Africa's Infrastructure: A Time for Transformation.* Africa Development Forum. Washington, DC: World Bank.

Galindo, L., J. Samaniego, J. Alatorre, J. Ferrer Carbonell, and O. Reyes. 2015. "Meta-analysis of the Income and Price Elasticities of Gasoline Demand: Public Policy Implications for Latin America." *CEPAL Review* 117: 7–25.

Gandhi, S., M. E. Kahn, R. Kochhar, S. V. Lall, and V. Tandel. 2022. "Adapting to Flood Risk: Evidence from a Panel of Global Cities." Working Paper 30137, National Bureau of Economic Research, Cambridge, MA.

GCA (Global Center on Adaptation) and WRI (World Resource Institute). 2019. *Adapt Now: A Global Call for Leadership on Climate Resilience.* Rotterdam: GCA.

Gendron-Carrier, N., M. Gonzalez-Navarro, S. Polloni, and M. A. Turner. 2022. "Subways and Urban Air Pollution." *American Economic Journal: Applied Economics* 14 (1): 164–96.

Glaeser, E. L. 2012. *Triumph of the City: How Our Greatest Invention Makes Us Richer, Smarter, Greener, Healthier, and Happier.* New York: Penguin Press.

Glaeser, E. L. 2022. "Urban Resilience." *Urban Studies* 59 (1): 3–35.

Gregory, J. 2017. "The Impact of Post-Katrina Rebuilding Grants on the Resettlement Choices of New Orleans Homeowners." Unpublished manuscript.

Harvey, F. 2022. "Truthful Climate Reporting Shifts Viewpoints, but Only Briefly, Study Finds." *Guardian*, June 20, 2022. https://www.theguardian.com/environment/2022/jun/20/truthful-climate-reporting-shifts-viewpoints-but-only-briefly-study-finds.

Hastings, J. S., B. C. Madrian, and W. L. Skimmyhorn. 2013. "Financial Literacy, Financial Education, and Economic Outcomes." *Annual Review of Economics* 5 (1): 347–73.

Heger, M., D. Wheeler, G. Zens, and C. Meisner. 2019. *Motor Vehicle Density and Air Pollution in Greater Cairo: Fuel Subsidy Removal and Metro Line Extension and Their Effect on Congestion and Pollution.* Washington, DC: World Bank.

Henderson, J. V., and M. Turner. 2020. "Urbanization in the Developing World: Too Early or Too Slow?" *Journal of Economic Perspectives* 34 (3): 150–73.

Hoekstra, A. Y., J. Buurman, and K. C. H. van Ginkel. 2018. "Urban Water Security: A Review." *Environmental Research Letters* 13 (5): 053002.

Hopkins, F., J. Ehleringer, S. Bush, R. Duren, C. Miller, C. Lai, Y. Hsu, et al. 2016. "Mitigation of Methane Emissions in Cities: How New Measurements and Partnerships Can Contribute to Emissions Reduction Strategies." *Earth's Future* 4: 408–25.

IPCC (Intergovernmental Panel on Climate Change). 2021. *Climate Change 2021: The Physical Science Basis.* Contribution of Working Group I to the Sixth Assessment Report of the Intergovernmental Panel on Climate Change. Cambridge, UK: Cambridge University Press.

IPCC (Intergovernmental Panel on Climate Change). 2022. "Summary for Policymakers." In *Climate Change 2022: Impacts, Adaptation, and Vulnerability*, edited by H.-O. Pörtner, D. C. Roberts, M. Tignor, E. S. Poloczanska, K. Mintenbeck, A. Alegría, M. Craig, et al. Cambridge, UK: Cambridge University Press.

Jiang, H., and L. Quintero. 2022. "Can't Stand the Heat: Climate Stress on Labor Productivity in 16 Latin American and Caribbean Countries." Background paper prepared for this report, World Bank, Washington, DC.

Kahn, M. 2010. "Climatopolis: How Will Climate Change Impact Urbanities and Their Cities?" *VOX-EU Blog*, September 11, 2010, Center for Economic Policy Research, London.

Kahn, M. E., and P. Li. 2020. "Air Pollution Lowers High Skill Public Sector Worker Productivity in China." *Environmental Research Letters* 15 (8): 084003.

Karlan, D., A. L. Ratan, and J. Zinman. 2014. "Savings by and for the Poor: A Research Review and Agenda." *Review of Income and Wealth* 60 (1): 36–78.

Lai, D., W. Liu, T. Gan, K. Liu, and Q. Chen. 2019. "A Review of Mitigating Strategies to Improve the Thermal Environment and Thermal Comfort in Urban Outdoor Spaces." *Science of the Total Environment* 661 (April): 337–53.

Lall, S. V., J. Kaw, S. B. Murray, and F. Shilpi. Forthcoming. *Vibrant Cities: Priorities for Green, Resilient, and Inclusive Urban Development.* Washington, DC: World Bank.

Landrigan, J., R. Fuller, N. J. R. Acosta, O. Adeyi, R. Arnold, N. Basu, A. Bibi Baldé, et al. 2017. "The *Lancet* Commission on Pollution and Health." *Lancet* 391 (10119): 462–512.

Lindsey, R., and L. Dahlman. 2021. "Climate Change: Global Temperature." Climate.gov, March 15, 2021. National Oceanic and Atmospheric Administration, Washington, DC.

Lusardi, A., and O. S. Mitchell. 2014. "The Economic Importance of Financial Literacy: Theory and Evidence." *Journal of Economic Literature* 52 (1): 5–44.

Madden, R. A., and V. Ramanathan. 1980. "Detecting Climate Change due to Increasing Carbon-Dioxide." *Science* 209: 763–68.

Michaels, G., D. Nigmatulina, F. Rauch, T. Regan, N. Baruah, and A. Dahlstrand. 2021. "Planning Ahead for Better Neighborhoods: Long-Run Evidence from Tanzania." *Journal of Political Economy* 129 (7): 2112–56.

Mukim, M. 2018. *Freetown Urban Sector Review: Options for Growth and Resilience.* Washington, DC: World Bank.

Nakagawa, M., M. Saito, and H. Yamaga. 2007. "Earthquake Risk and Housing Rents: Evidence from the Tokyo Metropolitan Area." *Regional Science and Urban Economics* 37 (1): 87–99.

Narayan, S., M. W. Beck, B. G. Reguero, I. J. Losada, B. van Wesenbeeck, N. Pontee, J. N. Sanchirico, et al. 2016. "The Effectiveness, Costs and Coastal Protection Benefits of Natural and Nature-Based Defences." *PLoS ONE* 11 (5): e0154735.

Park, J., and M. Roberts. 2023. "Urban Resilience and Weather Shocks: A Global Nighttime Lights Analysis." Background paper prepared for this report, World Bank, Washington, DC.

Pascale, S., S. B. Kapnick, T. L. Delworth, and W. F. Cooke. 2020. "Increasing Risk of Another Cape Town 'Day Zero' Drought in the 21st Century." *Proceedings of the National Academy of Sciences* 117 (47): 29495–503.

Patankar, A. M. 2015. "The Exposure, Vulnerability, and Ability to Respond of Poor Households to Recurrent Floods in Mumbai." Policy Research Working Paper 7481, World Bank, Washington, DC.

Pomponi, F., R. Saint, J. H. Arehart, N. Gharavi, and B. D'Amico. 2021. "Decoupling Density from Tallness in Analysing the Life Cycle Greenhouse Gas Emissions of Cities." *Urban Sustainability* 1: 33.

Raj, S., S. K. Paul, A. Chakraborty, and J. Kuttippurath. 2020. "Anthropogenic Forcing Exacerbating the Urban Heat Islands in India." *Journal of Environmental Management* 257: 110006.

Rentschler, J., P. Avner, M. Marconcini, R. Su, E. Strano, S. Hallegatte, L. Bernard, and C. Riom. 2022. "Rapid Urban Growth in Flood Zones: Global Evidence since 1985." Policy Research Working Paper 10014, World Bank, Washington, DC.

Rogers, D., and V. Tsirkunov. 2010. *Costs and Benefits of Early Warning Systems.* Global Assessment Report on Disaster Risk Reduction 2011. Washington, DC: World Bank.

Rossitti, G. 2022. "Who Is Affected? Which Segments of City Populations Are Most Exposed to Climate-Related Stresses?" Background paper prepared for this report, World Bank, Washington, DC.

Rubin, A. J., and S. Sengupta. 2018. "'Yellow Vest' Protests Shake France. Here's the Lesson for Climate Change." *New York Times*, December 6, 2018. https://www.nytimes.com/2018/12/06/world/europe/france-fuel-carbon-tax.html.

Santos, G., K. Button, and R. G. Noll. 2008. "London Congestion Charging." *Brookings-Wharton Papers on Urban Affairs* 2008: 177–234.

Singh, C., G. Jain, V. Sukhwani, and R. Shaw. 2021. "Losses and Damages Associated with Slow-Onset Events: Urban Drought and Water Insecurity in Asia." *Current Opinion in Environmental Sustainability* 50: 72–86.

Song, S., C.-C. Feng, and M. Diao. 2020. "Vehicle Quota Control, Transport Infrastructure Investment and Vehicle Travel: A Pseudo Panel Analysis." *Urban Studies* 57 (12): 2527–46.

Tan, Z., K. K.-L. Lau, and E. Ng. 2016. "Urban Tree Design Approaches for Mitigating Daytime Urban Heat Island Effects in a High-Density Urban Environment." *Energy and Buildings* 114: 265–74.

Varadhan, S. 2019. "Villagers Accuse City of Seizing Water as Drought Parches 'India's Detroit.'" Reuters, July 3, 2019.

Venkat, A., F. Dizon, and W. Masters. 2022. "The Impact of Climate Shocks and Stresses on Urban Food Prices." Background paper prepared for this report, World Bank, Washington, DC.

Votsis, A., and A. Perrels. 2016. "Housing Prices and the Public Disclosure of Flood Risk: A Difference-in-Differences Analysis in Finland." *Journal of Real Estate Finance and Economics* 53 (4): 450–71.

World Bank. 2013. *Inclusion Matters: The Foundation for Shared Prosperity*. New Frontiers of Social Policy. Washington, DC: World Bank.

World Bank. 2017. *Sovereign Catastrophe Risk Pools: World Bank Technical Contribution to the G20*. Washington, DC: World Bank.

World Bank. 2020. *Vietnam's Urbanization at a Crossroads: Embarking on an Efficient, Inclusive, and Resilient Pathway.* Washington, DC: World Bank.

World Bank. 2021a. *A Catalogue of Nature-Based Solutions for Urban Resilience*. Washington, DC: World Bank.

World Bank. 2021b. *Somalia Urbanization Review: Fostering Cities as Anchors of Development*. Washington, DC: World Bank.

Zaveri, E., J. Russ, A. Khan, R. Damania, E. Borgomeo, and A. Jagerskog. 2021. *Ebb and Flow Vol. 1: Water, Migration and Development.* Washington, DC: World Bank.

Introduction

Overview

For at least 50 years, the balance of scientific evidence has supported the view that the world is warming, and that human activity has spurred that warming (Benton 1970; Madden and Ramanathan 1980). Globally during this time, the number of people living in cities has increased by a factor of 3.8, from 1.19 billion in 1970 to 4.46 billion in 2021,[1] and the Earth's surface temperature has climbed by 1.19°C above its preindustrial levels.[2] Because of the prosperity they have helped generate, cities have been a major cause of this climate change (Kahn 2010). It is also in cities, however, that many of the solutions to the climate crisis—in terms of both adaptation and mitigation—will be found, not least because by 2050 almost 70 percent of the world's population will call cities their home. As such, cities are key to arguably the greatest public policy challenge of our times.

Nevertheless, urban economists have, with a few notable exceptions, been surprisingly silent in terms of their research on climate change.[3,4] In part, this report is an attempt to rectify that neglect. Even more important, the report provides a compass for policy makers on policies that can help cities thrive in the face of the perils of climate change. Climate change, however, is but one symptom of an even larger problem—the more general erosion of natural capital to which poorly managed urbanization contributes. That erosion, especially in many low- and middle-income countries, contributes, in turn, to dangerously poor air quality in many cities, detrimental competition for water between urban and rural areas, the unnecessary loss of fertile agricultural land, deforestation, and a damaging loss of biodiversity.[5] At the same time, these trends play out against a backdrop of high and rising levels of inequality in many cities globally and stalled progress in the worldwide fight against extreme poverty[6]—trends that themselves both interact with and reinforce stressors related to climate change—to affect the greenness, resilience, and inclusiveness of urban development (box I.1).

Box I.1

Defining greenness, resilience, and inclusiveness

In 2021, in response to the challenges posed by climate change, the more general degradation of the environment, the COVID-19 pandemic, stalled progress in the global fight against extreme poverty, and increasing inequality in many countries, the World Bank launched its GRID (green, resilient, and inclusive development) strategy (World Bank 2021). In keeping with that strategy, this report focuses on three broad but closely interrelated dimensions of a city's development.

- *Greenness* refers to a city's impacts on the environment, with a greener city having more beneficial or less negative environmental impacts. A city's greenness is reflected in its level of greenhouse gas emissions, including its carbon dioxide emissions. This report analyzes other dimensions of a city's greenness as well, including its level of air pollution, the extent to which it pollutes both its own water and that of surrounding areas, and a city's level of vegetation. These additional dimensions of greenness have important interrelationships with climate change. For example, a city's $PM_{2.5}$

BOX I.1 *continued*

emissions (that is, emissions of particulate matter of 2.5 microns or less in diameter) are strongly correlated with its carbon dioxide emissions, which implies that action to tackle local pollution tends to carry climate change mitigation co-benefits and vice versa. Meanwhile, increased vegetation can help mitigate the impacts of extreme urban heat associated with both climate change and the urban heat island effect. It can also help mitigate climate change itself through carbon sequestration.

- *Resilience* refers to how well a city withstands climate change–related shocks as measured by, for example, the total loss in output suffered and loss of population experienced. Resilience has two components: the size of the initial losses associated with a shock and how quickly a city returns to its preshock growth paths of output and population. A resilient city is one in which the initial impacts of a climate change–related shock are small and recovery is quick.

- *Inclusiveness* is broadly considered in terms of both (1) ability and opportunity and (2) outcomes. Inclusion is defined as the ability and opportunity for all who reside in a city to fully participate in markets, services, and spaces (including political, physical, cultural, and social), thereby enabling them to lead their lives with dignity (World Bank 2013). Consistent with that definition, this report variously discusses how cities differ globally in the access they provide to basic urban services, financial services, digital technologies, and labor market opportunities. It also shines a spotlight on multidimensional exclusion and touches on issues of voice. As for outcomes, the report analyzes, among other things, how cities vary globally in terms of their rates of poverty and levels of income inequality; the levels of socioeconomic mobility that they afford their residents, especially new migrants; gender-differentiated patterns of population displacement following climate-related natural disasters; and the differential impacts of exposure to extreme urban heat on segments of a city's workforce, including informal versus formal, female versus male, and older versus younger workers. Despite this broad coverage, however, the report is silent on certain important dimensions of inclusion. For example, because of the lack of adequate data, the report does not discuss the impacts of climate change on city dwellers who are living with disabilities or who belong to a racial or ethnic minority.

Although neither a city's prosperity nor its livability is included among the three dimensions just described, both critically depend on the greenness, resilience, and inclusiveness of a city's development. A city that, for example, has cleaner air, more green space, better access for its residents to both services and markets, and an ability to bounce back more quickly from climate change–related shocks is also likely to be a city that is both more prosperous and livable.

The primary audience for this report is high-level policy makers at both national and city levels whose decisions can affect the greenness, resilience, and inclusiveness of urban development. The report is also intended for those who advise these policy makers, as well as for technical staff across relevant government ministries and planning agencies. With that audience in mind, this report begins in part 1 by intertwining an original descriptive analysis of a wide variety of data sources with a review of the secondary literature, thereby taking stock of how green, how resilient, and how inclusive cities globally are today (chapter 1). It then presents a global typology of cities that identifies the severity of the greenness, resilience, and inclusiveness challenges they face and how those challenges intersect with future projected climate change–related hazards (chapter 2). In doing so, the report highlights how the stresses that urban economists have traditionally emphasized as being associated with urban growth—and which arise from the population pressures on cities' land and property markets, supplies of basic services, local infrastructure, and environment—interact with climate change–related stressors to determine how green, how resilient, and how inclusive a city's development is.

Part 2 of the report then presents the results of original empirical work, again intertwined with insights from the secondary literature. It examines the two-way interplay between climate change and cities and how that interplay affects development outcomes (chapters 3 and 4).

Finally, part 3 builds on the empirical insights of parts 1 and 2 to provide policy makers with a compass for policies that can help enhance the greenness, resilience, and inclusiveness of cities in a world confronted by climate change (chapter 5). In doing so, the report introduces a sequenced set of five broad types of policy instrument—information, incentives, insurance, integration, and investments (in short, the five I's)—that policy makers at the national and local levels have available to them (box I.2). And it provides guidance to help inform policy makers' selection of various combinations of those instruments.

In addition to the five main chapters, the report includes a spotlight on social exclusion and exposure to air pollution in Peruvian cities. That spotlight showcases a novel approach for estimating multidimensional exclusion.

Box I.2

The five I's: Information, incentives, insurance, integration, and investments

This report distinguishes five broad sets of instruments that policy makers can draw on in seeking to improve the greenness, resilience, and inclusiveness of a city's development in a world confronted by climate change.

- *Information.* Policies and measures to improve the timely provision of credible information that helps people, businesses, and local governments better understand climate change–related risks both across and within cities, and, in doing so, helps promote both mitigation and adaptation.

- *Incentives.* Policy instruments that provide incentives for individuals and businesses to internalize negative environmental externalities, as well as institutional and other types of reform that provide government officials with incentives to work better together to address green, resilient, and inclusive development challenges.

- *Insurance.* Policies and reforms that help people, businesses, and governments either to insure through the market or to self-insure against losses associated with climate change and other environmental shocks and stresses.

- *Integration.* Policy interventions and reforms that promote more compact cities and better integration of cities, both with each other and with rural areas, as a means of facilitating adaptation through both migration and trade.

- *Investments.* Investments by national and local governments in green, resilient, and inclusive urban infrastructure, including nature-based solutions, as well as measures to promote the crowding-in of private sector finance for such investments.

Chapter 5 of this report discusses these five sets of instruments in more detail, along with *who* wields these instruments (national or local governments) and *how* policy choices based on their use can be prioritized and sequenced for effective implementation.

A framework for assessing the greenness, resilience, and inclusiveness of a city's development

Inspired by insights from urban economic theory and the environmental and climate change literature, this report views the greenness, resilience, and inclusiveness of a city's development as jointly determined by the interaction of two opposing sets of forces (figure I.1).[7] On the one hand are the positive agglomeration economies to which a city's size and density give rise.[8] These agglomeration economies help generate prosperity, thereby facilitating resilience. They also promote inclusiveness by contributing to poverty reduction and lowering the average costs of providing the large-scale infrastructure that underpins not only many important basic services such as water, sewerage, and electricity, but also more complex services such as advanced medical services and modern digital networks. The greater prosperity associated with agglomeration economies, however, also leads to higher consumption of food—for example, beef and other meats, as well as dairy products—and goods whose production is intensive in greenhouse gas emissions.[9] And, because agglomeration economies help cities act as magnets for talent, they can contribute to higher income inequality in cities.

On the other hand, acting against these agglomeration economies, cities suffer from the negative, interacting stresses that arise from their own growth and from climate change. If not managed properly, these stresses can both dampen the prosperity gains that arise from agglomeration economies and undermine the greenness, resilience, and inclusiveness of urban development. In turn, the "five I" policy instruments affect these outcomes by influencing the strength of both the agglomeration economies and the interacting urban and climate change–related stresses.

The stresses that arise from a city's own growth—congestion forces, crowding effects, and diseconomies of agglomeration—stem from the pressure its population exerts on its land and property markets, local infrastructure, basic services, and environment. Therefore, if a city makes insufficient investment in infrastructure and basic urban services as it grows, their quality and per capita availability tend to deteriorate. If land and property markets fail to respond flexibly to a city's growth, housing becomes increasingly unaffordable, giving rise to overcrowding and slums, which can also facilitate the more rapid spread of infectious diseases such as COVID-19. And, if pressure on the environment is not managed appropriately, air quality can deteriorate, natural habitats can come under threat, and the conflict with rural areas over water sources may worsen.

Climate change both interacts with and exacerbates these stresses in a variety of ways. For example, the rise in sea level reduces the supply of land available for development in low-elevation coastal cities, thereby adding to the pressure on land and property markets (Balboni 2021). Droughts in areas supplying a city's water exacerbate pressures on its water supply

Figure I.1   Report framework and structure

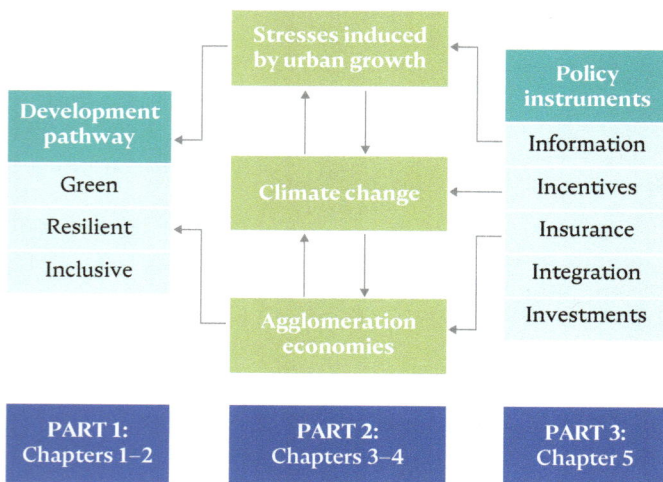

Source: World Bank staff.

system (Zaveri et al. 2021). And rising temperatures compound the so-called urban heat island effect (Deuskar 2022).

At the same time, the stresses that arise from a city's own growth influence both a city's contribution to climate change and the capacities of its residents to adapt to such change. For example, sprawl and traffic congestion resulting from failures in land and property markets, shortcomings in planning, and inadequate provision of high-quality public transportation increase the number of vehicle miles traveled and thus greenhouse gas emissions. Meanwhile, the widespread existence of poorly constructed slums, frequently in more hazard-prone areas, increases the exposure of the urban poor and vulnerable to the impacts of climate change. Climate change–induced migration into cities also adds to the stresses that cities experience but does not necessarily contribute to agglomeration economies.

Although more speculative, climate change may undermine the strength of agglomeration economies. For example, more frequent extreme weather could make it less likely that people can mingle, thereby reducing the likelihood of knowledge spillovers, or it could interrupt dense local supply chains.

Beyond its effects on agglomeration economies and other urban stresses, climate change has potential repercussions for the social optimality of a city's location. Although not shown in figure I.1, where urban development originally occurs within a country is largely determined by "locational fundamentals," which, in turn, depend on nature (Brakman, Garretsen, and van Marrewijk 2012). Historically, urban development has been more likely to occur where nature confers an advantage in terms of either production (such as an abundance of natural resources), trade (such as the existence of a natural harbor), or amenities (such as a stable and temperate climate). Climate change is, however, beginning to change the relative extent to which nature favors different locations. Nevertheless, because urban development has a strong inertia, rather than shifting to locations less affected, or possibly even favored, by climate change, that development continues in the same places.

Not only does the framework in figure I.1 help guide this report's analysis of the greenness, resilience, and inclusiveness of a city's development and the policy options for achieving better outcomes, but it also provides the report's three-part structure. Thus, part 1 describes where cities globally stand in terms of their current levels of greenness, resilience, and inclusiveness. Part 2 analyzes the two-way interplay between climate change and cities. And part 3 discusses the "five I" policy instruments, thereby providing policy makers with guidance on how to leverage and apply them.

Notes

1. All urban population data cited here are drawn from the following database: United Nations, Department of Economic and Social Affairs, World Urbanization Prospects 2018 (revision), https://population.un.org/wup/.

2. The surface temperature is averaged across land and water. The preindustrial period is defined as 1880–1900. Data are from Lindsey and Dahlman (2021).

3. The notable exceptions include Esteban Rossi-Hansberg of the University of Chicago, Matthew Kahn of the University of Southern California, and Stephane Hallegatte of the World Bank, who are among this report's expert technical advisers.

4. This is, however, beginning to change as evidenced, for example, by the conference program at the 2022 North American Meeting of the Urban Economics Association, which included two dedicated sessions on climate change (see https://urbaneconomics.org/meetings/uea2022/program.html).

5. Since 1900, the average abundance of native animal and plant species has declined by at least 20 percent globally, and about 1 million more species are now threatened with extinction (IPBES 2019).

6. Even before the onset of the COVID-19 pandemic, progress in the global fight against extreme poverty had slowed following the 2008 global financial crisis, and many cities in low- and middle-income countries had high inequality (World Bank 2021).

7. The urban part of this framework builds on the frameworks of Ellis and Roberts (2016) and Roberts, Gil Sander, and Tiwari (2019).

8. The concept of agglomeration economies originated in the work of Marshall (1890). Agglomeration economies arise from various sources, including the better matching of workers with jobs that occurs in cities than in rural areas, the wider variety of intermediate inputs into final production available from local suppliers in larger and denser cities, and the spillovers of knowledge that are a characteristic feature of large urban agglomerations (Duranton and Puga 2004; Marshall 1890). Further agglomeration benefits arise from the superior market access that larger cities tend to enjoy, which makes it easier for businesses to cover their start-up costs, thus stimulating increases in profits and productivity (Fujita, Krugman, and Venables 1999; Krugman 1991a, 1991b).

9. The use of cows, pigs, and other animals for food, as well as for the production of livestock feed, accounts for 57 percent of all food production–related greenhouse gas emissions globally, compared with 29 percent from the cultivation of plant-based foods (Xu et al. 2021).

References

Balboni, C. 2021. "In Harm's Way: Infrastructure Investments and the Persistence of Coastal Cities." Department of Economics, Massachusetts Institute of Technology, Cambridge, MA. https://economics.mit.edu/sites/default/files/publications/Catastrophe_Risk_and_Settlement_Location.pdf.

Benton, G. 1970. "Carbon Dioxide and Its Role in Climate Change." *Proceedings of the National Academy of Sciences* 67: 898–91.

Brakman, S., H. Garretsen, and C. van Marrewijk. 2012. *The New Introduction to Geographical Economics, 2nd edition*. Cambridge, UK: Cambridge University Press.

Deuskar, C. 2022. "Beating the Heat: Measuring and Mitigating Extreme Heat in East Asian Cities." Unpublished manuscript, World Bank, Washington, DC.

Duranton, G., and D. Puga. 2004. "Micro-Foundations of Urban Agglomeration Economies." In *Handbook of Regional and Urban Economics,* Vol.4, *Cities and Geography*, edited by J. V. Henderson and J.-F. Thisse, 2063–117. Amsterdam: Elsevier.

Ellis, P., and M. Roberts. 2016. *Leveraging Urbanization in South Asia: Managing Spatial Transformation for Prosperity and Livability*. Washington, DC: World Bank.

Fujita, M., P. Krugman, and A. J. Venables. 1999. *The Spatial Economy: Cities, Regions, and International Trade*. Cambridge, MA: MIT Press.

IPBES (Intergovernmental Science Policy Platform on Biodiversity and Ecosystem Services). 2019. *Global Assessment Report on Biodiversity and Ecosystem Services of the Intergovernmental Science Policy Platform on Biodiversity and Ecosystem Services*. Bonn: IPBES Secretariat. https://doi.org/10.5281/zenodo.3831673.

Kahn, M. 2010. "Climatopolis: How Will Climate Change Impact Urbanites and Their Cities?" *VOX-EU Blog*, September 11, 2010. https://cepr.org/voxeu/columns/climatopolis-how-will-climate-change-impact-urbanites-and-their-cities.

Krugman, P. 1991a. *Geography and Trade*. Cambridge, MA: MIT Press.

Krugman, P. 1991b. "Increasing Returns and Economic Geography." *Journal of Political Economy* 99 (3): 483–99.

Lindsey, R., and L. Dahlman. 2021. "Climate Change: Global Temperature." Climate.gov, March 15, 2021. National Oceanic and Atmospheric Administration, Washington, DC.

Madden, R. A., and V. Ramanathan. 1980. "Detecting Climate Change Due to Increasing Carbon-Dioxide." *Science* 209: 763–68.

Marshall, A. 1890. *Principles of Economics*. London: Macmillan.

Roberts, M., F. Gil Sander, and S. Tiwari, eds. 2019. *Time to ACT: Realizing Indonesia's Urban Potential*. Washington, DC: World Bank.

World Bank. 2013. *Inclusion Matters: The Foundation for Shared Prosperity*. New Frontiers of Social Policy. Washington, DC: World Bank.

World Bank. 2021. "From COVID-19 Crisis Response to Resilient Recovery: Saving Lives and Livelihoods while Supporting Green, Resilient, Inclusive Development." Paper presented to Development Committee at 2021 World Bank-IMF Spring Meetings, World Bank, Washington, DC.

Xu, X., P. Sharma, S. Shu, T. Lin, P. Ciais, F. N. Tubiello, P. Smith, N. Campbell, and A. K. Jain. 2021. "Global Greenhouse Gas Emissions from Animal-Based Foods Are Twice Those of Plant-Based Foods." *Nature Food* 2: 724–32.

Zaveri, E., J. Russ, A. Khan, R. Damania, E. Borgomeo, and A. Jagerskog. 2021. *Ebb and Flow Vol. 1: Water, Migration and Development*. Washington, DC: World Bank.

PART 1

Where Are We Now?

CHAPTER 1

The Stylized Relationships

*[W]e need to start focusing our support, both
financial and technical, on the green, resilient,
and inclusive transformations that will help
economies . . . brace against climate change. . . .*

**Axel van Trotsenburg, Managing Director of
Operations, World Bank Group, April 16, 2021**

MAIN FINDINGS

- As climate change has evolved globally, many cities have become subject to more
frequent and more intense extreme weather events, most notably, extreme heat and dry
events. By contrast, extreme cold events have become less frequent.

- Confronted with this changing climate, cities vary widely in terms of how green, how
resilient, and how inclusive they are. Nevertheless, some general patterns emerge, such
as the relationship of many indicators of greenness, resilience, and inclusiveness to
both a city's size and its level of development.

- Larger cities tend to be less green in terms of their carbon dioxide emissions, levels of
air quality, and average vegetation levels but, in many respects, are more inclusive. They
have lower poverty rates, provide better access to basic services, and have better average
outcomes on many health indicators.

- More-developed cities also tend to be less green in terms of carbon dioxide emissions;
however, beyond a certain income level, development correlates with both better air
quality and a higher average level of vegetation. More developed cities also have economies that are more resilient to unusual weather events, and they tend to be more inclusive when it comes to access to basic services and health outcomes. They also suffer
from less poverty and may have lower interhousehold income inequality.

- The greenness, resilience, and inclusiveness of cities are linked. A city's level of
inclusiveness is, for example, a key determinant of its resilience to both the short- and
longer-run stresses associated with climate change.

Introduction

It a well-worn but nevertheless empirically well-supported cliché that cities act as "engines of growth" at both the local and national levels. This expression stems in part from the better jobs found in cities than in rural areas and from the productivity and other welfare-enhancing benefits associated with urban size and density (Duranton and Puga 2020; World Bank 2009).

At the same time, as this report's overarching analytical framework makes clear, a city's growth can also give rise to a wide variety of stresses. These stresses—known as congestion forces, crowding effects, and diseconomies of agglomeration—arise from the pressure of a city's population on its supplies of land, housing, and basic services; stock of infrastructure; and environment.[1] If not well managed, these stresses can threaten not only a city's productivity and growth but also the *quality*—and, therefore, sustainability—of that growth, making the city less green, less resilient, and less inclusive. The results of these stresses are evident in the slums and sprawl, lack of access to basic services, gridlocked streets, choking air pollution, and contamination of water sources that characterize many cities in low- and middle-income countries today.

In thinking about these stresses, economists have traditionally assumed that a city's climate is fixed or changes only very slowly.[2] Climate change, however, has rendered this assumption increasingly untenable. It has emerged as an additional and growing source of stress on many cities, both adding to and interacting with many of the traditionally emphasized sources of stress, thereby further influencing the quality of a city's growth. It has also become clearly recognized that the nature of a city's spatial development has the potential to affect not only the global climate through its contribution to greenhouse gas (GHG) emissions but also its own local climate through the urban heat island effect.

In view of these issues, this chapter has the following main objectives:

- To take stock on a broad level of how green, how resilient, and how inclusive cities are today considering, among other things, (1) their contribution to climate change; (2) their economic resilience to various types of extreme weather events, the frequency and intensity of which are evolving with climate change; and (3) the strength of the other stresses they face because of the pressures of urban growth on a city's supplies of land, housing, and basic services; stock of infrastructure; and environment.

- To lay the groundwork for the development of the global typology of cities in chapter 2 that highlights the severity of urban- and climate change–related challenges faced by different types of cities, as well as their possible intersections.

To achieve these aims, this chapter first documents how different types of weather anomalies—hot, cold, wet, and dry events, along with tropical cyclones (such as hurricanes in the Atlantic)—have been evolving across cities globally in both frequency and intensity. It then presents stylized empirical relationships between key indicators of how green, how resilient, and how inclusive cities are and their basic characteristics with an emphasis on a city's size and level of development. The chapter also presents new empirical evidence on the short-run resilience of urban economies to weather anomalies and on how the level of this resilience varies with a city's size, level of development, and baseline climate.[3] In considering how green, how resilient, and how inclusive cities are today, it is important to recognize the interdependencies among these three broad outcomes. For example, a society's poverty rate, a key indicator of its inclusiveness, is an important determinant of its level of resilience.[4] Meanwhile, the average level of vegetation in a city, one indicator of its greenness, affects the strength of a city's urban heat island effect. Higher temperatures may, in turn, influence a city's level of spousal violence. Any increase in that violence further undermines a city's inclusiveness.

Finally, to the greatest extent possible, the chapter relies for its insights on a global sample of more than 10,000 consistently defined cities,[5] synthesizing both the original empirical analysis of this sample and the analysis of similarly defined urban areas by other authors (box 1.1). This synthesis is supplemented by insights from secondary literature and analysis of other data sources, some of which rely on other definitions of urban areas with the caveats of comparability that this reliance implies.

Box 1.1

Comparing apples with apples: How this report defines cities

How should a *city* be defined? This apparently fundamental question has, it turns out, no easy answer. Thus, countries around the world vary widely in how they define cities, using both different numbers and different combinations of criteria. For example, Senegal defines cities as "agglomerations of 10,000 inhabitants or more," and Albania defines them as "towns and other industrial centers with 400 inhabitants or more."[a] More generally, although some countries define cities based only on population, others also define them using criteria such as population density, the presence of certain types of infrastructure and basic services, and the share of their workforce that is employed outside of agriculture. In its official statistical definition, Indonesia even includes the presence of massage parlors and cinemas as some of the factors that help classify a place as urban. A large group of countries has no explicitly stated criteria by which they define cities. Rather, they simply either list their cities by name or designate administrative units that constitute cities (Roberts et al. 2017).

This wide variation in definitions poses huge challenges for any global analysis of cities. To avoid apples with oranges comparisons, the analysis reported here largely relies on a globally uniform definition of cities—*degree of urbanization*—that the European Commission devised in collaboration with several other international organizations (Dijkstra et al. 2021). This definition, officially endorsed in March 2020 by the United Nations Statistical Commission as a recommended method for making international comparisons of urban areas, identifies a city as a spatially contiguous, dense cluster of population grid cells in a global 1 square kilometer population grid. Thus, a *city* is a contiguous set of grid cells for which each cell has a population density of at least 1,500 people per square kilometer and the aggregate population of the set is at least 50,000.

Degree of urbanization also identifies *urban clusters*, which comprise both lower-density suburbs of cities and smaller urban areas or towns. In contrast to cities, these clusters are defined using a population density threshold of 300 people per square kilometer and an overall population threshold of 5,000. Although most of this chapter's analysis focuses on cities, some of it also considers urban clusters.

Other major World Bank reports have used the degree of urbanization definition of cities (notably, Ferreyra and Roberts 2018; Lall et al. 2021). This definition is fast becoming a globally accepted way of defining cities, not only by the international policy community but also by academic researchers publishing an increasing number of global data sets based on the definition, some of which this report uses.

Nevertheless, degree of urbanization has its shortcomings. For example, although the population density threshold of 300 people per square kilometer used to designate urban

Box 1.1 *continued*

clusters is reasonable for most countries, it implies implausibly high estimated urban shares of the population for countries and areas such as Bangladesh, the northeastern states of India, and Java (Indonesia) that have very high average population densities (Bosker, Park, and Roberts 2021). More generally, the degree of urbanization is only as good as the gridded population data used as its input, and the urban areas delineated are somewhat sensitive to the choice of such data (Dijkstra et al. 2021; Roberts et al. 2017).

Although several alternative methods for delineating urban areas have recently been developed and applied to individual countries (de Bellefon et al. 2021; Galdo, Li, and Rama 2021), these methods are much more computationally intensive than the degree of urbanization and have yet to be scaled to the global level. Furthermore, to a greater or lesser extent, global applications of these methods would still depend on the same gridded population data sets as the degree of urbanization, whose quality relies fundamentally on the quality of population data produced by national statistical offices through their population censuses. This being the case, the global data set of cities used in this report is the best currently available, especially in view of the number of other global data sets generated to match it.

a. "Data Sources and Statistical Concepts for Estimating the Urban Population" spreadsheet, United Nations' World Urbanization Prospects, https://population.un.org/wup/Download/.

A changing climate

Although weather and climate are temporally distinct but physically related concepts (a city's long-term climate condition is an aggregate of the short-term weather events it experiences), climate change has increasingly affected the frequency and intensity of abnormal weather events (or "anomalies"). This section provides an overview of the evolution of different types of weather anomaly—extreme heat, cold, wet, and dry events, as well as storm events—over the last six decades for this report's consistently defined global sample of cities.[6] A weather anomaly is defined relative to a city's own baseline climate considering the historic variability of its weather (box 1.2).

Extreme heat events have increased in frequency since the 1970s, whereas the opposite is true of extreme cold events

Globally, the average number of months a year a city's temperature was extremely hot relative to its own historical experience increased from 0.06 in the 1970s to 1.35 over the period 2010–20 (figure 1.1, panel a). Put differently, the average went from just under 2 days per year to more than 41 days per year—a staggering 21-fold increase in just four decades. Extreme heat events also increased in intensity over this period. In the 1970s, the average extreme heat event recorded a temperature almost 2.3 standard deviations above a city's own long-run average. Fast forward to 2010–20, and the intensity of the average extreme heat event had increased to just over 2.5 standard deviations (figure 1.1, panel b). As map 1A.1 in annex 1A illustrates, extreme heat events are particularly prevalent in southern India, Southeast Asia, upper parts of the Arab Republic of Egypt, and parts of Central America and Central Africa. When they do occur, these events are particularly intense in South Asia (see map 1A.2).

BOX 1.2

What is a weather anomaly, and how does this chapter define it?

In June 2021, countries throughout eastern Europe, including Belarus, Estonia, and Hungary, occupied the headlines as they set all-time high temperature records for the month. In Hungary, the temperature reached 40°C, whereas the country's average is typically between 12.8°C and 23.9°C, depending on the region. Although 40°C is hot by most standards, such a temperature would be nothing out of the ordinary for the residents of Kuwait City, where June daytime temperatures are typically 45°C–46°C.

In the climate literature, a *weather anomaly* is often defined as the absolute deviation of a measurable unit of weather, say degrees Celsius or millimeters of rain, over a certain period from a location's long-run average.[a] For a cross-city analysis on a global scale, however, such a definition is inadequate to characterize unusual weather because it does not fully consider the diverse climatological conditions to which people in different places have adapted.

Given its global focus, this chapter's analysis defines for any given month a city's weather anomaly in *standard deviations* from its own long-run average for that same month. Denoting x^w_{icmt} as the value of the weather variable (such as temperature or precipitation) in city i in country c in month m of year t, a weather anomaly, $Anomaly^w_{icmt}$, is defined as

$$Anomaly^w_{icmt} = \frac{x^w_{icmt} - \bar{x}^w_{icm}}{\sigma^w_{icm}}$$

where w refers to either temperature or precipitation, and $\bar{x}^w_{icm}$ and σ^w_{icm} to the city-specific long-run average and the standard deviation for month m, respectively. These long-run variables are calculated for the period January 1958–March 2012 using high spatial resolution monthly data from TerraClimate.[b]

This measure, by definition, captures unusual temperatures and precipitation in both positive (hotter or wetter than usual) and negative (colder or drier than usual) directions relative to a city's own climate over the long run (average and variability). For temperature, for example, the measure is equal to +1 if a city's temperature in a particular month is 1 standard deviation above its own long-run average for that same month. When the measure takes on an absolute value of 2 or more, a weather anomaly is considered extreme.

In interpreting the values of anomalies, however, one must keep in mind that—because the implications of an anomaly of a given size (say, −2) vary across cities according to their underlying climates—large values do not necessarily translate into severe weather events such as heat or cold waves, floods, or drought. For Kuwait City, any given June recording 2 standard deviations below the average reflects an unusually cool month, but it may still be warm in absolute terms. By contrast, for a city with a long-run average temperature of 5°C in December, such an extreme negative temperature anomaly will reflect an unusually cold winter in both relative and absolute terms.

Source: Based on Park and Roberts 2023.

a. National Oceanic and Atmospheric Administration, National Weather Service Glossary, https://forecast.weather.gov/glossary.php?word=ANOMALY.

b. Climatology Lab, TerraClimate, https://www.climatologylab.org/terraclimate.html.

Figure 1.1 Evolution of the frequency and intensity of extreme heat events for cities globally, 1958–69 to 2010–20

a. Frequency

b. Intensity

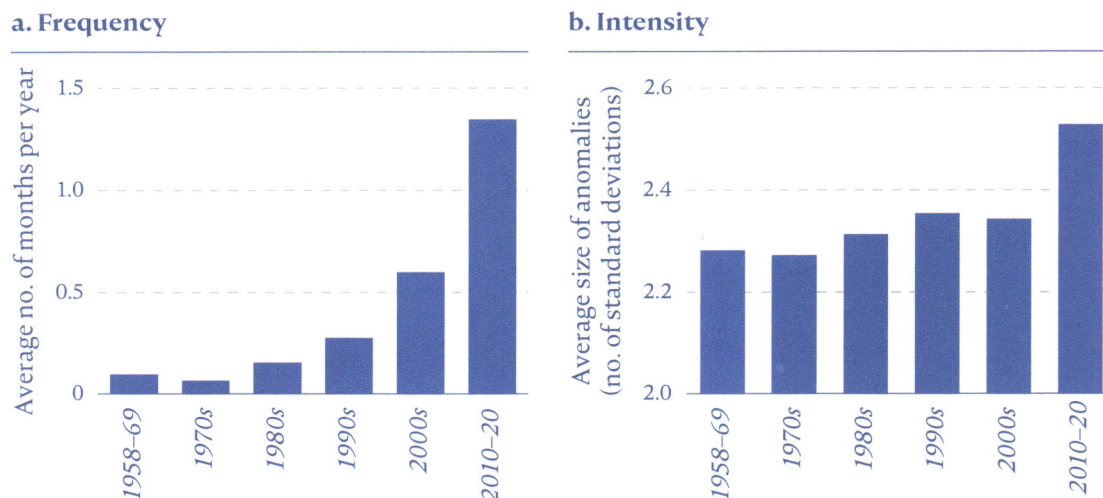

Sources: World Bank calculations based on Climatology Lab, TerraClimate (https://www.climatologylab.org /terraclimate.html); European Commission, Global Human Settlement (GHS) Urban Centre Database R2019 (https://ghsl.jrc.ec.europa.eu/ghs_stat_ucdb2015mt_r2019a.php).

Note: An *extreme hot month* is one in which a city's temperature for that month is at least 2 standard deviations higher than the month's city-specific historical norm, as calculated over the period January 1958–March 2012. Frequency is calculated as the number of extreme hot months per year. Intensity is calculated as the average size of the anomaly variable (as defined in box 1.2) during consecutive extreme hot months. Panel a presents the average frequency and panel b the average intensity across the global sample of urban centers that experienced an extreme hot month over the period January 1958–December 2020.

The increasing frequency and intensity of extreme heat anomalies are consistent with global warming, whereby a small increase in average temperature leads to a significantly increased number of days that are unusually hot by a city's own standards (IPCC 2021). The flip side is that, as a city's average temperature increases, the number of unusually cold days that it, again by its own standards, experiences decreases. It is not surprising, then, that the average number of months per year for which a city's temperature was extremely cold by its own long-run standards fell from 0.44 in the 1970s to 0.10 over the period 2010–20 (figure 1.2, panel a). Put differently, the average went from just over 13 days per year in the 1970s to slightly more than 3 days per year during 2010–20. However, although the frequency of extreme cold anomalies has dropped, the intensity of those anomalies, when they do occur, has increased since the 1980s (figure 1.2, panel b). As map 1A.3 in annex 1A shows, isolated geographic "hot spots" of more frequent extreme cold weather, relative to a city's own baseline climate, can be found, for example, around the state of Paraiba in Brazil, in East Africa, and in inland China. Meanwhile, when extreme cold events do occur, they tend to be very intense, especially in China and India (map 1A.4, annex 1A).

The trend in temperature anomalies, which because of climate change will continue in the coming decades, implies that heat waves will become an increasingly common problem for many cities, especially cities with tropical climates in which high baseline temperatures

Figure 1.2 Evolution of the frequency and intensity of extreme cold events for cities globally, 1958–69 to 2010–20

a. Frequency

b. Intensity

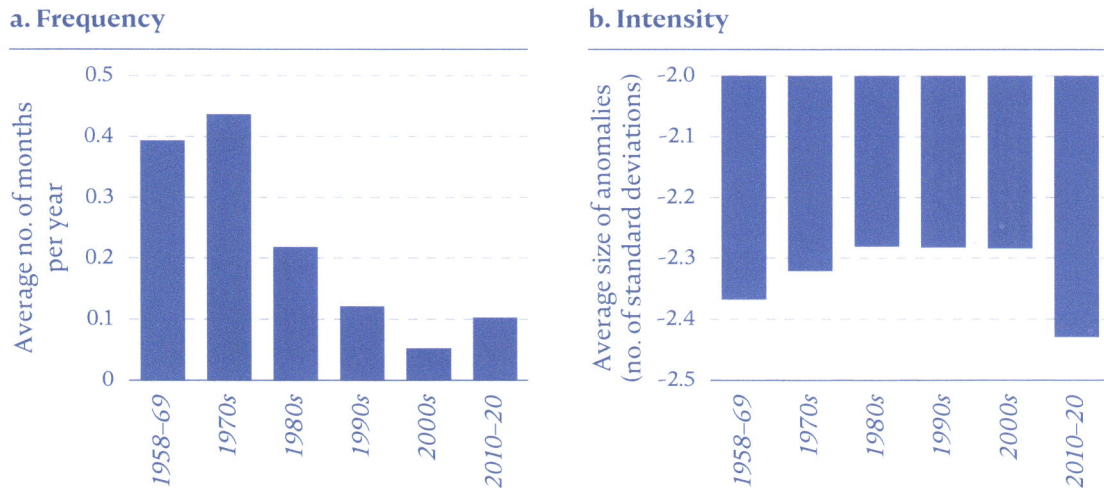

Sources: World Bank calculations based on Climatology Lab, TerraClimate (https://www.climatologylab.org /terraclimate.html); European Commission, Global Human Settlement (GHS) Urban Centre Database R2019 (https://ghsl.jrc.ec.europa.eu/ghs_stat_ucdb2015mt_r2019a.php).

Note: An *extreme cold month* is one in which a city's temperature for that month is at least 2 standard deviations below the month's city-specific historical norm, as calculated over the period January 1958–March 2012. Frequency is calculated as the number of extreme cold months per year. Intensity is calculated as the average size of the anomaly variable (as defined in box 1.2) during consecutive extreme cold months. Panel a presents the average frequency and panel b the average intensity across the global sample of urban centers that experienced an extreme cold month over the period January 1958–December 2020.

combine with high levels of humidity to create thermal discomfort. Without adequate adaptation, such heat waves will have negative consequences for a wide range of urban outcomes, including health, education, and learning outcomes, as well as worker productivity—see Deuskar (2022) for a review of the evidence. Evidence also shows that increased exposure to very hot temperatures significantly increases urban crime and violence, particularly in poorer neighborhoods with older housing stocks and little air-conditioning (see, among others, Heilmann and Kahn 2019). Consistent with these findings, the global annual average heat-related excess death ratio increased by 0.21 percentage points between 2000–2003 and 2016–19, reaching 0.91 percent of all global excess deaths in the latter period (Zhao et al. 2021). This figure is equivalent to 489,000 excess deaths per year, many concentrated in large, crowded, low-lying coastal cities in eastern and southern Asia and cities in eastern and western Europe.

At the same time, however, excess deaths due to cold far exceed those due to heat. Indeed, cold accounted for an annual average of almost 4.6 million excess deaths globally during 2016–19, more than nine times the number of heat-related excess deaths during the same period. And, because of the decreasing frequency of extreme cold events, the total number of excess deaths attributable to nonoptimal temperatures (that is, either too hot or too cold) has *declined* over the last two decades (Zhao et al. 2021). This finding implies that, despite increasing concern among urban policy makers about the impacts of extreme heat on human health, unusually cold weather does remain, and will remain for the foreseeable future, the bigger killer. Thus, policies to help residents adapt to cold spells remain important for many cities.

Extreme dry and, to a lesser extent, extreme wet events have also increased in frequency

This finding is most obviously true for extreme dry events. In the 1970s, the average number of months per year that cities experienced extremely low rainfall relative to their own historical experiences was 0.03, or an average of 0.91 days per year. By 2010–20, however, this average had more than tripled to almost 0.10 months (or 3.04 days) per year (figure 1.3, panel a). These extreme dry events are particularly common in Central Africa (see map 1A.5).[7]

The increasing frequency of extreme dry events globally has, in turn, contributed to the increasing numbers of cities experiencing near "day zero" events, whereby water supplies are only weeks or days from running out. Water supply systems typically are planned to meet a design standard for drought to maintain supplies without any restriction on use

Figure 1.3 **Evolution of the frequencies of extreme dry and wet events for cities globally, 1958–69 to 2010–20**

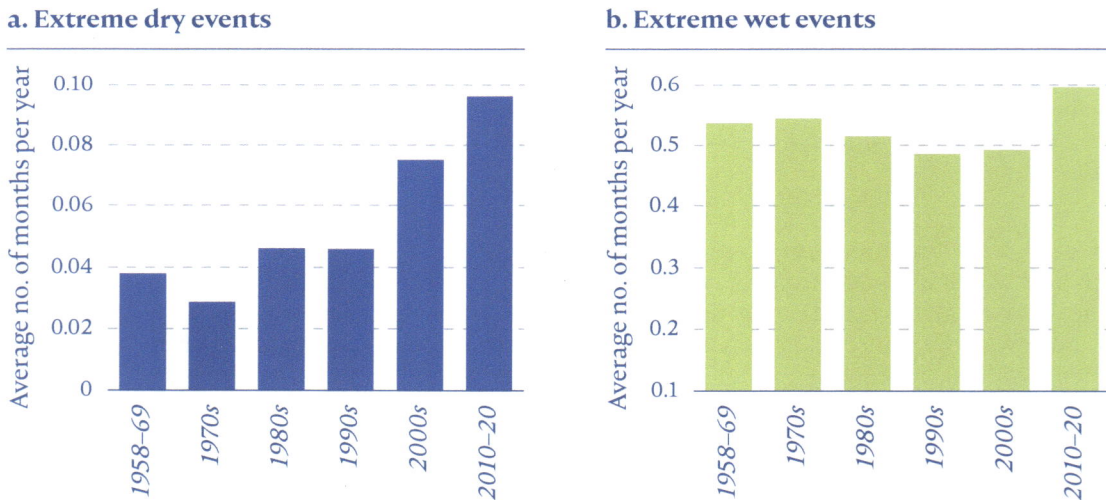

a. Extreme dry events

b. Extreme wet events

Sources: World Bank calculations based on Climatology Lab, TerraClimate (https://www.climatologylab.org /terraclimate.html); European Commission, Global Human Settlement (GHS) Urban Centre Database R2019 (https://ghsl.jrc.ec.europa.eu/ghs_stat_ucdb2015mt_r2019a.php).

Note: An extreme dry (wet) month is when a city's precipitation for that month is at least 2 standard deviations below (above) the month's city-specific historical norm, as calculated over the period January 1958–March 2012. Frequency is calculated as the number of extreme dry (wet) months per year. The graphs present the average annual frequency across the global sample of urban centers that experienced an extreme dry (wet) month during January 1958–December 2020.

(Watts et al. 2012; Zaveri et al. 2021). Although the length of the design drought that urban water systems can handle varies, experience worldwide has shown that long droughts lasting three or more years are typically more taxing for urban water supply systems and can lead to severe water use restrictions such as cuts or countdowns (Buurman, Mens, and Dahm 2017; Zaveri et al. 2021). Using this three-year period as a rule of thumb to capture both weather events and management responses, previous analysis has estimated that cumulative rainfall deficits, measured as the cumulative deviation of rainfall from long-run averages over three-year periods, can harm overall city growth when the magnitude falls below −3.5 standard deviations. In other words, when rainfall deficits are, on average, at least 1.2 standard deviations below the long-run average in each year over the three-year period, the negative impact on city growth becomes significant (Zaveri et al. 2021). Using a similar rule of thumb and threshold, figure 1.4 shows that these near–day zero events have become especially common in cities in low- and lower-middle-income countries.

As for extreme wet events, they declined steadily in average frequency from the 1970s up to 2000–2009, but their occurrence subsequently rebounded during the period 2010–20 (figure 1.3, panel b).[8] Increasingly frequent extreme rainfall since 2010 suggests an increased risk of urban flooding. As box 1.3 discusses, however, the occurrence of such flooding also critically depends on the characteristics of the built environment, including whether a city has adequate drainage infrastructure, and on the quality of its solid waste management.

Figure 1.4 **Share of cities, by deepest three-plus years of water deficits and country income group, that faced day zero–type events, 1992–2013**

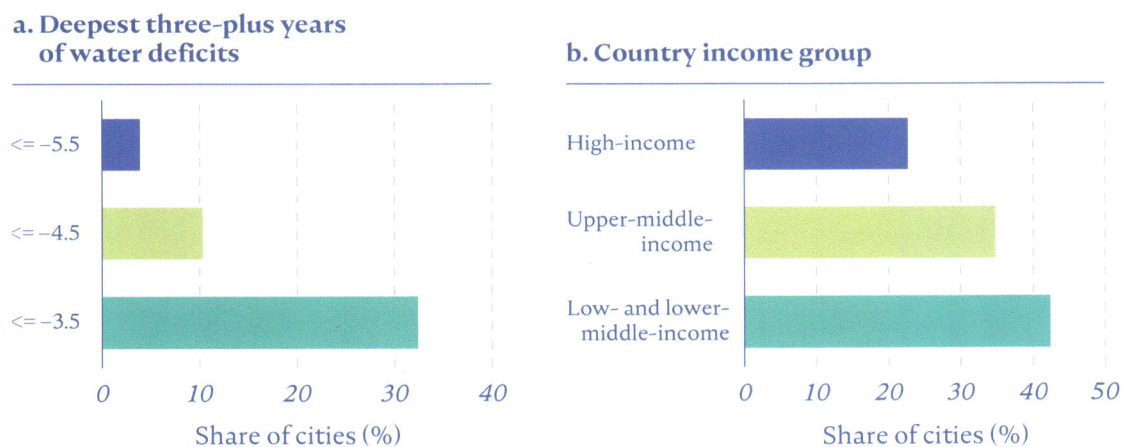

a. Deepest three-plus years of water deficits

b. Country income group

Sources: World Bank calculations based on Zaveri et al. 2021. Weather data: K. Matsuura and C. J. Willmott, Terrestrial Air Temperature and Precipitation: Monthly and Annual Time Series (1900–2017), University of Delaware, 2018; urban water sources data: Nature Conservancy and R. McDonald, "City Water Map (Version 2.2)," Knowledge Network for Biocomplexity, 2016 (doi:10.5063/).

Note: Panel a shows the share of all cities globally in the data set that experienced the deepest water deficit from 1992 to 2013, the period for which data are available. The deepest water deficit (measured on the vertical axis) is defined as a cumulative z-score of rainfall over each three-year period for each water point in the sample period. *Day zero events* are defined as those when the cumulative z-score of rainfall over each three-year period for each water point from 1992 to 2013 is less than −3.5 standard deviations.

Box 1.3

When does a wet event become a flood?

Accra, the capital of Ghana, experiences flooding every rainy season, but the flooding caused by heavy rainfall on June 3, 2015, was unprecedented in its magnitude and tragic consequences. The city's markets, normally crowded, came to a standstill as stormwater several feet deep destroyed traders' goods. The water flooded homes and trapped many people in their offices or cars. Twenty-five people died in the flood. Just when things seemed as though they could not get any worse, another disaster struck. In one of the city's busiest areas, dozens had gathered at a petrol station to shelter from the rain. As the floodwater rose, it mixed with fuel from a leaking petrol pump. A flame ignited the mixture, causing a massive explosion. Firefighters struggled to reach the blaze through the floodwater. Tragically, the inferno killed 150 people. In the mourning period that followed, residents and officials recognized that, despite the heavy rainfall, the underlying causes of the disaster were the inadequate drainage system, the solid waste that blocked drains, and the unplanned urban growth that obstructed natural drainage channels.

The US Federal Emergency Management Agency defines *urban flooding* as "the inundation of property in a built environment, particularly in more densely populated areas, caused by rain falling on increased amounts of impervious surfaces and overwhelming the capacity of drainage systems."[a] As the definition makes clear, flooding in cities results from a combination of factors both natural and human in origin. Although heavy rainfall may trigger flooding, characteristics of the built environment—such as the extent of impervious surfaces and the capacity of drainage infrastructure—also play a role. Urban flooding may occur anywhere, not just near water bodies. As chapter 3 discusses, such flooding often, but not always, disproportionately affects low-income residents, who are likelier to live in low-lying areas with insufficient drainage infrastructure and without flood protection insurance.

Sources: BBC News 2015; Karimi and Lett 2015; Weber 2019.

a. As cited in Hossain and Meng (2020).

Global sea-level rise also contributes to an increased risk of flooding for coastal cities

Global warming leads to a rise in sea level by causing seawater to expand and the ice over land to melt. Because of climate change, rises in sea level have accelerated in recent decades. According to the US National Ocean Service,[9] global tidal records from 1900 to 1990 reveal an estimated rise in the global mean sea level of 101.6–127.0 millimeters. In the 25 years from 1990 to 2015, however, the global sea level rose by 76.2 millimeters. Currently, sea levels are rising about 0.125 millimeters per year. And by 2100 they may have risen another 0.3–2.4 meters.

Historically, coastal locations have tended to enjoy advantages in terms of both trade and agriculture, making them natural locations for cities (Smith 1776). Globally, more than 300 million people, or 5 percent of the world's population, live in low-elevation coastal zones below 5 meters above sea level (CIESIN 2013). However, as analyzed in more detail in chapter 2, rising sea levels pose a growing threat of flooding for coastal cities globally.

Tropical cyclones have become increasingly frequent since the 1970s

Finally, in terms of weather anomalies, tropical cyclones (called "hurricanes" in the Atlantic Ocean and sometimes "typhoons" in the Pacific) that affect cities have become more frequent since the 1970s (figure 1.5). Between the 1970s and 2010–2020, the average number of tropical cyclones experienced by the global sample of cities increased more than fourfold, from 0.16 to 0.71.[10] Tropical cyclones form in all ocean basins, and cities in the Philippines are particularly prone to their strong impacts. Meanwhile, the hurricanes that form in the highly active North Atlantic basin affect cities throughout the Caribbean, eastern Mexico, and the eastern and southern United States. Tropical cyclones that form in the eastern Pacific can affect cities in western Mexico, whereas typhoons that form in the western Pacific are highly likely to hit cities in southern Asia, China, and Japan. The Asian nations along the Indian subcontinent are also prone to tropical cyclones from the Indian Ocean, and the Bay of Bengal is a hot spot for cyclonic activities. Finally, a tropical cyclone from the southwestern Indian Ocean can affect cities in Madagascar and other countries along the eastern coast of Africa, and one from the southeastern Indian Ocean could affect Australian cities.

Figure 1.5 Evolution of the frequency of tropical cyclones for cities globally, 1958–69 to 2010–20

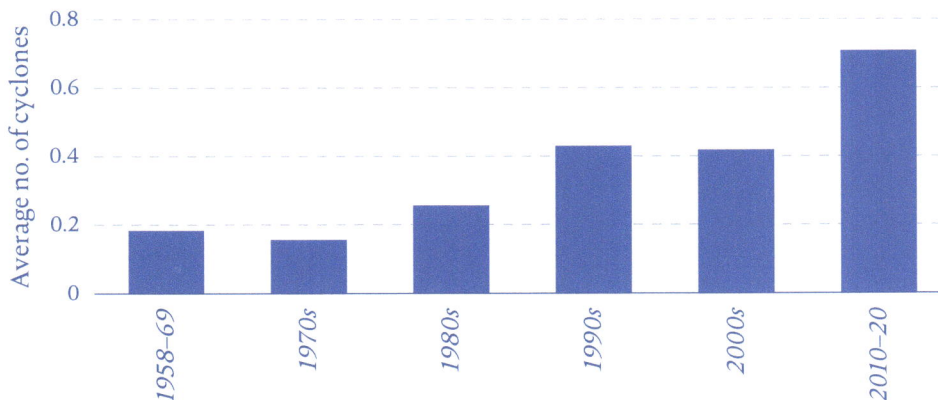

Sources: World Bank calculations based on Climatology Lab, TerraClimate (https://www.climatologylab.org/terraclimate.html); European Commission, Global Human Settlement (GHS) Urban Centre Database R2019 (https://ghsl.jrc.ec.europa.eu/ghs_stat_ucdb2015mt_r2019a.php).

Note: For any given month, a city is classified as being affected by a tropical cyclone if it had a storm with sustained winds of at least 96 miles per hour—that is, the storm was category 2 or stronger according to the Saffir-Simpson wind scale and was within 200 kilometers of the city's geographic center in that month. Frequency is calculated as the number of tropical cyclones a city experienced over each decade. The graph presents the average frequency across the global sample of urban centers that experienced a tropical cyclone at least once during January 1958–December 2020.

How green are cities today?

To what extent are cities responsible for the climate change that helps explain the evolution in weather anomalies they have experienced in recent decades? And, more generally, how "green" are cities today, not just in terms of their contributions to climate change but also in terms of, for example, their levels of outdoor air pollution and vegetation? To address these questions, this section analyzes data on carbon dioxide (CO_2) emissions, emissions of particulate matter of 2.5 microns or less in diameter ($PM_{2.5}$), and average vegetation levels (as detected in satellite imagery) for this report's consistently defined global sample of more than 10,000 cities. In doing so, and like subsequent sections of this chapter, it focuses on how these outcomes relate to basic city characteristics, including, most notably, a city's size and development level.

Although they have not typically made the link to climate change, urban economists have long emphasized that pollution, and therefore both CO_2 and $PM_{2.5}$ emissions, is among the key stresses that can arise from a city's growth. Fossil CO_2 emissions accounted for 77 percent of the world's anthropogenic GHG emissions in 2015. Since 2000, their increase has been the main source of the global increase in GHG emissions driving the Earth's warming (Crippa et al. 2019) and, with that increase, the global trends in the evolution of weather anomalies. Meanwhile, as a city's population increases, one might expect development pressures on open and green spaces to intensify, leading to a decrease in vegetation. A city's level of vegetation can also affect its local climate by influencing the strength of the urban heat island effect (box 1.4).

Box 1.4

Hot in the city: The causes and impacts of the urban heat island effect

Urban areas are *heat islands*—that is, they are hotter than the surrounding rural areas. Several factors contribute to this effect. Buildings and paved surfaces have high *thermal inertia*, meaning they absorb heat during the day and release it at night, which prevents cities from cooling. Buildings also trap heat and obstruct the flow of breezes. Cities typically have less vegetation than surrounding areas, so they benefit less from the shade and evaporative cooling that greenery provides. Heat from human sources (such as motor vehicles, factories, and air conditioners) also raises urban temperatures. The intensity of the urban heat island effect varies by season, time of day, and location within a city; but it can result in land surface temperatures that are more than 10°C higher than the equivalent rural land surface temperatures.

Exposure to extreme heat can result in higher mortality and morbidity, lower economic productivity, poorer educational outcomes, and higher rates of crime and violence, including sexual violence. Cities can mitigate urban heat by adding vegetation, using reflective materials on streets and buildings, and orienting buildings to maximize shade and breeze. They can also adapt to extreme heat events by preparing heat action plans, raising awareness about the health impacts of exposure to extreme heat, training public health workers to treat heat-related illnesses, and erecting cooling stations.

Source: Adapted from Deuskar 2022.

Cities as sources of climate change

Cities account for the majority of the world's CO$_2$ emissions

As a result of rapid urbanization, the world's population increasingly lives in cities. In 2015, 48 percent of the world's population lived in the consistently defined global sample of more than 10,000 cities examined here (Dijkstra et al. 2021). That percentage is close to the nearly 52 percent of the global population identified as living in cities in 2021 using official national definitions of urban areas—a share that is projected to increase to just over 68 percent by 2050 (United Nations 2019).[11] And an estimated 70 percent of global anthropogenic GHG emissions emanate from these cities (Hopkins et al. 2016).

Average per capita emissions across cities tend to increase with development, at least up to upper-middle-income status

Using data from the Global Human Settlement (GHS) Urban Centre Database of the European Commission, figure 1.6 shows how average production-based fossil CO$_2$ emissions differ across cities globally on a per capita basis at different levels of development and for different regions.[12] For emissions from the residential and transportation sectors—the sectors that urban planning and policies can most directly influence—the data tell a clear story: average emissions across cities increase with the level of development (figure 1.6, panel a).[13] The average per capita CO$_2$ emissions from these sectors for cities in high-income countries are therefore approximately 4 times those of cities in upper-middle-income countries, 10 times those of cities in lower-middle-income countries, and 76 times those of cities in low-income countries. Higher per capita transportation and residential emissions in higher-income country cities are consistent with higher levels of consumption of transportation and living space. On a regional basis, average per capita emissions from the residential and transportation sectors for North American cities dwarf those for cities in any other region; cities in Sub-Saharan Africa have the lowest average per capita emissions, followed by cities in South Asia—see figure 1.6, panel b.

However, when looking at average CO$_2$ emissions from all sectors—the residential and transportation sectors, as well as the energy, industrial, and agricultural sectors—the picture becomes more complicated because the GHS Urban Centre Database fails to distinguish missing values and zeroes in its reporting of the CO$_2$ data. If these values, which are common in the energy sector data, are treated as zeroes, then the qualitative patterns for average overall emissions per capita resemble those for average emissions per capita from the residential and transportation sectors. Thus, average overall emissions per capita across cities increase with the level of development, with emissions highest in cities in high-income countries and lowest in cities in low-income countries (figure 1.6, panel a). Meanwhile, on a regional basis North American cities are the biggest per capita emitters overall, followed by cities in the East Asia and Pacific and Europe and Central Asia regions. Cities in Sub-Saharan Africa are, again, the lowest per capita emitters (figure 1.6, panel b).

If, however, such values are treated as missing and the associated cities are dropped from the sample, the picture changes. Thus, although average per capita overall emissions again increase with the level of development, they do so only up to upper-middle-income status. Cities in high-income countries have lower per capita overall emissions than do cities in upper-middle-income countries (figure 1.6, panel a). On a regional basis, East Asia and Pacific rather than

Figure 1.6 Average CO$_2$ emissions per capita, by country income group and geographic region, 2015

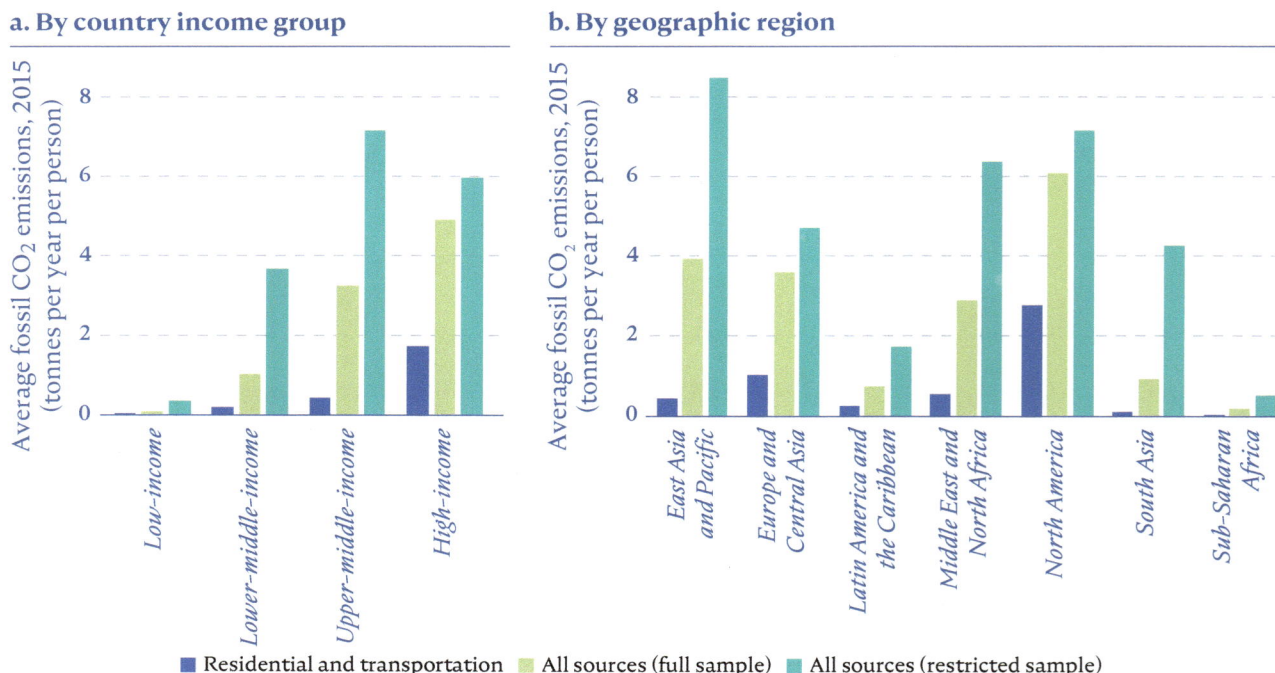

a. By country income group

y-axis: Average fossil CO$_2$ emissions, 2015 (tonnes per year per person)

x-axis categories: Low-income, Lower-middle-income, Upper-middle-income, High-income

b. By geographic region

y-axis: Average fossil CO$_2$ emissions, 2015 (tonnes per year per person)

x-axis categories: East Asia and Pacific, Europe and Central Asia, Latin America and the Caribbean, Middle East and North Africa, North America, South Asia, Sub-Saharan Africa

Legend: ■ Residential and transportation   ■ All sources (full sample)   ■ All sources (restricted sample)

Source: World Bank analysis based on data for 10,179 cities from the European Commission's Global Human Settlement (GHS) Urban Centre Database R2019 (https://ghsl.jrc.ec.europa.eu/ghs_stat_ucdb2015mt_r2019a.php), which derives its CO$_2$ emissions data from the European Commission's Emissions Database for Global Atmospheric Research (EDGAR v5.0).

Note: Each bar shows the unweighted average of long-cycle (fossil) CO$_2$ emissions per capita (measured in tonnes per year per person) of cities grouped by country income group (panel a) and World Bank region (panel b). From left to right, the first bar is based only on residential and transportation sources of CO$_2$ emissions. The middle bar is based on all sources, assuming that the missing information on CO$_2$ emissions from the agriculture, energy, and industrial sectors indicates that such emissions are zero. The last bar, a more conservative approach, is based only on a reduced sample of 3,148 cities for which CO$_2$ emissions data for all sectors are reported. CO$_2$ = carbon dioxide.

North American cities are the largest per capita emitters, while cities in Sub-Saharan Africa remain the lowest per capita emitters on average (figure 1.6, panel b).

These differences in results are likely explained by the fact that the CO$_2$ emissions data in the GHS Urban Centre Database cover only Scope 1 emissions, which are generated directly by activity within a city's boundaries (box 1.5). Crucially, such emissions do not include indirect emissions from the generation of purchased energy, known as Scope 2 emissions. These indirect emissions are instead attributed to the location of the energy-supplying power plants. Dropping cities with missing or zero values from the sample thus implies dropping cities that do not have power plants within their boundaries. If power plants within cities in upper-middle-income countries produce more CO$_2$ emissions per capita than power plants within cities in high-income countries, that could help explain why overall emissions per capita are higher in the former than in the latter.

Box 1.5

Greenhouse gas accounting and the four scopes of emissions

Greenhouse gas accounting identifies four scopes of emissions:

- *Scope 1.* Emissions directly generated by activity within a city's boundaries.

- *Scope 2.* Indirect emissions arising from the use of energy generated outside of a city's boundaries, including emissions from the use of grid-supplied electricity generated by power plants located in either other cities or rural areas.

- *Scope 3.* All other indirect emissions from outside a city's boundaries due to activities within the city, including emissions that occur in value chains associated with firms located in a city.

- *Scope 4.* Avoided emissions attributable to the use of a product and that occur outside of that product's life cycle or value chain, as well as policy choices or investment decisions that help avoid emissions that would have otherwise occurred. Fuel-saving tires are an example of a product that may help avoid emissions; a congestion charging scheme that successfully reduces vehicle miles traveled is an example of a policy that helps avoid emissions.

In formulating greenhouse gas inventories, most countries and cities have tended to focus on Scope 1 and Scope 2 emissions (Wiedmann et al. 2021); however, the future is likely to see a greater move toward preparing complete greenhouse gas inventories covering at least Scopes 1, 2, and 3, but potentially also tracking Scope 4.

In addition to Scope 1 and Scope 2 emissions, GHG accounting also conceptually defines Scope 3 and Scope 4 emissions (box 1.5). An important related distinction exists between production- and consumption-based emissions estimates, which raises the important question of whether a city's CO_2 emissions should be adjusted for international and internal trade (box 1.6).

In absolute terms, cities in upper-middle-income countries and in East Asia contribute the most to global CO_2 emissions

Moving from per capita to absolute production-based emissions, the data tell a consistent story regardless of how missing values are treated. Thus, for aggregate emissions from all sectors, cities in upper-middle-income countries contribute most to global fossil CO_2 emissions, accounting for about 55 percent of the total emissions generated in cities (figure 1.7, panel a). They are followed by cities in high-income countries, which account for about 31 percent of global emissions generated in cities. By contrast, cities in lower-middle-income countries account for only about 13 percent of emissions generated in cities, and cities in low-income countries for a meager 0.21 percent. The fact that cities in upper-middle-income countries account for a greater share of emissions than cities in high-income countries despite their lower per capita emissions (the case when missing values are treated as zeroes) is a result of their collectively larger population.[14] Meanwhile, on a regional basis cities in the East Asia and Pacific region account for about 50 percent of global CO_2 emissions generated in cities,

Box 1.6

Should a city's carbon dioxide emissions be adjusted for international and internal trade?

A consumption-based approach to carbon dioxide emissions accounting—one that assigns emissions to the point of final consumption of goods, services, and energy—offers a very different picture of a city's emissions than does one based on production. Consumption-based accounting includes emissions associated with goods, services, and energy imported and consumed locally, but excludes emissions associated with exported goods, services, and energy (or imported only to add value before exporting for final consumption elsewhere). It also excludes emissions associated with businesses serving visitors, such as emissions from hotels and tour operators serving tourists (Seto et al. 2021). Consumption-based emissions may, then, be higher or lower than production-based emissions, depending on the nature of trade, including internal trade with both other cities and rural areas in the same country, and tourism in the city.

Most global emissions data use a production-based approach, including the Emissions Database for Global Atmospheric Research (EDGAR) data included in the Global Human Settlement (GHS) Urban Centre Database. Moran et al. (2018), however, estimate consumption-based emissions for the same set of cities as the GHS Urban Centre Database (and therefore as this report's global sample). Their model uses urban versus rural consumption patterns and purchasing power as the main predictors of per capita carbon dioxide emissions, so it is agnostic on the point of origin of goods, services, and energy consumed. On this basis, Moran et al. find that a relatively small number of cities account for a disproportionate share of the world's carbon footprint. For example, the top 100 cities by carbon footprint are responsible for 18 percent of global consumption-based emissions.

Most of the cities in the top 200 are in high-income countries with high national carbon footprints; however, 41 of the top 200 are large cities—for example, Cairo, Dhaka, and Lima—in countries that otherwise have low carbon footprints. These cities have high total carbon footprints because of both their size and the relative affluence of their residents. Most of the world's largest cities and small cities, as well as most medium-size cities in high-income countries, have higher consumption-based than production-based emissions. The opposite is true for medium-size cities in low- and middle-income countries, presumably because they are more oriented toward manufacturing for export, while their own residents have relatively low consumption levels.

In formulating greenhouse gas inventories and therefore their approaches to net zero emissions, countries and cities have tended to adopt a production-based accounting perspective. This perspective naturally encourages an infrastructure-focused approach to climate action. Sweden, however, recently broke with this trend. In April 2022, its political parties agreed to include consumption-based emissions in the country's climate targets—the first country to do so. Sweden will thus have to not only look at its territorial emissions but also account for emissions imported into Sweden (Morgan 2022). Other countries and cities seeking to be at the forefront of climate action will likely follow Sweden's lead. C40 Cities, a global network of mayors, recently conducted a study of its member cities and finds that they represent 10 percent of global greenhouse gas emissions when accounting for consumption-based emissions (C40 Cities Climate Leadership Group, Arup, and University of Leeds 2019). The study also finds that action on consumption in the network's member cities could contribute to large reductions in emissions by 2050 for key consumption categories, including clothing and textiles (66 percent), food (60 percent), and aviation (55 percent).

followed by cities in the Europe and Central Asia region and North America, which together account for about 25 percent. Sub-Saharan African cities, by contrast, account for only about 1.6 percent of overall emissions (figure 1.7, panel b).

For the residential and transportation sectors, cities in high-income countries contribute the most to global CO_2 emissions

By contrast, for the residential and transportation sectors—again, the sectors urban planning and policies can most directly influence—cities in high-income countries account for the largest share of global CO_2 emissions generated in cities (figure 1.7, panel a). Although cities in the East Asia and Pacific region, collectively, remain the biggest emitters, the share of global emissions they generate in these sectors is, at about 33 percent, much smaller than their share

Figure 1.7 **Share of global CO_2 emissions generated in cities, by country income group and geographic region, 2015**

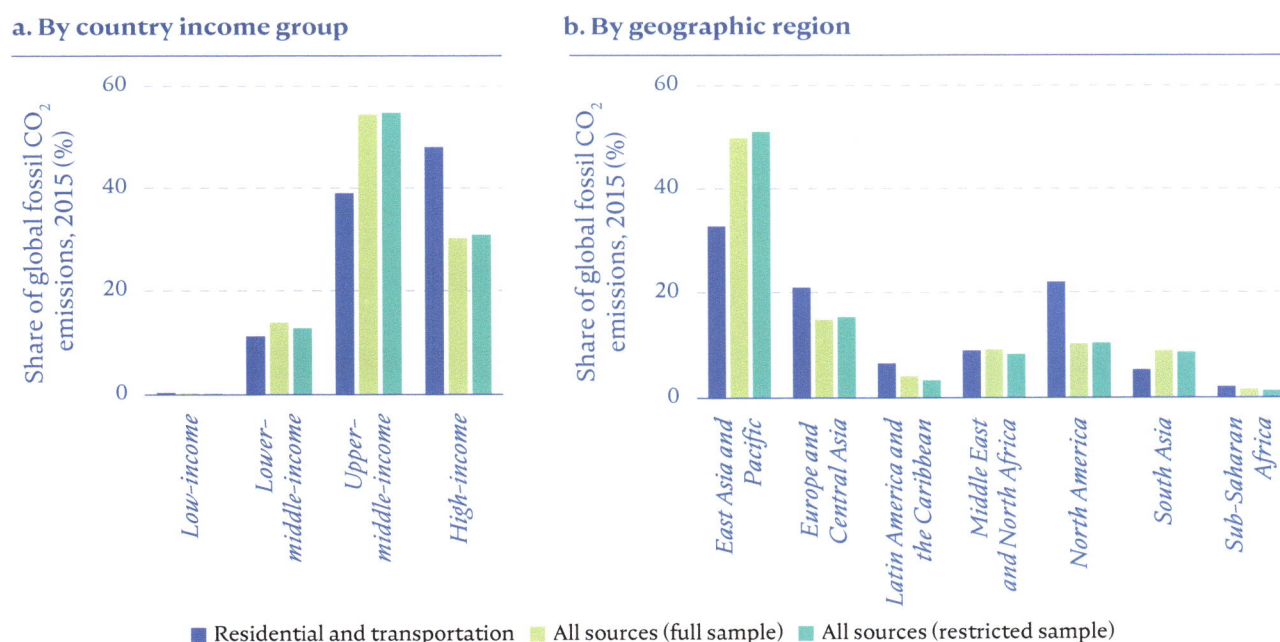

a. By country income group

b. By geographic region

Legend: Residential and transportation ■ All sources (full sample) ■ All sources (restricted sample)

Source: World Bank analysis based on data for 10,179 cities with complete information on residential and transportation CO_2 emissions from the European Commission's Global Human Settlement (GHS) Urban Centre Database R2019 (https://ghsl.jrc.ec.europa.eu/ghs_stat_ucdb2015mt_r2019a.php), which derives its CO_2 emissions data from the European Commission's Emissions Database for Global Atmospheric Research (EDGAR v5.0).

Note: Each bar shows the share of global long-cycle (fossil) CO_2 emissions generated in cities classified by income group and World Bank region. From left to right, the first bar is based only on residential and transportation sources of CO_2 emissions. The middle bar is based on all sources, assuming that the missing information on CO_2 emissions from the agriculture, energy, and industrial sectors indicates that such emissions are zero. The last bar, a more conservative approach, is based only on a smaller sample of 3,148 cities for which CO_2 emissions data for all sectors are reported. CO_2 = carbon dioxide.

of global urban emissions from all sectors. Meanwhile, cities in North America and Europe and Central Asia account for about 43 percent of the global residential and transportation sector emissions generated in cities (figure 1.7, panel b).

As cities develop, the sources of CO_2 emissions change

As cities develop, not only do their levels of CO_2 emissions tend to change but so, too, do the sources of those emissions (figure 1.8). Thus, emissions from energy and industry are more important for cities in middle-income countries than for those in low-income countries. However, although these sources remain large in absolute terms, they are relatively less important for cities in high-income countries than for those in middle-income countries. By contrast, the residential and transportation sectors are more important sources of emissions for cities in high-income countries in both absolute and relative terms.

These patterns are consistent with the pattern of structural transformation that tends to accompany development. Stereotypically, this pattern involves the emergence of industry

Figure 1.8 **Average shares of long-cycle CO_2 emissions sources for cities, by country income group, 2015**

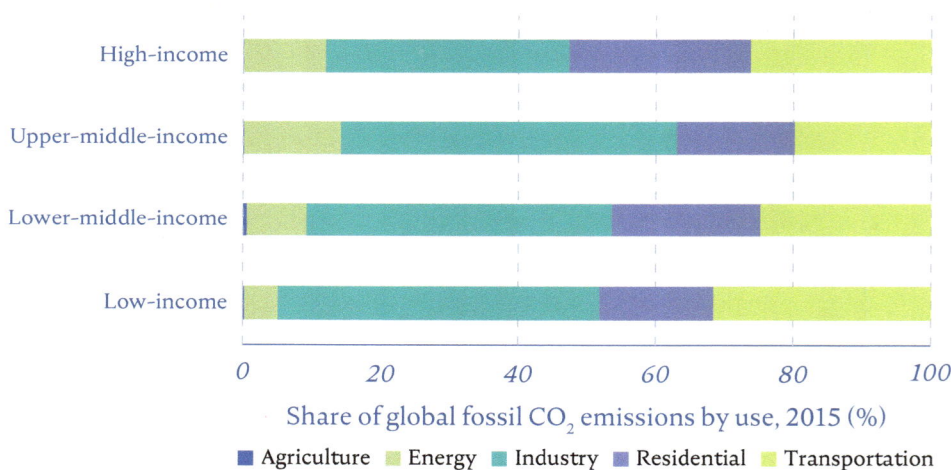

Source: World Bank analysis based on data for 10,179 cities with complete information on residential and transport CO_2 emissions from the European Commission's Global Human Settlement (GHS) Urban Centre Database R2019 (https://ghsl.jrc.ec.europa.eu/ghs_stat_ucdb2015mt_r2019a.php), which derives its CO_2 emissions data from the European Commission's Emissions Database for Global Atmospheric Research (EDGAR v5.0).

Note: Each bar shows the unweighted average percentage contribution of each of the five sectors to the total long-cycle (fossil) CO_2 emissions across cities in each income class. It is assumed that missing information on CO_2 emissions from the agriculture, energy, and industrial sectors indicates that such emissions are zero. Results are qualitatively identical if cities with missing values are instead dropped from the sample. CO_2 = carbon dioxide.

in cities at an early stage of development, followed by industry's subsequent move to the peripheries of cities and more rural areas, as well as overseas, as development evolves (World Bank 2009). More generally, cities increasingly become centers of consumption rather than of production as development progresses, again raising the question of whether a city's CO_2 emissions should be adjusted for international and internal trade (box 1.6).

Larger and more developed cities have higher levels of residential and transportation CO_2 emissions

Focusing again on the residential and transportation sectors, regression analysis reveals that, in the global sample, larger and more developed cities have larger CO_2 emissions (figure 1.9). Thus, in both sectors the size of a city's population, built-up area, and gross domestic product (GDP) per capita of the country in which it is located are all significantly positively related to its level of CO_2 emissions.

Figure 1.9 **Determinants of CO_2 emissions for cities globally, residential and transportation sectors, 2015**

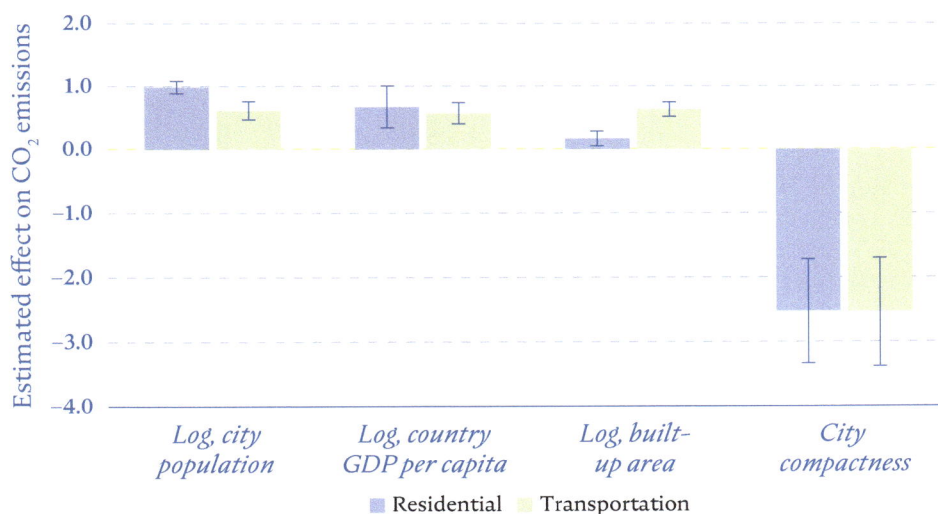

Source: World Bank analysis based on data for 2015 for 2,785 cities with population of over 200,000 from the European Commission's Global Human Settlement (GHS) Urban Centre Database R2019 (https://ghsl.jrc.ec.europa.eu/ghs_stat_ucdb2015mt_r2019a.php), which derives its CO_2 emissions data from the European Commission's Emissions Database for Global Atmospheric Research (EDGAR v5.0).

Note: For each sector, the graph presents estimated coefficients, together with the associated 95 percent confidence intervals, from a regression of a city's log CO_2 emissions on the log of its population, the log of the GDP per capita of the country in which the city is located, the log of its built-up area, and a measure of the city's compactness (the Polsby-Popper Ratio). The regressions, which also control for a city's climate (precipitation, temperature, biome, and elevation), are based on cross-sectional data for 2015 with robust standard errors. CO_2 = carbon dioxide.

More compact, less sprawling urban development may offset higher levels of residential and transportation CO_2 emissions

The regression results also reveal that, controlling for a city's size and level of development, more-compact cities have lower production-based CO_2 emissions from the residential and transportation sectors (figure 1.9 and figure 1.10).[15] This effect is strong in both sectors. In the residential sector, a 1-standard-deviation increase in a city's compactness is associated with a 77 percent reduction in emissions and in the transportation sector with an 81 percent reduction. These results are consistent with the hypothesis that urban planning and policies that enable better management of land and property market stresses lead to lower CO_2 emissions. Lower emissions could stem, for example, from more infill as opposed to leapfrog development and less reliance on personal motorized vehicles. This hypothesis is consistent, in turn, with findings that denser cities, which also tend to be more compact, have less commuting and car use, as well as lower levels of domestic energy consumption (Ahlfeldt and Pietrostefani 2019).

The results are also in line with the idea that encouraging tall buildings through, for example, the relaxation of restrictive floor area ratios, may have beneficial environmental effects. When considering the environmental impacts of tall buildings, however, the lower CO_2 emissions associated with a more compact urban form must be weighed against the higher embedded emissions associated with the construction of those buildings (see chapter 4).

Air pollution in cities

Poor air quality and climate change are closely linked

Of the various air pollutants, one of the most concerning, and the one on which this section focuses, is $PM_{2.5}$. $PM_{2.5}$ can penetrate deep into the lungs, increasing the likelihood of asthma, lung cancer, severe respiratory illness, and heart disease. Furthermore, black carbon, a short-lived climate pollutant, constitutes a major part of $PM_{2.5}$. Thus, not only are $PM_{2.5}$ emissions strongly correlated with CO_2 emissions (figure 1.11), but $PM_{2.5}$ emissions themselves also contribute to climate change.[16] This finding implies that urban policies that mitigate climate change also could significantly improve air quality (and vice versa). Better air quality would produce not only health benefits but also productivity benefits, because studies have shown that poor air quality harms worker productivity (Kahn and Li 2020).

Larger and less compact cities have more pollution than do smaller and more compact ones

Like the equivalent CO_2 emissions, a city's residential and transportation sector $PM_{2.5}$ emissions are significantly positively related to its population size, controlling for, among other things, the GDP per capita of the country in which the city is located and its built-up area (figure 1.12).[17] In other words, for a given level of development, larger cities tend to have more air pollution. This finding is consistent with those of two previous studies that find, using different data sources, a positive relationship between a city's size and its annual mean

Figure 1.10 **Relationship between city compactness and CO$_2$ emissions across cities globally, residential and transportation sectors, 2015**

a. Residential sector

Log of fossil CO$_2$ emissions, 2015 (tonnes/year)

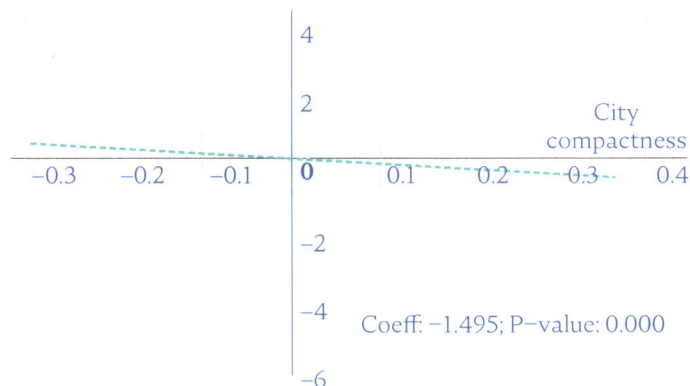

Coeff: −1.495; P−value: 0.000

b. Transportation sector

Log of fossil CO$_2$ emissions, 2015 (tonnes/year)

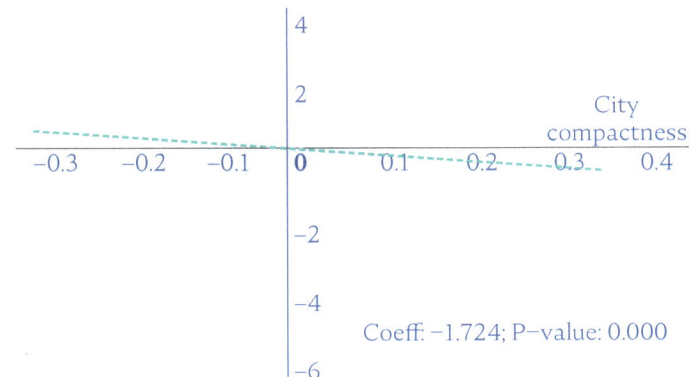

Coeff: −1.724; P−value: 0.000

Source: World Bank analysis based on data for 2,785 cities with a 2015 population of over 200,000 from the European Commission's Global Human Settlement (GHS) Urban Centre Database R2019 (https://ghsl.jrc.ec.europa.eu/ghs_stat_ucdb2015mt_r2019a.php), which derives its data on CO$_2$ emissions from the European Commission's Emissions Database for Global Atmospheric Research (EDGAR v5.0).

Note: Graphs are partial scatterplots of log CO$_2$ emissions in 2015 on a measure of city compactness (the Polsby-Popper Ratio) controlling for the log of a city's population, the log of its built-up area, a city's climate (precipitation, temperature, biome) and elevation, and country fixed effects. CO$_2$ = carbon dioxide.

Figure 1.11 Relationship between CO_2 and $PM_{2.5}$ emissions across cities globally, residential and transportation sectors, 2015

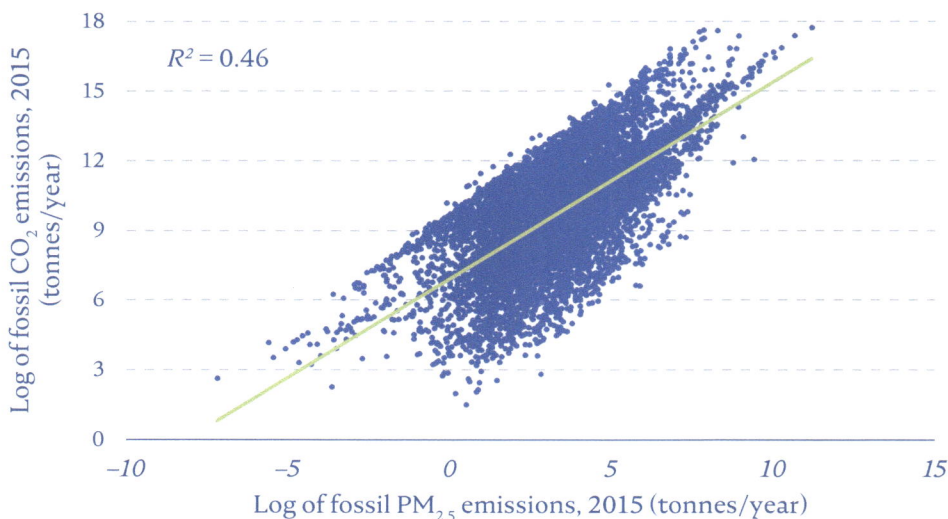

Source: World Bank analysis based on data for 10,179 cities with complete information on residential and transportation CO_2 and $PM_{2.5}$ emissions from the European Commission's Global Human Settlement (GHS) Urban Centre Database R2019 (https://ghsl.jrc.ec.europa.eu/ghs_stat _ucdb2015mt_r2019a.php), which derives its emissions data from the European Commission's Emissions Database for Global Atmospheric Research (EDGAR v5.0).

Note: The graph is a scatterplot of the log of the sum of residential and transportation long-cycle CO_2 emissions in 2015 on the log of the sum of residential and transportation $PM_{2.5}$ emissions in the same year. The slope of the fitted line implies that a halving of a city's $PM_{2.5}$ emissions in the residential and transportation sectors is associated with a roughly 43 percent reduction in CO_2 emissions. CO_2 = carbon dioxide; $PM_{2.5}$ = particulate matter of 2.5 microns or less in diameter.

concentration of $PM_{2.5}$ for a more limited sample of 381 cities in low- and middle-income countries (Ellis and Roberts 2016; Ferreyra and Roberts 2018).[18]

Also mirroring the findings for CO_2 emissions, more compact cities have significantly lower $PM_{2.5}$ emissions from the residential and transportation sectors (figure 1.12). This finding suggests that more compact urban development, by promoting less reliance on cars, not only reduces a city's contribution to climate change but also reduces local air pollution, thereby producing positive effects on health and well-being. Evidence for India and Latin America and the Caribbean also suggests that more compact urban development may be associated with higher productivity levels and growth rates (Duque et al. 2021; Tewari and Godfrey 2016). This possibility stems not only from improved air quality but also from the fact that more compact development increases the likelihood of knowledge spillovers, thereby strengthening agglomeration economies.

Figure 1.12 Determinants of PM$_{2.5}$ emissions for cities globally, residential and transportation sectors, 2015

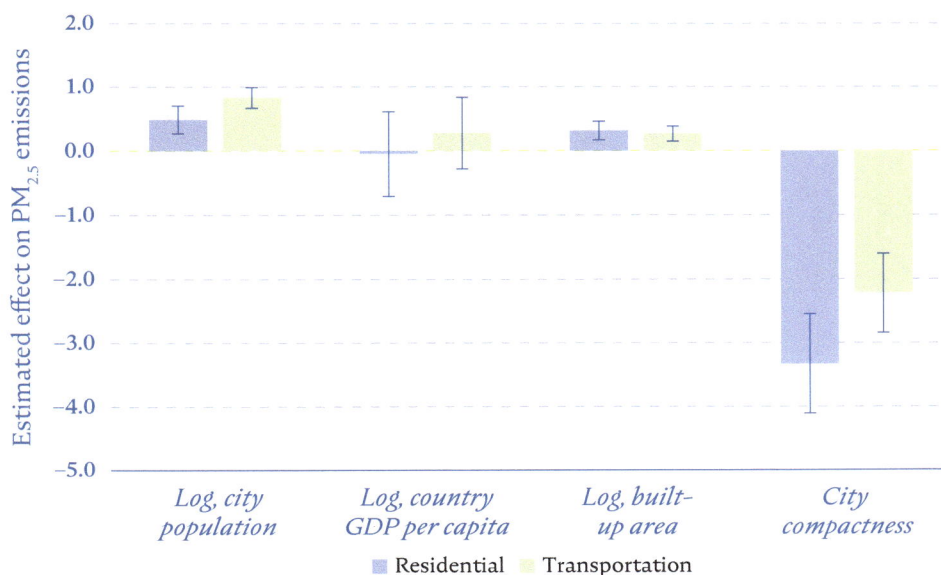

Source: World Bank analysis based on data for 2,785 cities with a 2015 population of over 200,000 from the European Commission's Global Human Settlement (GHS) Urban Centre Database R2019 (https://ghsl.jrc.ec.europa.eu/ghs_stat_ucdb2015mt_r2019a.php), which derives its data on PM$_{2.5}$ emissions from the European Commission's Emissions Database for Global Atmospheric Research (EDGAR v5.0).

Note: For each sector, the graph presents estimated coefficients, together with the associated 95 percent confidence intervals, from a regression of a city's log PM$_{2.5}$ emissions on the log of its population; the log of the GDP per capita of the country in which the city is located, as well as its interaction with a dummy variable that takes the value 1 if the country is upper-middle- or high-income; the log of its built-up area; and a measure of the city's compactness (the Polsby-Popper Ratio). The regressions, which also control for a city's climate (precipitation, temperature, biome) and elevation, are based on cross-sectional data for 2015 with robust standard errors. PM$_{2.5}$ = particulate matter of 2.5 microns or less in diameter.

Pollution first increases with development, then (eventually) declines

Thus, overall PM$_{2.5}$ concentrations are higher, on average, for cities in lower-middle-income countries than for cities in low-, upper-middle-, and high-income countries (figure 1.13). In cities in high-income countries, the average concentration is even lower than that for cities in low-income countries. This finding suggests the so-called environmental Kuznets curve relationship.

Many factors could explain the tendency of air pollution in cities to decline as countries move from lower-middle- to upper-middle- and then to high-income status. More prosperous countries tend to specialize more in services whose production is less polluting than the production

Average of PM$_{2.5}$ concentrations across cities, by country income group, 2000 and 2015

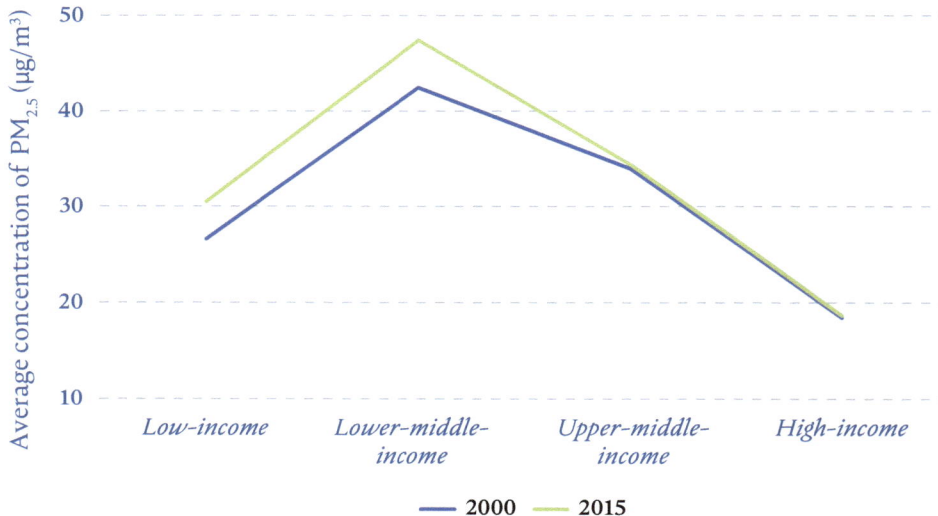

Source: World Bank analysis based on data for 10,303 cities from the European Commission's Global Human Settlement (GHS) Urban Centre Database R2019 (https://ghsl.jrc.ec.europa.eu/ghs_stat _ucdb2015mt_r2019a.php), which derives its data on PM$_{2.5}$ concentrations from the Global Burden of Disease (GBD) 2017 database on ambient air pollution.

Note: The graph shows the weighted average of PM$_{2.5}$ concentrations across cities in each income classification, where the weights are given by city population. µg/m³ = micrograms per cubic meter; PM$_{2.5}$ = particulate matter of 2.5 microns or less in diameter.

of manufactured goods, which they have a greater tendency to import. Although the consumption of imported manufactured goods in more developed countries may still be associated with air pollution, that pollution occurs in other countries (Feng, Hubacek, and Yu 2019; Wiedmann and Lenzen 2018). More prosperous countries also often have a greater capacity and resources to monitor pollution and to enact and enforce regulations (Awe et al. 2015; Dasgupta et al. 2004). Moreover, cleaner fuels and technologies are more affordable in richer countries. For example, people in poorer countries use inexpensive but highly polluting biomass fuels such as wood and coal for household cooking and heating (Bruce, Perez-Padilla, and Albalak 2000).

Meanwhile, residents of more developed countries tend to have higher environmental health literacy because they have higher levels of education and better access to information. As a result, they are more aware of the adverse impacts of poor air quality and thus likelier to demand policy action in response (Raufman et al. 2020). Wealthier and better-educated people are also more willing to pay for improvements in air quality (Mariel, Khan, and Meyerhoff 2022).

Better urban air quality should not, however, be considered an automatic outcome of a country's evolution from lower-middle- to higher-income levels.[19] As the history of London demonstrates (box 1.7), the introduction of policies that helped improve air quality in many of today's most developed cities have often encountered stiff political resistance from vested interest groups. Sometimes, only a crisis has catalyzed decisive political action.

BOX 1.7

How did London get rid of (most of) its smog?

The problem of industrial air pollution in London was recognized as early as 1661, if not before, when a government official, John Evelyn, presented King Charles II with a treatise titled *Fumifugium: or the Inconvenience of the Aer and Smoake of London Dissipated*. In 1819, a committee appointed to study the problem concluded that the city's smoke-filled air was bad for residents' health. However, it was not until enactment of the Smoke Nuisance Abatement (Metropolis) Acts of 1853 and 1856 that London's police were empowered to act against industrial emitters of smoke. These regulations, enacted despite opposition from industrial interests claiming that smoke had health benefits, were not enough. Because most of London's smoke came not from industrial sources but from the chimneys of private houses, which used a coal fire for heating, London's air quality hardly improved.

The turning point came about a century later when the Great Smog of 1952 suffocated London. Weather conditions caused unprecedented levels of smoke and sulfur dioxide to concentrate in London's air, leading to an estimated 3,500–4,000 deaths. Although the government initially claimed that no new regulations were needed, it eventually succumbed to pressure and opened an inquiry into the problem of air pollution. The recommendations of the inquiry led to passage of the Clean Air Act of 1956, which was extended in 1968. This act regulated pollution from residential, commercial, and industrial sources and provided grants for retrofitting houses to burn smokeless fuels. It also created "smokeless zones" covering half of Greater London, in which only smokeless fuels were permitted for domestic heating. As a result, London's air pollution declined rapidly. The widespread adoption of central heating, along with further legislation in subsequent decades, further contributed to this decline.

Despite these improvements, thousands of Londoners died each year from causes linked to air pollution exposure—even as recently as 2016. A series of regulations since then, including a ban on the entry of polluting vehicles into central London's Ultra Low Emissions Zone, and technological improvements to bus and taxi fleets have had dramatic results. For example, the number of Londoners living in areas exceeding the legal limit for nitrogen oxide concentrations fell by 94 percent between 2016 and 2019. Even after this improvement in air quality, however, nearly all of London still exceeds the World Health Organization's guideline limit for particulate matter of 2.5 microns or less in diameter.

London's experience offers three lessons. First, improvements in air quality do not automatically go hand in hand with development. Rather, they result from deliberate policy actions, often enacted in the face of stiff opposition from vested interest groups. Second, although obviously better avoided, a disaster such as the Great Smog of 1952 can present an opportunity for decisive action to tackle serious environmental ills that might otherwise linger. And, third, the battle to address urban stresses never ends. Even in the most developed of cities, policy makers need to continually seek policy improvements to keep at bay the stresses that arise from the pressure of a city's population on its land and housing markets, its supplies of basic services and infrastructure, and the environment.

Sources: Based on Greater London Authority 2002, 2020.

Green cover: To what extent are cities literally green?

The greenery in cities—that is, the trees and other vegetation in parks and elsewhere—comes with important benefits for a city's residents. Not only does greenery have an inherent amenity, but its presence can also play an important role in mitigating the urban heat island effect (see box 1.4 and Deuskar 2022). Despite those benefits, the demand for land that comes with the growth of urban population can place development pressure on green spaces within a city, adding to the other stresses of urbanization.

To capture a city's average greenness, this section draws on data derived from satellite imagery for this report's global sample of more than 10,000 cities and, in particular, on a measure of average greenness based on the color of the pixels within each city's area.[20]

More populous cities have lower average greenness, and average greenness first declines with development before increasing

Regression analysis reveals a negative relationship between a city's average greenness and its population size, controlling for both its level of development and aspects of its geography and climate that may be correlated with both greenness and size (figure 1.14, panel a). Like the results for CO_2 and $PM_{2.5}$ emissions, this finding is consistent with the existence of stronger stresses for larger cities.

By contrast, mirroring the results for air pollution, a city's average greenness first tends to decrease as development of the country in which it is located advances before subsequently increasing (figure 1.14, panel b). This relationship holds for the three years—1990, 2000, and 2014—for which data are available but has shifted over time. Although in 1990 cities in lower-middle-income countries had the lowest levels of average greenness, in 2000 and 2014 cities in upper-middle-income countries did.

Most cities have become greener in recent decades, although probably not because of deliberate greening policies

Panel b of figure 1.14 also reveals that between 1990 and 2000 average greenness increased, on average, across cities at all levels of development, then stabilized between 2000 and 2014. For the entire 1990–2014 period, however, most cities globally exhibited an increase in their average greenness (map 1.1). The most notable exceptions to this trend were the cities on China's eastern seaboard, which grew extremely rapidly over the sample period, and those in South America. Beijing has responded to these trends with deliberate policies aimed at (re-)greening the city (box 1.8).

Although the widespread increases in average greenness over the last three decades may seem like an encouraging development, it is unlikely that, with some exceptions, adoption of greening policies by cities has driven the trend. Indeed, on a global scale greenness is more strongly affected by changes in CO_2 concentrations than by land use changes (Schut et al. 2015). This effect does not mean that climate change is beneficial in terms of vegetation. To the contrary, climate change increases the stressors that undermine plant resilience and disrupt both forest structure and ecosystem services. Rising temperatures

Figure 1.14 Relationship between average greenness and population size across cities globally, 2014, and average greenness and level of development across cities globally, 1990, 2000, and 2014

a. Average greenness, by population size

b. Average greenness, by country income group

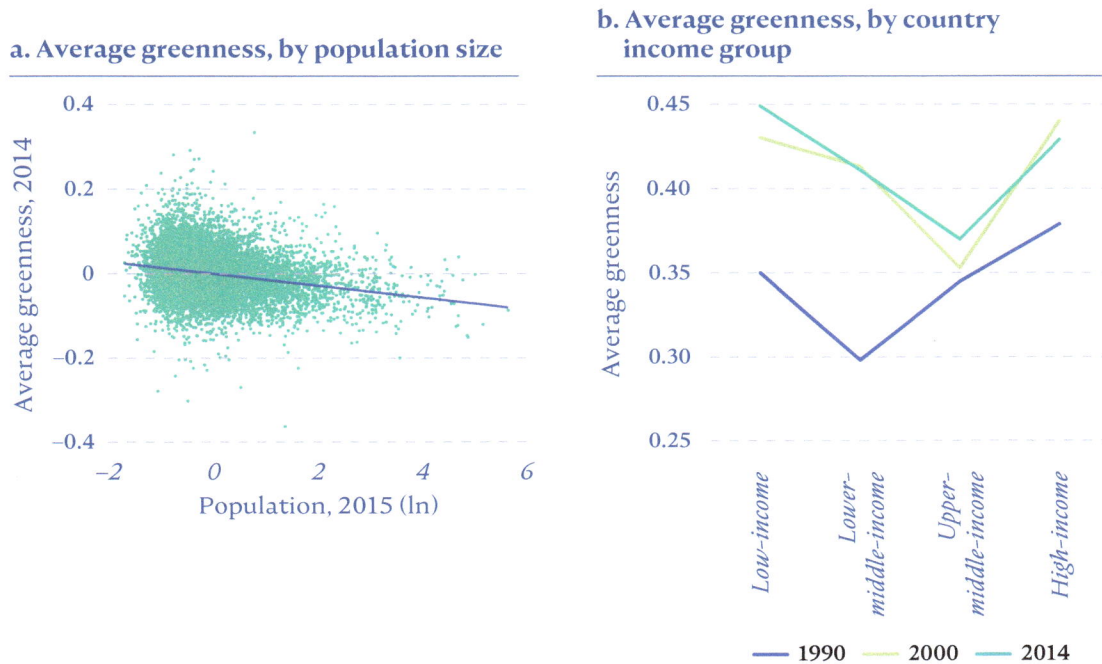

Source: World Bank analysis based on data for 8,893 cities from the European Commission's Global Human Settlement (GHS) Urban Centre Database R2019 (https://ghsl.jrc.ec.europa.eu/ghs_stat_ucdb2015mt_r2019a.php).

Note: Panel a is a partial scatterplot of a city's average greenness in 2014 against the natural log of its population in 2015 controlling for its GDP per capita level, latitude and longitude, elevation, average levels of rainfall and temperature in 2014, biome zone, and country fixed effects. Panel b shows the unweighted mean of average greenness across cities by country income group. ln = natural log.

also increase the frequency of droughts, wildfires, and invasive pest outbreaks, leading to the loss of plant species.[21]

How resilient are cities today?

Now that it is clearer how green cities are globally, this section turns to the question of their resilience. To see what lessons might emerge about cities' resilience to climate change–related shocks, it first considers evidence from the urban economics literature on the long-run resilience of cities to large-scale shocks to their stocks of both physical and human capital. It then presents, for this report's global sample of cities, new empirical evidence on the short-run

Map 1.1   Percentage change in average greenness across cities globally, 1990–2014

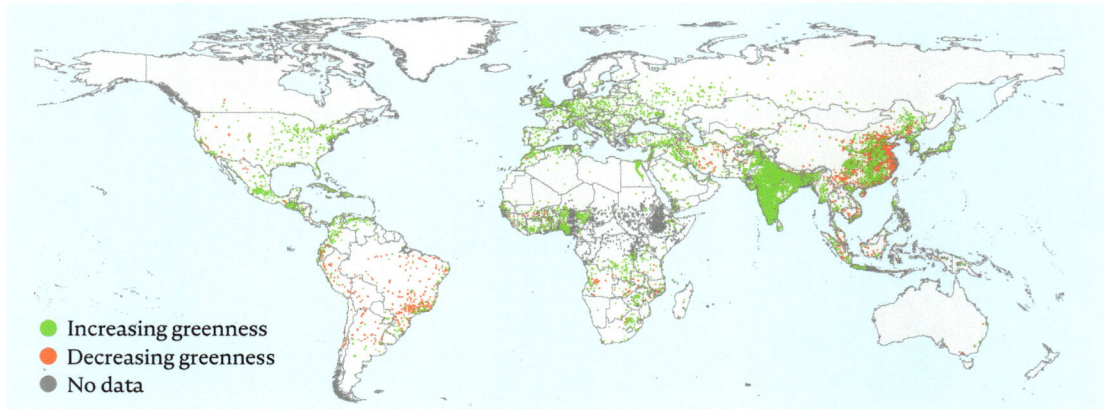

- ● Increasing greenness
- ● Decreasing greenness
- ● No data

Source: World Bank analysis based on data on the level of average greenness for 10,660 cities, as defined in box 1.1, from the European Commission's Global Human Settlement (GHS) Urban Centre Database R2019 (https://ghsl.jrc.ec .europa.eu/ghs_stat_ucdb2015mt_r2019a.php).

Note: The percentage change in average greenness between 1990 and 2014 is calculated as $[(Avg.Green_{BU,2014} - Avg.Green_{BU,1990})/Avg.Green_{BU,1990}] \times 100$, where $Avg.Green_{BU,x}$ denotes the level of average greenness in a city's built-up area in year x.

Box 1.8

Beijing's afforestation miracle

Beijing—a megacity of 22 million people that suffers from air pollution, the urban heat island effect, and a host of other environmental problems—might not be expected to offer a positive example of urban greening. Between 2012 and 2016, however, the city undertook a massive urban afforestation program, the One Million Mu Plain Afforestation Project (a *mu* is equivalent to 1/15 of a hectare). The project involved planting 54 million trees over an area of 700 square kilometers. Much of the afforested area lies between the city's central districts and new city centers on the periphery. The urban forest ecosystem now includes large forests, ecological corridors, nine "wedges" of green space, green belts, and parks of various sizes. Because of this initiative, tree cover in the Beijing plain increased by 42 percent.

Independent studies of Beijing's afforestation initiative find that it successfully increased the city's green cover. Nevertheless, the locations in which afforestation occurred were not always laid out as specified in the original plans. Although the initiative originally intended to avoid afforesting agricultural land, almost 80 percent of the newly forested area covers former cropland. Studies also observe the need for greater civic participation, which includes giving voice to otherwise excluded or marginalized members of society, in the initiative's planning and implementation.

Sources: FAO 2018; Jin, Sheppard, and Wang 2021; Yao, Xu, and Zhang 2019.

resilience of economic activity to the various types of weather anomalies—hot, cold, wet, and dry events, as well as tropical cyclones—whose evolution in response to climate change was examined earlier in this chapter. In doing so, this section also considers how a city's resilience varies with its size, level of development, and baseline climate.

Evidence on the long-run resilience of cities to the destruction of many forms of physical, and even human, capital provides some grounds for optimism

A large empirical literature has emerged over the last two decades documenting the long-run resilience of cities—defined here as the ability of cities to recover their population levels and economic vitality following an adverse shock—to many forms of extreme physical destruction. For example, Schencking (2006, 833) describes the great Tokyo earthquake of 1923, which left more than 120,000 dead and just over 1.5 million homeless, as "one of the most devasting and disruptive natural disasters of the 20th century." Yet not only did Tokyo survive the earthquake, but it also went on to thrive. By 1925, just two years after the earthquake, the population of Tokyo prefecture had reached 4.49 million, an increase of 64 percent over that in 1920, a few years before the earthquake. By 1940, its popula-tion had further climbed to 7.35 million, almost double its pre-earthquake level in 1920 (Glaeser 2022).

Similarly, Ager, Eriksson, and Lonstrup (2020) find that the 1906 San Francisco earthquake, which destroyed 28,000 buildings, killed about 3,000 people, and left more than 225,000 homeless, did not spell the city's end. Quite the contrary—between 1900 and 1910, San Francisco's population grew at a faster rate than between both 1890 and 1900 and 1910 and 1920. Moreover, San Francisco grew faster than cities such as Boston and Philadelphia, which were among its main competitors at the time. More recently, although Hurricane Katrina was associated with a large drop in the population of both the city and metropolitan area of New Orleans after it hit in 2005, the population of the metropolitan area has since largely recovered (Glaeser 2022).

These findings of cities' long-run resilience to the physical destruction caused by earthquakes and tropical cyclones also carry over to other sources of major physical destruction, including the Great Fire of London of 1666, the Boston Fire of 1872, and the Chicago Fire of 1871 (Glaeser 2022). Indeed, the latter two fires, both of which caused devastating short-term physical damage, seem to have generated longer-term economic benefits by allowing the cities to build back better (Glaeser 2012; Hornbeck and Keniston 2017). In Chicago, a clutch of talented architects were attracted to the city by its continued population growth, which implied a huge demand for floor space, and the empty land left when physical structures at the city's center burned. According to the renowned urban economist Edward Glaeser (2022, 10), "This agglom-eration of talent both rebuilt the city, and invented the skyscraper, which would reshape city skylines worldwide, in the process."

Historically, even large-scale bombing, such as that experienced by German and Japanese cities during World War II and Vietnamese cities during the Vietnam war, seems to have done little to undermine cities' long-run economic prospects (Brakman, Garretsen, and Schramm 2004; Davis and Weinstein 2002). Indeed, although flattened in 1945 by the atomic bombs that forced Japan's eventual surrender in World War II, Nagasaki and Hiroshima had returned to their prewar population growth paths by 1960 and the mid-1970s, respectively (Davis and Weinstein 2002).

This evidence of long-run resilience of cities to shocks that destroy large portions of their physical capital is mirrored by evidence of long-run resilience to shocks that destroy significant portions of their human capital stocks. Thus, in considering the potential long-run impacts of the COVID-19 pandemic on cities, Glaeser (2022, 10) notes, "The Black Death, Yellow Fever, Cholera and the 1918–1919 Influenza Pandemic are the most direct antecedents of the COVID-19 pandemic. Yet there is little evidence that any of these terrible killers did much to deter urban growth, at least in the west, and at least since 1200 CE."

More generally, Glaeser (2022) argues that, in the long run, a city will tend to recover, in terms of both population and economic vitality, from even the most devastating shocks to its physical and human capital stocks, provided its underlying fundamentals remain sound—in particular, if it remains an attractive location for workers, especially skilled workers, and for businesses. So long as this is the case, the demand for urban (residential and commercial) floor space will be more than sufficient to cover the costs of rebuilding. And with rebuilding comes the opportunity to build back better. Moreover, the demand for urban floor space will likely remain sufficiently buoyant in a rapid urbanizing context, like that characterizing the developing world.

Climate change will, however, threaten a city's long-run fortunes if it precipitates a major economic or political shock

These findings offer grounds for optimism that, from a long-run perspective, cities in low- and middle-income countries will be able not only to survive but also to thrive in the face of the ever-harder punches they can expect from mother nature because of climate change. The major exceptions may occur if climate change makes a city's climate so unpleasant or its location so hazardous that large numbers of people no longer wish to live there. The city's decline would, then, need to be managed. One historical example of this possibility is Port Royal in southeastern Jamaica, which was once the largest city in the Caribbean. It is now known to postmedieval archaeologists as the "city that sank" following a devastating earthquake in 1692 that liquified the ground on which it was built (Lanthier 2007). At its height, just before the earthquake, Port Royal had a population ranging from 6,500 to 10,000 (Buisseret 1966; Claypole 1972; Pawson and Buisseret 1975; Taylor 1688). In 2011, its population stood at just 884.[22]

Other major exceptions may occur if climate change itself precipitates a major economic or political shock to a city.[23] For example, climate change could lead to a loss of comparative advantage in the production of the goods or services in which a city specializes, or it might exacerbate inequalities to such an extent that it leads to strong political discord and maybe even violence, which, in turn, leads to the flight of segments of a city's population. The cities that face perhaps the greatest risk of loss of comparative advantage are those that specialize in the extraction of fossil fuels, such as the coal mining towns of eastern Europe, which can expect to be directly hit by the energy transition (see chapter 5 for further discussion).

The short- to medium-term impacts of climate change–related shocks on cities may be significant and, for many households, devastating

The observation that cities have tended to exhibit remarkable long-run resilience is not to deny, however, that negative shocks associated with climate change can cause potentially severe, aggregate economic losses to a city in the short to medium term. Nor is it to deny that, in the face of an increased frequency of shocks, these losses will accumulate over time unless a city becomes more fully adapted to such shocks. Furthermore, although a city may survive and even thrive in response to one or more climate change–related shocks, households may suffer devastating losses from any given shock.

A full analysis of the factors that determine resilience at the household and neighborhood level is beyond the scope of this report. It is possible, however, to offer some new empirical evidence on how short-run aggregate economic resilience varies across this report's global sample of cities in the face of different types of weather anomaly, the frequency and intensity of which have been evolving—and will continue to evolve—with climate change. This evidence comes from background research for this report by Park and Roberts (2023), who examine the impacts of various types of weather anomaly on a city's level of economic activity. Using data for the period April 2012–December 2020, their research analyzes how a weather anomaly (as defined in box 1.2) in any given month affects a city's aggregate economic activity in that same month. Because of the absence of high-frequency GDP data for cities, the research follows the now standard practice of using the intensity of a city's nighttime lights as a proxy for its aggregate level of economic activity.[24]

When confronted by abnormal weather events, both small and large cities in low- and lower-middle-income countries suffer more than cities in upper-middle- and high-income countries

Table 1.1 summarizes the estimates by Park and Roberts (2023) of the impacts of five different types of weather anomalies—hot, cold, wet, and dry anomalies, and tropical cyclones—on a city's nighttime lights. In their analysis, Park and Roberts distinguish between estimated impacts for small and large cities in all income groups, with a small (large) city defined as one whose population in 2015 was below (above) the global median of 371,885.[25] In the cases of hot, cold, wet, and dry anomalies, the table also distinguishes between the estimated impacts of anomalies of any size (Extreme = —) and those of extreme anomalies (Extreme = Y). For the anomalies of any size, the cells report the estimated impact of a 1-standard-deviation change in the relevant weather variable (temperature or precipitation) from a city's long-run average for that variable on its nighttime light intensity. For extreme anomalies, the table reports the estimated impact of a 2-standard-deviation or greater anomaly. Finally, for tropical cyclones, the cells report the estimated impact of a category 2 or stronger cyclone that occurs within 200 kilometers of a city's geographic center.

Table 1.1 **Estimated impacts of various types of weather anomaly on the intensity of a city's nighttime lights, by country income group, April 2012–December 2020**

Type of anomaly	Extreme	All cities		Cities, developing countries		Cities, developed countries	
		Small cities	Large cities	Small cities	Large cities	Small cities	Large cities
Hot	—	−0.007	−0.008	−0.009	−0.015	−0.003	−0.003
	Y	−0.005	−0.009	−0.017	−0.024	0.008	0.004
Cold	—	0.025	0.016	0.024	0.005	0.026	0.029
	Y	0.072	0.042	0.079	0.025	0.055	0.061
Wet	—	−0.002	−0.004	−0.001	−0.004	−0.005	−0.004
	Y	−0.025	−0.021	−0.024	−0.021	−0.026	−0.020
Dry	—	−0.009	−0.004	−0.030	−0.015	0.013	0.005
	Y	−0.034	−0.053	−0.065	−0.052	0.026	−0.051
Cyclone	—	−0.12	−0.09	−0.21	−0.30	−0.05	−0.000

Significant at ▢ 1 % ▢ 5 % ▢ 10 %

Sources: Derived from Park and Roberts 2023. Results are based on the analysis of monthly composites of nighttime lights derived from VIIRS (Visible Infrared Imaging Radiometer Suite) satellite data (https://payneinstitute.mines.edu/eog-2/viirs/), monthly weather data from Climatology Lab, TerraClimate (https://www.climatologylab.org/terraclimate.html), and tropical cyclone data from International Best Track Archive for Climate Stewardship (https://www.ncdc.noaa.gov/ibtracs/).

Note: The numbers in the cells indicate the estimated impact of a 1-standard-deviation change in each weather variable from its historical norm; for extreme anomalies (Extreme = Y), the numbers indicate the estimated impact if the weather variable deviates by 2 standard deviations or more from its historical norm. "Extreme = —" indicates hot, cold, wet, and dry anomalies of any size; the impacts of tropical cyclones are estimated using a dummy variable, which takes the value of 1 if a city experienced a category 2 or stronger cyclone (based on the Saffir-Simpson wind scale) within 200 kilometers of its center. "Cities, developing countries" are in countries classified by the World Bank as either low- or lower-middle-income. "Cities, developed countries" are those in countries classified by the World Bank as either upper-middle-income or high-income. Small (large) cities are those with a 2015 population below (above) the sample median.

Park and Roberts estimate that all types of weather anomalies, except for cold anomalies, will have negative impacts on a city' lights in the month in which the anomaly occurs—in both small and large cities in low- and lower-middle-income countries, and regardless of whether all or only extreme anomalies are considered. Furthermore, except for wet anomalies in small cities in these countries, all estimated negative impacts are statistically significant. The estimated negative impacts of tropical cyclones are particularly large—a category 2 or stronger cyclone reduces nighttime light intensity by 21 percent in a small city in low- and lower-middle-income countries and by 30 percent in a large city in this income group. Extreme dry shocks also have quite severe negative estimated impacts on local economic activity—dimming a small city's lights in a low- or lower-middle-income country by 6.5 percent and those in a large city in such a country by 5.2 percent. By contrast, both wet and hot anomalies, even if extreme, are estimated to have much smaller, although still statistically significant, negative impacts.

In marked contrast to the results for cities in low- and lower-middle-income countries, the estimated impacts of weather anomalies on economic activity for cities in upper-middle- and high-income countries are generally statistically insignificant and/or nonnegative. The major exception is extreme wet shocks. If a large city in an upper-middle- or high-income country experiences extreme rainfall during a month, the intensity of its lights for that month is reduced by an estimated 2 percent. For a small city in this income group, the estimated reduction is larger—2.6 percent. These estimated negative impacts of extreme rainfall are comparable to those for cities in low- and lower-middle-income countries.

The fact that, in general, weather anomalies have much more severe estimated negative impacts for cities in lower- than in higher-income countries is consistent with a greater level of resilience on the part of the latter. The results provide just a partial picture of resilience, however, because they consider only the immediate impacts of a weather shock and remain silent on the subsequent path of recovery of economic activity or lack thereof. Nevertheless, related research that also uses lights data suggests a quicker rebound of economic activity for a city in an upper-middle- or high-income country than for a city in a low- or lower-middle-income country. Thus, although a city in a higher-income country may restore economic activity to its preshock level within one month, a city in a lower-income country needs two months (Gandhi et al. 2022; Lall et al. forthcoming). In turn, their greater resilience is likely due to investments in basic services and urban infrastructure, not to mention emergency preparedness, that leave cities in higher-income countries better placed to handle especially extreme anomalies. This finding suggests that both economic development and inclusiveness are vital to building resilience.

Interestingly, and in contrast to all other types of weather anomaly, Park and Roberts (2023) estimate the impacts of cold anomalies to be positive for small cities in both lower- and higher-income countries, regardless of size.

For cities in low- and lower-middle-income countries, their baseline climate matters

In lower-income countries, cities with warmer baseline climates drive the estimated positive impact of cold anomalies on urban economic activity. Thus, in hot cities a cold anomaly leads to a significant brightening of lights in the same month, whereas such an anomaly has no significant impact on the lights of cities with cold baseline temperatures. This result is consistent with the idea that cold anomalies make the weather in hot cities unusually pleasant, and it seems plausible that this benefit could stimulate more economic activity. However, because climate change has contributed to a declining frequency of cold anomalies across cities globally since the 1970s, cooler, more pleasant evenings in cities in lower-income countries with hot baseline climates have become, and will likely continue to become, increasingly rare.

More generally, and especially for cities in low- and lower-middle-income countries, weather anomalies are estimated to have more severe impacts on economic activity when they go in the same direction as a city's baseline climate. Thus, hot, wet, and dry anomalies have larger negative impacts in cities with hot, wet, and dry baseline climates—with impacts particularly evident for dry anomalies in cities in lower-income countries with dry baseline climates (figure 1.15). Because both dry and hot anomalies have increased in frequency over time, these results are especially worrying for cities with dry or hot baseline climates in these income groups. Unless these cities can better adapt to dry and hot anomalies, they will accumulate greater losses in aggregate economic activity over time. However, the analysis by Park and Roberts (2023) does provide some cautious reasons for optimism on this front. Implicit in the construction of their weather anomaly variable, and therefore in their results, is the idea that cities will adjust over time to long-run changes in their climates. Their variable defines anomalies relative to a city's own long-run average temperature/precipitation level, while also

Figure 1.15 Estimated impacts of hot, cold, wet, and dry anomalies on cities in low- and lower-middle-income countries with hot, cold, wet, and dry baseline climates, April 2012–December 2020

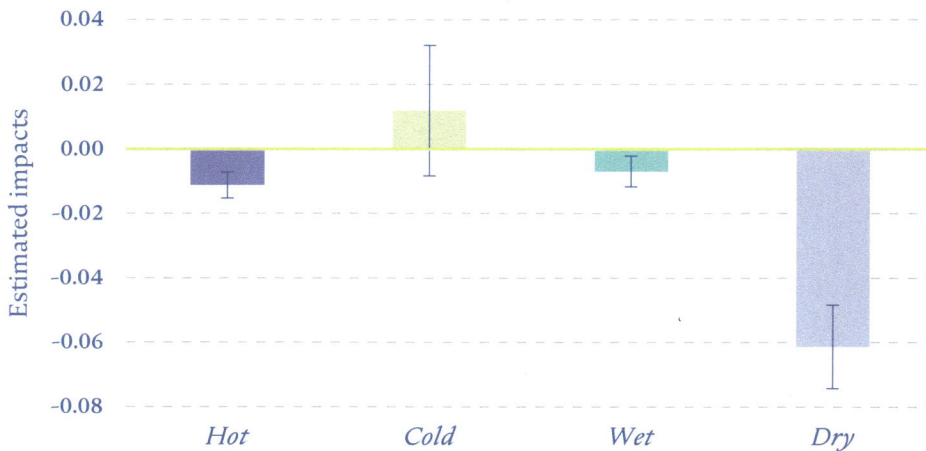

Sources: Derived from Park and Roberts 2023. Results are based on the analysis of Visible Infrared Imaging Radiometer Suite (VIIRS) nighttime lights monthly composites (https://payneinstitute .mines.edu/eog-2/viirs/) and monthly weather data from Climatology Lab, TerraClimate (https://www.climatologylab.org/terraclimate.html).

Note: Each bar shows the estimated impact of a 1-standard-deviation weather anomaly, where anomalies are calculated following the methodology described in box 1.2. Each vertical black line indicates the upper and lower bounds of the 95 percent confidence interval associated with the corresponding estimated impact. Hot (cold) cities are in the top (bottom) half of the global distribution of long-run mean monthly temperature. Wet (dry) cities are in the top (bottom) half of the global distribution of long-run mean monthly precipitation.

considering the city's own long-run variability around that average. As climate change shifts the long-run average and level of variability, the meaning of an anomaly also changes. A key question, however, is how fast such adaptation occurs and whether policy can do anything to speed it up. Chapter 5 picks up on this question.

How inclusive are cities today?

Inclusion figures prominently in the World Bank's GRID (green, resilient, and inclusive development) strategy launched in 2021 in response to the challenges posed by climate change, the more general degradation of the environment, and other factors (World Bank 2021). This section focuses on the inclusion dimension of a city's development, recognizing that, as mentioned at the chapter's outset, a city's greenness and resilience are linked to its level of inclusiveness and vice versa.

Inclusion has many important, and frequently overlapping, dimensions. They include but are not limited to gender, disability status, socioeconomic status, employment status, religion, age, sexual orientation, residency or citizenship status, race, marital status, ethnicity, and location. Unfortunately, lack of data makes it difficult to consider and do justice to all these dimensions in this report. Thus, this section focuses mainly on five measures of inclusion for which city-level data are available: poverty, access to basic services, spousal violence as an indicator of (lack of) gender inclusion, intracity household income inequality, and health outcomes. It acknowledges, however, that other important aspects of inclusion are either not well covered or not covered at all. Spotlight 1 (which appears after chapter 2) presents a more detailed analysis of inclusion in Peruvian cities, showcasing an innovative multidimensional approach to assessing inclusion. Chapter 3, as part of its more general discussion of the impacts of climate change on cities, discusses the results of various analyses that relate to inclusion. They include an analysis of the gender-differentiated impacts of tropical cyclones on displacement from cities and how various climate change–related stressors affect a city's areas with slums versus areas without slums and neighborhoods with different socioeconomic characteristics.

In focusing on poverty, access to basic services, spousal violence, intracity household income inequality, and health outcomes, this section draws on work by a variety of authors—Combes et al. (2022); Ferreyra and Roberts (2018); Henderson and Turner (2020); and Roberts, Gil Sander and Tiwari (2019). Except for Ferreyra and Roberts (2018) and Roberts, Gil Sander, and Tiwari (2019), these authors define urban areas using the degree of urbanization approach (see box 1.1). Instead of considering different sizes of urban centers (cities), however, their analyses focus on the differences between cities, less densely populated and smaller urban clusters (towns and suburbs), and rural areas. The samples considered are also not fully global, which suggests caution in generalizing the derived insights.

Box 1.9 presents a more globally comprehensive analysis of levels of social inclusion, but the analysis focuses only on aggregate urban–rural differences. The inclusion measures considered here represent more the outcomes of the interaction of agglomeration economies and urban stresses, and how well these stresses are managed, than the stresses themselves. A city's poverty rate offers an obvious example. A concept related to but distinct from that of social inclusion is social cohesion. Box 1.10 presents analysis of aggregate differences in social cohesion (which may also condition the impacts of climate change) between urban and rural areas across countries.

Larger and more developed urban areas have lower poverty rates

As revealed in figure 1.16, all seven low- and lower-middle-income countries—Angola, Bangladesh, the Arab Republic of Egypt, Ethiopia, Ghana, Tanzania, and Vietnam—analyzed by Combes et al. (2022) have lower poverty rates in urban than in rural areas based on the same globally consistent definition of cities used elsewhere in this report. The figure shows that, at both the extreme global poverty line of US$1.90 a day and the middle-income global poverty line of US$3.20 a day, poverty rates are lower in more densely populated larger cities (urban centers) than in less densely populated smaller towns and suburbs (urban clusters). In turn, towns and suburbs have lower poverty rates than rural areas. The one exception to this pattern is Egypt, where the US$1.90-a-day poverty rate is slightly higher for cities than for towns and suburbs.[26]

Although they use national definitions of both urban areas and poverty rates rather than globally consistent definitions, Ferre, Ferreira, and Lanjouw (2012) also find clear evidence that poverty rates tend to be lower in larger urban settlements in a further eight low- and middle-income countries: Albania, Brazil, Kazakhstan, Kenya, Mexico, Morocco, Sri Lanka, and Thailand. Meanwhile, Roberts, Gil Sander, and Tiwari (2019) provide evidence that in

BOX 1.9

Comparing levels of social inclusion in urban versus rural areas

The analysis in this report reveals that more populous urban areas tend to be more inclusive on several indicators: poverty rate, access to various types of basic services, and basic health outcomes such as infant mortality. The analysis, however, is based only on various subsamples of countries or on selected regions. For a more comprehensive global analysis, this box presents the results from the construction of a new index of social inclusion that captures, for a sample of 79 countries, access to markets; services such as financial ones, which may affect a person's ability to (self-)insure against climate change–related shocks and stresses; and digital spaces, which could, for example, be important in helping spread information on climate change–related hazards. This index leverages the Social Sustainability Global Database recently developed by the World Bank.[a]

Although the data do not permit the construction of the index for individual cities or size classes of cities, or disaggregation for specific vulnerable individuals and groups, they do allow analysis of overall urban–rural differences across countries for circa 2020 and how these differences vary with a country's level of development. More precisely, for any given country the social inclusion index takes a value of between 0 and 1, with higher values signifying higher average levels of access to markets, services, and digital spaces. The index is constructed separately for each country's urban and rural populations, and is based on the equal weighting of six indicators: labor force participation rate, share of the population with a bank account, share of households with access to adequate sanitation, share of households with access to electricity, secondary school enrollment rate, and share of households with access to the internet.[b] As figure B1.9.1, panel a, shows, the index indicates higher social inclusion in urban than in rural areas in all World Bank regions. More specifically, access to markets, services, and digital spaces is, on average, higher in urban areas than in rural areas. It is in that sense that urban areas are found to be more inclusive. This urban advantage is largest in Sub-Saharan Africa and South Asia, and smallest in Europe and Central Asia and the Middle East and North Africa. Consistent with this finding, the urban advantage tends to decline with a country's development level (figure B1.9.1, panel b) because, as countries develop, the provision of basic services tends to spread increasingly from urban to rural areas, leading to catch-up even while provision continues to improve in cities (World Bank 2009).

What drives the overall gap between urban and rural areas globally? It turns out that higher access to internet, electricity, and adequate sanitation acts as the main driver. Differences in financial inclusion and (secondary) education between cities and rural areas are less marked. Rural populations report higher access to labor markets as captured by labor market participation rates. The fact that higher access to internet, electricity, and sanitation drives the overall gap is consistent with the lower average costs of supplying infrastructure networks in densely populated areas, which can spread over a greater number of users the large up-front fixed costs of constructing such networks. The spreading of these large up-front fixed costs is a source of agglomeration economies that benefits not only productivity but also social inclusion.

BOX 1.9 *continued*

Figure B1.9.1 **Social inclusion index for urban and rural areas, by geographic region, and relationship between urban–rural gap in social inclusion index and level of development across countries, circa 2020**

a. Social inclusion index, by geographic region

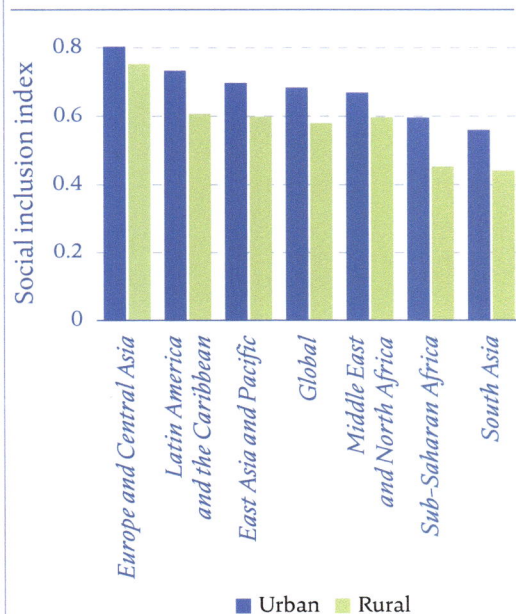

b. Relationship between urban–rural social inclusion index gap and GDP per capita

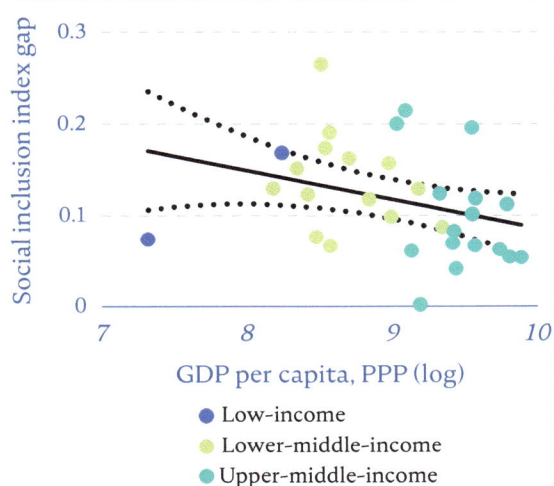

Low-income
Lower-middle-income
Upper-middle-income

Urban   Rural

Source: World Bank calculations based on data from World Bank, Social Sustainability Global Database; World Bank 2022a. Also see World Bank 2022b.

Note: The vertical axis in panel a is the value of the social inclusion index; in panel b it is the difference in the value of the index in a country's urban and rural areas. The social inclusion index is calculated as the average of six indicators: labor force participation rate, share of population with a bank account, share of households with access to adequate sanitation, share of households with access to electricity, secondary school enrollment rate, and share of households with access to the internet. The index is constructed with the latest value for each indicator between 2016 and 2020. The GDP per capita values in panel b are for 2020. The solid and dotted lines in panel b respectively indicate the fitted line and 95 percent confidence intervals based on all countries included in the calculation. PPP = purchasing power parity.

a. World Bank, Social Sustainability Global Database 2022a.

b. Results are robust to the number of indicators used and to alternative choices of the indicators. See Cuesta, Madrigal, and Pecorari (forthcoming) for a detailed discussion of these robustness checks.

Indonesia poverty rates are lower in the cores of large metropolitan areas than in their urbanized peripheries, whose rates are, in turn, lower than those in smaller, less densely populated nonmetro urban areas.

The tendency for poverty rates to be lower in larger and more developed urban areas of lower-income countries is consistent with the tendency of these areas to provide both more formal and higher-paying jobs. In turn, larger and more developed urban areas tend to provide better jobs because, compared with smaller and less developed urban areas, they tend to be home to higher-valued-added industries and because agglomeration economies make workers in these areas more productive (Roberts, Gil Sander, and Tiwari 2019; World Bank 2009). Thus cities provide "escalators out of poverty" for in-migrants (Glaeser 2012). Chapter 4 assesses whether climate change–related shocks and stresses are slowing down these escalators.

Although the cross-country data on urban poverty rates are not sufficient to allow for a meaningful analysis of their correlation with national levels of GDP per capita, national rates of overall poverty tend to decline with a country's level of development at both the US$1.90 and US$3.20 global poverty lines. Indeed, globally a 1 percent increase in a country's level of urbanization, which has a strong positive correlation with its GDP per capita, is associated with a

Box 1.10

Cities tend to have slightly lower levels of social cohesion than rural areas

Although this report focuses on issues of inclusion, a distinct but related concept is that of social cohesion—that is, a sense of shared purpose, trust, and willingness to cooperate among members of a group, between members of different groups, and between people and government. More cohesive societies are expected to be better prepared to withstand climate change–related shocks, avoid conflict, redistribute income and wealth toward vulnerable and marginalized populations, and leave no one behind (Chatterjee, Gassier, and Myint, forthcoming).

A social cohesion index was constructed to compare the social cohesion of urban and rural populations across a global sample of countries. This index uses the equal weighting of five indicators that capture the extent to which residents trust each other, trust their government, tolerate minorities, have not been the victim of a crime, and actively participate in political and civic spaces.[a] The index takes a value between 0 and 1, with higher values indicating more cohesive societies.

The results show that, in a reversal of the pattern seen for social inclusion (see box 1.9), rural areas are slightly more cohesive than urban areas both globally and in all World Bank regions (figure B1.10.1, panel a). Social cohesion in rural areas exceeds that in cities by the largest proportion in the East Asia and Pacific region and Sub-Saharan Africa, and by the smallest proportion in the Middle East and North Africa. Rural areas have, on average, higher confidence in governments and residents who are more likely to participate in elections, to be members of an organization, and to report lower victimization rates. By contrast, residents in urban areas have slightly higher trust in people and tolerance of (racial) minorities. Furthermore, as societies become richer and more urbanized, the rural social cohesion edge diminishes (figure B1.10.1, panel b). This finding suggests that, as a country develops, its cities should also become at least as cohesive as its rural areas.

Box 1.10 *continued*

Figure B1.10.1   Social cohesion index for urban and rural areas, by geographic region, and relationship between urban–rural gap in social cohesion index and level of development across countries, circa 2020

a. Social cohesion index, by geographic region

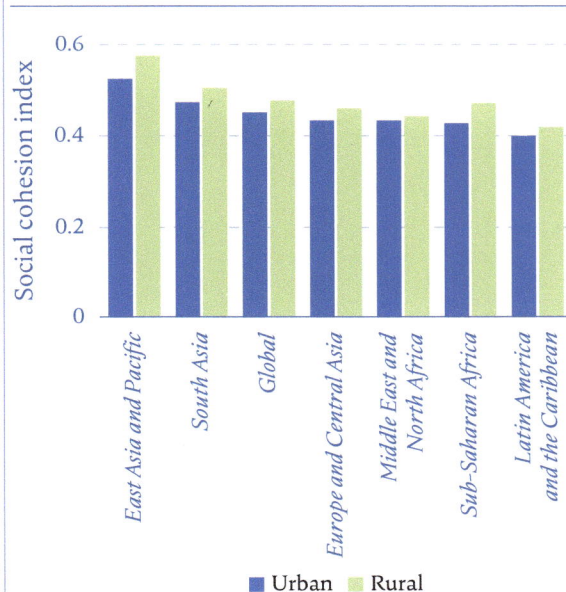

b. Relationship between the urban-rural social cohesion index gap and GDP per capita

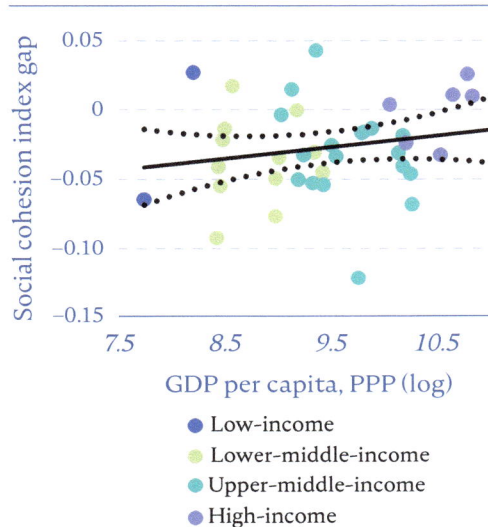

Source: World Bank calculations based on data from World Bank, Social Sustainability Global Database; World Bank 2022a. Also see World Bank 2022b.

Note: The vertical axis in panel a is the value of the social cohesion index; in panel b it is the difference in the value of the index in a country's urban and rural areas. The social cohesion index is calculated as the average of five indicators: share of population that (1) says most people can be trusted, (2) has confidence in government, (3) voted in the last national election, (4) is an active member of any organization, and (5) has not been a victim of a crime. The index is constructed with the latest value for each indicator between 2016 and 2020. The GDP per capita values in panel b are for 2020. The solid and dotted lines in panel b respectively indicate the fitted line and 95 percent confidence intervals based on all countries included in the calculation. PPP = purchasing power parity.

a. Data on these indicators come from World Bank, Social Sustainability Global Database 2022, https://worldbankgroup.sharepoint.com/:u:/r/teams/SSI-DataandAnalytics-WBGroup/Shared%20Documents/Global%20Dataset/Global%20database%20versions/Base%2003222022/final_24.dta?csf=1&web=1&e=Ym2tDU. Also see World Bank 2022.

Figure 1.16   Poverty rates (US$1.90 and US$3.20) for three types of urban and rural areas, selected countries, 2015

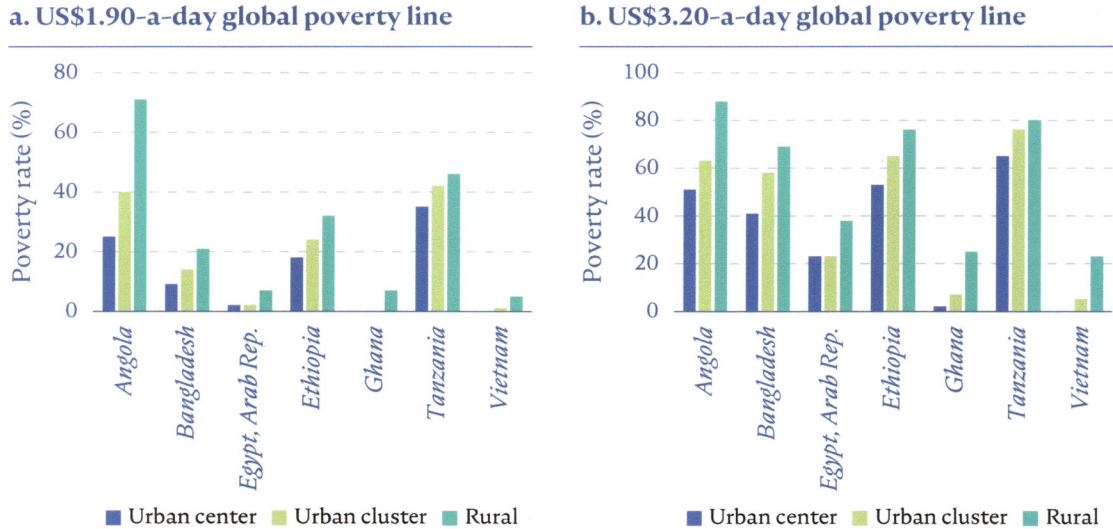

a. US$1.90-a-day global poverty line

b. US$3.20-a-day global poverty line

Source: Combes et al. 2022, based on WorldPop gridded population data for 2015 and household budget survey data for circa 2015.

Note: Urban centers (cities), urban clusters (towns and suburbs), and rural areas are defined using the degree of urbanization methodology outlined in box 1.1. Both the US$1.90 and US$3.20 global poverty lines are defined in 2011 constant international prices at purchasing power parity exchange rates using country-specific spatial price deflators.

1 percent decline in the share of its population living on less than US$3.20 per day (Roberts, Gil Sander, and Tiwari 2019). It seems likely, therefore, that urban poverty rates at both lines also fall as countries develop.

Residents of cities tend to have better access to basic services and better health outcomes than do residents of towns and suburbs

Not only do poverty rates tend to be lower in cities than in towns and suburbs—whose poverty rates, in turn, tend to be lower than those in rural areas—but access to basic services also tends to be better, as do many health outcomes. For example, as shown in figure 1.17, panel a, households in cities in Latin America and the Caribbean, South Asia, Southeast Asia, and Sub-Saharan Africa have better access to safely managed drinking water than do households in towns and suburbs, which, in turn, have better access than rural households (Henderson and Turner 2020).[27] Meanwhile, infant mortality rates in the four regions tend to follow a reverse pattern—lower in cities than in towns and suburbs, and lower in towns and suburbs than in rural areas. Exceptions are Latin America and the Caribbean and Southeast Asia, where cities

Figure 1.17 **Household access to safely managed drinking water and infant mortality rates, by urban and rural areas, selected regions, circa 2015**

a. Households with access to safely managed drinking water

b. Infant mortality rates

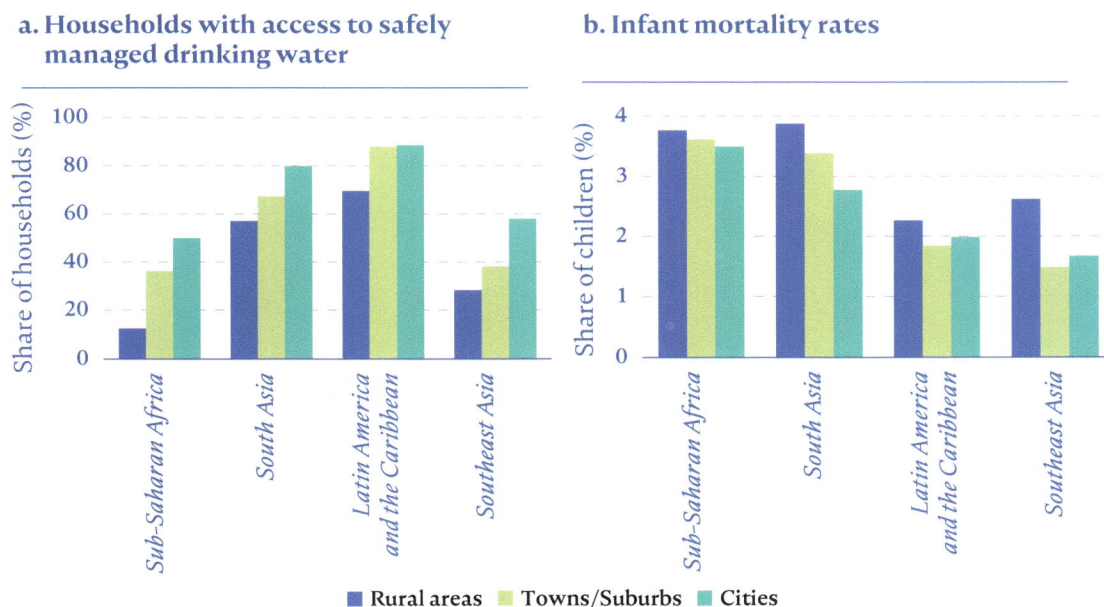

■ Rural areas   ■ Towns/Suburbs   ■ Cities

Source: World Bank calculations using data from Henderson and Turner 2020 and downloaded from https://doi .org/10.7910/DVN/YZ46FJ. The underlying data from the Demographic and Health Surveys cover different survey years across countries from 2010 to 2016.

Note: Urban centers (cities), urban clusters (towns and suburbs), and rural areas are defined using the degree of urbanization methodology outlined in box 1.1. In panel a, safely managed drinking water is defined as all improved water sources that take zero minutes to collect or are on the premises. Improved water sources include all piped water and packaged water, in addition to protected wells or springs, boreholes, and rainwater. In panel b, infant mortality is defined as child death within three months of birth among those born from three months to three years before the survey was administered.

have slightly higher infant mortality rates than do towns and suburbs. The same patterns hold for access to a wide range of other basic services, including schooling, electricity, and improved sanitation, as well as for child health outcomes, such as the share of children for whom diarrhea is reported. Although they use a different definition of urban areas, Roberts, Gil Sander, and Tiwari (2019) likewise report patterns of better access to basic services and health outcomes in larger cities than in smaller ones in Indonesia. Such patterns have also been reported for numerous other low- and middle-income countries in the World Bank's series of Urbanization Reviews.[28]

Using once more the examples of access to safely managed drinking water and infant mortality, figure 1.18 shows that access to basic services and many basic health outcomes in cities tend to improve as development occurs. Thus, although for Latin America and the Caribbean, South Asia, Southeast Asia, and Sub-Saharan Africa the share of households in a country's cities with access to safely managed drinking water is positively correlated with its level of GDP per capita, the rate of infant mortality in cities is negatively correlated.

Figure 1.18 **Relationship between a city's level of development and its access to safely managed drinking water and its infant mortality rate, selected regions, circa 2015**

a. Households with access to safely managed drinking water

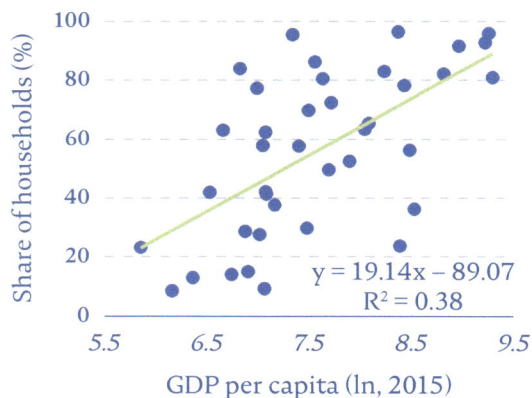

b. Infant mortality rates

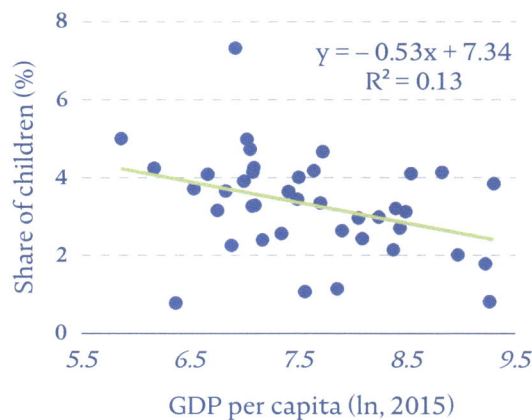

Source: World Bank calculations using data on household access to safely managed drinking water and infant mortality from Henderson and Turner 2020 and downloaded from https://doi.org/10.7910/DVN/YZ46FJ. The underlying data from the Demographic and Health Surveys cover different survey years across countries from 2010 to 2016; data on gross domestic product (GDP) and population are from the European Commission's Global Human Settlement (GHS) Urban Centre Database R2019 (https://ghsl.jrc.ec.europa.eu/ghs_stat_ucdb2015mt_r2019a.php).

Note: In both panels, GDP per capita and the percentage values are calculated for cities in 40 countries (3 in Southeast Asia, 5 from Latin America and the Caribbean, 3 from South Asia, and 29 from Sub-Saharan Africa). Panel a excludes Cambodia because of limited data. The term *cities* refers to urban centers as defined in box 1.1. In panel a, safely managed drinking water is defined as all improved water sources that take zero minutes to collect or are on the premises. Improved water sources include all piped water and packaged water, in addition to protected wells or springs, boreholes, and rainwater. In panel b, infant mortality is defined as child death within three months of birth among those born three months to three years before the survey was administered. ln = natural log.

Cities in some regions tend to have lower prevalence of spousal violence

In South Asia and Southeast Asia, the share of currently married women who report having ever experienced spousal violence is lower in cities than in towns and suburbs (figure 1.19, panel a). In both regions, a lower share of married women in towns and suburbs than in rural areas also reports having ever experienced spousal violence. Even in cities, however, reported rates of spousal violence remain very high. The pattern of less spousal violence in larger and denser areas reverses for Latin America and the Caribbean—that is, the share of married women who report ever having experienced spousal violence is higher in cities than in towns and suburbs. That share is, in turn, higher than that in rural areas. In Sub-Saharan Africa, the share of married women who report ever having experienced spousal violence is roughly the same in cities as in rural areas, but married women in towns and suburbs report less spousal violence.

Figure 1.19 **Reported levels of spousal violence experienced by currently married women and of women who believe wife beating is justified, by type of urban and rural area, selected geographic regions, circa 2015**

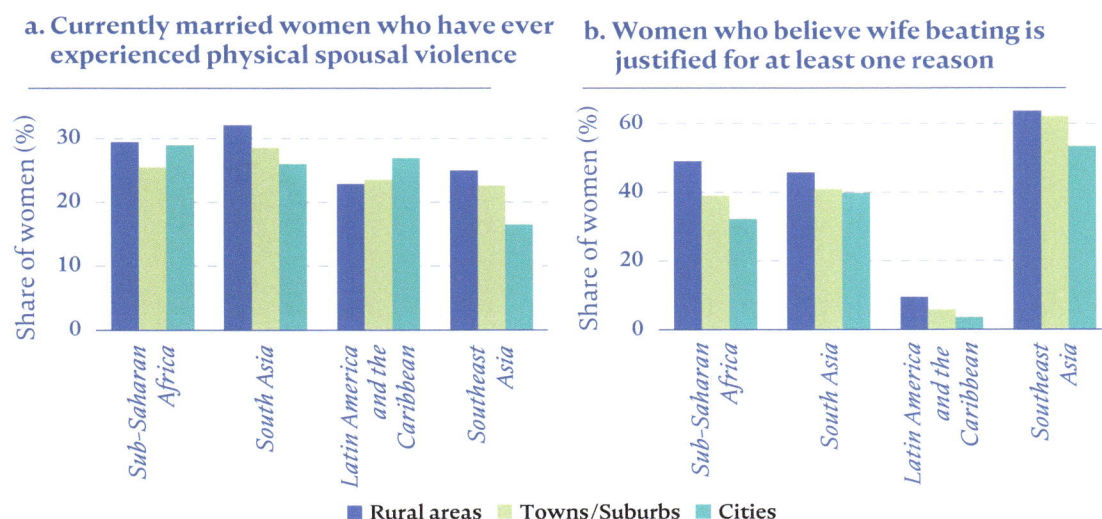

a. Currently married women who have ever experienced physical spousal violence

b. Women who believe wife beating is justified for at least one reason

■ Rural areas   ■ Towns/Suburbs   ■ Cities

Source: World Bank calculations using data from Henderson and Turner 2020 and downloaded from https://doi .org/10.7910/DVN/YZ46FJ. The underlying data from the Demographic and Health Surveys cover different survey years across countries from 2010 to 2016.

Note: Urban centers (cities), urban clusters (towns and suburbs), and rural areas are defined using the degree of urbanization methodology outlined in box 1.1.

In general, the share of women who believe wife beating is justified for at least one reason is lower in cities than in towns and suburbs, and lower in towns and suburbs than in rural areas. Although Southeast Asia has the lowest level of reported spousal violence among currently married women, it has the highest share of women who say they believe wife beating is justified. More generally, even in cities the share of women who believe wife beating is justified for at least one reason is shockingly high, especially outside of Latin America and the Caribbean, ranging from more than 3 in 10 women in Sub-Saharan Africa to more than 5 in 10 women in Southeast Asia. Using data on South Africa, Bruederle, Peters, and Roberts (2017) estimate that a 1-standard-deviation increase in temperature is correlated with an 8.6 percent increase in sexual crimes. Meanwhile, for Madrid, Spain, Sanz-Barbero et al. (2018) report a positive correlation between heat waves (temperatures over 34°C) and the incidence of intimate partner violence.

Larger cities, especially in lower-income countries, tend to have higher intracity household income inequality

In low- and middle-income countries, income equality between households within a city tends to increase with a city's size—see figure 1.20 for 16 countries in Latin America and the Caribbean (panel a) and for Indonesia (panel b). Such a positive relationship is consistent with a greater concentration of households with skilled workers in larger cities than in smaller

Figure 1.20 **Relationship between income inequality and city size in 16 Latin American and Caribbean countries, circa 2014, and in Indonesia, 2017**

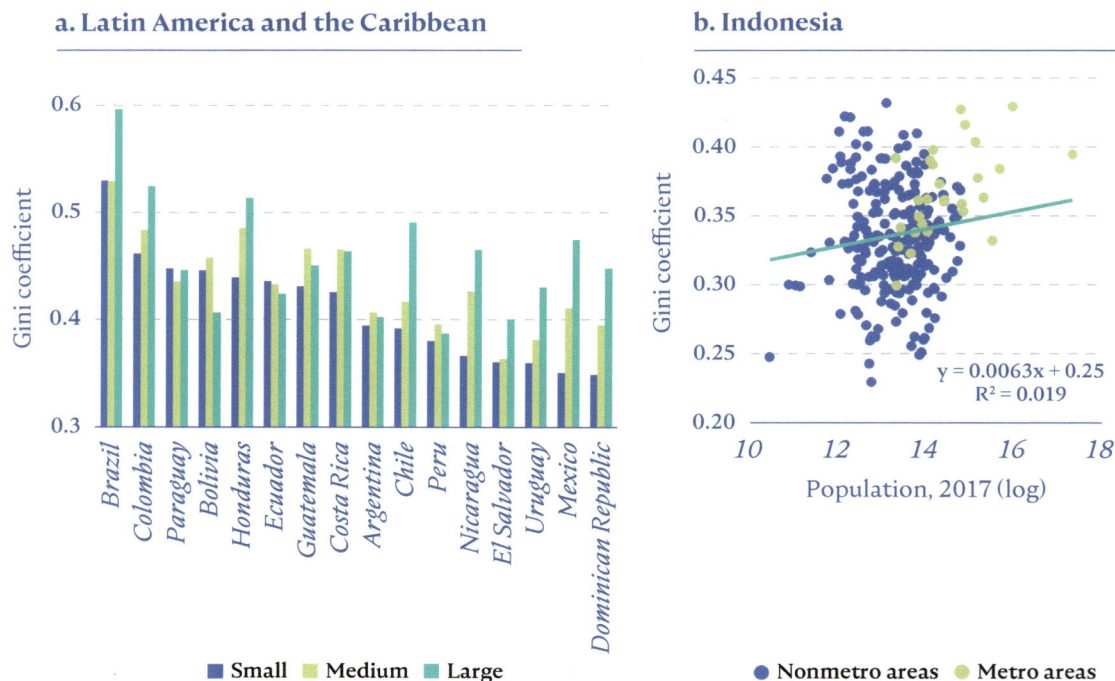

a. Latin America and the Caribbean

b. Indonesia

$$y = 0.0063x + 0.25$$
$$R^2 = 0.019$$

■ Small ■ Medium ■ Large   ● Nonmetro areas ● Metro areas

Sources: Panel a: Ferreyra and Roberts 2018, with calculations based on data from Socio-Economic Database for Latin America and the Caribbean (SEDLAC) for countries other than Brazil and Integrated Public Use Microdata Series (IPUMS) for Brazil; panel b: Roberts, Gil Sander, and Tiwari 2019, with calculations based on data from the 2017 round of Indonesia's National Socio-Economic Survey (SUSENAS).

Note: Panel a shows, for each size class of city, the weighted average Gini coefficient across cities, where the weights are equal to city sizes. The classification of city size follows the country-specific thresholds defined in Ferreyra and Roberts (2018). In panel b, the unit of analysis is districts. For multidistrict metro areas, the Gini coefficient and population are calculated over all districts in the metro area.

cities because of skill-selective migration and better learning outcomes in larger cities. Thus, for both Indonesia and Latin America and the Caribbean, a large portion of the higher income inequality that exists in larger cities can be explained by the income gap between skilled and unskilled households. Households in small cities consist mainly of relatively unskilled workers; therefore, relatively low incomes generally prevail. By contrast, large cities have a mix of households with both skilled and unskilled workers, leading to higher income inequality. Moreover, the evidence for Indonesia and Latin America and the Caribbean suggests that skilled workers benefit more than unskilled workers in terms of both productivity and wages from agglomeration, which further reinforces the divide between them (Ferreyra and Roberts 2018; Roberts, Gil Sander and Tiwari 2019).

Large cities, then, will likely have greater income inequality when their countries provide uneven access to high-quality education and when these cities present their residents with uneven education and learning opportunities. Unequal access to basic services will also likely feed into uneven human capital accumulation in cities, thereby contributing to higher income inequality. In the United States, however, despite higher income inequality in larger cities than in smaller cities (Behrens and Robert-Nicoud 2015), the relationship between inequality and city size is not as strong as for either Indonesia or countries in Latin America and the Caribbean (Ferreyra and Roberts 2018). This finding stems, at least in part, from the better general access to education in the United States and the higher levels of access to basic services that feed into human capital accumulation in cities.

Uneven access to basic services and learning opportunities not only contributes to present-day inequality within cities but also can undermine intergenerational mobility

Two types of intergenerational mobility can be distinguished: *absolute mobility*, which refers to the extent to which children tend to be richer or more educated than their parents, and *relative mobility*, which refers to the extent to which children tend to occupy a higher rung on the income or socioeconomic ladder than their parents.[29] Evidence on intergenerational mobility is sparse for lower-income countries and generally restricted to education levels. But the evidence that does exist suggests that, although the share of adults in those countries who are more educated than their parents has increased over time, absolute intergenerational mobility remains higher in high-income countries. Furthermore, although almost 62 percent of adults born in 1960 in lower-income countries have more education than their parents, less than 57 percent of adults born in 1980 do. Thus, in lower-income countries, relative intergenerational mobility has declined over time. As for whether the urban areas of those countries provide for higher levels of mobility than the rural areas, the evidence is mixed. In Latin America and the Caribbean, mobility tends to be higher in larger cities, whereas Indonesia has no difference in mobility between urban and rural areas. Meanwhile, in India mobility in urban areas is slightly lower than in rural areas, although urban areas saw a larger improvement in mobility in the 1980s and 1990s (Lall et al. forthcoming).

Residents in larger cities suffer more from illnesses associated with modern lifestyles, and shortcomings of urban food systems may exacerbate this problem

Finally, in addition to having higher inequality, cities tend to have greater prevalence of illnesses associated with modern lifestyles than do towns and suburbs. These illnesses are, in turn, more prevalent in towns and suburbs than in rural areas—see figure 1.21 for evidence on obesity and hypertension (Henderson and Turner 2020). These patterns likely arise because of the higher incomes that tend to prevail in larger and more densely populated urban areas: higher incomes are often associated with less healthy diets, including the consumption of more meat and more processed food products with higher fat and sugar contents. Higher consumption of meat (especially beef) also contributes to higher greenhouse gas emissions. According to one recent study, the production of 1 kilogram of beef results in greenhouse gas emissions that are 28 times higher than those associated with the production of 1 kilogram of wheat. More generally, the use of cows, pigs, and other animals for food, as well as livestock feed, accounts for 57 percent of all food production–related greenhouse gas emissions globally, compared with 29 percent from the cultivation of plant-based foods (Xu et al. 2021). Shortcomings in urban food systems further exacerbate the prevalence of less healthy diets in cities, particularly among the poor (box 1.11).

Figure 1.21 Obesity, by geographic region, and hypertension in India, by type of urban and rural area, circa 2015

a. Obese respondents, by geographic region

b. Household members age 25 and up with high blood pressure, India

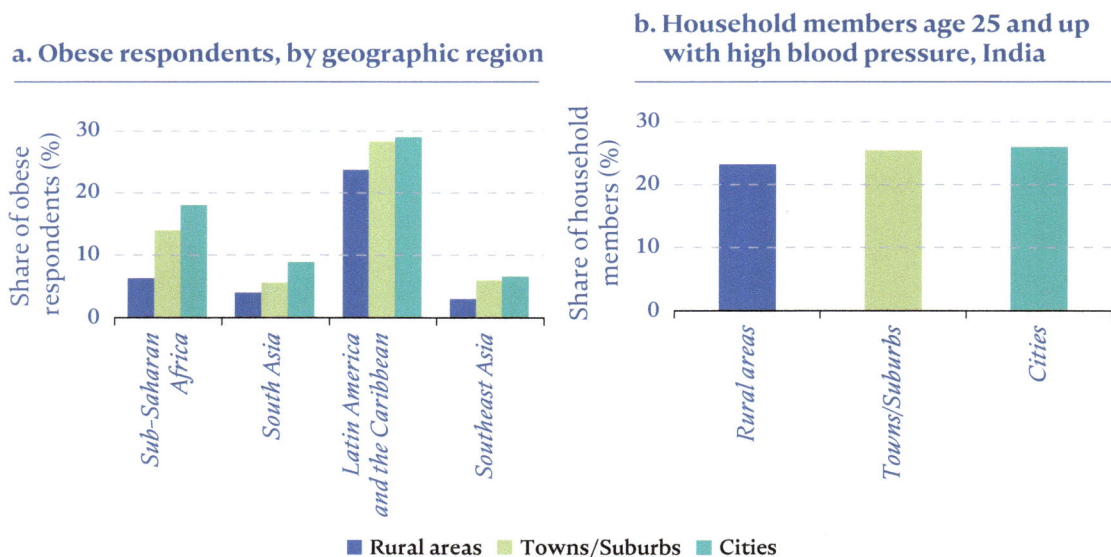

■ Rural areas ■ Towns/Suburbs ■ Cities

Source: World Bank calculations using data from Henderson and Turner 2020 and downloaded from https://doi.org/10.7910/DVN/YZ46FJ. The underlying data from the Demographic and Health Surveys cover different survey years across countries from 2010 to 2016.

Note: Urban centers (cities), urban clusters (towns and suburbs), and rural areas are defined using the degree of urbanization methodology outlined in box 1.1.

Box 1.11

Unhealthy diets and poorly governed food systems for urban consumers

The demographic and socioeconomic changes associated with urbanization are causing large shifts in dietary and activity patterns. Urban consumers eat more fruits and vegetables than rural consumers do (figure B1.11.1), but they also consume more processed meats and sugary drinks. Urban consumers with lower socioeconomic status (low maternal education) have the poorest diets. They have low levels of vegetable consumption—almost as low as those for rural consumers with lower socioeconomic status. At the same time, they have high levels of soda consumption—almost as high as that for urban consumers with higher socioeconomic status.

Globally, the cost of healthy diets could be prohibitive—a healthy diet costs US$3.75 per day, making it out of reach for about 3 billion people (Herforth et al. 2020). At the same time, unhealthy foods are largely affordable. The price per calorie of fats and oils, sugar, soft drinks, and salty snacks is 0.67, 0.83, 5.26, and 2.54 times, respectively, the price per calorie of a basket of staples. By contrast, the price per calorie of foods rich in vitamin A

Box 1.11 *continued*

Figure B1.11.1 **Intake of food groups, by urban and rural and maternal education, 187 countries**

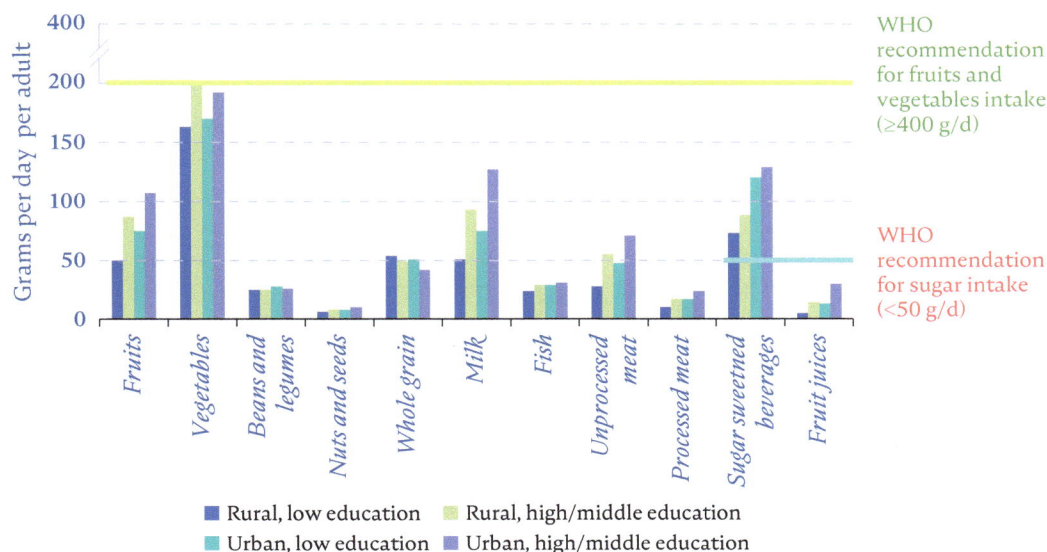

WHO recommendation for fruits and vegetables intake (≥400 g/d)

WHO recommendation for sugar intake (<50 g/d)

■ Rural, low education   ▪ Rural, high/middle education
■ Urban, low education   ■ Urban, high/middle education

Source: World Bank staff calculations based on data from the 2018 Global Dietary Database (GDD) (https://www.globaldietarydatabase.org/).

Note: The GDD provides intakes for 11 food categories for 187 countries. Its data come from more than 300 dietary nationally representative surveys of 1.75 million individuals representing 89 percent of the global adult population. g/d = grams per day; WHO = World Health Organization.

and dark green leafy vegetables is 7.74 and 16.12 times, respectively, the price per calorie of a basket of staples (Headey and Alderman 2019).

At the country level, urbanization and improved connectivity between rural and urban areas lower the cost of nutrient-adequate diets (Bai et al. 2021). Within countries, although healthier diets could be more expensive in urban areas, they are typically more affordable to urban consumers with higher incomes in countries such as Bangladesh, India, and Myanmar (Dizon, Wang, and Mulmi 2021; Herforth et al. 2020).

Poor urban diets largely result from poor governance of urban food systems (Acharya et al. 2021). Such systems have complex governance, involving disparate actors (such as the ministries of agriculture and health, food safety authorities, and market development authorities) and a broad range of decisions (on, for example, land use zoning, water and sanitation, waste management, urban transport and logistics, and public infrastructure). Given their complexity, governance structures of urban food systems are often weak. A survey of 170 cities in South and East Asia finds that many of them exhibit reactive, fragmented, and exclusionary food policies, whereas only a few have food policies that are proactive, forward-looking, integrative, and inclusive (Acharya et al. 2021).

Summary and conclusions

This chapter has taken stock of how green, how resilient, and how inclusive cities globally are today, revealing that many indicators relate to both a city's size and its level of development. Although less green in terms of their CO_2 emissions, levels of air quality, and average vegetation levels, more populous cities are in many respects more inclusive, as evidenced by their lower poverty rates, better levels of access to basic services, and better average outcomes on many health indicators. Beyond a certain income level, development also correlates with both better air quality and a higher average level of vegetation. Furthermore, more developed cities are more resilient to extreme weather events, the frequency and intensity of which are, except for extreme cold events, increasing with climate change.

These results suggest that a city's resilience to climate change–related shocks and stresses and its economic development go together, and that economic development is, at least beyond some level, also associated with more positive outcomes on many dimensions of greenness and inclusiveness. An exception is a city's level of CO_2 emissions and therefore its contribution to climate change. Thus, for cities in low- and lower-middle-income countries, the key challenge, from a climate change perspective, is how to develop on a lower CO_2 emissions trajectory than that historically followed by today's cities in upper-middle and high-income countries. Although putting this responsibility on lower-income countries may seem unfair, the fact that, for example, lower CO_2 emissions are strongly correlated with better local air quality, which, in turn, carries positive health and productivity benefits, suggests that this challenge comes with an opportunity. By implementing policies that help improve local air quality, cities in lower-income countries can not only avoid calamities such as London's Great Smog but also perhaps follow a more climate-friendly—and faster—growth path. The results also suggest that the greenness, resilience, and inclusiveness challenges that cities face vary with their sizes and evolve as cities develop. Thus, there can be no blanket policy prescriptions. Instead, policies need to be tailored according to both a city's size and its level of development, as well as the climate change–related hazards it faces.

Annex 1A: Spatial distributions of extreme weather anomalies

Map 1A.1 **Frequency of extreme hot months per year, 2011–20**

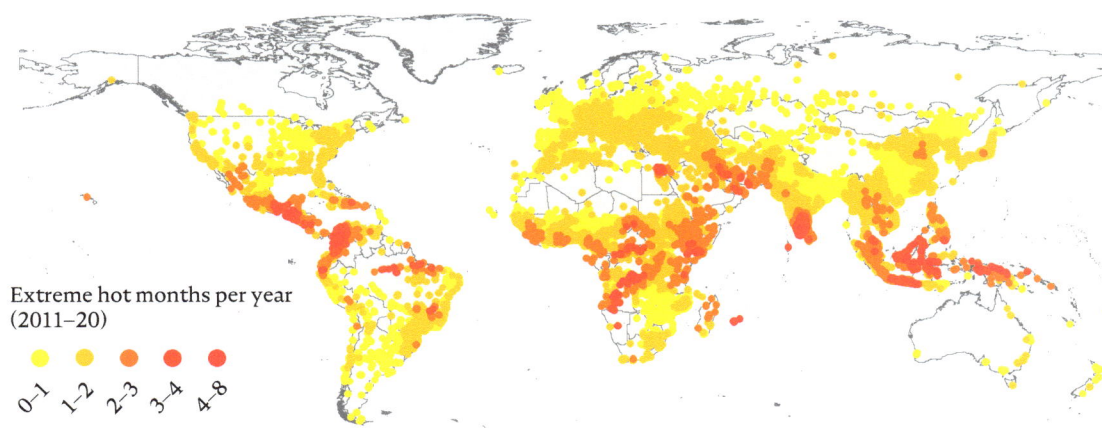

Extreme hot months per year
(2011–20)

0–1 1–2 2–3 3–4 4–8

Source: World Bank calculations based on Climatology Lab, TerraClimate (https://www.climatologylab.org
/terraclimate.html); European Commission, Global Human Settlement (GHS) Urban Centre Database R2019
(https://ghsl.jrc.ec.europa.eu/ghs_stat_ucdb2015mt_r2019a.php).

Note: An extreme hot month is one in which a city's temperature anomaly variable (as defined in box 1.2) records a
value of at least 2. Frequency is defined as the number of extreme hot months per year. The map presents the average
annual frequency from January 2011 to December 2020 for each city in the global sample.

Map 1A.2 **Intensity of extreme hot months, 2011–20**

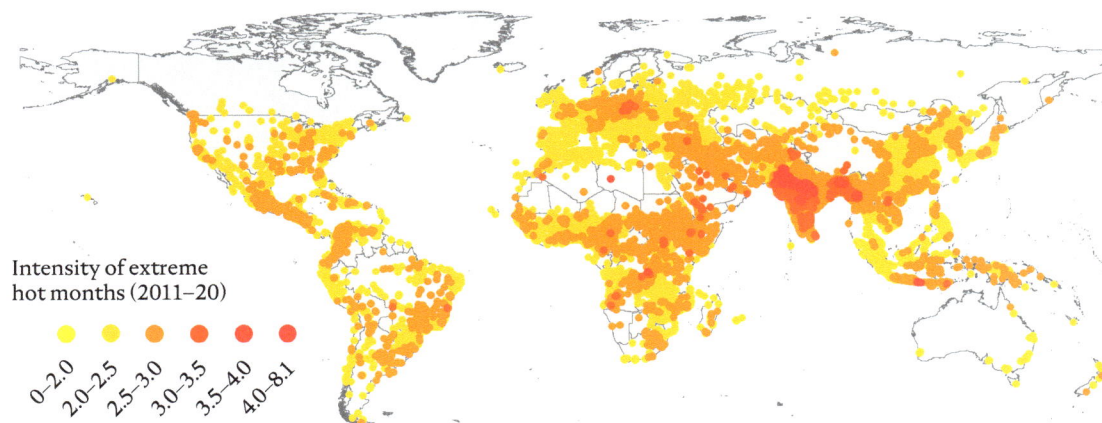

Intensity of extreme
hot months (2011–20)

0–2.0 2.0–2.5 2.5–3.0 3.0–3.5 3.5–4.0 4.0–8.1

Sources: World Bank calculations based on Climatology Lab, TerraClimate (https://www.climatologylab.org
/terraclimate.html); European Commission, Global Human Settlement (GHS) Urban Centre Database R2019
(https://ghsl.jrc.ec.europa.eu/ghs_stat_ucdb2015mt_r2019a.php).

Note: An extreme hot month is when a city's temperature anomaly value (as defined in box 1.2) records a value of at
least 2. Intensity is calculated as the average size of the anomaly variable during consecutive extreme hot months.
The map shows the average intensity from January 2011 to December 2020 for each city in the global sample.

Map 1A.3   Frequency of extreme cold months per year, 2011–20

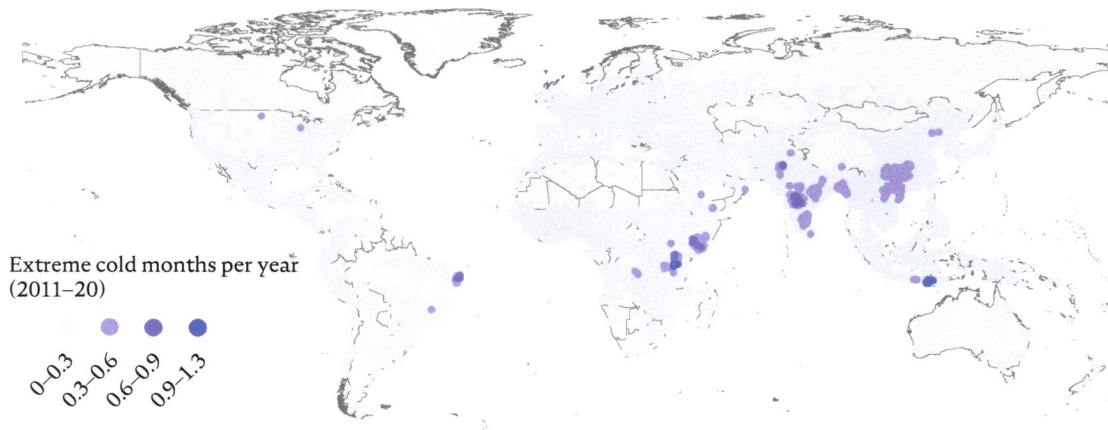

Extreme cold months per year
(2011–20)

0–0.3 0.3–0.6 0.6–0.9 0.9–1.3

Sources: World Bank calculations based on Climatology Lab, TerraClimate (https://www.climatologylab.org /terraclimate.html); European Commission, Global Human Settlement (GHS) Urban Centre Database R2019 (https://ghsl.jrc.ec.europa.eu/ghs_stat_ucdb2015mt_r2019a.php).

Note: An extreme cold month is when a city's temperature anomaly variable (as defined in box 1.2) records a value of –2 or lower. Frequency is defined as the number of extreme cold months per year. The map presents the average annual frequency from January 2011 to December 2020 for each city in the global sample.

Map 1A.4   Intensity of extreme cold months, 2011–20

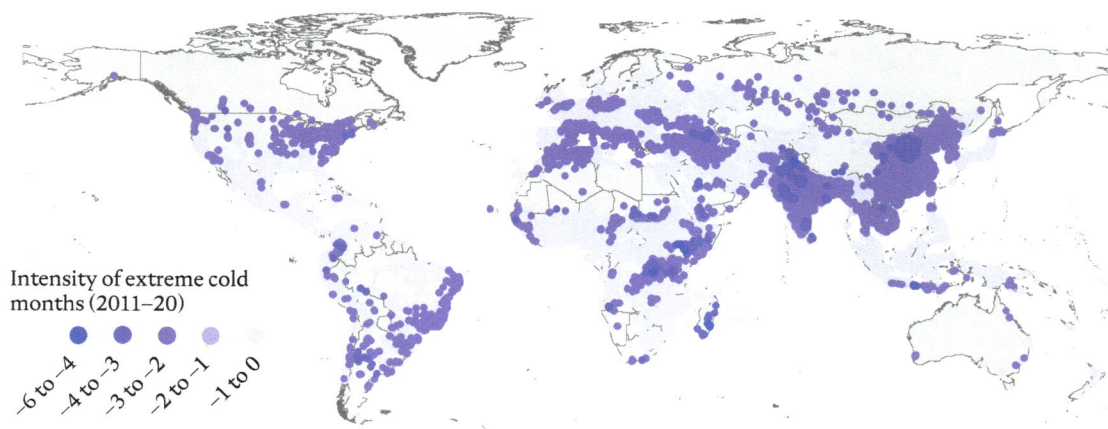

Intensity of extreme cold
months (2011–20)

–6 to –4 –4 to –3 –3 to –2 –2 to –1 –1 to 0

Sources: World Bank calculations based on Climatology Lab, TerraClimate (https://www.climatologylab.org /terraclimate.html); European Commission, Global Human Settlement (GHS) Urban Centre Database R2019 (https://ghsl.jrc.ec.europa.eu/ghs_stat_ucdb2015mt_r2019a.php).

Note: An extreme cold month is when a city's temperature anomaly variable (as defined in box 1.2) records a value of –2 or lower. Intensity is calculated as the average size of the anomaly variable during consecutive extreme cold months. The map shows the average intensity from January 2011 to December 2020 for each city in the global sample.

Map 1A.5   Frequency of extreme dry months per year, 2011–20

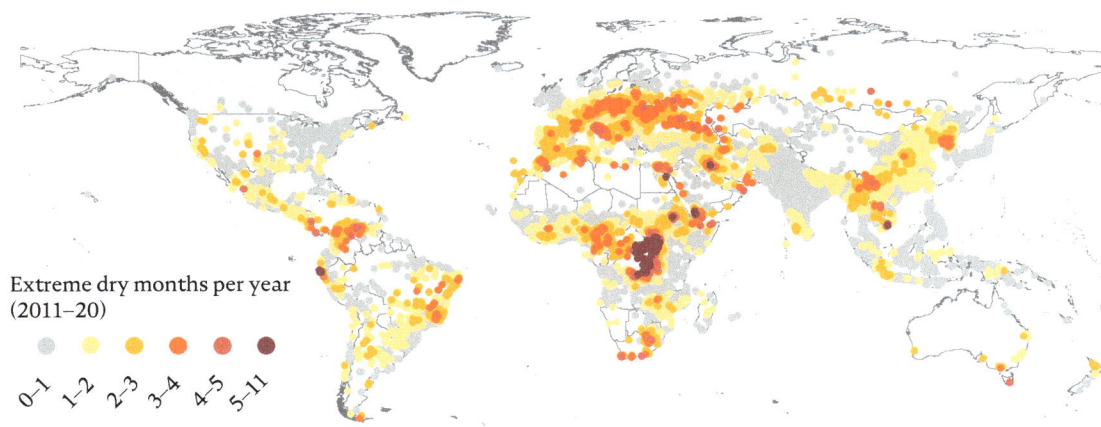

Extreme dry months per year
(2011–20)

0–1   1–2   2–3   3–4   4–5   5–11

Sources: World Bank calculations based on Climatology Lab, TerraClimate (https://www.climatologylab.org
/terraclimate.html); European Commission, Global Human Settlement (GHS) Urban Centre Database R2019
(https://ghsl.jrc.ec.europa.eu/ghs_stat_ucdb2015mt_r2019a.php).

Note: An extreme dry month is when the value of the Standardized Precipitation-Evapotranspiration Index (SPEI)
is –1.5 or below. Frequency is defined as the number of extreme dry months per year. The map presents the average
annual frequency from January 2011 to December 2020 for each city in the global sample.

Map 1A.6   Intensity of extreme dry months, 2011–20

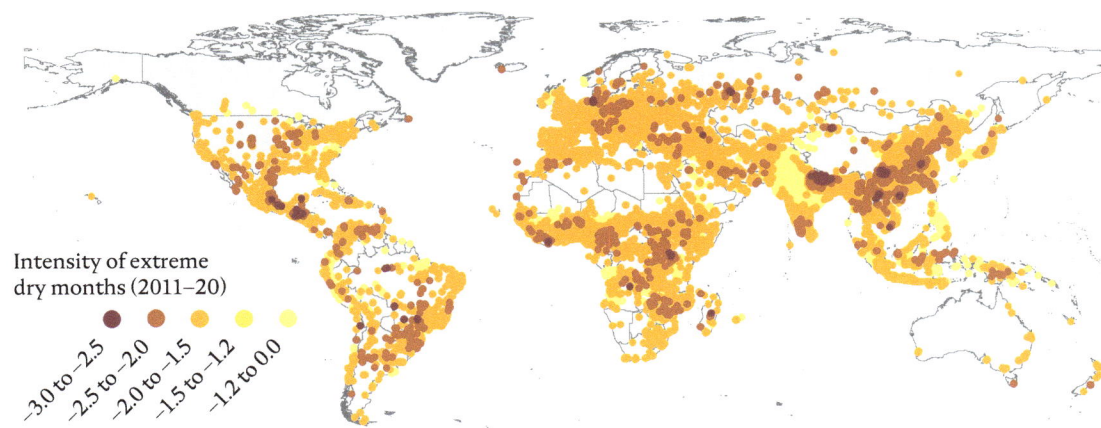

Intensity of extreme
dry months (2011–20)

–3.0 to –2.5   –2.5 to –2.0   –2.0 to –1.5   –1.5 to –1.2   –1.2 to 0.0

Sources: World Bank calculations based on Climatology Lab, TerraClimate https://www.climatologylab.org
/terraclimate.html; European Commission, Global Human Settlement (GHS) Urban Centre Database R2019
(https://ghsl.jrc.ec.europa.eu/ghs_stat_ucdb2015mt_r2019a.php).

Note: An extreme dry month is when the value of the Standardized Precipitation-Evapotranspiration Index (SPEI) is
–1.5 or below. Intensity is calculated as the average value of SPEI during consecutive extreme dry months. The map
shows the average intensity from January 2011to December 2020 for each city in the global sample.

Map 1A.7   Frequency of extreme wet months per year, 2011–20

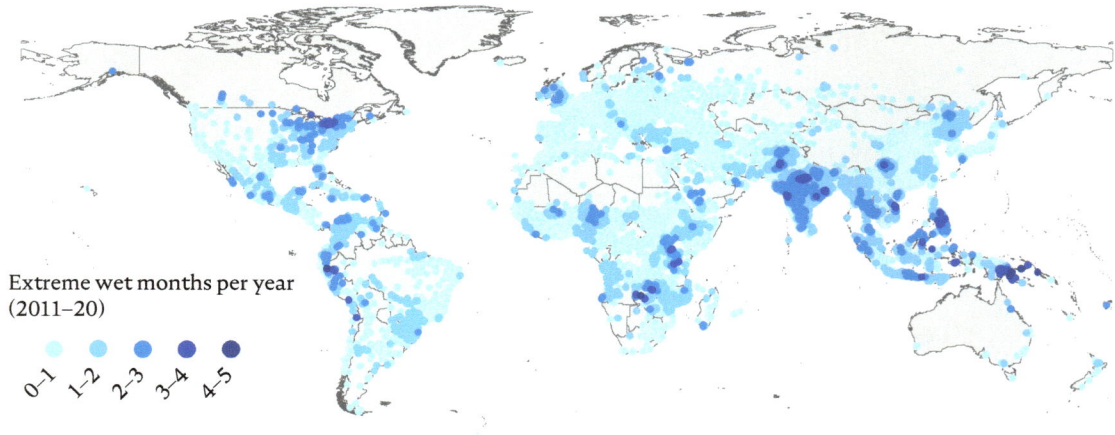

Extreme wet months per year
(2011–20)

0–1   1–2   2–3   3–4   4–5

Sources: World Bank calculations based on Climatology Lab, TerraClimate (https://www.climatologylab.org
/terraclimate.html); European Commission, Global Human Settlement (GHS) Urban Centre Database R2019
(https://ghsl.jrc.ec.europa.eu/ghs_stat_ucdb2015mt_r2019a.php).

Note: An extreme wet month is when the value of the Standardized Precipitation-Evapotranspiration Index (SPEI)
is +1.5 or above. Frequency is defined as the number of extreme wet months per year. The map presents the average
annual frequency from January 2011 to December 2020 for each city in the global sample.

Map 1A.8   Intensity of extreme wet months, 2011–20

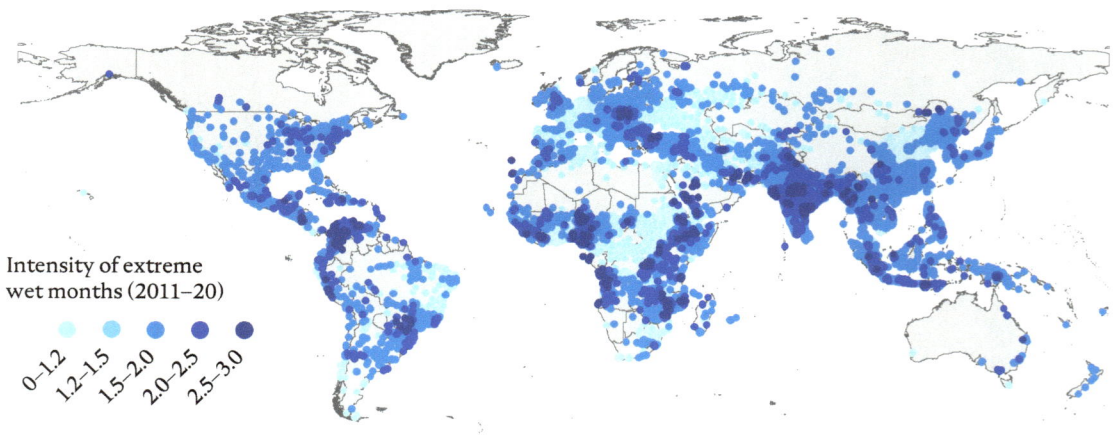

Intensity of extreme
wet months (2011–20)

0–1.2   1.2–1.5   1.5–2.0   2.0–2.5   2.5–3.0

Sources: World Bank calculations based on Climatology Lab, TerraClimate (https://www.climatologylab.org
/terraclimate.html); European Commission, Global Human Settlement (GHS) Urban Centre Database R2019
(https://ghsl.jrc.ec.europa.eu/ghs_stat_ucdb2015mt_r2019a.php).

Note: An extreme wet month is when the value of the Standardized Precipitation-Evapotranspiration Index (SPEI) is
+1.5 or above. Intensity is calculated as the average value of SPEI during consecutive extreme wet months. The map
shows the average intensity from January 2011 to December 2020 for each city in the global sample.

Notes

1. Urban stresses traditionally emphasized by economists also include negative externalities associated with urban density, such as a heightened risk of crime and more rapid spread of infectious diseases (see, for example, Glaeser 2012). The fact that urban density may give rise to the more rapid spread of infectious diseases has received more attention recently because of the COVID-19 pandemic. Despite this attention, evidence on the role of density in driving the pandemic is mixed (Fang and Wahba 2020; Lall and Wahba 2020).

2. Urban and spatial economists distinguish between the "first-nature" and "second-nature" advantages of locations. First-nature advantages are associated with a location's physical geography and climate, and second-nature advantages arise from agglomeration economies (Brakman, Garretsen, and van Marrewijk 2012; Krugman 1991). First-nature advantages tend to be taken as exogenously fixed, independent of the processes of urban growth, whereas second-nature advantages are modeled as both a cause and a consequence of urban growth.

3. This new empirical evidence, which leverages fine spatial resolution and high frequency satellite imagery, is based on background research for this report by Park and Roberts (2023).

4. See also Hallegatte et al. (2017), among others. The interdependencies between how green, how resilient, and how inclusive societies are is a key theme of the original World Bank (2021) paper that introduced the GRID (green, resilient, and inclusive development) concept.

5. The European Commission's Urban Centre Database R2019, on which this chapter heavily relies, provides data for 10,303 cities after discarding both false positive and uncertain detections of cities—for more details, see Florczyk et al. (2019). The exact sample size used in both this chapter and the report more generally varies according to the variable being analyzed.

6. Chapter 2 includes a look forward at how climate and the associated hazards that cities face are projected to evolve in the coming decades.

7. Map 1A.6 shows the global spatial distribution of the intensity of extreme dry events when they do occur for the period 2011–20.

8. Maps 1A.7 and 1A.8 in annex 1A show, respectively, the global spatial distributions of the frequency of extreme wet events and the intensity of extreme wet events when they do occur for the period 2011–20.

9. From the US National Ocean Service web page, "How Is Sea Level Rise Related to Climate Change?" https://oceanservice.noaa.gov/facts/sealevelclimate.html.

10. No evidence exists that tropical cyclones per se have been increasing in frequency. In fact, a growing literature suggests that the opposite might be more likely the case (Chand et al. 2022; Knutson et al. 2020). Evidence does suggest, however, that their tracks have been migrating toward coasts as well as poleward (Wang and Toumi 2021). Although further investigation is needed, this migration presumably explains the increased exposure of cities globally to tropical cyclones over time shown in figure 1.5.

11. Custom data were acquired via the United Nations' World Urbanisation Prospectis: 2018 Revision website, https://population.un.org/wup/.

12. The GHS Urban Centre Database derives its CO_2 emissions data from the European Commission's Emissions Database for Global Atmospheric Research (EDGAR). The data cover "All human activities leading to climate relevant emissions . . . , except biomass/biofuel combustion (short-cycle carbon) in the power, industry, buildings, transport and agricultural sectors, large-scale biomass burning and land use, land-use change and forestry" (Crippa et al. 2019, 24).

13. Following EDGAR, the GHS Urban Centre Database distinguishes five sectors—agriculture, energy, industry, residential, and transportation—from which CO_2 emissions originate. Residential sector emissions include emissions associated with energy for buildings and waste. All sectors are defined using the 1996 codes of the Intergovernmental Panel on Climate Change (Florczyk et al. 2019).

14. Cities in upper-middle-income countries in the global sample had an aggregate population of approximately 1.3 billion in 2015, whereas cities in high-income countries had an aggregate population of about 0.57 billion.

15. A city's compactness is measured using the Polsby-Popper Ratio, which ranges from 0 to 1, with 1 indicating the maximal level of compactness. The Polsby-Popper Ratio is equal to the ratio of a city's actual area to that of a circle with circumference equal to the perimeter of the area (Polsby and Popper 1991).

16. From the United Nations Economic Commission for Europe's web page, "Improving Air Quality While Fighting Climate Change," https://unece.org/unece-and-sdgs/improving-air-quality-while-fighting-climate-change.

17. Results similar to those reported in this section hold for both a city's population and GDP per capita of the country in which a city is located, if overall $PM_{2.5}$ concentrations as opposed to $PM_{2.5}$ emissions from the residential and transportation sectors are examined.

18. Ellis and Roberts (2016) reveal that this relationship is stronger for South Asian cities than for other cities in low- and middle-income countries. They attribute this finding to the particularly "messy" nature of urbanization in South Asia, which has severe sprawl and very high levels of traffic congestion.

19. Equally, worse urban air quality should not be considered an automatic outcome of a country's evolution from low- to lower-middle-income status. Whether urban air quality deteriorates or improves as any given country develops will depend, at least to a certain extent, on policy choices at the national and local levels within the country.

20. For more details on this measure of average greenness, see Corbane et al. (2020) and Florczyk et al. (2019). In addition to average greenness, chapter 2 also analyzes the share of a city's area that is "high green"—that is, covered by dense vegetation corresponding to gardens, parks, and urban forests.

21. From the US National Park Service web page, "Plants and Climate Change," https://www.nps.gov/articles/000/plants-climateimpact.htm.

22. Based on census data from citypopulation.de.

23. In 1431, Angkor, the capital of the Khmer empire, began a rapid decline. The decline followed the sacking and looting of the city by Ayutthaya invaders, but it also coincided with a series of natural disasters and a time of drastic climate change (such as monsoon rains followed by drought). Although the sacking and looting of the city seem unassociated with the disasters

and climate change of the time, this example does demonstrate the possible risks to a city's long-run fortunes should climate change itself spark a major economic or political shock.

24. The use of nighttime lights to proxy for a city's level of economic activity has become widespread since the seminal articles by Henderson, Storeygard, and Weil (2011, 2012), demonstrating that movements in national GDP are strongly correlated with movements in nighttime light intensity.

25. The analysis by Park and Roberts (2023) is restricted to cities that had a 2015 population of at least 200,000.

26. When, instead of degree of urbanization, Combes et al. (2022) adopt an alternative "dartboard" methodology for the globally consistent definition of urban areas, they also find evidence of lower poverty rates in cities than in towns and suburbs, whose rates are, in turn, lower than those in rural areas. Their results are also robust when different gridded population data sets serve as input in the definition of urban areas.

27. Data used for the calculations in this section cover 3 countries in Southeast Asia (Cambodia, Myanmar, Timor-Leste); 5 in Latin America and the Caribbean (Colombia, Dominican Republic, Guatemala, Haiti, Honduras); 3 in South Asia (Bangladesh, India, Nepal); and 29 in Sub-Saharan Africa (East Africa: Burundi, Comoros, Ethiopia, Kenya, Malawi, Mozambique, Rwanda, Tanzania, Uganda, Zambia, Zimbabwe; West Africa: Benin, Burkina Faso, Côte d'Ivoire, Ghana, Guinea, Liberia, Mali, Nigeria, Senegal, Sierra Leone, Togo; Central Africa: Angola, Cameroon, Chad, Democratic Republic of the Congo, Gabon; southern Africa: Lesotho, Namibia).

28. World Bank, "Urbanization Reviews" (dashboard), https://www.worldbank.org/en/topic/urbandevelopment/publication/urbanization-reviews.

29. The discussion in this paragraph is largely based on that contained in a new World Bank report, *Vibrant Cities: Priorities for Green, Resilient, and Inclusive Urban Development* (Lall et al., forthcoming).

References

Acharya, G., E. Cassou, S. Jaffee, and E. K. Ludher. 2021. *RICH Food, Smart City: How Building Reliable, Inclusive, Competitive, and Healthy Food Systems Is Smart Policy for Urban Asia*. Washington, DC: World Bank.

Ager, P., K. Eriksson, and L. Lonstrup. 2020. "How the 1906 San Francisco Earthquake Shaped Economic Activity in the American West." *Explorations in Economic History* 77: 101342.

Ahlfeldt, G., and E. Pietrostefani. 2019. "The Economic Effects of Density: A Synthesis." *Journal of Urban Economics* 111: 93–107.

Awe, Y., J. Nygard, S. Larssen, H. Lee, H. Dulal, and R. Kanakia. 2015. "Clean Air and Healthy Lungs: Enhancing the World Bank's Approach to Air Quality Management." Environment and Natural Resources Global Practice Discussion Paper No. 3, World Bank, Washington, DC.

Bai, Y., R. Alemu, S. Block, D. Headey, and W. Masters. 2021. "Cost and Affordability of Nutritious Diets at Retail Prices: Evidence from 177 Countries." *Food Policy* 99 (February): 101983.

BBC News. 2015. "Ghana Petrol Station Inferno Kills about 150 in Accra." *BBC News*, June 5, 2015. https://www.bbc.com/news/world-africa-33003673.

Behrens, K., and F. Robert-Nicoud. 2015. "Agglomeration Theory with Heterogeneous Agents." In *Handbook of Regional and Urban Economics, Volume 5: Cities and Geography*, edited by G. Duranton, J. V. Henderson, and W. Strange, 171–245. Amsterdam: Elsevier.

Bosker, M., J. Park, and M. Roberts. 2021. "Definition Matters. Metropolitan Areas and Agglomeration Economies in a Large-Developing Country." *Journal of Urban Economics* 125: 103275.

Brakman, S., H. Garretsen, and M. Schramm. 2004. "The Strategic Bombing of German Cities during World War II and Its Impact on City Growth." *Journal of Economic Geography* 4(2): 201–18.

Brakman, S., H. Garretsen, and C. van Marrewijk. 2012. *The New Introduction to Geographical Economics*. Cambridge, UK: Cambridge University Press.

Bruce N., R. Perez-Padilla, and R. Albalak. 2000. "Indoor Air Pollution in Developing Countries: A Major Environmental and Public Health Challenge." *Bulletin of the World Health Organization* 78 (9): 1078–92.

Bruederle, A., J. Peters, and G. Roberts. 2017. "Weather and Crime in South Africa." Ruhr Economic Papera 739. RWI–Leibniz Institut für Wirtschaftsforschung, Ruhr-University Bochum, TU Dortmund University, University of Duisburg-Essen.

Buisseret, D.J. 1966. "Port Royal 1655–1725." *Jamaican Historical Review* 6: 21–28.

Buurman, J., M. J. Mens, and R. J. Dahm. 2017. "Strategies for Urban Drought Risk Management: A Comparison of 10 Large Cities." *International Journal of Water Resources Development* 33 (1): 31–50.

C40 Cities Climate Leadership Group, Arup, and University of Leeds. 2019. *The Future of Urban Consumption in a 1.5°C World*. C40 Cities Headline Report. https://www.c40knowledgehub.org/s/article/The-future-of-urban-consumption-in-a-1-5-C-world?language=en_US.

Chand, S., K. Walsh, S. Camargo, J. Kossin, K. Tory, M. Wehner, J. Chan, et al. 2022. "Declining Tropical Cyclone Frequency under Global Warming." *Nature Climate Change* 12: 655–61.

Chatterjee, S., M. Gassier, and N. Myint. Forthcoming. "Leveraging Social Cohesion for Development Outcomes." A Framing Paper, Social Sustainability and Inclusion Global Practice, World Bank, Washington, DC.

CIESIN (Center for International Earth Science Information Network). 2013. "Low Elevation Coastal Zone Urban-Rural Population and Land Area Estimates, Version 2." Technical report, CIESIN, Columbia University; NASA Socioeconomic Data and Applications Center, Palisades, NY.

Claypole, W. A. 1972. "The Merchants of Port Royal, 1655 to 1700." Unpublished master's thesis, University of the West Indies, Kingston, Jamaica.

Combes, P. P., S. Nakamura, M. Roberts, and B. Stewart. 2022. "Estimating Urban Poverty Consistently across Countries." World Bank Poverty and Equity Notes, World Bank, Washington, DC.

Corbane, C., P. Martino, P. Panagiotis, F. Aneta, M. Michele, F. Sergio, S. Marcello, et al. 2020. "The Grey-Green Divide: Multi-Temporal Analysis of Greenness across 10,000 Urban Centres

Derived from the Global Human Settlement Layer (GHSL)." *International Journal of Digital Earth* 13 (1): 101–18.

Crippa, M., G. Oreggioni, D. Guizzardi, M. Muntean, E. Schaaf, E. Lo Vullo, E. Solazzo, et al. 2019. *Fossil CO$_2$ and GHG Emissions of All World Countries*. EUR 29849 EN. Luxembourg: Publications Office of the European Union.

Cuesta, J., L. Madrigal, and N. Pecorari. Forthcoming. "Social Sustainability, Poverty and Income: An Empirical Exploration." Policy Research Working Paper, World Bank, Washington, DC.

Dasgupta, S., K. Hamilton, K. Pandey, and D. Wheeler. 2004. "Air Pollution during Growth: Accounting for Governance and Vulnerability." Policy Research Working Paper 3383, World Bank, Washington, DC.

Davis, D., and D. Weinstein. 2002. "Bones, Bombs, and Break Points: The Geography of Economic Activity." *American Economic Review* 92 (5): 1269–89.

de Bellefon, M. P., P. P. Combes, G. Duranton, L. Gobillon, and C. Gorin. 2021. "Delineating Urban Areas Using Building Density." *Journal of Urban Economics* 125: 103226.

Deuskar. 2022. "Beating the Heat: Measuring and Mitigating Extreme Heat in East Asian Cities." Technical Working Paper 1: Literature Review, World Bank, Washington, DC.

Dijkstra, L., A. Florczyk, S. Freire, T. Kemper, M. Melchiorri, M. Pesaresi, and M. Schiavina. 2021. "Applying the Degree of Urbanisation to the Globe: A New Harmonised Definition Reveals a Different Picture of Global Urbanisation." *Journal of Urban Economics* 125: 103312.

Dizon, F., Z. Wang, and P. Mulmi. 2021. "The Cost of a Nutritious Diet in Bangladesh, Bhutan, India, and Nepal." Policy Research Working Paper 9578, World Bank, Washington, DC.

Duque, J. C., N. Lozano-Gracia, J. E. Patino, and P. Restrepo. 2021. "Urban Form and Productivity: What Shapes Are Latin-American Cities?" *Environment and Planning B: Urban Analytics and City Science* 49 (1): 131–50.

Duranton, G., and D. Puga. 2020. "The Economics of Urban Density." *Journal of Economic Perspectives* 34 (3): 3–26.

Ellis, P., and M. Roberts. 2016. *Leveraging Urbanization in South Asia: Managing Spatial Transformation for Prosperity and Livability*. Washington, DC: World Bank.

Fang, W., and S. Wahba. 2020. "Urban Density Is Not an Enemy in the Coronavirus Fight: Evidence from China. Sustainable Cities." *Sustainable Cities* (blog), April 20, 2020. https://blogs.worldbank .org/sustainablecities/urban-density-not-enemy-coronavirus-fight-evidence-china.

FAO (Food and Agriculture Organization of the United Nations). 2018. *Forests and Sustainable Cities: Inspiring Stories from Around the World*. FAO Forestry Department. Rome: FAO.

Feng, K., K. Hubacek, and Y. Yu. 2019. *Local Consumption and Global Environmental Impacts: Accounting, Trade-Offs and Sustainability*. London: Routledge.

Ferre, C., F. Ferreira, and P. Lanjouw. 2012. "Is There a Metropolitan Bias? The Relationship between Poverty and City Size in a Selection of Developing Countries." *World Bank Economic Review* 26 (3): 351–82.

Ferreyra, M. M., and M. Roberts, eds. 2018. *Raising the Bar for Productive Cities in Latin America and the Caribbean*. Washington, DC: World Bank.

Florczyk, A., J. M. Melchiorri, C. Corbane, M. Schiavina, M. Maffenini, M. Pesaresi, P. Politis, et al. 2019. "Description of the GHS Urban Centre Database 2015, Public Release 2019, Version 1.0." Publications Office of the European Union, Luxembourg.

Galdo, V., Y. Li, and M. Rama. 2021. "Identifying Urban Areas by Combining Human Judgment and Machine Learning: An Application to India." *Journal of Urban Economics* 125: 103229.

Gandhi, S., M. E. Kahn, R. Kochhar, S. V. Lall, and V. Tandel. 2022. "Adapting to Flood Risk: Evidence from a Panel of Global Cities." Working Paper 30137, National Bureau of Economic Research, Cambridge, MA.

Glaeser, E. L. 2012. *Triumph of the City: How Our Greatest Invention Made Us Richer, Smarter, Greener, Healthier and Happier.* New York: Penguin Press.

Glaeser, E. L. 2022. "Urban Resilience." *Urban Studies* 59 (1): 3–35.

Greater London Authority. 2002. *50 Years On: The Struggle for Air Quality in London since the Great Smog of December 1952.* London: Greater London Authority.

Greater London Authority. 2020. *Air Quality in London, 2016–2020. London Environment Strategy: Air Quality Impact Evaluation.* London: Greater London Authority.

Hallegatte, S., A. Vogt-Schilb, M. Bangalore, and J. Rozenberg. 2017. *Unbreakable: Building the Resilience of the Poor in the Face of Natural Disasters.* Washington, DC: World Bank.

Headey, D., and H. Alderman. 2019. "The Relative Caloric Prices of Healthy and Unhealthy Foods Differ Systematically across Income Levels and Continents." *Journal of Nutrition* 149: 2020–33.

Heilmann, K., and M. E. Kahn. 2019. "The Urban Crime and Heat Gradient in High and Low Poverty Areas." Working Paper 25961, National Bureau of Economic Research, Cambridge, MA.

Henderson, J. V., A. Storeygard, and D. N. Weil. 2011. "A Bright Idea for Measuring Economic Growth." *American Economic Review* 101 (3): 194–99.

Henderson, J. V., A. Storeygard, and D. N. Weil. 2012. "Measuring Economic Growth from Outer Space." *American Economic Review* 102 (2): 994–1028.

Henderson, J. V., and M. Turner. 2020. "Urbanization in the Developing World: Too Early or Too Slow?" *Journal of Economic Perspectives* 34 (3): 150–73.

Herforth, A., Y. Bai, A. Venkat, K. Mahrt, A. Ebel, and W. A. Masters. 2020. "Cost and Affordability of Healthy Diets across and within Countries." Background paper prepared for *The State of Food Security and Nutrition in the World 2020.* FAO Agricultural Development Economics Technical Study No. 9. Rome: Food and Agriculture Organization of the United Nations.

Hopkins, F., J. Ehleringer, S. Bush, R. Duren, C. Miller, C. Lai, Y. Hsu, et al. 2016. "Mitigation of Methane Emissions in Cities: How New Measurements and Partnerships Can Contribute to Emissions Reduction Strategies." *Earth's Future* 4: 408–25.

Hornbeck, R., and D. Keniston. 2017. "Creative Destruction: Barriers to Urban Growth and the Great Boston Fire of 1872." *American Economic Review* 107 (6): 1365–98.

Hossain, M. K., and Q. Meng. 2020. "A Fine-Scale Spatial Analysis of the Assessment and Mapping of Buildings and Population at Different Risk Levels of Urban Flood." *Land Use Policy* 99 (December): 104829.

IPCC (Intergovernmental Panel on Climate Change). 2021. *Climate Change 2021: The Physical Science Basis.* Contribution of Working Group I to the Sixth Assessment Report of the Intergovernmental Panel on Climate Change. Cambridge, UK: Cambridge University Press.

Jin, J., S. Sheppard, and C. Wang. 2021. "Planning to Practice: Impacts of Large-Scale and Rapid Urban Afforestation on Greenspace Patterns in the Beijing Plain Area." *Forests* 12 (3): 316.

Kahn, M. E., and P. Li. 2020. "Air Pollution Lowers High Skill Public Sector Worker Productivity in China." *Environmental Research Letters* 15 (8): 084003.

Karimi, F., and C. Lett. 2015. "Ghana Explosion: People Fleeing Heavy Rain Are among 150 Killed in Accra." CNN.com, June 5, 2015. https://www.cnn.com/2015/06/05/africa/ghana-explosion -floods/index.html.

Knutson, T., S. Camargo, J. Chan, K. Emanuel, C.-H. Ho, J. Kossin, M. Mohapatra, et al. 2020. "Tropical Cyclones and Climate Change Assessment. Part II: Projected Response to Anthropogenic Warming." *Bulletin of the American Meteorological Society* 101 (3): E303–22.

Krugman, P. 1991. "Increasing Returns and Economic Geography." *Journal of Political Economy* 99 (3): 483–99.

Lall, S. V., J. Kaw, S. B. Murray, and F. Shilpi. Forthcoming. *Vibrant Cities: Priorities for Green, Resilient, and Inclusive Urban Development.* Washington, DC: World Bank.

Lall, S. V. M. Lebrand, H. Park, D. M. Sturm, and A. J. Venables. 2021. *Pancakes to Pyramids: City Form to Promote Sustainable Growth.* Washington, DC: World Bank.

Lall, S. V., and S. Wahba. 2020. *No Urban Myth: Building Inclusive and Sustainable Cities in the Pandemic Recovery.* Sustainable Development Series. Washington, DC: World Bank. https://www.worldbank.org/en/news/immersive-story/2020/06/18 /no-urban-myth-building-inclusive-and-sustainable-cities-in-the-pandemic-recovery.

Lanthier, N. 2007. "Talk Tells Story of Jamaican 'Underwater City.'" *Vancouver Sun*, March 24, 2007.

Mariel, P. M., A. Khan, and J. Meyerhoff. 2022. "Valuing Individuals' Preferences for Air Quality Improvement: Evidence from a Discrete Choice Experiment in South Delhi." *Economic Analysis and Policy* 74: 432–47.

Moran, D., R. Wood, E. Hertwich, K. Mattson, J. Rodriguez, K. Schanes, and J. Barrett. 2018. "Carbon Footprints of 13,000 Cities." *Environmental Research Letters* 13 (2018).

Morgan, S. 2022. "Sweden Set to Be World's First Country to Target Consumption-Based Emission Cuts." *Climate Home News*, April 8, 2022.

Park, J., and M. Roberts. 2023. "Urban Resilience and Weather Shocks: A Global Nighttime Lights Analysis." Background paper prepared for this report, World Bank, Washington, DC.

Pawson, M., and D. J. Buisseret. 1975. *Port Royal, Jamaica.* Oxford, UK: Clarendon Press.

Polsby, D. D., and R. D. Popper. 1991. "The Third Criterion: Compactness as a Procedural Safeguard against Partisan Gerrymandering." *Yale Law and Policy Review* 9 (2): 301–53.

Raufman, J., D. Blansky, D. W. Lounsbury, E. W. Mwangi, Q. Lan, J. Olloquequi, and H. D. Hosgood. 2020. "Environmental Health Literacy and Household Air Pollution-Associated Symptoms in Kenya: A Cross-Sectional Study." *Environmental Health* 19 (1): 89.

Roberts, M., B. Blankespoor, C. Deuskar, and B. Stewart. 2017. "Urbanization and Development. Is Latin America and the Caribbean Different from the Rest of the World?" Policy Research Working Paper 8019, World Bank, Washington, DC.

Roberts, M., F. Gil Sander, and S. Tiwari, eds. 2019. *Time to ACT: Realizing Indonesia's Urban Potential.* Washington, DC: World Bank.

Sanz-Barbero, B., C. Linares, C. Vives-Cases, J. L. González, J. J. López-Ossorio, and J. Díaz. 2018. "Heat Wave and the Risk of Intimate Partner Violence." *Science of the Total Environment* 644 (December): 413–19. https://doi.org/10.1016/j.scitotenv.2018.06.368.

Schencking, J. C. 2006. "Catastrophe, Opportunism, Contestation: The Fractured Politics of Reconstructing Tokyo following the Great Kantô Earthquake of 1923." *Modern Asian Studies* 40 (4): 833–73.

Schut, A. G., T. E. Ivits, J. G. Conijin, B. ten Brink, and R. Fensholt. 2015. "Trends in Global Vegetation Activity and Climate Drivers Indicate a Decoupled Response to Climate Change." *PLoS ONE* 10 (10): e0138013.

Seto, K., G. Churkina, A. Hsu, M. Keller, P. Newman, B. Qin, and A. Ramaswami. 2021. "From Low- to Net-Zero Carbon Cities: The Next Global Agenda." *Annual Review of Environment and Resources* 46: 377–415.

Smith, A. 1776. *The Wealth of Nations.* London: W. Strahan and T. Cadell.

Taylor, J. 1688. "Second Part of the Historie of His Life and Travels in America." Manuscript on file, Institute of Jamaica, Kingston.

Tewari, M., and N. Godfrey. 2016. *Better Cities, Better Growth: India's Urban Opportunity.* The New Climate Economy, Global Commission on the Economy and Climate. Washington, DC: World Resources Institute; London: Overseas Development Institute; New Delhi: Indian Council for Research on International Economic Relations.

United Nations. 2019. *World Urbanization Prospects: The 2018 Revision.* New York: Department of Economic and Social Affairs, Population Division, United Nations. https://population.un.org/wup/publications/Files/WUP2018-Report.pdf.

Wang, S., and R. Toumi. 2021. "Recent Migration of Tropical Cyclones toward Coasts." *Science* 371: 514–17.

Watts, G., B. von Christierson, J. Hannaford, and K. Lonsdale. 2012. "Testing the Resilience of Water Supply Systems to Long Droughts." *Journal of Hydrology* 414: 255–67.

Weber, A. 2019. "What Is Urban Flooding?" *Natural Resources Defense Council Expert Blog,* January 15, 2019. https://www.nrdc.org/experts/anna-weber/what-urban-flooding.

Wiedmann, T., and M. Lenzen. 2018. "Environmental and Social Footprints of International Trade." *Nature Geoscience* 11: 314–21.

Wiedmann, T., G. Chen, A. Owen, M. Lenzen, M. Doust, J. Barrett, and K. Steele. 2021. "Three-Scope Carbon Emissions Inventories of Global Cities." *Journal of Industrial Ecology* 25: 735–50.

World Bank. 2009. *World Development Report 2009: Reshaping Economic Geography.* Washington, DC: World Bank.

World Bank. 2021. *Green, Resilient, and Inclusive Development.* Washington, DC: World Bank.

World Bank. 2022a. *Social Sustainability Global Database 2022*. Washington, DC: World Bank.

World Bank. 2022b. *Social Sustainability Global Database 2022 Codebook*. Washington, DC: World Bank.

Xu, X., P. Sharma, S. Shu, T. Lin, P. Ciais, F. N. Tubiello, P. Smith, et al. 2021. "Global Greenhouse Gas Emissions from Animal-Based Foods Are Twice Those of Plant-Based Foods." *Nature Food* 2: 724–32.

Yao, L., Y. Xu, and B. Zhang. 2019. "Effect of Urban Function and Landscape Structure on the Urban Heat Island Phenomenon in Beijing, China." *Landscape and Ecological Engineering* 15: 379–90.

Zaveri, E., J. Russ, A. Khan, R. Damania, E. Borgomeo, and A. Jagerskog. 2021. *Ebb and Flow Vol. 1: Water, Migration and Development*. Washington, DC: World Bank.

Zhao, Q., Y. Guo, T. Ye, A. Gasparrini, S. Tong, A. Overcenco, A. Urban, et al. 2021. "Global, Regional, and National Burden of Mortality Associated with Non-optimal Ambient Temperatures from 2000 to 2019: A Three-Stage Modelling Study." *Lancet Planetary Health* 5 (7): E415–25.

CHAPTER 2

A Global Typology of Cities

Climate change . . . does not respect who
you are—rich and poor, small and big.

Ban Ki-Moon, Secretary-General of the United Nations
Remarks, "Momentum for Change" Initiative, December 2011

MAIN FINDINGS

- Cities can be usefully classified using a typology of two dimensions, population size and level of development of the country in which they are located. Such a typology distinguishes between nine types of cities: small, medium, and large cities in low-, middle-, and high-income countries.

- Across these nine types of cities, the mix and severity of greenness, resilience, and inclusiveness challenges vary widely. Likewise, cities vary in both the mix and the severity of the climate change–related hazards they will face in the next two decades.

- Looking forward to 2030–40, cities in low-income countries and large cities worldwide will more likely have greater exposure to climate change–related hazards. Thus, although cities in middle- and high-income countries are responsible for the bulk of the world's urban carbon dioxide emissions, cities in low-income countries—if not well prepared—will likely bear the brunt of climate change.

- Small island developing states in the Caribbean and the Pacific are projected to be worst positioned to withstand climate change–related hazards, in part because they cannot adapt through internal migration.

- Although the quality and breadth of climate data have improved dramatically in recent decades, high levels of uncertainty and coverage gaps on more local scales highlight the importance of further investments in information on the climate change–related risks that cities globally face. Such information is an indispensable input into better policy making.

Introduction

As chapter 1 revealed, cities across the globe vary widely in terms of how green, how resilient, and how inclusive they are currently. They differ not only in physical geography and climate but also in their capacities to manage the stresses arising from the pressure their populations put on their land, housing, basic services, infrastructure, and environment. Thus, the challenges faced by a well-planned wealthy city with a highly productive service economy differ significantly from those confronting a fast-growing lower-income city with a large manufacturing sector.

Although these differences make it difficult to identify the challenges that confront each city globally, a typology of cities can provide useful information to cities that share similar characteristics. Indeed, multiple initiatives have recently emerged from global city networks with the aim of improving cities' capacity for climate change mitigation and adaptation through collaboration and knowledge sharing.[1] Although a universal upscaling of effective measures and interventions is difficult, understanding some general patterns emerging from similar cities elsewhere can help in identifying common policy needs, which is crucial to transferring good or best practices successfully (Sterzel et al. 2020).

In view of these issues, this chapter has the following main objectives:

- Define a global typology of cities that provides a high-level overview of the mix and severity of greenness, resilience, and inclusiveness challenges that a *typical* city of a given type faces.
- Present the heterogeneities in the mix and severity of climate-related hazards to which different types of cities are projected to be exposed in 2030–40.

To achieve these objectives, the chapter builds on the insights from chapter 1 that various indicators of greenness, resilience, and inclusiveness are related to both a city's size and the level of development of the country in which it is located. Such a typology is undeniably crude, but it does give a broad sense of how urban challenges vary across cities globally and how these challenges may evolve both as cities grow—or in some cases shrink—and as countries move from one level of development up to another.

To present the heterogeneities in climate exposure, this chapter overlays this typology with city-specific information on the levels of exposure to climate-related hazards projected for a global subsample of more than 2,200 cities in 2030–40. This exercise not only reveals how the mix and severity of these hazards vary across types of cities but also highlights unique challenges that cities in small island nations face in terms of limited adaptation strategies. Together with the analytical insights generated in part 2 of this report on how climate change–related stresses affect cities (chapter 3) and how cities affect the environment (chapter 4), this analysis provides crucial input into the high-level policy guidance provided in part 3 (chapter 5) of the report.

Defining a global typology of cities

The goal of defining a global typology of cities is to group together cities that resemble one another in their current challenges related to greenness, resilience, and inclusiveness, while ensuring broad applicability. Fulfilling this goal requires confronting the following fundamental problems.

- *The curse of dimensionality.* Chapter 1 explored multiple indicators for assessing how green, how resilient, and how inclusive cities are currently. However, grouping cities based on multiple indicators to form a typology presents a multidimensional and highly complex clustering problem.
- *Missing data.* This problem applies especially to indicators that capture aspects of the inclusiveness of cities. For that reason, the stylized relationships presented in chapter 1 are based on either combining insights from the secondary literature derived from samples of cities or analyzing dichotomous urban–rural differences in outcomes across countries at different levels of development.

The curse of dimensionality can be overcome by taking advantage of the fact that, as shown in chapter 1, the intensity of many of the greenness, resilience, and inclusiveness challenges confronting cities vary with a city's size and the level of development of a city's parent country. The curse can then be addressed by defining a global typology along those two dimensions. Although this approach may raise concerns that it misses important dimensions of a city's characterization, the existing literature, which attempts to quantify the intensity of various urban challenges, suggests that population (either size or density) is a primary determinant of the strength of challenges across development stages.[2]

The missing data problem can be overcome by primarily focusing, at least in defining the city size and development categories used in the typology, on the greenness indicators, which are available for this report's full global sample of more than 10,000 cities. The emerging typology is then also applied to assess the severity of resilience and inclusiveness challenges to the largest extent possible (box 2.1).

BOX 2.1

Defining and applying the global typology of cities

The approach uses three steps to define the global typology of cities and subsequently to assess the associated severity of current greenness, resilience, and inclusiveness challenges. Annex 2A provides a more detailed description.

Step 1. Define eight possible typologies, each of which combines the three categories of city size and the three categories of development level.

There are multiple plausible ways of defining whether a city is small, medium, or large and, similarly, whether the country in which a city is located should be classified as low-, middle- or high-income. To incorporate these multiple definitions, eight alternative typologies were initially defined. They are based on four competing definitions of the three city size categories (small, medium, and large) and two competing definitions of the three development level categories (low-, middle-, and high-income). The first and second definitions of city size categories are based on the terciles of the global and the within-country distributions of city populations, respectively, whereas the third and fourth are based on the Organisation for Economic Co-operation and Development's urban area classification. The two competing definitions of development level categories are derived from the World Bank's country income classifications for fiscal year 2021/22.

Step 2. Identify the typology that best accounts for the variation in greenness indicators across the global sample of cities.

This step identifies, among the eight typologies defined in step 1, the typology that best accounts for the variation in the greenness indicators. This step is carried out by applying analysis of covariance techniques to the six greenness indicators: (1) total fossil carbon dioxide emissions; (2) per capita fossil carbon dioxide emissions; (3) total emissions of particulate matter of 2.5 microns or less in diameter; (4) total concentrations of particulate matter of 2.5 microns or less in diameter; (5) a city's average level of vegetation; and (6) the share of a city's area that is "high green"—that is, covered by dense vegetation corresponding to gardens, parks, and urban forests. The typology best able to account for the statistical variation across cities in these six indicators is selected as the "winning" typology.

Box 2.1 *continued*

Step 3. Assess each type of city in terms of the relative severity of the current urban challenges.

The final step is to distinguish the *relative* levels of severity associated with greenness, resilience, and inclusiveness challenges facing the types of cities, on average. Although statistical methods and underlying data sets vary across types of challenges, depending on the data structure and availability, the approach to classifying the relative level of severity essentially comprises four substeps. First, estimate the mean *absolute* level of each indicator for each type of city (such as the mean fossil carbon dioxide emissions). Second, assign each type of city a level of severity (high, medium, or low) based on the order of the means. If two types of cities have mean absolute levels of an indicator that are not statistically different in pairwise comparisons, the severity of the challenge is classified as being the same. Third, because each type of challenge is represented by multiple indicators (for example, six indicators for the greenness challenge), calculate the unweighted mean level of severity across all indicators as the overall level of severity for each type of challenge. Fourth, fill the remaining gaps in classifying the levels of severity by making inferences based on what is known about such challenges from the secondary literature.

Nine types of cities globally emerge

Applying steps 1 and 2 of the methodology described in box 2.1 results in a preferred global typology in which small, medium, and large cities correspond to the Organisation for Economic Co-operation and Development's categories of small cities (population of 50,000–199,999), metropolitan areas and medium cities (population of 200,000–1.499 million), and large metropolitan areas (population of at least 1.5 million), respectively. Meanwhile, low-income countries correspond to countries that the World Bank classifies as either low- or lower-middle-income, and middle-income countries correspond to those that the World Bank classifies as upper-middle-income. High-income countries remain as classified by the World Bank (table 2.1). On average, this typology accounts for 32 percent of the variation across indicators. Map 2.1 shows the global distribution of the types of cities.

Table 2.1 **Categories of city size and level of development used to define global typology of cities**

Development level	GNI per capita range	City size	Population range
Low-income	<US$4,096	Small	50,000–199,999
Middle-income	US$4,096–US$12,695	Medium	200,000–1.499 million
High-income	>US$12,695	Large	1.5 million or more

Sources: World Bank analysis based on population data from the European Commission's Global Human Settlement (GHS) Urban Centre Database R2019 (https://ghsl.jrc.ec.europa.eu/ghs_stat_ucdb2015mt_r2019a.php). Per capita GNI data come from the World Bank's World Development Indicators database (http://wdi.worldbank.org).

Note: Cities are defined as urban centers following the degree of urbanization methodology (see box 1.1, chapter 1). The population ranges are based on the populations of these urban centers in 2015. GNI per capita is measured in current 2020 US dollars and calculated using the World Bank Atlas method. GNI = gross national income.

Map 2.1   Global typology of cities

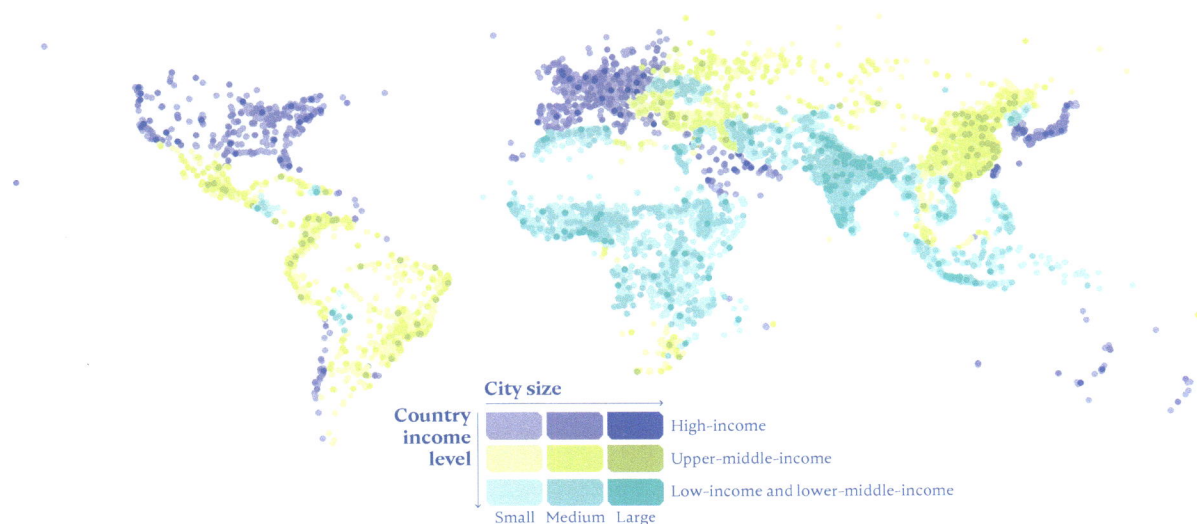

Source: World Bank calculations based on data from the European Commission's Global Human Settlement (GHS) Urban Centre Database R2019 (https://ghsl.jrc.ec.europa.eu/ghs_stat_ucdb2015mt_r2019a.php).

Note: Cities are defined as urban centers following the degree of urbanization methodology. Types of cities are defined using the methodology described in box 2.1 and annex 2A.

Each type covers a broad spectrum of cities

Low-income countries

This group comprises 5,344 cities from 76 countries, or more than half the cities covered by the global sample. Of these, 42 percent are in South Asia, with India alone accounting for 36 percent. Sub-Saharan Africa follows, with 7.3 percent and 4.4 percent of low-income country cities in Nigeria and Ethiopia, respectively. By contrast, Europe and Central Asia and Latin America and the Caribbean account for only 4 percent of cities in low-income countries (figure 2.1). The low-income group consists of the following categories.

- *Low-income small cities (type 1)* account for almost a third (about 26 percent) of the total population of cities in low-income countries (figure 2.2). Cities of this type include agricultural market towns (such as Pirganj, Bangladesh), natural resource industry centers (such as Luwuk, Indonesia), tourist destinations (such as Battambang, Cambodia), transportation hubs (such as Galle, Sri Lanka), satellite cities adjacent to a larger city but falling under a separate administrative unit (such as Demak, Indonesia), and capitals of island states (such as Honiara, Solomon Islands). Nevertheless, their median gross domestic product per capita levels imply that cities of this type are the least productive (table 2.2).

Figure 2.1 In global typology, number of cities, by region and country income group

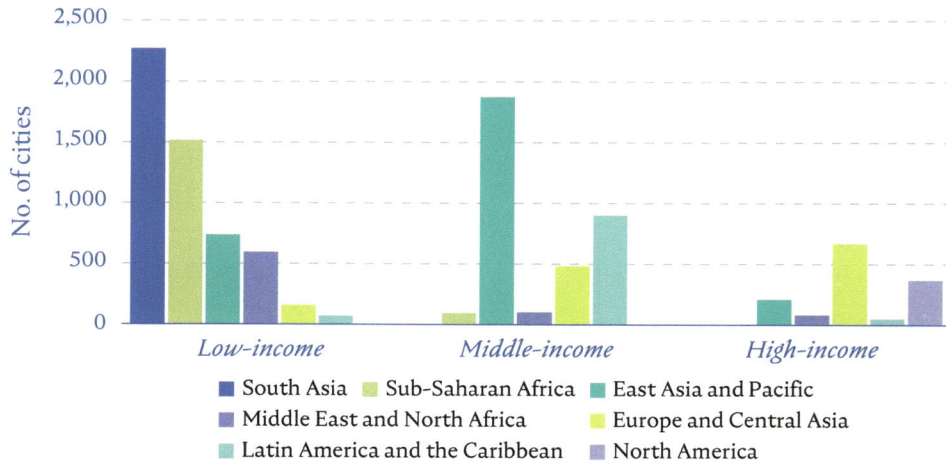

Source: World Bank analysis based on data drawn from the European Commission's Global Human Settlement (GHS) Urban Centre Database R2019 (https://ghsl.jrc.ec.europa.eu/ghs_stat _ucdb2015mt_r2019a.php).

Note: Cities are defined as urban centers following the degree of urbanization methodology (see box 1.1, chapter 1). The income classes are based on the World Bank country classifications for fiscal year 2021/22. Low-income countries correspond to low- and lower-middle-income countries, and middle-income countries to upper-middle-income countries.

- *Low-income medium cities (type 2)* are home to almost 550 million people in about 1,300 cities, accounting for 35.4 percent of the population of cities in low-income countries (figure 2.2). As expected from the wide range of population size (200,000–1.499 million), this type of city also covers a broad spectrum of functionality, depending on the size of the hosting country. For example, national capitals of many African countries, including Abuja, Nigeria, and Monrovia, Liberia, and those of smaller countries, such as Bishkek, Kyrgyz Republic, and Ulaanbaatar, Mongolia, belong to this group. Subnational capitals (such as Raipur, India) and regional economic centers (such as Marrakesh, Morocco; Odessa, Ukraine; Shiraz, Islamic Republic of Iran; and Sylhet, Bangladesh) belong to this type as well. This group also includes cities—such as Muzaffarpur, India—whose economic base is still mainly provided by the large-scale primary sector.

- *Low-income large cities (type 3)* include metropolitan areas—such as Delhi, Dhaka, Jakarta, and Mumbai—in emerging economies. These 134 cities are home to just over 600 million people, or nearly 40 percent of the city population in low-income countries (figure 2.2). In addition to national primate cities, this group includes secondary cities with functional specialty, such as gateway cities that account for a significant portion of a country's international trade (among them, Chittagong, Bangladesh), major information and communication technology service centers (notably, Bangalore and Hyderabad, India), and international tourism destinations such as Denpasar, Indonesia. Despite their size and importance to their national economies, however, the median gross domestic product per capita across type 3 cities falls far behind that of even small cities in middle-income countries. At the same time, almost half of these cities are located within 100 kilometers of the nearest coastline, implying possible vulnerability to, for example, tropical cyclones and higher sea levels (figure 2.3).

Figure 2.2 In global typology, distribution of population, by city size and country income group

a. Number of persons

b. Share of population

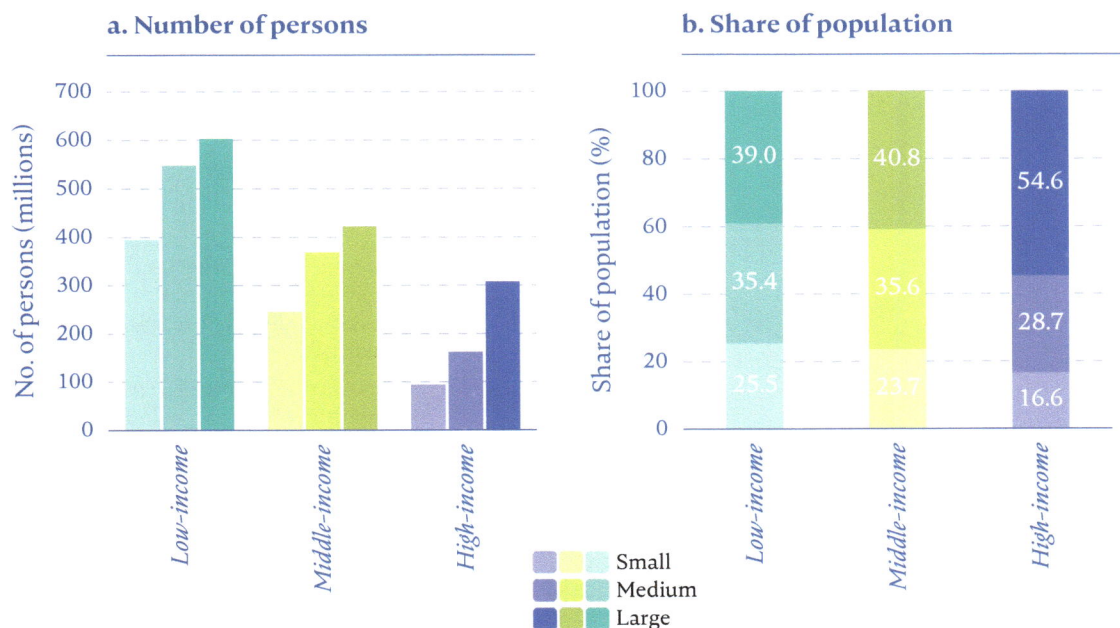

Small
Medium
Large

Source: World Bank analysis based on population data from the European Commission's Global Human Settlement (GHS) Urban Centre Database R2019 (https://ghsl.jrc.ec.europa.eu/ghs_stat_ucdb2015mt_r2019a.php).

Note: Cities are defined as urban centers following the degree of urbanization methodology (see box 1.1, chapter 1). A city is categorized as small, medium, or large when its population is between 50,000 and 199,999; between 200,000 and 1.499 million; or at least 1.5 million, respectively. The income classes are based on the World Bank country classifications for fiscal year 2021/22. Low-income countries correspond to low- and lower-middle-income countries and middle-income countries to upper-middle-income countries.

Table 2.2 Summary of global typology of cities

Income group	City size	Number of cities	Median city size	Median GDP per capita	Five most populous cities
Low-income	Small	3,913 (38.5%)	91,216	US$2,426	Pirganj (Bangladesh); Pleiku (Vietnam); Baraut (India); Turbat (Pakistan); Siguiri (Guinea)
	Medium	1,297 (12.8%)	327,342	US$3,022	Abuja (Nigeria); Muzaffarpur (India); Raipur (India); Kharkiv (Ukraine); Monrovia (Liberia)
	Large	134 (1.3%)	2,700,292	US$3,879	Jakarta (Indonesia); Delhi (India); Dhaka (Bangladesh); Mumbai (India); Quezon City–Manila (Philippines)

(Continued)

Table 2.2 *continued*

Income group	City size	Number of cities	Median city size	Median GDP per capita	Five most populous cities
Middle-income	Small	2,538 (25.0%)	85,346	US$7,087	Wenshan (China); Shanghai (China); Gangyu (China); Xinchang (China); Cabo Frio (Brazil)
	Medium	820 (8.1%)	357,205	US$8,475	Basra (Iraq); Huizhou (China); Pretoria (South Africa); Liuzhou (China); Yinchuan (China)
	Large	94 (0.9%)	3,087,354	US$11,118	Mexico City (Mexico); São Paulo (Brazil); Beijing (China); Bangkok (Thailand); Istanbul (Türkiye)
High-income	Small	980 (9.6%)	82,763	US$19,723	Arnhem (The Netherlands); Santa Clarita (United States); Appleton (United States); Moreno Valley (United States); Newcastle (Australia)
	Medium	327 (3.2%)	359,117	US$23,729	San Antonio (United States); Gwangju (Republic of Korea); Valencia (Spain); Brussels (Belgium); Baltimore (United States)
	Large	66 (0.6%)	3,118,764	US$28,438	Tokyo (Japan); Seoul (Republic of Korea); New York (United States); Osaka (Japan); Los Angeles (United States)
Overall		10,169	111,958	US$5,152	Jakarta, Tokyo, Delhi, Dhaka, Mumbai

Source: World Bank analysis based on data from the European Commission's Global Human Settlement (GHS) Urban Centre Database R2019 (https://ghsl.jrc.ec.europa.eu/ghs_stat_ucdb2015mt_r2019a.php).

Note: Cities are defined as urban centers following the degree of urbanization methodology (see box 1.1, chapter 1). Types of cities are defined using the methodology described in box 2.1 and annex 2A. Percentages are the share of the total number of cities used to derive the typology of cities (10,169). GDP per capita is measured in constant 2007 US dollars at purchasing power parity exchange rates.

Middle-income countries

China hosts 52 percent of the 3,452 cities in this category. Apart from China, cities in Latin America and the Caribbean account for 25 percent of this group (901 cities), followed by cities in Europe and Central Asia, which account for about 14 percent of this group (figure 2.1). Except for Iraq and South Africa, countries in the Middle East and North Africa and in Sub-Saharan Africa make few contributions to this group. The middle-income country group consists of the following categories:

• *Middle-income small cities (type 4)* are home to over 245 million people in 2,538 cities. Among those people, 132 million (54 percent) are spread over 1,343 Chinese cities, which can be roughly characterized as the lowest-tier cities and towns with agricultural bases or a cultural or ecological connotation, or with an integrated function of industrial production, tourism, and residence (such as Wenshan and Xinchang). Because of the Chinese government's effort to make small cities more attractive for rural migrants by, for example, eliminating the *hukou* (household registration) system, these cities could expand rapidly in the coming years (Zhang 2019). Outside of China, type 4 cities include regional market towns (such as Itabuna, Brazil), industrial cities in former Soviet states (such as Babruysk, Belarus; Karaganda and Oskemen, Kazakhstan; and Komsomolsk-on-Amur, Russian Federation),

Figure 2.3 **In global typology, distribution of large coastal and inland cities, by location and country income group, and share of coastal cities, by city size and country income group**

a. Global distribution of large coastal and inland cities

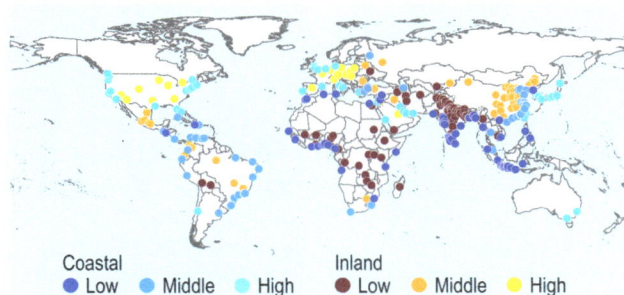

b. Share of coastal cities

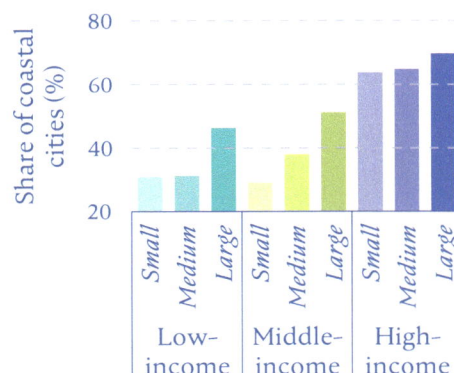

Sources: World Bank analysis based on data from the European Commission's Global Human Settlement (GHS) Urban Centre Database R2019 (https://ghsl.jrc.ec.europa.eu/ghs_stat_ucdb2015mt_r2019a.php) and World Coastline polyline data (https://datacatalog.worldbank.org/int/search/dataset/0038272/World-Bank-Official-Boundaries).

Note: A coastal city is defined as one whose geographic center is within 100 kilometers of the nearest coastline. The percentage of coastal cities is calculated from the total number of cities by type. Cities are defined as urban centers following the degree of urbanization methodology (see box 1.1, chapter 1). Types of cities are defined using the methodology described in box 2.1 and annex 2A.

tourism destinations in the East Asia and Pacific and Latin America and the Caribbean regions (such as Taiping, Malaysia, and Cabo Frio, Brazil), and small cities specializing in primary production and processing (such as Rio Verde, Brazil, and Tulu, Colombia).

- *Middle-income medium cities (type 5)* represent about 12 percent of the population in the global sample. As with small cities, Chinese cities make up by far the largest portion of this group, accounting for nearly 50 percent of the aggregate population. Notable examples are Anshan, Liuzhou, and Yantai, all of which serve as regional industrial centers. Similarly, major industrial cities in other countries, including national capitals with strong manufacturing bases, fall into this group. Such cities include Bucaramanga, Colombia; Campinas, Brazil; Córdoba, Argentina; Gaziantep, Türkiye; Novosibirsk, Russia; Toluca, Mexico; and the capital cities Nur-Sultan, Kazakhstan, and Yerevan, Armenia.

- *Middle-income large cities (type 6)* house 422 million people, or around 41 percent of the population of cities in middle-income countries, in only 94 cities (see table 2.2 and figure 2.2).[3] Although some type 6 cities, such as Beijing, have already reached a postindustrial phase with economies dominated by the tertiary sector, most remain in the transition stage or as key players in manufacturing and heavy industry. Like large cities in low-income countries, just over half of large cities in middle-income countries are near coastlines (figure 2.3).

High-income countries

This group consists of 1,373 cities in 53 countries. Although 76 percent of these cities are in Western Europe and North America, cities from oil-rich countries in Latin America and the Caribbean and the Middle East and North Africa also make up part of this group (figure 2.1). Cities in high-income countries exhibit two distinctive features relative to low- and middle-income country cities. First, more people are concentrated in large cities: 55 percent of the population in high-income countries lives in large cities as opposed to about 40 percent in lower-income countries (figure 2.2). Second, more cities are located near coastlines. Whereas the majority of low- and middle-income cities are more than 100 kilometers away from coastlines, the opposite is true for high-income cities (figure 2.3). The high-income country group consists of the following categories:

- *High-income small cities (type 7)* are home to over 93 million people, accounting for about 17 percent of the population of cities in high-income countries (figure 2.2). Most of these cities are in Western Europe and North America (77 percent) and can be broadly characterized as provincial or regional capitals that are part of midsize metropolitan areas with aggregate populations of less than a million. Notable examples are Arnhem, the Netherlands; Appleton, United States; Clermont-Ferrand, France; Heidelberg, Germany; Messina, Italy; and Regina, Canada. Outside of these two regions, the following cities have similar characteristics: Abha, Saudi Arabia; Beersheba, Israel; and Newcastle, Australia.

- *High-income medium cities (type 8)*, which host some 162 million people in 327 cities globally, are also mostly located in Western Europe and North America (see table 2.2 and figure 2.2, panel a). These cities can be characterized as the core city and neighboring municipalities of metropolitan areas. Depending on the size of the country, the core city can be the national capital, a provincial capital, or a major regional city. Examples are the capital regions of northwestern European countries (except France, Germany, and the United Kingdom) and, outside of Europe, Auckland, New Zealand; Manama, Bahrain; and Montevideo, Uruguay. US cities such as Baltimore, Orlando, San Antonio, and some cities in the Midwest are part of this category as well. Among the most populous cities in this category are Gwangju, Republic of Korea; Valencia, Spain; Mecca, Saudi Arabia; Liverpool, United Kingdom; Perth, Australia; Hiroshima, Japan; and Lyon, France.

- *High-income large cities (type 9)* host 307 million people in 66 cities globally, largely in East Asia and Pacific, North America, and Western Europe (see figure 2.1 and figure 2.2, panel a). The cities range from national or regional economic centers with populations of just over 1.5 million (for example, Cologne, Germany; Doha, Qatar; and Katowice, Poland) to global megacities hosting 10 million or more people, including London, Los Angeles, New York, Osaka, Paris, Seoul, and Tokyo. These cities appear to be at high risk of coastal hazards because they are located close to coastlines (figure 2.3).

How current challenges vary across different types of cities

Using the methodology outlined in step 3 of box 2.1, table 2.3 provides an overview of how the severity of current urban challenges related to greenness, resilience,[4] and inclusiveness vary across the nine types of cities. The upper part of the table employs a traffic light system (red, yellow, and green) to distinguish the level of *relative* severity (high, moderate, and low) of each type of challenge. The lower part of the table lists the challenges identified as severe and moderate for a typical city of each type. For example, in a high-income country take a typical large city with a population of at least 1.5 million such as Atlanta in the United States or Tokyo in Japan. Relative to other types of cities globally, such a city faces severe challenges

Table 2.3 In global typology, severity of challenges, by city size and country income group

Income group	Low-income			Middle-income			High-income		
City size	Small	Medium	Large	Small	Medium	Large	Small	Medium	Large
G Carbon									
Pollution									
Vegetation									
R Resilience									
I Poverty									
Inequality									
Services									
Severe challenges	Resilience Poverty Services	Resilience Poverty Services	Pollution Resilience Services	Poverty Inequality	Vegetation Inequality	Carbon Pollution Vegetation Inequality			Carbon Inequality
Moderate challenges	Pollution Inequality	Pollution	Carbon Vegetation Poverty	Pollution Vegetation Resilience Services	Carbon Pollution Resilience Poverty Services	Resilience Poverty Services	Carbon Resilience Inequality	Carbon Vegetation Resilience Inequality	Pollution Vegetation

Severity: High   Moderate   Low

Sources: World Bank analysis based on the following sources: (1) carbon dioxide emissions, pollution, and vegetation: European Commission, Global Human Settlement (GHS) Urban Centre Database R2019 (https://ghsl.jrc.ec.europa.eu/ghs_stat_ucdb2015mt_r2019a.php); (2) resilience indicator: Visible Infrared Imaging Radiometer Suite (VIIRS) nighttime lights satellite data (https://payneinstitute.mines.edu/eog-2/viirs/); International Best Track Archive for Climate Stewardship tropical cyclone data (https://www.ncdc.noaa.gov/ibtracs/); (3) inequality indicator: compiled from Roberts, Gil Sander, and Tiwari 2019 for Indonesia; Behrens and Robert-Nicoud 2015 for the United States; Ferreyra and Roberts 2018 for 16 countries in Latin America and the Caribbean; and (4) basic services indicators: Henderson and Turner 2020 and https://doi.org/10.7910/DVN/YZ46FJ.

Note: Cities are defined as urban centers following the degree of urbanization methodology (see box 1.1, chapter 1). Types of cities are defined using the methodology described in box 2.1 and annex 2A. G = greenness; I = inclusiveness; R = resilience.

in reducing the size of its overall carbon footprint and intracity inequality,[5] and moderate challenges in reducing air pollution and expanding its green cover. By contrast, in a low-income country a typical small city with a population of between 50,000 and 199,999 faces severe challenges in reducing poverty, increasing access to basic services, and strengthening economic resilience to climate change–related shocks and stresses, as well as moderate challenges in tackling air pollution and inequality.

For small and medium cities in low-income countries, poverty and access to basic services are severe challenges, dampening resilience against climate change–related stresses as well

As discussed in chapter 1, urban areas tend to provide better standards of living and access to basic services than rural areas do. Yet, for cities in low-income countries, the challenges associated with limited access to services remain significant, especially in small and medium cities. For countries with adequate data, evidence also suggests that poverty in low-income countries is deeper and more prevalent in small and medium cities than in large cities.

Poverty is normally compounded by serious deprivation in access to basic services. Analysis of cities in 41 low- and middle-income countries reveals that access to improved sanitation is more pressing for small and medium cities in low-income countries, whereas access to safely managed drinking water is a common severe challenge for cities of different sizes in low-income countries. Thus, 20 percent of households in small and medium cities still lack access to improved sanitation, and safely managed drinking water is unavailable for about 30 percent of households (figure 2.4).

Partly because of inadequate basic services and infrastructure more generally, small and medium cities in low-income countries suffer more severely than other types of cities when confronted by weather variations, even routine changes in weather. Thus, when a typical medium city in a low-income country is hit by any weather that is hotter, wetter, or drier than usual, the city's overall level of economic activity, as measured by nighttime lights intensity, falls by nearly 1.5 percent (figure 2.5, panel a). The average size of impact reaches nearly 26 percent when a tropical cyclone hits the country.[6] Because of their limited resources and capacity to adapt to emerging challenges, small cities in low-income countries are also likely to find resilience to climate change-related stresses a severe challenge.[7]

For a typical small or medium city in a low-income country (which is most likely in an early stage of industrialization or still heavily dependent on the primary sector), greenhouse gas emissions, measured by production-based fossil carbon dioxide (CO_2) emissions (figure 2.6, panels a and b), and lack of green space (figure 2.6, panels e and f) are less urgent challenges than for larger cities or those in higher-income countries. Lower CO_2 emissions and more green space do not necessarily translate into clean air, however, in part because of the unaffordability of cleaner fuels for cooking, heating, and lighting, as well as less stringent and less well-enforced regulations on air quality and vehicle emissions. Thus, pollution poses a moderate challenge for small and medium cities in low-income countries. Their average annual $PM_{2.5}$ (particulate matter of 2.5 microns or less in diameter) concentrations of more than 40 micrograms per cubic meter ($\mu g/m^3$) of air (figure 2.6, panel d) far exceed the safe air guidelines of the World Health Organization (WHO).[8]

Finally, analysis of 4,574 cities from Indonesia, the United States, and 16 countries in Latin America and the Caribbean[9] identifies intracity inequality, measured by the Gini coefficient of income or consumption, as a moderate challenge for small cities in low-income countries

Figure 2.4 **In global typology, level of severity, by city size and country income group: Inclusiveness indicators**

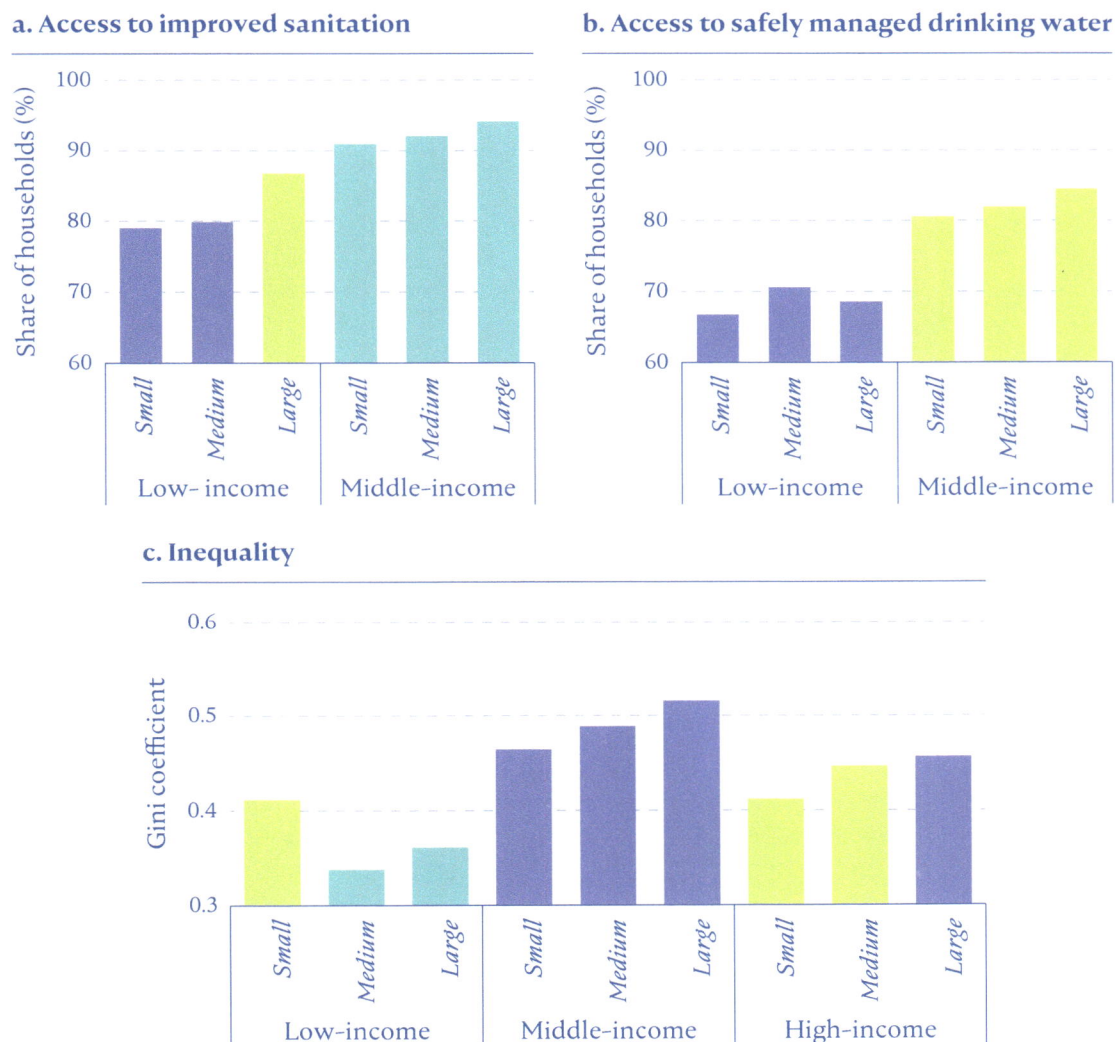

a. Access to improved sanitation

b. Access to safely managed drinking water

c. Inequality

Sources: World Bank analysis based on the following sources: (1) inequality indicator: compiled from Roberts, Gil Sander, and Tiwari (2019) for Indonesia; Behrens and Robert-Nicoud (2015) for the United States; Ferreyra and Roberts (2018) for 16 countries in Latin America and the Caribbean; (2) services indicator: Henderson and Turner (2020) and https://doi.org/10.7910/DVN/YZ46FJ.

Note: For the service indicators (access to improved sanitation and access to safely managed drinking water), cities are defined as urban centers following the degree of urbanization methodology (see box 1.1, chapter 1). For inequality, cities are defined as (1) metropolitan statistical areas for the United States; (2) the types of districts (level-2 administrative units) derived from Roberts, Gil Sander, and Tiwari (2019) for Indonesia; and (3) urban clusters following the cluster algorithm (Dijkstra and Poelman 2014). Types of cities are defined using the methodology described in box 2.1 and annex 2A. The measure of inequality, the Gini coefficient, is calculated on the basis of per capita expenditure for Indonesia and of income elsewhere. The green, light green, and blue bars indicate low, moderate, and high levels of severity, respectively.

Figure 2.5 In global typology, level of severity, by city size and country income group: Resilience indicators

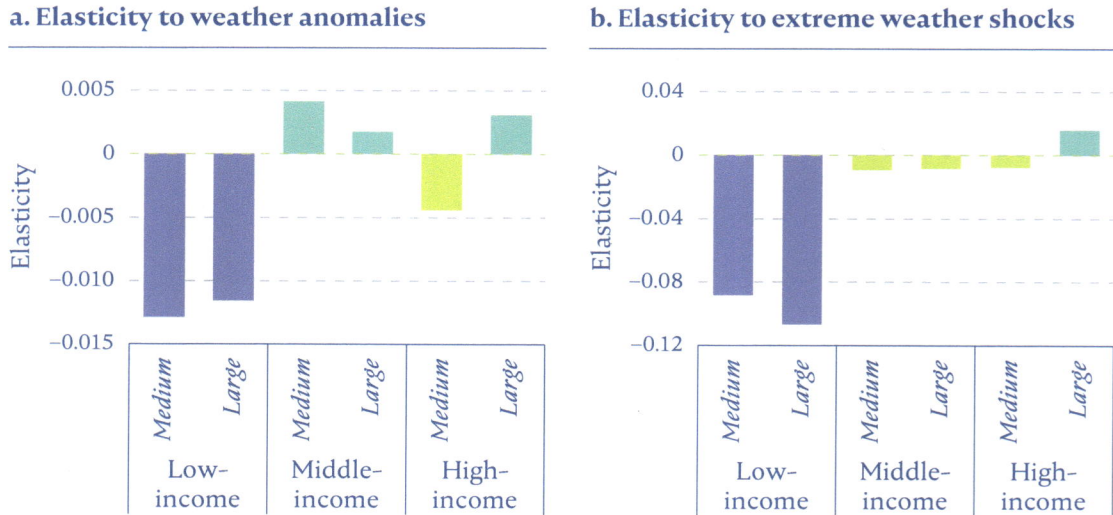

a. Elasticity to weather anomalies

b. Elasticity to extreme weather shocks

Sources: World Bank analysis based on data derived from monthly composites of Visible Infrared Imaging Radiometer Suite (VIIRS) nighttime lights satellite data (https://payneinstitute.mines.edu/eog-2/viirs/), monthly weather data from Climatology Lab, TerraClimate (https://www.climatologylab.org /terraclimate.html), and tropical cyclone data from International Best Track Archive for Climate Stewardship tropical cyclone data (https://www.ncdc.noaa.gov/ibtracs/).

Note: The elasticity for each type of city is calculated as the unweighted average elasticity across the hot, wet, and dry anomalies in panel a, and across the extreme hot, extreme wet, and extreme dry anomalies as well as tropical cyclones in panel b. Because the purpose of this section is to assess the severity of urban challenges, the calculations exclude cold anomalies and extreme cold shocks, the elasticities of which are positive for all types of cities. Cities are defined as urban centers following the degree of urbanization methodology (see box 1.1, chapter 1). Types of cities are defined using the methodology described in box 2.1 and annex 2A. The green, light green, and blue bars indicate low, moderate, and high levels of severity, respectively.

(figure 2.4, panel c).[10] Such inequality can potentially have adverse consequences including low local economic growth, high crime, and social unrest (Ferreira and Schoch 2020; Glaeser, Resseger, and Tobio 2009). This finding, albeit based on data with limited geographic coverage, is driven by small cities in Latin America and the Caribbean, a region well-known for its high levels of income inequality (Busso and Messina 2020; Ferreyra and Roberts 2018).

Large cities in low-income countries face severe challenges in reducing pollution, strengthening resilience, and improving access to services

Large cities in low-income countries struggle with poor air quality, a lack of resilience, and inadequate access to basic services. Thus, of all types of cities, they record the second-highest level of severity in terms of both $PM_{2.5}$ emissions and (lack of) air quality, as measured by total $PM_{2.5}$ concentration (figure 2.6, panels c and d). When hit by extreme weather events, this type of city also appears even more vulnerable than smaller cities (figure 2.5, panel b). And, despite

Figure 2.6 **In global typology, level of severity, by city size and country income group: Greenness indicators**

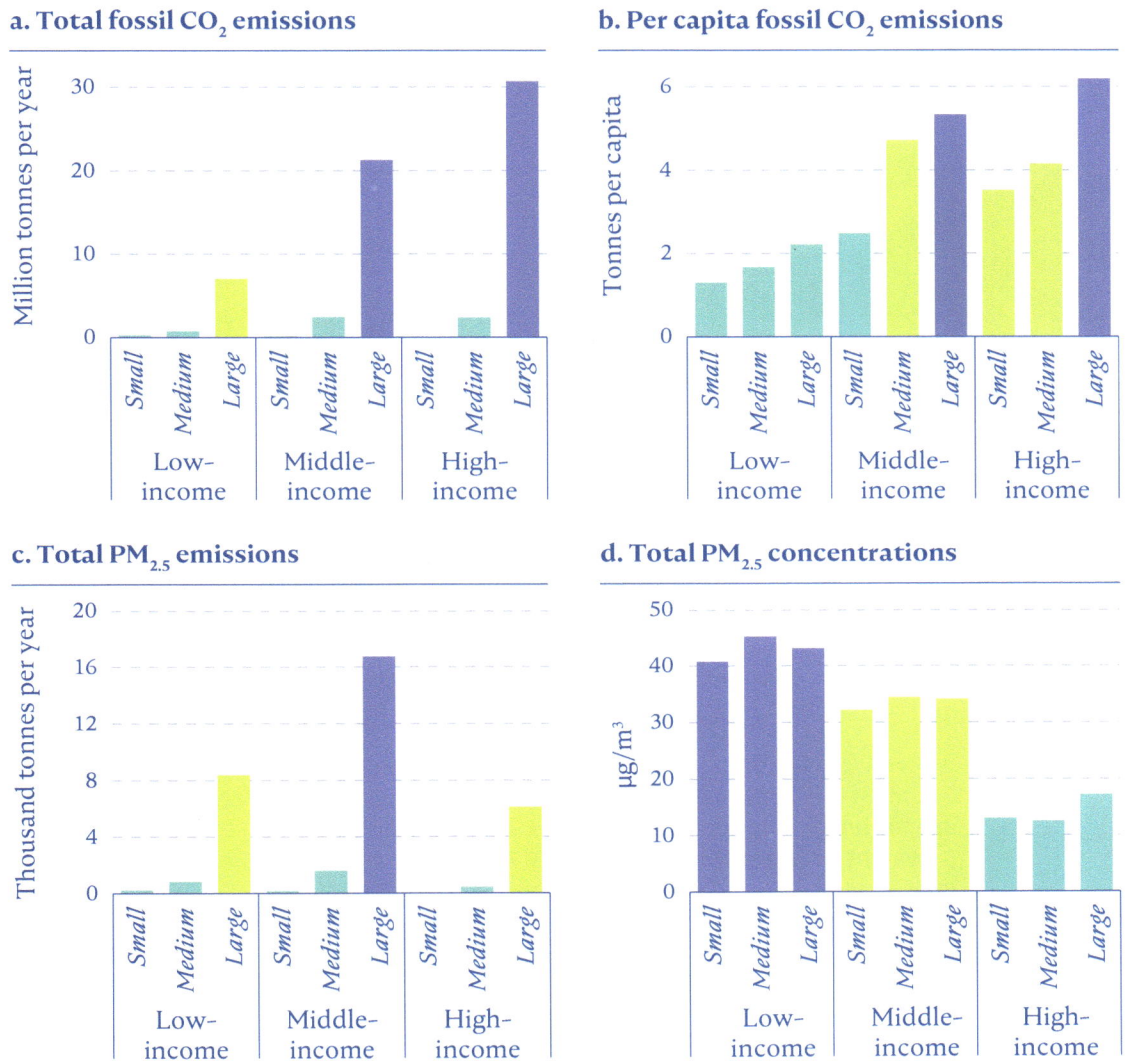

a. Total fossil CO_2 emissions

b. Per capita fossil CO_2 emissions

c. Total $PM_{2.5}$ emissions

d. Total $PM_{2.5}$ concentrations

(Continued)

Figure 2.6 *continued*

e. Average greenness index

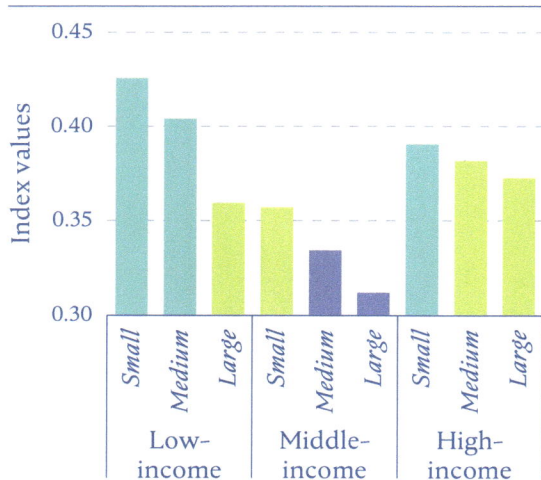

f. Share of high green area

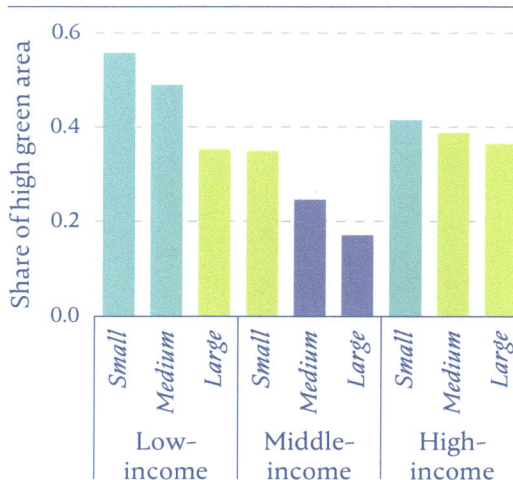

Source: World Bank analysis using data from the European Commission's Global Human Settlement (GHS) Urban Centre Database R2019 (https://ghsl.jrc.ec.europa.eu/ghs_stat_ucdb2015mt_r2019a.php).

Note: Cities are defined as urban centers following the degree of urbanization methodology (see box 1.1, chapter 1). Types of cities are defined using the methodology described in box 2.1 and annex 2A. The green, light green, and blue bars indicate low, moderate, and high levels of severity, respectively. CO_2 = carbon dioxide; µg/m³ = microgram per cubic meter; $PM_{2.5}$ = particulate matter of 2.5 microns or less in diameter.

better access to improved sanitation in large cities, access to safely managed drinking water is almost as poor as in small cities in low-income countries (figure 2.4, panel b). Based on the discussion in chapter 1, it can also be assumed that, although extreme poverty may be less prevalent in larger cities than in smaller cities, significant pockets nevertheless continue to exist in large cities in low-income countries.

Unlike smaller cities in low-income countries, large cities in these countries also make quite significant contributions to global warming. Thus, even though their levels of per capita fossil CO_2 emissions remain far lower, their aggregate emissions exceed those of small and medium cities in higher-income countries (figure 2.6, panel a). Because of poorly managed development pressures, large cities in low-income countries experience significantly greater stresses on green space than do smaller cities in those countries (figure 2.6, panels e and f).

Small cities in middle-income countries experience severe inequality, and poverty (presumably) persists

Severe income inequality is an acute issue for small cities in middle-income countries. Analysis of cities in Latin America and the Caribbean reveals that the average Gini coefficient of income for this type of city is 0.46, which is higher than that of cities in high-income countries (figure 2.4, panel c). Cities in Brazil, Colombia, and Costa Rica stand out in this regard. Also, cities of this type likely face severe challenges dealing with poverty because they predominately consist of the lowest-tier Chinese cities and towns—which represent less developed parts of China—as well as small cities in Latin America and the Caribbean and in former Soviet states (Fay 2005; Slay 2009; Xu et al. 2021).

Pollution, lack of vegetation, and inadequate access to basic services, meanwhile, present moderate challenges for this type of city. Although air pollution is not as severe as in cities in low-income countries, the overall level of $PM_{2.5}$ concentrated in the air (=32 µg/m^3) is still considered unsafe according to WHO's guideline. Likewise, as both the average level of greenness and the share of high green area indicate, green space is much less prevalent than in small cities in low-income countries (figure 2.6, panels e and f). This finding is consistent with a shrinkage of such space in cities as countries move from low- to middle-income status. In terms of basic services, about 20 percent of households still do not have access to safe drinking water, according to analysis drawing on a subsample of cities from 41 low- and middle-income countries (figure 2.4, panel b). Judging by the results for medium cities in middle-income countries (figure 2.5, panel b), small cities in those countries also likely face moderate challenges in strengthening economic resilience to climate change–related shocks and stresses.

Medium and large cities in middle-income countries face severe greenness challenges

As discussed earlier, medium and large cities in middle-income countries mainly rely on the secondary sector. Thus, these types of cities have relatively high levels of carbon emissions and pollution, together with less green space. Large cities have a much higher level of severity, which is not surprising because these cities include key players in manufacturing and heavy industry domestically as well as globally.

Even without two extreme outliers (Guangzhou and Shanghai), large cities in middle-income countries emit, on average, about two-thirds as much fossil CO_2 as, and far more $PM_{2.5}$ than, cities of equivalent size in high-income countries (figure 2.6, panels a and c). Meanwhile, medium cities in middle-income countries have per capita fossil CO_2 emissions approaching those of large cities in those countries, although their relatively small sizes allow total emissions to obscure this finding. Air quality is by no means satisfactory in either medium or large cities in middle-income countries. Moreover, with economies generally specializing in land-intensive activities, these types of cities face a very serious lack of green space, which is particularly pronounced in large cities (figure 2.6, panels e and f).

At the same time, large cities in middle-income countries are the most unequal among all types of cities, followed by medium cities in those countries. They have average Gini coefficients of 0.52 and 0.49, respectively, both higher than the 0.46 for large cities in high-income countries (figure 2.4, panel c). Likewise, Chen, Liu, and Lu (2017) find severe income inequality in larger Chinese cities mainly because these cities tend to have more low-skilled (low-income) migrants. These findings suggest that medium and large cities in middle-income countries must still address pockets of poverty. Meanwhile, these types of cities face moderate challenges in providing universal basic services (figure 2.4, panels a and b).

Small and medium cities in high-income countries fare best overall, but still face moderate challenges related to carbon emissions, resilience, and inequality

As discussed earlier, small and medium cities in high-income countries include secondary cities in larger developed countries and the national capitals of smaller countries. These cities tend to be relatively well governed and have access to adequate resources and technical capacity, making them less susceptible than cities in lower-income countries to greenness, resilience, and inclusiveness challenges. Nevertheless, they have moderate levels of CO_2 emissions per person, mainly from transportation-related activities and electricity consumption (figure 2.6, panel b; see the sources of emissions discussed in chapter 1 as well).

Moreover, medium cities in high-income countries are economically less resilient to weather shocks than their larger counterparts. Unlike for large cities, the average estimated impact of weather anomalies on economic activity is significantly negative for medium cities regardless of whether those anomalies are extreme (figure 2.5). Although further investigation of the underlying mechanisms behind the relationship between city size and economic resilience is beyond the scope of this report, previous studies point out that resilience planning and action are often built around the needs and interests of large metropolitan areas, and tend to overlook smaller cities. Thus, even in high-income countries, small and medium cities likely have limited access to the necessary financial and human resources, as well as weaker governance, constraining their preparedness and adaptive capacity for climate shocks and stresses.[11]

Finally, intracity income inequality presents a common moderate challenge for small and medium cities in high-income countries. Because of their level of development, these cities likely host populations with more uniform levels of education and skill relative to those in cities of similar size in middle-income countries. Nevertheless, small cities in high-income countries remain quite unequal, as reflected in the average Gini coefficient of 0.41 calculated using the data for 363 US metropolitan statistical areas. Medium cities exhibit higher levels of income inequality—nearly as high as those of larger cities in the sample (figure 2.4, panel c).

Large cities in high-income countries grapple with severe inequality, alongside persistently high CO_2 emissions

Large cities in high-income countries have by far the highest levels of fossil CO_2 emissions both in absolute terms and on a per capita basis (figure 2.6, panels a and b). Although their economic activities have mostly shifted to human capital–intensive tertiary industry, they still emit the greatest quantities of CO_2, largely generated by transportation-related activities, as well as by energy consumption by residential and commercial buildings (see the discussion in chapter 1).

In addition, large cities in high-income countries have very high levels of intracity inequality. Although not as high as in medium and large cities in Latin America and the Caribbean, the average Gini coefficient across large cities in high-income countries, represented by large US metropolitan areas, is 0.46 (figure 2.4, panel c). Furthermore, among high-income countries, a high level of income inequality in large cities is not unique to the United States. Boulant, Brezzi, and Veneri (2016) and Castells-Quintana, Royuela, and Veneri (2020) find evidence that income inequality tends to increase with city size for a more general sample of Organisation for Economic Co-operation and Development countries as well.[12]

Compared with cities of comparable size in middle-income countries, however, large cities in high-income countries find pollution and lack of vegetation only moderately challenging. Although the average amount of $PM_{2.5}$ they emit is not trivial, it is roughly a third of the average amount emitted by large cities in middle-income countries. Air quality (measured by $PM_{2.5}$ concentration) appears to be significantly better than that in lower-income cities, although it still does not meet WHO's safety standard. Consistent with this finding, these cities have more green space than comparably sized cities in middle-income countries, although they remain less green in terms of vegetation than small cities in high-income countries (figure 2.6, panels e and f).

How climate change–related hazards vary across cities globally

Following on the previous overview of a typical city of each type and the severity of its current urban challenges related to greenness, resilience, and inclusiveness, this section uses the same nine types of cities to look at each type's *exposure* to six climate change–related hazards—floods, heat stress, tropical cyclones, sea level rise, water stress, and wildfires—as well as its weighted exposure to combined climate change–related hazards. The data, provided by Moody's ESG Solutions,[13] include city-level scores on a scale of zero to 100, from less to more exposed (table 2.4). The data set covers more than 2,200 cities from the full global sample of more than 10,000 cities examined in this report. Figure 2.7 shows the distribution of cities, by type, in the Moody's data set.

Exposure scores for each city are calculated by bringing together spatially explicit physical hazard and socioeconomic data projected to 2030–40. For physical hazard data, estimates are based on the highest emission pathway—Representative Concentration Pathway 8.5. Emissions pathways do not vary significantly within the time frame selected because of the delayed implications of potentially divergent policy responses, making the selection appropriate for near-term planning purposes. For socioeconomic data, estimates of potential exposure are derived from spatially explicit data of a city's important assets, including population, gross domestic product (measured using exchange rates adjusted for purchasing power parity), and agricultural area. Shared Socioeconomic Pathway 2 (SSP2), a middle-of-the-road SSP, is used for 2040 socioeconomic projections. SSP2 was selected as the most realistic depiction of future growth patterns because, of the SSPs, it makes the fewest overall assumptions.[14]

Although the quality and breadth of climate and socioeconomic data have improved dramatically in recent decades, high levels of uncertainty and coverage gaps on a more localized scale remain, limiting the ability of city stakeholders to make informed policy and investment decisions. Furthermore, although the scores provide a baseline understanding of socioeconomic exposure to climate change–related hazards, they do not account for *vulnerability*—conditions that increase one's susceptibility to the impact of a hazard—and so should not be conflated with climate change–related risk. Vulnerability to climate change–related hazards can be informed by several factors, such as sensitivity to harm and capacity to cope and adapt, that together constitute an important component of climate risk (IPCC 2022b). Thus, high exposure scores may not necessarily translate into a significant impact on cities and their populations. This information gap highlights the importance of ongoing investment in data collection that would facilitate a better understanding of climate change–related vulnerability and risk at the city level.

For this analysis, seven indicators—the six identified climate change–related hazards plus the weighted overall hazard—are regressed on the nine types of cities. To ensure that the analysis includes only the cities' relevant hazards, it excludes hazards identified as not affecting a city.

Table 2.4 Methodological reference table for projected climate change–related exposure scores, 2030–40

	No exposure	Low exposure	Medium exposure	High exposure	Red flag
Combined climate change–related hazard Average of all exposure scores	n.a.	Not significantly exposed to historical and/or projected hazards	Exposed to some historical and/or projected hazards	Exposed to high historical and/or projected hazards	Exposed to extremely high historical and/or projected hazards
Floods One-in-100-year flood (rainfall- and riverine-based) Wet days (>10 millimeters) Very wet days (>95th percentile) Rainfall intensity	n.a.	Population minimally exposed to flooding; future rainfall intensification	Population moderately exposed to flooding; future rainfall intensification	Population highly exposed to flooding; future rainfall intensification	Population extremely highly exposed to flooding; future rainfall intensification
Heat stress Energy demand Extreme heat days Extreme temperature	n.a.	Changes in heat extremes are relatively less severe	Changes in heat extremes are within range of global average	Changes in heat extremes are relatively more severe	Changes in heat extremes are much more severe
Tropical cyclones Cumulative wind speed	No known historical occurrence	Possible tropical cyclone activity but infrequent and/or less severe	Infrequent but possibly severe tropical cyclone activity	Frequent and possibly severe tropical cyclone activity	Frequent severe tropical cyclone activity
Sea-level rise One-in-100-year flood (coastal-based)	Not coastal or near coastal waterways	Population minimally exposed to coastal flooding	Population moderately exposed to coastal flooding	Population highly exposed to coastal flooding	Population extremely highly exposed to coastal flooding
Water stress Current baseline water stress Current interannual variability Future water supply and demand Water supply and demand change	n.a.	Water supply and/or demand changes relatively small	Water supply and/or demand changes likely to increase	Current water stress likely already high, and supplies diminishing	Competition for water resources extreme, and future water supply failure possible
Wildfires Total and change in days with high wildfire potential Total and change in maximum wildfire potential	Not burnable based on land type	Low wildfire potential, little change in severity, relatively fewer high-hazard days	Moderate wildfire potential, with some degree of change in future severity	High wildfire potential with sizable increases in future severity	Very high wildfire potential and at least several additional weeks of high-hazard days

Source: Adapted from Moody's ESG Solutions, Sub-Sovereign Physical Climate Risk Scores Methodology, October 2021, https://esg.moodys.io/climate-solutions.

Note: n.a. = not applicable. We do not present a specific score range associated with each level of exposure, because the range varies by the type of hazard.

Figure 2.7 Distribution of cities in climate change–related exposure data set, by city size and country income group

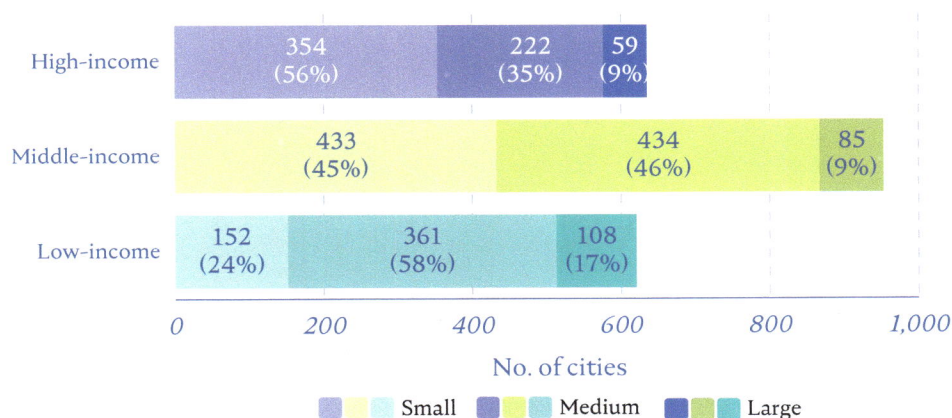

Source: World Bank analysis based on data from Moody's ESG Solutions, Sub-Sovereign Physical Climate Risk Scores, October 2021 (https://esg.moodys.io/climate-solutions).

Note: The percentages in parentheses are calculated by income group. Cities are defined as urban centers following the degree of urbanization methodology (see box 1.1, chapter 1). Types of cities are defined using the methodology described in box 2.1 and annex 2A. Low-income numbers add up to 99 rather than 100 due to rounding.

The analysis provides predicted estimates of scores for each of the nine types of cities, conditional on exposure to an existing hazard. This exercise allows examination of whether a given type of city is expected to have more or less exposure than other types of cities to the various hazards.

Underlying geographic factors, such as a city's climate zone or proximity to coastline, provide important context for understanding potential exposure to certain climate change–related hazards (Li et al. 2018). Although the relationship between city typology and geolocation is not analyzed, many "red flag" cities are clustered in coastal and tropical areas and are more likely to be severely exposed or highly exposed to one or more climate change–related hazards (map 2.2). An example of a red flag city is Sylhet, Bangladesh, which is highly exposed to both heat stress and floods. Climate shocks and stresses can act together to exacerbate the overall impact, even in the most resilient cities (Simpson et al. 2021; Zscheischler et al. 2018).

Overall, cities in low-income countries are more exposed than other cities of all types to climate change–related hazards

Overall, cities in low-income countries—types 1, 2, and 3—are more exposed to climate change–related hazards. These three types of cities show the highest average scores across all income groups for such hazards (figure 2.8). When segmented by hazard, floods, heat stress, sea-level rise, and wildfires demonstrate a similar exposure bias toward cities in low-income countries. Notable exceptions are water stress, which does not show a noticeable trend, and tropical cyclones, which show an inverse trend (figure 2.9). The results highlight the additional challenges that many low-income cities face in adapting to a changing climate because of a preexisting exposure bias to climate change–related hazards.

Map 2.2 Geographic distribution of overall climate change–related exposure, by city size and country income group

Low-income Middle-income High-income

Small / Medium / Large

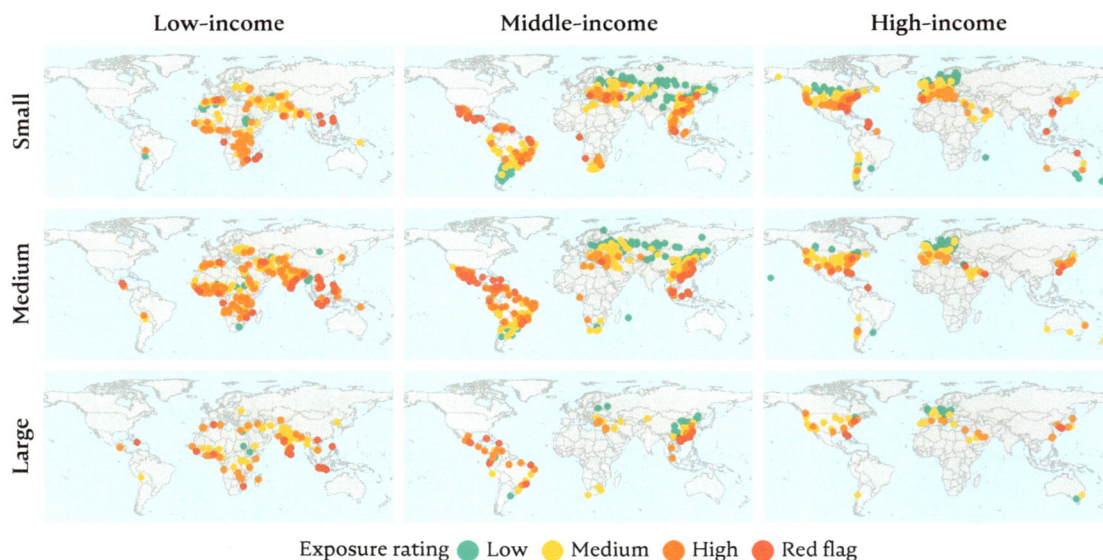

Exposure rating ● Low ● Medium ● High ● Red flag

Sources: World Bank analysis based on data from Moody's ESG Solutions, Sub-Sovereign Physical Climate Risk Scores, October 2021 (https://esg.moodys.io/climate-solutions), and the European Commission's Global Human Settlement (GHS) Urban Centre Database R2019 (https://ghsl.jrc.ec.europa.eu/ghs_stat_ucdb2015mt_r2019a.php).

Note: The exposure rating for each city is determined using the methodology outlined in table 2.4. Cities are defined as urban centers following the degree of urbanization methodology (see box 1.1, chapter 1). Types of cities are defined using the methodology described in box 2.1 and annex 2A.

Proportionally, larger cities are more exposed to overall climate change–related hazards

At each income level, a trend also shows proportionally higher overall climate change–related exposure for larger cities. This trend is most defined for cities in middle-income countries—types 4, 5, and 6—with the average score moving from 51 to 56 to 61 as city size increases from small to medium to large (figure 2.8). When segmented by the type of hazard, the trends often diverge. For floods, results indicate that in low-income countries large cities have higher levels of exposure than small cities, whereas in high-income countries small cities have higher levels of exposure than large cities. The results highlight the vast challenges that large cities in low-income countries—type 3—face in terms of managing flood risk (figure 2.9, panel a). These challenges can be exacerbated when paired with rapid urbanization and highlight the need to support large cities in low-income countries, which can act as engines of sustainable growth for countries and regions in the areas of resilient urban planning and development.

Figure 2.8 **Average weighted overall climate change–related hazard exposure, by city size and country income group**

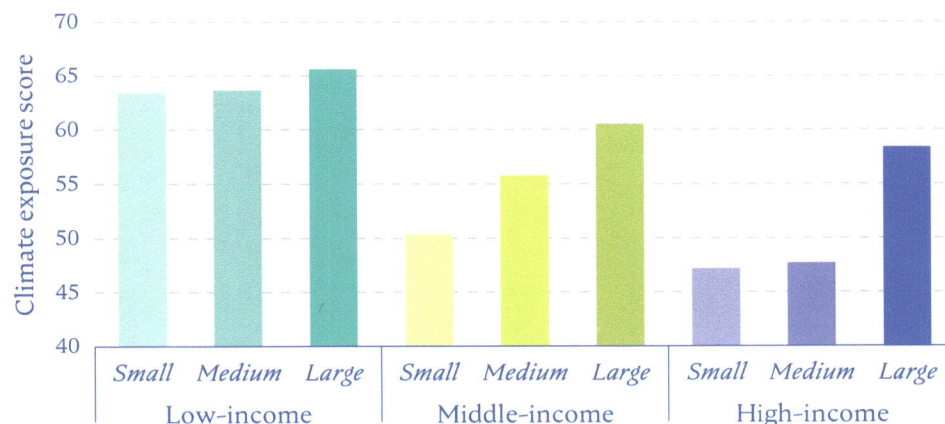

Source: World Bank analysis based on data from Moody's ESG Solutions, Sub-Sovereign Physical Climate Risk Scores, October 2021 (https://esg.moodys.io/climate-solutions).

Note: The values reported in the figure are the mean climate exposure scores for cities that belong to a given type. The mean scores are estimated by regressing a city's climate exposure score on a series of dummy variables for the different types of cities. Cities are defined as urban centers following the degree of urbanization methodology (see box 1.1, chapter 1). Types of cities are defined using the methodology described in box 2.1 and annex 2A.

For water stress, cities in middle- and high-income classes face increasingly higher levels of exposure as they become larger, whereas the distribution of exposure in low-income class cities is relatively uniform across city size (figure 2.9, panel b). This finding highlights the challenges that many cities face in managing water resources for large populations when shocks, such as prolonged drought, affect a system. Water crises, such as the one experienced by Cape Town in 2017 and 2018, may become increasingly common in the face of a changing climate. To adapt, large cities, particularly those with more resources in middle- and high-income countries, must strengthen the resilience of their water supply systems by enhancing their robustness—such as by promoting water reuse and source diversification—and strengthen their abilities to cope.

Intersection with urban challenges exacerbates the impact of climate shocks and stresses

When intersected with urban challenges, such as those identified in table 2.3, cities with high exposure scores are more likely to sustain significant damage or impacts from climate change–related shocks and stresses. This analysis finds proportionally higher levels of exposure for low-income and large city typologies. Unfortunately, the same city typologies also face higher levels of severity for many urban challenges, exacerbating the challenges they face in adapting to a changing climate. Table 2.5 provides examples of how the relative severity of a city's urban challenges can either blunt or exacerbate the impacts of climate shocks and stresses.

Figure 2.9 Average climate exposure scores for six climate change–related hazards, by city size and country income group

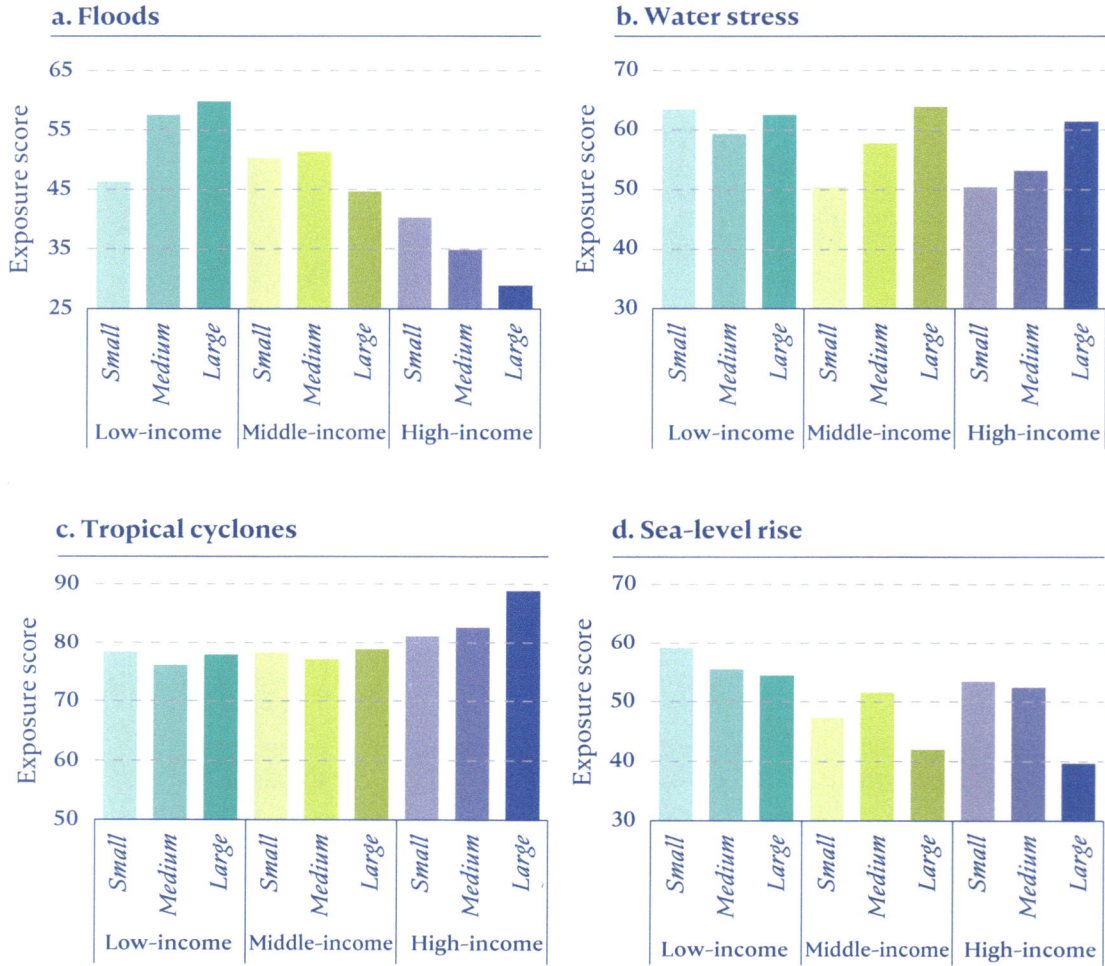

a. Floods

b. Water stress

c. Tropical cyclones

d. Sea-level rise

(Continued)

Figure 2.9 *continued*

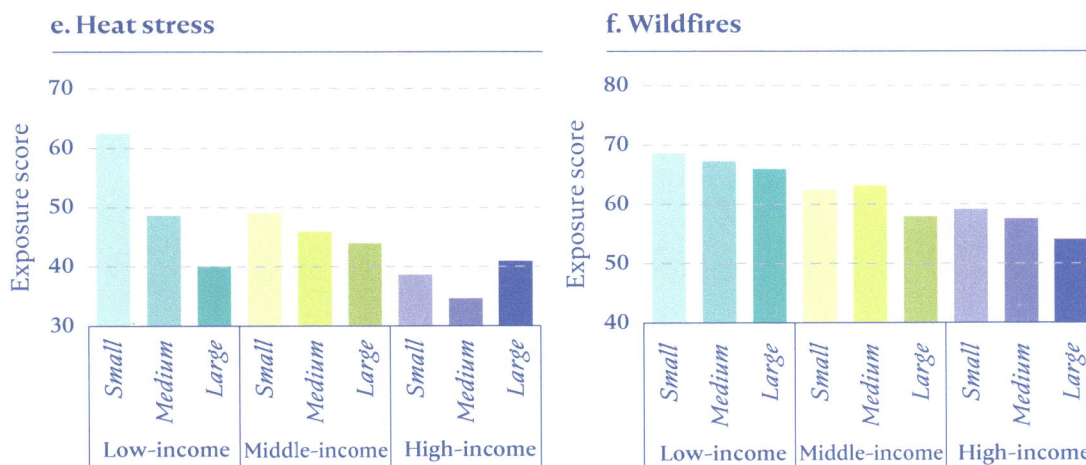

e. Heat stress

f. Wildfires

Source: World Bank analysis based on data from Moody's ESG Solutions, Sub-Sovereign Physical Climate Risk Scores, October 2021 (https://esg.moodys.io/climate-solutions).

Note: In each figure, the reported values (vertical axis) are the mean climate exposure scores for cities that belong to a given type. The means are estimated by regressing a city's exposure score associated with each type of climate hazard on a series of dummy variables for the different types of cities. Cities are defined as urban centers following the degree of urbanization methodology (see box 1.1, chapter 1). Types of cities are defined using the methodology described in box 2.1 and annex 2A.

Table 2.5 **Intersection between urban challenges and climate shocks and stresses**

Urban challenges		Intersection with climate shocks and stresses
Greenness	Carbon	High emissions in global cities will increase the severity of certain climate change–related hazards felt at the local scale (such as sea-level rise), whereas low-carbon investments offer opportunities for adaptation co-benefits. For example, tree cover can reduce heat stress while also lowering the energy demand for cooling (IPCC 2022a; Seddon et al. 2020).
	Pollution	High pollution levels lower the health of populations, making them more vulnerable to hazards such as heat stress (O'Lenick et al. 2019). High pollution levels also undermine worker productivity (Deuskar 2022), thereby damaging the resilience of cities to climate change–related shocks and stresses.
	Vegetation	Vegetation and nature-based solutions can blunt the impact of storm surges from tropical cyclones, provide retention for floods, and reduce ambient heat (Debele et al. 2019; Deuskar 2022; World Bank 2021).
Resilience	Resilience	Resilient cities experience lower economic losses from climate change–related shocks and stresses because of fewer disruptions of basic services and quicker recovery (Hallegatte, Rentschler, and Rozenberg 2019; Qiang, Huang, and Xu 2020), and as shown by this report's analysis of nighttime lights data based on the work of Park and Roberts (2023).

(Continued)

Table 2.5 *continued*

Urban challenges		Intersection with climate shocks and stresses
Inclusiveness	Poverty	Poor populations may face an exposure bias to climate change–related hazards such as floods by, for example, living in slums in floodplains and to heat stress by having less access to air-conditioning and less green space in poor areas, among other things (Hsu et al. 2021; Winsemius et al. 2015—see also the discussion in chapter 3).
	Inequality	Poor populations may incur disproportionately higher losses when affected by shocks and stresses (Hallegatte et al. 2017).
	Services	Lack of basic services is a cross-cutting challenge that can exacerbate the impacts of shocks such as floods (lack of drainage), as well as water stress (lack of drinking water supply) and heat stress (lack of energy for air-conditioning)—see Baker 2012.

Source: World Bank.

Small and isolated island states have fewer options for internal climate migration

Building on the analysis of city typologies, city scores within each country were averaged to better understand a country's overall urban exposure and capacity to adapt to long-term climate exposure through internal migration. The results of the analysis highlight the unique struggles faced by smaller island and coastal nations such as those in the Caribbean and the Pacific (figure 2.10). In addition, in several larger island and coastal countries, such as Indonesia and Vietnam, exposure to climate change–related hazards is pervasive across all cities being analyzed. By contrast, in the United States a city such as Miami has a high score for overall exposure to climate change–related hazards, but other cities with lower exposure such as Minneapolis or Pittsburgh counter that score. When scores are averaged, lower-income countries face higher levels of exposure to climate change–related risk (table 2.6).

Summary and conclusions

Building on the insights in chapter 1, this chapter classifies the global sample of cities analyzed in this report into nine types based on the population size of the cities (small, medium, and large) and the level of development of the countries in which they are located (low-, middle-, and high-income). The resulting typology highlights the heterogeneity across different types of cities in the mix and severity of their current urban challenges, as well as in the level of exposure to climate change–related hazards projected forward to 2030–40.

Although cities in high-income countries face moderate to severe challenges in reducing CO_2 emissions and intracity inequality, those in low- and middle-income countries are confronted with moderate to severe challenges in dealing with air pollution, poverty, and universal access to basic services, as well as economic resilience to climate shocks and stresses. Consistent with that lack of access and low economic resilience, the analysis of data from Moody's ESG Solutions predicts that, over the next two decades, the lower a city's level of development the higher its exposure will be to the overall level of climate change–related hazards.

Figure 2.10 Urban exposure to combined climate change–related hazards, selected countries, by country income group

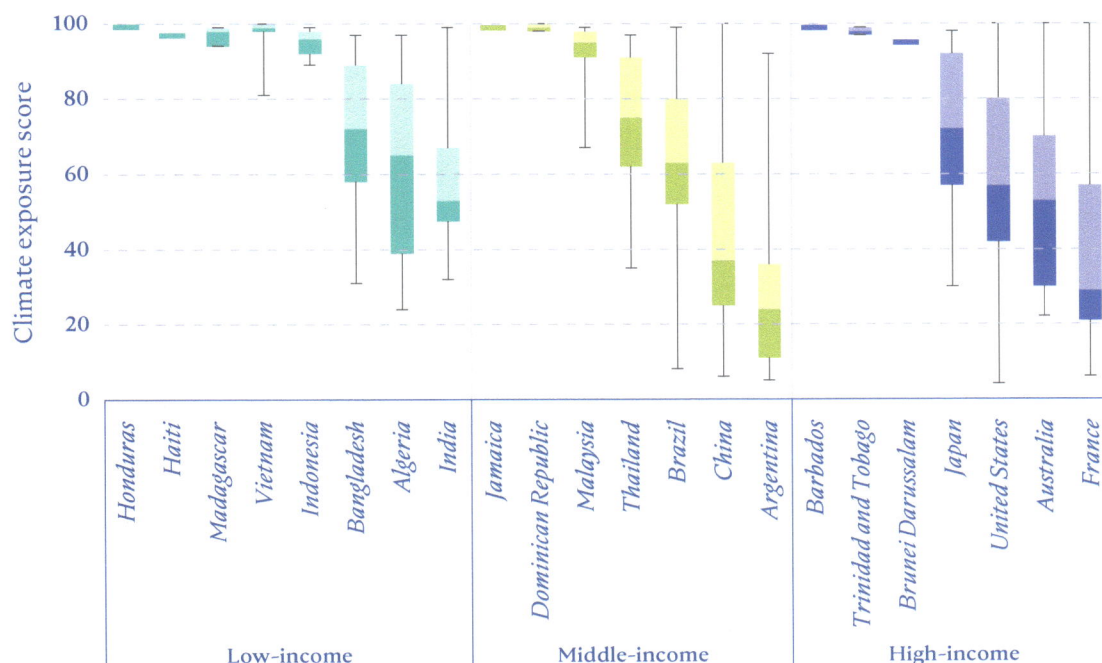

Source: World Bank analysis based on data from Moody's ESG Solutions, Sub-Sovereign Physical Climate Risk Scores, October 2021 (https://esg.moodys.io/climate-solutions).

Note: The figure is organized in descending order of the mean climate exposure scores in each income group. The upper and lower bars indicate the maximum and the minimum scores, respectively, for each country. The bottom of the box, the border of two colors, and the top of the box, respectively, depict the first, second (median), and third quartiles of the scores in each country. The horizontal bars indicate the climate exposure scores for countries with only one city being analyzed except for Honduras, which has two cities with the same score. Cities are defined as urban centers following the degree of urbanization methodology (see box 1.1, chapter 1).

Table 2.6 Urban exposure to combined climate-related hazard, by country income group

Income group	Average country score	Five most highly exposed countries
Low-income	64.0	Honduras, Liberia, Sri Lanka, Haiti, and Madagascar
Middle-income	53.7	Dominican Republic, Jamaica, Guyana, Cuba, and Suriname
High-income	48.4	Bahamas, Barbados, Trinidad and Tobago, Brunei, and Taiwan, China

Source: World Bank analysis based on data from Moody's ESG Solutions, Sub-Sovereign Physical Climate Risk Scores, October 2021 (https://esg.moodys.io/climate-solutions).

Note: Average country score is calculated as the unweighted average score across all cities within each income group, with cities defined as urban centers following the degree of urbanization methodology (see box 1.1, chapter 1).

Moreover, the overall level of climate change–related hazards, alongside CO_2 emissions, increases as cities become more populated. Thus, larger cities at the same level of development are expected to be more afflicted with climate shocks and stresses over the coming decades. This trend is particularly pronounced when it comes to water stress and geographic exposure to tropical cyclones, on top of which exposure to floods is projected to place an additional burden on larger cities in low-income countries.

Water stress and threats to long-term habitability are major drivers of internal climate migration (Clement et al. 2021). Unfortunately, the small island states in the Caribbean and the Pacific, having few options for internal migration, are the worst-positioned to withstand future climate hazards. In the developing world, such limited adaptation options, compounded by inadequate financial and social capacities, may reduce the opportunities for households to move out of poverty and build resilient livelihoods. The chapters that follow delve into how climate change–related shocks and stresses affect cities (chapter 3) and vice versa (chapter 4). Chapter 5 then elaborates on the tailored policy guidance for the unique challenges facing each type of city.

Annex 2A: Methodology for defining a global typology of cities

The global typology of cities described in this chapter is defined according to two dimensions: the size of a city and the level of development represented by the income group of the country in which the city is located. The dimensions are identified in chapter 1 as important in characterizing the intensity of current urban challenges related to greenness, resilience, and inclusiveness. Restricting the dimensions at the outset simplified a complex clustering problem.

Based on the two dimensions, the study team split the global sample of cities into nine types so that (1) each type has a low variance of severity—that is, cities within the same type are relatively homogeneous; and (2) each type has a distinctive mean level of severity. The derivation of the typology and assessment of the severity of current urban challenges proceeded in the following steps.

Step 1. Generate eight typologies according to the combination of city size and income class.

The team generated eight typologies of cities by combining four options for three city sizes (small, medium, and large) and two for the three income groups (low, middle, and high). Table 2A.1 describes the criteria for the categorization, as well as the population ranges and per capita gross national income for each group.

Step 2. Identify the typology that accounts for the largest variation in urban challenge indicators.

Among the eight typologies generated in step 1, the team chose as the global typology of cities the one that produces the most effective way of distinguishing cities in terms of severity of urban challenge. To make an objective judgment about the best combinations of grouping, the

Table 2A.1   Criteria for deriving a global typology of cities

Dimension		Criteria	Group	Population and income ranges
City size	1	Terciles of global population distribution Three groups with equal number of cities	Small Medium Large	50,007–76,560 76,562–142,264 142,276–36,312,540
	2	Terciles of national population distribution Three groups with equal number of cities	Small Medium Large	50,007–164,795 55,126–354,778 78,040–36,312,540
	3	Based on OECD classification of urban areas Metros and large metros combined as large cities	Small Medium Large	50,000–199,999 200,000–499,999 >= 500,000
	4	Based on OECD classification of urban areas Metros and medium cities combined as medium cities	Small Medium Large	50,000–199,999 200,000–1,499,999 >= 1,500,000
Income group	1	World Bank country classification for fiscal year 2021/22: upper-middle- and lower-middle-income combined as middle-income	Low Middle High	<1,046 1,046–12,695 >12,695
	2	World Bank country classification for fiscal year 2021/22: low- and lower-middle-income combined as low-income	Low Middle High	<4,096 4,096–12,695 >12,695

Source: Population data from the European Commission's Global Human Settlement (GHS) Urban Centre Database R2019 (https://ghsl.jrc.ec.europa.eu/ghs_stat_ucdb2015mt_r2019a.php).

Note: Cities are defined as urban centers following the degree of urbanization methodology (see box 1.1, chapter 1). Population is as of 2015. Income ranges are based on gross national income per capita in current US dollars calculated using the World Bank Atlas method for exchange rates in 2020. For countries with fewer than three cities in the global sample, the categories based on the national distribution are replaced with the ones based on the global distribution. The Organisation for Economic Co-operation and Development (OECD) classification of urban areas is available at https://data.oecd.org/popregion/urban-population-by-city-size.htm.

team employed an analysis of covariance. Thus, it first separately regressed each of the urban challenge indicators on each of the eight categorical variables of typology while controlling for the effects of other relevant variables. It then identified the typology that produces the highest adjusted R^2 across the estimated models.

In deriving the typology, the team focused exclusively on six indicators that characterize greenness challenges: aggregate fossil CO_2 emissions and per capita fossil CO_2 emissions for carbon footprint, aggregate $PM_{2.5}$ emissions and total $PM_{2.5}$ concentration for pollution, and average greenness (index) and the share of high green area for vegetation.[15] This focus stemmed primarily from the fact that the data on those greenness indicators cover the full sample of cities, unlike the data on the resilience and inclusiveness indicators.

Previous studies suggest that a city's climate and geography are correlated with the greenness indicators. Thus, in the regressions of carbon emissions and pollution, the team controlled for the potential effects of temperature and precipitation (both in annual mean), as well as the mean elevation and the major type of biome within the spatial domain of each city. For vegetation, the mean elevation, longitude, latitude, and their squares were controlled alongside those controlled in the regressions of carbon footprint and pollution.

Figure 2A.1 Comparisons of adjusted R^2 across combinations of city size and country income group

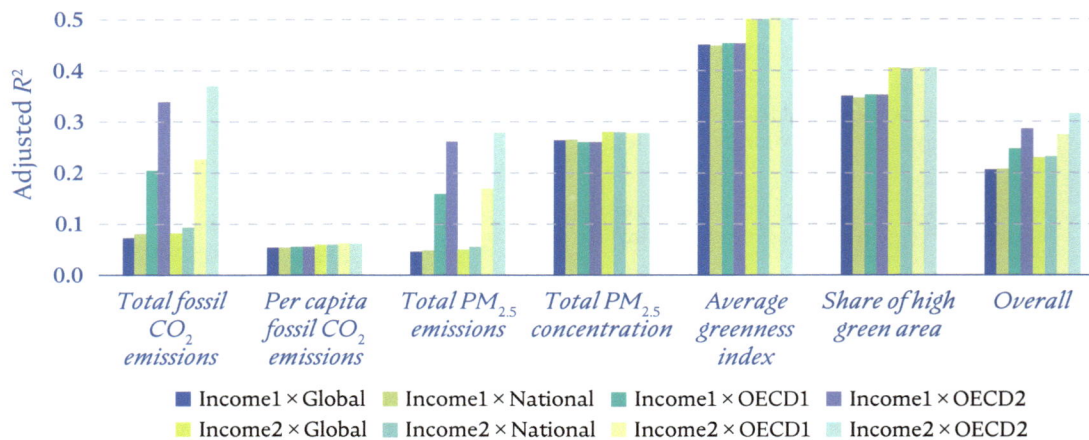

Source: World Bank analysis based on data drawn from the European Commission's Global Human Settlement (GHS) Urban Centre Database R2019 (https://ghsl.jrc.ec.europa.eu/ghs_stat_ucdb2015mt_r2019a.php).

Note: Cities are defined as urban centers following the degree of urbanization methodology (see box 1.1, chapter 1). Income1 and Income2 refer to the groupings of income class based on the World Bank classification. In Income1, upper-middle- and lower-middle-income classes are combined as middle-income. In income2, lower-middle- and low-income classes are combined as low-income. Global and National refer to the groupings of city size based on global and national terciles, respectively. OECD1 and OECD2 refer to the groupings based on the Organisation for Economic Co-operation and Development's classification of urban areas. In OECD1, large metros and metro areas are combined as large cities. In OECD2, large metros by themselves constitute large cities, whereas metro areas and medium urban areas are combined as medium cities. CO_2 = carbon dioxide; $PM_{2.5}$ = particulate matter of 2.5 microns or less in diameter.

Figure 2A.1 compares the R^2 across the estimated models, which led to the choice of typology combining city size option 4 (grouping small urban areas as small, metros and medium cities as medium, and large metros as large, drawing on the Organisation for Economic Co-operation and Development's classification) and income class option 2 (combining low- and lower-middle-income as low-income, while designating upper-middle-income as middle-income and high-income as high-income).

Step 3. Assess each type of city in terms of the severity of current urban challenges.

The assessment of each indicator broadly proceeded in the following steps:

3.1. Obtain the means across the nine types of cities.

3.2. Based on pairwise comparisons, group the pairs of city types that are not statistically different at the significance level of 0.1.

3.3. Assign one of three levels of severity—high (3), medium (2), and low (1)—considering the ranking of the means obtained in step 3.1 and the grouping derived in step 3.2. Thus, the same level of severity is assigned to the pairs whose means are statistically indistinguishable.

3.4. Calculate the aggregate level of severity for each type of challenge by taking the unweighted mean level of severity across multiple indicators—for example, the carbon footprint by total and per capita fossil CO_2 emissions.

Table 2.3 in the main text presents the outcome of step 3. Essentially, the same set of steps was applied in the context of analysis of covariance to all but the resilience indicators for which the data are in the panel structure.[16] Although the assessment of greenness indicators covers the full sample of cities, the same global coverage was not feasible for other dimensions. Data on resilience indicators, for example, address about 2,700 medium and large cities for which the proxy measure of a city's economic activity—nighttime lights intensity—is available. Similarly, the severity of lack of access to basic services was drawn from the analysis of 1,970 cities in 41 low- and middle-income countries.[17] For inequality, limited data on income or consumption at the city level did not allow construction of a measure, especially for cities outside high-income countries. Thus, data used for previous studies were consolidated to cover 4,574 cities in Indonesia, the United States, and 16 countries in Latin America and the Caribbean.[18] A caveat here is that cities are delineated differently across the regions, all of which differ from urban centers identified by the degree of urbanization methodology.[19] Finally, the remaining gaps in empirical evidence, including the missing results for poverty, are addressed by consultations with World Bank experts, as well as by reviews of the existing literature, including the World Bank's series of Urbanization Reviews.

Notes

1. Such initiatives include the C40 Cities Climate Leadership Group, the World Mayors Council on Climate Change, and the Urban Climate Change Research Network.

2. For more on the relationships between various greenness indicators and a city's size, see chapter 1, as well as Corbane et al. (2020); Huang et al. (2014); Kennedy et al. (2009); and Marcotullio et al. (2013).

3. The analysis that defines the global typology excludes Guangzhou and Shanghai, the two largest type 6 cities, because they are extreme outliers in terms of both CO_2 and $PM_{2.5}$ emissions. As such, their inclusion would considerably skew the average picture.

4. The measure of resilience used in this chapter is rather narrow in that it does not explicitly measure a city's capacity to absorb, recover, and prepare for future shocks. Nevertheless, this chapter does not distinguish between the terms *vulnerability* and *resilience* because the baseline analysis (Park and Roberts 2023) implicitly captures a city's ability to absorb an (extreme) weather shock in the month that it occurs, which, in turn, is also closely related to how prepared the city is for such a climate change–related stress.

5. The measure of inequality, the Gini coefficient, is calculated on the basis of per capita expenditure for Indonesia and worker income for the United States and 16 countries in Latin America and the Caribbean.

6. Panel b of figure 2.5 presents the average elasticity calculated across different types of extreme weather shocks (hot, wet, and dry), as well as tropical cyclones. Thus, the figure does not explicitly show the estimated elasticity referred to here. See chapter 1 for a complete set of individual results for five types of extreme weather shocks, including tropical cyclones.

7. Throughout this section, the discussions around resilience challenges are based on the results for some 2,700 medium and large cities. Empirical evidence for small cities is lacking because the data on nighttime lights intensity—the proxy measure for a city's economic activity—are available only for cities with populations of over 200,000.

8. The WHO guideline level for safe air is an annual mean $PM_{2.5}$ concentration of 5 µg/m³ or a 24-hour mean of 15 µg/m³.

9. The 16 countries included in the analysis are Argentina, Bolivia, Brazil, Chile, Colombia, Costa Rica, Dominican Republic, Ecuador, El Salvador, Guatemala, Honduras, Mexico, Nicaragua, Peru, Paraguay, and Uruguay.

10. Specifically, countries in Latin America and the Caribbean classified as low-income in the sample are Bolivia, El Salvador, Honduras, and Nicaragua. Small cities in all but El Salvador exhibit average Gini coefficients of income higher than 0.4.

11. For Europe, see, for example, the relevant discussions in Häußler and Haupt (2021); Otto et al. (2021); and Reckien et al. (2015). For the United States, see Climate Resilience Consulting (2018).

12. These studies analyze income data from 18 countries, of which Mexico is the only non-high-income country.

13. Moody's ESG Solutions, https://esg.moodys.io/climate.

14. See box 4.5 in chapter 4 for a description the five different SSPs.

15. The high green area corresponds to a densely vegetated area, such as a forest or garden (Florczyk et al. 2019).

16. For details of the estimation process, see chapter 1 and the background paper by Park and Roberts (2023).

17. The data come from Henderson and Turner (2020), https://doi.org/10.7910/DVN/YZ46FJ, and cover the East Asia and Pacific, Latin America and the Caribbean, South Asia, and Sub-Saharan Africa regions.

18. Data for Indonesia come from Roberts, Gil Sander, and Tiwari (2019); for the United States from Behrens and Robert-Nicoud (2015); and for 16 countries in Latin America and the Caribbean from Ferreyra and Roberts (2018).

19. Specifically, level-2 administrative units are used for Indonesia, metropolitan statistical areas for the United States, and urban clusters identified by the clustering algorithm (Dijkstra and Poelman 2014) for countries in Latin America and the Caribbean.

References

Baker, J. L. 2012. *Climate Change, Disaster Risk, and the Urban Poor: Cities Building Resilience for a Changing World*. Washington, DC: World Bank.

Behrens, K., and F. Robert-Nicoud. 2015. "Agglomeration Theory with Heterogeneous Agents." In *Handbook of Regional and Urban Economics, Volume 5: Cities and Geography*, edited by G. Duranton, J. V. Henderson, and W. Strange, 171–245. Amsterdam: Elsevier.

Boulant, J., M. Brezzi, and P. Veneri. 2016. "Income Levels and Inequality in Metropolitan Areas: A Comparative Approach in OECD Countries." Regional Development Working Paper 2016/06, Organisation for Economic Co-operation and Development, Paris.

Busso, M., and J. Messina, eds. 2020. *The Inequality Crisis: Latin America and the Caribbean at the Crossroads*. Washington, DC: Inter-American Development Bank.

Castells-Quintana, D., V. Royuela, and P. Veneri. 2020. "Inequality and City Size: An Analysis for OECD Functional Urban Areas." *Papers in Regional Science* 99: 1045–64.

Chen, B., D. Liu, and M. Lu. 2017. "City Size, Migration, and Urban Inequality in the People's Republic of China." Working Paper Series No. 723, Asia Development Bank Institute, Mandaluyong, Philippines.

Clement, V., K. K. Rigaud, A. de Sherbinin, B. Jones, S. Adamo, J. Schewe, N. Sadiq, et al. 2021. *Groundswell Part 2: Acting on Internal Climate Migration*. Washington, DC: World Bank.

Climate Resilience Consulting. 2018. "Does Climate Resilience Matter for Small-Town America?" *Climate Resilience Consulting Blog*, October 1, 2018. https://www.climateresilienceconsulting.com/blog/does-climate-resilience-matter-for-small-town-america.

Corbane, C., P. Martino, P. Panagiotis, F. Aneta, M. Michele, F. Sergio, S. Marcello, et al. 2020. "The Grey-Green Divide: Multi-Temporal Analysis of Greenness across 10,000 Urban Centres

Derived from the Global Human Settlement Layer (GHSL)." *International Journal of Digital Earth* 13 (1): 101–18.

Debele, S. E., P. Kumar, J. Sahani, B. Marti-Cardona, S. B. Mickovski, L. S. Leo, F. Porcu, et al. 2019. "Nature-Based Solutions for Hydrometeorological Hazards: Revised Concepts, Classification Schemes and Databases." *Environmental Research* 179 (B): 108799.

Deuskar, C. 2022. "Beating the Heat: Measuring and Mitigating Extreme Heat in East Asian Cities." Technical Working Paper 1: Literature Review, World Bank, Washington, DC.

Dijkstra, L., and H. Poelman. 2014. "A Harmonised Definition of Cities and Rural Areas: The New Degree of Urbanization." Regional Working Paper, Directorate-General for Regional and Urban Policy, European Commission, Brussels.

Fay, M. 2005. *The Urban Poor in Latin America.* Directions in Development Series. Washington, DC: World Bank.

Ferreira, F., and M. Schoch. 2020. "Inequality and Social Unrest in Latin America: The Tocqueville Paradox Revisited." *World Bank Blogs*, February 24, 2020. https://blogs.worldbank.org /developmenttalk/inequality-and-social-unrest-latin-america-tocqueville-paradox-revisited.

Ferreyra, M. M., and M. Roberts, eds. 2018. *Raising the Bar for Productive Cities in Latin America and the Caribbean.* Washington, DC: World Bank.

Florczyk, A. J., M. Melchiorri, C. Corbane, M. Schiavina, M. Maffenini, M. Pesaresi, P. Politis, et al. 2019. "Description of the GHS Urban Centre Database 2015, Public Release 2019, Version 1.0." Publications Office of the European Union, Luxembourg.

Glaeser, E. L., M. Resseger, and K. Tobio. 2009. "Inequality in Cities." *Journal of Regional Science* 49 (4): 617–46.

Hallegatte, S., J. Rentschler, and J. Rozenberg. 2019. *Lifelines: The Resilient Infrastructure Opportunity.* Washington, DC: World Bank.

Hallegatte, S., A. Vogt-Schilb, M. Bangalore, and J. Rozenberg. 2017. *Unbreakable: Building the Resilience of the Poor in the Face of Natural Disasters.* Washington, DC: World Bank.

Häußler, S., and W. Haupt. 2021. "Climate Change Adaptation Networks for Small and Medium-Sized Cities." *SN Social Sciences* 1: 262.

Henderson, J. V., and M. Turner. 2020. "Urbanization in the Developing World: Too Early or Too Slow?" *Journal of Economic Perspectives* 34 (3): 150–73.

Hsu, A., G. Sheriff, T. Chakraborty, and D. Manya. 2021. "Disproportionate Exposure to Urban Heat Island Intensity across Major US Cities." *Nature Communications* 12: 2721.

Huang, Y., H. Shen, H. Chen, R. Wang, Y. Zhang, S. Su, Y. Chen, et al. 2014. "Quantification of Global Primary Emissions of PM2.5, PM10, and TSP from Combustion and Industrial Process Sources." *Environmental Science and Technology* 48 (23): 13834–43.

IPCC (Intergovernmental Panel on Climate Change). 2022a. "Chapter 6: Cities, Settlements and Key Infrastructure." In *Climate Change 2022: Impacts, Adaptation, and Vulnerability.* Contribution of Working Group II to the Sixth Assessment Report of the Intergovernmental Panel on Climate Change, edited by H.-O. Pörtner, D. C. Roberts, M. Tignor, E. S. Poloczanska, K. Mintenbeck, A. Alegría, M. Craig, S. Langsdorf, et al. Cambridge, UK: Cambridge University.

IPCC (Intergovernmental Panel on Climate Change). 2022b. "Summary for Policymakers." In *Climate Change 2022: Impacts, Adaptation, and Vulnerability*. Contribution of Working Group II to the Sixth Assessment Report of the Intergovernmental Panel on Climate Change, edited by H.-O. Pörtner, D. C. Roberts, M. Tignor, E. S. Poloczanska, K. Mintenbeck, A. Alegría, M. Craig, et al. Cambridge, UK: Cambridge University Press.

Kennedy, C., J. Steinberger, B. Gason, Y. Hansen, T. Hillman, M. Havranck, D. Pataki, et al. 2009. "Greenhouse Gas Emissions from Global Cities." *Environmental Science and Technology* 43 (19): 7297–302.

Li, D., S. Wu, L. Liu, Y. Zhang, and S. Li. 2018. "Vulnerability of the Global Terrestrial Ecosystems to Climate Change." *Global Change Biology* 24 (9): 4095–106.

Marcotullio, P. J., A. Sarzynski, J. Albrecht, N. Schulz, and J. Garcia. 2013. "The Geography of Global Urban Greenhouse Gas Emissions: An Exploratory Analysis." *Climate Change* 121: 621–34.

O'Lenick, C. R., O. V. Wilhelmi, R. Michael, M. H. Hayden, A. Baniassadi, C. Wiedinmyer, A. J. Monagham, et al. 2019. "Urban Heat and Air Pollution: A Framework for Integrating Population Vulnerability and Indoor Exposure in Health Risk Analyses." *Science of the Total Environment* 660: 715–23.

Otto, A., K. Kern, W. Haupt, P. Eckersley, and A. H. Thieken. 2021. "Ranking Local Climate Policy: Assessing the Mitigation and Adaptation Activities of 104 German Cities." *Climate Change* 167: 5.

Park, J., and M. Roberts. 2022. "Urban Resilience and Weather Shocks: A Global Nighttime Lights Analysis." Background paper prepared for this report, World Bank, Washington, DC.

Qiang, Y., Q. Huang, and J. Xu. 2020. "Observing Community Resilience from Space: Using Nighttime Lights to Model Economic Disturbance and Recovery Pattern in Natural Disasters." *Sustainable Cities and Society* 57: 102115.

Reckien, D., J. Flacke, M. Olazabal, and O. Heidrich. 2015. "The Influence of Drivers and Barriers on Urban Adaptation and Mitigation Plans—An Empirical Analysis of European Cities." *PLoS One* 10 (8): e0135597.

Roberts, M., F. Gil Sander, and S. Tiwari, eds. 2019. *Time to ACT: Realizing Indonesia's Urban Potential*. Washington, DC: World Bank.

Seddon, N., A. Chausson, P. Berry, C. A. J. Girardin, A. Smith, and B. Turner. 2020. "Understanding the Value and Limits of Nature-Based Solutions to Climate Change and Other Global Challenges." *Philosophical Transactions of the Royal Society* B 375 (1794): 20190120.

Simpson, N. P., K. J. Mach, A. Constable, J. Hess, R. Hogarth, M. Howden, J. Lawrence, et al. 2021. "A Framework for Complex Climate Change Risk Assessment." *One Earth* 4 (4): 489–501.

Slay, B. 2009. *Poverty, Inequality, and Social Policy Reform in the Former Soviet Union*. New York: United Nations Development Programme.

Sterzel, T., M. K. B. Ludeke, C. Walther, M. T. Kok, D. Sietz, and P. L. Lucas. 2020. "Typology of Coastal Urban Vulnerability under Rapid Urbanization." *PLoS One* 15 (1): e0220936.

Winsemius, H., B. Jongman, T. Veldkamp, S. Hallegatte, M. Bangalore, and P. Ward. 2015. "Disaster Risk, Climate Change, and Poverty: Assessing the Global Exposure of Poor People to Floods and Droughts." Policy Research Working Paper 7480, World Bank, Washington, DC.

World Bank. 2021. *A Catalogue of Nature-Based Solutions for Urban Resilience*. Washington, DC: World Bank.

Xu, X., C. Wang, S. Ma, and W. Zhang. 2021. "China's Special Poor Areas and Their Geographical Conditions." *Sustainability* 13: 8636.

Zhang, Z. Y. 2019. "China Is Relaxing Hukou Restrictions in Small and Medium-Sized Cities." China-Briefing.com, April 17, 2019. https://www.china-briefing.com/news /china-relaxing-hukou-restrictions-small-medium-sized-cities.

Zscheischler, J., S. Westra, B. van den Hurk, S. Seneviratne, P. Ward, A. Pitman, A. Aghakouchak, et al. 2018. "Future Climate Risk from Compound Events." *Nature Climate Change* 8: 469–77.

Multidimensional Exclusion and Exposure to Air Pollution in Peruvian Cities

Introduction

A sustainable city is built on interacting economic, environmental, and social pillars.[1] If well balanced, these pillars contribute to well-functioning cities in which the intertwined stresses associated with urban growth and climate change are well managed and people lead fulfilling lives. By contrast, imbalances among the pillars can translate into exclusion, thereby undermining the quality of life that a city offers. Peru presents a good case study of this possible imbalance.

In recent decades, the outdoor air quality in Peru's cities, especially in Lima-Callao, seems to have improved (Sanchez-Triana 2017). By 2021, however, Peru still faced a high economic cost, equivalent to some US$1.5 billion a year (IEc 2021), from outdoor and indoor air pollution. The impact of poor-quality air on the health of Peru's urbanites is compounded by their exclusion from labor and financial markets, basic services, and opportunities to accumulate human capital, as well as from civil participation, equality of law, and freedom of speech. Other manifestations of exclusion are lack of government accountability and the declining resilience of Peruvian citizens to human and environmental shocks.

This spotlight describes multidimensional exclusion in Peru's cities and its overlap with exposure to air pollution. Multidimensional exclusion is measured along three dimensions: (1) economic inclusion, (2) resilience and social cohesion, and (3) empowerment, voice, and accountability.[2] Air pollution is measured using data on ground-level fine particulate matter of 2.5 microns or less in diameter ($PM_{2.5}$).[3]

Methodology

The counting approach used to measure multidimensional poverty (Alkire and Foster 2011; Alkire et al. 2015) is adapted here to analyze the joint distribution of exclusion in 2019 across the three dimensions just noted.[4] In doing so, the analysis here measures multidimensional exclusion using the number of indicators from which a person is simultaneously excluded. This measurement of multidimensional exclusion is achieved by applying a cross-dimensional threshold that defines the number of (weighted) indicators of simultaneous exclusion a person must experience to be classified as multidimensionally excluded.[5]

The methodology focuses on the adjusted headcount ratio (M_0). This index encompasses both the incidence (H) and intensity (A) of multidimensional exclusion. *Incidence* refers to the share of the population that falls above the cross-dimensional threshold, whereas *intensity* refers to the degree to which people are excluded.[6] M_0 is additively decomposable by subgroup, facilitating analysis of the multidimensional exclusion profiles by location.

Measurement

Appraisal of economic inclusion considers five indicators that capture access to labor markets, financial services, basic services, and human capital (education and health) services. Resilience and social cohesion are measured by four indicators capturing a person's number of income sources, confidence in government institutions, experience with discrimination, and experience as a victim of crime. Finally, empowerment, voice, and accountability are captured by four indicators that assess civil participation, freedom of speech, government effectiveness, and equality of the law. All indicators are equally weighted within a dimension.[7]

Profiles of multidimensional exclusion

Profiling of multidimensional exclusion is based on a cross-dimensional threshold of 33 percent[8]—that is, a person is multidimensionally excluded if that person experiences exclusion on a third of the 13 indicators. According to this threshold, 84 percent of Peruvians are multidimensionally excluded (H = 84 percent) and, on average, they experience exclusion on 7 of the 13 indicators (intensity rate, A)—see figure S1.1. The incidence of multidimensional exclusion is higher in rural areas (91 percent) than in urban areas (82 percent). And it is more prevalent and intense in coastal areas than in rainforest areas and the highlands.

The profiling of experiences of exclusion is also quite heterogenous across cities within a given type of natural region. Thus, experiences with exclusion vary more among people living in coastal cities, with incidence rates ranging from 68 to 88 percent. By contrast, incidence

Figure S1.1   **Adjusted headcount ratio (M_0), incidence (H), and intensity (A) of multidimensional exclusion, by type of area of Peru, 2019**

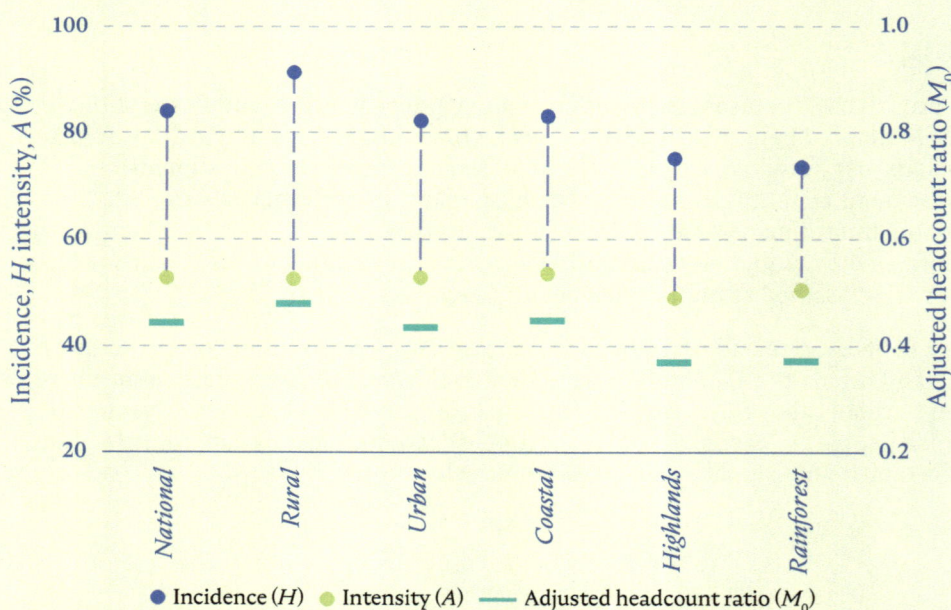

Source: World Bank calculations based on data from Peru's National Household Survey.

rates across cities in rainforest areas vary much less—between 72 and 78 percent. Cities in the highlands exhibit the lowest degree of multidimensional exclusion.

Which cities in Peru are the most excluding? Lima-Callao and Tacna in coastal areas, Puerto Maldonado in a rainforest area, and Arequipa in the highlands have the highest levels of multidimensional exclusion (figure S1.2). Lima-Callao, Peru's capital and most populated city, has the country's highest rates of both incidence and intensity. Puerto Maldonado, a much smaller city, has an intensity rate above the national average but an incidence similar to the national average. Clearly, the extent to which people experience multidimensional exclusion is very diverse across Peru's cities.

Experience with multidimensional exclusion and exposure to outdoor air pollution

How does experience with multidimensional exclusion overlap with exposure to outdoor air pollution across Peruvian cities? This spotlight focuses on air pollution because of the strong correlation between $PM_{2.5}$ emissions and carbon dioxide (CO_2) emissions (highlighted in chapter 1). Figure S1.3 presents a categorization by levels of multidimensional exclusion (MDE) and outdoor air pollution (OAP). Low (or high) levels are defined as rates of exclusion

Figure S1.2 **Incidence (*H*) versus intensity (*A*) of multidimensional exclusion across Peru's cities**

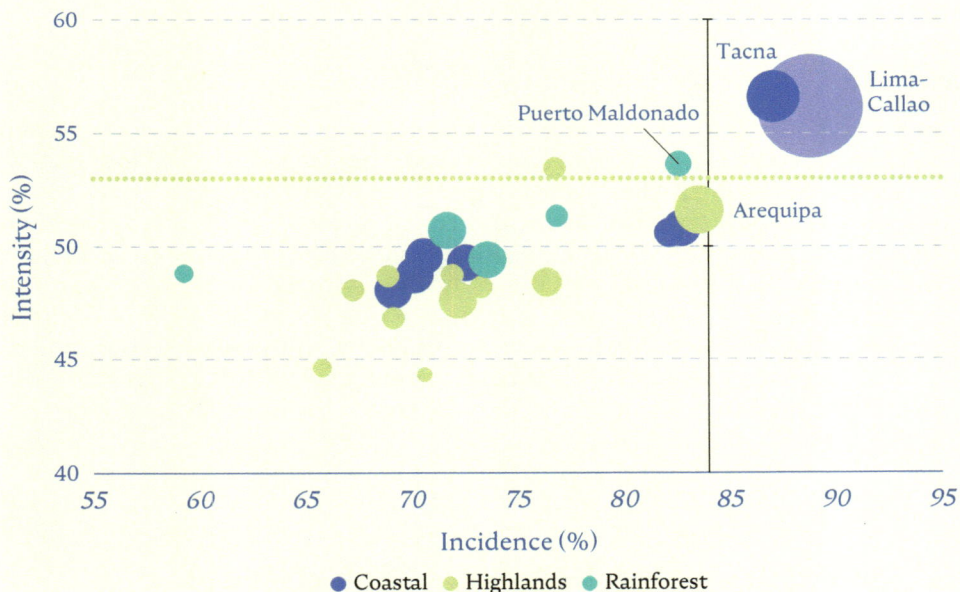

Source: World Bank calculations based on data from Peru's National Household Survey.

Note: Bubble sizes are proportional to city populations. National rates of intensity and incidence are indicated by the intersection of the vertical and horizontal dashed lines at 84 percent and 53 percent, respectively.

Figure S1.3 Multidimensional exclusion and outdoor air pollution: A typology by city, Peru, 2019

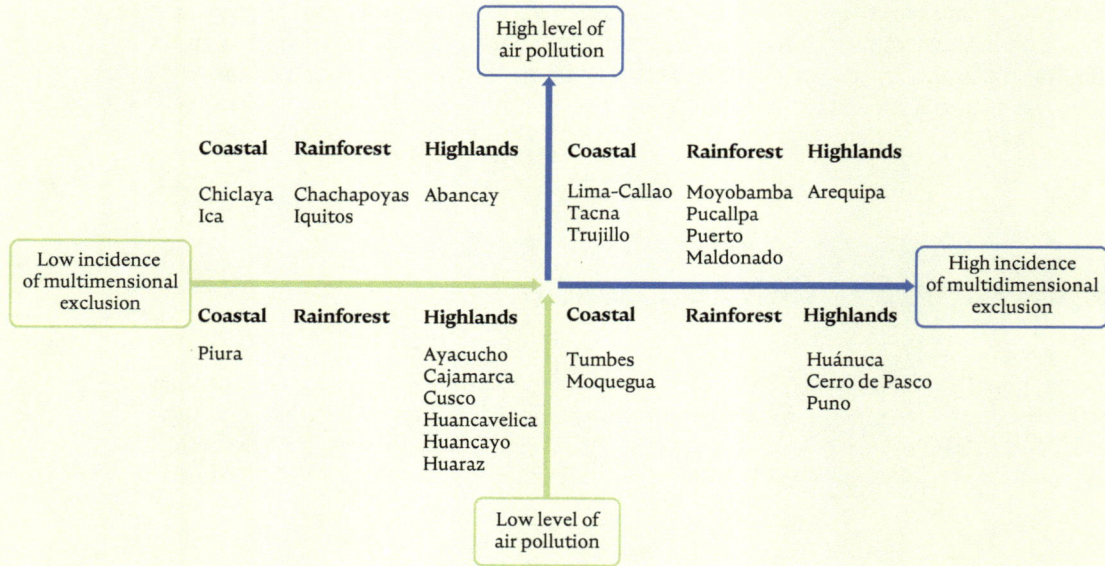

Source: World Bank calculations based on data from Peru's National Household Survey and National Aeronautics and Space Administration Socioeconomic Data and Applications Center.

Note: "Low level" refers to cities with rates below the median, and "high level" refers to cities with rates above the median.

and pollution that are below (or above) the median of the respective distributions. This definition results in a classification of four groups: high MDE–high OAP, low MDE–low OAP, and mismatches. The high MDE–high OAP group consists of Arequipa, Lima-Callao, Moyobamba, Puerto Maldonado, Pucallpa, Tacna, and Trujillo, drawn from all three of Peru's natural regions. By contrast, the low MDE–low OAP group includes cities from the coastal and highland areas, but not from the rainforest areas. Cities showing low levels of exclusion but high pollution are Chiclayo and Ica in coastal areas, Chachapoyas and Iquitos in rainforest areas, and Abancay in the highlands. Cities with low pollution but high exclusion are Tumbes and Moquegua in coastal areas and Cerro de Pasco, Huánuco, and Puno in highlands areas. Policies aimed at addressing exclusion should account for the links with pollution and climate change.

Notes

1. This spotlight was prepared by Paola Ballon and Jose Cuesta.

2. These three dimensions are anchored in the World Bank's Social Sustainability Strategy 2021 (World Bank 2021).

3. These data come from Hammer et al. (2022)

4. The assessment is carried out using data from Peru's National Household Survey.

5. Two types of threshold are used to identify the multidimensionally excluded: a set of indicator-specific thresholds and a threshold across dimensions. The indicator-specific thresholds identify a person as excluded on a particular indicator if that person falls below the relevant threshold. The cross-dimensional threshold specifies how widely excluded a person must be to be identified as multidimensionally excluded.

6. This incidence rate indicates on how many indicators, on average, those who are above the threshold (the multidimensionally excluded) experience exclusion.

7. A more detailed description of the indicators is available upon request. The indicator-specific thresholds used to identify exclusion follow the definitions used in the United Nations' Sustainable Development Goals.

8. Results are robust to the alternative use of thresholds of 50 and 75 percent.

References

Alkire, S., and J. Foster. 2011. "Counting and Multidimensional Poverty Measurement." *Journal of Public Economics* 95 (7–8): 476–87.

Alkire, S., J. M. Roche, P. Ballon, J. Foster, JM. E. Santos, and S. Seth. 2015. *Multidimensional Poverty Measurement and Analysis*. Oxford, UK: Oxford University Press.

IEc (Industrial Economics Incorporated). 2021. "Assessing the Mortality Burden of Air Pollution in Lima-Callao." Final report prepared for the US Environmental Protection Agency. IEc, Cambridge, MA.

Hammer, M. S., A. van Donkelaar, C. Li, A. Lyapustin, A. M. Sayer, N. C. Hsu, R. C. Levy, M. J. Garay, et al. 2022. "Global Annual PM2.5 Grids from MODIS, MISR and SeaWiFS Aerosol Optical Depth (AOD), 1998-2019, V4.GL.03." National Aeronautics and Space Administration Socioeconomic Data and Applications Center, Palisades, NY. https://doi.org/10.7927/fx80-4n39.

Sanchez-Triana, E. 2017. "Access to Quality Information Is Crucial to Tackle Peru's Environmental Problems." *World Bank Blogs,* January 31, 2017. World Bank, Washington, DC.

World Bank. 2021. *Time to Champion Social Sustainability and Inclusion.* Social Sustainability and Inclusion Global Practice, Washington, DC: World Bank.

PART 2

What Do We Know?

CHAPTER 3

The Impacts of Climate and Environmental Change on Cities

The future is always uncertain, yet it seems clear that cities will grow, and that climate will change, although disparately.

Natural Hazards, UnNatural Disasters:
The Economics of Effective Prevention, World Bank (2010)

MAIN FINDINGS

- From the growing exposure to climate hazards, to shortages of food and natural resources, to fatalities, the effects of climate change are vast yet variable. Cities must, then, plan accordingly.

- Because cities concentrate people, activities, and infrastructure geographically, they are particularly vulnerable to the direct effects of climate change events—both rapid-onset shocks and slower-onset stressors.

- Rural and urban areas are linked economically, socially, and environmentally. Moreover, the effects of climate events occurring outside of cities can spill over to them.

- Spillover could occur by way of migration of people, affecting the pace and level of urbanization (and urban form) and of economic sectors within cities, and by way of the movement of goods and services via trade.

- Climate events affect groups of people differently, and those who are already more vulnerable have less ability to cope with or mitigate the effects.

Introduction

The trends are clear: All countries will urbanize; they may do it in their own ways and at their own pace, but urbanize they will. And climate will also change, bringing with it various complex, compounding, and cascading impacts on places and people. The latest report by the Intergovernmental Panel on Climate Change predicts that the worsening impacts of climate change, especially heat stress, floods, and higher sea levels, will be felt acutely in cities (IPCC 2022).

This chapter reviews the secondary literature on how each of the climate change–related stresses described and analyzed in chapters 1 and 2 has affected urban development. Analysis undertaken in preparation for this report complements that review to fill in some of the existing gaps. Specifically, the chapter looks more closely at how climate change–related stresses affect cities directly, through their impacts on urban areas, and indirectly, through their impacts outside urban areas. It also describes the heterogeneous impacts on different populations in cities. Chapter 4 then assesses how cities affect the climate (and, more generally, the environment) through their urban form and investments in, for example, public transportation, as well as the repercussions of urban expansion for agricultural systems and competition for water. Although climate change is expected to make cities more vulnerable over time, important uncertainties remain about the magnitude of its effects and their persistence over time, the heterogeneity of the effects across socioeconomic groups, the conditions under which they cause more or less harm, and the effectiveness of interventions in dealing with them. This chapter tackles the effects and conditions, leaving a discussion of the interventions to chapter 5.

This chapter has the following objectives:

- Review the evidence on how climate change–related stresses of various types already affect different types of cities globally and how these effects further affect the sustainability of existing and new urban construction.

- Investigate how climate change stresses affect cities through their impacts on nonurban locations.

- Examine how different groups of populations in cities are affected similarly or differentially by these impacts.

- Set the stage for the next chapter, which will tackle the second part of the two-way relationship between cities and climate—that is, how urban development affects climate change.

How does climate change affect cities directly?

In all cities and urban areas, the risks faced by people and assets from the hazards associated with climate change have increased

As cities grow, their urban landscapes will increasingly feel the effects of acute climate shocks and chronic climate stressors (box 3.1). Seventy percent of cities globally are already dealing with climate change, and nearly all are at risk. The cultural, demographic, and economic characteristics of urban residents, city governments, built environment, ecosystem services, and human-induced stresses such as overexploitation of resources and environmental degradation define the vulnerability of cities to climate-related disasters. Meanwhile, climate change will continue to amplify the existing social and environmental risks and create novel risks for cities at the intersection of climate hazards and the vulnerability, exposure, and resilience of urban social-ecological systems and populations (Gencer et al. 2018).

Climate shocks—sudden-onset events

Extreme heat. About 250 cities (home to 200 million people) currently experience extreme heat conditions arising from three-month average maximum temperatures of about 35°C. By 2050, 950 cities (1.6 billion people) will likely be exposed to extreme summer temperatures (UCCRN 2018). Urban centers and cities are often several degrees warmer than surrounding areas because of the presence of heat-absorbing materials, reduced evaporative cooling caused

Box 3.1

How do climate shocks and stressors differ?

A *climate shock* is an unpredictable weather event that damages the sustainability of a community. Examples are heat waves, floods, cyclones, and wildfires. *Climate stressors*, or slow-onset events, unfold gradually over time. Examples are higher sea levels, climbing temperatures, ocean acidification, glacial retreat and related impacts, salinization, land and forest degradation, biodiversity loss, and desertification. Some meaningful relationships exist between rapid-onset and slow-onset events. Drought, for example, is an extreme weather event but is also closely linked to slow-onset, incremental climatic change. Interactions among rapid-onset and slow-onset events may result in the crossing of thresholds. For example, a study in Florida finds that, once the sea reached a critical level, the transition from a landscape characterized by upland forests and freshwater wetlands to one dominated by mangroves occurred suddenly following a single storm surge event (Ross et al. 2009). Changes in climate parameters—for example, temperature, precipitation, and their associated impacts such as water availability and crop productivity changes—occur over long periods.

by lack of vegetation, and waste heat production. Many cities in the southern hemisphere are already familiar with extremely high temperatures for sustained periods, but cities in higher latitudes are not, and will for the first time face heat extremes. In urban areas, exposure to heat island effects is uneven, with some populations— including low-income communities, children, the elderly, the disabled, and ethnic minorities—more at risk than others. For example, socio-economically disadvantaged populations are more likely to live in the hotter parts of cities associated with higher-density residential land use and in dwellings built of poorer or older construction materials such as insulation (Inostroza, Palme, and de la Barrera 2016). Extreme heat affects the built environment and city infrastructure through material expansion and corrosion, thereby damaging roads, buildings, and infrastructure.

Extreme cold. Cities also feel the effects of extreme cold events. The events, whose impacts may be more delayed than those of extreme heat, are more likely to affect cities located in warmer climates. Smith and Sheridan (2019) find a strong correlation between latitude and extreme cold event mortality for cities in the United States, as well as higher mortality rates for events early in the cold season. Even though heat-related mortality is expected to increase with climate change, extreme cold events will continue to pose a public health problem (Broadbent, Krayenhoff, and Georgescu 2020).

Heavy precipitation and floods. Rainfall is spatially heterogeneous, much more so than temperature. Thus, fully understanding the effects of precipitation will require spatially disaggregated analyses. Between 1985 and 2015, settlements worldwide grew by 85 percent, to over 1.28 million square kilometers. During the same period, settlements exposed to the highest flood hazard level increased by 122 percent, and 36,500 square kilometers of settlements were built in the world's highest-risk zones, 82 percent of them in low- and middle-income countries (Rentschler et al. 2022). Fully understanding the effects of precipitation, however, will require spatially disaggregated analyses. Heavy precipitation and the consequent floods disrupt urban settlements, stagnate trade and commerce, interrupt transportation networks, and place immense pressure on urban infrastructure.

Coastal flooding. Almost 11 percent of the global population—approximately 896 million people—lives in coastal cities and settlements, and that number is expected to exceed 1 billion by 2050 (IPCC 2022). Coastal flooding (often coupled with inundation and erosion) arises from severe storm-induced surges, wave overtopping, and rainfall runoff. Under a high-emissions scenario, by 2050 an estimated 340 million people will live below the projected high tide line (Kulp and Strauss 2019).

Coastal cities are often important nodes for global trade supply chains, and they play an essential role in national economies. With changing climate, coastal cities and their associated assets and infrastructure will continue to face escalating risks linked to higher sea levels and coastal flooding. In fact, coastal flooding not only strains critical urban infrastructure but also has significant effects on peri-urban coastal cultural heritages and resources (Choy et al. 2016). Moreover, population and asset growth, climate change, and subsidence will all likely contribute to a drastic increase in global average flood losses, from US$6 billion per year in 2005 to over US$60 billion per year in 2050, assuming all cities undertake proactive adaptation actions (Hallegatte et al. 2013). Higher sea levels will also allow storm surges to reach further inland (IPCC 2018).

Wildfires. Hotter, drier regions tend to experience wildfires affecting cities at the wildland-urban interface (WUI)—that is, the transition zone where woodland and dense vegetation meet human development (Bento-Gonçalves and Vieira 2020). In the United States, the WUI grew rapidly between 1990 and 2010 (Radeloff et al. 2018). In fact, it was the fastest-growing land use type in the United States after urbanization and urban sprawl trends. Land defined as WUI in California grew between 1990 and 2010 and now encompasses 6.4 percent of the state's total land area. WUI growth often results in more wildfire ignitions, putting more lives and settlements at risk. During California's 2020 fire season, nearly 11,500 structures—more than 6,000 residences and 700 commercial structures—were destroyed. Apart from the rare possibility of wildfires annihilating cities, the direct impact of wildfires on cities is the severe burden of smoke on public health. The Bay Area alone saw a three-month average Air Quality Index above 100 in 2020. In South Africa, regularly occurring wildfires have caused significant damage to cities and towns along the country's Garden Route, which depend primarily on agriculture and tourism. In 2017, wildfires swept through the Southern Cape, destroying critical infrastructure, displacing more than 1,500 households, and directly affecting 134 businesses

Wind-related disasters (hurricanes, cyclones, and typhoons). Wind disasters contribute to significant economic losses and human casualties in cities by destroying buildings and infrastructure, damaging vegetation, and inducing respiratory disease (He, Thies, et al. 2021). Also in cities, extreme wind events have had devastating effects on poor building stock, including low-income houses in African cities (Okunola 2019). In Timor-Leste, for example, Cyclone Seroja destroyed over 25,000 homes (more than 50 percent of all households) in the capital, Dili, in 2021. The cost of repairing and replacing the housing assets affected was estimated at US$70 million (World Bank 2021b).

Climate stressors—slow-onset events

Drought. An estimated 350.0 million additional people in urban areas will be exposed to water scarcity from severe droughts if warming of 1.5°C occurs—and that estimate increases to 410.7 million if warming of 2°C occurs (Dodman et al. 2022). Another estimate predicts that more than 2 billion people living in urban areas (including 284 cities) will face water scarcity by 2050 (He, Wu, et al. 2021). The impacts of drought on urban areas emerge gradually and less visibly. Water scarcity can be driven by drought and heightened by competing water users. The higher concentration of people in naturally arid cities results in water scarcity, especially during a drought. As urbanization skyrockets, demand and competition for limited water resources will increase, and drought will exacerbate these pressures.

Air pollution. Exposure to air pollution is higher in denser cities. The analysis by Anenberg et al. (2019) of the world's 250 most populous cities estimates that concentrations of particulate matter of 2.5 microns or less in diameter ($PM_{2.5}$) are highest in cities in Africa, East Asia, South Asia, and the Middle East. Air pollution in many cities in the Middle East and North Africa results mainly from windblown dust, whereas that in East Asia and South Asia is mainly anthropogenic in origin. Air pollutants emitted by one city can be moved by airflow and traced in neighboring areas (Abas et al. 2019). Undoubtedly, air pollution harms human health and affects global warming. Exposure to ambient air pollution increases morbidity[1] and mortality, and contributes to the global disease burden (Cohen et al. 2017). From 2000 to 2017, residents of European cities were exposed to $PM_{2.5}$ and ozone levels that surpassed the World Health Organization limits, despite a marked reduction in emissions (Sicard et al. 2021). According to Croitoru, Chang, and Akpokodje (2020), the cost of mortality and morbidity in Lagos due to air pollution from $PM_{2.5}$ exposure is an estimated US$2.1 billion, or 0.5 percent of Nigeria's gross domestic product in 2018. Beyond $PM_{2.5}$, urban populations are exposed to ground-level ozone, nitrogen dioxide, and other combustion-related air pollutants.

Land degradation. Urbanization affects natural ecosystems by removing forests and creating a new built environment. Changes in land cover continue to affect city-scale climate by altering the flow of energy, water, and greenhouse gases between the land and the atmosphere. The Intergovernmental Panel on Climate Change defines *land degradation* as a negative trend in land condition stemming from human-induced processes (IPCC 2019a). The processes lead to a long-term reduction in or loss of the land's biological productivity, ecological integrity, and value to humans.

Changes in land use, such as developing in floodplains, also constitute a stressor. For example, pressure to build in flood-prone areas may arise from lower real estate values and limited land for expansion. In their study of 55 African countries, Li et al. (2016) reveal a correlation between urban expansion, flood disasters, loss, and damage. These alterations can directly reinforce and contribute to the negative impacts of climate change. Of the many examples, an increase in impervious surfaces increases flood risk through stormwater runoff (Hamilton, Coops, and Lokman 2021); too many dark surfaces (such as pavement and tar roofs) increase the urban heat island effect (Santamouris and Yun 2020); cutting down trees contributes to greater flooding and the urban heat island effect (Qin 2020); destruction of natural mangrove forests reduces a natural buffer to coastal storms (Dasgupta et al. 2019); and subsidence from overpumping of groundwater leads to increased flooding (Erban, Gorelick, and Zebker 2014).

Rising sea levels. The future rise in the global mean sea level stemming from thermal expansion, melting of glaciers and ice sheets, and changes in land water storage will depend strongly on which Representative Concentration Pathway emission scenario is followed (IPCC 2019b). Rising sea levels threaten populations, critical infrastructure, and valuable assets in coastal floodplains, coastal cities, urban atoll islands, arctic communities, and densely populated deltas. For example, buildings and communities in the urban atolls of Majuro in the Marshall Islands are at high risk of inundation from a rise in sea level. Without any form of adaptation, 37 percent of Majuro's building stock, mainly concentrated in Delap-Uliga-Djarrit, is at risk of permanent inundation from a 1-meter rise in sea level (World Bank 2021a). Rising sea levels also increase the salinity of surface and groundwater sources and coastal aquifers through saltwater intrusion, thereby affecting urban drinking water supplies. Increases in sea level and in tropical cyclone storm surge and rainfall intensity will raise the probability of coastal city flooding, with more than a billion people located in low-lying cities and settlements expected to be at risk from coastal-specific climate hazards by 2050 (IPCC 2022).

The compounding, cascading, and indirect effects of climate change

The climate-related shocks and stressors that affect cities do not occur in isolation but often interact with and intensify each other, making their possible impacts on cities even more uncertain and potentially disastrous. For that reason, the compound risks of climatic shocks are receiving greater scrutiny. For example, cyclones and heat waves can occur concurrently, adding complexity to their effects on local populations and assets (Ford et al. 2018). Removal of urban trees could compound the effects of heat waves and floods. Food supplies will be affected by production losses from heat and drought, compounded by heat-induced falloffs in the productivity of workers (as discussed later in this chapter). Risks can also be transmitted across populations, places, and sectors, leading to cascading impacts. For example, rural migrants fleeing a drought can settle in precarious informal settlements in urban floodplains, with cascading risks for other groups of people and locations. Wildfires in agricultural regions can increase urban air pollution, while disrupting the supply, and thus prices, of essential food items (Zscheischler et al. 2018). Meanwhile, in cities, critical infrastructure, such as transportation systems and power grids, is generally interdependent, so the failure of one element or node could result in a cascade of adverse events. Thus, storm surges and extreme heat could lead to power outages.

Indeed, the impacts of climate change are pervasive. For example, urban residents will suffer financially through higher demand for electricity for air-conditioning, medical costs, and missed work (see box 3.8 later in this chapter). Transportation networks in urban areas are especially vulnerable to weather-related hazards. Nearly all transportation modes are at risk from extreme events such as extensive floods (Rebally et al. 2021), which can reduce the capacity of a road transportation network by rendering it impassable, thereby creating severe traffic congestion. The tangible impacts of the physical destruction of transportation infrastructure such as roads and bridges can be quantified in monetary terms.[2]

Some low-income countries clearly show the relationship between rainfall and growth of gross domestic product. In their study of the impacts of large-scale urban floods between 2003 and 2008 on 1,868 cities in 40 mainly low-income countries, Kocornik-Mina et al. (2019) find that low-elevation urban areas, which tend to concentrate more economic activity per square kilometer, experience flooding more frequently. On average, flooding reduces a city's economic activity by 2–8 percent in the flood year. This effect masks the medium- to longer-term damages that could include the costs of restoring damaged infrastructure, the opportunity cost of adults pulled away from productive work, and the loss of human capital as children are withdrawn from schools. Most cities with the highest relative coastal flood losses are in South and Southeast Asia, and they are projected to suffer US$52 billion in flood losses per year by 2050 (Hallegatte et al. 2016). Low-lying cities such as Ho Chi Minh City, Vietnam, or Lagos, Nigeria, are especially vulnerable. Desmet et al. (2021) evaluate the costs of coastal flooding using a spatially disaggregated dynamic model and find that real global gross domestic product could fall by 4.5 percent without a dynamic migration and investment response.

Although wildfires may break out in peri-urban or even rural areas, cities bear their economic burdens. The total direct and indirect economic impacts of wildfires on cities include the cost of damages, health costs, and indirect losses from power shutoffs, business closures, travel cancellations, and supply chain disruptions. The economic losses of Cape Town's 2021 wildfires were estimated at US$1.5 million , affecting businesses and agricultural yield. The wildfires across California in 2018 produced US$7.8 billion in estimated health costs in the Bay Area, upticks in hospital admissions, and a shift in the housing market, with rents jumping more than 40 percent (Bellisario, Cowan, and Raisz 2021).

Bertinelli and Strobl (2013) find that hurricane strikes reduce income growth by 1.5 percent, on average, at the local level. Indaco, Ortega, and Taspinar (2021) studied the effects of Hurricane Sandy on firms in New York, finding that flooding led to reductions in employment of about 4 percent and average wages of about 2 percent among affected businesses. The effects were heterogeneous across boroughs, reflecting the severity of flooding, building types, and industry composition. Adaptation also involved migration, with some firms relocating to other neighborhoods. Shughrue, Werner, and Seto (2020) find that cities are vulnerable to economic harm even if they are geographically distant from the direct impacts of cyclones, and that vulnerability to secondary impacts such as material shortages and price spiking is highest in cities that depend strongly on the global trade network but have relatively fewer suppliers.

Changes in water availability and in the intensity and frequency of drought will have dire consequences for cities in terms of water resources and water management systems. One in four cities globally, with a total of US$4.2 trillion in economic activity, is classified as water stressed (McDonald et al. 2014). A drought affects a city's power infrastructure, reducing overall activity. In 2016, 18 thermal power plants across Indian cities experienced significant operational disruptions and shutdowns caused by water shortages, costing India 1 percent of its annual power output (WRI 2017). A drought can also lead to higher concentrations of pollutants, lack of adequate water flow for sewerage, and flood-related damage to physical assets. Deficits in the urban water supply will greatly affect the future availability and cost of water in cities and peri-urban areas. During droughts, health conditions worsen and, following the absence of adequate sanitation, cities with higher population densities suffer the rapid spread of disease, reducing the probability of employment (Desbureaux and Rodella 2019). Droughts, more than floods, reduce worker productivity and labor income and may have a longer-lasting, severer impact on workers and firms (Damania et al. 2017).

Underlying non-climate-related stresses in urban areas can also exacerbate the effects of climate change. For example, high rates of informal dumping of waste exacerbate pluvial floods as refuse piles up in drains, waterways, and open spaces (Jha, Bloch, and Lamond 2012). Studies have looked at how a rise in sea level and heavy rainfall may affect urban drainage systems (Grip, Haghighatafshar, and Aspegren 2021) and the effects that a combination of daytime and nighttime heat extremes may have on urban areas (Wang et al. 2021). Air pollution also can act as a stressor on urban residents, especially when combined with the heat-related effects of climate change (Harlan and Ruddell 2011). Other stressors, such as global pandemics, will push cities to manage compound risks (Phillips et al. 2020) and force cities to understand their links, such as how pandemics may affect shared transportation (Moraci et al. 2020) and air pollution (and vice versa). For example, some cities experienced reduced air pollution during the COVID-19 pandemic, whereas cities with more pollution had higher caseloads of COVID-19 (Ching and Kajino 2020). According to the Intergovernmental Panel on Climate Change, multiple climate hazards will continue to occur simultaneously, with interaction across multiple climate and nonclimate risks, thereby compounding the overall risk and causing risks to cascade across sectors and regions (IPCC 2022). Thus, predicting the medium- to long-term effects of climate change on cities is challenging, to say the least.[3]

Measurement of effects is not always straightforward

Global warming[4] is a protracted global phenomenon with heterogeneous local effects, making the assessment of such effects complex (see box 3.2 for a brief overview of these challenges). The difficulty in mapping the physical impacts of extreme weather events is compounded by the nonlinearities in the climate system, across both space[5] and time.[6] Economic geographers have thus introduced spatial dynamic assessment models to take into account the temporal and spatial dimensions of the economic impacts of climate change (see Balboni 2021; Desmet and Rossi-Hansberg 2011, 2012, 2015; Desmet et al. 2021). Some models also emphasize the role of economic adaptation through migration, trade, and innovation. Cruz and Rossi-Hansberg (2021) allow changes in local temperatures to influence three characteristics: local productivity, local amenities, and the differences between birth and death rates. They find that the spatial heterogeneity of the impact of global warming is stark—welfare losses globally of 5 percent—but that the world's poorest regions lose substantially more—as much as 15 percent. Their estimates suggest that an increase of 1°C in local temperatures implies a decline in amenities of about 2.5 percent in the world's hottest areas and a commensurate increase in the world's coldest areas. The effects of temperature on productivity are larger and asymmetric: an increase of 1°C in local temperatures leads to a 15 percent decline

---

Box 3.2

Measurement issues

Because of the broad uncertainties about how the effects of climate change may play out over time, the best approach to predictions may be to understand how the current effects might change under different scenarios. Those scenarios will need to include the effects of climate change across different future warming estimates—that is, 1.5°C, 2.0°C, or 3.0°C. In addition, scenario planning will have to consider urbanization, land use changes (Avashia and Garg 2020), and uncertainty. These scenarios would also be affected by assumptions about other key driving forces, such as the rate of technological change and prices. Even when direct impacts can be estimated with some level of confidence, the indirect effects are more complex to assess.

Direct effects from climatic shocks or exposure to prolonged stressors include loss of life, ecosystem degradation, and economic losses. With new advances in attribution science, it is now possible to assess the likelihood that climate change caused, or intensified, an event. This possibility applies to several types of shocks: flooding, tropical storms (Reed et al. 2020), drought (Philip et al. 2018a, 2018b), heat waves (Vautard et al. 2020), and fires (van Oldenborgh et al. 2021). Despite these advances, attributing to climate change lives lost still does not occur commonly, nor does assessing the environmental consequences. Several studies, however, have placed dollar values on the economic losses from both flooding and drought (Frame, Rosier, et al. 2020; Frame, Wehner, et al. 2020). An assessment of indirect effects is particularly important in urban areas because these areas concentrate so much activity, functioning as integrated systems with various sectors and infrastructures closely interlinked. These indirect effects have impacts on cities down to the individuals who live in them and in adjacent areas. At times, indirect effects can have global impacts, such as on mental health and conflicts (Evans 2019), and can cause trade interruptions and reductions in gross domestic product (Botzen, Deschenes, and Sanders 2019).

in productivity in the warmest regions and a 10 percent increase in the coldest regions. Trade and migration can act as substitutes for adaptation mechanisms. Conte et al. (2021), using a spatial dynamic model of the world economy, extend the spatial growth theory of Desmet et al. (2021) to include multiple sectors, with sectoral productivity depending on temperatures and with production leading to emissions that feed back into the atmospheric stock of carbon. They find that agriculture becomes more spatially concentrated; however, regions that lose agriculture do not replace it with productive nonagricultural (manufacturing or services) sectors.

Urban industrial hubs face additional challenges because they rely on key inputs such as water, timber, or energy for the production process, or because they may suffer from disruptions in supply chains. Global trade means that a tsunami in Japan or floods in Thailand can result in significant losses for automobile manufacturers in Ontario, Canada, because of shortages of parts and delivery delays (Kovacs and Thistlethwaite 2014). In the United States, in 2021 freezing temperatures in Texas led to an energy blackout, which then forced major semiconductor plants to close, exacerbating the semiconductor shortage triggered by the global pandemic and further slowing the production of microchip-dependent cars in several countries (Fitch 2021). Thus, weather and climate events increasingly disrupt supply chains that rely on specialized commodities and key infrastructure. Of course, cities not only host manufacturers and storage and distribution facilities, but also serve as principal demand points. As Gomez et al. (2021) find, extreme weather events transmit food production or distribution losses through supply chains to other locations, usually with cities bearing the brunt of the shocks.

Changing climate risks are expected to interact with the already intense competition for land and housing in urban areas. The desire to live close to jobs and amenities means that even areas with high flood or landslide risks often host large communities. Because housing prices often reflect the risks, the poorest often live in the most hazardous areas (a subject discussed in more detail later in the chapter). Those settled in vulnerable locations face repeated damage to their homes and may need to bear the brunt of retrofitting to enhance resilience. Homeowners also face rising insurance rates as the insurance industry better understands the risks of hazards. Because the market for housing is not static, households can migrate in response to repeated disaster events and with the advent of improved hazard information. For example, in Cali, Colombia, poorer residents decided to move away from inner-city neighborhoods to informal settlements on the periphery (see the detailed analysis by Campos Garcia et al. 2011). Over time, housing markets may also reflect heterogeneity in beliefs about long-run climate risks. Baldauf, Garlappi, and Yannelis (2020) find that housing prices in the United States exhibit different elasticities to climate risk and to measures of beliefs about climate change. In effect, in zones increasingly at risk of floods, houses in neighborhoods with high levels of belief in climate change risks sell at a discount compared with houses in neighborhoods with high levels of denial.

Climate change could also affect cities by undermining the fiscal health of local governments

Climate impacts could have fiscal consequences for local governments, primarily through declines in certain sources of revenues and growing expenditures related to climate hazards (see box 3.3 for a brief overview). Gilmore, Kousky, and St. Clair (2022) demonstrate the pathways by which climate shocks and stresses drive local government fiscal stress by affecting specific categories of revenue and expenditures. Declines in revenue can result, for example, not only from the destruction of property but also from a drop in property values. An analysis of real estate transactions across the United States shows that frequent tidal flooding caused by the rise in sea level resulted in a US$15.9 billion loss in home value appreciation in just over a decade (see Bernstein, Gustafson, and Lewis 2019). Households and firms respond to physical impacts by relocating (either temporarily or permanently) or by changing their consumption of and payment for basic services, further affecting revenue sources.

On the expenditure side, local governments are increasingly at the forefront of responses to climate shocks via funding emergency services, investing in climate adaptation, or dealing with the chronic or cumulative impacts on people and assets. In the Philippines, local government units are the primary first responders during a disaster, and the national government provides financing and technical assistance when local capacity is limited or overwhelmed. However, as demonstrated by studies on public expenditure reviews (World Bank 2020b) and parametric catastrophic risk insurance programs (World Bank 2021e), lack of coordination and low capacity by local agencies have resulted in slow responses. Although the national government contributed from 66 percent to 100 percent of total postdisaster expenditures in the Philippines between 2015 and 2018, that contribution did not account for all spending by the local governments, including for preparedness and risk reduction. Jerch, Kahn, and Lin (2021) provide evidence that exposure to hurricanes jeopardizes local provision of public goods in the longer term. Their look at 2,000 local governments in US Atlantic and Gulf states hit by hurricanes finds reductions in tax revenues and expenditures and increases in the cost of debt in the decade following exposure. They also find that municipalities with a higher proportion of racial minorities suffered higher expenditure losses (twofold) and higher debt default risks (eightfold). The results imply that hurricane-induced declines in current financial resources can translate into lower future investments.

City budgets bear the brunt of climate events

In low- and middle-income countries, local governments are often forced to redirect finances from other service delivery accounts in order to finance recovery activities, thereby undermining not just the fiscal position of local authorities but also the delivery of basic services. Funds provided by national or provincial governments in the wake of disasters, including programs for adaptation, can provide an important source of budgetary assistance for local governments. In many countries, however, a substantial funding shortfall exists, even for the most urgent of needs. The World Bank's *South Africa Disaster Risk Financing Diagnostic* (forthcoming) collates findings from case studies of floods in eThekwini (previously, Durban) and drought in Cape Town. It finds that both metropolitan governments were forced to reprioritize spending away from core service delivery toward disaster response. Ninety-eight percent of the estimated damage from the 2019 floods in eThekwini was unfunded, and the budget was found from grants previously allocated for education infrastructure, maintenance of provincial roads, and development of human settlements. In addition, although metropolitan cities have access to financing instruments to fund disaster responses, the application process is too onerous and the funds come with high levels of oversight, discouraging their use.

Climate change is transforming the sustainability of urban construction—for the worse

Future climate change may render many of the world's cities unsustainable or even unlivable. If people can migrate and if capital depreciates quickly enough, risk could be transferred easily across locations. As this section describes, the migration of individuals in response to climate shocks and stressors is already an established phenomenon. Much of this migration takes place from rural to urban areas and within national borders. However, the migration of capital—specifically, capital that is embedded in durable structures and thus depreciates very slowly—is a whole different matter.

As part of the background research conducted for this report, Desmet and Jedwab (2022) investigated to what extent the most expensive (and very durable) real estate structures—skyscrapers—are not being built in locations that would become increasingly unlivable because of extreme heat. They focus on tall buildings for two reasons. First, urban planners and policy makers are encouraged to increase density, including by building higher, to meet the growing demand for space by households and firms. Second, tall buildings are built to last, making them very durable over time and thus less likely to reallocate capital in response to changing climate risks. The authors use the Emporis data set, an inventory of all the world's buildings exceeding 55 meters in height, which includes information on their year of construction and height.[7] This study encompasses 12,877 urban agglomerations in 182 countries, which together account for 90 percent of the world's current urban population.

Desmet and Jedwab hypothesize that, as the information about the growing risks of climate change increases, over time the construction of durable structures (that is, those with embedded capital that cannot be easily reallocated over space) should slow in "future bad locations."[8] In economic terms, if a set of locations becomes unlivable in the not-too-distant future, the assumption is that a government, acting as a dynamic social planner,[9] would discourage the construction of expensive and very durable structures in these locations. Such an approach should, at the very least, lower the rate of construction of such buildings in future bad locations. Desmet and Jedwab find the opposite, however: countries are not necessarily avoiding construction of expensive and durable structures in locations that in the future are potentially unsustainable or even unlivable, implying that the world could see a growing dynamic spatial misallocation of capital over time. Despite the fact that climate change conferences—Kyoto (1997), Doha (2012), and Paris (2015)—put the spotlight on the risks associated with future climate change, this information does not seem to be associated with any changes in building patterns. Evidence also exists that less democratic countries are more likely to build durable skyscrapers in less-livable locations.

Public policy could encourage settlement in more hazard-prone areas

Moral hazard—a term applied to engagement in reckless behavior because one does not have to fully bear the cost of that behavior—is widely accepted as one of the leading causes of the 2008 global financial crisis. Bank managers pushed for reckless lending to increase profits (and consequently their bonuses) under the implicit guarantee that if things went wrong the government (taxpayers) would bail them out to avoid a systemic effect on the economy. That example perfectly captures the issue as presented in the seminal paper by Kydland and Prescott (1977), who explain that the optimal time to apply a policy is often inconsistent. That is, government would want to discourage reckless behavior by avoiding any commitment to bail out large banks, but it would want to rescue them once they are bankrupt.[10] Kydland and Prescott (1977) focus on monetary policy (which is more effective when it is a surprise) but provide an example of time inconsistency involving flood insurance. Very much like bank bailouts, government subsidies of flood insurance would encourage building in risk-prone areas; after a disaster a government normally offers some monetary relief, thereby acting as a de facto insurer and providing an implicit guarantee that may encourage building in flood-prone areas.

A large US-based literature has studied the effects of subsidized flood insurance and relief aid (Deryugina 2014; Gregory 2017; Kousky, Luttmer, and Zeckhauser 2006). Deryugina (2014) points out that flood insurance benefits risk-averse individuals and those who are credit-constrained, but it discourages the provision of private insurance and increases the willingness of people to live in disaster-prone areas. Moreover, she points out another type of moral hazard: because unemployment insurance premiums do not take into account disaster risk, they subsidize activity in riskier areas.. The same pattern emerges for other types of disasters. Baylis and Boomhower (2019) estimate that fire insurance in the form of free federal fire protection may have increased construction in areas at high risk of fire in the western United States by 2.5 percent overall, and by an even higher percentage in the highest-risk areas.

Despite the increase in risky behavior, however, insurance and postdisaster aid policies may still be optimal in welfare terms. Evaluating a large US disaster relief program (Louisiana Road Home) in locations affected by Hurricane Katrina, Gregory (2017) finds that the distortion caused by an ex ante promise of postdisaster aid is not large enough to justify committing to less generous relief. Even the most conservative estimate finds that the excess burden due to risky location choices is more than one order of magnitude smaller than the welfare gains from guaranteed postdisaster transfers. The deadweight loss from actuarially unfair (not accounting for relative risk) disaster relief is estimated to be only 4 percent of the total yearly relief expenditure.

Two solutions to the moral hazard location issue are to forbid construction in riskier areas (via zoning) and to create actuarially fair relief insurance. However, both solutions face political, social, and technical challenges because urban land is often in short supply, and flood risk is hard to determine precisely (especially in countries with poor administrative capacities). Avner and Hallegatte (2019) explain that, when most of a city is flood-prone, subsidized insurance improves welfare, and the same applies to areas with a low risk of flooding. Zoning becomes feasible only in the presence of geographically limited areas at very high risk.

How does climate change affect cities indirectly?

Climate shocks in rural areas lead to faster urbanization

When extreme climate events hit, people in the countryside can seek shelter in cities, which have stronger infrastructure and more hospitals and other essential services. In Sub-Saharan Africa, for example, manufacturing towns have grown after droughts in the agricultural hinterlands (Henderson, Storeygard, and Deichmann 2017). Burzynski et al. (2019) predict that climate change will induce both voluntary and forced displacement of 200 million–300 million people over the course of the twenty-first century, although only 20 percent of that movement will involve cross-border migration. In another recent study, Benveniste, Oppenheimer, and Fleurbaey (2020) find substantially smaller numbers, estimating excess climate-induced cross-border migration flows in 2100 at 75,000. Most people displaced by natural disasters eventually return to their place of origin, but not all do. Some settle in the suburbs or on the outskirts of cities, placing further stress on urban infrastructure, services, and resources.

About 40 percent (14 million) of the residents of Bangladesh's capital, Dhaka, live in informal settlements, and 70 percent of those were forced to leave their homes because of phenomena related to climate change, including cyclones and coastal and riverbank erosion (Lombraña and Dodge 2021).

Understanding these patterns remains paramount because poorer countries tend to urbanize faster and earlier than developing states of the past. With that in mind, investigators are turning their attention to the push factors (Barrios, Bertinelli, and Strobl 2006; Maurel and Tuccio 2016), including the changing climate (Kaczan and Orgill-Meyer 2020).

A background global analysis conducted for this report by Chlouba, Mukim, and Zaveri (2022) shows that from 1985 to 2014 periods of extended drought resulted in faster urban growth, providing further evidence of the importance of push factors. The findings indicate an unambiguous positive relationship between drought in areas surrounding cities and urban expansion. The study focuses on the share of the calendar year that an area experienced drought and the size of territories classified as urban land in the World Settlement Footprint database. The results indicate that, if an area spent the previous year under drought conditions, nearby cities would experience a 15 percent increase in urban land use. Although drought rarely extends to an entire year, the relationship between drought and urban growth remains substantial. This result echoes patterns suggested by recent studies (such as Castells-Quintana, Krause, and McDermott 2021), but the approach taken by Chlouba, Mukim, and Zaveri (2022) offers several key improvements. Most crucially, their approach captures the effects of drought specifically on crops that matter most for local economies rather than studying the effects of mere changes in temperature or precipitation. Similarly, they employ a novel and highly disaggregated measure of built-up areas using remotely sensed data from the World Settlement Footprint. This approach allows for a global scope of analysis rarely attempted in the existing literature.

Although local migration flows are difficult to measure accurately, evidence suggests that migration to cities is one of the key coping mechanisms in drought-stricken regions (Castells-Quintana, Lopez-Uribe, and McDermott 2018). For example, migration could occur gradually as a response to cumulative changes in water variability. Recent work has shown that migration is a significant response to persistent drought, particularly for households strongly dependent on agriculture. Evidence also suggests that climate migrants are often from the lower end of the skill distribution (Sedova and Kalkuhl 2020; Zaveri et al. 2021). Indeed, estimates suggest that those escaping drought often migrate to nearby cities and are frequently less advantaged than typical migrants, raising important implications for the migrants themselves and the receiving urban areas (Kleemans and Magruder 2018).

Chlouba, Mukim, and Zaveri (2022) do not offer much insight into the exact decision-making calculus of migrating families and individuals; nevertheless, their results line up convincingly with evidence gathered in specific contexts. For example, crop conditions emerge as a leading factor pushing Somalis out of their homes. The *Somalia Urbanization Review* measured crop conditions using the normalized difference vegetation index—a remotely sensed measure of land greenness—to investigate how Somalis react to drought (World Bank 2021c). The report finds that, when crops suffer from lack of water, people move, many of them to cities. Following a drought in 2017, many Somalis did precisely this, increasing the number of internally displaced persons (IDPs) in Baidoa and Mogadishu. The significance of drought decreases with time, suggesting that the decision to migrate is often reached rather quickly, at least in the Somali context.

According to Chlouba, Mukim, and Zaveri (2022), the relationship between drought and urban growth is particularly pronounced in low- and middle-income countries, hinting at a likely explanation for the rapid urbanization in these countries (Glaeser 2014). Of the noticeable heterogeneity, the effects are strongest in poorer countries—that is, countries that depend more on agriculture for national income. Between 1985 and 2014, industrialized countries saw an average effect that was nine times smaller than the effect of drought on urban growth observed in nonindustrialized countries.[11] The effects are also strongest for smaller and less developed urban areas—that is, those characterized by lower baseline shares of urban land and as measured by nighttime light intensity, respectively. Although cities in high-income countries are somewhat immune to drought-induced urban growth (likely because of both their location and a greater ability to cope with harsh climatic conditions), the phenomenon is hard to miss in middle-income and, above all, low-income countries. Not surprisingly, the most affected regions are the Middle East and North Africa and Sub-Saharan Africa. South of the Sahara, a single year spent under drought conditions is predicted to increase the share of urban land within each 55 × 55 kilometer cell by 5 percent. In Sub-Saharan Africa, low-income countries—where rain-fed agriculture continues to be a crucial source of subsistence for much of the population—are more affected by drought than middle-income countries. The effect of drought on the share of urban land among the poorest countries in Sub-Saharan Africa is about three times as large as the average effect estimated for the entire African continent. Again, this finding supports the impression that the impacts of climate change are strongest in regions dependent on subsistence agriculture (Cattaneo et al. 2019). Thus, it is no wonder that when the climate changes so, too, do people's livelihoods.

The drought–urban growth nexus is clearest in contexts where drought remains a persistent problem. One of the common forms of adaptation to changing climate is crop migration—that is, when conditions for agriculture become too poor in one region, farmers move their crops to another one. In regions where drought has been a persistent issue, however, this mechanism is not always available because fewer potentially productive areas remain. Chlouba, Mukim, and Zaveri (2022) show this problem empirically. The effect of droughts is stronger in locations below the global precipitation median. In other words, areas that are, on average, more humid (and wet) than the global median do not experience urban growth at nearly as fast a pace as areas that normally are generally dry. In these contexts, epitomized by the Sahel region, some of the fastest-growing informal settlements at the outskirts of large cities have been observed over the last few decades.

The research also suggests that in rapidly urbanizing environments dry spells most strongly affect urban growth. Many countries in the developing world, most notably in Africa, remain predominantly rural countries but have precipitous rates of urbanization. In Burundi, for example, 87 percent of the population continues to reside in rural areas, making the country one of the least urbanized globally. At the same time, Burundi has one of the fastest urban growth rates in its region—5.7 percent between 2000 and 2019 (Mukim 2021). In countries like Burundi, the effect of drought on urbanization is particularly noticeable. The background analyses conducted for this report indicate that the effect of drought on urban land in areas that were below the global median in terms of share of urban land in 1985 is more than 10 times bigger when compared with areas above the median in 1985. In other words, drought appears to be driving migration to cities, especially in locations that had relatively little urban land only four decades ago. The Somali city of Galkayo is a case in point. Thought to host more than 100,000 IDPs across dozens of settlements, Galkayo has tripled its spatial footprint since 1985. The 2017 drought in Galkayo's surrounding areas brought in tens of thousands of new arrivals (World Bank 2021c).

The challenge of climate-driven displacement is compounded by the fact that many migrants remain "invisible" in official statistics. One reason for that invisibility is the difficulty in untangling the nexus of climate change, conflict, and economic migration; and national governments (not to mention, host cities) are not well equipped to count and categorize displaced populations. Policies aimed at assisting IDPs often paint them with a broad brush, neglecting to differentiate between migrants who seek to integrate themselves into local economies and stay for the long term and displaced individuals who merely seek shorter-term protection from temporary natural disasters in their locations of origin. Urban IDPs who stay with their families and relatives escape official statistics, even though their arrival puts additional pressure on resource-stricken service delivery systems. Finally, authorities in countries such as Burundi do not always recognize domestic political reasons as a sufficient motive for displacement and so do not register certain IDPs.

Climate-induced migration is associated with growing urban sprawl

Drought-driven urban growth often takes the form of expanding informal settlements where service delivery remains a challenge. When climate migrants arrive in urban areas, they often cluster in peripheral areas that are underprepared for hosting large numbers of people. Rather than seamlessly integrating into the host communities and economies, these migrants often join the community of the displaced already there. Such communities are invariably found in urban peripheries, which have limited job opportunities, lack basic infrastructure, and have service delivery systems that remain in their infancy. The World Bank's *Burundi Urbanization Review* describes the clustering of IDPs around the Bujumbura airport, hardly an ideal location for the growing city's new inhabitants (Mukim 2021). In Liberia, the Peace Island Camp established on the outskirts of Monrovia during the country's civil wars offers an example of a refugee camp that evolved into a permanent settlement (World Bank 2020a). Informal settlements established in suboptimal locations increase the likelihood of evictions and forced relocation, creating a phenomenon known as secondary displacement. In such circumstances, new arrivals run the risk of long-term displacement when integration in host cities remains difficult and return to climate-decimated rural areas is no longer a viable option. Map 3.1 illustrates the degree to which urban growth in the last four decades has taken the form of expanding informal settlements, only some of which subsequently formalize. The map shows how Niamey, the capital of Niger, has expanded since 1985. Most new neighborhoods at the outskirts of the city contain a substantial share of informal housing.

Climate-induced displacement to rapidly growing cities can severely undermine the inclusivity of urban development, leaving some of the most vulnerable members of society at the outskirts, both figuratively and literally. Evidence from various sources suggests that women and children are overrepresented in the population of individuals displaced to cities by climate shocks. For example, women and children make up nearly a third of all displaced individuals in Burundi. As alarming as this proportion may be, these sorts of demographic disparities are even more pronounced in hot conflict zones. In countries such as Afghanistan, the Democratic Republic of Congo, and Somalia, women and children account for nearly two-thirds of those displaced (World Bank 2020a). The disproportionate representation of women and children displaced to cities in conflict zones compounds the pressure placed on service delivery because these IDPs often have less mobility once they arrive yet require greater access to the health care and education sectors. People displaced to urban locations may be less able to rely on the coping mechanisms available to rural-to-rural migrants, such as support from their extended families or from customary institutions. Thus, the burden of climate-driven displacement to growing cities often falls hardest on vulnerable populations.

Map 3.1   Urban expansion in Niamey, Niger, by share of informal settlements, 1985–2021

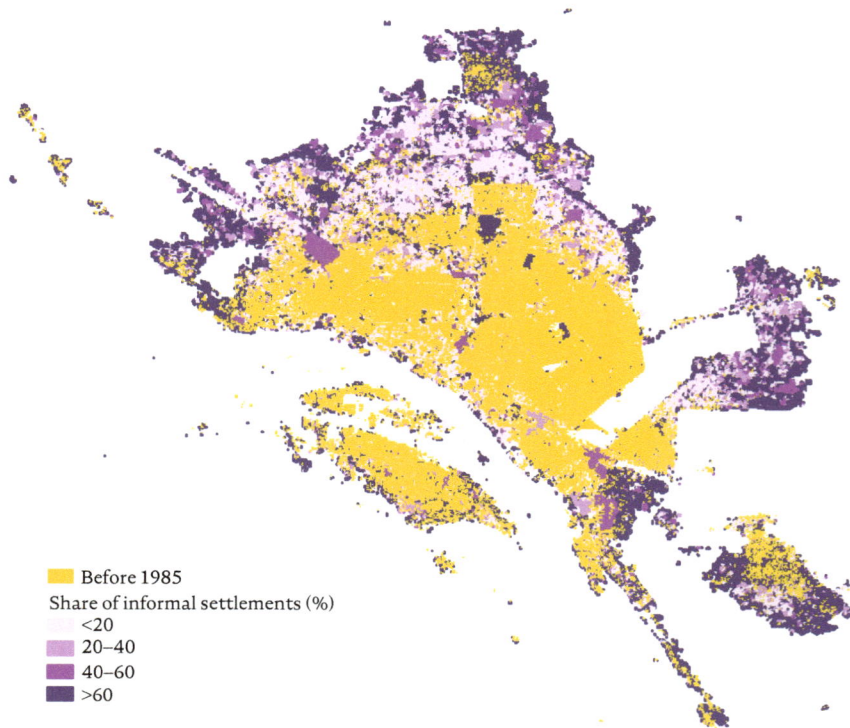

Before 1985

Share of informal settlements (%)
- <20
- 20–40
- 40–60
- >60

Source: Chlouba, Mukim, and Zaveri 2022.

Rapid urban growth induced by climate change can strain service delivery, but it can also fuel urban economies by providing a steady flow of new laborers to growing sectors such as manufacturing, construction, hospitality, communication, and transportation. Urban environments also could break down traditional gender barriers by bringing women into professions previously reserved for their male counterparts. The *Somalia Urbanization Review* finds that nearly half of Somali firms in the manufacturing, retail, and service sectors in Bosaso and Mogadishu tried to hire new employees in the preceding two years (World Bank 2021c). For example, 45.6 percent of manufacturing firms surveyed in Bosaso and Mogadishu reported new hires in the preceding fiscal year. Despite persistent security challenges, the firms that operate in Somali cities experienced rapid growth in sales, even when compared with regional peers such as the Democratic Republic of Congo and Rwanda. The opportunities enjoyed by urban-specific economic sectors notwithstanding, notable bottlenecks limit the ability of climate migrants to get new jobs. For one thing, job seekers often lack the abilities required by employers, including interpersonal, problem-solving, computer, and managerial skills. In cities across the developing world, ethnic and sectarian cleavages also often continue to limit job seekers' ability to look for jobs for which they are qualified. Furthermore, government and educational institutions do not always provide sufficient job assistance to link prospective employees with suitable employers. As for expanding firms, limited financial intermediation, the high cost and unavailability of land, unfavorable tax rates, and the price volatility of imported products represent some of the most important bottlenecks (World Bank 2021c).

Using country-level data on climate, conflict, emigration, and immigration in 126 countries for 1960–2000, Bosetti, Cattaneo, and Peri (2021) look into whether climate-induced migration could act as a possible driver of social unrest in the areas of destination. They do not find any evidence that inflows of climate migrants had a significant effect on conflicts in the receiving regions. Even following migration away from climate-stressed regions to urban areas, evidence suggests that rural migrants may have replaced one set of risks with another. In their case study of rural migrants arriving in the Bhola slum in Bangladesh's capital, Dhaka, McNamara, Olson, and Rahman (2016) find that the erstwhile rural migrants were now dealing with urban floods, outbreaks of cholera, fire hazards, and lack of access to basic services, including potable water.

Although most people displaced or migrating because of climate impacts stay in their countries of origin, the accelerating trend of global displacement related to climate impacts can increase cross-border movements, particularly where climate change interacts with conflict and violence (see box 3.4 for more details).

Water stresses also affect cities—even from afar

Cities have always relied on imported water (also see chapter 4). From ancient Rome and Los Angeles in the early twentieth century to modern-day initiatives in Mexico City and Kathmandu, Nepal, water imports have offered a path to urban water security (Garrick et al. 2019; Hoekstra, Buurman, and Van Ginkel 2018). But the scale and intensity of need have undergone rapid change, with cities of today often relying on dozens of water sources located hundreds of kilometers outside their municipal boundaries (McDonald et al. 2014). According to some estimates, the urban water infrastructure of large cities now moves approximately 500 billion liters of water daily across nearly 27,000 kilometers. More disruptive is when the reach of urban water infrastructure extends over larger areas and across basins, such as when it transports water from rural regions. A systematic review of the global experience by Garrick et al. (2019) finds that such transfers serve 69 cities that in 2015 had a total population of almost 400 million and that the transfers involve reallocating approximately 16 billion cubic meters of water each year.

It is therefore critical to account for this localized nature of water availability when studying the impacts of water stress on urban areas (see box 3.5). For example, a climatic shock such as a drought far away from a city can have profound impacts, whereas a drought just outside of the city, or even within the city itself, may be benign (Zaveri et al. 2021). Consistent with this example, recent research has found that drought impinging on water sources in often distant locations affects city growth because of the pressures such a situation exerts on a city's water supply system. Estimates suggest that dwindling urban water supplies due to prolonged drought in locations from which a city's water supply originates can reduce a city's gross domestic product by up to 12 percentage points (Zaveri et al. 2021).[12]

Upstream contributing areas can also affect the raw water quality and quantity of surface water sources (McDonald et al. 2014). Across local watersheds and even thousands of kilometers away, forests alter the movement, quality, and availability of water by regulating flow, absorbing water when it is plentiful, and releasing it when it is scarce (Damania et al. 2017; Zaveri et al. 2021). Although large cities occupy only 1 percent of the Earth's land surface, their source watersheds cover 41 percent of that surface. As a result, the raw water quality of large

Box 3.4

Does climate change lead to violence and migration?

An emerging literature over the last few years has attempted to explore the relationship among climate change, conflict, and migration. The nexus of these three forces has long been anecdotally invoked as a stylized fact seeking to explain, for example, phenomena such as the Arab Spring and subsequent waves of both conflict and migration. Yet the scholarship has yielded divergent findings (Mach et al. 2020); contrary to common belief, the evidence linking climatic risks to conflict and forced displacement, especially in regions such as the Middle East and North Africa, is not unequivocal (Borgomeo et al. 2021).

Focusing on the relationship between climate and violence broadly construed, Burke, Hsiang, and Miguel (2015) attempt to summarize the existing findings related to both interpersonal conflict, such as domestic violence, and intergroup strife, such as riots, civil wars, and coups. The authors surveyed 55 econometric studies in a meta-analysis, finding that, for every standard deviation rise in temperature, the frequency of interpersonal conflict increased by 2.4 percent. Some studies in their review also suggested that deviations in either direction increased the likelihood of conflict, extreme heat, or extreme cold. Extreme rainfall seems to be associated with the rising probability of intergroup conflicts.

Harari and La Ferrara (2018) suggest that climate-induced violence is particularly pronounced in regions traditionally dependent on rain-fed agriculture, such as Sub-Saharan Africa. As a case in point, McGuirk and Nunn (2021) argue that drought can fatally disrupt the arrangement between transhumant pastoralists, who need land to graze their animals, and sedentary agriculturalists, who need arable land for crop farming during the wet season. Persistent drought forces pastoralists to migrate before the harvest, leading to conflict with sedentary farmers.

A smaller strand of studies points to climate-induced conflict as a driver of subsequent migration. Poor water management together with increasing drought and multiyear crop failures have been shown to accelerate mass migration of rural households to urban areas (Kelley et al. 2015). Abel et al. (2019) exploit data on asylum applications from 157 countries between 2006 and 2015 to show that local climate, through its impact on both drought severity and armed conflict, played a pivotal role in explaining the volume of asylum applications between 2011 and 2015. Several of the World Bank's Urbanization Reviews have provided evidence of the climate-conflict-migration nexus at the subnational levels in some of the world's poorest countries. Evidence from the *Burundi Urbanization Review* shows that, even though most climate migrants tend to remain in their home provinces, they flock disproportionately to local urban centers (Mukim 2021). Once they arrive in growing cities, internally displaced populations do not automatically integrate into local economies, thereby contributing to the growth of informal settlements and putting extra pressure on local service delivery. In Somalia, three-quarters of internally displaced persons are thought to live in urban areas, most of them displaced by a combination of persistent conflict and difficult climate conditions (World Bank 2021c).

How water supplies from proximate natural sources are struggling to keep up with the needs of nearby cities and towns

The background paper prepared for this report by the Gauteng City-Region Observatory cites South African cities as good examples of major agglomerations that have effectively run out of water (GCRO 2022). South Africa is a water-scarce country and receives only half of the average global rainfall—495 millimeters compared with the world average of 1,033 millimeters.

Among other cities experiencing water supply extremes like those in Cape Town and the Nelson Mandela Bay Metropolitan Municipality, Johannesburg faced a critical water deficit during a severe dry spell in 2015–16. Far from any major water body and built on gold-rich grasslands, Greater Johannesburg and its 16 million residents face inevitable crises because of the city's unusual geographic position at the pinnacle of a continental watershed. The city first emerged in an area called Witwatersrand ("ridge of white waters"), suggesting a plentiful water supply from local springs and streams flowing from the ridge. Presently, however, all water flows out and away from the core of the region toward the Indian Ocean on one side and the Atlantic Ocean on the other. In fact, much of the water consumed in the city is supplied by the Lesotho Highlands Water Scheme across the Lesotho–South Africa border. Without increasing dam capacity and in view of the growing environmental uncertainties arising from climate change, this water may not be sufficient to meet the future needs of residents and industry in the region.

cities also depends on the land use in this much larger area (McDonald et al. 2014). For 33 of the world's 105 largest cities, nearby protected forest lands are a primary factor in drinking water availability and quality (Dudley and Stolton 2003; Zaveri et al. 2021).[13]

Climate stresses and shocks influence urban food prices

High food prices negatively affect the diets and nutrition of urban consumers, particularly in poorer countries and for the urban poor, who spend a larger share of their incomes on food. Food expenditures in low- and lower-middle-income countries represent about 40 percent of household income, whereas those in upper-middle- and high-income countries are 29 and 15 percent, respectively (Graf von Luckner, Holston, and Reinhart 2022). Urban residents, especially the more disadvantaged, already have less healthy diets (see chapter 1). Higher food prices increase poverty and vulnerability and lead to poorer diets and nutrition, with potential longer-term and largely irreversible consequences for the poor, particularly for mothers and children (Baez et al. 2017; Green et al. 2013; Ivanic, Martin, and Zaman 2012).

In already vulnerable contexts, climate change–related shocks and stressors affect rural food-producing areas. These impacts spill over to urban areas via higher urban food prices (Venkat, Dizon, and Masters 2022). According to analysis that combines food prices and climate change–related shocks and stressors for a subset of vulnerable countries, various types of shocks in rural areas increase food prices in cities (Bai et al. 2021; Florczyk et al. 2019; Pesaresi et al. 2019).[14] These impacts vary by the type of shock or stressor and by the type of food (such as more nutrient-dense perishables versus calorie-dense nonperishables).

Better transportation networks help mitigate the impact of shocks and stressors, allowing for potentially more resilient food supply chains (Venkat, Dizon, and Masters 2022).[15] Roads and road quality reduce poverty and increase consumption, reduce price volatility, and help households cope with shocks (Dercon et al. 2009; Moctar, d'Hôtel Elodie, and Tristan 2015; Nakamura, Bundervoet, and Nuru 2019; Shively and Thapa 2016). Roads are important for food security in times of disaster. Economic losses from transportation disruptions increase linearly with the duration of disruptions, which calls for quick repairs but also flexible procurement strategies (Colon, Hallegate, and Rozenberg 2021).

How does climate change affect different populations in cities?

Cities are large ecosystems composed of many different groups of people. Because income and education levels, service provision, and amenities often vary dramatically within the boundaries of a city, the same should be expected of exposure to natural hazards. If diverse types of inequalities are correlated, vulnerabilities are compounded because those who face higher risk will also be more vulnerable and less able to adopt mitigation strategies. Moreover, by increasing the likelihood and frequency of adverse events, climate change has the power to exacerbate inequality (Hallegatte et al. 2016).

It is important to understand the relative exposure dynamics in cities because those dynamics may differ considerably from country-level ones. Recent World Bank studies have used global hazard maps to build a general understanding of exposure to climate change by country (Hallegatte, Bangalore, and Vogt-Schilb 2016a, 2016b; Park et al. 2018; Rentschler and Salhab 2020; Winsemius et al. 2018). Findings based on larger subnational units, such as the Demographic and Health Surveys, do not always translate into what happens at the city level. For example, in Vietnam the poor are not systematically overexposed to floods (Narloch and Bangalore 2016); however, Bangalore, Smith, and Veldkamp (2019) find that the slums in Ho Chi Minh City are relatively more exposed than the rest of the city.

The poor are not universally more exposed than the well-off to climate risks

Precise information on individual or household income is often not available for cities in the developing world. Information on the location of slums, however, can help identify pockets of deprivation in cities. Matching data on slums with environmental risk maps can shed light on which slum dwellers are more highly exposed to stressors. Urban slums are often found in unsafe locations—that is, on steep slopes, on floodable land, or near open drains and sewers (Fay 2005; Hallegatte et al. 2016). Bangalore, Smith, and Veldkamp (2019) find that 64 percent of Ho Chi Minh City faces a yearly flood risk of 1 percent, but that figure rises to 80 percent for slums. Elsewhere, slums in Medellín, Colombia (Restrepo Cadavid 2011), as well as in Caracas, República Boliariana de Venezuela, and Rio de Janeiro, Brazil (Fay 2005; Lall and Deichmann 2012), are in peripheral city locations on steep slopes and close to water bodies, whereas slums in Dhaka, Mumbai, and Pune are mostly exposed to floods and polluted locations (Hallegatte et al. 2016). Although this body of evidence establishes the exposure of poor people in cities, it does not fully speak to relative exposure because most of the studies did not set out to make an empirically robust comparison with formal residential areas. Accordingly, the calculations by Patankar (2015) of flood exposure for each ward in Mumbai do not show clearly that informal residential areas are more exposed than formal ones.

The poor, however, are not universally more exposed than the well-off to climate risks, despite being more exposed in some cities (see box 3.6). In Bogotá, Colombia, residents in the bottom 20 percent of the income distribution are more likely than richer residents to live in areas at higher risk of earthquake (Lall and Deichmann 2012). Similarly, Erman et al. (2019),

Box 3.6

Intensifying urban heat in Johannesburg will disproportionately affect the poor

Johannesburg, known for a historically mild climate, faces a sharp increase in temperatures over coming decades that will disproportionately affect poorer neighborhoods whose physical form has a stronger tendency to absorb and store heat. The Highveld region has already seen a 1.2°C increase in average temperatures over preindustrial levels and will warm by a further 1.2–1.7°C by 2050, shifting from a temperate to a hot and dry climate zone. Detailed heat maps, produced through a community monitoring campaign, show that Johannesburg already faces a strong urban heat island effect: most neighborhoods are 3–4°C warmer at night than nearby rural areas; and neighborhoods like Alexandra, Katlehong, Soweto, and Tembisa, as well as the Central Business District, are up to 6.5°C hotter (map B3.6.1). The highest heat intensities occur in historically marginalized neighborhoods, which are home to nonwhite and low-income communities, and which have high building and population density as well as very low levels of vegetation and tree cover. These neighborhoods often contain many low-cost dwellings that tend to overheat, and their inhabitants have limited capacity to adapt to excessive heat, such as through air conditioning.

Historical factors including apartheid-era land use practices have contributed to sharp disparities in heat, which may intensify in coming decades. Urban climate modeling suggests that by 2050 the number of hot nights per year (nights when the temperature remains above 20°C) will increase from 10 to 40 for much of the city but from 40 to 100 for the hottest neighborhoods—primarily poorer and majority black township areas. The heat exposure results from physical characteristics of these neighborhoods that absorb solar radiation and reemit it at night, including dense housing, lack of green features, and use of heat-trapping materials such as corrugated iron roofs. Extreme heat will affect the health and livelihoods of poorer communities. Modeling suggests an increase in the heat-related excess mortality rate by 2050, resulting in several hundred additional deaths per year. Health risks are higher for the elderly, people with tuberculosis or HIV/AIDS, and people whose homes absorb and retain heat. Indoor heat measurements conducted by volunteers in February 2022 confirmed that indoor temperatures in wood-frame, corrugated iron dwellings can be 15°C higher than in nearby brick and concrete homes. Labor productivity for outdoor and informal sector workers will also likely diminish as outdoor heat stress reaches high or very high categories for more hours per day.

The cities of Ekurhuleni and Johannesburg have already integrated cooling measures into their climate action plans. One aspect addresses the phenomenon of "green apartheid," whereby low-income areas have a vegetation cover rate of 0–15 percent compared with 30–60 percent for well-off areas. For the 2010 World Cup, Johannesburg planted some 200,000 trees. Further building on these efforts, interventions for cooler places—such as targeting greening and implementing cool building designs for homes, schools, and clinics—and interventions to protect vulnerable people—such as provision of heat wave early warning alerts and community cooling centers—offer cost-effective ways to adapt to rising temperatures.

BOX 3.6 *continued*

MAP B3.6.1   **Residents of hotter neighborhoods face daytime temperatures that are up to 6.5°C higher, Johannesburg, South Africa**

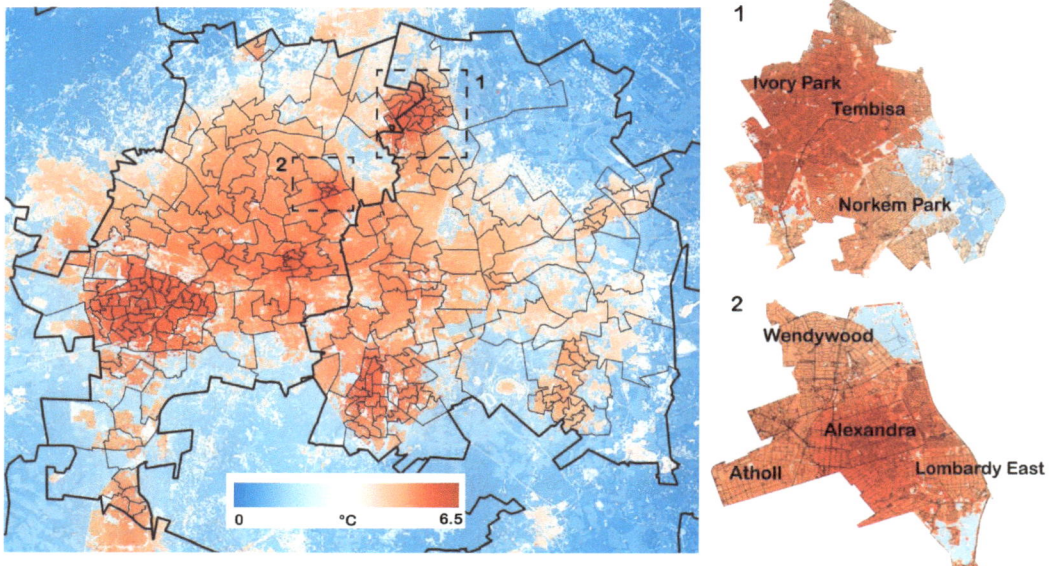

Source: Souverijns et al. 2022.

Note: Map shows the present-day urban heat island intensity (that is, average daytime temperature as compared with nearby rural areas) corrected for topographical (surface height) effects. Insets 1 and 2 show Tembisa and Alexandra, respectively.

using responses to a household survey on the April 2018 floods, find that the share of directly affected households in Dar Es Salaam, Tanzania, generally decreases as income quartile goes up (from 29 percent in the first quartile to 15 percent in the fourth quartile). By contrast, a survey conducted in Greater Accra, Ghana, on the 2015 floods finds no difference in exposure between richer and poorer households (Erman et al. 2020).

In a background paper for this report, Rossitti (2022) provides results of a novel analysis revealing that slums in developing world cities are, on average, not more exposed to floods or excessive heat but face a higher probability of a high-risk flood event. Rossitti employs global land use data for 18 cities in the South Asia and Sub-Saharan Africa regions[16] to identify poverty clusters and determine their relative exposure to climate hazards, and derives information on slums' locations from aerial imagery.[17] The author finds that, in general, the average results conceal large differences among cities. Regression analysis suggests that, in 8 of the 18 cities in the sample, slums are more exposed to floods, whereas half show an exposure bias in terms of excessive heat. A different sample of cities may therefore yield different average results.[18] Rossitti concludes that, although in many cities the poor appear to be more exposed to climate hazards, this finding cannot be generalized because the presence of exposure bias often depends on individual city characteristics.

Location sorting may offer one explanation

Location sorting[19] can explain why in some cities the poor are overexposed to climate risks: they choose to live in hazard-prone areas because they, like households in slums affected by recurrent floods in Mumbai (Patankar 2015) and those living in areas with higher earthquake risk in Bogotá (Lall and Deichmann 2012), prefer to trade safety for better access to jobs, services, and economic activity. Financial constraints may also explain sorting into high-risk areas. Because poor households often have less leverage and find it difficult to borrow money in the financial marketplace, they may borrow against their location asset by choosing to live in a worse location with low housing costs but relatively poor work and education opportunities (Bilal and Rossi-Hansberg 2021). Heblich, Trew, and Zylberberg (2021) provide clear evidence of this mechanism using a historical time series of neighborhood-level data on employment and pollution in British cities. The current income distribution depends, in part, on how poorer residents sorted during the industrial revolution in the eastern areas of the cities because those areas had more exposure to industrial coal pollution.

A different but not mutually exclusive mechanism for location sorting is information asymmetries, which also may play a role in the residential location choices of the poor in cities. It is possible that poorer households are less able to acquire information on the environmental risks of a specific location, or that migrants from rural areas do not have access to such information before settling on a location.[20] It is also possible that risk-averse low-income households that would value safety over accessibility still sort in risky locations because they lack information on environmental hazards. Even if prospective dwellers do have information on the risks associated with different locations, that information may not be accurate (Bakkensen and Barrage 2021; Votsis and Perrels 2016). Because poverty involves a series of distractions that reduce productivity as well as the chances to acquire information (Banerjee and Mullainathan 2008), poorer, less educated individuals may face a higher cost of acquiring hazard-proneness information than do their richer counterparts.[21]

Household survey data from Bamako also suggest that the poor face a trade-off between accessibility and environmental risk. Rossitti (2022) uses information on migration status from Mali's 2018 household income and expenditure survey in Bamako[22] to provide evidence supporting the location-sorting mechanisms. Although poor households do not appear to be relatively more exposed to either floods or excessive heat, poor and uneducated migrants face 1.24 more days of excessive heat than do poor and uneducated nonmigrants. At the same time, nonmigrants and highly educated migrants appear to have no difference in exposure. These findings could be explained by a combination of sorting and information mechanisms. Moreover, the data highlight the trade-off between being in a central location and the environmental risk faced by the most deprived households, as shown in figure 3.1. Low-income or poorly educated households that live close to the city center face a higher risk than those living farther away. For the wealthier or more educated, by contrast, distance is a weaker predictor of exposure.

Figure 3.1 **Marginal effects of remote location within a city on exposure to excessive heat, by education level and consumption per capita, Bamako, Mali**

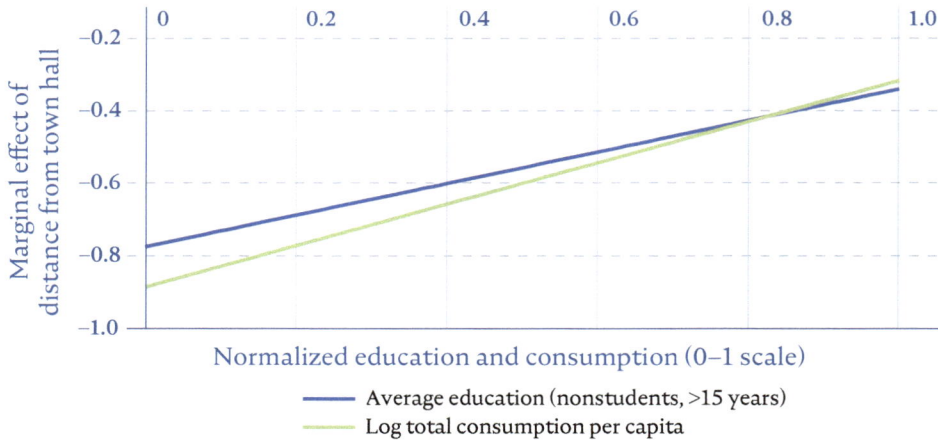

Source: Rossitti 2022.

Note: The graph shows the marginal effects of the distance from the notional city center of Bamako (proxied by location of the town hall) on the average yearly number of days of excess heat measured for each household (see box 3.7 on measuring environmental risk). The regression includes average household education levels (of members older than 15) and log consumption per capita (both variables normalized on a 0–1 scale); the distance from the town hall in kilometers; and the respective interactions, migration status, and altitude at the location where the household lives.

The poor are the hardest-hit by disasters

The poor often lose more when hit by a disaster. Although the presence of exposure bias depends on the specific city considered, more evidence supports the presence of vulnerability bias in cities—that is, when hit by a disaster, poor urban dwellers lose more than their richer counterparts. In absolute terms, the rich often lose more because their assets are worth more; however, in relative terms, the opposite holds true (Hallegatte, Bangalore, and Vogt-Schilb 2016b). Patankar (2015) reports that, during the Mumbai floods in 2005, households below the poverty line suffered losses equal to six times their monthly income, higher in relative terms than the losses by all other income groups.[23] In Ho Chi Minh City, Vietnam, disasters have relatively larger negative impacts on the poor in terms of health, employment, and income (Hallegatte, Bangalore, and Vogt-Schilb 2016b).[24] Erman et al. (2020) find similar evidence in Accra, Ghana. Poorer households also suffer disproportionally from the indirect effects of natural hazards when infrastructure disruptions, for example, cut households off from roads, their water supply (Erman et al. 2019), or public transit (He, Liu, et al. 2021).

Not only do poor urban dwellers suffer higher losses from environmental hazards, but they also have impaired ability to deal with those hazards. In general, poorer households have less access to financial markets (Erman et al. 2019) and insurance markets (which are also less developed in lower-income countries). Moreover, without subsidies and tenant protection laws, poorer households are less likely to benefit from property owners' investments in mitigation structures because such investments will likely lead to higher property prices (Nakagawa, Saito, and Yamaga 2007), which will, in turn, force poor households out of now safer areas of the city. Finally, many poor households engage in recurrent self-financed short-term measures (such as temporary structural improvements) that impose a large financial burden on the poorest urban dwellers with the lowest-quality housing (Patankar 2015).

Beyond its physical and financial impacts, climate change can also adversely affect mental health (Evans 2019). Because the brunt of climate change shocks, such as flooding, disproportionately affects the poor (Hallegatte et al. 2016), a climate shock may severely lower their income and their ability to earn a living wage, likely increasing the incidence of stress. A review of studies linking heat and mental health finds a higher suicide rate related to heat in 15 of the 35 studies reviewed (Thompson et al. 2018). Studies have also found a link between flooding, especially repeated flooding, and mental health disorders such as post-traumatic stress disorder (Evans 2019).

Evidence suggests that some social groups are affected more than others

Although this section has concentrated on the exposure bias of the poor, environmental risks in cities may also disproportionately affect vulnerable populations such as women and the less educated. Erman et al. (2019) find that floods compound women's challenges because, according to gender norms, women are responsible for cleaning up in the aftermath and for taking care of children during school closures. Following the floods in Dar Es Salaam, Tanzania, in 2018, of all those who had to stay home and miss work, the majority (60 percent) were women.

The World Bank report *Healthy Cities* (forthcoming a) outlines the ways in which climate stresses in urban areas affect health directly and indirectly. Storms and flooding cause injuries, exposure to toxins, and disease outbreaks. The increased frequency and intensity of extreme heat can cause heat stroke, worsen chronic conditions, and, as noted earlier, affect mental health. Climate change–caused shifts in wildlife habitats have also led to greater opportunities for the emergence of zoonotic diseases such as COVID-19. Meanwhile, drought can have longer-term impacts on nutrition and health, and wildfires can affect long-term heart and lung issues. The *Healthy Cities* report also looks at how some of these health impacts disproportionately affect marginalized population groups. For example, urban heat island effects are far worse for more vulnerable groups such as migrants, racial minorities, children, the elderly, those with chronic illnesses, and those whose livelihoods require them to work outdoors (Madrigano et al. 2015; Mashhoodi 2021; Shahmohamadi et al. 2011; Voelkel et al. 2018).

Rossitti (2022) suggests a strong relationship between environmental hazards and educational level in the largest Indonesian metropolitan areas (map 3.2). He bases his finding on a large data set of 5,821 village (*desa*)-level observations from the eight largest multi-metro agglomerations in Indonesia on average educational attainment.[25] In terms of environmental hazards, his analysis considers fluvial and pluvial flood, and excessive heat, measured as described in box 3.7. Regression analysis confirms that, within cities, more deprived areas (where deprivation is proxied by a lower education level) are more exposed.[26]

Map 3.2 Educational attainment and environmental risk within Indonesian multidistrict metros

a. Denpasar

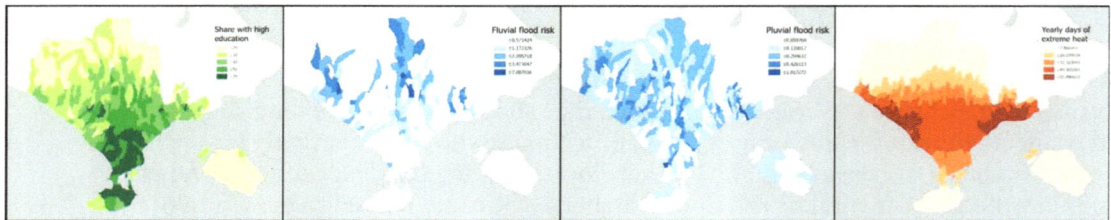

b. Jakarta

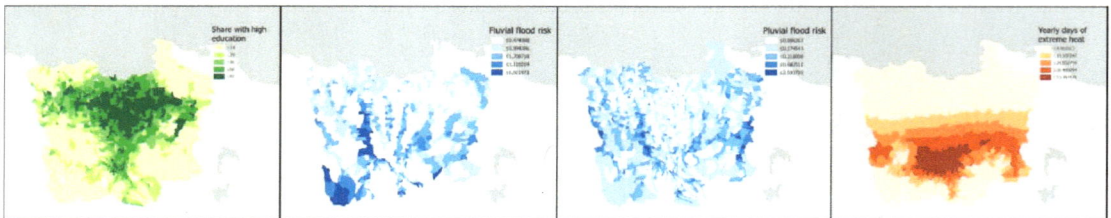

c. Medan

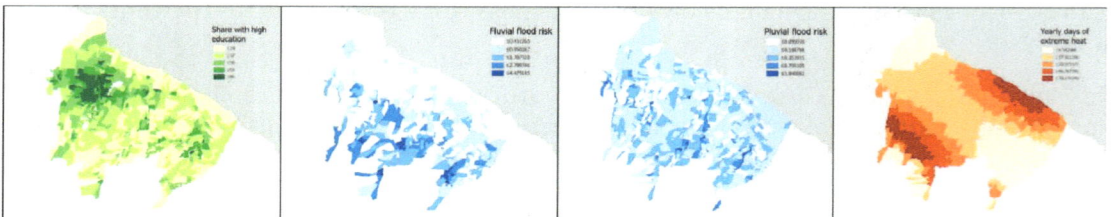

d. Pasuruan

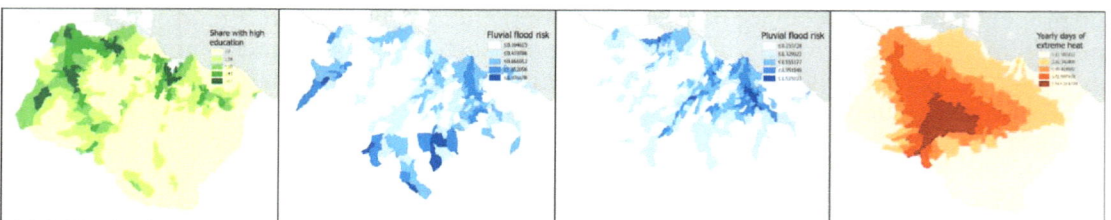

Continued

Map 3.2 *continued*

e. Probolinggo

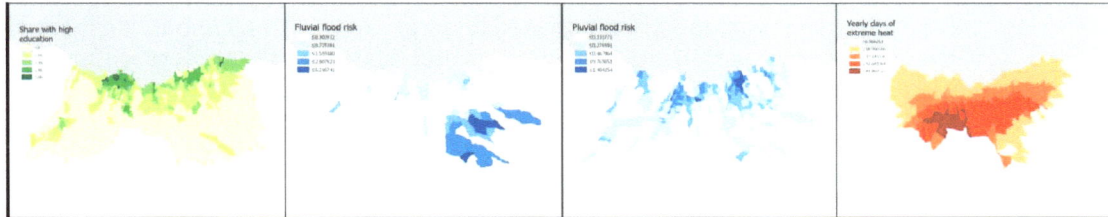

f. Semarang

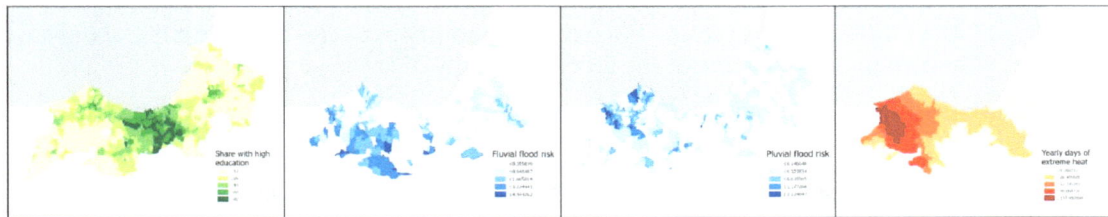

g. Surabaya

h. Yogyakarta

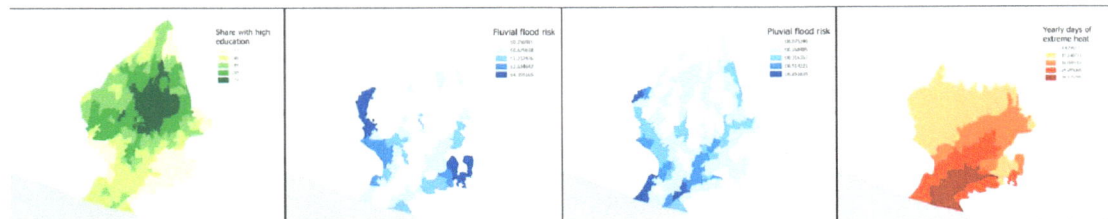

Source: Rossitti 2022.

Note: For each multidistrict metro, maps show from left to right the share of individuals with a tertiary education degree (a darker color equals a more highly educated population), fluvial (riverine) flood risk, pluvial (surface water) flood risk, and the total number of days each year with excessive heat (a darker color indicates higher exposure to the environmental hazard considered). All variables are averaged at the village (desa) level. See box 3.7 for a detailed description of the environmental risk variables. Metro areas are defined as in Roberts, Gil Sander, and Tiwari (2019).

BOX 3.7

Measuring environmental risk in cities

Many of the climate hazard and disaster data that have informed understanding of the spatial variation of environmental risk cannot be used to study relative exposure *within* cities. Event data are mostly catalogued for large areas (cities, regions), so measuring relative exposure within cities requires smaller-scale data that reflect within-city variation. For this reason, Rossitti (2022) focuses on floods and heat—for which high-resolution gridded data are available—to study exposure within cities.

Flood risk data are obtained from the national grids of Fathom Flood Hazard Data and Maps (Sampson et al. 2015). Fathom data report both fluvial (riverine) and pluvial (surface water) maximum flood depth at 3-arcsecond (~90-meter) resolution for several return periods.[a] A return period indicates the probability associated with the event. For example, a Fathom record of 0.4 with a 1-in-100-years return indicates a yearly 1 percent probability of a 40-centimeter flood event. For consistency, the analysis uses the 1-in-100-years return (1 percent probability per year) because it is the only available return period for some of the cities in the global land use sample.[b]

For a given return period, it is also possible to categorize flood events by level of risk. Although FATHOM classifies very minor events, these events may not carry any environmental risk. Rentschler and Salhab (2020) classify events with flood depth under 15 centimeters as minor and those over 0.5 meter as high risk. A flood with a depth from 0.5 meter to 1.5 meters carries a very high risk and is likely to create extensive damage. Following their categorization, part of the analysis focuses only on the existence of high risk, testing the hypothesis that, although the poor are not necessarily more exposed, on average, within cities, they may be more likely to face a high-risk event.

Exposure to temperature-related hazards is measured as the number of days of extreme heat each year (using a 2000–16 average to control for potential outlier years). The daily temperature is obtained from a CHELSA global high-resolution (250 meters to 1 kilometer) land surface temperature grid (Karger et al. 2021). A day of extreme heat is a day in which the temperature exceeds 35°C.

Sources: Karger et al. 2021; Sampson et al. 2015.

a. Fluvial flood data are further broken down into defended and undefended (data that do not account for modeled river barriers). For consistency, the analysis uses undefended fluvial flood risk data because defended data are unavailable for some countries.
b. The last iteration of the national grids for Bangladesh and India (version 1, May 2016) does not include data for other return periods than 1 in 100 years and fluvial defended flood depth. All the other cities in the analysis use version 2 data (June 2020).

Climate shocks affect different types of workers and in different ways

A warming world could affect livelihoods and socioeconomic outcomes through its impacts on labor productivity (see box 3.8 describing new research commissioned for this report). Climate stressors could directly affect worker productivity by, for example, circumscribing the time available for work or, conversely, through the health impacts linked to laboring in high temperatures (Shayegh, Manoussi, and Dasgupta 2021). Extreme temperatures reduce performance during working hours because workers slow down (Parsons 2014), take more breaks to rehydrate and cool off, and make more mistakes (Dasgupta et al. 2019, 2021; Park et al. 2020). This effect is higher in jobs exposed more directly to weather conditions (Orlov et al. 2020), such as agriculture and construction. The least perceptible but most widespread effects arise, however, from slow-onset events that may not be enough to keep people from work but that could affect their performance (Kahn et al. 2021).

Box 3.8

The economic and societal consequences of urban heat are pervasive

A background paper prepared for this report by Jiang and Quintero (2022) evaluates the effects of high temperatures on labor productivity across thousands of cities in eight countries in Latin America and the Caribbean. Jiang and Quintero use successive rounds of household survey microdata that, apart from Brazil, come from the Socio-Economic Database for Latin America and the Caribbean (SEDLAC).[a] Because comparability presents an important obstacle in assessing labor productivity across a large set of countries, one of the great advantages of SEDLAC is that it provides harmonized microdata collected from over 300 household surveys. It ensures strong comparability of the data across time and countries by using similar definitions of variables in each country and year, and by applying consistent methods of processing the data (CEDLAS and World Bank 2014).

The paper by Jiang and Quintero (2022) builds on Quintero and Roberts (2022) to clean the data and build wage variables. In each country, the location analyzed changes slightly according to the lowest possible administrative division that can be identified in the surveys. The paper also includes city characteristics from a geospatial database constructed by the University of Southampton's GeoData center.[b] The number of hot days[c] in the year and average temperature from MODIS Terra Land Surface Temperature are proxies for climate stressors. The analysis focuses on a broad sample of workers covering both the formal and informal sectors if wages are reported. A worker's wage is assumed to be the nominal hourly wage earned in the primary occupation.

Jiang and Quintero (2022) find that both hot days and high temperatures reduce the labor productivity of workers, as measured by wages. The results are statistically significant for most countries. Estimated coefficients imply, for example, that, if the number of hot days in a temperate city like Medellín increases by 1 percent a year, average wages would fall by 0.8 percent. On average, an annual temperature increase of 1°C is associated with a 1 percent decline in wages. The effect of hot days is particularly strong in countries with warmer climates such as Colombia, Mexico, Panama, and Peru. By contrast, results are weaker and the point estimates much smaller in countries with more distinct seasons, which could indicate better adaptation. It could also be explained by the distribution of sectoral activity in countries.

197

Box 3.8 *continued*

To understand the impacts across different groups of workers, Jiang and Quintero pool data across countries and study workers by demographic characteristics including, age, gender, education, and sector (private or public, formal or informal).[d] It turns out that the impact of climate stressors on productivity are not homogeneous across the population. Younger workers are more affected than older workers, probably because of disparities in working conditions and sector of occupation. Similarly, informal workers, and those with lower educational attainment, are also more strongly affected by higher temperatures. These results are consistent with the lower implementation of adaptation measures in informal sectors. Those in the private sector are also more affected. Thus, Jiang and Quintero find that climate stresses negatively affect labor productivity in cities across large groups of countries. Furthermore, the effects are heterogeneous, with more vulnerable workers worse affected and with further evidence of exacerbating inequalities.

a. This database was jointly constructed by the Center for Distributive, Labor and Social Studies (CEDLAS) at the Universidad National de La Plata and the World Bank.

b. This database was constructed for this report to align the research with the identifiers for subnational areas in SEDLAC.

c. Hot days are constructed as the average number of hot days per year measured during the day, weighted by the pixel population using LandScan 2012 population. A day is considered hot if the average daily temperature exceeds 35°C. This threshold for hot days is supported by the literature on the temperature above which workability is affected (Andrews et al. 2018).

d. SEDLAC provides two indicators for whether a worker is considered informal (CEDLAS and World Bank 2014). The first, based on a productive definition of informality, identifies a worker as informal if the worker belongs to any of the following categories: unskilled self-employed, salaried worker in a small private firm, or zero-income worker. The second, based on a legalistic or social protection notion of informality, identifies a salaried worker as informal if that worker does not have the right to a pension linked to employment when retired. Jiang and Quintero use the first indicator because surveys more frequently provide this information. The sample already excludes self-employed workers, and doing so equates informal employment with employment by very small private firms (five or fewer employees).

Climate stressors can further affect labor productivity indirectly through their effect on capital investment (Somanathan et al. 2021), population loss, macroeconomic conditions (Cashin, Mohaddes, and Raissi 2017), and the productivity of other production factors (Letta and Tol 2019). Because adaptation takes time, deviations from historical temperatures could be more harmful than higher temperatures per se (Kahn et al. 2021).

Evidence also exists that these effects will have negative distributional impacts. For one thing, the effects are likely to be concentrated in low- and middle-income countries. Lower-income countries often depend more on agriculture and sectors focused on outdoor work. More important, they are less able to implement adaptation measures. Adaptation measures such as air-conditioning in the workplace could decouple high temperatures from work productivity, but such measures can be relatively expensive. Moreover, sharper reductions in the incomes of informal and rural workers, who already have lower levels of income, will exacerbate inequality within countries.

Water scarcity has a disproportionate impact on vulnerable groups

Globally, although the provision of water and sanitation services has greatly improved, urban areas still face several challenges. These challenges arise in large part because urban population growth has continued to outpace the ability to adequately meet the water and sanitation needs of growing peri-urban and marginalized areas.[27] And marginalized groups often carry the disproportionate burden of the impacts of water scarcity.

Even though piped utility water is the least expensive option for most households, many still lack access (Mitlin et al. 2019). Poorer households, often located in areas not served by utilities, are most affected because they must buy poor-quality water from water vendors at prices much higher than those paid by users connected to piped water supplies (Borgomeo et al. 2021). Across Africa, water deficits in peri-urban, slum, and informal urban areas are well documented (Keener, Luengo, and Banerjee 2010). These areas must pay a higher cost for water scarcity because they are more likely to rely on off-site standpost water and unregulated markets of informal water resellers or alternative service providers who charge higher prices. For example, vendor-delivered water in Nairobi costs 10 times more than household piped water—and nearly 30 times as much in Dar es Salaam (Azunre et al. 2022). In urban Ethiopia, which has substantially expanded coverage of piped water, richer households are almost four times more likely than poorer ones to have piped water. In smaller Ethiopian towns, weaker infrastructure makes it difficult to connect households; in larger cities, poorer households simply lack the means to pay for services (Das 2020; World Bank 2017). In India, only 38 percent of households among the poorest fifth of the country's urban population have access to indoor piped water, compared with 62 percent of the richest fifth (Frumkin et al. 2020). Informal areas in Lima, Peru, also exemplify the impact of urban growth and inequality. Many of the 1.5 million who are underserved (Howson 2015) live in growing peri-urban settlements, rely on informal water tankers, and must pay up to US$6 per cubic meter, compared with US$0.40 per cubic meter from the formal water system (Ritter 2018). Because water from informal sources is often untreated, it also increases the cost of household treatment and poses health risks. Meanwhile, indigenous people migrating to urban areas often face severe shortfalls of access to basic water services, along with marginalization (UN 2018). In Latin America, indigenous migrants in urban areas are twice as likely as nonindigenous migrants to end up living in informal settlements with limited access to basic services, including water (World Bank 2015; Zaveri et al. 2021).

Climate change has exacerbated these impacts

Cities affected by disaster or fragility have additional challenges. They are more likely to rely on the resale of informal water, thereby compounding their vulnerability. Haiti, prone to both disaster and conflict, saw a drop in the provision and uptake of safe drinking water between 1990 and 2015. The decline was particularly noticeable in urban areas, where, among other reasons, residents did not trust the quality of publicly provided water (Das 2020; World Bank 2017).

Water scarcity and climate-related drought further exacerbate these structural gaps and are felt most keenly in underserved informal areas. For example, in Uganda residents are more likely to pay user fees during a drought and spend 13 percent more time fetching water—an increase of 1.9 hours a week—than in a nondrought year (Kamei 2020). Women and girls disproportionately bear this burden, and so have less time to devote to education and productive endeavors.

Although women in cities spend less time, on average, collecting water than do women in rural areas, in many places they still have responsibility for that task. In the urban areas of Africa, for example, the differential between men and women who spend a minimum of 30 minutes a day collecting water is large in many countries. In 18 out of 24 African countries studied, women have responsibility for most of the water collection in urban areas; and, in most countries where women do not have the primary responsibility, it falls on children in a majority of households (Graham, Hirai, and Kim 2016).

Climate change has negative knock-on effects on already vulnerable populations

The need to spend more time fetching water can lead to more gender-based violence and less time to engage in other activities such as education or income-generating activities. One study calculates that in Khayelitsha, an urban township of Cape Town, South Africa, doubling the number of toilets to reduce the distance from the household could decrease the incidence of sexual assault by 30 percent (Gonzalves, Kaplan, and Paltiel 2015). Other studies suggest that reducing the time needed to collect water frees up time for leisure and child-rearing activities and reduces stress levels and intrahousehold conflict (Devoto et al. 2012). Where women have a higher likelihood of fetching water, children's participation in school is affected because they help with domestic chores. Thus, improvements in household access to piped water can also lead to better schooling outcomes for children, although the effect depends on the country-specific context (Das 2017; Koolwal and Van de Walle 2013). For example, a study finds that halving the time it takes to carry water in Ghana would increase enrollment rates by about 7 percentage points for girls, with similar effects for boys (Nauges and Strand 2017). In the Sundarbans in Bangladesh and West Bengal, India, saline water and lack of access to improved water sources increase the chances of girls dropping out of school and becoming responsible for water collection. For boys, however, there is little difference among the households with different water quality and water sources (Das 2017; Komatsu and Joseph 2016).

Reducing the distance to access safely managed water became even more important during the COVID-19 pandemic because the need for better hygiene increased the burden that women and children faced in poorer regions. This burden and, conversely, the potential benefits of reducing the gap have unfolded among existing inequalities, so that groups already facing a deficit in access to clean and safe drinking water experienced the most acute impacts. Surveys of female refugees and displaced persons in 15 African countries during the pandemic highlighted harassment and sexual violence encountered on the way to and at water collection points (Abwola and Michelis 2020).

Although they bear a higher burden in securing water for their households, women and other marginalized groups are substantially underrepresented in the workforce and decision-making roles in the water sector (Das 2014; World Bank 2019).[28] As a result, their needs and opinions are not considered when planning for the provision of water services to water-scarce informal urban areas, in resilience planning, or in devising recovery measures. A 2013 survey of 65 countries reveals that only 15 percent of countries had a gender policy in their water ministry, and only 35 percent of countries included gender considerations in their water policies and programs. Furthermore, only 22 percent of surveyed water ministries had gender focal points (Fauconnier et al. 2018), and only 16 percent of national water plans mention women as key stakeholders or primary participants in climate adaptation (UNESCO 2015). Urban water and sanitation utilities and water resources management institutions are also staffed predominantly by men (World Bank 2019). A survey of about 64 water utilities in 28 low- and middle-income countries finds that women make up less than 20 percent of employees and are significantly underrepresented in technical and managerial roles (World Bank 2019).[29] One in three surveyed utilities did not have a single female engineer, and one in six had no female managers (World Bank 2019). Such egregious disparities reflect a broader trend of female underrepresentation in the labor force (Jayachandran 2021; Klasen 2019).

This lack of voice presents not only a problem of equity but also a barrier to devising sustainable solutions to water scarcity. Because women are the key clients of water and sanitation utilities, their presence in a more gender-diverse workforce can help utilities better understand and respond to the concerns and needs of their female clients. Women also often teach children about water use and water conservation, and country-level studies have pointed to the higher value women place on protecting water quality; water management issues are a policy priority raised by women (Chattopadhyay and Duflo 2004; Chaturvedi, Das, and Mahajan 2021). Research from India has shown that, when women occupy leadership positions, they tend to give priority to issues valued more highly by women relative to men, such as access to toilets, clean drinking water, and water control and harvesting. Women, therefore, remain important change agents in communities when it comes to improving water resource management.

The gender-differentiated causes and impacts of displacement

The Internal Displacement Monitoring Center recorded 18.8 million new displacements associated with disasters in 2017; as of the end of that year, nearly 40 million people in more than 50 countries were living in internal displacement because of conflict or violence (IDMC 2018b). In 2020, the total global economic loss due to internal displacement was US$20.5 billion (IDMC 2021). Because of the growing frequency and intensity of natural hazards, the social and economic impacts of disaster-driven displacement are expected to continue rising globally. In addition to its economic costs, displacement may have many negative socioeconomic effects, such as separating the displaced culturally and socially from their original communities, less security, worse sanitary conditions with degradation of housing quality, interrupted education for many children, and less access to health care (IDMC 2018a).

Moreover, postdisaster displacement is a gendered process. Multiple socio-cultural factors such as income, education, health, and access to natural resources affect women's adaptive capacities, which in turn affect their likelihood of displacement (Chindarkar 2012). Studies in Bangladesh find that cultural norms could prevent women from leaving home during emergencies (Nelson et al. 2002), whereas in high-income countries such as the United States women evacuate to fulfill family obligations and caregiving duties (Bateman and Edwards 2002). In low-income countries like Nepal, women tend to have a low capacity to adapt to displacement, and their low nutritional status could exacerbate postdisaster recovery (Cannon 2002). Women's low education levels could push them into labor-intensive and low-paying jobs (Kakissis 2010), and women are more likely to be permanently displaced because they lack housing ownership (Willinger 2008) and employment opportunities. Moreover, women face greater risks of gender-based violence and distress because of social disintegration (Mitchell, Tanner, and Lussier 2007).

To achieve more inclusive disaster risk management policies, governments should take into account gender differences in the effects of hazards. The studies just noted point out gender-differentiated impacts in various disaster contexts. Because of limitations in conventional data such as surveys, however, these studies lack regional-scale and temporally granular analysis. Some questions remain unanswered: What factors determine gender differences in initial and long-term displacement rates and travel distances? Do men and women choose migration destinations differently, and, if so, how? Novel mobility data provide valuable opportunities to shed light on such questions.

Mobility data for disaster displacement analysis

Efforts to quantitatively understand the movement of large populations within and across cities before, during, and after disaster events use large-scale GPS location data sets (mobility data) collected from smartphones and mobile phones. These sources present an advantage because they provide real-time data and do so more cost-efficiently than surveys. For policy interventions, mobility data collected with high spatial and temporal granularity offer better monitoring, forecasting, and understanding of mass population movements across a longer time horizon. With careful handling of the data and adequate safeguards to protect users' privacy, mobility data hold immense potential for helping disaster relief agencies and policy makers build inclusive, sustainable, and resilient cities (World Bank 2021f).

In the aftermath of a disaster, such analyses of mobility data could provide support for rapidly directing resources to the hardest-hit areas. In their seminal paper, Lu, Bengtsson, and Holme (2012) used call detail record data collected from mobile phones to study the predictability of displacement mobility patterns after the 2010 Haiti earthquake. Based on data collected from 1.9 million mobile phone users over the period from 42 days before the shock to 341 days after the shock, the study estimated that 23 percent of the population in Port-au-Prince had been displaced by the earthquake. Despite the substantial displacement, they also found that the destinations of the displaced were highly correlated with their pre-earthquake mobility patterns. This finding shows the possibility of predicting postdisaster mobility patterns and has significant implications for relief operations, including the predisaster positioning of distribution centers and evacuation shelters.

Another disaster, the Gorkha earthquake—which measured 7.8 on the moment magnitude scale when it struck Nepal in 2015—also highlights the use of mobile phone location data. Wilson et al. (2016) rapidly analyzed the displacement movements of 12 million de-identified mobile phone users within nine days of the earthquake. During that period, an estimated 390,000 people left the Kathmandu Valley. On a longer time scale, Lu et al. (2016) used call detail record data for three months during and two years following Cyclone Mahasen to quantify the magnitude, direction, duration, and seasonality of migration in Bangladesh.[30]

Toward gender-differential displacement analysis

Despite the increasing use of large-scale mobility data for analyzing disaster-induced movement patterns, gender-differentiated impacts have been difficult to assess because of the lack of gender-labeled data. To overcome this data gap, the Data for Good team at Facebook (now Meta), in collaboration with the Internal Displacement Monitoring Center, produced Data for Good Displacement maps, which provide gender-aggregated and anonymized estimates of displacement based on information from Facebook users who have enabled location history. The goal of these maps is to help humanitarian organizations understand the origins and destinations of displaced people, and when those people can return to their homes. The maps use inverse probability weighting to correct potential biases in the Facebook user group and to improve the population data set's representativeness of the true underlying sociodemographic and economic characteristics.[31]

Map 3.3 **Displacement mobility patterns following Cyclone Yaas, east coast of India and the Bengal area of Bangladesh, May 2021**

a. Males

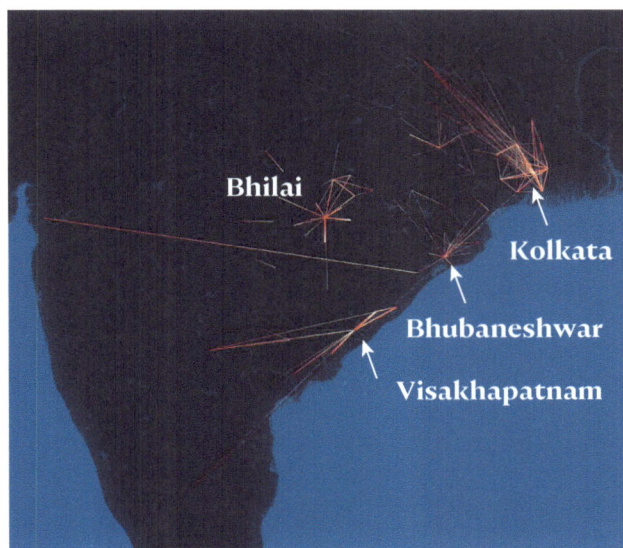

b. Females

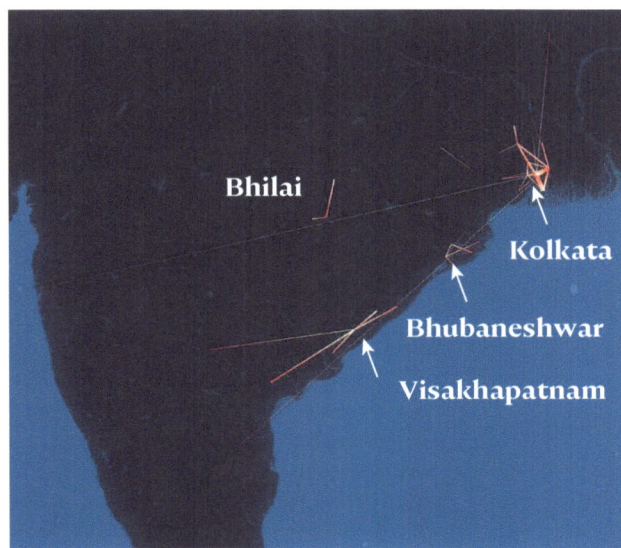

Source: World Bank analysis using data from kepler.gl.

Note: Comparison of maps reveals that displaced males move farther away than displaced females.

Using Meta's displacement data, Yabe et al. (2022), in a background paper prepared for this report, analyze the displacement behavioral differences across gender both during and after Cyclone Yaas, which struck the east coast of India in May 2021. The data used in their study provide estimates of the number of males and females displaced from one city to another, covering more than 100 cities in the region. Map 3.3 shows the origins and destinations of displaced people after the cyclone. In 55–60 percent of the cities affected by the cyclone, more men than women were displaced, both over the short term (14 days) and long term (50 days after landfall of the cyclone), and they traveled farther. Kolkata was the largest major city affected by the cyclone, with 4.0 percent of males and 2.1 percent of females displaced in the two weeks following landfall.

Further quantitative analysis of displacement destinations using regression models reveals that displaced males and females differ significantly in how they choose their destinations. Distance to destination, distance from coastline, and inequality of wealth in the destination city were all significant factors in the choice of destination for male displaced populations, whereas the social connectedness index (computed by the density of friend ties on Facebook between two cities) was most significant in the choices of displaced females. This finding is consistent with previous findings that women suffer more than men from disintegration of social ties (Mitchell, Tanner, and Lussier 2007) and that social ties (friends and family) can provide a major source of support for women because of their lack of economic independence (Kaya 2018).

Such insights could help better design programs aimed at supporting and empowering displaced women in undertaking economic independence and recovery (UN OCHA 2019). Moreover, if data agreements and analytical pipelines are prepared beforehand, near real-time analysis of gender-differentiated displacement patterns could aid decision-makers in effectively delivering disaster relief aid and financial support. An important future step would be to expand the study to multiple disaster events worldwide to evaluate gender-differentiated effects in regions with different cultural backgrounds and under different levels of disruptions caused by a hazard.

Climate change may be slowing the urban escalator out of poverty

By providing economic opportunities and amenities, urban areas can support poverty reduction. The urban–rural gaps in poverty and living standards remain stark. As shown in figure 3.2, when both poverty and urban areas are measured in a globally consistent manner, poverty rates in urban areas—particularly cities with a higher population density—tend to be lower than in rural areas (Combes et al. 2022). Nonmonetary living standards also tend to be better in denser areas (Gollin, Kirchberger, and Lagakos 2021).[32] Beyond such static comparisons, urban areas have proven to facilitate poverty reduction if the urban poor have escaped from poverty over time, if rural-to-urban migrants have escaped from poverty, and if the rural poor benefit from urban areas through, for example, a higher demand for agricultural products and higher remittances from urban areas. Indeed, despite the prevalence of chronic poverty in Sub-Saharan Africa, upward mobility is higher in urban areas than in rural areas (Dang and Dabalen 2019).

Figure 3.2   **Poverty rates at US$1.90 per day, by degree of urbanization classification, selected countries**

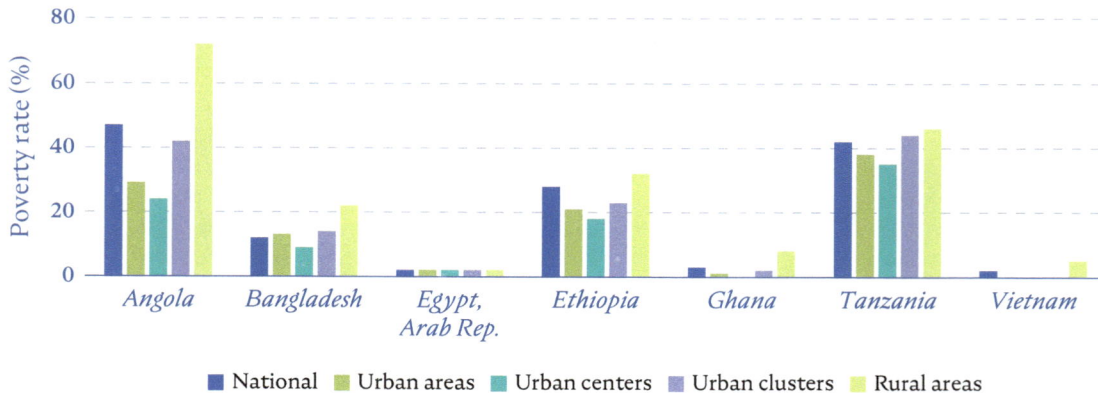

Legend: ■ National   ■ Urban areas   ■ Urban centers   ■ Urban clusters   ■ Rural areas

Source: Combes et al. 2022.

Note: Poverty is measured using the international poverty line of US$1.90 per day, 2011, purchasing power parity–adjusted. Because of the modifications in consumption aggregates and spatial price deflators, the national-level poverty rates do not match the official international poverty rates. Urban centers, urban clusters, and rural areas are classified using the degree of urbanization definition applied to WorldPop data. See Combes et al. (2022) for details.

Although poverty, measured by monetary income or consumption, constitutes an important dimension of inclusiveness, it provides only a static picture of the distribution of welfare outcomes across segments of a city's population at a particular time. In this context, arguably even more important to inclusiveness is the extent to which a city can facilitate the upward movement of households in the income distribution over time, especially the extent to which the city's environment provides the conditions to facilitate a household's escape from poverty and, from there, up into the middle class. According to the prominent urban economist Edward Glaeser (2012), existing empirical evidence suggests that cities provide an "escalator out of poverty." Moreover, that escalator operates faster in larger cities, even though those cities tend to have higher levels of income inequality.[33]

As the incidence of climatic shocks continues to rise, however, cities may fail to fulfill their potential as the escalator out of poverty. Urban residents remain vulnerable or chronically poor if deprived of access to economic opportunities and amenities in, for example, informal settlements (Marx, Stoker, and Suri 2013). It is also possible that high migration costs prevent all but a limited share of people from migrating to urban areas (Lagakos 2020). Moreover, the lack of space and affordable housing in urban destinations limits the number of migrants that can be accommodated or forces them to live in peripheral and possibly environmentally hazardous areas, leaving them trapped in poverty and squalor. Meanwhile, urban economies may have no spillover effects to rural economies if they are not integrated by adequate connective infrastructure. The impacts of climate and environmental shocks exacerbate such failures. For example, flooding could worsen vulnerability and chronic poverty in urban areas because the poor have a limited financial buffer to cope with shocks. In addition, as described in earlier sections, poor people in cities tend to live in areas prone to flooding, so their assets are more exposed to shocks. Thus, climate change–related and other environmental stresses, especially in interaction with the other stresses associated with urban population growth, could slow down, or even halt completely, a city's poverty escape escalator.

Chile and Colombia are two examples of countries in which climatic risks appear to have weakened upward mobility in urban areas. A background paper prepared for this report by Abanokova et al. (2022) analyzes the transitions in households' poverty status by applying a synthetic panel analysis as used in Dang et al. (2014).[34] Their analysis reveals that in the two countries many people have escaped from poverty in urban areas. In Colombia, 13 percent of the urban poor escaped from poverty between 2008 and 2010, and, in Chile, almost 65 percent between 2011 and 2015. In both countries, people in larger cities were more likely to escape from poverty (figure 3.3); however, as flood risks rose in large cities, the transition from poor to nonpoor essentially halted. In cities with large populations, households in high flood-risk areas have a substantially lower predicted probability of escaping from poverty than those in low-risk areas.

A similar pattern is observed in Indonesia, where climate shocks have lessened the ability of urban areas to reduce poverty. An empirical analysis conducted for this report using panel data from the Indonesia Family and Life Survey, and building on a study by Setiawan, Tiwari, and Rizal (2018), confirms that from 1993 to 2014 people moving to large metro areas had a higher chance of escaping poverty (figure 3.4). In those areas, however, flood risks appear to have reduced such upward mobility; the predicted probability of escaping from poverty was low in large metro areas experiencing extreme rainfalls. Thus, climate shocks in urban areas may make an escape from poverty less likely. In other words, cities more exposed to and less able to manage these stresses will be less inclusive in terms of the opportunities they provide for moving up the welfare ladder.

Figure 3.3 Predicted probability of escaping poverty, by town population size and flood risk, Colombia and Chile

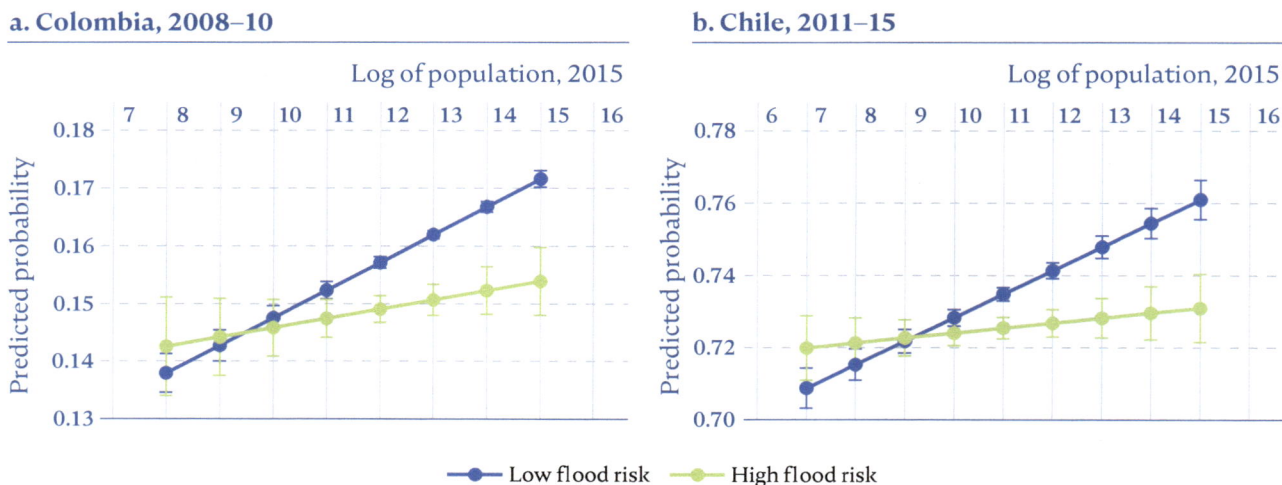

a. Colombia, 2008–10

b. Chile, 2011–15

— Low flood risk — High flood risk

Source: Abanokova et al. 2022.

Note: The vertical axis indicates the probability of a change from poor to nonpoor predicted for each household by the synthetic panel analysis. Poverty is measured by the upper-middle-income poverty line of US$5.50 per day, 2011, purchasing power parity–adjusted. The horizontal axis indicates the log of town populations. The flood risk is classified high for municipalities (Colombia) and ***comuna*** (Chile), within a 100-year flood return period, with the top 25 percent flood depth in each country.

Figure 3.4 Predicted probability of escaping poverty, by location, Indonesia, 1993–2014

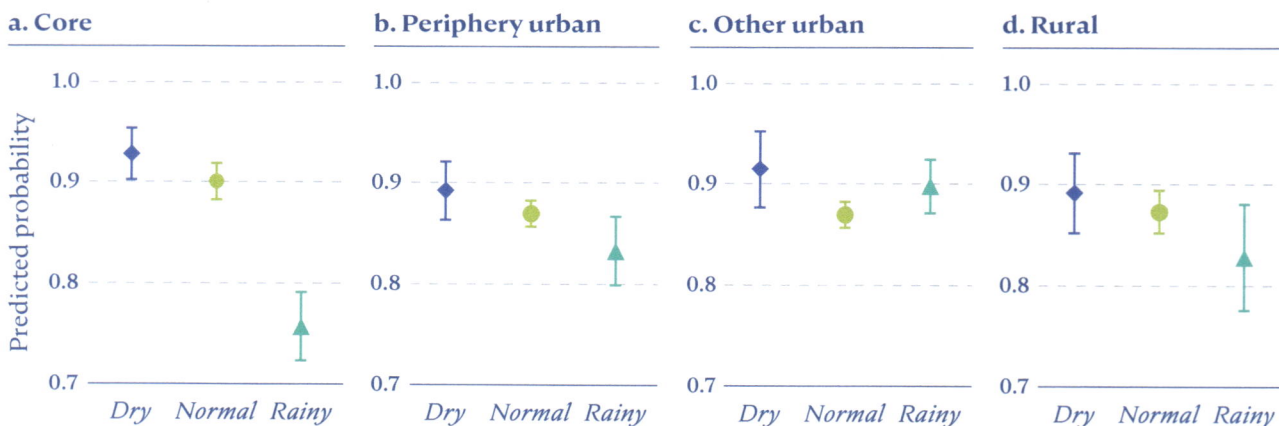

a. Core

b. Periphery urban

c. Other urban

d. Rural

Source: Abanokova et al. 2022.

Note: The probability of being nonpoor is predicted for each household based on the two-way fixed-effects regression model using the five rounds of the Indonesia Family and Life Survey panel data. Locations are classified by core (multidistrict metro cores), periphery urban (urban noncore districts), other urban (single-district metros or nonmetro urban districts), and rural districts. See Roberts, Gil Sander, and Tiwari (2019) for details. The rainy year district is identified with a Standardized Precipitation-Evapotranspiration Index (SPEI) score of 2 or greater.

Summary and conclusions

The effects of a changing climate on cities are heterogeneous across places, sectors, and people. Because cities concentrate people, activities, and infrastructure, they can experience intense direct effects of climate shocks and stressors. These direct effects include rapid-onset events— such as extreme heat and cold, floods, and wildfires—and slow-onset events—such as drought, air pollution, and land degradation. But these impacts do not occur in isolation; they interact and compound, making the effects more uncertain and potentially more disastrous. Yet investments in durable construction (representing capital that would be very difficult to reallocate) continue in locations that may become unlivable over time. The patterns of displacement in response to sudden shocks illustrate gender-differentiated characteristics, suggesting the existence of many poorly understood facets of response that require attention.

Cities function as part of a larger environment. Climate shocks in rural areas lead to faster urbanization because local-level migration represents an important coping mechanism, particularly in poorer countries. Such climate-induced migration is also associated with growing urban sprawl, often expanding informal settlements where service delivery remains a challenge. Droughts in rural areas affect cities not only via migration but also by directly affecting the urban water supply. Cities rely on rural areas for many natural resources—water is paramount, but food is also important. Climate shocks affect agricultural production and productivity, with impacts spilling over to urban areas through higher and more volatile food prices.

Climate change affects population groups in cities differently. In many cities, the poor, though not all of them, are more exposed to climate hazards. This increased exposure could result from sorting and information asymmetries and because the urban poor trade safety for better access to jobs or services. Even if not the most exposed, the poor are hardest-hit by climate shocks and are the most vulnerable because they are least able to mitigate the effects of hazards, such as through access to financial or insurance markets. In addition, those with lower levels of education or working in informal jobs will likely feel more significant effects through sharper falls in their productivity. For these reasons, climate change may be slowing the urban escalator out of poverty.

Notes

1. The cost of morbidity includes resource costs (the financial costs of avoiding or treating pollution-associated illnesses), opportunity costs (the indirect costs of loss of time for work and leisure), and disutility costs (the cost of pain, suffering, or discomfort)—see World Bank (2020c).

2. By contrast, the intangible impacts, such as disruptions of commuters' travel routes, are difficult to quantify. According to He, Liu, et al. (2021), clusters of low-income residents incur a large share of the effects of disruptions. Their study reveals that the regular floods in Kinshasa, Democratic Republic of Congo, affected transportation services (increasing public transit headways, forcing transit rerouting, and decreasing travel speeds) and job accessibility (causing travel delays resulting in losses in accessibility).

3. This complexity is equally, if not more, relevant to how responses to climate events are framed. For example, water management would have to respond simultaneously to intensifying droughts and floods—a subject addressed in more detail in chapter 5.

4. *Global warming* is a shorthand term. Climate models predict that some places may become warmer, some cooler, some wetter, some drier, and some stormier or less stormy.

5. Because of differences in ocean dynamics and tectonics, sea level does not rise uniformly across space. A 1°C rise in global temperatures could result in more than a 2°C rise in some northern latitudes, but only a 0.5°C rise in some equatorial regions.

6. Warming trends are nonlinear. Warming accelerated over most of the twentieth century, but the trend has been much stronger since 1980 (Franzke 2014).

7. Emporis data cover 693,855 completed buildings, along with their exact geographical coordinates, year of construction, and date of demolition. The data set mostly captures buildings over 55 meters tall. Skyscrapers are defined as buildings more than 100 meters tall.

8. The study uses the mean of the max (daytime) temperatures during the hottest season as a proxy for whether a city is a "future bad location."

9. If a country has only bad locations in the future, one consideration is whether the government may want to hedge its real estate portfolio by encouraging its economic agents (those who influence capital markets and the economy at large) to invest in real estate abroad.

10. The US Congress enacted the Dodd-Frank Act in July 2010 to tackle this specific issue. Similar legislation was then enacted in the European Union and the United Kingdom.

11. For simplicity's sake, *industrialized countries* are defined as those in which agriculture's share of national income in 1985 was greater than 30 percent.

12. This finding is based on analysis of nighttime lights data.

13. An early example is an innovative decision by New York City to acquire land in the nearby Catskills region to filter and store water in natural ecosystems, saving the city US$6 billion in capital costs related to building a water filtration plant (Damania et al. 2017).

14. These studies are based on spatial analysis of the impact of rural shocks on urban food prices, controlling for international commodity prices (based on the commodity price index of the

Food and Agriculture Organization of the United Nations) and differentiating by type of food group—that is, perishable and nonperishable food items.

15. Assessment of the mitigation of the impact of shocks and stressors is based on travel time to the nearest city, which depends on the type and quality of the road network (Meijer et al. 2018; Nelson et al. 2019).

16. South Asia: Jalalabad and Kabul (Afghanistan); Chittagong (Bangladesh); Auraiya, Amritsar, and Kanpur (India); Karachi (Pakistan); Colombo and Kandy (Sri Lanka). Sub-Saharan Africa: Bujumbura (Burundi); Ougadougou (Burkina Faso); Bangui (Central African Republic); Bamako (Mali); Niamey (Niger); N'djamena (Chad); Bulawayo, Harare, and Mutare (Zimbwabwe).

17. The South Asian data were produced in World Bank projects in 2014 and 2015 from surveying high-resolution imagery to determine land use categories for city parcels. The data for African cities are at a higher resolution and were assembled for this report. Formal residential areas are predicted using an unsupervised machine learning algorithm (Chlouba, Mukim, and Zaveri 2022).

18. Accordingly, when the sample is split by region, slums in Sub-Saharan Africa are, on average, less exposed to both hazards, whereas the opposite is true in South Asia.

19. This refers to the sorting of different types of workers across locations due to employment opportunities or differences in amenities (Couture et al. 2019; Diamond 2016; Moretti 2013).

20. The literature on rural-urban migration confirms the existence of such informational gaps but points to an opposite effect: the lack of information on higher returns in urban areas discourages advantageous migration (Aker, Clemens, and Ksoll 2011; Baseler 2021; Bryan, Chowdhury, and Mobarak 2014).

21. For example, a rich body of literature in development economics documents how the poor possess lower financial literacy; thus, their acquisition of financial information can have substantial positive welfare effects, among others (Hastings, Madrian, and Skimmyhorn 2013; Karlan, Ratan,and Zinman 2014; Lusardi and Mitchell 2014).

22. The Harmonized Survey on Household Living Conditions (Enquête Harmonisée sur les Conditions de Vie des Ménages) is conducted in West African Economic and Monetary Union member states to provide governments with reliable statistics to underpin their poverty reduction efforts. Data collection took place in two rounds: October 17–December 31, 2018, and April 1– June 30, 2019. The results are representative at the subnational level and across Bamako in both urban and rural areas (World Bank 2021d).

23. Those below the poverty line had losses four to five times higher than the monthly income of low-income households, three times higher those of middle-income households, and two times higher than those of the high-income group. Patankar and Patwardhan (2016) also find that poor people have lost 60 percent more of their estimated wealth relative to nonpoor people.

24. Originally from World Bank and Australian AID (2014). The survey conducted in Ho Chi Minh City reveals that 86 percent of surveyed poor households had more health problems stemming from polluted flood water, compared with 64 percent of nonpoor ones. Sixty-nine percent of the poor were affected in terms of employment and 67 percent in terms of income, compared with 56 percent and 40 percent, respectively, of the nonpoor.

25. The agglomerations are Denpasar in Bali; Jakarta (Jabodetabek), Pasuruan, Probolinggo, Semarang, Surabaya, and Yogyakarta in Java; and Medan in Sumatra. Educational attainment

refers to the highest level of schooling or qualification that a worker has acquired, ranging from incomplete primary school to tertiary degrees. (Roberts, Gil Sander, and Tiwari 2019).

26. The empirical analysis consists of regressing the relevant measure of environmental risk (either pluvial or fluvial flood risk or excessive heat) on the average level of education in the village and city fixed effects, thereby capturing the variation within cities.

27. Almost one-fourth of the world's urban population, over a billion people, lives in informal settlements or slums with 80 percent in East and Southeast Asia, Sub-Saharan Africa, and Central and South Asia, https://unstats.un.org/sdgs/report/2019/goal-11/.

28. This includes their underrepresentation in (1) water supply and sanitation utilities and ministries; (2) agencies allocating emergency or postdisaster recovery assistance; (3) firms and businesses that stand to benefit from emergency relief; and (4) increasingly important upstream decisions on water allocations and technical options for more sustainable water management (UNICEF 2016).

29. These surveys constitute the first industrywide global database on gender diversity in water institutions. Additional surveys will expand the database through the Equal Aqua platform, a collaborative initiative launched by the World Bank to deepen the dialogue on gender diversity and inclusion in water sector jobs. See World Bank Water Data for summaries of past and ongoing surveys, https://wbwaterdata.org/breakingbarriers/home/.

30. For a comprehensive review on the scientific literature and the usage of mobility data for disaster response and recovery, see Yabe et al. (2022).

31. Facebook Data for Good, Displacement Maps: Methodology, 2021, https://dataforgood.facebook.com/dfg/docs/methodology-displacement-maps.

32. Examples of the nonmonetary dimensions of urban poverty include squalid living conditions, risks from the dis-amenities of urbanization (poor sanitation, air pollution, crime and violence, traffic accidents), and increasing disaster risks.

33. For evidence of this for Indonesian cities, see chapter 4 in Roberts, Gil Sander, and Tiwari (2019).

34. The synthetic panel analysis creates pseudo-panel data from a repeated cross-sectional household survey data set, by which the changes in poverty status among the sample households for two time points can be analyzed.

References

Abanokova, K., H.-A. Dang, S. Nakamura, S. Takamatsu, C. Pei, and D. Prospere. 2022. "Is Climate Change Slowing the Urban Escalator out of Poverty? Evidence from Indonesia and LAC." Background paper prepared for this report, World Bank, Washington, DC.

Abas, N., M. S. Saleem, E. Kalair, and N. Khan. 2019. "Cooperative Control of Regional Transboundary Air Pollutants." *Environmental Systems Research* 8 (1): 1–14.

Abel, G. J., M. Brottrager, J. C. Cuaresma, and R. Muttarak. 2019. "Climate, Conflict and Force Migration." *Global Environmental Change* 54: 239–49.

Abwola, N., and I. Michelis. 2020. *What Happened? How the Humanitarian Response to COVID-19 Failed to Protect Women and Girls*. International Rescue Committee, New York.

Aker, J. C., M. A. Clemens, and C. Ksoll. 2011. "Mobiles and Mobility: The Effect of Mobile Phones on Migration in Niger." *Proceedings of the German Development Economics Conference*, Berlin.

Andrews, O., C. Le Quéré, T. Kjellstrom, B. Lemke, and A. Haines. 2018. "Implications for Workability and Survivability in Populations Exposed to Extreme Heat under Climate Change: A Modelling Study." *Lancet Planetary Health* 2 (12): e540–47.

Anenberg, S. C., P. Achakulwisut, M. Brauer, D. Moran, J. S. Apte, and D. K. Henze. 2019. "Particulate Matter–Attributable Mortality and Relationships with Carbon Dioxide in 250 Urban Areas Worldwide." *Scientific Reports* 9 (1): 1–6.

Avashia, V., and A. Garg. 2020. "Implications of Land Use Transitions and Climate Change on Local Flooding in Urban Areas: An Assessment of 42 Indian Cities." *Land Use Policy* 95: 104571.

Avner, P., and S. Hallegatte. 2019. "Moral Hazard vs. Land Scarcity: Flood Management Policies for the Real World." Policy Research Working Paper 9012, World Bank, Washington, DC.

Azunre, G. A., O. Amponsah, S. A. Takyi, H. Mensah, and I. Braimah. 2022. "Urban Informalities in Sub-Saharan Africa (SSA): A Solution for or Barrier against Sustainable City Development." *World Development* 152: 105782.

Baez, J. E., L. Lucchetti, M. E. Genoni, and M. Salazar. 2017. "Gone with the Storm: Rainfall Shocks and Household Well-Being in Guatemala." *Journal of Development Studies* 53 (8): 1253–71.

Bai, Y., L. Costlow, A. Ebel, S. Laves, Y. Ueda, N. Volin, M. Zamek, A. Herforth, and W. Masters. 2021. "Review: Retail Consumer Price Data Reveals Gaps and Opportunities to Monitor Food Systems for Nutrition." *Food Policy* 104: 1021–48.

Bakkensen, L. A., and L. Barrage. 2021. "Going Underwater? Flood Risk Belief Heterogeneity and Coastal Home Price Dynamics." *Review of Financial Studies* 35 (8): 3666–709.

Balboni, C. 2021. "In Harm's Way? Infrastructure Investments and the Persistence of Coastal Cities." Department of Economics, Massachusetts Institute of Technology, Cambridge, MA.

Baldauf, M., L. Garlappi, and C. Yannelis. 2020. "Does Climate Change Affect Real Estate Prices? Only if You Believe in It." *Review of Financial Studies* 33 (3): 1256–95.

Banerjee, A. V., and S. Mullainathan. 2008. "Limited Attention and Income Distribution." *American Economic Review* 98 (2): 489–93.

Bangalore, M., A. Smith, and T. Veldkamp. 2019. "Exposure to Floods, Climate Change, and Poverty in Vietnam." *Economics of Disasters and Climate Change* 3 (1): 79–99.

Barrios, S., L. Bertinelli, and E. Strobl. 2006. "Climate Change and Rural-Urban Migration: The Case of Sub-Saharan Africa." *Journal of Urban Economics* 26: 656–73.

Baseler, T. 2021. "Hidden Income and the Perceived Returns to Migration." http://dx.doi .org/10.2139/ssrn.3534715.

Bateman, J. M., and B. Edwards. 2002. "Gender and Evacuation: A Closer Look at Why Women Are More Likely to Evacuate for Hurricanes." *Natural Hazards Review* 3 (3): 107–17.

Baylis, P., and J. Boomhower. 2019. "Moral Hazard, Wildfires, and the Economic Incidence of Natural Disasters." NBER Working Paper 26550, National Bureau of Economic Research, Cambridge, MA. https://ssrn.com/abstract=3504434.

Bellisario, J., G. Cowan, and A. Raisz. 2021. *The True Cost of Wildfires: Analyzing the Impact of Wildfires on the California Economy*. Berkeley, CA: Bay Area Council Economic Institute.

Bento-Gonçalves, A., and A. Vieira. 2020. "Wildfires in the Wildland-Urban Interface: Key Concepts and Evaluation Methodologies." *Science of the Total Environment* 707: 135592.

Benveniste, H., M. Oppenheimer, and M. Fleurbaey. 2020. "Effect of Border Policy on Exposure and Vulnerability to Climate Change." *Proceedings of the National Academy of Sciences* 117 (43): 26692–702.

Bernstein, A., M. T. Gustafson, and R. Lewis. 2019. "Disaster on the Horizon: The Price Effect of Sea Level Rise." *Journal of Financial Economics* 134 (2): 253–72.

Bertinelli, L., and E. Strobl. 2013. "Quantifying the Local Economic Growth Impact of Hurricane Strikes." *Journal of Applied Meteorology and Climatology* 52 (8): 1688–97.

Bilal, A., and E. Rossi-Hansberg. 2021. "Location as an Asset." *Econometrica* 89 (5): 2459–95.

Borgomeo, E., A. Jägerskog, E. Zaveri, J. Russ, A. Khan, and R. Damania. 2021. *Ebb and Flow, Volume 2: Water in the Shadow of Conflict in the Middle East and North Africa*. Washington, DC: World Bank.

Bosetti, V., C. Cattaneo, and G. Peri. 2021. "Should They Stay or Should They Go? Climate Migrants and Local Conflicts." *Journal of Economic Geography* 21 (4): 619–51.

Botzen, W. W., O. Deschenes, and M. Sanders. 2019. "The Economic Impacts of Natural Disasters: A Review of Models and Empirical Studies." *Review of Environmental Economics and Policy* 13 (2): 167–88.

Broadbent, A. M., E. S. Krayenhoff, and M. Georgescu. 2020. "The Motley Drivers of Heat and Cold Exposure in 21st Century US Cities." *Proceedings of the National Academy of Sciences* 117 (35): 21108–17.

Bryan, G., S. Chowdhury, and A. M. Mobarak. 2014. "Underinvestment in a Profitable Technology: The Case of Seasonal Migration in Bangladesh." *Econometrica* 82 (5): 1671–748.

Burke, M., S. M. Hsiang, and E. Miguel. 2015. "Climate and Conflict." *Annual Review of Economics* 7: 577–617.

Burzynski, M., C. Deuster, F. Docquier, and J. de Melo. 2019. "Climate Change, Inequality, and Human Migration." Discussion Paper Series 13997, Centre for Economic Policy Research, London.

Campos Garcia, A., N. Holm-Nielsen, C. Diaz G., D. M. Rubiano V., C. R. Costa P., F. Ramirez C., and E. Dickson. 2011. *Analysis of Disaster Risk Management in Colombia: A Contribution to the Creation of Public Policies*. Washington, DC: World Bank.

Cannon, T. 2002. "Gender and Climate Hazards in Bangladesh." *Gender and Development* 10 (2): 45–50.

Cashin, P., K. Mohaddes, and M. Raissi. 2017. "Fair Weather or Foul? The Macroeconomic Effects of El Niño." *Journal of International Economics* 106: 37–54.

Castells-Quintana, D., M. Krause, and T. K. J. McDermott. 2021. "The Urbanising Force of Global Warming: The Role of Climate Change in the Spatial Distribution of Population." *Journal of Economic Geography* 21: 531–56.

Castells-Quintana, D., M. d. P. Lopez-Uribe, and T. K. J. McDermott. 2018. "Adaptation to Climate Change: A Review through a Development Economics Lens." *World Development* 104: 183–96.

Cattaneo, C., M. Beine, C. Fröhlich, D. Kniveton, I. Martínez-Zarzoso, M. Mastrorillo, K. Millock, et al. 2019. "Human Migration in the Era of Climate Change." *Review of Environmental Economics and Policy* 13: 189–206.

CEDLAS (Center for Distributive, Labor and Social Studies) and World Bank. 2014. *A Guide to SEDLAC—Socio-Economic Database for Latin America and the Caribbean*. Washington, DC: World Bank.

Chattopadhyay, R., and E. Duflo. 2004. "Women as Policy Makers: Evidence from a Randomized Policy Experiment in India." *Econometrica* 72 (5): 1409–43.

Chaturvedi, S., S. Das, and K. Mahajan. 2021. "The Importance of Being Earnest: What Explains the Gender Quota Effect in Politics?" Working Paper No. 52, Department of Economics, Ashoka University, Haryana, India.

Chindarkar, N. 2012. "Gender and Climate Change–Induced Migration: Proposing a Framework for Analysis." *Environmental Research Letters* 7 (2): 025601.

Ching, J., and M. Kajino. 2020. "Rethinking Air Quality and Climate Change after COVID-19." *International Journal of Environmental Research and Public Health* 17 (14): 5167.

Chlouba, V., M. Mukim, and E. Zaveri. 2022. "How Do Climate Change-Related Stressors Affect Urban Form?" Background paper prepared for this report, World Bank, Washington, DC.

Choy, D. L., P. Clarke, S. Serrao-Neumann, R. Hales, O. Koschade, and D. Jones. 2016. "Coastal Urban and Peri-Urban Indigenous People's Adaptive Capacity to Climate Change." In *Balanced Urban Development: Options and Strategies for Liveable Cities*, vol. 72, edited by B. Maheshwari, B. Thoradeniya, and V. P. Singh, 441–61. Capital Region of Denmark: Cham Springer.

Cohen, A. J., M. Brauer, R. Burnett, H. R. Anderson, J. Frostad, K. Estep, K. Balakrishnan et al. 2017. "Estimates and 25-Year Trends of the Global Burden of Disease Attributable to Ambient Air Pollution: An Analysis of Data from the Global Burden of Diseases Study 2015." *Lancet* 389: 1907–18.

Colon, C., S. Hallegate, and J. Rozenberg. 2021. "Criticality Analysis of a Country's Transport Network via an Agent-Based Supply Chain Model." *Nature Sustainability* 4: 209–15.

Combes, P-P., S. Nakamura, M. Roberts, and B. Stewart. 2022. "Estimating Urban Poverty Consistently across Countries." World Bank Poverty and Equity Notes, World Bank, Washington, DC.

Conte, B., K. Desmet, D. Nagy, and E. Rossi-Hansberg. 2021. "Local Sectoral Specialization in a Warming World." *Journal of Economic Geography* 21 (4): 493–530.

Couture, V., C. Gaubert, J. Handbury, and E. Hurst. 2019. "Income Growth and the Distributional Effects of Urban Spatial Sorting." NBER Working Paper 26142, National Bureau of Economic Research, Cambridge, MA.

Croitoru, L., J. C. Chang, and J. Akpokodje. 2020. "The Health Cost of Ambient Air Pollution in Lagos." *Journal of Environmental Protection* 11: 753–65.

Cruz, J-L., and E. Rossi-Hansberg. 2021. "The Economic Geography of Global Warming." NBER Working Paper 28466, National Bureau of Economic Research, Cambridge, MA.

Damania, R., S. Desbureaux, M. Hyland, A. Islam, S. Moore, A.-S. Rodella, J. Russ, and E. Zaveri. 2017. *Uncharted Waters: The New Economics of Water Scarcity and Variability.* Washington, DC: World Bank.

Dang, H.-A. H., and A. L. Dabalen. 2019. "Is Poverty in Africa Mostly Chronic or Transient? Evidence from Synthetic Panel Data." *Journal of Development Studies* 55 (7): 1527–47.

Dang, H.-A. H., P. Lanjouw, J. Luoto, and D. McKenzie. 2014. "Using Repeated Cross-Sections to Explore Movements into and out of Poverty." *Journal of Development Economics* 107: 112–28.

Das, M. B. 2017. *The Rising Tide: A New Look at Water and Gender.* Washington, DC: World Bank.

Das, M. B. 2020. "Dry Cities Can't Be Healthy without Reducing Inequalities." *BMJ Opinion* (blog), November 16, 2020. https://blogs.bmj.com/bmj/2020/11/16/dry -cities-cant-be-healthy-without-reducing-inequalities/.

Das., P. 2014. "Women's Participation in Community-Level Water Governance in Urban India: The Gap between Motivation and Ability." *World Development* 64: 206–18.

Dasgupta, S., M. S. Islam, M. Huq, Z. Huque Khan, and M. R. Hasib. 2019. "Quantifying the Protective Capacity of Mangroves from Storm Surges in Coastal Bangladesh." *PLoS One* 14 (3): E0214079.

Dasgupta, S., N. van Maanen, S. N. Gosling, F. Piontek, C. Otto, and C-F. Schleussner. 2021. "Effects of Climate Change on Combined Labour Productivity and Supply: An Empirical, Multi-Model Study." *Lancet Planetary Health* 5 (7): E455–65.

Dercon, S., D. O. Gilligan, J. Hoddinott, and T. Woldehanna. 2009. "The Impact of Agricultural Extension and Roads on Poverty and Consumption Growth in Fifteen Ethiopian Villages." *American Journal of Agricultural Economics* 91 (4): 1007–21.

Deryugina, T. 2014. "The Fiscal Cost of Hurricanes: Disaster Aid versus Social Insurance." *American Economic Journal: Economic Policy* 9 (3): 168–98.

Desbureaux, S., and A.-S. Rodella. 2019. "Drought in the City: The Economic Impact of Water Scarcity in Latin American Metropolitan Areas." *World Development* 114: 13–27.

Desmet, K., and R. Jedwab. 2022. "Are We Over-building in 'Bad' Locations Globally? Future Climate Change and Durable Real Estate." Background prepared paper for this report, World Bank, Washington, DC.

Desmet, K., and E. Rossi-Hansberg. 2011. "Spatial Development." NBER Working Paper 15349, National Bureau of Economic Research, Cambridge, MA.

Desmet, K., and E. Rossi-Hansberg. 2012. "On the Spatial Economic Impact of Global Warming." NBER Working Paper 18546, National Bureau of Economic Research, Cambridge, MA.

Desmet, K., and E. Rossi-Hansberg. 2015. "The Geography of Development: Evaluating Migration Restrictions and Coastal Flooding." NBER Working Paper 21087, National Bureau of Economic Research, Cambridge, MA.

Desmet, K., R. E. Kopp, S. A. Kulp, D. K. Nagy, M. Oppenheimer, E. Rossi-Hansberg, and B. H. Strauss. 2021. "Evaluating the Economic Cost of Coastal Flooding." *American Economic Journal: Macroeconomics* 13 (2): 444–86.

Devoto, F., E. Duflo, P. Dupas, W. Parienté, and V. Pons. 2012. "Happiness on Tap: Piped Water Adoption in Urban Morocco." *American Economic Journal: Economic Policy* 4 (4): 68–99.

Diamond, R. 2016. "The Determinants and Welfare Implications of US Workers' Diverging Location Choices by Skill: 1980-2000." *American Economic Review* 106 (3): 479–524.

Dodman, D., B. Hayward, M. Pelling, V. Castan Broto, W. Chow, E. Chu, R. Dawson, et al. 2022. "Cities, Settlements and Key Infrastructure." In *Climate Change 2022: Impacts, Adaptation, and Vulnerability*, Contribution of Working Group II to the Sixth Assessment Report of the Intergovernmental Panel on Climate Change. Cambridge, UK: Cambridge University Press.

Dudley, N., and S. Stolton. 2003. *Running Pure: The Importance of Forest Protected Areas to Drinking Water*. Washington, DC: World Bank/WWF Alliance for Forest Conservation and Sustainable Use.

Erban, L. E., S. M. Gorelick, and H. A. Zebker. 2014. "Groundwater Extraction, Land Subsidence, and Sea-Level Rise in the Mekong Delta, Vietnam." *Environmental Research Letters* 9 (8): 084010.

Erman, A., M. Tariverdi, M. Obolensky, X. Chen, R. C. Vincent, S. Malgioglio, J. Rentschler, et al. 2019. "Wading Out the Storm: The Role of Poverty in Exposure, Vulnerability and Resilience to Floods in Dar es Salaam." Policy Research Working Paper 8976, World Bank, Washington, DC.

Erman, A., E. Motte, R. Goyal, A. Asare, S. Takamatsu, X. Chen, S. Malgioglio, A. Skinner, N. Yoshida, and S. Hallegatte. 2020. "The Road to Recovery: The Role of Poverty in the Exposure, Vulnerability and Resilience to Floods in Accra." *Economics of Disasters and Climate Change* 4 (1): 171–93.

Evans, G. W. 2019. "Projected Behavioral Impacts of Global Climate Change." *Annual Review of Psychology* 70: 449–74.

Fauconnier, I., A. Jenniskens, P. Perry, S. Fanaian, S. Sen, V. Sinha, and L. Witmer. 2018. *Women as Change-Makers in the Governance of Shared Waters*. Gland, Switzerland: International Union for Conservation of Nature.

Fay, M. 2005. *The Urban Poor in Latin America*. Washington, DC: World Bank.

Fitch, A. 2021. "Texas Winter Storm Strikes Chip Makers, Compounding Supply Woes." *Wall Street Journal*, February 17, 2021. https://www.wsj.com/articles/texas -winter-storm-strikes-chip-makers-compounding-supply-woes-11613588617.

Florczyk, A. J., M. Melchiorri, C. Corbane, M. Schiavina, M. Maffenini, M. Pesaresi, P. Politis, et al. 2019. "Description of the GHS Urban Centre Database 2015." Public Release 2019, Version 1.0, Publications Office of the European Union, Luxembourg.

Ford, J. D., T. Pearce, G. McDowell, L. Berrang-Ford, J. S. Sayles, and E. Belfer. 2018. "Vulnerability and Its Discontents: The Past, Present, and Future of Climate Change Vulnerability Research." *Climatic Change* 151 (2): 189–203.

Frame, D. J., S. M. Rosier, I. Noy, L. J. Harrington, T. Carey-Smith, S. N. Sparrow, D. A. Stone, and S. M. Dean. 2020. "Climate Change Attribution and the Economic Costs of Extreme Weather Events: A Study on Damages from Extreme Rainfall and Drought." *Climatic Change* 162 (2): 781–97.

Frame, D. J., M. F. Wehner, I. Noy, and S. M. Rosier. 2020. "The Economic Costs of Hurricane Harvey Attributable to Climate Change." *Climatic Change* 160 (2): 271–81.

Franzke, C. L. E. 2014. "Nonlinear Climate Change." *Nature Climate Change* 4: 423–24.

Frumkin, H., M. B. Das, M. Negev, B. C. Rogers, R. Bertollini, C. Dora, and S. Desai. 2020. "Protecting Health in Dry Cities: Considerations for Policy Makers." *BMJ* 2020: 371.

Garrick, D., L. De Stefano, L. Turley, I. Jorgensen, I. Aguilar-Barajas, B. Schreiner, R. de Souza Leão, et al. 2019. *Dividing the Water, Sharing the Benefits: Lessons from Rural-to-Urban Water Reallocation*. Washington, DC: World Bank.

GCRO (Gauteng City-Region Observatory). 2022. "Not Enough in the Right Place, Too Much in the Wrong Place: Understanding and Managing the Gauteng City-Region's Coupled Long-Term Water Challenges." Background paper prepared for this report, World Bank, Washington, DC.

Gencer, E., R. Folorunsho, M. Linkin, X. Wang, C. E. Natenzon, S. Wajih, N. Mani, et al. 2018. "Disasters and Risk in Cities." In *Climate Change and Cities: Second Assessment Report of the Urban Climate Change Research Network*, edited by C. Rosenzweig, W. Solecki, P. Romero-Lankao, S. Mehrotra, S. Dhakal, and S. Ali Ibrahim, 61–98. New York: Cambridge University Press.

Gilmore, E. A., C. Kousky, and T. St. Clair. 2022 "Climate Change Will Increase Local Government Fiscal Stress in the United States." *Nature Climate Change* 12: 210–18.

Glaeser, E. L. 2012. *Triumph of the City: How Our Greatest Invention Made Us Richer, Smarter, Greener, Healthier and Happier*. New York: Penguin Press.

Glaeser, E. L. 2014. "A World of Cities: The Causes and Consequences of Urbanization in Poorer Countries." *Journal of the European Economic Association* 12: 1154–99.

Gollin, D., M. Kirchberger, and D. Lagakos. 2021. "Do Urban Wage Premia Reflect Lower Amenities? Evidence from Africa." *Journal of Urban Economics* 121: 103301.

Gomez, M., A. Mejia, B. L. Ruddell, and R. R. Rushforth. 2021. "Supply Chain Diversity Buffers Cities against Food Shocks." *Nature* 595: 250–54.

Gonzalves G. S., E. H. Kaplan, and A. D. Paltiel. 2015. "Reducing Sexual Violence by Increasing the Supply of Toilets in Khayelitsha, South Africa: A Mathematical Model." *PLoS One* 10 (4): e0122244.

Graf von Luckner, C., K. Holston and C. Reinhart (2022, April 15). "Is Another Food Crisis Unfolding? Let's Talk Development." https://blogs.worldbank.org/developmenttalk/another -food-crisis-unfolding

Graham, J. P., M. Hirai, and S. S. Kim. 2016. "An Analysis of Water Collection Labor among Women and Children in 24 Sub-Saharan African Countries." *PLoS One* 11 (6): e0155981.

Green, R., L. Cornelsen, A. D. Dangour, R. Turner, B. Shankar, M. Mazzocchi, and R. D. Smith. 2013. "The Effect of Rising Food Prices on Food Consumption: Systematic Review with Meta-Regression." *BMJ* 346: f3703.

Gregory, J. 2017. "The Impact of Post-Katrina Rebuilding Grants on the Resettlement Choices of New Orleans Homeowners." Unpublished manuscript.

Grip, I. L., S. Haghighatafshar, and H. Aspegren. 2021. "A Methodology for the Assessment of Compound Sea Level and Rainfall Impact on Urban Drainage Networks in a Coastal City under Climate Change." *City and Environment Interactions* 12: 100074.

Hallegatte, S., M. Bangalore, L. Bonzanigo, M. Fay, T. Kane, U. Narloch, J. Rozenberg, et al. 2016. "Shock Waves: Managing the Impacts of Climate Change on Poverty." Washington, DC: World Bank.

Hallegatte, S., M. Bangalore, and A. Vogt-Schilb. 2016a. "Assessing Socioeconomic Resilience to Floods in 90 Countries." Policy Research Working Paper 7663, World Bank, Washington, DC.

Hallegatte, S., M. Bangalore, and A. Vogt-Schilb. 2016b. "Socioeconomic Resilience: Multi-Hazard Estimates in 117 Countries." Policy Research Working Paper 7886, World Bank, Washington, DC.

Hallegatte, S., C. Green, R. J. Nicholls, and J. Corfee-Morlot. 2013. "Future Flood Losses in Major Coastal Cities." *Nature Climate Change* 3: 802–06.

Hamilton, B., N. C. Coops, and K. Lokman. 2021. "Time Series Monitoring of Impervious Surfaces and Runoff Impacts in Metro Vancouver." *Science of the Total Environment* 760: 143873.

Harari, M., and E. La Ferrara. 2018. "Conflict, Climate, and Cells: A Disaggregated Analysis." *Review of Economics and Statistics* 100 (4): 594–608.

Harlan, S. L., and D. M. Ruddell. 2011. "Climate Change and Health in Cities: Impacts of Heat and Air Pollution and Potential Co-benefits from Mitigation and Adaptation." *Current Opinion in Environmental Sustainability* 3 (3): 126–34.

Hastings, J. S., B. C. Madrian, and W. L. Skimmyhorn. 2013. "Financial Literacy, Financial Education, and Economic Outcomes." *Annual Review of Economics* 5 (1): 347–73.

He, C., Z. Liu, J. Wu, X. Pan, Z. Fang, J. Li, and B.A. Bryan. 2021. "Future Global Urban Water Scarcity and Potential Solutions." *Nature Communications* 12 (1): 1–11.

He, Y., S. Thies, P. Avner, and J. Rentschler. 2021. "Flood Impacts on Urban Transit and Accessibility—A Case Study of Kinshasa." *Transportation Research Part D: Transport and Environment* 96: 102889.

He, Y., B. Wu, P. He, W. Gu, and B. Liu. 2021. "Wind Disasters Adaptation in Cities in a Changing Climate: A Systematic Review." *PLoS One* 16 (3): e0248503.

Heblich, S., A. Trew, and Y. Zylberberg. 2021. "East-Side Story: Historical Pollution and Persistent Neighborhood Sorting." *Journal of Political Economy* 129 (5): 1508–52.

Henderson, J. V., A. Storeygard, and U. Deichmann. 2017. "Has Climate Change Driven Urbanization in Africa?" *Journal of Development Economics* 124: 60–82.

Hoekstra, A. Y., J. Buurman, and K. C. Van Ginkel. 2018. "Urban Water Security: A Review." *Environmental Research Letters* 13 (5): 053002.

Howson, A. 2015. "Thirsty Lima Uses Robust Planning to Address Its Future Water Needs." *World Bank News*, October 5, 2015.

IDMC (Internal Displacement Monitoring Centre). 2018a. *The Ripple Effect: Economic Impacts of Internal Displacement; Multidimensional Impacts of Internal Displacement*. Geneva: IDMC.

IDMC (Internal Displacement Monitoring Centre). 2018b. *The Ripple Effect: Economic Impacts of Internal Displacement; Research Agenda and Call for Partners*. Geneva: IDMC.

IDMC (Internal Displacement Monitoring Centre). 2021. *The Ripple Effect: Economic Impacts of Internal Displacement; Unveiling the Cost of Internal Displacement*. Geneva: IDMC.

Indaco, A., F. Ortega, and S. Taspinar. 2021. "Hurricanes, Flood Risk and the Economic Adaptation of Businesses." *Journal of Economic Geography* 21 (4): 557–91.

Inostroza, L., M. Palme, and F. de la Barrera. 2016. "A Heat Vulnerability Index: Spatial Patterns of Exposure, Sensitivity and Adaptive Capacity for Santiago de Chile." *PLoS One* 11 (9): e0162464.

IPCC (Intergovernmental Panel on Climate Change). 2018. "Summary for Policymakers." In *Global Warming of 1.5°C: An IPCC Special Report on the Impacts of Global Warming of 1.5°C above Pre-Industrial Levels and Related Global Greenhouse Gas Emission Pathways, in the Context of Strengthening the Global Response to the Threat of Climate Change, Sustainable Development, and Efforts to Eradicate Poverty*. Geneva, Switzerland: World Meteorological Organization.

IPCC (Intergovernmental Panel on Climate Change). 2019a. "Summary for Policymakers." In *Climate Change and Land: An IPCC Special Report on Climate Change, Desertification, Land Degradation, Sustainable Land Management, Food Security, and Greenhouse Gas Fluxes in Terrestrial Ecosystems*. Geneva, Switzerland: World Meteorological Organization.

IPCC (Intergovernmental Panel on Climate Change). 2019b. "Summary for Policymakers." In *IPCC Special Report on the Ocean and Cryosphere in a Changing Climate*. Cambridge, UK and New York: Cambridge University Press.

IPCC (Intergovernmental Panel on Climate Change). 2022. "Summary for Policymakers." In *Climate Change 2022: Impacts, Adaptation and Vulnerability. Contribution of Working Group II to the Sixth Assessment Report of the Intergovernmental Panel on Climate Change*. Cambridge, UK: Cambridge University Press.

Ivanic, M., W. Martin, and H. Zaman. 2012. "Estimating the Short-Run Poverty Impacts of the 2010–11 Surge in Food Prices." *World Development* 40: 2302–17.

Jayachandran, S. 2021. "Social Norms as a Barrier to Women's Employment in Developing Countries." *IMF Economic Review* 69 (3): 576–95.

Jerch, R., M. E. Kahn, and G. C. Lin. 2021. "Local Public Finance Dynamics and Hurricane Shocks." NBER Working Paper 28050, National Bureau of Economic Research, Cambridge, MA.

Jha, A. K., R. Bloch, and J. Lamond. 2012. *Cities and Flooding: A Guide to Integrated Urban Flood Risk Management for the 21st Century*. Washington, DC: World Bank.

Jiang, H., and L. Quintero. 2022. "Can't Stand the Heat: Climate Stress on Labor Productivity in 16 Latin American and Caribbean Countries." Background paper prepared for this report, World Bank, Washington, DC.

Kaczan, D. J., and J. Orgill-Meyer. 2020. "The Impact of Climate Change on Migration: A Synthesis of Recent Empirical Insights." *Climatic Change* 158: 281–300.

Kahn, M. E., K. Mohaddes, R. N. C. Ng, M. H. Pesaran, M. Raissi, and J.-C. Yang. 2021. "Long-Term Macroeconomic Effects of Climate Change: A Cross-Country Analysis." *Energy Economics* 104: 105624.

Kakissis, J. 2010. "Environmental Refugees Unable to Return Home." *New York Times*, January 3, 2010. http://www.nytimes.com/2010/01/04/world/asia/04migrants.html.

Kamei, A. 2020. "Who Walks for Water? Water Consumption and Labor Supply Response to Rainfall Scarcity in Uganda." http://dx.doi.org/10.2139/ssrn.4013213.

Karger, D. N., S. Lange, C. Hari, C. P. O. Reyer, and N. E. Zimmermann. 2021. *CHELSA-W5E5 v1.1: W5E5 v1.0 downscaled with CHELSA v2.0*. ISIMIP Repository. https://doi.org/10.48364/ISIMIP.836809.1.

Karlan, D., A. L. Ratan, and J. Zinman. 2014. "Savings by and for the Poor: A Research Review and Agenda." *Review of Income and Wealth* 60 (1): 36–78.

Kaya, Z. 2018. "Resilience Policy and Internally Displaced Women in Iraq: An Unintentionally Flawed Approach." Working Paper Series 13/2018, LSE Women, Peace and Security.

Keener, S., M. Luengo, and S. G. Banerjee. 2010. "Provision of Water to the Poor in Africa: Experience with Water Standposts and the Informal Water Sector." Policy Research Working Paper 5387, World Bank, Washington, DC.

Kelley, C. P., S. Mohtadi, M. A. Cane, R. Seager, and Y. Kushnir. 2015. "Climate Change in the Fertile Crescent and Implications of the Recent Syrian Drought." *Proceedings of the National Academy of Sciences* 112 (11): 3241–46.

Klasen, S. 2019. "What Explains Uneven Female Labor Force Participation Levels and Trends in Developing Countries?" *World Bank Research Observer* 34 (2): 161–97.

Kleemans, M., and J. Magruder. 2018. "Labour Market Responses to Immigration: Evidence from Internal Migration Driven by Weather Shocks." *Economic Journal* 128 (613): 2032–65.

Kocornik-Mina, A., T. McDermott, G. Michaels, and F. Rauch. 2019. "Flooded Cities." *American Economic Journal: Applied Economics* 12 (2): 35–66.

Komatsu, H., and G. Joseph. 2016. *Drinking Water Salinity, Burden of Water Collection and School Attendance of Girls: Evidence from Bangladesh and West Bengal*. Washington, DC: World Bank.

Koolwal, G., and D. Van de Walle. 2013. "Access to Water, Women's Work and Child Outcomes." *Economic Development and Cultural Change* 61 (2): 369–405.

Kousky, C., E. Luttmer, and R. Zeckhauser. 2006. "Private Investment and Government Protection." *Journal of Risk and Uncertainty* 33 (1): 73–100.

Kovacs, P., and J. Thistlethwaite. 2014. "Industry." In *Canada in a Changing Climate: Sector Perspectives on Impacts and Adaptation*, edited by F. J. Warren and D. S. Lemmen, 135–58. Ottawa, ON: Government of Canada.

Kulp, S. A., and B. H. Strauss. 2019. "New Elevation Data Triple Estimates of Global Vulnerability to Sea-Level Rise and Coastal Flooding." *Nature Communications* 10 (1): 1–12.

Kydland, F. E., and E. C. Prescott. 1977. "Rules Rather than Discretion: The Inconsistency of Optimal Plans." *Journal of Political Economy* 85 (3): 473–92.

Lagakos, D. 2020. "Urban-Rural Gaps in the Developing World: Does Internal Migration Offer Opportunities?" *Journal of Economic Perspectives* 34 (3): 174–92.

Lall, S. V., and U. Deichmann. 2012. "Density and Disasters: Economics of Urban Hazard Risk." *World Bank Research Observer* 27 (1): 74–105.

Letta, M., and R. S. J. Tol. 2019. "Weather, Climate and Total Factor Productivity." *Environmental and Resource Economics* 73 (1): 283–305.

Li., C.-J., Y-Q. Chai, L.-S. Yang, and H.-R. Li. 2016. "Spatio-Temporal Distribution of Flood Disasters and Analysis of Influencing Factors in Africa." *Natural Hazards* 82: 721–31.

Lombraña, L. M., and S. Dodge. 2021. "Whatever Climate Change Does to the World, Cities Will Be Hit Hardest." *Bloomberg*, April 19, 2021. https://www.bloomberg.com/graphics /2021-cities-climate-victims/.

Lu, X., L. Bengtsson, and P. Holme. 2012. "Predictability of Population Displacement after the 2010 Haiti Earthquake." *Proceedings of the National Academy of Sciences* 109 (29): 11576–81.

Lu, X., D. J. Wrathall, P. R. Sundsøy, M. Nadiruzzaman, E. Wetter, A. Iqbal, and L. Bengtsson. 2016. "Unveiling Hidden Migration and Mobility Patterns in Climate Stressed Regions: A Longitudinal Study of Six Million Anonymous Mobile Phone Users in Bangladesh." *Global Environmental Change* 38: 1–7.

Lusardi, A., and O. S. Mitchell. 2014. "The Economic Importance of Financial Literacy: Theory and Evidence." *Journal of Economic Literature* 52 (1): 5–44.

Mach, K. J., W. N. Adger, H. Buhaug, M. Burke, J. D. Fearon, C. B. Field, C. S. Hendrix, et al. 2020. "Directions for Research on Climate and Conflict." *Earth's Future* 8 (7): e2020EF001532.

Madrigano, J., K. Ito, S. Johnson, P. L. Kinney, and T. Matte. 2015. "A Case-Only Study of Vulnerability to Heat Wave–Related Mortality in New York City (2000–2011)." *Environmental Health Perspectives* 123 (7): 672–78.

Marx, B., T. Stoker, and T. Suri. 2013. "The Economics of Slums in the Developing World." *Journal of Economic Perspectives* 27 (4): 187–210.

Mashhoodi, B. 2021. "Environmental Justice and Surface Temperature: Income, Ethnic, Gender, and Age Inequalities." *Sustainable Cities and Society* 68 (February): 102810.

Maurel, M., and M. Tuccio, 2016. "Climate Instability, Urbanisation and International Migration." *Journal of Development Studies* 52: 735–52.

McDonald, R. I., K. Weber, J. Padowski, M. Flörke, C. Schneider, P. A. Green, T. Gleeson, et al. 2014. "Water on an Urban Planet: Urbanization and the Reach of Urban Water Infrastructure." *Global Environmental Change: Human and Policy Dimensions* 27 (July): 96–105.

McGuirk, E. F., and N. Nunn. 2021. "Transhumant Pastoralism, Climate Change, and Conflict in Africa." NBER Working Paper 28243, National Bureau of Economic Research, Cambridge, MA.

McNamara, K. E., L. L. Olson, and M. A. Rahman. 2016. "Insecure Hope: The Challenges Faced by Urban Slum Dwellers in Bhola Slum, Bangladesh." *Migration and Development* 5 (1): 1–15.

Meijer, J. R., M. A. J. Huijbregts, C. G. J. Schotten, and A. M. Schipper. 2018. "Global Patterns of Current and Future Road Infrastructure." *Environmental Research Letters* 13: 064006.

Mitchell, T., T. Tanner, and K. Lussier. 2007. *We Know What We Need: South Asian Women Speak Out on Climate Change Adaptation*. Brighton, UK: ActionAid and Institute of Development Studies at the University of Sussex.

Mitlin, D., V. A. Beard, D. Satterthwaite, and J. Du. 2019. "Unaffordable and Undrinkable: Rethinking Urban Water Access in the Global South." World Resources Institute, Washington, DC.

Moctar, N., M. d'Hôtel Elodie, and L. C. Tristan. 2015. "Maize Price Volatility: Does Market Remoteness Matter?" Policy Research Working Paper 7202, World Bank, Washington, DC.

Moraci, F., M. F. Errigo, C. Fazia, T. Campisi, and F. Castelli. 2020. "Cities under Pressure: Strategies and Tools to Face Climate Change and Pandemic." *Sustainability* 12 (18): 7743.

Moretti, E. 2013. "Real Wage Inequality." *American Economic Journal: Applied Economics* 5 (1): 65–103.

Mukim, M. 2021. *Burundi Urbanization Review.* Washington, DC: World Bank.

Nakagawa, M., M. Saito, and H. Yamaga. 2007. "Earthquake Risk and Housing Rents: Evidence from the Tokyo Metropolitan Area." *Regional Science and Urban Economics* 37 (1): 87–99.

Nakamura, S., T. Bundervoet, and M. Nuru. 2019. "Rural Roads, Poverty, and Resilience Evidence from Ethiopia." Policy Research Working Paper 8800, World Bank, Washington, DC.

Narloch, U. G., and M. Bangalore. 2016. "Environmental Risks and Poverty: Analyzing Geo-spatial and Household Data from Vietnam." Policy Research Working Paper 7763, World Bank, Washington, DC.

Nauges, C., and J. Strand. 2017. "Water Hauling and Girls' School Attendance: Some New Evidence from Ghana." *Environmental and Resource Economics* 66 (1): 65–88.

Nelson, A., D. J. Weiss, J. van Etten, A. Cattaneo, T. S. McMenomy, and J. Koo. 2019. "A Suite of Global Accessibility Indicators." *Scientific Data* 6 (1): 1–9.

Nelson, V., K. Meadows, T. Cannon, J. Morton, and A. Martin. 2002. "Uncertain Predictions, Invisible Impacts, and the Need to Mainstream Gender in Climate Change Adaptations." *Gender and Development* 10 (2): 51–59.

Okunola, O. 2019. "Spatial Analysis of Disaster Statistics in Selected Cities of Nigeria." *International Journal of Emergency Management* 15 (4): 299–315.

Orlov, A., J. Sillmann, K. Aunan, T. Kjellstrom, and A. Aaheim. 2020. "Economic Costs of Heat-Induced Reductions in Worker Productivity due to Global Warming." *Global Environmental Change* 63: 102087.

Park, J., M. Bangalore, S. Hallegatte, and E. Sandhoefner. 2018. "Households and Heat Stress: Estimating the Distributional Consequences of Climate Change." *Environment and Development Economics* 23 (3): 349–68.

Park, R. J., J. Goodman, M. Hurwitz, and J. Smith. 2020. "Heat and Learning." *American Economic Journal: Economic Policy* 12 (2): 306–39.

Parsons, K. 2014. *Human Thermal Environments. The Effects of Hot, Moderate, and Cold Environment on Human Health, Comfort, and Performance*, 3d ed. Boca Raton, FL: CRC Press.

Patankar, A., and A. Patwardhan. 2016. "Estimating the Uninsured Losses due to Extreme Weather Events and Implications for Informal Sector Vulnerability: A Case Study of Mumbai, India." *Natural Hazards* 80 (1): 285–310.

Patankar, A. M. 2015. "The Exposure, Vulnerability, and Ability to Respond of Poor Households to Recurrent Floods in Mumbai." Policy Research Working Paper 7481, World Bank, Washington, DC.

Pesaresi, M., A. Florczyk, M. Schiavina, M. Melchiorri, and L. Maffenini. 2019. "GHS Settlement Grid, Updated and Refined REGIO Model 2014 in Application to GHS-BUILT R2018A and GHS-POP R2019A, Multitemporal (1975-1990-2000-2015), R2019A." Joint Research Centre, European Commission, Brussels.

Philip, S., S. F. Kew, G. J. van Oldenborgh, E. Aalbers, R. Vautard, F. Otto, K. Haustein, et al. 2018a. "Validation of a Rapid Attribution of the May/June 2016 Flood-Inducing Precipitation in France to Climate Change." *Journal of Hydrometeorology* 19 (11): 1881–98.

Philip, S., S. F. Kew, G. J. van Oldenborgh, F. Otto, S. O'Keefe, K. Haustein, A. King, et al. 2018b. "Attribution Analysis of the Ethiopian Drought of 2015." *Journal of Climate* 31 (6): 2465–86.

Phillips, C. A., A. Caldas, R. Cleetus, K. A. Dahl, J. Declet-Barreto, R. Licker, L.D. Merner, et al. 2020. "Compound Climate Risks in the COVID-19 Pandemic." *Nature Climate Change* 10: 586–88.

Qin, Y. 2020. "Urban Flooding Mitigation Techniques: A Systematic Review and Future Studies." *Water* 12 (12): 3579.

Quintero, L., and M. Roberts. 2022. "Cities and Productivity: Evidence from 16 Latin America and Caribbean Countries." Unpublished manuscript.

Radeloff, V. C., D. P. Helmers, H. Anu Kramer, M. H. Mockrin, P. M. Alexandre, A. Bar-Massada, V. Butsic, et al. 2018. "Rapid Growth of the US Wildland-Urban Interface Raises Wildfire Risk." *Proceedings of the National Academy of Sciences* 115 (13): 3314–19.

Rebally, A., C. Valeo, J. He, and S. Saidi. 2021. "Flood Impact Assessments on Transportation Networks: A Review of Methods and Associated Temporal and Spatial Scales." *Frontiers in Sustainable Cities* 3: 10.3389/frsc.2021.732181.

Reed, K. A., A. M. Stansfield, M. F. Wehner, and C. M. Zarzycki. 2020. "Forecasted Attribution of the Human Influence on Hurricane Florence." *Science Advances* 6 (1): eaaw9253.

Rentschler, J., P. Avner, M. Marconcini, R. Su, E. Strano, S. Hallegatte, L. Bernard, and C. Riom. 2022. "Rapid Urban Growth in Flood Zones: Global Evidence since 1985." Policy Research Working Paper 10014, World Bank, Washington, DC.

Rentschler, J., and M. Salhab. 2020. "People in Harm's Way: Flood Exposure and Poverty in 189 Countries." Policy Research Working Paper 9447, World Bank, Washington, DC.

Restrepo Cadavid, P. 2011. "The Impacts of Slum Policies on Households' Welfare: The Case of Medellin (Colombia) and Mumbai (India)." *Economics and Finance*. École Nationale Supérieure des Mines, Paris.

Ritter, K. 2018. "Water Access in Lima Complicated by Inequality and Climate Uncertainty." *Circle of Blue* (blog), June 28, 2018. https://www.circleofblue.org/2018/south-america/water-access-in-lima-complicated-by-inequality-and-climate-uncertainty/.

Roberts, M., F. Gil Sander, and S. Tiwari, eds. 2019. *Time to ACT: Realizing Indonesia's Urban Potential*. Washington, DC: World Bank.

Ross, M. R., J. J. O'Brien, R. G. Ford, K. Zhang, and A. Morkill. 2009. "Disturbance and the Rising Tide: The Challenge of Biodiversity Management on Low-Island Ecosystems." *Frontiers in Ecology and the Environment* 7 (9): 471–78.

Rossitti, G. 2022. "Who Is Affected? Which Segments of City Populations Are Most Exposed to Climate-Related Stresses?" Background paper prepared for this report, World Bank, Washington, DC.

Sampson, C. C., A. M. Smith, P. D. Bates, J. C. Neal, L. Alfieri, and J. E. Freer. 2015. "A High-Resolution Global Flood Hazard Model." *Water Resources Research* 51 (9): 7358–81.

Santamouris, M., and G. Y. Yun. 2020. "Recent Development and Research Priorities on Cool and Super Cool Materials to Mitigate Urban Heat Island." *Renewable Energy* 161: 792–807.

Sedova, B., and M. Kalkuhl. 2020. "Who Are the Climate Migrants and Where Do They Go? Evidence from Rural India." *World Development* 129 (C): 104848.

Setiawan, I., S. Tiwari, and H. Rizal. 2018. "Economic and Social Mobility in Urbanizing Indonesia." Background paper prepared for *Time to ACT: Realizing Indonesia's Urban Potential*, edited by M. Roberts, F. Gil Sander, and S. Tiwari. World Bank, Washington, DC.

Shahmohamadi, P., A. I. Che-Ani, I. Etessam, K. N. A. Maulud, and N. M. Tawil. 2011. "Healthy Environment: The Need to Mitigate Urban Heat Island Effects on Human Health." *Procedia Engineering* 20 (January): 61–70.

Shayegh, S., V. Manoussi, and S. Dasgupta. 2021. "Climate Change and Development in South Africa: The Impact of Rising Temperatures on Economic Productivity and Labour Availability." *Climate and Development* 13 (8): 725–35.

Shively, G., and G. Thapa. 2016. "Markets, Transportation Infrastructure, and Food Prices in Nepal." *American Journal of Agricultural Economics* 99: 660–82.

Shughrue, C., B. Werner, and K. C. Seto. 2020. "Global Spread of Local Cyclone Damages through Urban Trade Networks." *Nature Sustainability* 3: 606–13.

Sicard, P., E. Agathokleous, A. De Marco, E. Paoletti, and V. Calatayud. 2021. "Urban Population Exposure to Air Pollution in Europe over the Last Decades." *Environmental Sciences Europe* 33 (1): 1–12.

Smith, E. T., and S. C. Sheridan. 2019. "The Influence of Extreme Cold Events on Mortality in the United States." *Science of the Total Environment* 647: 342–51.

Somanathan, E., R. Somanathan, A. Sudarshan, and M. Tewari. 2021. "The Impact of Temperature on Productivity and Labor Supply: Evidence from Indian Manufacturing." *Journal of Political Economy* 129 (6): 1797–1827.

Souverijns, N., K. De Ridder, N. Veldeman, F. Lefebre, F, Kusambiza-Kiingi, W. Memela, and N. Jones. 2022. "Urban Heat in Johannesburg and Ekurhuleni, South-Africa: A Meter-Scale Assessment and Vulnerability Assessment." Submitted to *Urban Climate*.

Thomson, R., R. Hornigold, L. Page, and T. Waite. 2018. "Associations between High Ambient Temperatures and Heat Waves with Mental Health Outcomes: A Systematic Review." *Public Health* 161: 171–91.

UCCRN (Urban Climate Change Research Network). 2018. *The Future We Don't Want: How Climate Change Could Impact the World's Greatest Cities*. Urban Climate Change Research Network Technical Report. New York: Columbia University.

UN (United Nations). 2018. "Indigenous Peoples and Ethnic Minorities: Marginalization Is the Norm." In *Promoting Inclusion through Social Protection: Report on the World Social Situation 2018*. New York: United Nations.

UN OCHA (United Nations Office for the Coordination of Humanitarian Affairs). 2019. "Gender-Based Violence: Financial Independence and Economic Empowerment Key to Survivors' Recovery." *UN OCHA News and Updates,* May 17, 2019. https://www.unocha.org/story /gender-based-violence-financial-independence-and-economic-empowerment-key -survivors-recovery.

UNESCO (United Nations Educational, Scientific and Cultural Organization). 2015. *Gender and Water Data: Project for Gender Sensitive Water Monitoring, Assessment and Reporting*. Perugia: United Nations World Water Assessment Programme.

UNICEF (United Nations Children's Fund). 2016. "Collecting Water Is Often a Colossal Waste of Time for Women and Girls." Press release, August 29, 2016. https://www.unicef.org /press-releases/unicef-collecting-water-often-colossal-waste-time-women-and-girls.

van Oldenborgh, G. J., F. Krikken, S. Lewis, N. J. Leach, F. Lehner, K. R. Saunders, M. van Weele, et al. 2021. "Attribution of the Australian Bushfire Risk to Anthropogenic Climate Change." *Natural Hazards Earth System Science* 21 (3): 941–60.

Vautard, R., M. van Aalst, O. Boucher, A. Drouin, K. Haustein, F. Kreienkamp, G. J. van Oldenborgh, et al. 2020. "Human Contribution to the Record-Breaking June and July 2019 Heatwaves in Western Europe." *Environmental Research Letters* 15 (9): 094077.

Venkat, A., F. Dizon, and W. Masters. 2022. "The Impact of Climate Shocks and Stresses on Urban Food Prices." Background paper prepared for this report, World Bank, Washington, DC.

Voelkel, J., D. Hellman, R. Sakuma, and V. Shandas. 2018. "Assessing Vulnerability to Urban Heat: A Study of Disproportionate Heat Exposure and Access to Refuge by Socio-Demographic Status in Portland, Oregon." *International Journal of Environmental Research and Public Health* 15 (4): 640.

Votsis, A., and A. Perrels. 2016. "Housing Prices and the Public Disclosure of Flood Risk: A Difference-in-Differences Analysis in Finland." *Journal of Real Estate Finance and Economics* 53 (4): 450–71.

Wang, J., Y. Chen, W. Liao, G. He, S. F. B. Tett, Z. Yan, P. Zhai, et al. 2021. "Anthropogenic Emissions and Urbanization Increase Risk of Compound Hot Extremes in Cities." *Nature Climate Change* 11 (12): 1084–89.

Willinger, B. A., ed. 2008. *Katrina and the Women of New Orleans*. New Orleans, LA: Newcomb College Center for Research on Women, Tulane University.

Wilson, R., E. Z. Erbach-Schoenberg, M. Albert, D. Power, S. Tudge, M. Gonzalez, S. Guthrie, et al. 2016. "Rapid and Near Real-Time Assessments of Population Displacement Using Mobile Phone Data Following Disasters: The 2015 Nepal Earthquake." *PloS Currents*, February 24, 2016. https://pubmed.ncbi.nlm.nih.gov/26981327/.

Winsemius, H. C., B. Jongman, T. I. Veldkamp, S. Hallegatte, M. Bangalore, and P. J. Ward. 2018. "Disaster Risk, Climate Change, and Poverty: Assessing the Global Exposure of Poor People to Floods and Droughts." *Environment and Development Economics* 23 (3): 328–48.

World Bank. 2010. *Natural Hazards, UnNatural Disasters: The Economics of Effective Prevention*. Washington, DC: World Bank.

World Bank. 2015. *Indigenous Latin America in the Twenty-First Century*. Washington, DC: World Bank.

World Bank. 2017. *Maintaining the Momentum while Addressing Service Quality and Equity: A Diagnostic of Water Supply, Sanitation, Hygiene, and Poverty in Ethiopia. WASH Poverty Diagnostic*. Washington, DC: World Bank.

World Bank. 2019. *Women in Water Utilities: Breaking Barriers*. Washington, DC: World Bank.

World Bank. 2020a. *Forced Displacement: An Agenda for Cities and Towns*. Washington, DC: World Bank.

World Bank. 2020b. *Public Expenditure Review: Disaster Response and Rehabilitation in the Philippines*. Washington, DC: World Bank.

World Bank. 2020c. *The Global Health Cost of Ambient PM$_{2.5}$ Air Pollution*. Washington, DC: World Bank.

World Bank. 2021a. "Adapting to Sea Level Rise in the Marshall Islands." *StoryMaps*, October 22, 2021. https://storymaps.arcgis.com/stories/8c715dcc5781421ebff46f35ef34a04d.

World Bank. 2021b. *Learning from Tropical Cyclone Seroja: Building Disaster and Climate Resilience in Timor-Leste*. Washington, DC: World Bank.

World Bank. 2021c. *Somalia Urbanization Review: Fostering Cities as Anchors of Development*. Washington, DC: World Bank.

World Bank. 2021d. *Strengthening the Link between Economic Growth and Poverty Reduction in Mali. A Poverty Assessment*. Washington, DC: World Bank.

World Bank. 2021e. *The Philippines Parametric Catastrophe Risk Insurance Program Pilot*. Washington, DC: World Bank.

World Bank. 2021f. *World Development Report 2021: Data for Better Lives*. Washington, DC: World Bank.

World Bank. Forthcoming a. *Healthy Cities*. Washington, DC: World Bank.

World Bank. Forthcoming b. *South Africa Disaster Risk Financing Diagnostic*. Washington, DC: World Bank.

World Bank and Australian AID (Agency for International Development). 2014. "Where Are We During Flooding? A Quantitative Assessment of Poverty and Social Impacts of Flooding in Selected Neighborhoods of HCMC." World Bank, Washington, DC.

WRI (World Resources Institute). 2017. "Droughts and Blackouts: How Water Shortages Cost India Enough Energy to Power Sri Lanka." *World Resources Institute Blog*, July 26, 2017. https://www.wri.org/insights/droughts-and-blackouts-how-water-shortages-cost-india-enough-energy-power-sri-lanka.

Yabe, T., N. K. Jones, P. S. C. Rao, M. C. Gonzalez, and S. V. Ukkusuri. 2022. "Mobile Phone Location Data for Disasters: A Review from Natural Hazards and Epidemics." *Computers, Environment and Urban Systems* 94: 101777.

Zaveri, E., J. Russ, A. Khan, R. Damania, E. Borgomeo, and A. Jagerskog. 2021. *Ebb and Flow Vol. 1: Water, Migration and Development*. Washington, DC: World Bank.

Zscheischler, J., S. Westra, B. J. J. M. Van Den Hurk, S. I. Seneviratne, P. J. Ward, A. Pitman, A. Agha Kouchak, et al. 2018. "Future Climate Risk from Compound Events." *Nature Climate Change* 8 (6): 469–77.

CHAPTER 4

The Impact of Cities on Climate and the Environment

City growth has caused climate change, but that growth is also what's going to get us out of it.

Matthew E. Kahn, Provost Professor of Economics and Spatial Sciences
University of Southern California
The Routledge Handbook on Spaces of Urban Politics (Ward et al. 2018)

MAIN FINDINGS

- Cities grow along three margins: horizontal expansion, infill development, and vertical layering. The relative importance of each varies with both a city's level of income and the costs of vertical development.

- When today's advanced countries began to develop and urbanize, they faced prohibitively high technological costs of vertical development. The elevator and other modern building technologies have lowered such costs for cities in today's lower-income countries. Yet cities in these countries tend to expand outward rather than upward because of the capital-intensive nature of vertical construction, failings in land and property markets, and regulations that constrain developers from building upward.

- Previous work has pointed to a city's productivity level as the main driver of whether it grows outward or upward, and theorized that cities that build upward also expand faster outward. New research undertaken for this report finds instead that more vertical development results in both a more compact, environmentally friendly urban form and higher incomes; however, lower carbon dioxide emissions associated with a more compact urban form must be weighed against the higher emissions embedded in the construction of taller buildings.

- In addition to their indirect impacts through a city's urban form, incentives and investments that encourage the use of public transportation and reduce dependence on private vehicles can also directly contribute to better air quality. The effects are, however, highly heterogeneous across cities globally, and poorly designed public transportation systems may contribute to more traffic congestion, leading to lower-quality air and higher greenhouse gas emissions.

- If not well managed, urban expansion threatens fertile agricultural land—with negative repercussions for urban food systems as well as for water pollution downstream of cities. Measures to enhance agricultural productivity and reduce food loss and waste can help offset the adverse impacts of urban expansion on food production, while contributing to reduced greenhouse gas emissions.

Introduction

As highlighted in chapter 1, cities are responsible for 70 percent of global anthropogenic greenhouse gas emissions (Hopkins et al. 2016). In 2019, about 86 percent of the world's urbanites lived in cities with dangerously high air pollution levels, which contributed to 1.8 million excess deaths worldwide (Southerland et al. 2022). In Asia, urban expansion has been a central driver of cropland loss and, according to one recent report, now poses "an existential threat to peri-urban agriculture—a leading source of nutritionally important fresh fruit and vegetables for many cities" (Acharya et al. 2021, xviii). Moreover, cities frequently compete with agricultural lands for water (Garrick et al. 2019), and farmland downstream of cities often must rely on contaminated urban wastewater for irrigation (Damania et al. 2019).

Although it is difficult to deny the negative environmental impacts of many cities, it is also important to be aware of their environmental benefits. Cities, after all, concentrate more than 50 percent of the world's population into less than 1 percent of its land area.[1] Econometric estimates indicate that higher urban density is associated with less commuting and car use and lower levels of domestic energy consumption (Ahlfeldt and Pietrostefani 2019). Chapter 1 of this report provided evidence of a striking negative correlation between the compactness of a city's development and its levels of carbon dioxide (CO_2) emissions and emissions of particulate matter of 2.5 microns or less in diameter ($PM_{2.5}$) in both the transportation and residential sectors.

Many factors contribute to determining the impact of a city's development on the environment, including, for example, practices of solid waste management, the energy efficiency of its buildings, and the local uptake of renewable forms of energy. Although action in all these areas is undoubtedly important to the mitigation of climate change, this chapter mainly focuses on an area in which it can provide new evidence and insights: the role played by the form that a city's development takes and, in particular, whether a city accommodates population growth by expanding outward like a pancake or upward like a pyramid (Lall et al. 2021). The tendency to grow outward or upward depends on how well urban policy makers can manage the stresses associated with a city's growth. These stresses put pressure on land and property prices in central areas, while also undermining the livability of those areas, thereby pushing both people and firms outward to a city's periphery (Ellis and Roberts 2016).

This chapter therefore has the following main aims:

- Investigate how the form of a city's development—especially how vertical that development is—affects both its consumption of land (and thus the compactness of its form) and its level of productivity and therefore prosperity.

- Review the evidence on the impacts on air pollution of incentives and investments that affect the use of different modes of urban transportation and that also play a key role in shaping the evolution of a city's form.

- Examine projections of how urban expansion will affect agricultural land and production under various policy scenarios.

- Discuss how urban expansion affects water pollution downstream of cities and competition for water between urban and rural areas.

To achieve the first of these aims, the chapter presents the results of empirical analysis undertaken for this report on the causal impacts of vertical development on both the areas and productivity levels of cities using the report's global sample of more than 10,000 cities (Ahlfeldt and Jedwab 2022). It combines this work, which draws on a unique global database of almost 700,000 tall buildings, with insights from secondary literature to derive the chapter's main insights.

Pancakes or pyramids—How do cities around the world evolve in form?

Modern cities can develop along three margins

A modern-day city can develop along three margins: horizontal expansion, infill development, and vertical layering (Lall et al. 2021). *Horizontal expansion* often manifests itself as low-density sprawl; *infill development* takes the form of inward additions of built-up area in the gaps left between existing structures; and *vertical layering* consists of building taller residential and commercial properties. Although no firm height definitions exist, these taller properties may consist of midrise buildings (6–14 stories), high-rise buildings (15–24 stories), or skyscrapers (25 stories or more).

Historically, cities could develop along only two of these margins—horizontal expansion and infill development. This limitation was due, in large part, to the absence of a safe, fast, and convenient means of moving between the floors of a building, which meant that the height of buildings was constrained by the willingness and ability of people to walk up flights of stairs. Until 1884, when the height of Ulm Minster in Germany was surpassed by that of the Washington Monument, the tallest structures in the world were cathedrals (figure 4.1).

With the introduction of the passenger elevator, however, the possibility of significant vertical development beyond a few stories became a reality.[2] Even so, the elevator got off to a slow start. The first passenger elevator, installed at the five-story Haughwout Department Store in

Figure 4.1   Evolution of tall buildings and structures since 1880

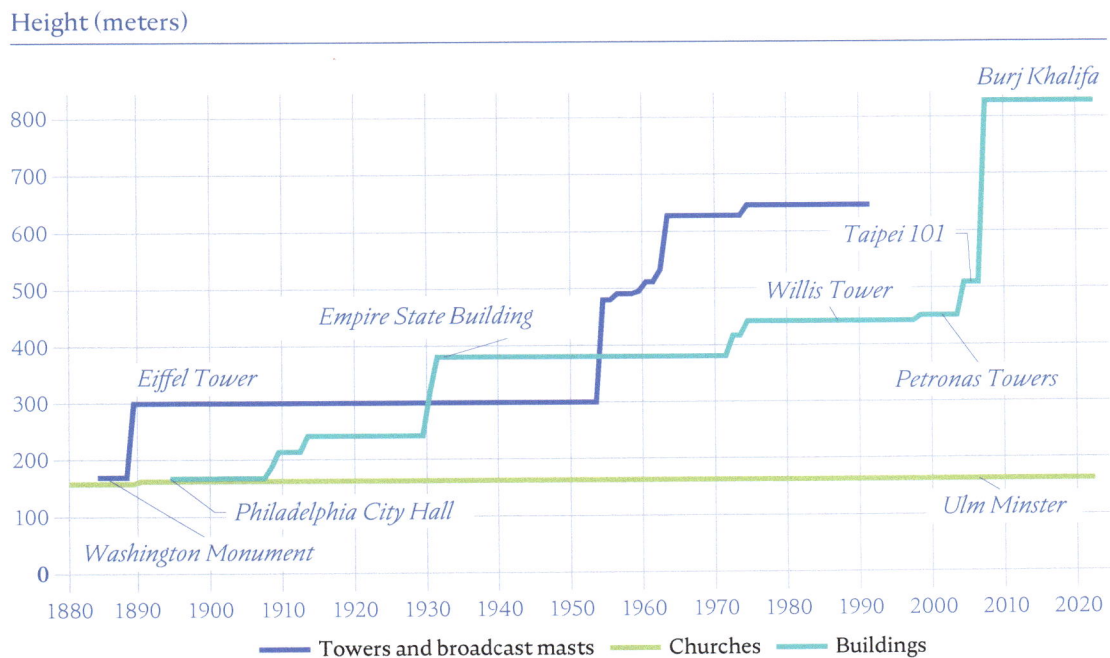

Source: World Bank elaboration based on data from Emporis and World Economic Forum (https://www.weforum.org/agenda/2019/09/tallest-historical-structures).

New York in 1857, was powered by a steam engine and, compared to today's fastest elevators that can ascend at speeds upward of 40 feet per second, traveled at a snail's pace of 40 feet per minute. After just three years, it ceased operations because the store's customers refused to use it. Only after passage of another decade and completion of the 130-foot, eight-story Home Insurance Building in downtown Manhattan was the elevator incorporated into the design of an office building. However, it was not until the opening in 1885 of the world's "first skyscraper"— the 10-story Home Insurance Building in Chicago—that the elevator became a mainstay of architectural office building design (Prisco 2019).[3] See box 4.1 for a brief history of the elevator.

Box 4.1

A brief history of the elevator or "vertical railway"

Although an unremarkable feature of today's many tall buildings, elevators are, in fact, a revolutionary means of mass transportation that allowed the emergence of midrises, high-rises, and skyscrapers (Gottmann 1966). The invention of the modern elevator opened up a new frontier of urban development, allowing cities to grow vertically beyond the limits of their scarce usable land.

The first patent for a so-called vertical railway was filed in 1859 by the engineer Otis Tuft. The well-known Otis Elevator Company, however, takes its name from American industrialist Elisha Otis. He held spectacular demonstrations at the 1853 World's Fair in New York at which he cut the elevator rope to showcase his invention, the safety brake, which would stop the elevator car from crashing to the ground.

The steam engine and Otis's safety brake created the conditions for the takeoff of elevators at the end of the nineteenth century. Because the first models were extremely slow and expensive, however, they were not widely adopted. Among the first users were luxury hotels, which featured richly decorated cars that offered an experience rather than a transportation service.

The evolution from steam engine–powered machines to hydraulic ones, and later to electric engines, increased the speed of elevators and so led to more widespread adoption. Manhattan's eight-story Equitable Life Building, completed in 1870, was the first commercial building designed with an elevator. Chicago's Home Insurance Building had four elevators. In the 1910s and 1920s, as tower after tower began to spring up in the New York skyline, many were fitted with Otis's elevators. The uptake in Europe, however, was slower, in part because of building height restrictions.

The 1920s also brought the first penthouses and the beginning of a cultural switch. Before elevators, the upper floors of buildings often came with the lowest rents because of their inaccessibility; after elevators, upper floors carried large price premiums because of their greater privacy and better views (Wong et al. 2011).

Elevators continue to evolve today. In the world's tallest buildings, they are an integral part of the advanced designs. For midrises, elevators add significantly to the cost of building, but their marginal cost is close to zero above the seventh floor.[a] The near future may see the evolution from electricity-powered elevators to magnetic ones, which take up less space and will further improve the land use efficiency of tall buildings.

Sources: Bernard 2014; Glaeser 2011; Prisco 2019.

a. The world's tallest skyscrapers, however, require multiple costly sets of elevators to cover their height. In Saudi Arabia, the 167-story Jeddah Tower, whose construction is currently on hold, requires very complex engineering solutions and costlier materials.

By dramatically reducing the costs of vertical transportation within a building, the development of the modern passenger elevator, aided by other advances in tall building construction (most notably, mass-produced steel and improved techniques for measuring and analyzing structural loads and stresses), has allowed cities to sprawl not just outward but also upward. Tall buildings[4] constructed around the world since 1885 have a combined height of more than 16,000 kilometers, equivalent to the combined height of almost 43,000 Empire State Buildings (Ahlfeldt and Jedwab 2022). Although, at least for the very tallest of these buildings, the main construction material was steel, since about 1964, it has been concrete (Jedwab, Barr, and Brueckner 2022).

Despite the lower costs of vertical transportation and construction, cities in low-income countries still mainly expand horizontally

Using the same global sample of more than 10,000 cities that underpins much of this report's analysis, Lall et al. (2021) address the extent to which modern cities develop along the three margins open to them—horizontal development, infill development, and vertical layering. On the basis of their analysis of the period 2000–15, Lall et al. draw a striking contrast between the development patterns of cities in low-income countries and those of cities in upper-middle- and high-income countries.[5] In cities in low-income countries, 91 percent of the built-up area growth experienced over this period was horizontal expansion and only 9 percent infill development. In cities in upper-middle- and high-income countries, infill development accounted for 35 percent of built-up area growth and horizontal expansion for 65 percent. At the same time, building heights in higher-income cities became taller and more peaked.

In view of their findings, Lall et al. describe cities in low-income countries as growing like "pancakes," whereas cities in more developed countries grow like "pyramids" because vertical growth accompanies their outward growth. The presence of both vertical and horizontal growth is consistent with predictions of the standard open city model of urban economics in which a city faces a completely elastic supply of labor. Therefore, any increase in the supply of floor space due to vertical layering that reduces rents results in a very large population inflow to the city, which also pushes its development outward (Ahlfeldt and Barr 2022).

Income growth appears to be the main driver of vertical layering, but that may not be the whole story

According to Lall et al. (2021), this striking difference in growth patterns is mainly explained by the fact that cities in higher-income countries are more productive than cities in lower-income countries. Because building tall is capital-intensive, it requires sufficient economic demand for new floor space. At low productivity levels, this demand is insufficient, and developers therefore fail to build upward.[6] Policy makers in low-income countries should therefore aim to create an enabling environment that will allow vertical layering to occur *once* a city becomes sufficiently productive. Doing so will facilitate the city's development as a pyramid rather than as a pancake.

Beyond productivity, the development experiences of cities in today's high-income countries suggest an extra dimension to the story. When Chicago's Home Insurance Building opened in 1885, the US gross domestic product (GDP) per capita was US$6,424 (in 2011 constant international dollars), less than Angola's GDP per capita (US$7,771) in 2018. By the time the

Empire State Building was completed in 1931, US GDP per capita was US$8,381, roughly equal to Morocco's GDP per capita (US$8,451) in 2018.[7] Whereas the 102-story Empire State Building is 1,454 feet tall, Morocco's tallest completed building—the Hassan II Mosque in Casablanca,[8] completed in 1993—is, at 690 feet, less than half the height of the Empire State Building.

In 1970, when its GDP per capita was US$9,250, Hong Kong SAR, China, embarked on an era of exponential growth in its stock of tall buildings (figure 4.2). Over the period 1975–85, the city added more height to its skyline than did New York over the entire century from 1885 to 1985. In doing so, it became the undisputed global leader in tall buildings. The evolution of the skyline in Hong Kong SAR, China, also appears to have encouraged other countries in East and Southeast Asia to become more pro-development. As a result, cities such as Bangkok, Kuala Lumpur, and Manila adopted tall buildings much earlier than did non-Asian countries with similar economic conditions (Ahlfeldt and Jedwab 2022).

The fact that many East and Southeast Asian cities, not to mention cities in the United States, began to build tall at a relatively early stage of development suggests considerable untapped demand for vertical layering in many developing, especially middle-income, countries.

Figure 4.2   **Evolution of total sum of tall building heights: Hong Kong SAR, China; New York; and Tokyo, 1890–2020**

Total height of tall buildings (km)

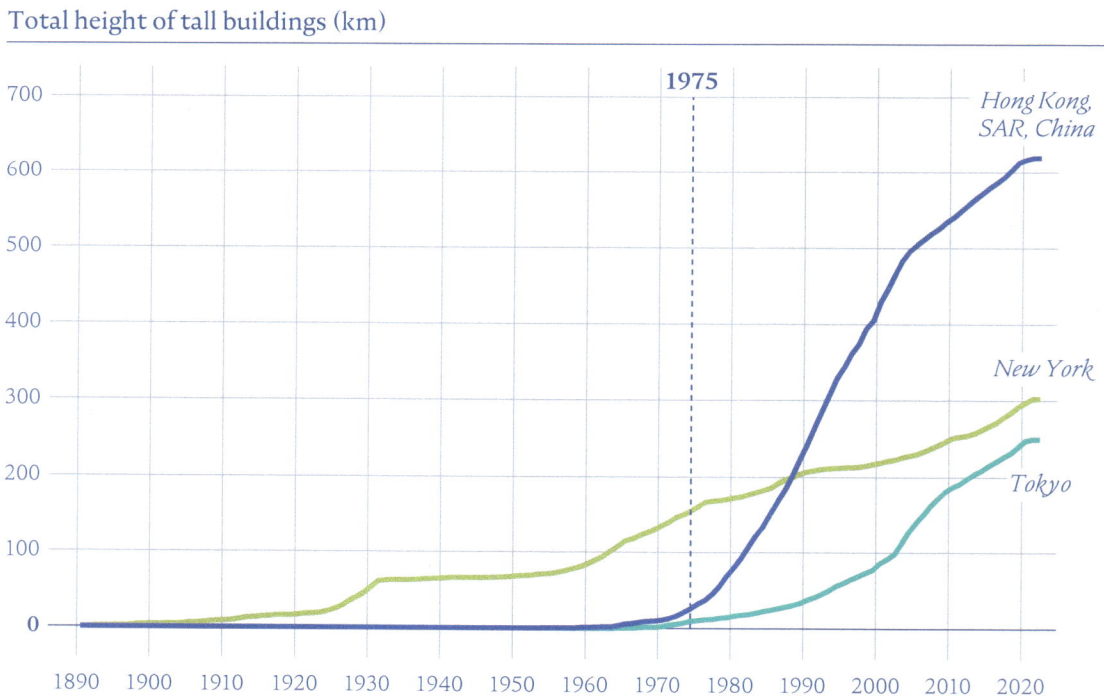

Source: Ahlfeldt and Jedwab 2022, based on data for tall buildings from Emporis.

Note: The figure shows the total sum of heights of tall buildings. Tall buildings are defined as having a height of at least 55 meters (approximately 15 stories). Tall buildings include high-rises (15–24 stories) and skyscrapers (more than 25 stories). km = kilometers.

Consistent with this suggestion, Jedwab, Barr, and Brueckner (2022) estimate, on the basis of a global analysis of tall buildings with a height of at least 80 meters, that the total height of tall buildings is less than predicted in several middle-income countries, including Armenia, Equatorial Guinea, India, Lesotho, Mauritius, Sri Lanka, and Uzbekistan.[9] For example, they estimate that in Sri Lanka a 261 percent increase in aggregated urban building heights would be required to make the country's building height stock equal to the total height predicted for a country at its level of urban development and with its level of agricultural rents.

Finally, although the experience of East and Southeast Asian cities that made an early start on building tall is consistent with the theory that income growth is a necessary precondition for vertical layering, the fact that the two went together allows a reverse possibility—in addition to being a consequence of economic development, building tall may also, at least in part, have caused it.

The impacts of vertical development on land consumption, the environment, and productivity

The idea that vertical development (development above low-rise levels) should result in more compact cities that consume less land is an intuitively plausible one. As mentioned earlier, however, the standard open city model of urban economics predicts that vertical layering will also lead to horizontal expansion because of its assumption of perfect labor mobility. In this standard model, the reduction in rents that results from tall building construction draws in people from the countryside, thereby bidding rents back up, until their utility (or "happiness") has returned to its original level. The result is a very large wave of in-migration with the implication that vertical expansion also causes horizontal expansion that neutralizes any welfare gains (Ahlfeldt and Barr 2022).

Migration is far from perfect in the real world, and research undertaken for this report demonstrates that the predictions of the standard open city model change once this imperfection is taken into account (Ahlfeldt and Jedwab 2022). Thus, under a canonical parameterization of the model, a reduction in the cost of height leads to an increase in the sum of heights across all buildings in the city. As in the standard model, this outcome stimulates net migration into the city, but that migration is accommodated by the taller buildings. Moreover, in the model the city's vertical expansion is partially offset by a horizontal contraction.[10] With the positive net effect on housing supply, the average rent on floor space falls. In the new equilibrium rents are lower and wages higher because of agglomeration economies, so the city also sees an overall welfare gain.

As this description implies, the model predicts that a reduction in the cost of height should not only lead to an increase in a city's population within a more compact urban form but also stimulate income growth and result in residents being better-off because of their higher welfare levels.

By leading to more compact urban forms and higher productivity, lower costs of vertical development could save fertile agricultural land and reduce pollution

How do the predictions of the model hold up in practice? To answer this question, Ahlfeldt and Jedwab (2022) draw on Emporis, a global database of 693,855 tall buildings. For each city in this report's global sample, Ahlfeldt and Jedwab construct a measure of its total height (that is, the sum of heights of all tall buildings) for all years since 1884, the year in which construction of the Home Insurance Building in Chicago started. In doing so, they confine their investigation to buildings with a height of at least 55 meters (150 feet) or approximately 15 floors—that is, high-rises and skyscrapers—judging the data as likely unreliable for buildings under this height. Their main findings, however, are robust to the measurement error that results from ignoring low- and midrise buildings.

Using these data, Ahlfeldt and Jedwab estimate the impact of a city's total height on its population, area, compactness, and productivity, as captured by the intensity of its nighttime lights per capita. To control for the expectation that causation will run in both directions, including from a city's productivity to its extent of vertical layering, Ahlfeldt and Jedwab employ three instrumental variable (IV) strategies.[11] The first strategy is based on the demonstration effect of the early start in building tall in Hong Kong SAR, China, which appears to have stimulated the adoption of more pro-development policies in other East and Southeast Asian countries. The second strategy exploits the variation across cities in bedrock depth, which affects the costs of vertical construction. And the third strategy exploits variation in earthquake risk across the global city sample, which similarly affects vertical construction costs.

Overall, the empirical results align with the theory. Depending on the estimation strategy adopted, a doubling of a city's total height is associated with a long-run increase in its population of between 5 percent (ordinary least squares estimation) and 23–24 percent (earthquake strategy), and a long-run decrease in its area of between 9 percent (ordinary least squares estimation) and 22–25 percent (bedrock strategy)—see figure 4.3. Averaging across the estimates that control for reverse causation, these findings imply that a doubling of a city's total height leads to a roughly 16 percent increase in its population and a 19 percent reduction in its land area relative to other cities. At the same time, a doubling of height is associated with an estimated 4 percent increase in the intensity of a city's nighttime lights per capita (figure 4.3). Although this increase may seem small, it is about the same order of magnitude as the estimates of the strength of agglomeration economies reported in the literature (Ahlfeldt and Pietrostefani 2019; Rosenthal and Strange 2004).[12]

The fact that an increase in a city's overall height is associated with a reduction, relative to other cities, in its area implies that lowering the costs of vertical construction could result in valuable savings in fertile agricultural land (discussed in more detail later in this chapter). Furthermore, a more compact urban form is also correlated with lower emissions of $PM_{2.5}$ and, therefore, cleaner, more breathable air, which can have beneficial impacts on both health and productivity.

Despite these results, "building tall" does not imply a policy recommendation to construct skyscrapers. Indeed, Ahlfeldt and Jedwab's measure of a city's height—the sum of heights across all tall buildings in a city—does not distinguish between, for example, construction of one 60-story skyscraper and four 15-story high-rise buildings. More generally, taller building heights are best seen as the result of a market response to lower costs of vertical construction. Government decisions to become directly involved in developing tall buildings may or may not be good for urban inclusion (box 4.2). Jedwab, Barr, and Brueckner (2022) provide evidence suggesting that several countries—most notably, the Democratic People's Republic of Korea and several Gulf states—may have engaged in excessive construction of tall buildings.

Figure 4.3 **Estimated elasticities of population, land area, and nighttime light intensity with respect to total sum of tall building heights**

Estimated elasticity with respect to building heights (%)

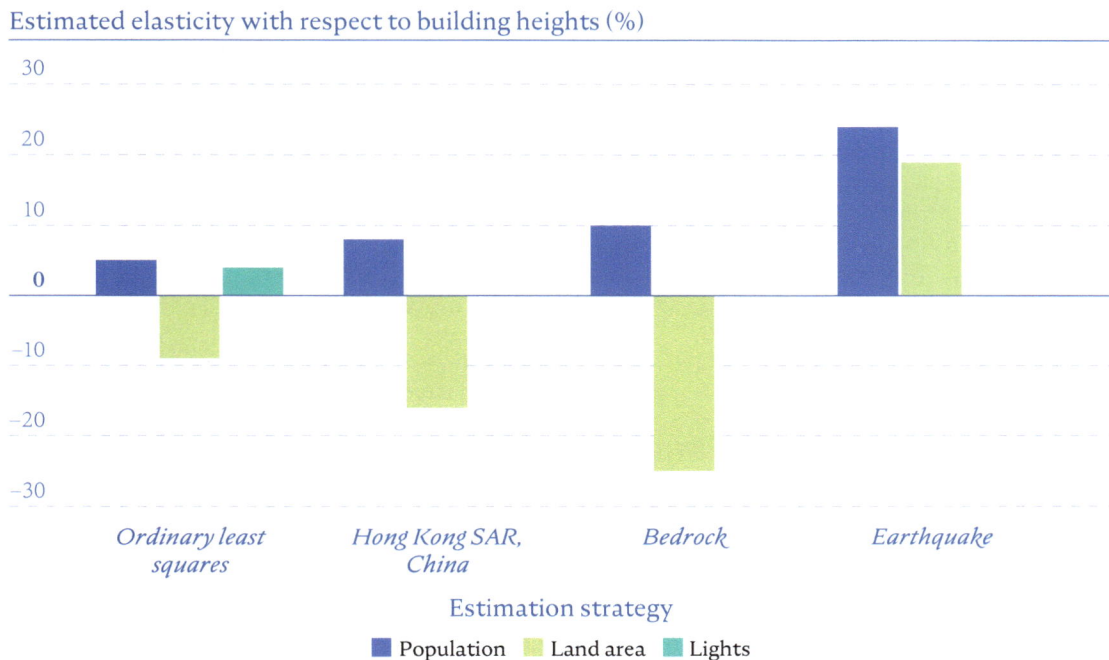

Source: World Bank based on results from Ahlfeldt and Jedwab 2022, whose data on tall buildings are based on data from Emporis.

Note: Figure shows the estimated percentage change in each variable resulting from a doubling of the total sum of tall building heights based on four econometric estimation strategies: ordinary least squares and three instrumental variable strategies ("Hong Kong SAR, China," "bedrock," and "earthquake"), a full description of which can be found in Ahlfeldt and Jedwab (2022). "Lights" refers to the intensity of nighttime lights per capita within a city's extent, where nighttime light intensity is measured using radiance calibrated data derived from Defense Meteorological Satellite Program satellite sensors.

Box 4.2

What do high-rise buildings mean for urban inclusion?

The question of whether high-rise construction is good for urban inclusion has no straightforward answer. Vertical development provides a means of achieving higher population densities, which, if well located, well designed, and coordinated with public transportation, can have a range of benefits for urban inclusion. Dense, transit-oriented development makes it more affordable for residents to access employment, education, and amenities. Denser construction increases housing supply in desirable locations, which, all else being equal, reduces housing prices. Ewing et al. (2016) find that in the United States low-density sprawl is associated with lower levels of upward income mobility (measured as the likelihood that a child born into the bottom fifth of the national income distribution reaches the top fifth by age 30), thereby suggesting that more compact vertical development may be good for such mobility.

BOX 4.2 *continued*

Despite their potential benefits, high-rise residential buildings, whether built by the private or the public sector, have not always succeeded in providing decent housing for the poor. In the absence of the kinds of reforms of land and property markets advocated in this report, high-rise construction in most low- and middle-income countries remains expensive, and thus unaffordable for much of the population. In the United Kingdom, United States, and Western Europe, high-rise public housing for low-income residents, once seen as a solution to their housing problems, is now widely perceived to be a failure (Hess, Tammaru, and van Ham 2018; Hunt 2018; White and Serin 2021). This style of public housing was eventually seen as simply concentrating poverty and crime, and the communal life that occurs at street level rarely flourishes in high-rises. The often poor construction and maintenance of such buildings has sometimes resulted in high-profile disasters such as the Grenfell Tower fire in London in 2017, which killed 72 people. Many cities have demolished their high-rise public housing.

Not all cities, however, have had bad experiences with publicly built high-rise housing. Vienna and especially Singapore have had relative success in building affordable high-rises, often designed to provide space for social interaction at multiple levels (Falk and Rudlin 2018; Samant and Hsi-En 2017). Their experiences suggest that the design, construction quality, and maintenance of buildings—rather than their height—determine their suitability as affordable housing.

Does vertical development also reduce a city's overall contribution to climate change?

Although more compact cities, at any given level of development, tend to have lower CO_2 emissions in both the residential and transportation sectors, construction of taller buildings tends to rely on materials such as concrete, steel, and glass, whose production entails high CO_2 emissions (Pomponi et al. 2021). Thus, a tall building constructed using current technologies embeds high up-front CO_2 emissions, which must be weighed against the future lower flow of CO_2 emissions associated with more compact urban development. Relative to a scenario of lower-rise development, it is not clear which of these two opposing effects dominates in the long run or under what conditions.[13] Because remarkably little research has been devoted to this issue, it is not possible to say whether vertical development is likely to lead to a net long-run reduction or an increase in a city's contribution to climate change. This is notwithstanding the beneficial impacts of more vertical development in terms of saving fertile agricultural land and in reducing local levels of air pollution and raising incomes.

Despite that uncertainty, it does seem clear that the net impact of more vertical development on a city's long-run contribution to climate change will more likely be beneficial if combined with complementary transportation investments and policies that both encourage a move toward less-polluting modes of transportation, including walking and cycling, and further promote compact and livable development. As discussed further shortly, cities will more likely see beneficial environmental impacts if their vertical development results in a more architecturally interesting urban landscape (see the subsection on urban design and land use diversity).

Vertical and infill development in cities in low- and middle-income countries is constrained by dysfunctional urban land markets, zoning, and restrictive building regulations

Given their apparent benefits, what factors prevent more cities in low- and middle-income countries from following the lead set by countries in East and Southeast Asia in the 1970s and 1980s in creating a more enabling environment for vertical and infill development? The answer lies in a combination of the dysfunctionality of urban land markets in many low- and middle-income countries and failures in planning. Weak formal institutions for titling and property transfer frequently deter investors from putting capital in formal structures, contributing to the persistence of slums (Lall et al. 2021). Meanwhile, current urban plans and planning institutions tend to lack effectiveness, failing to both coordinate market-driven investment in structures and manage the spatial form of cities in ways that promote their green, resilient, and inclusive development (Ellis and Roberts 2016; Lall et al. 2021).

In some cases, cities enact planning regulations in an explicit attempt to discourage vertical development. India is a classic example. Major cities such as Bangalore and Mumbai have historically used restrictive floor area ratios to deliberately limit vertical development (Bertaud and Brueckner 2004; Ellis and Roberts 2016). In part, policy makers feared that allowing more of such development would lead to an unmanageable inflow of population that would overwhelm already overstretched urban infrastructure. Instead, such regulations ended up promoting a "messy" pattern of urbanization, characterized by sprawl and slums, undermining both the prosperity and the livability of major Indian cities while also driving up the negative environmental impacts of urbanization. Many South Asian cities are also characterized by large, fragmented public land holdings, often in prime locations, that further complicate land assembly by private developers (Ellis and Roberts 2016). This situation further raises the cost of vertical development. In their global analysis of tall buildings, Jedwab, Barr, and Brueckner (2022) find that countries with a lower maximum floor area ratio and more stringent land use regulations have higher building height percentage change gaps. This finding indicates that, relative to a set of benchmark countries, the total height of a country's buildings is lower than expected given its levels of urban income and agricultural rents.

Addressing constraints could lead to pro-poor welfare gains, especially in larger cities

To assess the welfare implications of constrained vertical development, Ahlfeldt and Jedwab (2022), in their background research for this report, conducted a thought experiment using their calibrated theoretical model. What if all cities limited vertical development to a maximum of 15 floors? How much lower would welfare be than in a hypothetical world in which vertical development was completely unconstrained by regulation and able to respond freely to market demand?

They find that, in the completely unconstrained world, global welfare would be about 1.5 percent higher and worker welfare about 3.3 percent higher. These figures, then, provide estimates of the overall welfare potential of tall buildings. Ahlfeldt and Jedwab calculate that cities currently realize only about one-third of this potential, presumably because of the dysfunctionality of urban land markets in many low- and middle-income countries and the failures in planning discussed earlier.

Ahlfeldt and Jedwab also calculate that the welfare potential of tall buildings is highest for the largest cities, precisely the cities in low- and middle-income countries where one might expect the constraints to vertical development posed by dysfunctional land markets and failures in planning to have the biggest effects. Thus, for a city with a population of 3 million, constraining vertical development to 15 floors results in a 10 percent loss in worker welfare and an increase in aggregate land rent of more than 15 percent. The land rent increase also implies a welfare transfer from workers to landowners. This finding suggests not only that artificially constrained vertical development results in an aggregate net welfare loss but also that the poorest will likely suffer most from this welfare loss because of the higher than necessary rents they must pay.

A global aggregate unrealized welfare potential of 0.5 percent (1.0 percent for workers) may seem small, but it is important to note that these welfare calculations do not include the environmental benefits in terms of, for example, the lower air pollution generally associated with more compact urban development. A full accounting that includes these benefits would undoubtedly yield much higher estimates of the welfare costs imposed by the land and property market and planning failures that inflate vertical development costs in many low- and middle-income countries.

Urban design and land use diversity also matter for the walkability, associated carbon "carprints," and urban heat island effect of cities

Using detailed household survey data for French cities, Blaudin de Thé, Carantino, and Lafourcade (2021) point to the beneficial causal impacts not only of urban compactness but also of both urban design and the diversity of a city's economic activities on household fuel consumption for car use, which translates into significant CO_2 emissions savings. Urban design in this case refers to, among other things, accessibility to public transportation networks and a city's walkability, based on the fractal dimension of the local built-up area.[14] Whereas a high fractal dimension is typical of more historical French city centers developed through a quasi-random demolition and reconstruction process, a much lower fractal dimension describes the more homogeneous suburbs of these cities, which are characterized by regularly shaped housing compounds (map 4.1). A higher fractal dimension encourages walkability by providing both greater legibility (which makes a place comprehensible to an observer moving through it) and greater diversity of visual experience.

The lesson emerging from this analysis is that policies that reduce the costs of building tall may more likely benefit the environment if combined with urban and architectural design that makes the resulting built environment more interesting to pedestrians, thereby encouraging walking over car use. Conversely, if building tall leads to a more homogeneous—and therefore more boring, less pedestrian-friendly, and even potentially less safe built environment—then it will more likely have negative net environmental impacts. Increased walkability, which also critically depends on the quality of sidewalks and streetlighting, can also help promote better health outcomes, as can the reductions in air pollution that tend to go with reductions in CO_2 emissions.

Good urban design can also help combat the urban heat island effect (see box 1.4, chapter 1, for a more detailed description of this effect). The depth of street canyons—that is, the ratio of the height of buildings along a street to the width of the street—can affect air temperatures through its impact on shade and ventilation. The orientation of streets also affects both shade

Map 4.1   **Examples of more and less walkable urban environments**

a. Fractal dimension: 1.81 (Roubaix, France)

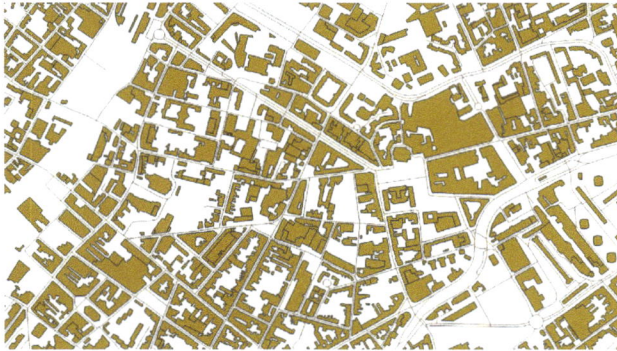

b. Fractal dimension: 1.65 (Créteil, France)

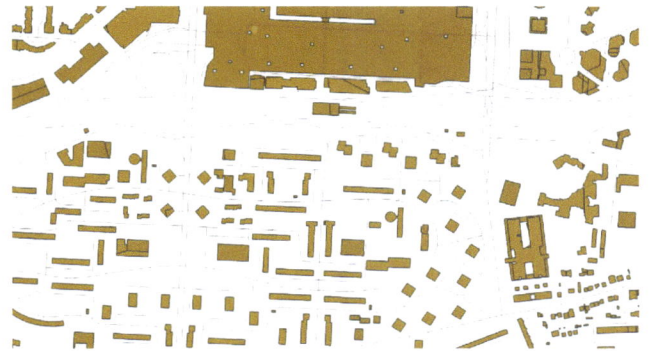

Source: Blaudin de Thé, Carantino, and Lafourcade 2021.

and ventilation: streets with an east-west orientation receive more prolonged exposure to the sun than those with other orientations and thus experience more heat, especially in cities close to the equator (Lai et al. 2019).

The overall shape of a city's built-up footprint can also affect the urban heat island effect. Research on European cities suggests that larger cities, more compact cities, and cities with more circular built-up footprints experience a more intense heat island effect (Pierer and Creutzig 2019; Zhou, Rybski, and Kropp 2017). By contrast, star-shaped cities, with transportation corridors radiating from a high-density core, can retain the transportation benefits of compactness while reducing heat effects. The design of green spaces also influences urban temperatures, although not only the quantity but also the configuration of vegetation matter. Pocket parks—small parks of about 1,000 square meters—placed at regular intervals are more effective than a single large park, especially in high-rise, high-density tropical regions (Giridharan and Emmanuel 2018).

What role does (horizontal) transportation play in shaping cities and their environmental impacts?

Along with income and other factors—technologies, institutions, and policies—that affect vertical development costs, a major determinant of a city's urban form is (horizontal) transportation technologies and systems—and the incentives that affect the modes of transportation that a city's residents choose to use. Moreover, investments in transportation systems and incentives that influence choices of transportation mode affect the environment. They do so not only indirectly by helping shape a city's form but also directly through the emissions of both CO_2 and air pollutants such as $PM_{2.5}$ to which different modes give rise.

A close and mutually reinforcing relationship also exists between transportation and land use. For example, the viability of mass transit systems depends heavily on land use and density.

On the supply side, the costs of providing mass public transit are higher in low-density settings because of the need to serve more distant locations. On the demand side, compact urban development in the form of infill and vertical development requires mass transit systems to support the resultant density. Consistent with this finding, in a meta-analysis of studies on the effects of density, Ahlfeldt and Pietrostefani (2019) find that metro rail density is positively associated with population density, whereas car use is negatively associated with population density. Policies to promote mass transit are therefore complementary to policies that promote vertical and infill development.

Cities that rely more on cars and less on mass transit systems are more sprawling

In the same vein, Ostermeijer et al. (2022) show, for a global sample of 123 cities, a strong negative relationship between a city's population and employment densities and its rate of car ownership. A similarly strong negative relationship exists across countries between average urban population density and average car ownership (figure 4.4). To address concerns of

Figure 4.4 Relationship between car ownership and urban population densities, by city level and country level

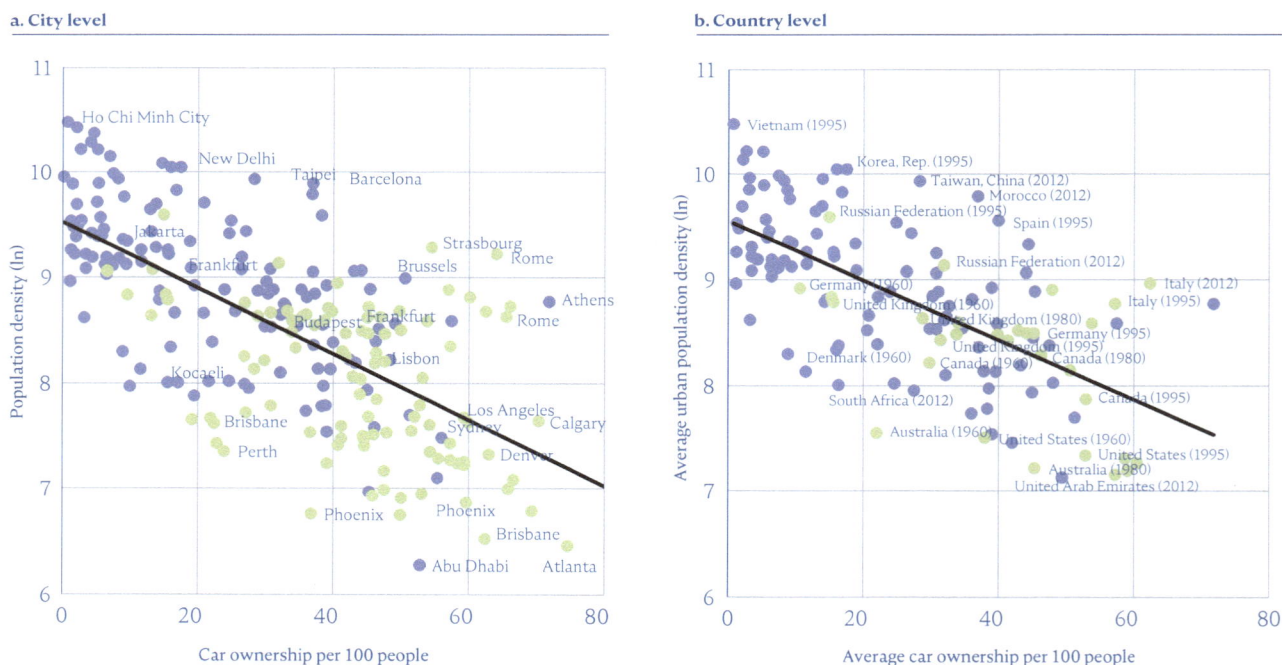

Source: Ostermeijer et al. 2022 using data for various years between 1960 and 2012 with multiple data points for some cities.

Note: Green markers indicate cities and countries with a domestic car manufacturer in 1920. City and country labels are based on minimum, median, and maximum population densities for each bin of 10 cars per 100 people. The solid line represents the estimated best fit linear regression line. ln = natural log.

reverse causality—that lower density development also encourages people to buy more cars—Ostermeijer et al. (2022) use an IV strategy. This strategy exploits the fact that cities that had a commercial car manufacturer in 1920, before the construction of modern highways in today's high-income countries and the rise of mass car ownership, more likely have higher car ownership today. A city's population density today, however, cannot explain the presence of a commercial car manufacturer in 1920, nor was a city's population density in 1920 related to the presence of a car manufacturer at the time. Using this strategy, Ostermeijer et al. estimate that an increase of 1 standard deviation in car ownership (equivalent to about 20 cars per 100 urban inhabitants) causes a long-run reduction in a city's population density of about 35 percent. This effect is mainly driven by an expansion in the size of a city's extent rather than a loss of population, suggesting that cars allow lower-density expansion into a city's periphery.

This evidence on the role of cars in driving sprawl is consistent with evidence that shows that the US interstate highway system contributed to suburbanization of the cities through which it passes (Baum-Snow 2007). Highways also contributed to the suburbanization of cities in China (Baum-Snow et al. 2016).

Part of the reason the presence of a car manufacturer in 1920 predicts car ownership in cities globally today is that, from the 1950s to the late twentieth century, large commercial car manufacturers lobbied strongly, especially in their domestic markets, for incentives and investments aimed at promoting car ownership, often at the expense of other transportation modes. Lobbyists sought to limit vehicle taxes, to increase road construction and parking in cities, and to quash investment in public transportation (Ostermeijer et al. 2022).[15]

The historic lobbying of major car manufacturers against investments in urban public transportation and mass transit suggests they believed such investments would limit car ownership. Evidence that this is indeed the case is provided for Greater Cairo by Heger et al. (2019). Using machine learning techniques to estimate, from high-resolution satellite imagery, the daily number of cars on Cairo's roads and inputting these estimates into an econometric model, Heger et al. find that the two-phased opening of Cairo's Metro Line 3 in February 2012 and July 2014 significantly reduced the number of cars on the city's roads.

Investments in mass transit systems may contribute directly to reducing air pollution, with significant health benefits

In a study of the 58 subway system openings that occurred in cities globally between August 2001 and July 2016, Gendron-Carrier et al. (2022) find that, for cities with higher initial pollution levels, subway openings reduced particulates by 4 percent in the area surrounding a city center. These effects persist for at least four years, the longest time horizon over which the authors' data permit them to estimate impacts. Furthermore, on the basis of observed subway ridership levels, Gendron-Carrier et al. find that these impacts can be plausibly explained "only if subways divert trips that would otherwise have occurred in particularly dirty vehicles or at particularly congested times" (Gendron-Carrier et al. 2022, 166). They go on to state on the same page, "This is consistent with evidence that public transit serves the poor and that subways are much more heavily used at peak times for vehicle traffic." Investments in public transit are therefore not only good for the environment but also pro-poor, thereby helping contribute to more inclusive cities.[16]

Substantial health benefits are associated with the reduction in particulate levels stemming from the launch of new subway systems in more polluted cities. Gendron-Carrier et al. calculate that, on average in such a city, a subway system opening prevents 22.5 infant deaths and

500 total deaths per year. Using standard income-adjusted life values, this averted mortality can be valued at roughly US$43 million and US$1 billion per year, respectively. As Gendron-Carrier et al. note, their estimates do not take into account the effects of reduced air pollution on morbidity or on productivity. Moreover, the estimates do not consider the potential external environmental and health benefits that could result from longer-run land use changes that mass public transit helps induce. These changes may contribute to a more compact urban form, which is correlated with lower CO_2 and $PM_{2.5}$ emissions (see the earlier discussion in this chapter and in chapter 1).

Looking at Greater Cairo, Heger et al. (2019) provide further evidence that subways help reduce air pollution with substantial health benefits for highly polluted cities. As mentioned earlier, Heger et al. estimate that Cairo's two-phased opening of its Metro Line 3 in February 2012 and July 2014 significantly reduced the number of cars on its roads. They further estimate that this reduction in traffic helped reduce by about 3 percent the city's concentrations of particulate matter with a diameter of 10 microns or less, generating estimated averted mortality gains valued at about US$98.7 million.

Removal of fuel subsidies can help reduce dependence on cars, with significant environmental and health benefits

In addition to estimating the impacts of the opening of Metro Line 3 on car use and pollution in Greater Cairo, Heger et al. (2019) studied the impacts of the Arab Republic of Egypt's fuel subsidy removal program. This program resulted in targeted fuel price increases in November 2016 and June 2017 that, depending on the fuel category and period, varied between 30 and 80 percent. Heger et al. estimate that, by reducing traffic below levels that otherwise would have prevailed, these increases led to a 4 percent reduction in concentrations in Greater Cairo of particulate matter with a diameter of 10 microns or less, on top of the 3 percent reduction associated with the opening of the metro line. In turn, this 4 percent reduction generated estimated averted mortality gains valued at roughly US$110.4 million. This finding suggests that, in addition to investments in public transportation systems, the removal of distortionary incentives that skew mode choices away from public transportation and toward private car use can have significant environmental benefits.

The same is also true of policies that go beyond just removing subsidies that artificially encourage car ownership and use by trying to address the negative congestion and environmental externalities that arise from private vehicle use. The most obvious such policy is congestion charging as applied in, for example, Durham and London in the United Kingdom, Gothenburg and Stockholm in Sweden, Milan in Italy, and Riga in Latvia. Other policies include those to encourage higher occupancy of vehicles, such as Jakarta's 3-in-1 policy in place between March 1992 and March 2016 (box 4.3), and those to discourage city center parking and, therefore, driving.

The use of demand-side policies that help correct for the congestion and environmental externalities arising from private vehicle use is important to stave off the risk of traffic congestion rebounding in the long run in response to any public transportation investment. In the absence of demand-side policies, such a long-run response is to be expected because, by reducing congestion in the short run, public transportation investments lower driving costs, which, in turn, stimulates more driving.[17] At the same time, policies to discourage private car use may matter less, from an environmental perspective, in the long run given the rapid growth of electric vehicles. Box 4.4 discusses the possibility that such vehicles could dramatically reduce transportation-related CO_2 emissions in cities.

Box 4.3

High-occupancy vehicle policy in Jakarta

Jakarta's 3-in-1 high-occupancy vehicle restriction, implemented in March 1992, required cars riding in both directions on the major corridors in Jakarta at specific times of day to have at least three passengers, including the driver. The penalty for not complying was a maximum fine of 500,000 Indonesian rupiah (about US$37.50) or two months in prison.

Because many affluent car users commuting into Jakarta did not meet the occupancy restriction, an informal market for professional passengers, or "jockeys," emerged. Jockeys would ride along from 3-in-1 access points for about US$1.20. The practice contributed to the termination of the 3-in-1 policy, temporarily in March 2016 and then permanently in May 2016.

The termination set back Jakarta's attempt to curb congestion. Despite the policy's problems, traffic worsened significantly when it was eliminated (Hanna, Kreindler, and Olken 2017). Delays increased by 39–45 percent during the morning peak period and by 69–85 percent during the evening peak period. The average speed fell from 28 kilometers per hour to 20 in the morning and from 21 kilometers per hour to 12 in the evening. In addition, negative knock-on effects occurred at other times of the day and on roads outside the regulated areas, mainly because of the increased number of cars on the road from eliminating the 3-in-1 policy.

This episode reveals several facts. First, drivers were willing to pay to access the city center by car—enough to sustain the informal jockey market. Second, the authorities' failure to anticipate driver willingness to pay contributed to the policy's limited impact on congestion. Third, faced with this evidence, the authorities responded by scrapping the policy rather than trying to improve it. The 3-in-1 experiment showed that, in the Jakarta area, some type of congestion pricing would better address the problem. Proceeds could then be used to fund urban mass transit or mobility for lower-income people.

Source: Adapted from Roberts, Gil Sander, and Tiwari 2019 and based on Hanna, Kreindler, and Olken 2017.

Box 4.4

Will electric cars save the day?

Automobiles with internal combustion engines were once acclaimed as the ecological saviors that would solve the great horse manure crisis afflicting London, New York, and other large cities at the turn of the twentieth century. Instead, automobiles brought toxic pollutants that, although less visible than manure, were no cleaner. Globally, transportation emissions, mainly generated by personal automobiles, represented about a quarter of all urban carbon dioxide (CO_2) emissions in 2015.[a]

The last decade, however, has seen the tremendous growth of electric vehicles (EVs) with global sales soaring from 130,000 in 2012 to 6.6 million in 2021. China's market, the largest, accounted for more than half of global EV sales in 2021. Meanwhile, in relative terms European countries lead the way—in 2021, EVs accounted for almost 75 percent of vehicle sales in Norway, and 45 percent in Sweden.[b]

Box 4.4 *continued*

By comparison, in the United States, only 4.5 percent of vehicles sold in 2021 were EVs. Nevertheless, even this share represents a doubling over that of 2020. Outside of China, Europe, and the United States, EVs currently have only meager market shares, including in countries such as Brazil, India, and Indonesia, although Brazil has annual sales increases of over 200 percent.

Higher prices present one important hurdle to the widespread adoption of EVs in lower-income countries. This problem will likely change as prices fall with a sharp and continuing decline in battery production costs—from US$1,000 per kilowatt-hour in 2007 to US$410 per kilowatt-hour in 2014. And, just as for smartphones, which had much faster adoption than forecast, lower-income countries are likely to closely follow richer ones. For example, Cherif, Hasanov, and Pande (2017) predict that, in a slow-adoption scenario, EVs will account for about 36 percent of all cars on the world's roads by the early 2040s. In a fast-adoption scenario, almost 90 percent of the world's total vehicle stock will be electric by the 2040s.

Nevertheless, although EVs are widely seen as being greener than conventional vehicles, the exact size of their environmental benefits is not clear. Thus, studies come to different conclusions about the reduction of CO_2 emissions associated with EV adoption, depending on the studies' assumptions about how dirty the electricity generation mix is,[c] whether they use average or marginal emissions in their calculations, and their assumptions about driving patterns and the weather. Despite similar emissions associated with the manufacturing of internal combustion engine cars and EVs, differences in life-cycle emissions between the two types of car depend on the fuel cycle, battery production, and tailpipe emissions. Because EVs lack the latter, results tend to show that they fare better than combustion engine vehicles, but the margins are finer when comparing EVs with hybrids.

Although the environmental advantages arising from EVs are marginal under some assumptions, there are reasons to be optimistic about EVs' potential contribution to reducing urban CO_2 emissions. Many countries are steadily decarbonizing their energy supplies, so the lifetime emissions of EVs have fallen sharply and are projected to keep falling. Moreover, because power plants burn fuel more efficiently than combustion engines do, an EV fleet powered by a 100 percent carbon energy mix would still generate less fuel cycle emissions than an equivalent fleet of internal combustion engine vehicles.

The benefits appear lower in low- and middle-income countries because renewable sources represent a smaller share of the energy mix. China, India, and countries in Sub-Saharan Africa, however, have picked up the pace of their energy transition. In some of these countries, the unreliability of the grid, which will necessitate substantial investments to sustain a large network of EVs, represents a serious obstacle to adoption. The need to build a sufficiently dense network of EV charging stations presents another challenge. The widespread use of motorcycles may be beneficial because their electrical counterparts, whose market is also growing very rapidly in Asia, have smaller batteries.

Box 4.4 *continued*

Effectively "computers on wheels," EVs offer very different capabilities from their predecessors, and could fundamentally shift the way people use vehicles. Although most projections assume a one-to-one replacement of motor vehicles with EVs, the simultaneous development of autonomous driving could move the world's cities toward a system of shared vehicles.

Sources: Cherif, Hasanov, and Pande 2017; Hall and Lutsey 2018; Hausfather 2019; Paoli and Gül 2022.

a. World Bank analysis based on CO_2 emissions data from the European Commission's Global Human Settlement (GHS) Urban Centre Database R2019, https://ghsl.jrc.ec.europa.eu/ghs_stat_ucdb2015mt_r2019a .php, which derives its CO_2 emissions data from the European Commission's Emissions Database for Global Atmospheric Research (EDGAR v5.0).

b. Passage of national legislation subsidizing ownership of EVs and setting strict emissions standards has encouraged and accelerated this surge of EV sales in Europe. Some large cities have hard deadlines for completely phasing out petrol and diesel cars.

c. In countries where energy production does not involve emissions—such as France (nuclear) and Norway (hydroelectric)—the fuel cycle emissions associated with EVs are almost zero (Hall and Lutsey 2018). *Fuel cycle emissions* refers to the diesel or petrol that powers an internal combustion engine vehicle or to the energy mix that generates the electricity for charging an EV's battery.

Mass transit systems are not a silver bullet for reducing congestion and pollution—good planning and design are crucial to success

Although Gendron-Carrier et al. (2022) report that subway openings have a significant negative *average* impact on air pollution in the more polluted cities, this result hides considerable heterogeneity of estimated impacts across cities. For 9 of the 28 cities in their sample that had levels of air pollution above the sample median, the opening of a subway system had a statistically significant *positive* impact on air pollution—that is, air pollution increased (figure 4.5).[18]

One potential explanation for higher pollution levels in these cities could be higher traffic congestion in the vicinity of new subway stations. For example, private cars and motorbikes, taxis, and ride-sharing vehicles stop to drop off and pick up passengers using the subway, particularly around peak hours. Consistent with this idea, Rao (2016) finds that the opening of London's "night tube" service in August 2016, which extended the weekend operating hours of the Central and Victoria lines on the city's metro system to also cover the hours 12:30 a.m. to 5:30 a.m., had a statistically significant positive impact on rideshare journeys in the neighborhoods in which night tube metro stations are located. Meanwhile, for Jakarta, Gaduha, Gračner, and Rothenberg (2022) estimate that the opening of TransJakarta, one of the world's largest bus rapid transit systems, had the unintended effect of *increasing* traffic congestion along service corridors. They attribute this outcome to failings in the implementation of the system. Gaduha, Gračner, and Rothenberg rely on counterfactual simulations performed using a quantitative spatial general equilibrium model to show how improvements in design could yield significant welfare improvements with only modest costs. These examples suggest that good design and planning are key to realizing the environmental and other benefits of mass public transportation systems.

Figure 4.5 Estimated impacts of subway system openings between August 2001 and July 2016 on air pollution levels, 58 cities

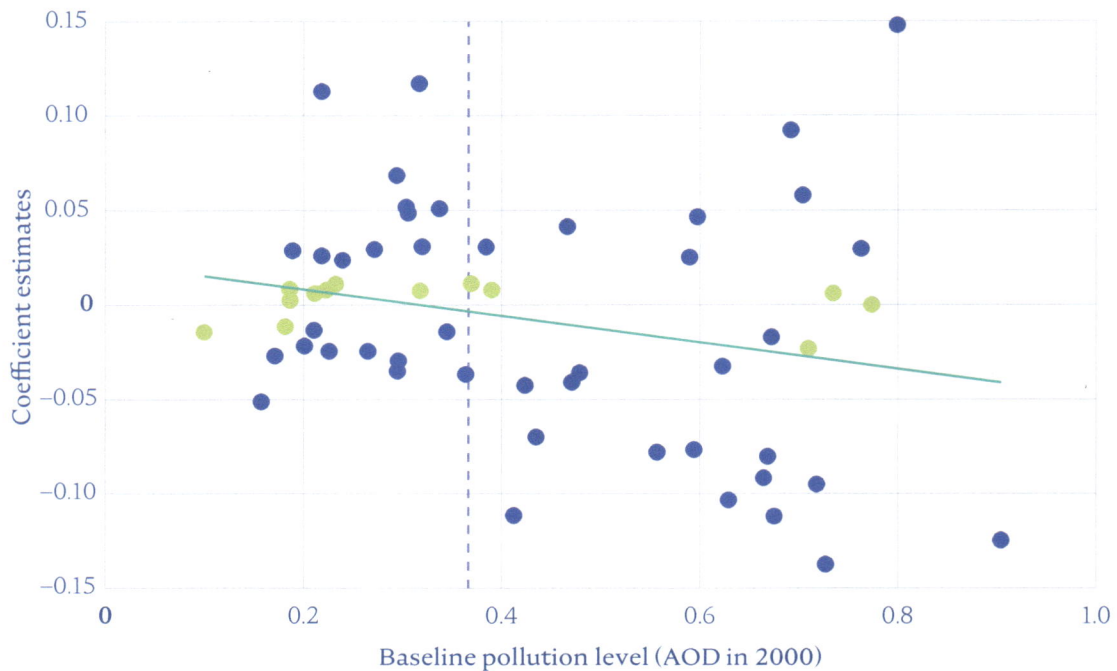

Source: Gendron-Carrier et al. 2022.

Note: Graph shows the estimated 58 city-specific subway effects as markers. Blue markers indicate estimates that are statistically significant at the 5 percent level; green markers indicate estimates that are statistically insignificant at the 5 percent level. The horizontal axis indicates the Aerosol Optical Depth (AOD) level, a measure of air pollution, in 2000, and the vertical axis indicates the coefficient estimates. The solid line shows a linear fit of the markers, and the vertical dashed line the partition of the sample into those below and above median initial AOD level. Standard errors are clustered at the city level.

How will urban expansion affect agricultural land and production?

How climate change is addressed will have important implications for land use

The growth of cities, and urbanization more generally, is intertwined with food systems and opportunities for their transformation. Because it gives rise to income growth, urbanization is associated with a rising and changing demand for food. It also leads to changes in land use that affect agriculture, and cities channel important finance, inputs, information, services, and off-farm employment opportunities to rural areas (Abu Hatab et al. 2019; de Bruin, Dengerink, and van Vliet 2021; World Bank 2009). Moreover, the interactions among climate change, urban expansion, land use, and food production exacerbate challenges for cities.

The world's approach to climate change adaptation and mitigation is, to an extent, determined by economic and demographic drivers, including population growth, the urban share of the population, and income per capita. In this context, the five Shared Socioeconomic Pathways (SSPs) represent scenarios of how the world might respond to climate change moving forward according to different projections of these drivers (box 4.5). The SSPs trace the projected trajectories of various outcomes, including energy use, land use, greenhouse gas (GHG) emissions, and climate change. Of the five SSPs, SSP1 is a largely positive scenario referred to as a "sustainability pathway," whereas SSP3 is a largely negative scenario called a "regional rivalry pathway" (Riahi et al. 2017).

A look at the underlying economic and demographic drivers reveals the following. First, total population will grow faster and the illiterate proportion of the population will decline more slowly under SSP3 than under SSP1. Population will peak around 2050 under SSP1, whereas it will continue to grow through 2100 under SSP3. Also under SSP3, the illiteracy rate will begin to grow by 2040. Second, the urban share of the population will increase under both scenarios, but it will do so much faster under SSP1 than under SSP3 because urbanization is assumed to link to better development outcomes. Third, GDP per capita grows exponentially under SSP1, whereas it remains stagnant under SSP3. Income inequality declines much faster under SSP1 than under SSP3.

Box 4.5

Five Shared Socioeconomic Pathways

The five Shared Socioeconomic Pathways (SSPs) are part of a new scenario framework established by the climate change research community to facilitate integrated analysis of future climate impacts, vulnerabilities, adaptation, and mitigation (Riahi et al. 2017). They involve three main sets of scenario drivers: (1) population and education; (2) urbanization, defined as the urban share of the population (Jiang and O'Neill 2017); and (3) gross domestic product per capita and interpersonal income inequality. The five SSPs are the following:

- *SSP1*: Sustainability—taking the green road (low challenges to adaptation and mitigation)
- *SSP2*: Middle of the road (medium challenges to mitigation and adaptation)
- *SSP3*: Regional rivalry (high challenges to mitigation and adaptation)
- *SSP4*: Inequality (low challenges to mitigation, high challenges to adaptation)
- *SSP5*: Fossil-fueled development (high challenges to mitigation, low challenges to adaptation)

The narrative for SSP1, for example, says that "the world shifts gradually, but pervasively, toward a more sustainable path, emphasizing more inclusive development that respects perceived environmental boundaries. Management of the global commons slowly improves, educational and health investments accelerate the demographic transition, and the emphasis on economic growth shifts toward a broader emphasis on human well-being. Driven by an increasing commitment to achieving development goals, inequality is reduced both across and within countries. Consumption is oriented toward low material growth and lower resource and energy intensity." (Riahi et al. 2017, 157).

Food production has significant negative impacts on climate. In 2015, GHG emissions from the global food system amounted to 18 gigatonnes of CO_2 equivalent or one-third of total GHG emissions. The largest contribution, 71 percent, came from agriculture and land use or land use change activities, with the remainder from supply chain activities, including retail, transportation, consumption, fuel production, waste management, industrial processes, and packaging (Crippa et al. 2021). Emissions associated with animal-based foods are twice as large as those associated with plant-based foods. Of the global GHG emissions from food production, 57 percent come from animal-based foods (including livestock feed), 29 percent from plant-based foods, and 14 percent from other uses (Xu et al. 2021). The two largest contributing plant- and animal-based commodities are rice (12 percent) and beef (25 percent).

Under a scenario of sustainability (SSP1), cropland would barely expand between 2010 and 2100, whereas pasture, suitable for livestock grazing, would decrease (figure 4.6, panels a and b). Meanwhile, forests and other natural land are projected to expand (figure 4.6, panel c). By contrast, under a regional rivalry pathway (SSP3), cropland and pasture would increase, whereas forests and other natural land would decline dramatically (Riahi et al. 2017). Under SSP1, therefore, sustainable food production implies the use of less land-intensive and more productive methods to feed a growing population. Under SSP3, the combination of population growth, deforestation, and unchecked livestock production will result in significantly increased risks, including a heightened risk for pandemics (box 4.6).

No matter the scenario, however, urban land is projected to expand—and more so, at least initially, under a scenario of sustainability than under one of regional rivalry. The assumed underlying growth trends in total population and in the urban population share will thus lead to an increase in the demand for urban land up to 2100 across all SSP pathways (Chen et al. 2020)—see figure 4.6, panel d. Under SSP1, the demand for urban land will increase but then decline after 2070, given the assumed eventual decline in population after 2050 under this scenario. Under SSP3, the demand for urban land will initially increase more slowly than under SSP1, given the assumed slow growth in the urban share of the population under SSP3. Because of the continued population growth to 2100 under SSP3, however, urban land demand will continue to expand to 2100 and will approach the same level as SSP1 by 2100.

These projections, however, do not account for the possibility of vertical and infill urban development, which, as discussed earlier in this chapter, can help cities accommodate the growing demand for urban land without having to expand as rapidly outward. To the extent that income per capita is projected to grow faster under SSP1 than under SSP3, vertical layering can, along with infill development, be expected to occur more quickly under the former than under the latter scenario. Policy and institutional reforms, which improve the functioning of urban land and property markets, thereby reducing vertical development costs, can likewise be expected to slow the horizontal expansion of cities, as can the relaxation of planning restrictions that constrain tall building development and foster car dependence.

Most urban expansion will be into cropland, followed by forests

Across all pathways, it is projected that most urban expansion will entail the conversion of particularly productive cropland, followed by forests and then grassland. By 2100, under SSP1, 55 percent of newly expanded urban land (63 percent under SSP3) is expected to have displaced current cropland, 27 percent (21 percent) forests, and 12 percent (6 percent) grassland. The conversion of cropland and grassland into urban land has important implications for crop and livestock production, and the conversion of forests will have negative implications for biodiversity and carbon sequestration (Chen et al. 2020). Urban expansion will therefore result in

Figure 4.6 **Projected changes in global land area devoted to crops, pasture, forests, and urban uses under five scenarios of climate change mitigation and adaptation, 2010–2100**

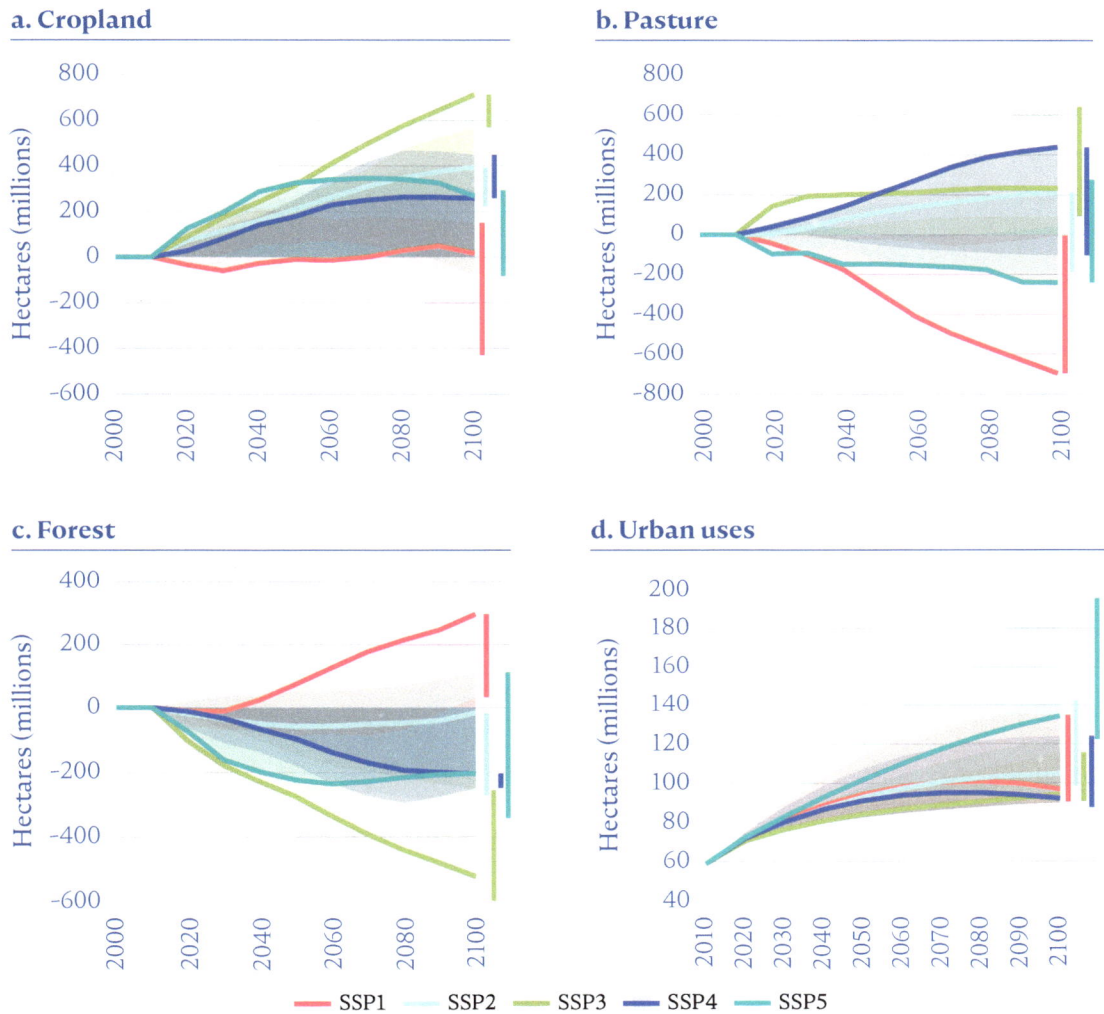

a. Cropland

b. Pasture

c. Forest

d. Urban uses

SSP1 SSP2 SSP3 SSP4 SSP5

Sources: Adapted based on data from Riahi et al. 2017 (panels a, b, and c) and Chen et al. 2020 (panel d).

Note: Panels a, b, and c depict changes in cropland, pasture, and forest for the five Shared Socioeconomic Pathways (SSPs) and their ranges. Changes are shown relative to the baseline year 2010 = 0. Panel d depicts projections of urban land demand under the SSP scenarios, with the shaded area representing 95 percent confidence intervals of projected urban land demand. km² = square kilometers.

Pandemic risks at the interface of humans, animals, and the environment

The continued periodic surges of COVID-19 highlight the urgent need to mitigate the risk of another pandemic, which may result in even more deaths and greater disruptions of economic activity. It is impossible to anticipate where the next pandemic will emerge because every region has experienced an increase in outbreaks of emerging infectious diseases (EIDs), with a growing prevalence of zoonotic and viral diseases.

Despite the global nature of pandemic risks and vulnerabilities, they are not distributed evenly. Most hot spots for EIDs are in low- and middle-income countries, where the biodiversity and abundance of animal hosts are high, and the behaviors and occupations that bring people and animals into contact are widespread. Diseases can spread rapidly in large cities, which can then serve as incubators for epidemics and pandemics. The low-quality housing and poor sanitation arising from poorly managed urbanization provide breeding grounds for various diseases. Poorly managed and unplanned urbanization can also lead to close encounters with wildlife as urban development intrudes on previously untouched ecosystems.

The best strategy in the face of uncertainties about EIDs and pandemic risks is to adopt a "One Health approach." This cross-sectoral approach centers around the connections among people, animals, plants, and their shared environment. It fosters mitigation of pandemic risk by preventing EIDs at the source.

Applying a One Health approach entails learning from past zoonotic outbreaks and focusing on hot spots where land use changes and food system characteristics involve certain high-risk practices.

- The most important reservoirs of pathogens with pandemic potential are mammals, particularly bats, rodents, and primates, as well as some birds and livestock such as pigs, poultry, and camels.

- High-risk practices in land use change include deforestation, mining practices, ecotourism practices, and the wildlife trade.

- High-risk practices in food systems include low biosecurity in livestock systems, uncontrolled intensification of animal production, livestock trade, slaughterhouses, and live animal markets.

- About 70 percent of EIDs (such as Ebola, Zika, and Nipah encephalitis) and almost all known pandemics (such as influenza, HIV/AIDS, COVID-19) are zoonoses, meaning they arise from microbes of animal origin. These microbes spill over to people after contact with wildlife and livestock.

Estimated costs of financing a One Health investment framework range from US$22 billion to US$31 billion, or roughly 1 percent of the global economic loss in 2020 from COVID-19. Such a framework would include investments to preserve key wildlife habitats and resources to avoid wildlife-human conflict; to improve housing conditions to avoid wildlife intrusions; to develop effective waste management systems; to implement community engagement, regulations, and enforcement to curb illegal or

Box 4.6 *continued*

unsafe wildlife trade; and to enhance markets (such as improved design of facilities, pest control, or off-site slaughter). Additionally, investments in biosecurity measures and technology for livestock facilities are crucial to prevent the spread of pathogens between livestock and from livestock to humans. Such investments may be led by different entities/bodies depending on the nature of the interventions and the responsibilities of the different entities (such as waste management, urban planning, and market supervision). They would, therefore, be best designed and supervised with the help of a One Health coordinating mechanism, such as a cross-sector platform that brings together the necessary technical expertise. Such preventive investment reduces the need for health sector–based prevention and preparedness measures, and generates environmental and health co-benefits from preventing deforestation and strengthening livestock production.

Source: Adapted from World Bank 2022.

a 1.8–2.4 percent reduction in global cropland by 2030, and 80 percent of this loss will likely take place in Africa and Asia. Moreover, expansion is expected to take place on cropland that is 1.77 times more productive than the global average (d'Amour et al. 2017).

This loss of crop and other land due to urban expansion is tied to a projected decline in cereal and vegetable production across all pathways. For the world's main cereals—rice, wheat, and maize—production declines of 2–3 percent, 1–3 percent, and 1–4 percent, respectively, are projected. Projected production reductions for vegetables are 2–4 percent and for potatoes 1–3 percent. These reductions correspond to the food needs of between 122 million and 1.39 billion people (Chen et al. 2020). Other global estimates similarly project a total crop production loss of about 3.7 percent, rising to losses of 5.6 percent for Asia and 8.9 percent for Africa (d'Amour et al. 2017).

Poorly managed urban expansion is also linked to a projected decline in other key crops and animal-source foods important for diets and nutrition. Under SSP1, by 2100, the largest projected declines among crops will occur for fruits, vegetables, and tubers/roots, and the smallest declines for oils, sugar, and pulses (relative to current levels of production)—see figure 4.7. These declines could potentially lead to less diverse diets. Although food production initially declines faster under SSP1 than under SSP3 to 2040, it then slows so that the projected decrease in food production by 2100 somewhat aligns for both the SSP1 and SSP3 scenarios. Under SSP1, by 2100, the number of livestock, important to the production of animal-source foods rich in protein, also faces a projected decline. The largest declines are for poultry (chickens and ducks) and pigs, with smaller declines for ruminants (cattle, sheep, and goats). This projection aligns with the notion that the production of poultry and pigs is more peri-urban than that of ruminants. The declines for crop and livestock production are largest under the SSP5 scenario. Finally, these projected impacts show important regional differences. Under SSP1 by 2100, the largest decline for cereals is in Europe, for vegetables in North America, and for poultry in Africa.

Figure 4.7 Projected crop and livestock losses from urban expansion under SSP scenarios by 2040 and 2100

a. Projected crop losses by 2040

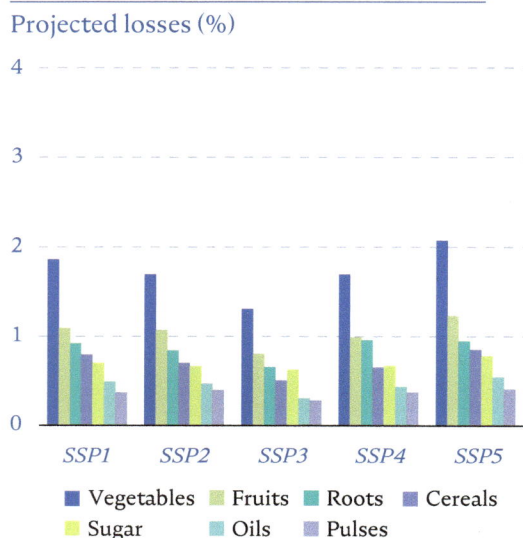

Projected losses (%)

b. Projected crop losses by 2100

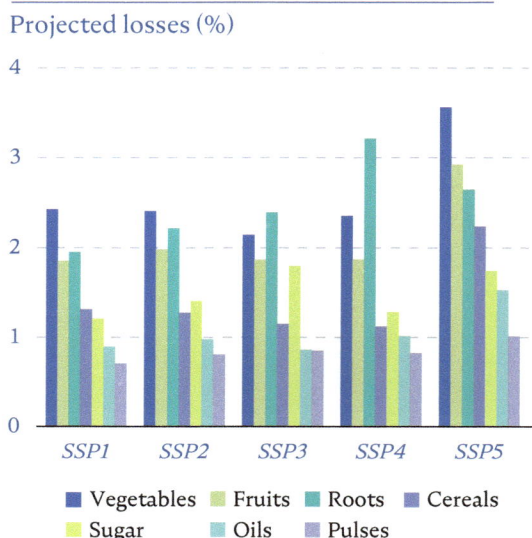

Projected losses (%)

Legend: Vegetables, Fruits, Roots, Cereals, Sugar, Oils, Pulses

c. Projected livestock losses by 2040

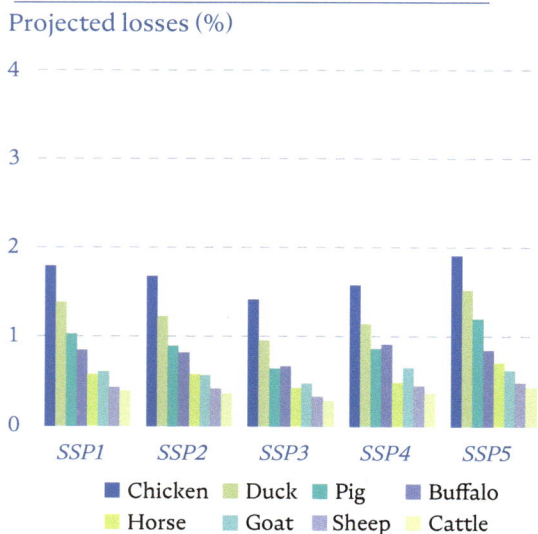

Projected losses (%)

e. Projected livestock losses by 2100

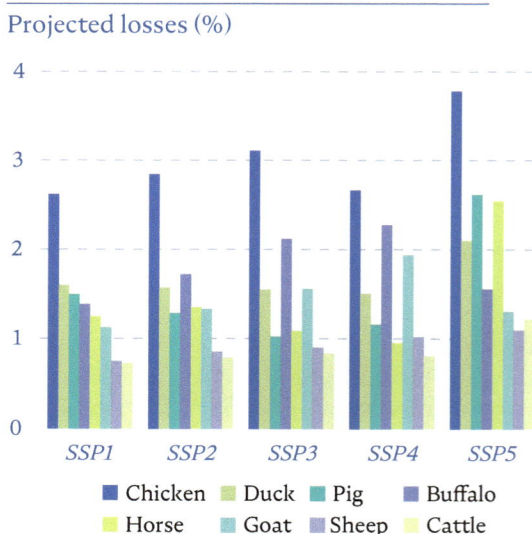

Projected losses (%)

Legend: Chicken, Duck, Pig, Buffalo, Horse, Goat, Sheep, Cattle

Source: World Bank Staff calculations based on Chen et al. 2020; Gilbert et al. 2018; International Food Policy Research Institute, "Global Spatially-Disaggregated Crop Production Statistics Data for 2010 Versi2.0," Harvard Dataverse, V4, 2019 (https://doi.org/10.7910/DVN/PRFF8V).

Note: SSP = Shared Socioeconomic Pathway.

The decline in food production projected to result from urban expansion reinforces the importance of policy measures and institutional reforms to promote more compact urban development. Because urban land expansion is projected to be faster and remain higher by 2100 under a sustainable pathway than under a regional rivalry pathway, the projected decline in food production is slightly larger under the sustainable pathway. If anything, such a finding places even more importance on measures to reduce the costs of vertical development and reduce car dependence under a sustainable pathway than under a regional rivalry pathway.

Along with encouraging more compact development, enhancing agricultural productivity and reducing food loss and waste also can offset the impacts of horizontal urban expansion. Sustainably improving agricultural productivity requires accelerated innovation, as opposed to increasing the use of land, water, and other production inputs. Innovation through the invention, adaptation, and dissemination of locally adapted new technologies will be key (Fuglie et al. 2019). In addition, reducing food loss and waste (for example, via agro-logistics, cold chains, improved infrastructure, easier access to markets, enhanced consumer awareness, and improved urban waste and landfill policies) not only reduces the carbon footprint and environmental stresses of the food system but also improves food security by making more food available in the supply chain and lowering prices (World Bank 2020).

Measures to enhance agricultural productivity are important also because, in addition to land constraints, agriculture faces climate change–related productivity losses and urbanization-related labor constraints. On the one hand, food systems have significant impacts on climate largely through agriculture and land use changes. On the other hand, climate change has slowed the global growth in agricultural productivity. Anthropogenic climate change has reduced global agricultural total factor productivity by an estimated 21 percent since 1961, equivalent to losing the last seven years of productivity growth (Ortiz-Bobea et al. 2021). These negative impacts are largest in Africa and Latin America and the Caribbean.

In addition to climate change–related productivity losses, an important corollary to increased urbanization (and structural transformation more broadly) is that the shrinking share of labor employed in food production must become much more productive to meet the growing and changing food demand of a much larger nonagricultural population.[19] Other indications suggest, however, that the movement of people from rural to urban areas may relax agricultural land constraints. Such movement would release rural lands for agriculture and make farms less fragmented and potentially more efficient (Wang et al. 2021). Finally, the rising need for food could be addressed through international trade, combined with productivity gains in countries that have such comparative advantages. Doing so must be balanced, however, by mitigating the risks associated with food production becoming concentrated in a narrower set of countries.

How will urban growth affect competition for water between cities and agricultural lands?

Competition between cities and agriculture for water supplies will likely grow

Since 1960, the global urban population has quadrupled, pushing up the demand for water by urban areas. In many cities, populations are growing faster than their water services. Recent headlines from Cape Town, South Africa; Chennai, Tamil Nadu, India; and

São Paulo, Brazil reveal that some of the world's megacities have begun to face "day zero" events, whereby water supplies become severely low (Zaveri et al. 2021).

Although these events have grabbed international attention, they are by no means unique. Scores of small cities throughout the world face similar water shortages (Zaveri et al. 2021). The many small urban centers closely tied to rural areas are surrounded by agricultural land experiencing very high levels of water stress or drought frequency (FAO 2020). Estimates suggest that 150 million people live in cities with perennial water shortages, defined as having less than 100 liters per person per day of sustainable surface water or groundwater. Many more people—885 million, roughly equivalent to four times the entire population of Brazil—live in cities with a seasonal water shortage (that is, with monthly water availability of less than 100 liters per person per day) and insufficient flows occurring in at least one month of the year (McDonald et al. 2011).

The expected addition of 2.5 billion urban dwellers by 2050 will accelerate this trend, increasing the urban water demand by a projected 50–80 percent (Flörke, Schneider, and McDonald 2018; Garrick et al. 2019; World Bank 2018). This increase will be fueled not only by the growing numbers of urban dwellers but also by lifestyles and consumption patterns that are more water-intensive. A large part of this increase will be driven by the consumption of more meat and dairy products, although such products can have vastly different water footprints, depending on how they are produced (FAO 2020). Such a dietary shift will therefore play a strong role in shaping water demand in an agriculture sector that will be called on to meet the greater demand for food, which, in turn, could fuel competition for water resources. As societies urbanize, demand from industry, energy, and other services could also increase. Evidence from Singapore suggests that industrial policies substantially increased the share of nondomestic water consumption to 55 percent (Hoekstra, Buurman, and van Ginkel 2018). Overall, by 2050 almost 1 billion urban dwellers globally will live in water-stressed cities (Damania et al. 2017).

Growing demands notwithstanding, the alteration of the global hydrologic cycle stemming from climate change is also leading to an increase in the number of extreme water shortage episodes, making water supplies less predictable (see also chapter 1). With climate change, water shortages will proliferate to other parts of the world, potentially affecting even more city dwellers. In a worst-case scenario, estimates suggest that a warming world could make events like the day zero drought 100 times more likely than they were in the early twentieth-century world in certain regions (Pascale et al. 2020).

Water shortages, and the restrictions put in place to deal with them, have high costs for both urban residents and businesses. Dwindling water supplies can cost a city up to a 12-percentage-point loss in GDP (Zaveri et al. 2021). Meanwhile, unreliable water supplies and water shortages adversely affect productivity by reducing workers' incomes, inducing lower sales for firms, and worsening health outcomes (Desbureaux and Rodella 2019; Islam and Hyland 2019), thereby reinforcing deep inequalities and trapping vulnerable households in cycles of poverty (see chapter 3). These findings highlight the critical importance of investing in policies and infrastructure that can enhance urban water resilience.

As cities grow, they often encroach on surrounding areas to satisfy their thirst

The encroachment of development into the flood banks of rivers, into wetlands, and upon natural infrastructure often occurs in response to the growing demand for scarce land in cities. Such encroachment destroys the natural storage and sponges that regulate cities' water supplies, largely because households and developers lack the incentive to preserve natural infrastructure as the private benefits derived from developing land do not fully reflect the benefits of these ecosystems to society (Taylor and Druckenmiller 2022). When renewable local water resources are insufficient to meet increasing demand and per capita consumption, the result may be overexploitation of surface water and groundwater resources (including the consumption of fossil groundwater) or the use of additional external water resources (Hoekstra, Buurman, and van Ginkel 2018; also see box 4.7). These pressures are especially exacerbated in areas of unplanned growth on the peripheries of cities, which suffer from a lack of municipal water connections and inadequate public service delivery. Overall, these trends create pressure and increase competition for water among cities, as well as between cities and rural areas.

Water reallocation from rural to urban areas is fast becoming a common strategy to meet fresh-water needs in ever-thirstier cities (Garrick et al. 2019; Zaveri et al. 2021). Globally, 69 cities with a population of 383 million receive water through reallocation projects that typically transfer water from surrounding rural areas (Garrick et al. 2019). Global estimates suggest that moving an estimated 16 billion cubic meters of water across nearly 13,000 kilometers is costly (Garrick et al. 2019). Reallocation can occur in other ways as well. When areas urbanize, reallocating water from agricultural to urban uses can occur organically and somewhat inconspicuously through land use change; however, other methods of reallocation can be more conspicuous. In some places, the failure of local utilities or the inadequacy of urban water supply infrastructure prompts informal water vendors to fill the gap by pumping water from surrounding agricultural tube wells. Elsewhere, reallocation occurs through expropriation of water rights, water grabbing by cities, or single-source water resource development.

For all these reasons, reallocation is politically complex because it may entail depriving farmers of a crucial livelihood resource and input. In the absence of equitable legal arrangements, transfers of water from rural areas can be coercive.[20] Most legal systems prioritize drinking water, and often industrial water, above agricultural water in allocation decisions. Such decisions can reduce the water available for irrigated urban and peri-urban agriculture (Hoekstra, Buurman, and van Ginkel 2018). Many countries also have poorly developed water rights systems, and adaptive allocation systems are still few and far between. Reallocations are often crisis-driven, ad hoc, and therefore very poorly designed. These trends suggest the need for capacity building to create the legal and institutional preconditions for more equitable arrangements.

Various other factors can also influence these transfers. Investments in efficient use of irrigation water and reuse of wastewater in irrigation can enable agricultural areas to grow more with less water. A 10 percent increase in the efficient use of irrigation water could free up enough water to reduce urban water deficits by 2.7 billion cubic meters by 2050, benefiting almost 240 million people (Flörke, Schneider, and McDonald 2018). Such effects will likely be most visible and relevant for cities in water-stressed basins highly dependent on irrigation. At the same time, it will be equally important to implement policies that encourage cities to use less water. Indeed, urban demand management will be critical. Dynamically efficient volumetric water pricing, for example, can adjust the price of water to better match the scarcity cities face. When cities allow utilities to carefully adjust the price of water according to its scarcity, the utilities can avoid the need to invest in water-augmenting technologies and thus save money, reduce water footprints, and keep water costs lower in the long run. Other technologies, such as smart water meters and water-saving and water-reusing appliances, can help households reduce their water footprint with little sacrifice (Zaveri et al. 2021).

Box 4.7

Sinking cities: Groundwater depletion and land subsidence

Urban water systems interact with many other systems and are affected in indirect ways. A clear example of complex interactions on an urban scale is when the land begins to slowly sink, a phenomenon known as land subsidence.

Land subsidence often results from unsustainable groundwater extraction to meet increasing demand or from drainage to make wetlands suitable for urban expansion (Hoekstra, Buurman, and van Ginkel 2018). High rates of groundwater extraction around major cities in the Americas, Asia, Europe, and the Middle East have led to localized depletion that, in many cases, has resulted in land subsidence. In these environments, groundwater depletion stems from high pumping rates and the reduction in recharge as the coverage of impervious surface areas increases. With continued urbanization, especially in coastal cities and cities in deltas, the trends of groundwater depletion and land subsidence will likely continue, with potentially higher susceptibility to flooding and groundwater salinization (Lall, Josset, and Russo 2020). New estimates suggest that 22 percent of the world's major cities are in potential subsidence areas, with 57 percent of these also located in flood-prone areas. (Herrera-García et al. 2021; Lall, Josset, and Russo 2020). Land subsidence also compromises the structural integrity of existing buildings. The risks posed by land subsidence can lead to lower property values and thus affect the income streams of property developers and tax revenues of local governments (World Bank 2021; Yoo and Perrings 2017). In the absence of well-functioning markets and institutions, these externalities are often not internalized.

One stark example of land subsidence is Jakarta, Indonesia, the world's fastest-sinking city. On average, it has subsided more than 3.5 meters since the 1980s and continues to sink at rates of up to 20 centimeters a year. The absence of access to reliable piped water, which forces users to resort to unregulated groundwater abstraction, is a major cause of groundwater overexploitation. Across Indonesia, government-owned water enterprises provide only 9 percent of total domestic water demand, and almost half of all households and most commercial and industrial premises rely on supplies from onsite groundwater (World Bank 2021).

Map B4.7.1 shows the comparative land subsidence rates across Indonesia and Asian megacities (World Bank 2021). Jakarta already lies significantly below sea level, and land subsidence increasingly exposes it to high coastal and inland flood risks, even without considering sea-level rise. Partly in response to the growing pressures, the Indonesian government, in a dramatic move in January 2022, passed a law to officially move the capital from Jakarta to an undeveloped jungle tract in East Kalimantan, Borneo.

Box 4.7 *continued*

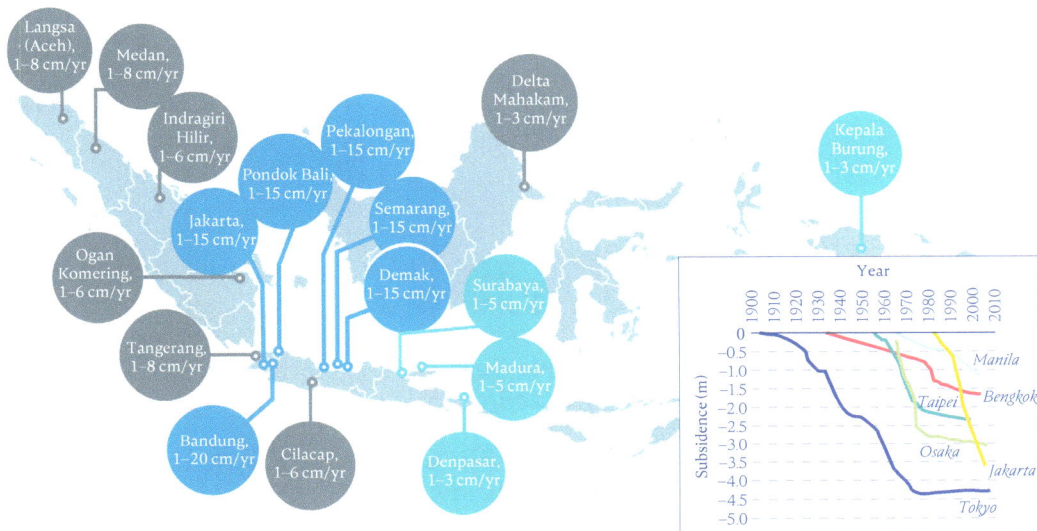

Map B4.7.1   Comparative land subsidence rates across Indonesia, 2000s, and Asian megacities, 1900–2010

Sources: World Bank 2021. Land subsidence rates across Indonesia from Andreas et al. 2018. Land subsidence rates in Asian megacities (inset graph at bottom right) from Kaneko and Toyota 2011 and Takagi et al. 2016.

Note: Rates for Indonesia in centimeters per year (cm/yr). Rates for Asian megacities in meters (m).

Cities also often use their surrounding regions as sinks for waste

Farmland downstream from cities often relies on contaminated urban wastewater for irrigation. Globally, 65 percent of all irrigated cropland within 40 kilometers downstream of cities relies heavily on wastewater flows (Thebo et al. 2017). In some ways, wastewater irrigation provides a triple win: it reduces the amount of water that needs to be extracted; it offers a solution to discharging urban wastewater, often without treatment; and some dissolved nutrients can act as a fertilizer to boost agricultural yields, which, in turn, can help meet the growing urban food demand (Damania et al. 2019).

Nevertheless, wastewater reuse for irrigation is not always a panacea. Urban wastewater can have high concentrations of heavy metals, particularly wastewater from cities in low- and middle-income countries where heavy industry is more likely to be present (Damania et al. 2019). If not carefully managed, wastewater irrigation can cause environmental damage, harm crop quality, and, in turn, potentially expose some 885 million urban residents who consume these agricultural products to serious health risks. The European Commission, the US Environmental Protection Agency, and the World Health

Organization all have minimum water quality requirements and guidelines for wastewater that should be properly enforced to foster best practices and implementation (Damania et al. 2019). Adopting fit for purpose treatment for wastewater—that is, treating waste-water according to the end users' needs—makes this resource a win-win and realistic option for nonconventional sources of water and nutrients for agriculture (Hoekstra, Buurman, and van Ginkel 2018). Because a significant share of urban water is used but not consumed, its reuse in agriculture after treatment has great potential, particularly in water-scarce countries (Hoekstra, Buurman, and van Ginkel 2018).

These examples highlight that water reallocation plays an important role in urban development. Questions remain, however, about how truly effective, equitable, and sustainable water reallocation is. A proper understanding of the range of interactions between urban areas and their local hinterlands is critical to fully understanding the long-run water security of cities.

Summary and conclusions

This chapter has analyzed some of the ways the development of cities can affect the climate and, more generally, the environment. In doing so, it has paid particular attention to the interrelated roles of urban form (that is, whether a city develops horizontally, as is typical of many lower-income country cities, or vertically through building taller) and choices of urban transportation mode. Policies and institutional reforms that improve the working of land and property markets, enhance urban planning, and encourage a move away from private internal combustion engine vehicles toward public transportation could help cities follow a more vertical and compact development trajectory. In addition to promoting productivity growth, such a trajectory can contribute to reductions in a city's CO_2 emissions and air pollutants such as $PM_{2.5}$, while helping to both prevent deforestation and conserve fertile agricultural land on the peripheries of cities that is a major source of food.

Such policies are more likely to be successful when vertical development is combined with good urban and architectural design, as well as with investments in street paving and lighting that promote walkability. And, when investments in mass transit systems are combined with demand-side policies that reduce the incentives to drive, the evidence suggests that such investments can, if well designed and well implemented, also help directly reduce pollution in highly congested and polluted cities. These investments are particularly relevant to large cities that currently lack mass transit systems. By contrast, no evidence exists to suggest that such investments have any direct impact on pollution in less congested and polluted cities; however, if these investments help promote more compact development in rapidly growing cities, they may have longer-term indirect benefits in terms of helping reduce pollution.

That said, a more vertical and compact development trajectory is not necessarily a panacea for the environmental stresses to which poorly managed urban growth can give rise. Building taller implies the use of more building materials whose production is itself highly carbon-intensive. Thus, a more vertical, compact city may embed more carbon in its buildings than a more horizontal, less compact city. Compact development, therefore, involves a trade-off between the large up-front CO_2 emissions involved in building taller and the long-term lower emissions associated with the more compact urban form. Current research is unclear about the conditions under which more compact development of a city will have net beneficial long-term impacts on its contribution to climate change. What is clear are the beneficial effects of more compact development on a city's productivity and resilience, the conservation of agricultural and forested land, and local air pollution levels.

Moreover, the calculus of the net long-term impacts of more compact development on a city's contribution to climate change will likely change over time, depending on technological progress in the construction and transportation sectors. As electric vehicles become more prevalent, some of the environmental benefits of more compact development—at least in terms of CO_2 emissions and local air pollution—are likely to wane. By contrast, any reduction in the carbon content of concrete, steel, and glass resulting from improved technologies and decarbonization of a country's energy supply will increase the net environmental benefits of more compact development. In thinking, then, about the future development of their cities, urban policy makers need to be cognizant of technological trends, especially because urban development is a highly path-dependent process whereby decisions that affect the built environment and urban form today can reverberate for decades, even centuries, to come.

Finally, this chapter has highlighted the stresses that poorly managed urbanization can place on a city's water supply and the resulting potentially harmful competition for water between urban and rural areas. Better management of urban water demand through scarcity pricing and behavioral as well as technological solutions that reduce water use within homes and by businesses are critical to helping reduce such conflict. Carefully managed reuse of urban wastewater for agriculture after treatment also has great potential, particularly in water-scarce countries.

Notes

1. Using the same definition of cities as this report, Lall et al. (2021) estimate that in 2015 the total built-up area of cities globally was 294,550 square kilometers, or 0.20 percent of the global land area. Other definitions of cities generate higher estimated shares of land area for cities globally, but they are, nevertheless, still small. For example, a nighttime lights–based definition of cities derived by the Center for International Earth Science Information Network implies that cities occupied 2.44 percent of the world's land area in 2010 (CIESIN 2013).

2. Other important technological advances in the late nineteenth century that enabled the construction of tall buildings were the ability to mass-produce steel and the development of better techniques for measuring and analyzing structural loads and stresses. During the 1920s and 1930s, the invention of electric arc welding and fluorescent light bulbs (whose bright light allowed people to work farther from windows and generated less heat than incandescent bulbs) further facilitated tall building construction (from the *How Products Are Made* web page, "Skyscraper," http://www.madehow.com/Volume-6/Skyscraper.html#ixzz7Re2detju).

3. By modern-day standards, it would be more accurate to describe the Home Insurance Building as a midrise building.

4. A tall building is defined as a building with a height of at least 55 meters.

5. The insights by Lall et al. (2021) on vertical layering are derived from a restricted global sample of 400 cities for which building height data are available. This sample is representative of the full global sample of more than 10,000 cities. Their building height data come from the German Aerospace Center's World Settlement Footprint 3D product, which provides estimates of building height at an aggregated 90-meter resolution derived from satellite imagery.

6. Cities in higher-income countries also have a stronger tendency to grow vertically because higher agricultural productivity makes land at a city's edge more expensive. Additionally, because wages are higher, the opportunity cost of commuting time is also higher in richer countries, which provides a further incentive for vertical, as opposed to horizontal, development (Jedwab, Barr, and Brueckner 2022).

7. The GDP per capita data quoted in this paragraph come from the Maddison Project Database 2020, https://www.rug.nl/ggdc/historicaldevelopment/maddison/releases/maddison-project-database-2020.

8. Once completed, the Mohamed VI Tower—currently under construction in Rabat, Morocco—will be the tallest in Africa. For more information, see the BESIX web page about the project, https://www.besix.com/en/projects/mohammed-vi-tower. At 820 feet (250 meters) and 55 stories, the tower will still be less than 60 percent of the height of the Empire State Building.

9. By contrast, for the Democratic People's Republic of Korea and several Gulf states, results from Jedwab, Barr, and Brueckner (2022) indicate excessive tall building construction given these countries' levels of urban development and agricultural rents.

10. Because urban land is rarely converted back into rural land, such a contraction should be thought of as being relative to what would have otherwise occurred—that is, horizontal expansion takes place at a slower pace than would have otherwise occurred, resulting in a city that is smaller in equilibrium relative to the counterfactual scenario.

11. An IV strategy is a standard econometric technique designed to control for various potential sources of endogeneity, including reverse causation.

12. In contrast to the results for population and area, the results for the impacts of a city's total height on its nighttime lights are based on ordinary least squares estimation only, which implies a potential upward bias due to, for example, possible reverse causation. In the results for population and area, however, using IV strategies to deal with reverse causation leads to higher estimated impacts of tall buildings in terms of both expanding population and conserving area. This result may occur because these strategies also help control for classical measurement error, which biases estimated coefficients toward zero (Wooldridge 2013).

13. Using data for 25 addresses in seven UK cities, Pomponi et al. (2021) conduct a simulation exercise that suggests that a high-density, low-rise pattern of urban development is associated with much lower life-cycle GHG emissions than a high-density, high-rise pattern. In addition to being based on a small number of UK addresses, however, their analysis does not account for the lower CO_2 emissions that tend to be associated with more compact development. Furthermore, a high-density, low-rise pattern of urban development is exactly what characterizes many cities in developing countries today. This pattern manifests itself in the form of slums and overcrowding, which are associated with poverty.

14. The fractal dimension is a measure of the "degree of inhomogeneity" of a geometric object (Mandelbrot 1982). It can be thought of as a measure of the complexity of a geometric object's shape.

15. As an example, Ostermeijer et al. (2022) cite the Streetcar Conspiracy of 1949, when General Motors and other car manufacturers were convicted of monopolizing the sale of buses and accused of controlling the transit system to dismantle existing streetcar networks.

16. In the United States, the construction of highways and, before that, railways through cities has contributed to greater segregation within cities by creating physical separation between neighborhoods, often reinforcing existing patterns of racial segregation (Ananat 2011; Badger and Cameron 2015).

17. The "iron law of congestion" asserts that any investment in infrastructure that reduces congestion and therefore the cost of driving in the short run will induce more driving, with the result that congestion eventually rebounds to its original level. Evidence of this outcome is provided by Chen and Klaiber (2020); Duranton and Turner (2011); Garcia-López, Pasidis, and Viladecans-Marsal (2020); and Hsua and Zhang (2014) for Chinese, US, European, and Japanese cities, respectively.

18. Gendron-Carrier et al. (2022) also find no evidence that subway system expansions affect (positively or negatively) levels of air pollution.

19. Historically, improved agricultural productivity has been thought of as a driver of urbanization (that is, labor-saving technological progress in agriculture releases labor from the land, thereby facilitating industrialization and urbanization).

20. When confronted by intermittent water supply, Indian cities such as Chennai draw on water resources from neighboring rural districts, often at the expense of farming communities, thereby fueling urban-rural tensions (Singh et al. 2021; Varadhan 2019; Zaveri et al. 2021).

References

Abu Hatab, A., M. Cavinato, A. Lindermer, and C. Lagerkvist. 2019. "Urban Sprawl, Food Security and Agriculture Systems in Developing Countries: A Systematic Review of Literature." *Cities* 94: 129–42.

Acharya, G., E. Cassou, S. Jaffee, and E. K. Ludher. 2021. *RICH Food, Smart City: How Building Reliable, Inclusive, Competitive, and Healthy Food Systems is Smart Policy for Urban Asia*. Washington, DC: World Bank.

Ahlfeldt, G. M., and J. Barr. 2022. "The Economics of Skyscrapers: A Synthesis." *Journal of Urban Economics* 129: 103419.

Ahlfeldt, G. M., and R. Jedwab. 2022. "The Global Economic and Environmental Effects of Vertical Urban Development." Background paper prepared for this report, World Bank, Washington, DC.

Ahlfeldt, G. M., and E. Pietrostefani. 2019. "The Economic Effects of Density: A Synthesis." *Journal of Urban Economics* 111: 93–107.

Ananat, E. O. 2011. "The Wrong Side(s) of the Tracks: The Causal Effects of Racial Segregation on Urban Poverty and Inequality." *American Economic Journal: Applied Economics* 3 (2): 34–66.

Andreas, H., H. Abidin, I. Gumilar, T. P. Sidiq, D. A. Sarsito, and D. Pradipta. 2018. "Insight into the Correlation between Land Subsidence and the Floods in Regions of Indonesia." In *Natural Hazards—Risk Assessment and Vulnerability Reduction,* edited by José Simão Antunes Do Carmo. IntechOpen.

Badger, E., and D. Cameron. 2015. "How Railroads, Highways and Other Man-Made Lines Racially Divide America's Cities." *Washington Post*, July 15, 2015.

Baum-Snow, N. 2007. "Did Highways Cause Suburbanization?" *Quarterly Journal of Economics* 122 (2): 775–805.

Baum-Snow, N., L. Brandt, V. Henderson, M. Turner, and Q. Zhang. 2016. "Highways, Market Access, and Urban Growth in China." IGC Working Paper C-89114-CHN-1, International Growth Centre, London.

Bernard, A. 2014. *Lifted: A Cultural History of the Elevator*. New York: New York University Press.

Bertaud, A., and J. K. Brueckner. 2004. "Analyzing Building Height Restrictions: Predicted Impacts, Welfare Costs, and a Case Study of Bangalore, India." Policy Research Working Paper 3290, World Bank, Washington, DC.

Blaudin de Thé, C., B. Carantino, and M. Lafourcade. 2021. "The Carbon 'Carprint' of Urbanization: New Evidence from French Cities." *Regional Science and Urban Economics* 89 (C).

Chen, G., X. Li, X. Liu, Y. Chen, X. Liang, J. Leng, X. Xu, et al. 2020. "Global Projections of Future Urban Land Expansion under Shared Socioeconomic Pathways." *Nature Communications* 11: 537.

Chen, W., and H. A. Klaiber. 2020. "Does Road Expansion Induce Traffic? An Evaluation of Vehicle-Kilometers Traveled in China." *Journal of Environmental Economics and Management* 104: 102387.

Cherif, R., F. Hasanov, and A. Pande. 2017. "Riding the Energy Transition: Oil Beyond 2040." IMF Working Paper WP/17/120, International Monetary Fund, Washington, DC.

CIESIN (Center for International Earth Science Information Network). 2013. "Low Elevation Coastal Zone Urban-Rural Population and Land Area Estimates, Version 2." Technical report, CIESIN, Columbia University, Palisades, NY.

Crippa, M., E. Solazzo, D. Guizzardi, F. Monforti-Ferrario, F.N. Tubiella, and A. Leip. 2021. "Food Systems Are Responsible for a Third of Global Anthropogenic GHG Emissions." *Nature Food* 2: 198–209.

Damania, R., S. Desbureaux, M. Hyland, A. Islam, S. Moore, A.-S. Rodella, J. Russ, et al. 2017. *Uncharted Waters: The New Economics of Water Scarcity and Variability*. Washington, DC: World Bank.

Damania, R., S. Desbureaux, A. S. Rodella, J. Russ, and E. Zaveri. 2019. *Quality Unknown: The Invisible Water Crisis*. Washington, DC: World Bank.

d'Amour, C. B., F. Reitsma, G. Baiocchi, S. Barthel, B. Güneralp, K. Erb, H. Haberl, et al. 2017. "Future Urban Land Expansion and Implications for Global Croplands." *Proceedings of the National Academy of Sciences* 114 (34): 8939–44.

de Bruin, S., J. Dengerink, and J. van Vliet. 2021. "Urbanization as Driver of Food Systems Transformation and Opportunities for Rural Livelihoods." *Food Security* 13: 781–98.

Desbureaux, S., and A. Rodella. 2019. "Drought in the City: The Economic Impact of Water Scarcity in Latin American Metropolitan Areas." *World Development* 114: 13–27.

Duranton, G., and M. Turner. 2011. "The Fundamental Law of Road Congestion: Evidence from US Cities." *America Economic Review* 101 (6): 2616–52.

Ellis, P., and M. Roberts. 2016. *Leveraging Urbanization in South Asia: Managing Spatial Transformation for Prosperity and Livability*. Washington, DC: World Bank.

Ewing, R., S. Hamidi, J. B. Grace, and Y. D. Wei. 2016. "Does Urban Sprawl Hold Down Upward Mobility?" *Landscape and Urban Planning* 148 (April): 80–88.

Falk, N., and J. Rudlin. 2018. "Learning from International Examples of Affordable Housing." Shelter/The URBED Trust.

FAO (Food and Agriculture Organization of the United Nations). 2020. *The State of Food and Agriculture 2020. Overcoming Water Challenges in Agriculture*. Rome: FAO.

Flörke, M., C. Schneider, and R. McDonald. 2018. "Water Competition between Cities and Agriculture Driven by Climate Change and Urban Growth." *Nature Sustainability* 1: 51–58.

Fuglie, K., M. Gautam, A. Goyal, and W. Maloney. 2019. *Harvesting Prosperity: Technology and Productivity Growth in Agriculture*. Washington, DC: World Bank.

Gaduha, A., T. Gračner, and A. D. Rothenberg. 2022. "Life in the Slow Lane: Unintended Consequences of Public Transit in Jakarta." *Journal of Urban Economics* 128: 103411.

Garcia-López, M. À., I. Pasidis, and E. Viladecans-Marsal. 2020. "Congestion in Highways when Tolls and Railroads Matter: Evidence from European Cities." Working Papers 2020/11, Institut d'Economia de Barcelona (IEB).

Garrick, D., L. De Stefano, W. Yu, I. Jorgensen, E. O'Donnell, L. Turley, I. Aguilar-Barajas, et al. 2019. "Rural Water for Thirsty Cities: A Systematic Review of Water Reallocation from Rural to Urban Regions." *Environmental Research Letters* 14 (4): 043003.

Gendron-Carrier, N., M. Gonzalez-Navarro, S. Polloni, and M. A. Turner. 2022. "Subways and Urban Air Pollution." *American Economic Journal: Applied Economics* 14 (1): 164–96.

Gilbert, M., G. Nicolas, G. Cinardi, T. P. Van Boeckel, S. O. Vanwambeke, G. R. William Wint, and T. P. Robinson. 2018. "Global Distribution Data for Cattle, Buffaloes, Horses, Sheep, Goats, Pigs, Chickens and Ducks in 2010." *Scientific Data* 5 (1): 180227. https://doi.org/10.1038/sdata.2018.227.

Giridharan, R., and R. Emmanuel. 2018. "The Impact of Urban Compactness, Comfort Strategies and Energy Consumption on Tropical Urban Heat Island Intensity: A Review." *Sustainable Cities and Society* 40 (July): 677–87.

Glaeser, E. 2011. "How Skyscrapers Can Save the City." *Atlantic*, March 2011. https://www.theatlantic.com/magazine/archive/2011/03/how-skyscrapers-can-save-the-city/308387/.

Gottmann, J. 1966. "Why the Skyscraper?" *Geographical Review* 56: 190–212.

Hall, D., and N. Lutsey. 2018. "Effects of Battery Manufacturing on Electric Vehicle Life-Cycle Greenhouse Gas Emissions." International Council on Clean Transportation, Washington, DC.

Hanna, R., G. Kreindler, and B. A. Olken. 2017. "Citywide Effects of High-Occupancy Vehicle Restrictions: Evidence from "Three-in-One" in Jakarta." *Science* 357 (6346): 89–93.

Hausfather, Z. 2019. "Factcheck: How Electric Vehicles Help to Tackle Climate Change." *Eco-Business*, May 14, 2019. https://www.eco-business.com/news/factcheck-how-electric-vehicles-help-to-tackle-climate-change/.

Heger, M., D. Wheeler, G. Zens, and C. Meisner. 2019. *Motor Vehicle Density and Air Pollution in Greater Cairo: Fuel Subsidy Removal and Metro Line Extension and Their Effect on Congestion and Pollution*. Washington, DC: World Bank.

Herrera-García, G., P. Ezquerro, R. Tomás, M. Béjar-Pizarro, J. López-Vinielles, M. Rossi, R.M. Mateos, et al. 2021. "Mapping the Global Threat of Land Subsidence." *Science* 371 (6524): 34–36.

Hess, D. B., T. Tammaru, and M. van Ham. 2018. "Lessons Learned from a Pan-European Study of Large Housing Estates: Origin, Trajectories of Change and Future Prospects." In *Housing Estates in Europe: Poverty, Ethnic Segregation and Policy Challenges*, edited by D. B. Hess, T. Tammaru, and M. van Ham, 3–31. Cham, Switzerland: Springer International Publishing.

Hoekstra, A. Y., J. Buurman, and K. C. H. van Ginkel. 2018. "Urban Water Security: A Review." *Environmental Research Letters* 13 (5): 053002.

Hopkins, F., J. Ehleringer, S. Bush, R. Duren, C. Miller, C. Lai, Y. Hsu, et al. 2016. "Mitigation of Methane Emissions in Cities: How New Measurements and Partnerships Can Contribute to Emissions Reduction Strategies." *Earth's Future* 4: 408–25.

Hsua, W., and H. Zhang. 2014. "The Fundamental Law of Highway Congestion Revisited: Evidence from National Expressways in Japan." *Journal of Urban Economics* 81: 65–76.

Hunt, D. B. 2018. "Public Housing in Urban America." *Oxford Research Encyclopedia of American History*. Oxford, UK: Oxford University Press.

Islam, A., and M. Hyland. 2019. "The Drivers and Impacts of Water Infrastructure Reliability— A Global Analysis of Manufacturing Firms." *Ecological Economics* 163 (C): 143–157.

Jedwab, R., J. Barr, and J. Brueckner. 2022. "Cities Without Skylines: Worldwide Building-Height Gaps and their Possible Determinants and Implications." https://www.remijedwab.com/_files /ugd/ea9b22_1310bef406ba40b3be2ba5e98ecf441d.pdf.

Jiang, L., and B. O'Neill. 2017. "Global Urbanization Projections for the Shared Socioeconomic Pathways." *Global Environmental Change* 42: 193–99.

Kaneko, S., and T. Toyota. 2011. "Long-Term Urbanization and Land Subsidence in Asian Megacities: An Indicators System Approach." In *Groundwater and Subsurface Environments: Human Impacts in Asian Coastal Cities*, edited by Makota Taniguchi. Springer Science & Business Media.

Lai, D., W. Liu, T. Gan, K. Liu, and Q. Chen. 2019. "A Review of Mitigating Strategies to Improve the Thermal Environment and Thermal Comfort in Urban Outdoor Spaces." *Science of the Total Environment* 661 (April): 337–53.

Lall, U., L. Josset, and T. Russo. 2020. "A Snapshot of the World's Groundwater Challenges." *Annual Review of Environment and Resources* 45: 171–94.

Lall, S., M. Lebrand, H. Park, D. Sturm, and A. Venables. 2021. *Pancakes to Pyramids: City Form to Promote Sustainable Growth*. Washington, DC: World Bank.

Mandelbrot, B. 1982. *The Fractal Geometry of Nature*. San Francisco: W. H. Freeman and Co.

McDonald, R. I., I. Douglas, C. Revenga, R. Hale, N. Grimm, J. Grönwall, and B. Fekete. 2011. "Global Urban Growth and the Geography of Water Availability, Quality, and Delivery." *Ambio* 40 (5): 437–46.

Ortiz-Bobea, A., T. R. Ault, C. M. Carrillo, R. G. Chambers, and D. B. Lobell. 2021. "Anthropogenic Climate Change Has Slowed Global Agricultural Productivity Growth." *Nature Climate Change* 11: 306–12.

Ostermeijer, F., H. R. A. Koster, J. van Ommeren, and V. M. Nielsen. 2022. "Automobiles and Urban Density." *Journal of Economic Geography* 22 (5): 1073–95.

Paoli, L., and T. Gül. 2022. "Electric Cars Fend Off Supply Challenges to More than Double Global Sales." International Energy Agency, Paris.

Pascale, S., S. B. Kapnick, T. L. Delworth, and W. F. Cooke. 2020. "Increasing Risk of Another Cape Town 'Day Zero' Drought in the 21st Century." *Proceedings of the National Academy of Sciences* 117 (47): 29495–503.

Pierer, C., and F. Creutzig. 2019. "Star-Shaped Cities Alleviate Trade-Off between Climate Change Mitigation and Adaptation." *Environmental Research Letters* 14 (8): 085011.

Pomponi, F., R. Saint, J. H. Arehart, N. Gharavi, and B. D'Amico. 2021. "Decoupling Density from Tallness in Analysing the Life Cycle Greenhouse Gas Emissions of Cities." *Urban Sustainability* 1: 33.

Prisco, J. 2019. "A Short History of the Elevator." *CNN Style*, February 2, 2019. https://www.cnn .com/style/article/short-history-of-the-elevator/index.html.

Rao, S. 2016. "London's New Late Night Alternative: The Night Tube + Uber." *Uber Under the Hood*, October 7, 2016. https://medium.com/uber-under-the-hood/londons -new-late-night-alternative-the-night-tube-uber-8f38e56de983.

Riahi, K., D. P. van Vuuren, E. Kriegler, J. Edmonds, B. C. O'Neill, S. Fujimori, N. Bauer, et al. 2017. "The Shared Socioeconomic Pathways and Their Energy, Land Use, and Greenhouse Gas Emissions Implications: An Overview." *Global Environmental Change* 42: 153–68.

Roberts, M., F. Gil Sander, and S. Tiwari, eds. 2019. *Time to ACT: Realizing Indonesia's Urban Potential*. Washington, DC: World Bank.

Rosenthal, S. S., and W. C. Strange. 2004. "Evidence on the Nature and Sources of Agglomeration Economies." In *Handbook of Urban and Regional Economics*, vol. 4, edited by J. V. Henderson and J. Thisse, 2119–71. New York: North-Holland.

Samant, S., and N. Hsi-En. 2017. "A Tale of Two Singapore Sky Gardens." *Council on Tall Buildings and Urban Habitat (CTBUH) Journal* 3: 26–31.

Singh, C., G. Jain, V. Sukhwani, and R. Shaw. 2021. "Losses and Damages Associated with Slow-Onset Events: Urban Drought and Water Insecurity in Asia." *Current Opinion in Environmental Sustainability* 50: 72–86.

Southerland, V. A., M. Brauer, A. Mohegh, M. S. Hammer, A. van Donkelaar, R. V. Martin, J. S. Apte, et al. 2022. "Global Urban Temporal Trends in Fine Particulate Matter ($PM_{2.5}$) and Attributable Health Burdens: Estimates from Global Datasets." *Lancet Planetary Health* 6 (2): E139–146.

Takagi, H., M. Esteban, T. Mikami and D. Fujii. 2016. "Projection of Coastal Floods in 2050 Jakarta." *Urban Climate* 17: 135–45.

Taylor, C. A., and H. Druckenmiller. 2022. "Wetlands, Flooding, and the Clean Water Act." *American Economic Review* 112 (4): 1334–63.

Thebo, A. L., P. Drechsel, E. F. Lambin, and K. L. Nelson. 2017. "A Global, Spatially-Explicit Assessment of Irrigated Croplands Influenced by Urban Wastewater Flows." *Environmental Research Letters* 12 (7): 074008.

Varadhan, S. 2019. "Villagers Accuse City of Seizing Water as Drought Parches 'India's Detroit.'" Reuters, July 2, 2019. https://www.reuters.com/article/us-india-water-chennai /villagers-accuse-city-of-seizing-water-as-drought-parches-indias-detroit-idUSKCN1TX1BF.

Wang, S., X. Bai, X. Zhang, S. Reis, D. Chen, J. Xu, and B. Gu. 2021. "Urbanization Can Benefit Agricultural Production with Large-Scale Farming in China." *Nature Food* 2 (3): 183–91.

Ward, K., A. E. G. Jonas, B. Miller, and D. Wilson, eds. 2018. *The Routledge Handbook on Spaces of Urban Politics*. Abingdon, UK: Routledge.

White, J., and B. Serin. 2021. "High-Rise Residential Development: An International Evidence Review." UK Collaborative Centre for Housing Evidence, Glasgow, UK.

Wong, S. K., K. W. Chau, Y. Yau, and A. K. C. Cheung. 2011. "Property Price Gradients: The Vertical Dimension." *Journal of Housing and the Built Environment* 26 (1): 33–45.

Wooldridge, J. M. 2013. *Introductory Econometrics: A Modern Approach*. Mason, OH: South-Western.

World Bank. 2009. *World Development Report 2009: Reshaping Economic Geography*. Washington, DC: World Bank.

World Bank. 2018. *Water Scarce Cities: Thriving in a Finite World*. Washington, DC: World Bank.

World Bank. 2020. *Addressing Food Loss and Waste: A Global Problem with Local Solutions*. Washington, DC: World Bank.

World Bank. 2021. *Indonesia Vision 2045: Toward Water Security*. Washington, DC: World Bank.

World Bank. 2022. "Putting Pandemics behind Us: Investing in One Health to Reduce Risks of Emerging Infectious Diseases." One Health report, October, World Bank, Washington, DC.

Xu, X., P. Sharma, S. Shu, T. Lin, P. Ciais, F. N. Tubiello, P. Smith, et al. 2021. "Global Greenhouse Gas Emissions from Animal-Based foods Are Twice Those of Plant-Based Foods." *Nature Food* 2: 724–32.

Yoo, J., and C. Perrings. 2017. "Modeling the Short-Run Costs of Changes in Water Availability in a Desert City: A Modified Input-Output Approach." *International Review of Applied Economics* 31 (4): 549–64.

Zaveri, E., J. Russ, A. Khan, R. Damania, E. Borgomeo, and A. Jagerskog. 2021. *Ebb and Flow Vol. 1: Water, Migration and Development*. Washington, DC: World Bank.

Zhou, B., D. Rybski, and J. P. Kropp. 2017. "The Role of City Size and Urban Form in the Surface Urban Heat Island." *Scientific Reports* 7: 4791.

PART 3

How Do We Get It Done?

CHAPTER 5

Policies for Promoting Green, Resilient, and Inclusive Urban Development

No matter where you are in life, there is always a long journey ahead.

Nelson Mandela

MAIN FINDINGS

- The World Bank's GRID (green, resilient, and inclusive development) approach adds a sustainability lens to its pursuit of the twin goals of ending extreme poverty and creating shared prosperity. This report aligns with the GRID approach—in its description of how green, how resilient, and how inclusive cities are and in the analytics of how climate change affects cities and vice versa. This prescriptive chapter mirrors that alignment.

- Because of the complexity of the subject, this chapter presents the general conclusions in the form of three questions that policy makers should answer: What policy instruments are available? Who wields these instruments? How can policy choices based on the use of these instruments be prioritized and sequenced for effective implementation?

- WHAT: Policy options take form of five I's: information, incentives, insurance, integration, and investments. Their order represents a sequencing of bundles of interventions. In many instances, the interdependencies between these sets of instruments play out in complementary ways, wherein policies across the bundles strengthen impact when implemented together.

- WHO: Because traditional urban stresses interact with climate change–related stresses to determine outcomes, local governments are well placed to drive climate action. Cities, working with other stakeholders—including national governments, the private sector, and civil society—have a large policy wedge at their disposal.

- HOW: Policy makers will need to toggle between and sandwich together the bundles of policy options described in this chapter to arrive at the GRID outcomes. The combination of interventions, their sequencing, and the prioritization of outcomes will vary depending on the characteristics of cities, including primarily their level of risk, level of development, and size.

Introduction

Even in ancient times, changing climate conditions had catastrophic effects on some cities. The preindustrial city of Angkor, the Khmer Empire's center of political and economic power and home to more than 1 million inhabitants at its peak, was known for its elaborate temples, modern water system, advanced tax administration, and ambitious building projects. Between 1300 and 1400 CE, the city experienced extreme weather anomalies, with severe floods that caused the reservoirs and canals to collapse and prolonged droughts that strained food production. These events may have contributed to the collapse of the city's civilization that followed its sacking and looting by Ayutthaya invaders (Buckley et al. 2010). Other ancient cities were also victims of catastrophic climate change effects. The decline of the Indus Valley—known for its urban settlements, agricultural production, and trade prowess—was precipitated by extensive periods of drought, which intersected with increasing levels of interpersonal violence and disease (Schug et al. 2013).

Fast forward to today. Using the 2021 assessments of the Intergovernmental Panel on Climate Change, Climate Central provides maps of cities expected to find themselves under water because of rising sea levels.[1] The cities include Bangkok, Thailand; Georgetown, Guyana; Kolkata, India; and New Orleans, United States. The panel's *Sixth Assessment Report* projects that more than 1 billion people located in low-lying cities and settlements will be at risk from coastal-specific climate hazards (IPCC 2022). Cities will, of course, face more than just sea-level rise; they will also have to contend with a multitude of sudden-onset shocks and slower-onset stressors.

With these challenges in mind, the World Bank's GRID (green, resilient, and inclusive development) approach adds a sustainability lens to its pursuit of the twin goals of eliminating extreme poverty and creating shared prosperity (World Bank 2021a).[2] The GRID approach sets out a framework for the urgent investments needed in human, physical, natural, and social capital—that is, in keystone systems: energy, food and land use, transportation, and urban systems. Such investments need to be balanced with policies for labor and capital markets to safeguard the vulnerable, compensate those who may lose from these policies, and deliver a just transition. Urbanization offers a critical opportunity to advance GRID in response to the pressures of climate change–related stresses.

This prescriptive chapter mirrors the alignment of the World Bank's goals with the GRID approach. Building on the analysis of previous chapters, this chapter lays out a systematic approach to policy formulation that focuses on what can be done, by whom, and how. In doing so, the chapter demonstrates how strides can be made beyond timid, temporizing policies. Given the complexity of the subject, the chapter lays out its general conclusions in three questions that policy makers should consider: *What* policy instruments are available? *Who* wields these instruments? *How* can policy choices be prioritized, sequenced, and financed for effective implementation? The experiences of various countries and cities qualify some of the general conclusions. Therefore, the chapter interprets the uniqueness of experiences across different contexts and provides a framework for thinking through how policy may tackle the challenges currently facing different types of cities, building on the global typology of cities laid out in chapter 2.

What are the choices?

To tackle the myriad challenges, and in some cases opportunities, associated with climate change, the policy makers of cities will have to make informed, astute choices across an array of possible policies. This section describes the large variety of policy instruments at the disposal of policy makers, coupled with the tools they need in order to think through the choices and their sequencing. These instruments fall into five broad groups, which together make up a sequenced set:

1. Information

2. Incentives

3. Insurance

4. Integration (within and between cities)

5. Investments

Information

Information helps people and firms better understand, and therefore better adapt to, climate risks both across and within cities

Information can take many forms involving various policy instruments. For example, risk management strategies or participatory initiatives could allow ordinary citizens to relay local information to local, regional, and national authorities and policy makers. Or information could take the form of responsive monitoring and early warning mechanisms. Other examples include regularly updated urban planning documents, building codes, and zoning regulations. Information guides decisions by both households and businesses on prevention, mitigation, and adaptation; yet aspects of the collection and sharing of information continue to suffer from shortcomings.

The climate vector embodies ambiguous risks. The probability of extreme events has increased. Fortunately, climate scientists are making significant progress toward rigorously modeling climate-related effects, and it is becoming cheaper to spread locally specific information about impending risks. Even so, policy makers, especially at the subnational level, may find it difficult to determine precisely the potential impacts or to define investment priorities on the basis of these projections. Meanwhile, need is growing for understandable, reliable information paired with no-regrets policy measures that involve key stakeholders, including both local communities and firms. Despite remarkable scientific progress, some of the most vulnerable communities in climate-threatened cities remain poorly informed about both looming disasters and slow-moving changes that affect everyday life. Some of the reasons for this shortcoming— such as insufficient state capacity or lack of trust in government institutions in conflict-affected areas—have been around for a long time. The problem is often not just the dearth of information but also the asymmetry of information across national and local actors, or across sector agencies.[3] Nevertheless, the opportunities for getting accurate and time-sensitive information to those who need it most are far from exhausted. Investments in research and analytical capacities within relevant institutions, for example, remain in their infancy.

Information critical to climate adaptation, such as the results of climate modeling and weather forecasts, is a public good, providing a strong rationale for government provision or subsidization. The diffusion of accurate risk information facilitates better decision-making by households, firms, and local governments. It also provides the facts that citizens need in order to hold their locally elected officials accountable. In the age of machine learning and artificial intelligence, costly surveys to identify changing risks across locations could give way to algorithms that provide cheap, up-to-date data with high degrees of accuracy. Such techniques have been used, for example, to assess wildfire risks in Bulgaria,[4] seasonal predictions of drought across several regions,[5] and even risk financing for host communities in Uganda.[6]

Early warning systems[7] can save lives and, if activated sufficiently in advance, property. Access to early warning systems is, however, lower among poorer populations, who also usually have the least access to other tools to mitigate or transfer risk (Hallegatte et al. 2017). Often, the benefits of early warning systems can be maximized when coupled with other preventative investments. For example, Hong Kong SAR, China, has invested in housing improvements that allow sheltering at home during tropical cyclones, and early warning allows people to return safely to their homes using storm-adaptive public transportation (Rogers and Tsirkunov 2010). Even modest investments in such systems can have high returns. A report from the Global Center on Adaptation and World Resources Institute (2019) finds that early warning systems provide a 10-fold return on investment—the highest of any adaptation measure considered.

When it comes to emerging climate risks, perception versus reality is important

It is not only access to information that matters, but also how that information influences behavior and policy making. Even if well informed, people and businesses may engage in myopic behaviors that can create market failures. For example, although most studies find that information on flood risks reduces land and property prices,[8] others find either mixed or weak evidence of property flood risk discounting (Beltrán, Maddison, and Elliott 2018; Hino and Burke 2021). Likewise, several studies find evidence that land and housing markets adjust in the aftermath of natural disasters but "forget" about the risk several years down the road. Bin and Landry (2013), for example, find strong evidence of properties in North Carolina being sold at a discount in the aftermath of Hurricanes Fran (1996) and Floyd (1999), but document as well that, consistent with myopic behavior, the discount slowly vanishes over time.

Another important dimension is the ambiguous effect of land prices that reflect information on disaster risks. On the one hand, this information signals higher costs to retrofit structures in the aftermath of disasters or to build to higher and more costly standards. This effect tends to depress the demand for the risky locations and reduce construction density, which, in turn, should reduce damages from disasters. On the other hand, lower land prices increase locational affordability for the poorest, allowing them to settle in risky but otherwise advantageous areas. Rentschler et al. (2022) document that the growth of settlements in flood-prone areas is outpacing growth in low-risk areas, with much of the increase in risk consumption happening in low- and middle-income countries. The study hypothesizes that as urban areas grow so, too, does land scarcity, pushing people to settle in areas previously avoided. Damages incurred by the destruction of dwellings occupied by the poor in such areas may be low in monetary terms—because the poor have fewer assets to lose—but will still dramatically reduce their medium- to long-term economic prospects. Some will be forced to resort to short-term coping mechanisms that will jeopardize their future well-being. Erman et al. (2020) find that a significant share of households affected by the 2015 flood in Accra, Ghana, had not recovered two years after the event.

Informational and other prevailing market failures can also slow down the transition toward a carbon-neutral economy. Such failures contribute to the mispricing of climate risks in financial markets. For example, environmental ratings for green bonds and other financial instruments are often inconsistent, incomparable, and, at times, unreliable, reflecting the absence of granular data in the construction of such indexes. The outcome may be "greenwashing," wherein green bonds do not necessarily translate into comparatively low or falling carbon emissions at the firm level (Ehlers, Mojon, and Packer 2020). Demands from the market, ranging from supervisory guidance to strong disclosure standards for stakeholders, can help identify gaps and vulnerabilities and improve the quality of climate-related finance disclosures. This problem has relevance for cities because an increasing number of them use green bonds to finance low-carbon projects.[9]

It is also useful to consider cities' land and real estate, labor, and capital markets. Because the price of land is the primary element driving efficient land use, both appraisers and the public need reliable information on the risks affecting locations and the value of land. A standard economic prescription is to provide transparent information that helps ensure that market prices accurately reflect risk. For example, in the United States several real estate platforms now provide neighborhood-level climate change–related risk information for prospective home buyers. Better information on land markets could also contribute to climate mitigation efforts by lowering the costs of vertical construction, thereby helping promote more compact urban forms (see chapter 4). For land and property prices to accurately convey information in turn requires strong property right and land administration systems.

Migration responds to pull factors, such as access to better labor market outcomes in destination locations, and push factors, such as adverse shocks to livelihoods in origin locations. Through its influence on these factors, climate change acts as an important driver of migration (see chapter 3). Informational nudges can act as a powerful impetus to migration (Wilson 2021). Better information on climate risks could encourage people to increase investments, either for in situ adaptation to risks or to fund migration to areas with lower risks. In countries that have large variation in climate risks across cities, this investment could help the overall resilience of the urban system (see chapter 2).

A shared understanding is important for credible policies

The more credible policies are, the more effective they are. Thus, planning regulations that limit new developments in high-risk areas will work if the information on risks is credible and if there is a credible commitment to enforcement. Only with a shared theory of how program inputs relate to outputs can the inputs be credible, especially when commitments are made over a long period to what may be painful and unpopular policies. For example, European countries are now seeing steep rises in energy prices because of the supply shortages arising from the war in Ukraine. Time will tell, then, whether climate change commitments to diversification away from fossil fuel energy sources will hold steady in the coming months and years.

Policies are also more likely to be credible and accepted if policy-making processes are transparent and involve citizens. For example, so-called procedural justice can be used to integrate fairness and equity into decarbonization approaches. Procedural justice, which entails formally involving citizens in the process of designing policies, is, at its core, about inclusive and transparent processes to build trust and better policies (World Bank, forthcoming a).

Finally, even when information is available, the political will to embrace it may be lacking. For example, according to the report *Natural Hazards, UnNatural Disasters: The Economics of Effective Prevention*, even when the US Federal Emergency Management Agency regularly updated coastal flood maps, households and firms in more than 100 US Gulf communities did not accept the maps as trusted information, thereby preventing the local adjustment of property prices (World Bank 2010).

Incentives

Incentives will encourage people and firms to properly factor in climate change risks, and government officials to address the challenges of pursuing green, resilient, and inclusive development

Although information helps households and businesses to factor climate change–related risks into their decisions, information, in and of itself, may not be sufficient to motivate them to take into account the impacts of their own decisions, good or bad, on the environment and others. Motivating households and businesses to consider the environmental effects of their actions requires incentives.

Incentives come in various guises, such as taxes, charges, subsidies, and tradable permits. Whatever the incentive, attention must be paid to equity because, although incentive policies raise overall welfare, for any given policy some people or firms may gain more than others. As a result, some economic or social groups could lose in absolute terms. Failure to take into account the distributional impacts of new incentives, and more generally of any policy intended to help address climate change and other environmental issues, may result in insurmountable political opposition to the policy. One recent high-profile example was the French government's freezing of its carbon pricing policy following the Yellow Vests protest movement of 2018 (Rubin and Sengupta 2018).

Because the atmosphere is a global common, no country (or city) has an individual interest to do much about greenhouse gas (GHG) emissions. How then does one incentivize lower emissions? Because a unit of GHG emissions has the same effect regardless of where it occurs, market-oriented approaches are well suited to controlling emissions. The additional flexibility provided through market approaches to the emitter in determining how to reduce emissions could also incentivize efficiency and innovation in meeting the regulatory requirement. Specific market-oriented approaches for GHG reductions include tradable permits (such as cap-and-trade programs) that set a specific cap on total emissions and allocate or auction the number of pollution permits or allowances needed to meet that goal. Another approach, emission taxes, provides incentives for polluters to find cost-effective solutions to emissions control. Subnational regions have often been at the forefront of such programs. For example, in 2010 Tokyo set up the first urban cap-and-trade program that focused on urban buildings. In 2013, China launched its own pilot in several cities aimed at reducing the emissions intensity of coal- and gas-fired energy plants (Nogrady 2021). Citing Japanese cities, Domon et al. (2022) find that congestion tolls could be highly effective (far more so than emissions taxes) in reducing urban carbon dioxide (CO_2) emissions from commuting and housing energy—with reductions of 22 percent and 3 percent, respectively.

More generally, however, regulations and standards provide more certainty about emission levels and could be preferable when information or other barriers prevent producers and consumers from responding to price signals. Indeed, some regulations, such as those for vehicle emissions, usually at the national level, have proven impressive in achieving reductions. The United States and countries in the European Union have been regulating emissions since the 1970s, and widespread evidence suggests that they have reduced vehicle emissions and improved air quality significantly in most large cities—see Winkler et al. (2018) for an overview. Quota control policies can also be effective but must be carefully designed. The analysis by Song, Feng, and Diao (2020) of Singapore's vehicle quota control finds that vehicle quotas have substantially limited vehicle ownership and usage. The desire to maximize return on investment, however, can partially offset mitigation effects because of higher usage by existing car owners.

Bans are often a low-hanging fruit—several Asian countries, including Bangladesh, the Philippines, and Sri Lanka, have national regulations or bans on single-use plastic; and, where no national policies exist, local governments have taken it upon themselves to regulate plastic waste. Through phased implementation and strict enforcement, the city of San Fernando in the Philippines maintains 98 percent compliance with single-use plastic bans. In 2021, France passed a Climate and Resilience Bill to tackle climate change. The bill encompasses bans, incentives, and quotas on transportation, housing, and consumption intended to lower carbon emissions, improve energy efficiency, and cut waste. The bans range from preventing landlords from renting poorly insulated buildings, to a 2025 target to curb single-use food packaging, to a blanket ban on short-haul flights that could be replaced by a four-hour train trip.

Although clearer rules and definitions are useful, they are not likely to be sufficient. To correct for missing markets and to set in motion a process whereby firms and households reduce their energy use and make a permanent shift to cleaner energy sources will require carbon pricing, cap-and-trade programs, and other market-based policies.[10] In Vietnam, the World Bank is supporting the establishment of a domestic carbon finance market for cities by linking them to international markets. This arrangement allows large cities to aggregate many small actions—such as improving the energy efficiency of buildings, upgrading to light-emitting diode streetlights, installing rooftop solar panels, and upgrading to e-motorbikes—that amount to enough emission reductions to transact on the market. Such an approach would enable a city to upgrade its own assets to increase efficiency and renewable energy generation capacity, while catalyzing action by the owners of private assets through the provision of technical support and incentive payments.

Land use regulation, a typical urban policy, can affect energy demand and congestion externalities by inducing changes in urban form and the spatial distribution of residents, thereby changing the total commuting distance and congestion levels. In addition, when floor space per household changes, household energy consumption of lighting, cooling, and heating also changes. As chapter 3 discusses, land use and other policies (including building height and floor area ratio regulations) that affect the costs of vertical construction, the walkability of cities, and, more generally, the choice of transportation mode can alter both city density and the degree of sprawl. Such changes, in turn, have implications for emissions of both CO_2 and local air pollutants such as particulate matter 2.5 microns or less in diameter ($PM_{2.5}$).

According to the latest Intergovernmental Panel on Climate Change report, in 2019 buildings accounted for 31 percent of global energy demand, 18 percent of electricity demand, and 30–40 percent of global CO_2 emissions (IPCC 2022). Operations of buildings (that is, not including the carbon embodied in materials and construction) accounted for a large proportion of annual global emissions. Existing buildings are especially important for effective GHG mitigation simply because they are long-lived assets. Incentives to retrofit housing to increase energy efficiency could therefore have long-term beneficial impacts on emissions. Weiss, Dunkelberg, and Vogelpohl (2012) studied the impacts of various incentives to motivate homeowners in German cities to carry out energy-efficient refurbishments. They found that, although financial incentives (such as grants and tax rebates) led to better results than regulatory standards alone, random audits also helped ensure compliance. Better communication of the benefits of making the energy-saving changes also promoted higher take-up.

Finally, fiscal incentives to households to retrofit and upgrade their properties can also be effective in reducing the risks they face from climate change–related and other natural hazards. For example, the government of Türkiye provides families with financial support to upgrade or retrofit residential units at risk of damage or collapse in the event of an earthquake or other hazard. This support comes in the form of either an interest rate buy-down for a loan from a commercial bank or rental support for a period of up to 18 months. The interest rate buy-down is more favorable for those households that include higher standards of energy efficiency in the reconstruction process. Such approaches can both bring down buildings-related emissions and increase resilience to natural hazards.

Local governments respond to incentives

International experience has shown that local governments respond to incentives and that national authorities can shape these incentives to achieve results. Incentives for local governments to act on climate might take the form of offering them grants conditional on developing a climate mitigation or adaptation plan, or of granting cities with sufficient capacity (such as sufficiently staffed planning and utility management teams) greater authority in areas relevant to local climate action. Some governments have begun to experiment with such incentives. For example, British Columbia, Canada, introduced a Climate Action Revenue Incentive Program, a conditional grant scheme that requires local governments to sign on to the province's Climate Action Charter to access additional funding.[11] These efforts are still young, but experimentation, adoption, and knowledge exchanges will eventually provide evidence on the effectiveness of such mechanisms for local government–led climate action.

Some incentives aim at adaptation

Cities must assess, and adjust as necessary, their building siting, design, and construction practices to avoid or withstand the increased force and frequency of hydro-meteorological hazards such as extreme wind, flood, storm surge, and sea-level rise. They should base assessments and adjustments on hazard data and the calculation of expected hazard loads on structures. Although it is not possible to build a completely storm- or earthquake-proof house, construction of resilient housing is both technically and economically feasible (World Bank 2019b). Financial incentives can help homeowners and developers move toward integrating adaptation measures into housing construction. For example, in Canada the city of Toronto launched in 2009 the Eco-Roof Incentive Program that provides grants to property owners for the construction of both green roofs that support vegetation and cool roofs that reflect the sun's thermal energy and manage water runoff. A green roof reduces the amount of heat transferred to the building below, keeping the building cooler and at a more constant temperature.[12] Insurance premiums for risk coverage can also incentivize homeowners to reduce their premium by reducing their risk. For example, homeowners could install fire alarms, raise electrical equipment or heating and cooling systems above potential flood levels, or install a new roof.

Closing the loop on water use within a household can go a long way toward solving water challenges and making cities more water-resilient. One initiative leading the way in this effort is the 50 Liter Home Coalition spearheaded by Procter & Gamble and supported by the World Economic Forum, the 2030 Water Resources Group, and the World Business Council for Sustainable Development. The coalition, which emerged from Cape Town's "day zero" event when household water use was restricted to 50 liters of water per day, aims to demonstrate that living on 50 liters of water per day is not only feasible but also can be done at little sacrifice to the household. The coalition is developing methods to treat water at its point of use to make it reusable. In this way, some wastewater can be treated to become drinkable and other water can be treated for reuse, such as shower water repurposed for toilet reuse (Zaveri et al. 2021). See box 5.1 for a discussion of cities and green innovation, and box 5.3 later in the chapter for examples of incentives, including pricing, in water-secure cities.

Box 5.1

Can cities be incubators of green innovation?

Nobel Prize–winning economists Michael Kremer and Paul Romer have both suggested that over the long term the size of a population is related to its speed of technological advance (Kremer 1993; Romer 1990). Small, isolated communities see technological stagnation, whereas large, integrated populations foster rapid innovation. As Kahn (2010) argues, climate change brings with it the potential for endogenous technological advances that could play an important role in spurring mitigation and adaptation. In a 2016 study, Fei et al. also discuss the interdependent relationship between cities and green innovations.

That interdependence arises because densely populated metropolitan areas are often vulnerable to the effects of climate change and face the biggest demand for green areas and ecosystem services (Oijstaeijen, Passel, and Cools 2020). In Vietnam, the city of Hue responded to such a demand by increasing green spaces and vegetation in one of its historic colonial districts that serves as a residential area and tourist attraction. In Malaysia, the city of Melaka is developing innovative public infrastructures that use solar power and other renewable energy as a part of the Melaka Green City Action Plan.[a]

Many green innovations in urban areas occur at the institutional level and are implemented through central and local authorities. For example, as a major developing country that aims at absolute reductions in greenhouse gas emissions, Brazil has adopted a series of subnational- and city-level green fiscal policies, such as fiscal incentives and subsidies for innovations and sustainable practices. Evidence from 24 manufacturing sectors confirms that these green fiscal policies have helped promote green innovations in Brazil and contributed to the country's transition to a green economy (Gramkow and Anger-Kraavi 2018). In the Arab Republic of Egypt, by implementing green policies, three new cities have substantially improved their environmental performance and urban management (Hegazy, Seddik, and Ibrahim 2017). Such cities can provide guidelines for other Egyptian cities and help authorities select the proper policies to establish green urban systems in the country.

Sustainable and nonconventional commercial products represent another crucial aspect of green innovation. In recent years, the development of sustainable green products has increased as many firms begin to realize the tangible advantages of and profits from addressing environmental impacts in product design decisions (Lenox, King, and Ehrenfeld 2000). These innovations often take place in cities and spread with urbanization. For example, in recognition of the potential to greatly reduce the carbon footprint of the high-emission transportation sector, sales of electric vehicles increased in recent years. In the United States, the adoption of electric vehicles has been closely associated with urbanization.[b]

Another example of an innovative green commercial product is plant-based meat, whose production emits 30–90 percent less greenhouse gas than the production of conventional meat (Good Food Institute 2021a). The plant-based meat industry has been expanding globally. Among the top 10 plant-based meat brands by sales, most of them are headquartered in large cities such as Chicago, Los Angeles, and Seattle (Good Food Institute 2021b).

BOX 5.1 *continued*

Thus, metropolises act as cradles of brands that produce sustainable, innovative products. Green innovations increase a firm's profit while reducing energy costs for society (Fei et al. 2016). Therefore, such innovations are expected to continue increasing in metropolitan areas and play an essential role in the transition toward more sustainable, energy-efficient urban environments.

a. From Asian Development Bank, "Green Cities," https://www.adb.org/green-cities/.
b. Electric vehicle registration per 10,000 people in US metro counties ranges from 10 to more than 100, whereas that in nonmetro counties is less than 5 or even zero in many cases (Tolbert 2021).

Insurance

People, firms, and governments can insure against losses associated with climate change and against unavoidable environmental shocks and stresses

How do people and firms behave when confronted with risk? The answer matters greatly for policy. An economic agent—here, an individual or a firm—could take several actions, none of them cost-free. They could purchase insurance to guarantee receiving funds when a disaster occurs. If market insurance is not available, such as in many lower-income countries, individuals or firms can either self-insure or self-protect. To self-insure, they set aside savings to mitigate the potential costs of future disasters. To self-protect, they take actions to reduce risk exposure by, for example, migrating away from risky areas, taking proactive steps to protect their dwelling or business, or diversifying their sources of revenue. Seminal work by Ehrlich and Becker (1972) provides an elegant treatment of the optimal insurance decision when faced with the options of market insurance, self-insurance, and self-protection.

Urbanization shifts the balance of prevention from individual measures to collective action. Governments, both local and national, will have a larger role to play in removing the constraints on individuals and complementing individual adaptation strategies. National governments could play an important role by augmenting both market insurance *and* self-protection. The growth of global insurance giants offers opportunities for insurers to expand in the developing world by offering policies and diversifying their risk exposure using instruments such as catastrophe bonds (box 5.2). In this sense, the rise of global financial markets helps protect more and more individuals from the ex post losses associated with place-based climate shocks. Meanwhile, if global insurers offer a good premium on coverage, then policy buyers will invest less in self-insurance. Using the example of indexed disaster funds in Mexico, Del Valle, de Janvry, and Sadoulet (2020) describe how public and private coordination in insurance markets, which allowed the easing of weak rules and the supplementation of administrative capacity by easing liquidity constraints, led to considerable acceleration of postdisaster economic recovery.

Disaster risk finance and insurance instruments aim to minimize the financial impacts of disasters and to secure access to postdisaster financing before an event strikes, thereby ensuring the rapid availability of cost-effective resources to finance recovery and reconstruction efforts. Typically, governments seek financial protection for four groups: national and local governments, homeowners and small and medium enterprises, farmers, and the poorest

Box 5.2

Subnational cat bonds—Do they work?

A *catastrophe bond* (cat bond) is a risk transfer instrument that functions like insurance. It is structured as a fixed income security that holds the principle in escrow, pays periodic coupons to the investor during the life of the bond, and effectively insures the sponsor of the bond against a predefined set of losses from hazards such as earthquakes or hurricanes. If a covered event occurs during the bond's life, the sponsoring country retains the bond principal without any debt obligation to fund emergency relief and reconstruction work. Cat bonds are most effective as part of a larger disaster risk management strategy that invests in risk reduction and adaptation efforts, in addition to other risk transfer and financing instruments. Many countries, including Chile, Colombia, Jamaica, Mexico, Peru, and the Philippines, have used cat bonds to transfer risks related to disasters from developing countries to the capital markets.

Cat bonds can also be issued at the subnational level to transfer risk from local governments and utility companies in the event of a natural disaster. For example, in 2020 and 2021 the Los Angeles Department of Water and Power secured two cat bonds in the amounts of US$50 million and US$30 million for wildfire insurance coverage. Similarly, the New York Metropolitan Transit Authority (MTA) has relied on cat bonds to transfer risk from storm surges and, more recently, earthquakes. The MTA issued its first cat bond in 2013 for US$200 million to transfer the risk of storm surges after Hurricane Sandy hit New York City, leading to US$4 billion in damage to MTA assets and infrastructure. In 2020, the MTA collateralized reinsurance protection against storm surges resulting from storms and earthquake risks within the New York metropolitan area on a parametric trigger and per occurrence basis for a three-year term. In short, cat bonds have the potential to help cities move some of their risk into capital markets. Deploying such bonds systematically in developing country contexts, however, will require more information and sophisticated data to help bring them to market.

segments of the population. Risk transfer solutions targeting households were deployed most recently in Türkiye with the use of catastrophe insurance pools. Türkiye is highly exposed to significant climate and disaster risks, especially in urban areas. In 1999 after the Marmara earthquake, the government established the Turkish Catastrophe Insurance Pool (TCIP) to set up long-term reserves to finance future earthquake losses and alleviate the financial burden of earthquakes on the government budget. Sold separately from fire and other indemnity insurance, TCIP provides households with compulsory earthquake insurance with affordable insurance premiums. TCIP is a nonprofit public entity with private financing. Its funding has primarily depended on insurance premiums paid by homeowners. With its coverage expanding over time, in 2021 TCIP reached about 10.5 million households nationwide (Afet and Kurumu 2021; Gurenko et al. 2006).

Local and national governments can also take advantage of risk transfer solutions. For example, in July 2017 the government of the Philippines purchased for US$205.9 million its first parametric insurance policy under the Philippine Parametric Catastrophe Risk Insurance Program. In doing so, it successfully transferred some of its disaster risk to the international reinsurance markets. In 2018, it purchased a second insurance policy (renewal) under the program, approximately doubling the amount of coverage offered by the first policy. The policy covered 25 local governments against emergency losses from major typhoons and covered national government agencies against emergency losses from major typhoons and earthquakes (World Bank 2020b).

Second-best options are sometimes the best options

Economists often tout market insurance, which reflects disaster risks, as the first-best option to internalize risks and minimize disaster impacts. Implementing risk-based insurance, however, requires overcoming major technical, social, and political challenges. It is, then, not always realistic, especially in the developing world. But there are other options. Using a theoretical urban economics model and numerical simulations, Avner and Hallegatte (2019) investigate the costs and benefits of two "second-best" ex ante flood management strategies, subsidized insurance and zoning, and compare them with risk-based insurance.

Subsidized insurance, which allows household compensation in the aftermath of a flood event, has the benefit of reducing housing scarcity because building decisions are then unaffected by the possibility of floods. Such an instrument reduces housing rents, but it also entails moral hazard because excessive construction takes place with no regard for risk. Land use zoning, if implemented correctly, ensures that damages from floods are zero, but it also reduces housing floor space because land becomes scarcer. Risk-based insurance incorporates disaster risk into construction decisions and reduces the housing stock more than subsidized insurance does. Flood zoning is close to optimal when flood-prone areas are small, floods are frequent, and housing quality is low. Subsidized insurance is close to optimal when a large fraction of a city is flood-prone, floods are rare, and housing quality is high. When the implementation of risk-based insurance is unrealistic, a combination of zoning in high-risk areas and subsidized insurance for low-risk areas may offer a good alternative. Although the cost of implementing a second-best policy generally remains low except in some extreme cases, the cost of implementing the wrong second-best policy (that is, zoning instead of subsidized insurance or vice versa) can be very high.

Equity is an important consideration when introducing insurance programs. Blickle and Santos (2022) demonstrate how quasi-mandatory flood insurance in the United States reduces mortgage lending because banks gravitate toward borrowers with higher incomes, which affects housing affordability for some of the poorest households. In addition, because the poorest are more likely to live in areas more exposed to hazards (see chapter 3 and Rossitti 2022), they would face the highest risk premium. As a result, those who need insurance the most often have the least access to it and the protection it affords (Hallegatte et al. 2017). The answer, however, is to avoid pricing insurance premiums too low; when insurance premiums are mispriced, that, too, can lead to overbuilding in risker places. This finding suggests that policies that provide more affordable housing in less risky locations would help not only address traditional urban stresses but also reduce risk exposure.

The unintended consequences of subsidized insurance policies could, perversely, magnify the harm of climate change. Moral hazard occurs when insurance spurs households and firms to take riskier actions than if not insured. If the national government subsidizes disaster insurance, individuals will more likely invest less in their own self-protection. For example, the US national flood insurance program has often paid to rebuild a flooded home multiple times in the same location.[13] Findings from Peralta and Scott (2018) suggest that insuring people against potential flood losses contributes directly to population growth in flood-prone US counties; the availability of flood insurance increases the population by 5 percent for every 1-standard-deviation increase in flood risk. Nevertheless, rapidly growing cities that face land and housing scarcity may see some benefits from overconstruction in the form of lower prices for floor space. Although always dominated in terms of efficiency by market-based insurance, subsidized insurance can under certain conditions serve as a useful second-best because it is much easier to implement and entails limited welfare costs (Avner and Hallegatte 2019).

Finally, social safety nets can also be an important source of social insurance for the poorest to help manage the risk of natural hazards. Safety nets can be deployed ex ante to prevent and mitigate the impact of a natural disaster. For example, Bangladesh's preplanned flood and cyclone response includes several social safety net programs to reduce vulnerability (Hassan et al. 2013). Ethiopia's safety net programs are scalable in response to shocks. For example, in 2011, in response to drought, the government managed to expand these programs to support 9.6 million people. Safety nets can also be deployed after a disaster shock to cope with its impacts. A safety net would take the form of labor or public works programs to aid recovery and to support shifts to more productive and alternative livelihoods, or it could take the form of cash transfers. For example, Malawi included a shock-responsive social protection mechanism in its 2019 National Disaster Risk Finance Strategy. In the event of a drought, this mechanism enables the existing social cash transfer program to reach additional households or top up payments to existing beneficiaries (GRiF 2020). Developing countries, however, often have low coverage of social protection, and even more so in urban regions because most programs tend to have a rural focus (Devereux and Cuesta 2021).

Integration

Within cities, integrated planning promotes more compact energy-efficient development

Plans are worthless—observed US President Eisenhower, drawing on his military experience—but planning is everything. When a city grows, the pressure on its land and housing markets, its supplies of basic services and infrastructure, and its environment grows as well. If not well managed, this pressure can undermine the greenness, resilience, and inclusiveness of development. Flexible and versatile urban planning, coordinated with investments in infrastructure, can ensure that cities are not locked into suboptimal physical forms and investments that exacerbate this pressure. Examples of such lock-ins include energy- or water-intensive building technologies, urban settlements in areas exposed to natural hazards, and sprawling and car-dependent paths of development. The findings in chapters 1 and 4 suggest that more compact development, which involves the growth of cities vertically rather than horizontally, is associated with reductions in both CO_2 and $PM_{2.5}$ emissions, as well as with less conversion of fertile agricultural land. As discussed under the fifth "I" (investments), although retrofitting infrastructure and buildings will be essential to greener and more resilient growth, doing so can be costly and could be avoided with early efforts at integrated planning.

Reforming land administration and urban planning in rapidly growing cities can go a long way toward ensuring greater compactness. Land administration services in low- and middle-income countries are frequently excessively centralized and, as a result, unresponsive to changing conditions. One possible solution is to decentralize land certification services by allowing existing local structures to verify ownership. For example, in 2011 Burundi reformed its land administration system to allow its 97 Communal Land Services offices to issue land certificates. Previously, land registration was handled by much less accessible land registration services under the Ministry of Justice (Mukim 2021). Other examples such as Ethiopia and Indonesia illustrate the benefits of decentralized land registration processes managed by local governments in a participatory manner. In Indonesia, the community-supported Land Administration Project paved the way to formalizing millions of previously unregistered parcels (Deininger, Selod, and Burns 2012). These cases also show, however, that decentralization increases the responsibilities of local governments, requiring commensurate increases in policy guidance and resources.

A decentralized approach to land administration also allows a degree of iterative policy experimentation. Selected primary and secondary cities can pilot important interventions such as creating inventories of all public land, buildings, and infrastructure. The findings from such pilots can then be used to inform both national urban master planning and local development plans that promote urban densification and regeneration over leapfrog development. Initiatives that succeed in selected cities can be scaled up, whereas failed attempts can be scuttled. Ideally, this dynamic will, in the longer term, result in cities of all sizes having functional land administration and planning services. Such an approach has been successful in Burundi. Its decentralized system of land certification emerged from a pilot project first implemented in four communes with the support of the Swiss Agency for Development and Cooperation and the European Union (World Bank 2014).

Integration is good for the poor—and good for budgets

Integration matters to the poor. They may be aware of the hazards they possibly face, but the poor depend more than the well-off on public services that are often inadequate. Policies that aim to move slum dwellers to less precarious locations via new housing developments, subsidies, or urban upgrades often fail to work well because poorer households often value accessibility to affordable services and amenities and proximity to jobs above safer homes. In places where land use and urban infrastructure and development decisions are not coordinated, households end up disconnected from labor markets and trading off safety for accessibility. Local governments often struggle to provide essential urban infrastructure, and, until they succeed in doing so, the poor will remain vulnerable. More secure land and property rights would encourage investment in upgrading and, therefore, self-protection.[14] Equally, however, the provision of land and affordable housing in safer areas with accessible jobs and essential services would go a long way toward lowering poor people's risk exposure.

Integration needs to be coordinated with risk assessments

City leaders may spend less time on long-term planning because they are often dealing with a series of emergencies. Interventions aimed at improving and increasing density can be delivered more easily and cost-effectively through investments before settlement. Estimates of the cost of affordable housing to accommodate the burgeoning population of Freetown, Sierra Leone, while reducing exposure to floods and landslides, find that proactive planning (for example, via investments in sites and services) would cost approximately US$375 million over the next decade. By contrast, the provision of a public housing scheme would cost almost nine times as much—US$3.2 billion (Mukim 2018b).

Rapid, unplanned urbanization in low- and middle-income countries is expected to exacerbate climate change and other shocks such as heat waves, flooding, and health emergencies. Integrating adaptation with good urban management will be an integral part of ameliorating climate change–related risks in cities. Such integration involves reducing not only the likelihood of impact on infrastructure and other assets but also the vulnerability across numerous interconnected systems. Multihazard risk assessments[15] could be deployed to better protect cities by better identification and understanding of risks. For example, more than 20,000 inhabitants benefited directly from such work carried out in the Moroccan municipalities of Fez and Mohammedia (World Bank 2020a). Such risk assessments can also help increase local capabilities, beyond those of public officials, by drawing in community stakeholders, including those from vulnerable communities. In Sierra Leone, city-level risk assessments conducted in Bo, Freetown, and Makeni used a participatory approach that included vulnerable communities. These assessments identified priority needs, investments, and feasibility studies to bolster resilience to flood risk and landslides. Following the 2017 flooding and landslides in Freetown that killed 493 people, left 600 more missing, and pushed a further 3,000 people into home-lessness, these risk assessments were deployed as part of postdisaster recovery programming (GFDRR 2014).

Multihazard risk assessments also inform land use planning and zoning. By understanding which areas of a city may be adversely affected by current and future hazards such as flooding and storm surges, policy makers can better plan for future urban growth and development (Hallegatte, Rentschler, and Rozenberg 2020). Colombia's framework law passed in 2018, for example, requires regional, municipal, and district authorities to incorporate climate change management into their development and land use plans.[16] Effective planning should also guide policies and choices for structural investments and community measures, ensuring that future urban development is compatible with changing risks. Such investments and measures to reduce risks could include erosion control and reforestation; retaining walls, drainage systems, dikes, spillways, or reservoirs; or investments in flood buffering zones such as wetlands and swamp areas (GFDRR 2012).

Such projects are often more effective when jointly developed and implemented alongside the communities that stand to benefit, so that they can appropriately manage behavior linked, for example, to littering, clearing of drainage canals, or heeding early warning systems. In Jamaica, coastal hazard mapping is under way to update land use regula-tion; in tandem, local authorities continue to successfully enforce minimally intrusive, low-cost hurricane straps for the roofs of residential buildings (GFDRR 2019). Nevertheless, risk-based land use planning presents challenges because of the potential negative impacts on the poor, who may reside in high-risk areas and require relocation support (Hallegatte et al. 2017).

Success requires coordination of planning with information and institutions

To be successful, land use planning requires effective implementation. Effective implementa-tion, in turn, often relies on cadastres, property rights, and other regulations and the willing-ness and capabilities of the public authorities who administer such regulations. For example, Hallegatte et al. (2017) point out that, although local authorities may have risk information readily available, incorporating such information into urban planning can pose a challenge because the costs could imply the immediate reduction of land values in areas identified as risky, and the benefits of planning (in the form of avoided losses) would accrue only in the unknowable future.

When land and housing markets work and information asymmetries are minimized, property values reflect the dis-amenities from hazard risks, guiding people's decisions on where to live and what prevention measures to take (see the earlier discussion on information). Conversely, lack of coordination, often the norm in many low- and middle-income countries, leads to perverse outcomes—mostly for poor people. In Bujumbura, Burundi, almost 60 percent of informal settlement growth between 1985 and 2019 took place in areas of urban expansion disconnected from existing agglomerations and at risk of flooding (Mukim 2021). The lack of planning standards and infrastructure that reflected the growing risks further exacerbated the physical vulnerabilities in these peri-urban areas. Thus, integrated urban planning, combined with well-designed and implemented regulations, including for facilitation of land and housing markets, can lead to greater compactness.

Integration within cities can have important benefits

Climate change is forcing individuals, families, and even whole communities to seek more viable and less vulnerable places to live (Rigaud et al. 2018). Migration becomes an adaption option for people when areas face adverse shocks, including from climate change. It also allows diversification of incomes in the face of shocks and increasing uncertainty. Vulnerable people have the fewest opportunities to adapt locally or to move away from risk and, when moving, often do so as a last resort. Those even more vulnerable will be unable to move, trapped in increasingly unviable areas. According to the *World Migration Report 2022*, the vast majority of people continue to live in the countries where they were born—only 1 in 30 migrates (McAuliffe and Triandafyllidou 2021).[17] When faced with a climate change–related shock, such as drought, as discussed in chapter 3, they often respond by migrating to urban areas. In 2016, the United Nations High Commissioner for Refugees reported that, between 2008 and 2016, an average of 21.5 million people were forcibly displaced each year by sudden-onset weather-related hazards, and thousands more by slow-onset hazards linked to climate change impacts.[18] Migration in response to climate impacts need not always be forced displacement in response to sudden events. It could also be linked to mobility as a proactive adaptation strategy.

Internal migration patterns are heterogeneous, with migration occurring simultaneously from rural to urban areas, between rural areas, and from urban to rural areas. Some governments have resorted to specific legislation, regulations, and policies to discourage or restrict domestic migration. Yet a growing body of evidence suggests that greater rural to urban migration could increase aggregate productivity and facilitate economic growth within countries (Lagakos 2020; Selod and Shilpi 2021). Migration away from shocks could also be associated with increasing remittances to affected areas, as illustrated by Gröger and Zylerberg (2016) who studied the impacts of a typhoon in Vietnam.

The overall economic effect of climate change–induced migration on the receiving city depends on local conditions and the capacity of the city to absorb a larger labor force of lower-skilled workers. Even though the policy mix will vary across counties, the fundamental approach to easing such migration transitions would likely remain unchanged. For example, decision-makers could seek to integrate migrants both to limit impacts on host communities and to ensure inclusive opportunities for new migrants (Zaveri et al. 2021).

Cities could invest as well in basic services such as water and sanitation, schools, health care, and safe housing for poor migrants in urban areas and broader city populations. Basic water and sanitation services are especially vital in slowing the spread of diseases, including COVID-19 (Zaveri et al. 2021). More broadly, proactive policies that promote shared economic progress and address social frictions between migrants and host populations will become even more critical (Borgomeo et al. 2021; Zaveri et al. 2021).

Human adaptation to the changing climate will always include migration. Climate and environmental stresses can act both as a driver (increased motivation to migrate) and as an inhibitor (reduced ability to migrate) in individuals' and households' decisions to migrate (Flores, Milusheva, and Reichert 2021; Quiñones, Liebenehm, and Sharma 2021; Zaveri et al. 2021). Thus, public policies should help relax some of the constraints to migration, including lifting regulations that purposefully restrict migrants' access to social and economic services in urban locations. At their origins or in contexts where land rights are contested, migrants also commonly face institutional barriers to out-migration, such as land tenure insecurity. Governments could help reduce the costs of migration by, for example, improving access to financial markets, lowering the barriers to assimilation in receiving areas, and providing better information on job opportunities.

Powerful social dynamics—such as communal and ethnic conflicts, some of which date back to the days before climate-induced migration—can also obstruct migration. In Somalia, for example, settlement patterns among newly arrived urban residents are highly segregated on the basis of clan membership (World Bank 2021c). This segregation complicates migrants' options when it comes to integrating into host communities and finding work; scarce jobs are often allocated to fellow clan members. Furthermore, migration can shift clan dynamics in destabilizing ways, pitting neighbor against neighbor. In Somalia, property disputes occur commonly in neighborhoods where land is scarce, and they can easily escalate when cross-pollinated with clan rivalries. The implications for policy makers navigating similar conditions are rather clear—they must ensure basic security, put in place clear land registration policies, and promote intergroup contact through peaceful means.

Trade and migration can act as substitutes when it comes to adaptation. Conte et al. (2021) evaluate changes in local specialization in agricultural and nonagricultural sectors and find that freer trade would increase the scope of local specialization, reducing losses from global warming but also weakening the incentives for people to migrate away from the world's poorest regions, which are more affected by climate change. Trade—both domestic and international—also plays a critical role in recovering from weather-related crises (Brenton and Chemutai 2021) by increasing access to food and attenuating price volatility. Movement of goods, medicines, and emergency workers can be critical to immediate recovery from a natural disaster and for rebuilding.

Investments

Investments in green, resilient, and inclusive infrastructure, including in nature-based solutions can help cities address climate change–related risks

Infrastructure investments, when well designed, constructed, and maintained, can help prevent and respond to disasters, reducing the loss of life and property. According to Fay et al. (2019), investment in infrastructure across low- and middle-income countries constitutes between 3.4 and 5.0 percent of their gross domestic product. Despite this spending, the infrastructure often cannot meet the needs of these countries' growing, and often swiftly urbanizing, populations. Climate stresses can exacerbate these challenges by leading to disruptions in the supply of services, including by damaging assets.[19] For example, urban floods often disrupt transportation services and knock out energy networks.

Important prevention measures such as flood control systems, shelters, and protection of environmental buffers can be embedded in infrastructure investments. Some infrastructure could serve multiple purposes, such as the schools in Bangladesh that also serve as community cyclone shelters. According to Hallegatte, Rentschler, and Rozenberg (2019), the extra cost of building resilience into existing infrastructure systems (power, water and sanitation, transportation, and telecommunications) would account for 3 percent of the overall investment needs, but each dollar invested would yield four in return.

The continued effectiveness of infrastructure depends on its quality. Spending on maintenance can be highly cost-effective. Rentschler et al. (2019) find that an additional US$1.00 spent on road maintenance in Organisation for Economic Co-operation and Development countries saves US$1.50 in new investments. Thus, investment outlays must not ignore maintenance because it boosts the resilience of infrastructure while reducing overall costs in the long run.

Investments are the last "I" because they are both costly and durable. Hallegatte (2009) estimates that a city's physical structures, once established, could remain in place for more than 150 years. As a result, infrastructure investments that affect land use and a city's urban form can have implications far into the future. For example, investments in roads that promote motor vehicle over public transportation use, thereby encouraging sprawl, can significantly and permanently increase the costs of delivering basic services such as water, sanitation and electricity, and social infrastructure (clinics and schools, among other things).[20]

Investing in basic services in cities in low-income countries—no matter their size—is a leap toward integration. Expanding investment in basic services such as water, sanitation, electricity, clean fuels for cooking, and digital connectivity, as well as ensuring access to financial, technical, and institutional resources, not only builds resilience in vulnerable communities but also enhances mobility by connecting smaller cities to medium and large cities and reducing migration barriers between them.

Because cities are threatened by climate change–related risks, decisions regarding urban construction have even more important ramifications. Private investment decisions linked to housing in hazard-prone areas will intensify risks and increase the negative effects of floods, landslides, storms, and other climate events. As Desmet and Jedwab (2022) point out in background research for this report, the most expensive real estate structures—skyscrapers— are highly durable. In a world with swiftly shifting and unpredictable effects associated with climate change, this durability can be a double-edged sword. Very durable investments could, perversely, increase the long-run costs of climate change.

Investments can help cities anticipate the challenges of growth

One of the great benefits of urban areas is that they create the density of demand that can justify large sunk investments, such as in public transportation, to guide settlements and manage disaster risks, the costs of which can be spread across numerous taxpayers. Public transportation systems, for instance, are key to transforming density into integrated labor markets that can foster better matches between employers and job seekers (Avner and Lall 2016; Peralta-Quiros, Kerzhner, and Avner 2019). Franklin (2018) finds in Addis Ababa that more affordable public transportation and lower job search costs resulted in more stable, better-paying, and more formal jobs for youth.

Public transportation systems are also a key lever in reducing urban transportation CO_2 emissions. Because of their high average occupancy rates, public transportation systems are typically less energy- and carbon-intensive modes of transportation per passenger-kilometer than individual cars or motorcycles. Such systems can also be electrified, making them very attractive contributors to CO_2 emission mitigation strategies if they can get people out of automobiles.

Investments can also help guide settlements spatially. Rentschler et al. (2022) document that urbanization in high-risk flood-prone areas is outpacing settlement growth in safe areas. One hypothesis is that land scarcity pushes households to settle where land is (or appears to be) available, often resulting in informal settlements with basic living conditions and high exposure to several hazards. Examples of such risky urban growth include urbanization in the periphery of Dakar, Senegal (World Bank 2016); settlements in low-lying areas, and even mangroves in Conakry, Guinea (World Bank 2019a); and encroachment into water beds in Cap Haitien, Haiti (Rentschler et al. 2022). Relocation or retrofitting of these neighborhoods is difficult, costly, and possibly sensitive. Instead, a much more effective and cost-efficient option involves anticipating urban growth and guiding it spatially.

How can this be done? Laying out basic infrastructure can act as a powerful signal for households to settle in areas that authorities have identified, away from high risks. In the early days of an area's development, it requires only the most basic infrastructure, essentially rights of way for roads and well-demarcated land plots. Upscaling of the infrastructure can happen in a second phase once households have settled in. Angel (2017) documents how this approach succeeded in a squatter community in Lima, Peru. And several recent papers have highlighted the long-lasting positive effects of sites and service projects implemented in the 1970s and 1980s—for example in India (Owens, Gulyani, and Rizvi 2018) and Tanzania (Michaels et al. 2021).

Finally, investments in disaster risk management not only help reduce disaster damages but also are an essential component of growth and development strategies. In addition to damage mitigation, such investments can deliver wider economic benefits in the form of increased productivity due to a reduction in background risk and other development co-benefits. Avner et al. (2022) show that flood mitigation in the central part of Buenos Aires, mainly in the form of stormwater drainage and retention capacity investments, can raise the value of land to a degree that covers, and probably exceeds, the flood protection investment costs, while allowing for better use of the previously affected location and reducing aggregate commuting costs. With increasing documentation of the wider economic benefits of disaster risk management investments, the approach should change from a reactive to a proactive one.

Investments can help cities secure water

Secure sources of water for cities are fundamental to development and well-being (Jensen et al., forthcoming; Saltiel et al., forthcoming). The world's cities increasingly face the difficult task of meeting the rising water and sanitation demands of their residents in a sustainable way. City planners will need to rethink urban planning, and water planners will need to factor urban planning into their own decision-making process (OECD 2015b). Through this process, it will be critical for decision-makers to look both outward and inward to increase urban water security and resilience. They will need to expand and increase the menu of water supply options while also managing water demand (Zaveri et al. 2021).

An emerging idea from China is to build cities like sponges so that they can absorb rainwater (Chan et al. 2018; Wishart et al. 2021). The system mimics the natural hydrological cycle and is designed to passively absorb, clean, and use rainfall in an ecologically friendly way. The idea is to restore wetlands and build green infrastructure to retain and store water. This system would not only deal with a sudden excess of stormwater but also reuse it to help mitigate the impact of drought (Zaveri et al. 2021). By 2030, China aims to have 80 percent of its urban areas be sponge-like (Jensen et al. forthcoming; Wishart et al. 2021). Cities must also look beyond their boundaries and invest in natural infrastructure. Such investment is critical because land use changes in upstream watersheds affect more than 90 percent of urban water sources, with degraded watersheds increasing water treatment operation costs in cities (McDonald et al. 2016).

As the challenge mounts to absorb the growing demands of urban populations and as shocks to water supplies increase, multilevel governance structures will play a critical role in ensuring urban water security (OECD 2015b; Saltiel et al., forthcoming). In that role, they must do the following:

- Recognize that urban water is part of a larger hydrological and economic system that encompasses rural and peri-urban areas.
- Recognize that an integrated, coordinated approach is needed to manage all sources of water supplies (surface and groundwater, nontraditional sources such as desalination, wastewater reuse, and stormwater retention) along with the uses of water in and outside the city.

- Recognize that achieving mutually beneficial water management objectives requires collaboration across administrative boundaries, such as with upstream catchment managers and downstream stakeholders affected by water use in the city and peri-urban areas.

- Recognize the need for policy, institutional, and regulatory reforms in service delivery in order to develop adequate incentives for achieving universal access and improved service delivery (World Bank 2018). The World Bank's new water-secure cities initiative aims to help decision-makers understand and address these interlinked problems and opportunities in urban water systems, so that cities can prioritize actions to achieve water security tailored to their specific conditions (see box 5.3 for a description of these interlinked challenges).

Box 5.3

Building water-secure cities: Using information, incentives, and investments

Cities can strengthen their water supplies and increase access by diversifying available water sources.[a] For example, cities can embrace the idea of reusing and recycling wastewater and harvesting stormwater as alternative sources of water supply. By returning water back into the economy, they can capture its full value—as a service, an input to processes, a source of energy, and a carrier of nutrients and other materials (Delgado et al. 2021).[b] Such an approach will help cities hedge against water risks while reducing resource extraction and environmental degradation.[c] Reused water can also benefit streams, rivers, lakes, wetlands, and aquifers, in part because the excess water returned to natural systems is of better quality than standard treated wastewater (Tortajada and van Rensburg 2020).

Although in some cases expanding the water supply through infrastructure (such as desalination plants) will be critical, truly solving this problem in the long term and in an efficient manner will require demand-side management or incentives (Saltiel et al., forthcoming; Zaveri et al. 2021). These will include scarcity pricing of water and technological solutions that reduce water use by homes and businesses. Few urban services are as subsidized as municipal water supplies. A recent World Bank study finds that subsidies in the water supply and sanitation sector were as much as 2.4 percent of gross domestic product (low-income economies are on the higher end), with urban expenditures accounting for 76 percent of this subsidy (Andres et al. 2019). Yet the poorest 20 percent of the population captured a mere 6 percent of water supply and sanitation subsidies, whereas the wealthiest 20 percent captured 56 percent. Instead of ensuring access, these subsidies push the price of water so low that inefficiency is incentivized, service sustainability is threatened, and resources are overexploited (Zaveri et al. 2021).

Subsidy reform in the water supply and sanitation sector is therefore critical. Cities will need to ensure affordable access to water while also discouraging the excess consumption that may result from low prices. One way policy makers can balance equity and conservation is to use targeted subsidies or bloc tariffs that can be strategically employed to ensure that the most vulnerable residents retain access to affordable water (Damania et al. 2017). Dynamically efficient volumetric water pricing, which incorporates the scarcity price of water into the current price, can also minimize the average water tariff paid by households over time (Grafton, Chu, and Kompas 2015; Zaveri et al. 2021).

One of the major challenges in offering incentives for lower water use is that, even with price incentives in place, behavioral change can occur slowly. Households may lack information

BOX 5.3 *continued*

on how much water they use and which activities require the most water, making it difficult for them to make decisions about limiting water use (Zaveri et al. 2021). New "smart" meters and other technological solutions offer a promising solution to this problem. Public awareness campaigns, educational programs in schools, and nudges to promote a culture of water conservation can help conservation efforts (World Bank 2015b).[d] Plugging leaky pipes can also go a long way toward conserving water. In some cities, more than half of the water losses in the distribution system are due to physical leaks (Jensen et al. forthcoming). Fixing pipes could soon become easier and cheaper thanks to robotic systems that, by sensing pressure changes around leaks, can detect and repair them while pipes are still in use (Balch 2014).

a. Singapore is a classic example. Despite being one of the world's scarcest freshwater locations, it has ensured adequate water provision by embracing a four-tap model. The first tap is the supply of water from local catchments. Most of the city is designed as a catchment with an integrated system of reservoirs and an extensive drainage system that collects rainwater and channels it into storage reservoirs. From the storage reservoirs, water treatment plants treat the rainwater to be supplied to the city as potable water. The second tap is imported water. The third tap is treated wastewater, which is treated to such high standards that it can be drunk. The fourth tap is desalination, whereby water from the sea is desalinated and supplied to the city (Zaveri et al. 2021).

b. Numerous cities reuse wastewater both to support industrial and nearby agricultural activity and to provide utilities with revenue. Examples include the sale of treated effluent to industrial users (Lingyuan City, China) and to a power plant's cooling towers (San Luis Potosi, Mexico); the use of recovered nutrients for fertilizer (Dakar, Senegal); and the outsourcing of municipal wastewater treatment to mining companies in exchange for the use of the resulting treated wastewater (Arequipa, Peru)—see Delgado et al. (2021).

c. In Windhoek, Namibia, one of the first cities to create a drinking water supply from reused water, the Goreangab Water Reclamation Plant contributes up to a third of the city's total water supply in times of drought when supplies from nearby reservoirs are especially meager (Tortajada and van Rensburg 2020).

d. In Bogotá, Colombia, a public information campaign that included publication of daily reports of water consumption in prominent newspapers, advertising, and minor sanctions on businesses with the highest consumption levels achieved long-term behavioral change (World Bank 2015b).

Investments can help cities retrofit

Past policies can weigh heavily on the present. For example, defects are difficult to detect and harder to remedy in many structures built earlier. Costa and Kahn (2011, 2013) document that homes built in the 1970s in California consumed more electricity than more recently built, observationally identical homes. Built when electricity prices were low, the 1970s homes were likely to be energy inefficient. Thus, retrofitting residential homes and buildings could have important impacts on greening through its effects on energy consumption. In fact, the International Energy Agency estimates that 75 percent of the total value created by building retrofits comes from public benefits that go well beyond the main goal of energy savings (IEA 2015). The positive spillovers include employment opportunities (often for local supply chains), higher property values and thus higher municipal revenue, health benefits, and additional benefits accruing to energy utilities.

The housing stock can also be retrofitted to increase its resilience to tropical cyclones, landslides, floods, and other hazards. Housing accounted for 93 percent of total private damages and losses from the 2013 flood in St. Vincent and the Grenadines and 44 percent following the 2010 tropical storm in Guatemala. However, retrofitting building structures and infrastructure in densely populated areas to help them adapt to natural hazard risks can also be a costly solution.[21] Hallegatte et al. (2017) estimate that retrofitting of an existing vulnerable structure could account for 10–50 percent of the structure's value. Evidence from Latin America suggests that retrofitting infrastructure after settlement has occurred can cost up to three times more than installation alongside housing construction (Fernandes 2011). Costs are not the only constraint to retrofitting buildings; incentives may not be aligned. Ghesquiere, Jamin, and Mahul (2006) demonstrate that landlords often have little incentive to retrofit buildings because they may not incorporate the potential costs to the tenant in terms of lost assets and lives. Information may be imperfect, so the risks of the natural hazard, or the costs and benefits of the investment, may not be well understood.

Often, the responses to a changing climate can be found in nature. Nature-based investments use natural or modified ecosystems to prop up resilience to disasters. From their survey of multiple nature-based projects aimed at defending coastal habitats, comparing them to investments in "gray infrastructure,"[22] Narayan et al. (2016) find that nature-based investments can be highly cost-effective for protecting coastal settlements. Trees, wetlands, green spaces, and rivers can alleviate the urban heat island effect (Raj et al. 2020; Tan, Lau, and Ng 2016). Nature-based solutions reduce the impact of natural hazards, such as flooding, erosion, landslides, and drought, in cities. They often do so by complementing gray infrastructure such as storm drains, embankments, and retaining walls (World Bank 2021b).

Avoiding some investments can increase resilience

Most risk reduction investments are no-regret actions because they save lives and reduce social and economic losses from disasters. Sometimes, however, resilience may be a function of not making an investment, such as in mitigation efforts that have the unintended consequence of increasing exposure to disaster risks. For example, building levees is often viewed as an effective way to reduce the impact of floods. Yet it can also lead to "the levee effect"—the paradox that building levees may increase losses from disasters because the protection creates a false sense of security and induces development and attracts more people to flood-prone areas (Georgic 2019; Hutton 2018).[23]

Not making investments also makes economic sense when the high investment costs yield low returns in risk reduction. According to Nicholls et al. (2019), although the total investment costs to build and upgrade defenses against sea-level rise and coastal flooding could reach US$18.3 trillion in the highest-cost scenario, these defenses protect only one-third or less of the world's coasts. Another study suggests that some flood protection infrastructures (such as levees, dams, and walls) could yield negative net benefits, with returns in flood risk reduction lower than their implementation and maintenance costs (World Bank 2021b). Alternatively, resilience could be improved by low-cost approaches or nature-based solutions, especially for communities in low-density areas, or by facilitating migration to less risky places (World Bank 2019b).

Sequencing of the five I's

The ordering of the five I's is deliberate and balances the need to maximize the desired effects of a policy and do it in the most economical way. Early and easy interventions linked to the provision of *information* could improve market outcomes. When households and firms have better access to information, they can better understand the benefits and costs of their actions, thereby stemming the need for expensive government interventions. In the same vein, well-implemented *incentives* can scale quickly (for example, by affecting behaviors) at relatively low costs. Economic incentives can have monetary implications that could lead to snowballing costs (such as with tax rebates or subsidies), but they could also be deployed to disincentivize behaviors through monetary fines, taxes, and the like. By transferring and mitigating risks, well-functioning markets for *insurance* could lower risks to a point that would minimize the need for expensive government interventions. *Integration* entails planning by cities, often before the urban settlements are built, and reducing barriers to migration. Because of the durability of urban investments, well-thought-through integration could have long-lasting benefits, not least for the balance sheet. Finally, *investments* in infrastructure often involve large public outlays, and in many cases are the primary (and very necessary) response following disasters. Durable investments in mitigation and adaptation strategies are crucially important because of their implications for longer-term outcomes.

The five I's represent a relatively simple approach to organizing the many policy instruments available into distinct bundles. Nevertheless, many interdependencies exist between these sets of instruments. In some cases, they play out in complementary ways—that is, policies across the bundles strengthen impact when implemented together. For example, information helps facilitate migration decisions and thus integration. Information also allows prices to better reflect risks, thereby better incentivizing behaviors. Large public investments themselves serve as an information signal to private firms and households regarding the direction of future development. And incentives via prices or regulation can drive the working of private and public insurance markets, affecting, in turn, investment decisions by private agents.

Thus, decisions across the five sets of I's should not be made in isolation of each other. For example, Avner, Rentschler and Hallegatte (2014) show how much more efficient, and acceptable, a carbon tax is when combined with a dense public transportation network—that is, combining incentives with investments. Similarly, Viguié and Hallegatte (2012) demonstrate how a series of policy options (a greenbelt, a land use zoning policy, and a transportation subsidy), representing information and incentives, if taken in isolation could help achieve a given policy goal yet be detrimental to the achievement of others. Combining these options, however, results in a policy package that helps the achievement of all objectives. The resilience and reliability of infrastructure assets and services can also be enhanced by well-designed regulations, construction codes, and procurement rules. Hallegatte, Rentschler, and Rozenberg (2019) demonstrate how these interventions—which usually require a small investment up front—could significantly improve the overall resilience of infrastructure systems and generate large benefits.

Who makes the choices?

Turning the five I's into actionable prescriptions will require effective institutions. There is widespread agreement that climate action will require multilevel involvement not only by city and national governments but also by nonstate actors such as multilateral institutions, large multinational corporations, small enterprises, and civil society groups. At the grassroots level, communities are often the ones in the lead on climate action.

City governments

With their knowledge of local context and the ability to mobilize their communities, cities and city governments will play a critical role in climate change mitigation and adaptation. In fact, many areas of local government policy relate closely to climate action—for example, infrastructure investments and service provision, land use regulations, and emergency planning. Because cities will likely bear an outsized share of climate impacts, city leaders are probably the most motivated political actors to take on climate change. Global credit agencies now consider the climate change preparedness of cities in assessing the risk of lending to them.[24] And many cities have adopted more ambitious greenhouse gas reduction targets than those of countries.

In 2017, overall commitments by cities amounted to 27 percent of greenhouse gas reductions, exceeding national commitments by almost 7 percent (Kona et al. 2018). The Covenant of Mayors for Climate and Energy already includes almost 11,000 local and regional government signatories from 505 countries with a total population of 340 million.[25]

The mayor's wedge

Local governments and city leaders can affect climate action by influencing and implementing climate policies put in place by higher levels of government; designing and implementing city-specific policies and initiatives; and, crucially, helping coordinate collective climate action in their cities (De Coninck et al. 2018). How local governments deliver on this role depends on their scope and their capacity. This so-called mayor's wedge consists of the range of policies that city leaders can hope to influence, including those predetermined by higher levels of government.[26] The first component—*scope*—is the administrative responsibility of the city authority to design and administer policies. The second component—*capacity*—is the availability of human, technical, organizational, and financial resources to plan and implement policies (World Bank 2015a).

Scope. Local government scope or administrative responsibility can be proxied by the level of fiscal decentralization. Figure 5.1 shows that the share of spending by local governments varies substantially across countries. Spending by local authorities is often correlated with their control over key aspects of service delivery, which are often linked to climate adaptation and mitigation. Nevertheless, spending does not equal ability to prioritize and redistribute financial resources, which in many countries come as ringfenced grants, such as in Uzbekistan (Sivaev et al. 2022).

Countries differ in the degree to which they centralize the design and implementation of climate policy. In China, climate policy targets are set in the National Climate Change Program as a part of the 11th Five-Year Plan and are then passed on to provincial leading groups for implementation. Although they have a say in the specific policy tools selected to implement the targets, the provinces are subject to national monitoring and oversight. India has adopted a somewhat less centralized approach that allows more subnational initiative. Along with the National Action Plan on Climate Change, each state has its own State Action Plan on Climate Change; these plans focus mostly on implementing national level targets, but they allow substantial flexibility in pursuing state-level concerns (Somanathan et al. 2014).

The authority of local governments to take climate action also depends on regulations and policies enacted by higher levels of government in specific sectors. The ability of local governments to design or implement such measures is closely related to the authority granted to them in traditional areas such as land use, transportation policy, and energy market regulations. Such authority differs between countries and can even differ widely across cities within the same country. For example, in the United States the de jure ability of local governments to act on various aspects of climate adaptation and mitigation depends on which state they are in (Blanchard 2021).

Capacity. The second component of the mayor's wedge, capacity, is critical for implementation. Institutional capacity is broadly recognized as a critical determinant of a local government's ability to plan and implement climate action (Seto et al. 2014). Capacity could also be endogenous. Reckien et al. (2015) suggest that higher exposure to climate risks (such as location in lower-lying areas, proximity to the coast, or higher summer temperatures) may be linked to a lower institutional capacity of local governments.

Even though no common metrics exist for measuring local government capacity, it could be approximated through local government size (number of employees), local tax extraction capacity, and the productivity of public employees (World Bank 2015a). Such a simple

Figure 5.1 **Share of government spending by local governments, by selected regions and countries**

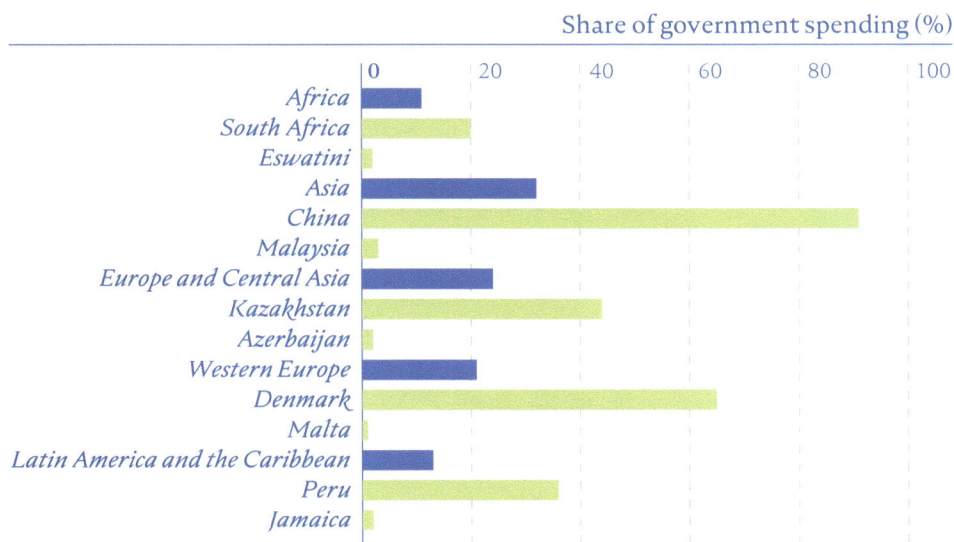

Source: Organisation for Economic Co-operation and Development and United Cities and Local Government (OECD-UCLG) World Observatory on Subnational Government Finance and Investment Database, 2016 (https://www.oecd.org/regional/observatory-on-subnational-government-finance-and-investment.htm).

approach—focusing mainly on staffing and fiscal capabilities—may be somewhat limited in proxying for the highly technical nature of the skills needed for climate action.

Countries and cities are often constrained by poor capacity—administrative, fiscal, technical—so it is critical that policy making take such constraints into account and acknowledge that some capacity constraints cannot be relaxed overnight. Baker et al. (2012) evaluate local climate adaptation plans in Southeast Queensland, Australia, and conclude that local governments were not effectively planning for the impacts of climate change. Although aware of expected impacts, these governments had limited capacity to use that information to develop geographically specific action plans. Mukim and Tingting (2018) study a countrywide process of county-to-city upgrading in China in the 1990s to identify whether extending the powers of urban local governments leads to better private sector performance. They find that a mismatch between the parameters of local government scope and capacity can lead to negative outcomes for private enterprises. Simply put, granting additional powers to local governments does not necessarily translate into better outcomes without the commensurate increases in capacity to use the additional authority.

Expanding scope and capacity. When cities run into the limits of their scope and capacity to act on their priorities (climate or otherwise), they can take action to expand them. Scope is often the prerogative of higher levels of government, so expanding it may require lobbying. Capacity, by contrast, can be expanded by seeking technical support or building partnerships locally, either with neighboring cities and municipalities or with the private sector and civic and academic leaders (World Bank 2015a). For example, building a public-private climate coalition could be a way to expand the influence of local governments (see box 5.4 for discussion of the public-private dialogue for climate).

Box 5.4

Adopting the public-private dialogue for local climate action

From developing green technology (Haselip et al. 2015) to transitioning to more sustainable business models (Burch et al. 2016), the private sector can contribute to action on climate change in many ways.

The Oxford Street Corridor Partnership in Greater Manchester, United Kingdom, is a good example of public-private engagement for climate adaptation. The Corridor Partnership board, made up of key local public actors, large private sector firms in the area, and local universities, led the effort to analyze the possible local climate change impacts. The partnership then announced forecasts of three climate pathways for the area: status quo, further intensification of development, and greening. After public discussion of these forecasts, local landowners committed to a program of greening the area that would help local climate adaptation and limit the potential heat island effect (Carter et al. 2015).

Experiences like the one in Manchester can be replicated using the public-private dialogue (PPD). PPD is a well-established approach for private sector engagement traditionally used in industrial development. The core strength of the PPD approach is its versatility and its adaptability to specific contexts and goals. Sivaev, Herzberg, and Manchanda (2015) draw on global experience to produce a set of observations on how to ensure the effectiveness of a local PPD (figure B5.4.1). For example, the optimal spatial scale of the dialogue should match the goal being pursued. If the goal is to improve walking and cycling infrastructure, just neighborhood engagement could produce results. But, if the goal is to limit greenhouse gas emissions from commuting by limiting journeys and changing the mode mix, then engagement of actors from across the urban agglomeration (or travel-to-work area) would be necessary.

Figure B5.4.1 Dimensions of adaptability of the public-private dialogue

National	Area	Local
Economywide	Scope	Sector-specific
Permanent institution	Institutionalization	Temporary initiative
Public-driven	Leadership	Private-driven
Third-party brokerage/support	Ownership	Locally driven/sustained
General orientations/Many goals	Focus	Specific changes/Specific goal
Many actors	Participation	Few actors

Source: Sivaev, Herzberg, and Manchanda 2015.

Local government actions for adaptation and mitigation

Because local governments are knowledgeable about local hazards and vulnerabilities, they can play a critical role in adaptation by not only raising awareness and issuing early warnings of hazards but also adopting land use planning and urban design that can substantially reduce the scale of future damage (Carter et al. 2015; Khan 2013). In fact, some local governments were among the first political actors to initiate climate action. Rotterdam, in the Netherlands, was one of the pioneers in adopting a comprehensive adaptation strategy (City of Rotterdam 2008). Almada, Portugal, has been implementing measures to protect the fragile coastal dune system for over a decade; and Burgas, Bulgaria, a city on the Black Sea coast, has been collaborating with local universities and nongovernmental organizations since 2013 to raise awareness of risks that threaten the community (European Union 2013).

The ability of local governments to influence mitigation is largely derived from their traditional urban functions. Local authorities oversee improvements in local public transportation services, including investments in local roads and cycling infrastructure, alongside zoning and land use. They can then effectively influence the urban layout of cities and determine density and influence commuting patterns—both parameters that drive compactness of cities and thus their emissions. And local governments can manage and regulate local utilities, which often shape energy consumption behaviors in the community (Gerda 2021). Meanwhile, local leaders can influence the choices and behaviors of residents through community engagement practices.

National governments

All this said, local governments have only a limited say in managing climate change. Because the causes of climate change and often the sources of impacts are external to cities, mayors and voters may be not inclined to set aside already scarce resources for mitigation measures that do not benefit them directly. Thus, higher levels of government may need to commit to policy and investment approaches that support local governments and give them incentives to better plan for and invest in addressing climate change impacts.

National governments provide strategic oversight, facilitate access to climate finance, and have the capacity and authority to drive climate action by creating a supportive enabling environment. Driving a sectoral approach, national governments can create plans that mainstream climate action (Somanathan et al. 2014). National programs on emissions and clean energy standards, carbon pricing mechanisms, appliance standards, and green financing are more likely to achieve economies of scale by creating larger markets for high- to low-tech cleaner technologies.

Because climate change will continue to generate significant disruptions, threatening livelihoods, national governments can impose climate change regulatory measures on the labor market. Through policy and regulatory interventions, the government could spur economic restructuring by managing transition and enabling green growth. The governments of industrialized countries are positioned to pursue green energy policies, moving jobs toward the renewables sector. Pestel (2019) points out the importance of considering big-picture policies and their impacts—both direct positive impacts (such as creating new jobs in the renewables sector) and indirect negative impacts on the labor market (such as stifling labor demand and imposing additional production costs). Environmental regulations that induce innovation often spur growth and employment (Horbach 2020).

National governments play the leading role in embedding social protection into climate plans and should focus on climate risks within social policies (Costella et al. 2021).

Moreover, they hold the key to setting policy frameworks for insurance and can provide coverage for high levels of physical and business risks. Aside from legislative and regulatory interventions, greater coverage can be achieved through subsidies and other financial incentives to promote the affordability of disaster insurance (OECD 2015a). Working with insurance stakeholders, government can monitor loss trends, improve hazard modeling, address causes of climate risk, and prepare for resilience (Gupta 2008).

At the nexus of major policy practices, national governments can unlock financial barriers. They can reduce the negative effects of climate change through disaster risk financing. By securing prearranged risk financing mechanisms, governments can empower subnational and local governments to avert and minimize the impacts of climate change (OECD 2015a). They can also remove political and institutional barriers because they hold the power to facilitate action by local governments and the private sector through their legislative, executive, and judiciary branches. Hsu and Rauber (2021) suggest that a national government can thus bridge the gap between the city, subnational, and national levels, and is positioned to set the stage for polycentric climate governance systems to ensure policy cohesion and integration and to avoid fragmentation that could undermine progress toward achieving climate action goals. In a polycentric climate governance system, a national government provides clear mandates to and ownership by subnational governments and cities, improves integration and coordination, and fast-tracks access to data and information.

Overall, although the role that national and local governments can play in climate adaptation and mitigation will depend on the national and local context, certain principles should help define that role. The first principle is that climate action in every country would require multilevel governance; even centralized states with limited local capacity should find avenues to engage local authorities and maximize the benefits of their local knowledge for climate adaptation and mitigation. Table 5.1 presents a summary list of other principles for national and city governments in defining their roles. The list in the table is not exhaustive, but rather is presented as guidance.

Table 5.1 Principles for defining the role of national and city governments in climate mitigation/adaptation

	National governments	City governments
Setting targets	• Define high-level greenhouse gas reduction and climate adaptation targets by sector and territory.	• Elaborate detailed local targets consistent with national goals based on local conditions, economic specialization, development challenges, major greenhouse gas contributors, and exposure to climate and other disaster risks.
Planning and implementation	• Establish critical national policy frameworks across all five I's.[a] • Establish regulations and incentives to drive adaptation and mitigation in sectors of critical importance for the climate: energy, transportation, construction and building management, agriculture, disaster risk management, and others.	• Maximize the use of traditional urban functions for climate adaptation and mitigation: land use and transportation planning, utilities management, urban infrastructure development and management, urban service provision, and disaster response planning and preparedness. • Engage the local community and businesses to drive behavior change and maximize their contributions to local targets.

(Continued)

Table 5.1   *continued*

	National governments	**City governments**
Financing	• Using national schemes for financing urban infrastructure and subnational grants, incentivize investments and programs that maximize adaptation and mitigation contributions. • Where possible, create financial incentives for local governments to drive climate action, such as through conditional grant schemes. • Develop a national legal framework to enable local governments to capture an increase of land value arising from investments in climate adaptation. • Create conditions and incentives to attract private financing of adaptation and mitigation investments and programs.	• Use all available options for maximizing financial resources for local climate action while ensuring the sustainability of municipal debt obligations. The following options should be considered (if appropriate): — Using land value capture schemes such as development fees, infrastructure levies, tax increment financing, and value-based land taxation. — Attracting private sector financing by implementing public-private partnership schemes through insurance or by providing financial incentives. — When appropriate, mobilizing financing from capital markets such as through issuance of green bonds.
Capacity building	• Set standards for local climate strategies and policies and provide sufficient technical and capacity-building support to help local governments achieve them. • Consider the use of performance-based grants and asymmetric decentralization tools to provide additional incentives for local climate action.	• Build public-private partnerships to leverage the capacities of the local private sector and academia for advancing local climate action. • Collaborate with neighboring jurisdictions to create conditions for residents and businesses across the agglomeration to adopt more sustainable practices and behaviors and promote adaptation to a changing climate. Collaboration specifically relates to transportation policy, land use and housing policy, utilities regulation and management, and business support and regulation.

Source: World Bank.

a. The five I's are five broad sets of policy instruments: information, incentives, insurance, integration, and investments.

The importance of transboundary coordination

Coordinated metropolitan area governance presents an opportunity, and a challenge, for improving local climate action. Coordination across local governments within a metro area is critical because effective adaptation and mitigation action demands more integrated planning, service delivery, and policies than individual local governments can provide. Coordination is also important because the decisions made by one municipality will directly affect its neighbors in an urban agglomeration (McCarney 2010).

With broad recognition of the importance of coordinated governance for climate action, positive examples are emerging. For example, more than two-thirds of metro areas in member countries of the Organisation for Economic Co-operation and Development have mechanisms for coordinated governance across municipal boundaries. Such arrangements range from special statuses granted by national legislation (for example, Daejeon, Republic of Korea, and 30 metro municipalities in Türkiye) and supra-municipal authorities (such as Portland Metro,

Oregon, United States), to informal coordination mechanisms (such as Delta Metropool, Amsterdam, and The Hague, Rotterdam, and Utrecht in the Netherlands)—see OECD 2015a. In Finland, the city of Tampere has launched a climate strategy with seven surrounding municipalities. This strategy covers coordinated action in areas of policy such as land use, traffic management, housing, and municipal services (McCarney et al. 2011). In 2007, the metropolitan region of Quito in Ecuador, which is governed by an elected metropolitan council and a metro mayor, adopted and implemented a climate strategy (Andersson 2015). This strategy centers around the challenges of managing water consumption in a city highly dependent on shrinking glaciers in the surrounding mountains (McCarney et al. 2011). Weak coordination mechanisms, such as in many cities in low- and middle-income countries, make it harder to tackle issues such as urban sprawl.

Financing

Municipal financing. Cities tend to rely on their own sources of revenue, intergovernmental fiscal transfers and grants, dedicated infrastructure, climate trust funds, and borrowing and leveraging instruments. As city capacity improves along with the enhancement of the overall enabling environment, cities can adopt more advanced tools. Enabling conditions are vital because certain climate finance instruments may not be available to cities struggling with low capacity, low agency, or higher political risk. The World Bank (2021d) suggests that perhaps the most promising area for unlocking resources for urban investments lies at the intersection of revenue enhancement, land value capture, and leveraging instruments. Borrowing and debt instruments can be out of reach for cash-strapped cities, but mechanisms that combine revenue generation with access to capital provide opportunities for climate financing, such as the sale of development rights and tax increment financing. Leveraging instruments and revenue generation, including special assessment districts, land value capture mechanisms, or tax increment schemes, can be used to mobilize additional sources of finance such as developer equity or in-kind value. In low- and middle-income countries, cities with lesser agency or weaker enabling conditions struggle to collect own-source revenue or compile investment plans. These cities should focus on strengthening expenditure-side systems alongside urban and capital investment planning systems, paving the way for progressive innovation on the revenue side through access to grants, impact fees, or development.

Although carbon markets will likely be most effective on a national or regional scale, enjoying greater liquidity and coverage of sectors, carbon pricing instruments have been gaining traction at the municipal level. To create the optimal enabling conditions, mobilizing urban climate finance at scale will require integration of the local and national levels and across urban planning and the built environment, capital investment planning, and municipal finance. The city of Vancouver and the province of British Columbia, in an example of the efficacy of Canada's carbon pricing system, worked vertically and horizontally to shift taxes away from labor and toward environmentally harmful activities. Working with eight cities, China's emissions trading pilots aim to cover 40 percent of national emissions and 12 percent of global emissions. China was the largest carbon market globally in 2021 (Zhang, Buote, and Acworth 2021).

Private financing. Private financial flows can contribute in several ways to tackling climate risks—from portfolio equity, to direct investments, to commercial bank lending, to bond finance.[27] Private capital could be aligned with decarbonization targets or net zero commitments.[28] The financial regulatory environment is also moving toward voluntary or mandatory disclosure of climate-related risks, with central banks and financial market supervisors playing a growing role. Initially, the focus was on the due consideration of climate-related risks;

however, since the 2015 speech in which Mark Carney, governor of the Bank of England, issued a warning about climate change ("break the tragedy of the horizon"), this focus has expanded to adjustment of market portfolios in line with sustainable development goals.[29] Subnational entities still struggle to access finance from capital markets—recent estimates by White and Wahba (2019) indicate that less than 20 percent of the largest 500 cities in low- and middle-income countries are deemed creditworthy, severely constricting their capacity to finance investments, including climate-linked investments in public infrastructure.

Private sector investment in adaptation is currently alarmingly low, however. The World Bank (2021e) finds that, of the US$30 billion spent on adaptation in 2017–18, only roughly US$500 million—a mere 1.6 percent—came from the private sector.[30] Most of this spending took place in higher-income countries and in sectors such as water and wastewater management and energy.[31] In addition, issues linked to investment risks—political or legal risks, currency risks, and credit risks, among others—could constrain private capital flows.

A crucial role remains, then, for public funds and support to help mobilize private investments. In this sense, public and private investments for climate action complement each other. Public funds could help mobilize private capital in several ways by, for example, co-financing individual projects (via grants, loans, and guarantees) or providing financial incentives (tax breaks, subsidies) or, more indirectly, via building technical capacity within the private sector and creating the right enabling conditions. Public investments could also reinforce private action. For example, building sea walls and sustaining tourism reinforce each other. Lack of coordination between the two, however, could lead to perverse outcomes—for example, in the absence of public sector incentives private (mal)adaptation could occur. Air-conditioning is a prime example of adaptive capacity contributing to future effects because of energy use (Davis and Gertler 2015).

Civil society organizations

Civil society organizations (CSOs), including nongovernmental organizations, are often a trusted source of information and can thus build awareness among communities of climate change and its likely impact on their lives, livelihoods, and habitats. Many of these organizations are simply an artifact of local communities organizing themselves to take on challenges that affect selected groups, neighborhoods, or sectors (see box 5.5 for an example of women's voice in influencing policy in the water sector). In fact, projects financed by the World Bank and other international organizations often work alongside CSOs to identify and map data on risks within urban areas and how these risks interact with underlying vulnerability and urban stresses. The World Bank has thus supported several cash-for-digital-work programs that employ vulnerable groups, including youth, in cities such as Bamako, Mali (Mukim 2018a), and Dar-Es-Salaam, Tanzania, to collect digital information to map risks across the urban space (see box 5.6 for examples of other participatory responses).

CSOs could also provide scientific and technical expertise to underpin implementation and monitoring of existing climate policy and act as advocates of new legislation to protect natural resources. For example, CSOs provide such functions in coastal zones in Mexico, in effect complementing the role of local governments (Baker, Ayala-Orozco, and García-Frapolli 2021). Similarly, CSOs in Islamabad promote green infrastructure through offering training programs for the local community, holding drives within schools, and helping build capacity in the city administration to establish policies and action plans (Mumtaz 2021). Such organizations can also go a long way toward mitigating risks by, for example, helping develop early warning systems and contingency plans, conducting drills, and responding to disasters.[32]

BOX 5.5

The importance of voice in decision-making

Women can be change agents in their communities. As chapter 3 demonstrated, women's needs and opinions are critical when planning for the provision of water services to water-scarce informal urban areas, in water resilience planning, and in water recovery measures. Yet women are still heavily underrepresented in the water workforce and in decision-making roles in water user associations and local governments, despite being disproportionately affected by inadequate water provision (Adams, Zulu, and Ouellette-Kray 2020; Das 2014).

Numerous international and national organizations have recognized the arguments for improving and increasing women's roles and have begun to make concerted efforts to increase women's influence on decision-making and diversity in the staffing of the water and sanitation sector. Togo encourages the involvement of women in the management of water points in semiurban areas through defined quotas that require local committees to have at least two women for every five members (GWP and UNEP-DHI 2021). In Vanuatu, a provision in the amended Water Resources Management Act requires 40 percent participation by women in all local water committees (GWP and UNEP-DHI 2021). Kenya has emphasized women's representation in water management organizations, with recommendations to maintain gender balance in water user associations and catchment advisory committees. Nicaragua has promoted the participation of women since 2012 as part of the multilevel water governance strategy (GWP and UNEP-DHI 2021).

Representation, however, is only the first step in moving toward a more diverse water workforce and better water resource management. Only when increased diversity translates into an ability to set agendas and influence decision-making can the full potential of representation be harnessed (Parthasarthy, Rao, and Palaniswamy 2019). An analysis of transcripts from Indian village assemblies revealed that, even when represented in local governance, women may participate in the deliberation at lower rates than men (Parthasarathy, Rao, and Palaniswamy 2019). Where communities have available transcripts of deliberations in water community governance, this kind of analysis using text-to-data methods may offer a promising way to detect imbalances in the participation of women and men. Moreover, this approach could help identify what features of discussion predict women's participation and thereby inform interventions (Blattner and Keener 2021).

A better understanding of interventions to increase women's participation in water governance will become even more critical as climate change and growing water scarcity increase the importance of sustainable water management practices and the maximization of upstream water conservation.

Box 5.6

Effectiveness of participatory responses to prepare for climate-related disasters

The Kenya Financing Locally Led Climate Action (FLLoCA) program is the first national-scale model of devolved climate finance. The program is based on the premise that locally led adaptation can be more effective than top-down interventions because local communities are more aware of the context and what is needed to drive change. FLLoCA supports partnerships between local governments and their citizens to assess climate risks and identify socially inclusive solutions tailored to local needs. With communities across Kenya also dealing with the impacts of the COVID-19 pandemic, FLLoCA takes a broad view of resilience and recognizes that communities have experience in managing multiple risks simultaneously. For example, investments may focus on activities that support livelihood diversification or community-level preparedness for multiple risks. Depending on what communities prioritize, investments may also promote water conservation and more efficient use of water, support natural resource management, rehabilitate degraded lands, or promote early warning systems.

FLLoCA builds on the Kenya Accountable Devolution Program, a pilot program funded by the World Bank, in addition to County Climate Change Funds piloted by the Adaptation Consortium. The County Climate Change Funds pilot projects financed some 100 public good investments prioritized by the communities through a highly consultative process, reaching more than 500,000 beneficiaries—most of whom were women—across five counties (Isiolo, Garissa, Kitui, Makueni, and Wajir). Investments included the rehabilitation of bore holes and installation of solar equipment; water harvesting, storage, and distribution systems; sanitation facilities; and governance activities. A large-scale household survey conducted in 2018 found that the investments resulted in 100 percent greater access to water for households and livestock.

A follow-up assessment of the program in 2019 found that the investments had additional direct and indirect benefits, including improved livelihoods, incomes, and food security; new economic opportunities; and fewer conflicts within households and communities and between neighboring villages. Overall, the pilots led to significant adaptation benefits for households and communities, while strengthening county institutions and improving the responsiveness to local needs, including of vulnerable and marginalized groups. The success of these pilots generated demand from other counties and support from Kenya's National Treasury to scale up the approach and make it available to all 47 counties, resulting in this new nationally scaled program.

Source: Arnold and Soikan 2021.

How to make choices?

How do policy makers choose between the different bundles of policies in a way that will produce the greatest positive impact for the most people in the most efficient manner? They must toggle between and sandwich together the bundles of policy interventions in the five I's to arrive at greener, more resilient, and more inclusive outcomes.

Cities can thrive in the shadow of an unpredictably changing climate only if programs and policies aim to combine as much as possible the objectives of combating climate change and furthering development, thereby aligning with the World Bank's GRID (green, resilient, and inclusive development) approach. That approach aims to promote economic growth that goes hand in hand with environmental goals and inclusion (World Bank 2021a).

How all cities should approach the GRID framework

How to green? Cities and countries, no matter their level of development, will face significant path dependencies in their investments. Even if reducing emissions is secondary to fostering resilience and inclusion, a business-as-usual approach to growth might entail choices that have higher costs in the future (entailing retrofitting, for example). Prices play a central role in allocating resources. Substitutability between building up (compact urban development) and building out (sprawl) will depend on their relative prices (accounting for land use, accessibility, and amenities). Misallocation and overuse (for example, of scarce resources such as energy or water) can result when prices are not attached to allocation. And, although they fall outside the authority of most cities, informational failures linked to the price of carbon can limit access to subnational borrowing for low-carbon investments.

How to increase resilience? Some cities will be much harder hit than others by climate shocks, but no city will remain unaffected. Thus, building resilience to the direct and indirect effects of climate events will be an important concern for most cities. Plugging information gaps is a modest intervention that can have high returns on investments and should be undertaken by all local and national governments. Risk information is a public good that is vital to the efficient functioning of land and urban housing markets. More targeted interventions, such as early warning systems, would have the greatest impact in locations at the highest risk and where the exact timing of climate shocks may be unpredictable. Easing movement of people across regions, including across borders, would also allow more dynamic reallocation of risks across places.

How to further inclusion? As the evidence in this report has emphasized, much of the risk associated with climate events will fall on poorer places and more vulnerable populations. Making things worse, these places and people are often the ones least able to mitigate or transfer the risks, and thus they often bear the full brunt of the impacts. Poor places and poor people are also found in rich countries. For example, the pockets of marginalized Roma populations in declining cities in Bulgaria or Romania are often the most affected by energy transitions. Thus, the provision of insurance to the most vulnerable, such as through urban safety nets, should be an almost universal practice. Better integration within cities, with better access to jobs and social services, will also provide large co-benefits to poorer populations, no matter what type of cities they reside in.

Taking contextual differences into account when choosing policies

In terms of policy choices, it matters where cities and countries are in terms of both their GRID challenges and their climate change–related risks (see chapter 2). The residents of cities in the poorest countries will suffer earliest and the most. Developing regions are at a geographic disadvantage because they are already warmer and suffer from high rainfall variability. Moreover, their low incomes and capabilities can make adaptation more difficult. Both local and national governments, however, can take several actions that take these issues into account.

In growth, some low- and middle-income countries are catching up by producing very explosive but sustained bursts of progress. Some countries continue to experience slower growth than the richest countries. And others have recently taken nosedives. The latest Intergovernmental Panel on Climate Change report calls for urgent and radical action to avert the potentially catastrophic effects of climate change (IPCC 2022). It also emphasizes, however, that such action cannot sidestep poverty reduction, equity, and development.

Stronger emphasis on greening. In many cities in higher-income countries, firms implemented ambitious green policies early on and took advantage of the economic opportunities that have sprung from climate policies. These opportunities in manufacturing (pollution control equipment and machinery, and renewable energy components), electricity generation (renewable energy), construction (green buildings), and services (tourism, recycling, and public transportation) will only grow; and many emerging economies are now banking on that growth. Greening cities by reducing air pollution and creating more green space (especially important in larger cities) will also have large positive spillovers for labor productivity and health outcomes. Greening could also reduce risks. For example, more permeable surfaces and green spaces can reduce flooding. Likewise, the analysis presented in chapter 4 suggests that policies to promote compactness do not just make cities greener but also boost overall economic activity and help address intracity inequalities.

Stronger emphasis on resilience. Mitigation in lower-income countries (fast-growing or not) will likely not be a priority. As highlighted in chapter 1, cities in low-income countries contribute less than 1 percent to global urban CO_2 emissions. Meanwhile, Chinese, Indian, and Indonesian cities may not be keen on diverting resources from their own development to reduce the greenhouse effect unless they find that the co-benefits, such as productivity gains, will be substantial. For cities in lower-income countries, the best defense against climate change and vulnerability to weather in general is their own development and investments in risk reduction and emergency preparedness measures. Furthermore, their immediate environmental problems—air and water pollution, poor sanitation, and disease—demand earlier attention. These challenges will also require big investments in risk reduction and emergency preparedness and response.

Stronger emphasis on inclusion. Countries already bearing the brunt of climate change and expecting these impacts[33] to increase over time are more likely to focus on adaptation. In countries already burdened with environmental and social challenges, climate shocks and stressors are expected to further exacerbate existing vulnerabilities. Brazilian, Sahelian, and South African cities are already seeing some of the effects of climate change in the form of increases in conflicts linked to agricultural and forest lands and water. In such places, close attention will need to be paid to redistribution, especially for policies that could have a regressive effect (such as withdrawal of public subsidies for fossil fuels and adaptation in place for wealthy beachfront properties).

The implications of city typologies might matter

Except for city-states such as Singapore, cities are not small countries. Therefore, they do not have all the tools available to countries to tackle climate-related challenges or exploit the opportunities. The diversity of cities also far exceeds that of countries, with even small countries displaying big differences among their urban regions. Thus, to be sensible, policy recommendations must capture multiple dimensions of cities. The examples that follow highlight some groupings of cities (based on the global typology from chapter 2) and the corresponding bundles of interventions that may best address their unique sets of challenges. The recommendations are aggregated in table 5.2.

Cities in low-income countries facing high levels of risk. In these cities, urgent needs and actions would have priority. Lower-cost policies, including those that could be financed in tandem with community investments, could be deployed more easily.

Although the exact timing of climate change–related shocks may not be easy to predict, because of their high risks and scarce resources, these cities, no matter their size, should pursue interventions aimed at better information. Such interventions could include putting in place early warning and information distribution systems for natural disasters and ensuring these systems reach poor households in isolated or remote areas. The relationship between high risk and low income also presents an opportunity to involve vulnerable households and communities in assessing and mapping disaster and environmental risks. Such a community-level, bottom-up approach could increase awareness and preparedness while providing small cash-for-work transfers to the poorest, thereby building community resilience and development, a key insurance mechanism for the urban poor.

In poor cities dealing with high-frequency and high-intensity climate events, governments, even if cash-strapped, can put in place incentives to increase local resilience. For example, ensuring the tenure security of the residents of informal settlements would help encourage them to invest in their properties (such as building dwellings with durable materials) or their neighborhoods (such as investing in small-scale infrastructure like gutters or paving). These investments should be combined with the provision of public assistance (such as cleaning and upgrading drainage canals) to help bolster resilience. Community-led development can also increase confidence in public officials, reduce neighborhood tensions, and put in place the preconditions for enhanced postdisaster responses.

For medium and large cities facing greater risks, the importance of addressing the traditional urban stresses that give rise to slums, gaps in basic service provision, and congestion takes on even greater urgency. These cities should focus on supporting more efficient, higher-density urban development in less risky areas. They could achieve such support by relying on a combination of urban planning instruments, including changing building regulations as needed, with investments in resilient infrastructure that help direct the location decisions of firms and households.

Cities in low-income countries facing low levels of risk. Because of their relatively low risk profile, these cities may need to account for faster growth in the future. They may have fewer pressing concerns and thus a larger window in which to plan.

Especially if measures to ensure better integration at the national level are being pursued, cities that might face lower risks of climate shocks could experience higher migration from rural or other urban locations, including those with a higher risk profile. Such cities would do well to tap opportunities linked with such migration. For example, they could ensure balanced development of the labor market by facilitating matching jobs with applicants via information mechanisms such as jobs fairs or local forums. More transparent information linked to the opportunities in urban destinations, including the changing profile of risks and the availability of potential support, could also help direct migration in line with policy makers' plans for urban development. In many such cities in low-income countries, delivery of basic public services usually lags needs, and private providers and actors fill the gap. In response to the growing attractiveness of the city, the focus of local governments in such circumstances, less hindered by frequent climate shocks, should be on ramping up accessibility and the quality of public goods and services provision.

The lower risk profile of these cities may also present them with a larger window of opportunity to plan for future urban development. Despite fewer resources, they could deploy policy reforms that set the stage up front for greener, more resilient, and more inclusive development. For example, the relaxation of building and planning regulations could give developers incentives to provide affordable units (particularly rental units) to low-income households in better-served and lower-risk neighborhoods. Cities could also use tax reductions or exemptions to incentivize such development, although these tools would have more claims on the fiscal purse. The development of affordable and resilient transportation, alongside coordinated investments in land use planning, would help enhance the accessibility of low-income households to economic opportunities and amenities. This type of planning will be particularly important for growing cities, whether starting out as small, medium, or large. It will also help reduce the likelihood of future urban fragmentation, segregated communities, and informal settlements.

Cities in middle- to high-income countries facing high levels of risk. These cities would have more space to put in place medium- to longer- term policies. The focus could be on policies that can help coordination among actors for common goals, including reforms and market mechanisms.

Cities that enjoy higher levels of income can deploy more resources to tackle the risks they face. They can wield additional policy instruments, and some may have more capable local governments. Thus, they might be in a better position to coordinate actors. For example, because of the variation in risk profiles (especially in larger cities), local governments in such cities should ensure that predicted environmental risk is included in cadastre systems and part of the mandatory disclosure of property characteristics. Households and firms could then make more informed location and investment decisions. At the same time, developers could be charged for the negative externalities generated by building in high-risk areas.

Financial incentives and programs could also help such cities mitigate the effects of disasters, plan for low-carbon development, and ensure that poor people are not left behind. The provision of social safety net programs for low-income households, including cash transfers and cash-for-work programs, would help mitigate the impacts of climate shocks and strengthen the city's "escalator out of poverty" function. Financial assistance, including subsidies, could also incentivize low-income households to invest in greener and more resilient upgrades of their properties. In parallel, national governments should create the conditions for the emergence of functional insurance markets. Government insurance schemes could provide discounts or make insurance conditional on actions intended to mitigate the impacts of extreme climate events.

Finally, with greater fiscal space for outlays, such cities would also be well equipped to coordinate their investments in land use and urban infrastructure. For example, they could subsidize housing for low-income residents in safer neighborhoods. At the same time, investments in transportation networks to low-risk areas could help mitigate the trade-offs that poorer residents might make between risk and accessibility.

Cities in middle- to high-income countries facing low levels of risk. These cities could serve as climate havens and help strengthen the stability of the urban system while exploiting the opportunities that such in-migration would provide.

Cities with low climate risk and more fiscal and technical capabilities could exploit several opportunities presented by a changing climate. They will be more attractive to in-migration, domestically and internationally, and could use this to their advantage. Such cities could support the inclusion of incoming migrants by, for example, rapidly providing identification to ensure access to services (health, education), establishing job training with job fairs, or improving the quality of public education (to facilitate intergenerational mobility). Such efforts would allow smaller or declining cities with these characteristics to serve as attractive destinations for climate migrants, thereby attracting talent and expanding their tax bases.

Many smaller, single-industry towns, including but not limited to mining, might also be affected because of efforts to support decarbonization and the move to renewable sources of energy (box 5.7). Countries might find migration to "climate havens" an effective insurance mechanism by allowing the dynamic spatial reallocation of people and capital away from riskier places, thereby ensuring greater stability of the urban system. Remittances from urban to rural areas could also contribute substantially to national poverty reduction. Thus, policies should be deployed to reduce barriers to migration. These policies could include those that help increase the supply of affordable housing in climate havens, reduce moving costs by improving transportation networks, and reduce skill mismatches by providing job training for low-skilled workers.

For cities in low-income countries, especially small and medium cities, addressing poverty and building resilience are key policy priorities and involve addressing the challenge of increasing access to basic services. In low-income countries, building institutional and individual capacity is a fundamental prerequisite to accelerating development. Meanwhile, for cities in middle-income countries the challenge, especially for small and medium cities, becomes one

Box 5.7

Are workers prepared for the green transition?

The transition to greener economic activities and the use of green technologies will depend on the skills of the population. The transition away from coal, combined with the ongoing technological disruption and digital transformation, will have a profound impact on the employment landscape over the coming years. Although some jobs will face redundancy and others will grow rapidly, many existing jobs will go through an important change in their required skill sets. The new types of jobs that emerge will likely require different types or higher levels of skills. Consequently, without adequate skills development measures in place to match labor supply and demand, unemployment may rise, dismissed workers may incur income losses, and migration trends may intensify toward the larger and more dynamic economic centers.

To assess workers' readiness for the green transition, the World Bank conducted a labor survey in multiple cities in Bulgaria (World Bank, forthcoming b). The survey identified and measured employability skills, movement across occupations, and typologies of groups of workers, including across mining and other carbon-intensive districts in the country. The results show that workers without specialized education, aging workers, and those employed in elementary occupations were at high risk of losing their livelihoods with little opportunity for transition. As a result, firms in transforming sectors would suffer from longer-term skill shortages and may be constrained in their productivity and avenues for growth.

of inequality rather than of poverty per se. This glaring commonality persists in cities of all sizes in high-income countries. Across the spectrum, cities should prioritize embedding social protection policies and programs to diminish risk.

The differences in challenges across types of cities also suggest that the focus for low- and middle-income country cities should be on adaptation, whereas for cities in high-income countries it must be on adaptation and mitigation. Pollution, however, is a key issue for large cities in both low- and middle-income countries, and addressing it comes with essential climate change mitigation co-benefits. Addressing greenhouse gas (GHG) emissions should be a priority for large cities in middle-income countries and for all cities in high-income countries. In low- and middle-income countries, the policy discourse should be on issues of air pollution, which then have the added benefit of also reducing GHG emissions.

Accounting for co-benefits and trade-offs

Making choices across bundles of interventions can be even more complicated because policy makers need to consider synergies (or co-benefits), trade-offs, and interactions between multiple objectives they may otherwise overlook. Such considerations are not new—urban policies have always had multiple goals, spanning social objectives, economic competitiveness, and environmental goals. A changing climate has simply supercharged the challenges, adding adaptation and mitigation to the mix—challenges that exacerbate the underlying ones (as described in the analytical framework for this report).

Adopting a co-benefit lens would help ensure that policy choices would aim to deliver simultaneously on multiple well-being objectives, including climate. Doing so would require an economywide perspective rather than a focus on a single or narrow range of output-related objectives, independent of others. Sometimes, the benefits accrue to the same or a similar set of stakeholders. For example, many investments in climate risk-reduction strategies can also support economic development, often within the same communities. Examining flood mitigation investments in Buenos Aires, Avner et al. (2022) find that, when land markets are functional, risk reduction can be captured through land value appreciation. In other cases, the benefits could spill over across multiple groups and geographies. For example, investments in public transit can reduce congestion, help tackle air pollution, and thus combine improvements in productivity with widespread benefits for health. Likewise, investments in renewable energy can reduce emissions and improve energy security.

The nature of climate risk also involves risks from responses themselves. Policy responses to climate change could entail their own opportunity costs, presenting themselves as trade-offs between GRID outcomes. For example, retrofitting buildings to improve energy efficiency increases costs for households and threatens housing affordability, potentially reducing inclusion. Avner and Hallegatte (2019) discuss the potential trade-offs between flood damage and housing scarcity and how they differ on the basis of flood management policies. Viguié and Hallegatte (2012) provide some early quantification of the trade-offs and synergies of selected urban climate policies. Using specific sets of policy packages for Paris, they quantify the interaction of interventions aimed at making the city greener, more resilient, and more inclusive. For example, a greenbelt policy that limits urban sprawl and protects natural areas could increase risk as more people move to flood-prone areas because of the greater scarcity of land. Their models suggest that a careful mix of several policies could mitigate the adverse consequences of each policy. In fact, for urgent actions, policy makers should explore options that seek to manage, minimize, or reverse the trade-offs for those places and people most affected.

Table 5.2 Tailored policy options, by type of city and instrument

Income class / Type of city	Low-income			Middle-income			High-income		
	Small	Medium	Large	Small	Medium	Large	Small	Medium	Large
Challenges	• Resilience (S) • Poverty (S) • Basic services (S)	• Resilience (S) • Poverty (S) • Basic services (S)	• Resilience (S) • Pollution (S) • Basic services (S)	• Poverty (S) • Inequality (S)	• Vegetation (S) • Inequality (S)	• GHG (S) • Pollution (S) • Vegetation (S) • Inequality (S)	• GHG (M) • Inequality (M) • Resilience (M)	• GHG (M) • Inequality (M) • Vegetation (M) • Resilience (M)	• GHG (S) • Inequality (S)
Instrument	**Information**								
	Early warning systems; hazard mapping and assessment								
	Build institutional capacity; Decentralized land administration services			• GHG emissions inventories					
Policy options	• Participatory risk awareness • Job fairs and local forums	• Participatory risk awareness • Job fairs and local forums	• Pollution monitoring • Better zoning of polluting industries • Urban planning documents	• Participatory risk awareness • Job fairs and local forums • Inclusionary zoning	• Urban planning documents • Urban design guidelines	• Pollution monitoring • Better zoning of polluting industries • Urban planning documents • Urban design guidelines • Building codes	• Urban planning documents • Urban design guidelines • Building codes • Disaster risk–informed land value	• Urban planning documents • Urban design guidelines • Building codes • Disaster risk–informed land value • Disaster-risk land development penalty	
Instrument	**Incentives**								
	Phase out fossil fuel subsidies								
						• Carbon taxes			
Policy options	• Cash transfers • Workfare programs • Subsidized housing	• Cash transfers • Workfare programs • Subsidized housing	• Congestion control schemes • Parking charges • Reforms to lower costs of vertical construction; relaxed height restrictions	• Cash transfers • Workfare programs • Subsidized housing • Inclusionary zoning	• Subsidized housing • Inclusionary zoning	• Congestion pricing • Parking reform • Lower costs of vertical construction; relaxed height restrictions • Density bonus • Expedited permitting • Building retrofit and clean energy subsidies and tax credits • EV tax credit • Inclusionary zoning	• Density bonus • Performance zoning • Expedited permitting • Building retrofit and clean energy subsidies and tax credits • EV tax credit • Inclusionary zoning	• Congestion pricing • Parking reform • Lower costs of vertical construction; relaxed height restrictions • Density bonus • Performance zoning • Expedited permitting and fast-track project review • Retrofit incentives • Air rights programs • Inclusionary zoning • Linkage fees	

(Continued)

Table 5.2 *(Continued)*

Income class →	Low-income			Middle-income			High-income		
Instrument / Type of city →	Small	Medium	Large	Small	Medium	Large	Small	Medium	Large
Insurance Policy options	• Social protection • Subsidized insurance (low-risk areas) • Catastrophe insurance			• Incorporate climate risk considerations in asset (re-)pricing, new insurance product launches, and underwriting process					
Integration *Integrate climate change adaptation and urban management; urban planning and regulation*									
Policy options	• Basic services; education • Laying out street networks	• Basic services; education • Laying out street networks		• Flexible urban planning • Compact growth	• Flexible urban planning • Compact growth	• Flexible urban planning • Compact growth	• Flexible urban planning • Compact growth	• Flexible urban planning • Compact growth	• Flexible urban planning • Compact growth
	• Connect to medium and larger cities • Lower migration barriers • Laying out of street network in anticipation of future expansion • Secure land and property rights	• Connect to medium and larger cities • Lower migration barriers • Laying out of street network in anticipation of future expansion • Secure land and property rights	• Integrated land use and transportation planning	• Connect to medium and large cities • Lower migration barriers • Laying out of street network in anticipation of future expansion	• Integrated land use and transportation planning	• Integrated land use and transportation planning	• Transit-oriented development • Connect to medium and large cities • Lower migration barriers	• Transit-oriented development	• Transit-oriented development
Investments Policy options	• Local bus services • Well-located affordable housing • Land provision • Improve building stock • Climate adaptation infrastructure • Nature-based solutions • Renewable energy	• Local bus services • Well-located affordable housing • Land provision • Improve building stock • Climate adaptation infrastructure • Nature-based solutions • Renewable energy	• Mass transit (BRT, MRT) • Well-located affordable housing • Climate adaptation infrastructure • Nature-based solutions • Renewable energy • Energy-efficient retrofits	• Local bus services • Well-located affordable housing	• Mass transit (BRT) • Well-located affordable housing • Urban green space	• Mass transit (BRT, LRT) • Mobility • Well-located affordable housing • Urban green space • Renewable energy • Energy-efficient retrofits	• Local bus services • Mobility • Well-located affordable housing • Climate adaptation infrastructure • Nature-based solutions • Renewable energy • Energy-efficient retrofits	• Mass transit (BRT, LRT) • Mobility • Well-located affordable housing • Climate adaptation infrastructure • Nature-based solutions • Urban green space • Renewable energy • Energy-efficient retrofits	• Mass transit (BRT, MRT) • Mobility • Well-located affordable housing • Renewable energy

Policy actions applied to: ■ All cities   ■ Cities in middle- or high-income countries   ■ Cities in low-income countries   □ One or two types of cities except for insurance

Source: World Bank.

Note: BRT = bus rapid transit; EV = electric vehicle; GHG = greenhouse gas; LRT = light rail transit; M = Moderate challenge; MRT = mass rapid transit; S = severe challenge.

Trade-offs across places

As discussed in chapter 3, climate change is expected to have heterogeneous local effects. Using a dynamic spatial equilibrium model, Cruz and Rossi-Hansberg (2021) find highly asymmetric effects of a 1°C increase in local temperature, with amenities and productivity declining in the world's hottest areas and increasing in the coldest. Balboni (2021) also demonstrates how the benefits of investing in selected regions in Vietnam—regions subject to the growing risk of coastal floods—diminishes rapidly with rising sea level. Although the model used by Cruz and Rossi-Hansberg (2021) is on a global scale and the one used by Balboni (2021) is on a country scale, the models have two characteristics in common. First, they demonstrate that the effects of climate change will be highly asymmetric across space, globally and within countries. Second, the future returns on current investments in more (negatively) affected regions are lower compared with returns in other regions. For governments, these findings imply making serious spatial choices in terms of where to invest, which, in turn, implies making trade-offs across places.

Places and ecological systems do not have an inexhaustible ability to adapt to climatic hazards. With rapidly shifting climate effects, risks and losses that may have been acceptable could become intolerable. A tipping point may, then, arise at which a good investment becomes a wasteful one. Without forward-looking policy and planning, and in the absence of credible choices or long-term pathways to viable alternatives, there is a risk that people will remain in places with deteriorating conditions. For example, about 20 million people in coastal Bangladesh already suffer the health effects of saltwater intrusion into drinking water supplies related to the rise in sea level. Remittances from family members working elsewhere can induce people in these areas to stay, possibly against their best interests. Seawalls can reduce impacts effectively in the short term, but they can also result in lock-ins and increased exposure to climate risks. Without appropriate policy interventions, perverse incentives to stay in place could greatly undermine community health and well-being. Nevertheless, standalone policies will have limited political acceptability. The existence of local networks, cultural preferences, and other socioeconomic factors may also affect the incentive to move away from riskier locations.[34] Thus, policies to limit future development in certain areas and potential resettlement away may also need to be paired with certain elements of adaptation.

Trade-offs across groups

Finally, climate policies will involve trade-offs among groups of people. Even benefits associated with the reduction of GHG emissions will accrue differentially across countries and populations. Some climate policies, however, can have regressive, albeit often unintended, effects. These policies could include carbon taxes, certain mandatory standards, subsidies, and regulatory tools, and might then require further corrective interventions. For example, Känzig (2021) finds that the European Union emissions trading systems has the intended effect of leading to a persistent fall in overall GHG emissions by means of a strong and immediate increase in energy prices, but that fall comes at the cost of a temporary drop in economic activity that is borne unequally. The paper finds that, although the expenditure of higher-income households falls only marginally, low-income households reduce their expenditure significantly and persistently.[35] Meanwhile, the widespread use of subsidies to achieve clean energy, such as for electric vehicles or rooftop solar, can benefit richer households disproportionately, at least in the short run because of higher take-up (Borenstein and Davis 2016). Vona (2021) provides a comprehensive overview of the distributional impacts of various climate and environmental policies.

The potentially adverse distributional impacts of climate policies suggest an important role for targeted fiscal policies to reduce the economic costs (that is, to shift their economic burden across population groups). Policy makers could do more. Policy measures could also be designed to reduce the adverse impacts or to expand the features that have progressive impacts. For example, Zachmann, Fredriksson, and Claeys (2018) suggest that certain policies are less regressive than others (such as fuel taxes compared with fuel efficiency standards or subsidies for public transportation versus subsidies for domestic air-conditioning systems) and that certain design elements could make policies less regressive (for example, auctioning emission permits instead of grandfathering them to polluters). Some policies, such as energy retrofits for social housing units, also actively benefit low-income households. Targeted compensation and well-designed climate policies with progressive impacts would also help increase public support.

Summary and conclusions

The challenges brought on by a changing climate may seem too intractable after reading this report. This chapter has looked at what can be done, by whom and how, and has demonstrated how strides can be made beyond timid, temporizing policies. Tackling the myriad challenges, and in some cases opportunities, associated with climate change will require making informed and astute choices.

This chapter presents a sequenced suite of policy instruments, the five I's—information, incentives, insurance, integration, and investments—at the disposal of policy makers. Information helps people and firms better understand, and therefore better adapt to, climate risks both across and within cities. Incentives allow people and firms to internalize environmental externalities and government officials to work better to address GRID challenges. Insurance allows people, firms, and governments to insure against losses associated with climate change and unavoidable environmental shocks and stresses that cannot be avoided. Integration allows more migration and trade. And, finally, investments are aimed at financing green, resilient, and inclusive infrastructure, including nature-based solutions.

Underpinning any policy response is the role of institutions. The five I's can be turned into actionable prescriptions only by those who get things done. Local governments could do so by ensuring balanced growth of their scope and capacity for adaptation and mitigation. National governments could provide strategic oversight, facilitate access to climate finance, and drive climate action by creating an enabling environment. Meanwhile, private financial flows—from portfolio equity to direct investments, to commercial bank lending, to bond finance—could contribute to tackling climate risks. Finally, civil society groups should not be overlooked. They are often a trusted source of information and can build awareness, provide technical expertise to underpin implementation and monitoring of existing climate policy, and act as advocates for new legislation.

Policy makers will need to move between and pull together the bundles of policy interventions presented in the five I's to arrive at the GRID outcomes. The combination of interventions, their sequencing, and the prioritization of outcomes will depend on the characteristics of cities—including primarily their level of risk, level of development, and size. All aspects of the GRID framework will apply to cities, no matter their characteristics, but the emphasis will depend strongly on the contextual differences. This is where the work on city typologies (as presented in chapter 2) will help clarify the pressures on a given city, the range of policy options available to it, and its ability to deploy its options over time. The mix of co-benefits and trade-offs will also guide the decision-making process to ensure that scarce resources can help deliver simultaneously on multiple well-being objectives, including climate action.

Notes

1. Available on Climate Central's website, https://www.climatecentral.org.

2. The World Bank defines shared prosperity using the annualized growth rate of the average per capita consumption or income of the poorest 40 percent (the bottom 40) of the population of a country.

3. Scientific institutions and insurance agencies often have the most detailed and accurate risk information and sophisticated modeling, yet local governments, communities, and businesses—who need that information the most—lack equivalent access and capabilities.

4. World Bank research in Bulgaria provided as part of Reimbursable Advisory Services.

5. See the overview of the World Bank's work on adaptive safety nets in Africa by Baez, Kshirsagar, and Skoufias (2020).

6. See the World Bank's development response to the Displacement Impact Project in Uganda (Mahony, Maher, and Haile 2021).

7. Such systems provide hazard warnings of different types (rapid or slow onset) and can vary in terms of the spatial scale (local, regional, national, or global) and the stakeholders (public authorities, media, communities, and so on).

8. Those studies include Bin, Kruse, and Landry (2008); Ortega and Taşpınar (2018); and Zhang and Leonard (2019). Likewise, detailed empirical work in Bogotá by World Bank (2010) shows that property values capitalized the exposure to seismic and other hazard risks, with lower values in riskier areas.

9. An oft-quoted example is the green bond issued by the city of Johannesburg, South Africa, in 2014 to introduce clean buses into its fleet.

10. The Stern Review argues that climate is the "greatest market failure," and mitigation requires placing a price on carbon so that the market has an incentive to shift to a low-carbon economy (Stern et al. 2006).

11. For more information, see the Government of British Columbia web page, "Climate Action Revenue Incentive Program," https://www2.gov.bc.ca/gov/content/governments/local-governments/grants-transfers/climate-action-revenue-incentive-program-carip.

12. From the Eco-Roof Incentive Program web page, https://www.toronto.ca/services-payments/water-environment/environmental-grants-incentives/green-your-roof.

13. However, a Federal Emergency Management Agency program, Building Resilient Infrastructure and Communities, now helps US cities buy out risky properties after a disaster, but it also requires a place for those residents to move so that they do not end up in another highly disaster-prone home.

14. For a recent overview of the literature on how tenure security affects investments in the physical resilience of homes, see Rentschler (2013).

15. These tools use geospatial data to identify and assess existing assets, concentration of population, location of critical infrastructure, and future areas of planned growth vis-à-vis historical hazard data (such as flood and seismic risk) and climate projections.

16. From the Grantham Research Institute on Climate Change and the Environment's "Climate Change Laws of the World" web page on Colombia, https://climate-laws.org/geographies /colombia/laws/law-no-1931-establishing-guidelines-for-the-management-of-climate-change.

17. The report estimates that international migrants totaled about 281 million in 2020, or 3.6 percent of the global population.

18. United Nations High Commissioner for Refugees, "Figures at a Glance" web page, https://www .unhcr.org/figures-at-a-glance.html.

19. Hallegatte, Rentschler, and Rozenberg (2019) find that natural shocks are among the leading causes of infrastructure disruptions and can cost between US$ 391 billion to US$ 647 billion in low- and middle-income countries.

20. For African cities, Foster and Briceno-Garmendia (2010) estimate that doubling urban density reduces the per capita cost of a package of infrastructure improvements by 25 percent or so.

21. Some simple solutions exist, such as the roof straps used in the Caribbean so roofs can withstand hurricane-force storms (Gibbs 2000).

22. *Gray infrastructure* refers to built structures and engineering equipment (such as reservoirs, embankments, canals, and so on) embedded within watersheds or coastal ecosystems.

23. This effect has been observed in low-income countries—see Ferdous et al. (2019) who study the effect of investments in flood protection along the Jamuna River in Bangladesh. It suggests that protective measures may need to be complemented with strict zoning restrictions, with better understanding of the expected risk exposure.

24. See the Covenant of Mayors for Climate and Energy's Urban Adaptation Support Tool, step 0-3, "Getting Started: Adaptation to Climate Change in Urban Areas," https://climate-adapt .eea:europa.eu/knowledge/tools/urban-ast/step-0-3.

25. See the Covenant of Mayors for Climate and Energy's web page "Covenant Initiative: Covenant in Figures," https://www.covenantofmayors.eu/about/covenant-initiative/covenant-in-figures .html.

26. But city leaders and governments can manage development effectively only if they have the functional mandate, revenue base, and capabilities to target such development.

27. Private financiers include banks, pension funds, insurance companies, corporations, impact investors, and other private actors. The private sector could also contribute by providing goods and services that facilitate adaptation or mitigation and by adapting their own operations and assets to be climate-resilient.

28. See the Net Zero Asset Managers initiative, https://www.netzeroassetmanagers.org/.

29. The speech argues that, just as the solution to the tragedy of the commons (a classic problem in environmental economics) lies in property rights and supply management, so, too, must central banks take the lead to combine data, technology, and expert judgment to measure and manage the risks.

30. To put this number in perspective, the United Nations Environment Programme estimates that the total cost of adaptation will reach US$140 billion–$300 billion a year by 2030 (UNEP 2021). Thus, actual spending still falls short of documented needs.

31. Because adaptation spending is often part of larger investments and because of issues of limited transparency, quantifying the current levels of private investment in adaptation is not a straightforward exercise.

32. See Amao et al. (2014) for examples from urban areas in Ghana and Kenya.

33. However, the impacts of disasters are often measured as the cost of the damages and losses, which, according to Hallegatte and Walsh (2021), does not properly reflect the real impact on low-income communities. Instead, Hallegatte and Walsh propose a new approach that measures the impact of a disaster at the household level, which would take into account distributional and poverty impacts. This approach could allow policy makers to better identify where and in which sectors to prioritize investments.

34. Henrique et al. (2022) provide an example of how residents in Southwest Australia trade off climate-induced losses against other values.

35. Two mechanisms account for this effect. Poorer households spend a larger share of their disposable income on energy, leaving less for other expenditures. And poorer households see a steeper drop in incomes because they tend to work in sectors that are more affected by a climate policy.

References

Adams, E. A., L. Zulu, and Q. Ouellette-Kray. 2020. "Community Water Governance for Urban Water Security in the Global South: Status, Lessons, and Prospects." *WIREs Water* 7 (5): e1466.

Afet, D., and S. Kurumu. 2021. "Faaliyet Raporu." https://www.dask.gov.tr/upload/Dask/FAALİYET%20RAPORLARI/2021_Faaliyet_Raporu.pdf.

Amao, O. B., D. Ettang, U. Okeke-Uzodike, and C. Tugizamana. 2014. "Revisiting the Utility of the Early Warning and Early Response Mechanisms in Africa: Any Role for Civil Society?" *Peace and Conflict Review* 8.1: 77–97.

Andersson, M. 2015. *Unpacking Metropolitan Governance for Sustainable Development*. Nairobi: UN-Habitat.

Andres, L. A., M. Thibert, C. Lombana Cordoba, A. V. Danilenko, G. Joseph, and C. Borja-Vega. 2019. *Doing More with Less: Smarter Subsidies for Water Supply and Sanitation*. Washington, DC: World Bank.

Angel, S. 2017. "Urban Forms and Future Cities: A Commentary." *Urban Planning* 2 (1): 1–5.

Arnold, M., and N. Soikan. 2021. "Kenya Moves to Locally Led Climate Action." World Bank Blogs, October 27, 2021. https://blogs.worldbank.org/nasikiliza/kenya-moves-locally-led-climate-action.

Avner, P., and S. Hallegatte. 2019. "Moral Hazard vs. Land Scarcity: Flood Management Policies for the Real World." Policy Research Working Paper 9012, World Bank, Washington, DC.

Avner, P., and S. V. Lall. 2016. "Matchmaking in Nairobi: The Role of Land Use." Policy Research Working Paper 7904, World Bank, Washington, DC.

Avner, P., J. E. Rentschler, and S. Hallegatte. 2014. "Carbon Price Efficiency: Lock-In and Path Dependence in Urban Forms and Transport Infrastructure." Policy Research Working Paper 6941, World Bank, Washington, DC.

Avner, P., V. Viguié, B. A. Jafino, and S. Hallegatte. 2022. "Flood Protection and Land Value Creation: Not All Resilience Investments Are Created Equal." *Economics of Disasters and Climate Change* 6: 417–49. https://doi.org/10.1007/s41885-022-00117-7.

Baez, J. E., V. Kshirsagar, and E. Skoufias. 2020. "Adaptive Safety Nets for Rural Africa: Drought-Sensitive Targeting with Sparse Data." Poverty and Equity Notes, World Bank, Washington, DC.

Baker, I., A. Peterson, G. Brown, and C. McAlpine. 2012. "Local Government Response to the Impacts of Climate Change: An Evaluation of Local Climate Adaptation Plans." *Landscape and Urban Planning* 107 (2): 127–36.

Baker, S., B. Ayala-Orozco, and E. García-Frapolli. 2021. "The Role of Civil Society Organisations in Climate Change Governance: Lessons from Quintana Roo, Mexico." *Journal of the British Academy* 9 (s10): 99–126.

Balboni, C. 2021. "In Harm's Way? Infrastructure Investments and the Persistence of Coastal Cities." Department of Economics, Massachusetts Institute of Technology, Cambridge, MA.

Balch, O. 2014. "Plugging the Leaks: How Digital Tools Can Prevent Water Loss." *The Guardian*, December 11, 2014. https://www.theguardian.com/sustainable-business/2014/dec/11/plugging-leaks-digital-tools--water-loss-leaks.

Beltrán, A., D. Maddison, and R. Elliott. 2018. "Is Flood Risk Capitalised into Property Values?" *Ecological Economics* 146: 668–85.

Bin, O., J. B. Kruse, and C. E. Landry. 2008. "Flood Hazards, Insurance Rates, and Amenities: Evidence From the Coastal Housing Market." *Journal of Risk and Insurance* 75 (1): 63–82.

Bin, O., and C. E. Landry. 2013. "Changes in Implicit Flood Risk Premiums: Empirical Evidence from the Housing Market." *Journal of Environmental Economics and Management* 65 (3): 361–76.

Blanchard, J. 2021. "Local Governments Can Use Their Power to Combat Climate Change." *Bloomberg Law*, June 3, 2021. https://news.bloomberglaw.com/environment-and-energy/local-governments-can-use-their-power-to-combat-climate-change-17.

Blattner, A., and S. Keener. 2021. "What Works? Assessing the Evidence Base on Gender and Inclusion." Research Note for the Water Global Practice, World Bank, Washington, DC.

Blickle, K., and J. A. C. Santos. 2022. "Unintended Consequences of 'Mandatory' Flood Insurance." FRB of New York Staff Report No. 1012, Federal Reserve Bank, New York.

Borenstein, S., and L. Davis. 2016. "The Distributional Effects of US Clean Energy Tax Credits." *Tax Policy and the Economy* 30 (1) 191–234.

Borgomeo, E., A. Jägerskog, E. Zaveri, J. Russ, A. Khan, and R. Damania. 2021. *Ebb and Flow, Volume 2: Water in the Shadow of Conflict in the Middle East and North Africa*. Washington, DC: World Bank.

Brenton, P., and V. Chemutai. 2021. *The Trade and Climate Change Nexus: The Urgency and Opportunities for Developing Countries*. Washington, DC: World Bank.

Buckley, B. M., K. J. Anchukaitis, D. Penny, R. Fletcher, E. R. Cook, M. Sano, L. C. Nam, et al. 2010. "Climate as a Contributing Factor in the Demise of Angkor, Cambodia." *PNAS* 107 (15): 6748–52.

Burch, S., M. Andrachuk, D. Carey, N. Frantzeskaki, H. Schroeder, N. Mischkowski, and D. Loorbach. 2016. "Governing and Accelerating Transformative Entrepreneurship: Exploring the Potential for Small Business Innovation on Urban Sustainability Transitions." *Current Opinion in Environmental Sustainability* 22: 26–32.

Carter, J., G. Cavan, A. Connelly, S. Guy, J. Handley, and A. Kazmierczak. 2015. "Climate Change and the City: Building Capacity for Urban Adaptation." *Progress in Planning* 95: 1-66.

Chan, F. K., J. Griffiths, E. Higgitt, S. Xu, F. Zhu, Y. T. Tang, Y. Xu, and C. Thorne. 2018. "'Sponge City' in China: A Breakthrough of Planning and Flood Risk Management in the Urban Context." *Land Use Policy* 76: 772–78.

City of Rotterdam. 2008. *Rotterdam Climate Proof: Adaptation Programmed.* Rotterdam Climate Initiative.

Conte, B., K. Desmet, D. Nagy, and E. Rossi-Hansberg. 2021. "Local Sectoral Specialization in a Warming World." *Journal of Economic Geography* 21(4): 493–530.

Costa, D. L., and M. E. Kahn. 2011. "Electricity Consumption and Durable Housing: Understanding Cohort Effects." *American Economic Review* 101 (3): 88–92.

Costa, D. L., and M. E. Kahn. 2013. "Energy Conservation 'Nudges' and Environmentalist Ideology: Evidence from a Randomized Residential Electricity Field Experiment." *Journal of the European Economic Association* 11 (3): 680–702.

Costella, C., A. McCord, M. van Aalst, R. Holmes, J. Ammoun, and V. Barca. 2021. "Social Protection and Climate Change: Scaling Up Ambition." Social Protection Approaches to COVID-19 Expert Advice Service (SPACE), Development Alternatives Incorporated (DAI) Global, LLC, Bethesda, MD.

Cruz, J-L., and E. Rossi-Hansberg. 2021. "The Economic Geography of Global Warming." NBER Working Paper 28466, National Bureau of Economic Research, Cambridge, MA.

Damania, R., S. Desbureaux, M. Hyland, A. Islam, A. S. Rodella, J. Russ, J., and E. Zaveri. 2017. *Uncharted Waters: The New Economics of Water Scarcity and Variability.* Washington, DC: World Bank.

Das, P. 2014. "Women's Participation in Community-Level Water Governance in Urban India: The Gap Between Motivation and Ability." *World Development* 64: 206–18.

Davis, L. W., and P. J. Gertler. 2015. "Contribution of Air Conditioning Adoption to Future Energy Use under Global Warming." *PNAS* 112 (19): 5962–67.

De Coninck, H., A. Revi, M. Babiker, P. Bertoldi, M. Buckeridge, A. Cartwright, W. Dong, et al. 2018. "Strengthening and Implementing the Global Response." In *Global Warming of 1.5°C,* edited by V. Masson-Delmotte, P. Zhai, H.-O. Pörtner, D. Roberts, J. Skea, P. R. Shukla, A. Pirani, et al. Geneva: Intergovernmental Panel on Climate Change.

Deininger, K., H. Selod, and A. Burns. 2012. *The Land Governance Assessment Framework: Identifying and Monitoring Good Practice in the Land Sector.* Washington, DC: World Bank.

Delgado, A., D. J. Rodriguez, C. A. Amadei, and M. Makino. 2021. *Water in Circular Economy and Resilience.* Washington, DC: World Bank.

Del Valle, A., A. de Janvry, and E. Sadoulet. 2020. "Rules for Recovery: Impact of Indexed Disaster Funds on Shock Coping in Mexico." *American Economic Journal: Applied Economics* 12 (4): 164–95.

Desmet, K., and R. Jedwab. 2022. "Are We Over-Building in 'Bad' Locations Globally? Future Climate Change and Durable Real Estate." Background paper prepared for this report, World Bank, Washington, DC.

Devereux, S., and J. Cuesta. 2021. "Urban-Sensitive Social Protection: How Universalized Social Protection Can Reduce Urban Vulnerabilities Post COVID-19." *Progress in Development Studies* 21 (4): 340–60.

Domon, S., M. Hirota, T. Kono, S. Managi, and Y. Matsuki. 2022. "The Long-Run Effects of Congestion Tolls, Carbon Tax, and Land Use Regulations on Urban CO_2 Emissions." *Regional Science and Urban Economics* 92: 103750.

Ehlers, T., B. Mojon, and F. Packer. 2020. "Green Bonds and Carbon Emissions: Exploring the Case for a Rating System at the Firm Level." *BIS Quarterly Review* (September): 31–47.

Ehrlich, I., and G. S. Becker. 1972. "Market Insurance, Self-Insurance, and Self-Protection." *Journal of Political Economy* 80 (4): 623–48.

Erman, A., E. Motte, R. Goyal, A. Asare, S. Takamatsu, X. Chen, S. Malgioglio, et al. 2020. "The Road to Recovery: The Role of Poverty in the Exposure, Vulnerability and Resilience to Floods in Accra." *Economics of Disasters and Climate Change* 4 (1): 171–93.

European Union. 2013. *Climate Change Adaptation: Empowerment of Local and Regional Authorities, with a Focus on Their Involvement in Monitoring and Policy Design.* Brussels: European Union.

Fay, M., H. I. Lee, M. Mastruzzi, S. Han, and M. Cho. 2019. "Hitting the Trillion Mark: A Look at How Much Countries Are Spending on Infrastructure." Policy Research Working Paper 8730, World Bank, Washington, DC.

Fei, J., Y. Wang, Y. Yang, S. Chen, and Q. Zhi. 2016. "Towards Eco-city: The Role of Green Innovation." *Energy Procedia* 104: 165–70.

Ferdous, M. R., A. Wesselink, L. Brandimarte, G. D. Baldassarre, and M. M. Rahman. 2019. "The Levee Effect along the Jamuna River in Bangladesh." *Water International* 44 (5): 496–519.

Fernandes, E. 2011. *Regularization of Informal Settlements in Latin America.* Cambridge, MA: Lincoln Institute of Land Policy.

Flores, F. M., S. Milusheva, and A. R. Reichert. 2021. "Climate Anomalies and International Migration: A Disaggregated Analysis for West Africa." Policy Research Working Paper 9664, World Bank, Washington, DC.

Foster, V., and C. Briceno-Garmendia. 2010. *Africa's Infrastructure: A Time for Transformation: A Time for Transformation.* Africa Development Forum. Washington, DC: World Bank.

Franklin, S. 2018. "Location, Search Costs and Youth Unemployment: Experimental Evidence from Transport Subsidies." *Economic Journal* 128 (614): 2353–79.

Georgic, W. 2019. "Vulnerability and Policy Response: Unintended Consequences." PhD dissertation, Ohio State University.

Gerda, N. 2021. "What Can Local Governments Do to Fight Climate Change? A Heck of a Lot, Say Experts." *Voice of OC*, April 8, 2021. https://voiceofoc.org/2021/04/what-can-local-governments -do-to-fight-climate-change-a-heck-of-a-lot-say-experts/.

GFDRR (Global Facility for Disaster Reduction and Recovery). 2012. *Analysis of Disaster Risk Management in Colombia: A Contribution to the Creation of Public Policies*. Washington, DC: World Bank.

GFDRR (Global Facility for Disaster Reduction and Recovery). 2014. *Understanding Risk in an Evolving World*. Washington, DC: World Bank.

GFDRR (Global Facility for Disaster Reduction and Recovery). 2019. *Building Regulation for Resilience: Program Brief*. Washington, DC: World Bank.

Ghesquiere, F., L. Jamin, and O. Mahul. 2006. *Earthquake Vulnerability Reduction Program in Colombia: A Probabilistic Cost-Benefit Analysis*. Washington, DC: World Bank.

Gibbs, T. 2000. *Detailing for Hurricanes*. Washington, DC: Organization of American States. https://www.oas.org/pgdm/document/mhbdc/b3_text.pdf.

Global Center on Adaptation and World Resources Institute. 2019. *Adapt Now: A Global Call for Leadership on Climate Resilience*. Global Center on Adaptation, World Resources Institute.

Good Food Institute. 2021a. *Plant-Based Meat for a Growing World*. Good Food Institute.

Good Food Institute. 2021b. *State of the Industry Report—Plant-Based Meat, Eggs, and Dairy*. Good Food Institute.

Grafton, R. Q., L. Chu, and T. Kompas. 2015. "Optimal Water Tariffs and Supply Augmentation for Cost-of-Service Regulated Water Utilities." *Utilities Policy* 34: 54–62.

Gramkow, G., and A. Anger-Kraavi. 2018. "Could Fiscal Policies Induce Green Innovation in Developing Countries? The Case of Brazilian Manufacturing Sectors." *Climate Policy* 18 (2): 246–57.

GRiF (Global Risk Financing Facility). 2020. *Annual Report July 1, 2019–June 30, 2020*. Washington, DC: World Bank.

Gröger, A., and Y. Zylberberg. 2016. "Internal Labor Migration as a Shock Coping Strategy: Evidence from a Typhoon." *American Economic Journal: Applied Economics* 8 (2): 123–53.

Gupta, A. 2008. "Climate Change and Insurance Markets." *Development Outreach* 10 (1): 30–34.

Gurenko, E., R. Lester, O. Mahul, and S. O. Gonulal. 2006. *Earthquake Insurance in Turkey*. Washington, DC: World Bank.

GWP (Global Water Partnership) and UNEP-DHI (United Nations Environment Programme–DHI Centre on Water and Environment). 2021. *Advancing towards Gender Mainstreaming in Water Resources Management*. Stockholm: GWP and UNEP-DHI Centre on Water and Environment.

Hallegatte, S. 2009. "Strategies to Adapt to an Uncertain Climate Change." *Global Environmental Change* 19 (2): 240–47.

Hallegatte, S., J. Rentschler, and J. Rozenberg. 2019. *Lifelines: The Resilient Infrastructure Opportunity*. Washington, DC: World Bank.

Hallegatte, S., J. Rentschler, and J. Rozenberg. 2020. *Adaptation Principles: A Guide for Designing Strategies for Climate Change Adaptation and Resilience*. Washington, DC: World Bank.

Hallegatte, S., A. Vogt-Schilb, M. Bangalore, and J. Rozenberg. 2017. *Unbreakable: Building the Resilience of the Poor in the Face of Natural Disasters, Climate Change, and Development*. Washington, DC: World Bank.

Hallegatte, S., and B. Walsh. 2021. "Natural Disasters, Poverty and Inequality." In *The Routledge Handbook of the Political Economy of the Environment*, edited by Éloi Laurent and Klara Zwickl. London: Routledge.

Haselip, J., U. E. Hansen, D. Puig, S. Trærup, and S. Dhar. 2015. "Governance, Enabling Frameworks and Policies for the Transfer and Diffusion of Low Carbon and Climate Adaptation Technologies in Developing Countries." *Climatic Change* 131 (3): 363–70.

Hassan, R., M. S. Islam, A. S. M. Saifullah, and M. Islam. 2013. "Effectiveness of Social Safety Net Programs on Community Resilience to Hazard Vulnerable Population in Bangladesh." *Journal of Environmental Science and Natural Resources* 6 (1): 123–29.

Hegazy, I., W. Seddik, and H. Ibrahim. 2017. "Towards Green Cities in Developing Countries: Egyptian New Cities as a Case Study." *International Journal of Low-Carbon Technologies* 12 (4): 358–68.

Henrique, K. P., P. Tschakert, C. Bourgault du Coudray, P. Horwitz, K. D. C. Krueger, and A. J. Wheeler. 2022. "Navigating Loss and Value Trade-Offs in a Changing Climate." *Climate Risk Management* 35: 100405.

Hino, M., and M. Burke. 2021. "The Effect of Information about Climate Risk on Property Values." *PNAS* 118 (17): e2003374118.

Horbach, J. 2020. "Impacts of Regulation on Eco-innovation and Job Creation." IZA World of Labor, Institute of Labor Economics, Bonn.

Hsu, A., and R. Rauber. 2021. "Diverse Climate Actors Show Limited Coordination in a Large-Scale Text Analysis of Strategy Documents." *Communications Earth and Environment* 2: 30.

Hutton, N. S. 2018. "The Levee Effect Revisited: Processes and Policies Enabling Development in Yuba County, California." *Flood Risk Management* 12 (3): e12469.

IEA (International Energy Agency). 2015. *Capturing the Multiple Benefits of Energy Efficiency*. Paris: IAE.

IPCC (Intergovernmental Panel on Climate Change). 2022. "Summary for Policymakers." In *Climate Change 2022: Impacts, Adaptation and Vulnerability*. Contribution of Working Group II to the Sixth Assessment Report of the Intergovernmental Panel on Climate Change. Cambridge, UK: Cambridge University Press.

Jensen, O., L. P. Weiss, S. Dahan, S. Fitzgerald, A. M. Khan, and F. Armendaris. Forthcoming. "Water Secure Cities: Position Paper." World Bank, Washington, DC.

Kahn, M. E. 2010. *Climatopolis: How Our Cities Will Thrive in a Hotter Future*. New York: Basic Books.

Känzig, D. R. 2021. "The Unequal Economic Consequences of Carbon Pricing." Department of Economics, London Business School. http://dx.doi.org/10.2139/ssrn.3786030.

Khan, M. R. 2013. *Toward a Binding Climate Change Adaptation Regime: A Proposed Framework*. Abingdon, UK: Routledge.

Kona, A., P. Bertoldi, F. Monforti-Ferrario, S. Rivas, and J. F. Dallemand. 2018. "Covenant of Mayors Signatories Leading the Way Toward 1.5 Degree Global Warming Pathway." *Sustainable Cities and Society* 41: 568–75.

Kremer, M. 1993. "Population Growth and Technological Change: One Million B.C. to 1990." *Quarterly Journal of Economics* 108 (3): 681–716.

Lagakos, D. 2020. "Urban-Rural Gaps in the Developing World: Does Internal Migration Offer Opportunities?" *Journal of Economic Perspectives* 34 (3): 174–92.

Lenox, M., A. King, and J. Ehrenfeld. 2000. "An Assessment of Design-for-Environment Practices in Leading US Electronics Firms." *Interfaces* 30 (3): 83–94.

Mahony, C., B. Maher, and Z. Haile. 2021. "Machine Learning in Uganda Brings the Power of Risk Financing to Strengthen Refugee and Host Community Resilience." *World Bank Blogs*, January 22, 2021. https://blogs.worldbank.org/nasikiliza/machine-learning-uganda-brings-power-risk-financing-strengthen-refugee-and-host.

McAuliffe, M., and A. Triandafyllidou, eds. 2021. *World Migration Report 2022*. Geneva: International Organization for Migration.

McCarney, P. 2010. "Conclusions: Governance Challenges in Urban and Peri-urban Areas." In *Peri-urban Water and Sanitation Services: Policy, Planning and Method*, 277–97. Berlin/Heidelberg: Springer Science Business Media.

McCarney, P., H. Blanco, J. Carmin, and M. Colley. 2011. "Cities and Climate Change." In *Climate Change and Cities: First Assessment Report of the Urban Climate Change Research Network*, edited by C. Rosenzweig, W. D. Solecki, S. A. Hammer, and S. Mehrotra, 249–69. Cambridge, UK: Cambridge University Press.

McDonald, R. I., K. F. Weber, J. Padowski, T. Boucher, and D. Shemie. 2016. "Estimating Watershed Degradation over the Last Century and Its Impact on Water-Treatment Costs for the World's Large Cities." *PNAS* 113 (32): 9117–22.

Michaels, G., D. Nigmatulina, F. Rauch, T. Regan, N. Baruah, and A. Dahlstrand. 2021. "Planning Ahead for Better Neighborhoods: Long-Run Evidence from Tanzania." *Journal of Political Economy* 129 (7): 2112–56.

Mukim, M. 2018a. *Bamako Urban Sector Review: An Engine of Growth and Service Delivery*. Washington, DC: World Bank.

Mukim, M. 2018b. *Freetown Urban Sector Review: Options for Growth and Resilience*. Washington, DC: World Bank.

Mukim, M. 2021. *Burundi Urbanization Review*. Washington, DC: World Bank.

Mukim, M., and J. Tingting. 2018. "Empowering Cities—Good for Growth?" *Asian Development Review* 35 (1): 175–95.

Mumtaz, M. 2021. "Role of Civil Society Organizations for Promoting Green and Blue Infrastructure to Adapting Climate Change: Evidence from Islamabad city, Pakistan." *Journal of Cleaner Production* 309: 127296.

Narayan, S., M. W. Beck, B. G. Reguero, I. J. Losada, B. van Wesenbeeck, N. Pontee, J. N. Sanchirico, et al. 2016. "The Effectiveness, Costs and Coastal Protection Benefits of Natural and Nature-Based Defences." *PLoS ONE* 11 (5): e0154735.

Nicholls, R. J., J. Hinkel, D. Lincke, and T. van der Pol. 2019. "Global Investment Costs for Coastal Defense through the 21st Century." Policy Research Working Paper 8745, World Bank, Washington, DC.

Nogrady, B. 2021. "China Launches World's Largest Carbon Market: But Is It Ambitious Enough?" *Scientific American*, July 21, 2021. https://www.scientificamerican.com/article/china-launches-worlds-largest-carbon-market-but-is-it-ambitious-enough/.

OECD (Organisation for Economic Co-operation and Development). 2015a. *Governing the City*. Paris: OECD.

OECD (Organisation for Economic Co-operation and Development). 2015b. *Water and Cities: Ensuring Sustainable Futures*. OECD Studies on Water. Paris: OECD.

Oijstaeijen, W. V., S. V. Passel, and J. Cools. 2020. "Urban Green Infrastructure: A Review on Valuation Toolkits from an Urban Planning Perspective." *Journal of Environmental Management* 267: 110603.

Ortega, F., and S. Taşpınar. 2018. "Rising Sea Levels and Sinking Property Values: Hurricane Sandy and New York's Housing Market." *Journal of Urban Economics* 106 (July): 81–100.

Owens, K. E., S. Gulyani, and A. Rizvi. 2018. "Success When We Deemed It Failure? Revisiting Sites and Services Projects in Mumbai and Chennai 20 Years Later." *World Development* 106 (June): 260–72.

Parthasarathy, R., V. Rao, and N. Palaniswamy. 2019. "Deliberative Democracy in an Unequal World: A Text-as-Data Study of South India's Village Assemblies." *American Political Science Review* 113 (3): 623–40.

Peralta, A., and J. B. Scott. 2018. "Moving to Flood Plains: The Unintended Consequences of the National Flood Insurance Program on Population Flows." Working paper. https://www .semanticscholar.org/paper/Moving-to-Flood-Plains-%3A-The-Unintended-of-the-on-Peralta -Scott/cf9e3987df6b77448ebc5207c97fa64b8952175f.

Peralta-Quiros, T., T. Kerzhner, and P. Avner. 2019. "Exploring Accessibility to Employment Opportunities in African Cities: A First Benchmark." Policy Research Working Paper 8971, World Bank, Washington, DC.

Pestel, N. 2019. "Employment Effects of Green Energy Policies." Centre for European Economic Research, IZA World of Labor, Bonn.

Quiñones, E. J., S. Liebenehm, and R. Sharma. 2021. "Left Home High and Dry—Reduced Migration in Response to Repeated Droughts in Thailand and Vietnam." *Population and Environment* 42 (4): 579–621.

Raj, S., S. K. Paul, A. Chakraborty, and J. Kuttippurath. 2020. "Anthropogenic Forcing Exacerbating the Urban Heat Islands in India." *Journal of Environmental Management* 257: 110006.

Reckien D., J. Flacke, M. Olazabal, and O. Heidrich. 2015. "The Influence of Drivers and Barriers on Urban Adaptation and Mitigation Plans—An Empirical Analysis of European Cities." *PLoS ONE* 10 (8): e0135597.

Rentschler, J. E. 2013. "Why Resilience Matters—The Poverty Impacts of Disasters." Policy Research Working Paper 6699, World Bank, Washington, DC.

Rentschler, J., P. Avner, M. Marconcini, R. Su, E. Strano, S. Hallegatte, L. Bernard, and C. Riom. 2022. "Rapid Urban Growth in Flood Zones: Global Evidence since 1985." Policy Research Working Paper 10014, World Bank, Washington, DC.

Rentschler, J., M. Kornejew, S. Hallegatte, J, Braese, and M. Obolensky. 2019. "Underutilized Potential: The Business Costs of Unreliable Infrastructure in Developing Countries." Policy Research Working Paper 8899, World Bank, Washington, DC.

Rigaud, K. K., A. de Sherbinin, B. Jones, J. Bergmann, V. Clement, K. Ober, J. Schewe, et al. 2018. *Groundswell: Preparing for Internal Climate Migration*. Washington, DC: World Bank.

Rogers, D., and V. Tsirkunov. 2010. *Costs and Benefits of Early Warning Systems*. Global Assessment Report on Disaster Risk Reduction 2011. Washington, DC: World Bank.

Romer, P. 1990. "Endogenous Technological Change." *Journal of Political Economy* 98 (5): 71–102.

Rossitti, G. 2022. "Who Is Affected? Which Segments of City Populations Are Most Exposed to Climate-Related Stresses?" Background paper prepared for this report, World Bank, Washington, DC.

Rubin, A. J., and S. Sengupta. 2018. "'Yellow Vest' Protests Shake France. Here's the Lesson for Climate Change." *New York Times,* December 6, 2018. https://www.nytimes.com/2018/12/06/world/europe/france-fuel-carbon-tax.html.

Saltiel, G., F. Zhang, A. Khan, D. Whittington, and R. Brears. Forthcoming. *Demand Management for Urban Water Security*. Washington, DC: World Bank.

Schug, G. R., K. E. Blevins, B. Cox, K. Gray, and V. Mushrif-Tripathy. 2013. "Infection, Disease, and Biosocial Processes at the End of the Indus Civilization." *PLoS ONE* 8 (12): e84814.

Selod, H., and F. Shilpi. 2021. "Rural-Urban Migration in Developing Countries: Lessons from the Literature." *Regional Science and Urban Economics* 91: 103713.

Seto K.C., S. Dhakal, A. Bigio, H. Blanco, G. C. Delgado, D. Dewar, L. Huang, et al. 2014. Human Settlements, Infrastructure and Spatial Planning. In *Climate Change 2014: Mitigation of Climate Change*. Contribution of Working Group III to the Fifth Assessment Report of the Intergovernmental Panel on Climate Change. Cambridge, UK: Cambridge University Press.

Sivaev, D., B. Herzberg, and S. Manchanda. 2015. "Public-Private Dialogue for City Competitiveness." Competitive Cities for Jobs and Growth, Companion Paper 7, World Bank, Washington, DC.

Sivaev, D., I. Kamilov, G. Rossitti, N. Orlova, and P. Vaggione. 2022. *The Time Is Now: How Can Uzbekistan Leverage Urbanization as a Driver of Sustainable Development?* Washington, DC: World Bank.

Somanathan E., T. Sterner, T. Sugiyama, D. Chimanikire, N. K. Dubash, J. Essandoh-Yeddu, S. Fifita, et al. 2014. "National and Sub-national Policies and Institutions." In *Climate Change 2014: Mitigation of Climate Change*. Contribution of Working Group III to the Fifth Assessment Report of the Intergovernmental Panel on Climate Change. Cambridge, UK: Cambridge University Press.

Song, S., C.-C. Feng, and M. Diao. 2020. "Vehicle Quota Control, Transport Infrastructure Investment and Vehicle Travel: A Pseudo Panel Analysis." *Urban Studies* 57 (12): 2527–46.

Stern, N., S. Peters, V. Bakhshi, A. Bowen, C. Cameron, S. Catovsky, D. Crane, et al. 2006. *Stern Review: The Economics of Climate Change*. London: HM Treasury.

Tan, Z., K. K.-L. Lau, and E. Ng. 2016. "Urban Tree Design Approaches for Mitigating Daytime Urban Heat Island Effects in a High-Density Urban Environment." *Energy and Buildings* 114: 265–74.

Tolbert, J. 2021. "Beyond Cities: Breaking Through Barriers to Rural Electric Vehicle Adoption." Environmental and Energy Study Institute. https://www.eesi.org/articles/view/beyond-cities-breaking-through-barriers-to-rural-electric-vehicle-adoption.

Tortajada, C., and P. van Rensburg. 2020. "Drink More Recycled Wastewater." *Nature* 577: 26–28.

UNEP (United Nations Environment Programme). 2021. *Adaptation Gap Report 2021: The Gathering Storm—Adapting to Climate Change in a Post-pandemic World*. Nairobi: UNEP.

Viguié, V., and S. Hallegatte. 2012. "Trade-Offs and Synergies in Urban Climate Policies: Nature Climate Change." *Nature Climate Change* 2 (5): 334–37.

Vona, F. 2021. "Managing the Distributional Effects of Environmental and Climate Policies: The Narrow Path for a Triple Dividend." Environment Working Paper 188, Organisation for Economic Co-operation and Development, Paris.

Weiss, J., E. Dunkelberg, and T. Vogelpohl. 2012. "Improving Policy Instruments to Better Tap into Homeowner Refurbishment Potential: Lessons Learned from a Case Study in Germany." *Energy Policy* 44: 406–15.

White, R., and Wahba, S. 2019. "Addressing Constraints to Private Financing of Urban (Climate) Infrastructure in Developing Countries." *International Journal of Urban Sustainable Development* 11 (3): 245–56.

Wilson, R. 2021. "Moving to Jobs: The Role of Information in Migration Decisions." *Journal of Labor Economics* 39 (4): 1083–128.

Winkler, S. L., J. E. Anderson, L. Garza, W. C. Ruona, R. Vogt, and T. J. Wallington. 2018. "Vehicle Criteria Pollutant (PM, NOx, CO, HCs) Emissions: How Long Should We Go?" *npj Climate and Atmospheric Science* 1: 26.

Wishart, M., T. Wong, B. Furmage, X. Liao, D. Pannell, and J. Wang. 2021. *Valuing the Benefits of Nature-Based Solutions: A Manual for Integrated Urban Flood Management in China*. Washington, DC: World Bank.

World Bank. 2010. *Natural Hazards, UnNatural Disasters: The Economics of Effective Prevention*. Washington, DC: World Bank.

World Bank. 2014. *Republic of Burundi. Fiscal Decentralization and Local Governance Managing Trade-Offs to Promote Sustainable Reforms. Burundi Public Expenditure Review*. Washington, DC: World Bank.

World Bank. 2015a. *Competitive Cities for Jobs and Growth*. Washington, DC: World Bank.

World Bank. 2015b. *World Development Report 2015: Mind, Society, and Behavior*. Washington, DC: World Bank.

World Bank. 2016. *Perspectives Urbaines: Villes Émergentes Pour Un Sénégal Émergent*. Washington, DC: World Bank.

World Bank. 2018. *Aligning Institutions and Incentives for Sustainable Water Supply and Sanitation Services*. Washington, DC: World Bank.

World Bank. 2019a. *Republic of Guinea—Planning, Connecting, Financing in Conakry*. Urban Sector Review. Washington, DC: World Bank.

World Bank. 2019b. *Resilient Housing Best Practices and Lessons Learned: United States and Japan*. Washington, DC: World Bank.

World Bank. 2020a. *Strengthening Urban Resilience in Morocco: Building Capacity and Identifying Risk to Better Protect Cities and Manage Disasters*. Results in Resilience Series. Washington, DC: World Bank.

World Bank. 2020b. *The Philippines Parametric Catastrophe Risk Insurance Program Pilot: Lessons Learned*. Washington, DC: World Bank.

World Bank. 2021a. *Green, Resilient, and Inclusive Development*. Washington, DC: World Bank.

World Bank. 2021b. *Investment in Disaster Risk Management in Europe Makes Economic Sense: Background Report. Economics for Disaster Prevention and Preparedness*. Washington, DC: World Bank.

World Bank. 2021c. *Somalia Urbanization Review: Fostering Cities as Anchors of Development*. Washington, DC: World Bank.

World Bank. 2021d. *The State of Cities Climate Finance: Part 2. The Enabling Conditions for Mobilizing Urban Climate Finance*. Washington, DC: World Bank.

World Bank. 2021e. "Unlocking Private Investment in Climate Adaptation and Resilience." *World Bank News*, March 4, 2021. https://www.worldbank.org/en/news/feature/2021/03/04 /unlocking-private-investment-in-climate-adaptation-and-resilience.

World Bank. Forthcoming a. *The Feasibility Frontier: Strategies to Make Policy for a Net Zero Future Possible*. Washington, DC: World Bank.

World Bank. Forthcoming b. *Territorial Decarbonization in Bulgaria*. Washington, DC: World Bank.

Zachmann, G., G. Fredriksson, and G. Claeys. 2018. *The Distributional Impacts of Climate Policies*. Bruegel Blueprint Series 28. Brussels: Bruegel.

Zaveri, E., J. Russ, A. Khan, R. Damania, E. Borgomeo, and A. Jägerskog. 2021. *Ebb and Flow: Volume 1. Water, Migration, and Development*. Washington, DC: World Bank.

Zhang, H., A. Buote, and W. Acworth. 2021. "China's Pilot Emission Trading Systems and Electricity Markets (Hubei and Shenzhen)." Case Study Report, German Environment Agency, Berlin.

Zhang, L., and T. Leonard. 2019. "Flood Hazards Impact on Neighborhood House Prices." *Journal of Real Estate Finance and Economics* 58 (4): 656–74.

www.ingramcontent.com/pod-product-compliance
Lightning Source LLC
Chambersburg PA
CBHW050806220326

41598CB00006B/130